Access® 2013
ALL-IN-ONE
FOR
DUMMIES®
A Wiley Brand

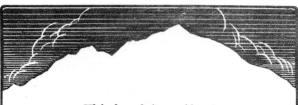

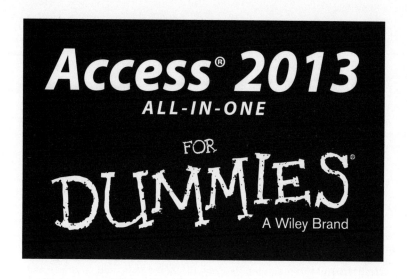

by Alison Barrows, Joseph C. Stockman,
and Allen G. Taylor

Access® 2013 All-in-One For Dummies®

Published by
John Wiley & Sons, Inc.
111 River Street
Hoboken, NJ 07030-5774

www.wiley.com

Copyright © 2013 by John Wiley & Sons, Inc., Hoboken, New Jersey

Published by John Wiley & Sons, Inc., Hoboken, New Jersey

Published simultaneously in Canada

Library of Congress Control Number: 2013932122

ISBN 978-1-118-51055-1 (pbk); ISBN 978-1-118-63737-1 (ebk); ISBN 978-1-118-52792-4 (ebk); ISBN 978-1-118-63747-0 (ebk)

Manufactured in the United States of America

10 9 8 7 6 5 4 3 2 1

About the Authors

Alison Barrows has authored or co-authored books on Windows, the Internet, Microsoft Access, WordPerfect, Lotus 1-2-3, and other topics. In addition to writing books, Alison writes and edits technical documentation and training material. In real life she hangs out with her "guys" — Parker, 6, and Mason, 4, and Evan, 2 — and tries to carve out some time to practice yoga. Alison lives with her family in central Massachusetts.

Joe Stockman has been using Microsoft Access since its initial release and has authored or co-authored several books on Access. He's also developed courseware in Access and VBA and has been on the speaker circuit for Microsoft Access seminars. Joe works as a consultant and software designer for Facilities Survey, Inc. in Pittsburgh, Pennsylvania. He also enjoys music, cooking, and anything else that lets him express his creative side.

Allen G. Taylor is a 30-year veteran of the computer industry and the author of over 20 books, including *SQL For Dummies*, *SQL All-in-One For Dummies*, and *Database Development For Dummies*. He lectures nationally on databases, innovation, and entrepreneurship. He also teaches database development through a leading online education provider. Allen is president of Goldfinger Global, LLC and can be reached at allen@goldfingerglobal.com.

Dedication

To Matt, Parker, Mason, and Evan. —Alison Barrows

To Mom, as always. —Joseph C. Stockman

To Marguerite Shelton, who gave me my life's greatest gift. —Allen G. Taylor

Authors' Acknowledgments

We would like to acknowledge the care of Kyle Looper, Blair Pottenger, Kathy Simpson, and all the others who shepherded this book through the editing and production process, as well as all the folks listed on the Publisher's Acknowledgments page who worked on this book. (It takes ALL of these people, not just those of us on the cover.) We'd also like to thank the folks at Microsoft for making Access a wonderful tool to create robust database applications.

Alison thanks Dotty, Christy, and Matt for taking great care of my guys so I can get work done. Matt (also known as Honey) gets special thanks as my hardware guru.

Joe thanks his mom and dad, for always encouraging but never pushing. Also thanks to Robin for her support and understanding of the time it took to finish this project.

Allen thanks all the folks at Wiley who made this book possible, but especially Kathy Simpson and Blair Pottenger, project editors, and Kyle Looper, acquisitions editor.

Publisher's Acknowledgments

We're proud of this book; please send us your comments at `http://dummies.custhelp.com`. For other comments, please contact our Customer Care Department within the U.S. at 877-762-2974, outside the U.S. at 317-572-3993, or fax 317-572-4002.

Some of the people who helped bring this book to market include the following:

Acquisitions and Editorial

Project Editors: Kathy Simpson, Blair J. Pottenger

Acquisitions Editor: Kyle Looper

Copy Editor: Kathy Simpson

Technical Editor: Brian Underdahl

Editorial Manager: Kevin Kirschner

Editorial Assistant: Annie Sullivan

Sr. Editorial Assistant: Cherie Case

Cover Photo: © Marcello Bortolino / iStockphoto

Composition Services

Project Coordinator: Katie Crocker

Layout and Graphics: Jennifer Creasey, Joyce Haughey

Proofreader: The Well-Chosen Word

Indexer: BIM Indexing & Proofreading Services

Publishing and Editorial for Technology Dummies

    Richard Swadley, Vice President and Executive Group Publisher

    Andy Cummings, Vice President and Publisher

    Mary Bednarek, Executive Acquisitions Director

    Mary C. Corder, Editorial Director

Publishing for Consumer Dummies

    Kathleen Nebenhaus, Vice President and Executive Publisher

Composition Services

    Debbie Stailey, Director of Composition Services

Contents at a Glance

Introduction 1

Book I: Getting Started with Access 2013 7
Chapter 1: Introducing Access 2013 9
Chapter 2: Getting Started, Getting Around 17
Chapter 3: Designing Your Database the Relational Way 37

Book II: Tables for Storing Your Data 65
Chapter 1: Creating and Modifying Tables 67
Chapter 2: Refining Your Table in Design View 105
Chapter 3: Sorting, Finding, and Filtering Data in a Datasheet 121
Chapter 4: Importing and Exporting Data...137
Chapter 5: Avoiding "Garbage In, Garbage Out" 157
Chapter 6: Relating Your Tables and Protecting Your Data.......................175

Book III: Queries (Or Getting Information from Your Data) 187
Chapter 1: Creating Select Queries...189
Chapter 2: Letting Queries Do the Math 221
Chapter 3: Doing Neat Things with Action Queries and Query Wizards 255
Chapter 4: Viewing Your Data from All Angles Using Crosstabs 277

Book IV: Forms for Editing Data 287
Chapter 1: Designing Custom Forms (and Reports)....................................289
Chapter 2: Jazzing Up Your Forms (and Reports)......................................313
Chapter 3: Creating Smarter Forms...339
Chapter 4: Doing Calculations in Forms and Subforms (and Reports)......365

Book V: Reporting in Words and Pictures............... 385
Chapter 1: Creating and Spiffing Up Reports..387
Chapter 2: Printing Beautiful Reports..415
Chapter 3: Creating Charts and Graphs from Your Data............................435

Book VI: Automation with Macros 457

Chapter 1: Making Macros Do the Work 459

Chapter 2: Making Macros Smarter 477

Book VII: Database Administration 497

Chapter 1: Database Housekeeping 499

Chapter 2: Sharing the Fun: Managing Multiuser Access 511

Chapter 3: Securing Your Data 523

Book VIII: Programming in VBA 535

Chapter 1: What the Heck Is VBA? 537

Chapter 2: Writing Code 557

Chapter 3: Writing Smarter Code 581

Chapter 4: Controlling Forms with VBA 605

Chapter 5: Using SQL and Recordsets 629

Chapter 6: Debugging Your Code 641

Book IX: Going Beyond Access 651

Chapter 1: Automation with Other Office Programs 653

Chapter 2: Using Access As a Front End to SQL Server 671

Chapter 3: Using Access with SharePoint 685

Appendix: Installing Microsoft Access 709

Index 717

Table of Contents

Introduction 1

About Access 2013 All-in-One For Dummies 1
Foolish Assumptions...2
How This Book Is Organized 3
    Book I: Getting Started with Access 2013 3
    Book II: Tables for Storing Your Data...3
    Book III: Queries (Or Getting Information from Your Data) 4
    Book IV: Forms for Editing Data...4
    Book V: Reporting in Words and Pictures 4
    Book VI: Automation with Macros..4
    Book VII: Database Administration..4
    Book VIII: Programming in VBA 4
    Book IX: Going Beyond Access..4
    Appendix: Installing Microsoft Access 5
What You Don't Have to Read..5
Icons Used in This Book 5
Conventions Used in This Book...6
Where to Go from Here..6

Book I: Getting Started with Access 2013 7

Chapter 1: Introducing Access 2013 9
Why Use a Database? 10
Plan, Plan, Plan...10
The Six Types of Access Objects..11
    Tables for storing your data 11
    Queries for selecting your data..12
    Forms for editing and displaying your data 12
    Reports for printing your data 13
    Macros for saving keystrokes 14
    Modules for writing your own programs 15
Essential Database Concepts 15

Chapter 2: Getting Started, Getting Around 17
Running Access...17
Opening a Database..19
    Opening oldies 21
    Saving in a different version 21
    I have that open already! 21
    Creating a sample database from a template....................................21

Making Friends with the Access Window..22
    The Ribbon 23
    The Quick Access toolbar...24
Introducing Mission Control: The Navigation Pane 25
    Choosing how database objects are grouped............................26
    Choosing size and details for Navigation Pane objects 27
    Sorting objects in the Navigation Pane.....................................29
    Searching for an object 29
Viewing Objects in Your Database 29
    Viewing lots of objects at the same time 30
    Switching views...30
Creating, Deleting, Renaming, Copying, and Printing Objects...............31
Introducing Backstage View...32
Using Wizards 33
Getting Help...34
Saving Time with Keyboard Shortcuts 34

Chapter 3: Designing Your Database the Relational Way 37

What Are Tables, Fields, and Keys? 37
    Data types 38
    Primary key fields for your tables 40
What Are Relationships? 40
    How relationships work..41
    One-to-many relationships 42
    One-to-one relationships...43
    Many-to-many relationships 44
Designing a Database 46
    Identifying your data 46
    Eliminating redundant fields 47
    Organizing fields into tables..47
    Adding tables for codes and abbreviations..............................51
    Choosing primary keys for each table 51
    Linking your tables 53
    Refining your links 54
    Seeing what's in a name 55
    Cleaning up the design..56
Choosing Field Types...57
    Choosing between Text and Yes/No fields 57
    Choosing between Short Text and Long Text fields.......................57
    Choosing between Text and Number (or Currency) fields 58
    Storing pictures and other files...59
    Storing names, money, codes, and other stuff..........................59
Storing Single Facts 60
Creating a Database 61
    Creating a database from scratch..61
    Creating a new database from a template 63

Book II: Tables for Storing Your Data **65**

Chapter 1: Creating and Modifying Tables .... .67

Viewing Your Tables 68
Creating the First Table for Your Data...70
Creating a new table using Datasheet view.....................................70
Entering data and creating fields..71
Choosing field names 72
Changing a field name 73
Saving your table 73
Working with Tables and Fields in Your Database 74
Finding other ways to create a table..74
Starting with table templates (aka Application Parts)..................75
Creating Fields 76
Creating fields by clicking a button...77
Quick-starting your table with field templates...............................78
Working with a Datasheet Full of Data..80
Looking at a datasheet 80
Navigating the data...81
Adding and Editing Records...82
Using keystrokes to enter data automatically................................83
Editing the data you have..84
Adding calculated fields to tables..85
Entering and editing hyperlinks...86
Using the Attachment data type 89
Deleting records..91
Entering special characters...91
Checking Your Spelling 92
Using AutoCorrect for Faster Data Entry..94
Formatting a Datasheet...96
Formatting a field 97
Changing the font..97
Taking advantage of Rich Text..97
Changing gridlines and background color.......................................98
Rearranging columns in a datasheet..99
Changing column width 99
Changing row height...100
Inserting and deleting columns..100
Hiding columns 101
Freezing columns 101
Changing default formatting for new tables 101
Taking Advantage of Subdatasheets 101
Adding a Total Row to the Datasheet 103

Chapter 2: Refining Your Table in Design View **105**

Creating Tables in Design View 105
Refining Your Table in Design View 107
Using the Caption property 109
Adding a field 109
Copying a field 109
Moving a field 110
Deleting a field 110
Choosing a data type 110
Formatting Fields with Field Properties 113
Formatting Number and Currency fields 113
Setting the field size 115
Formatting Date/Time fields 116
Formatting Text fields 116
Defining the Primary Key 117
Indexing Fields 118
Printing Table Designs 119

Chapter 3: Sorting, Finding, and Filtering Data in a Datasheet **121**

Sorting the Rows of a Datasheet 121
Finding (and Replacing) Data 123
Exploring the Find and Replace dialog box 124
Replacing the data you find 125
Filtering a Datasheet 125
Understanding filtering basics 126
Using different types of datasheet filters 127
Filtering with quick filters 128
Filtering by selection 129
Filtering multiple fields 130
Filtering with Advanced Filter/Sort 132

Chapter 4: Importing and Exporting Data **137**

Cutting, Copying, and Pasting 137
Using the Office clipboard 139
Cutting and pasting small to mediumish amounts of data 140
Moving data from Excel to Access 141
Importing or Linking to Data 142
Making data available 142
Understanding what applications are compatible with Access 143
Getting external data 144
Importing text or spreadsheet data 146
Importing with the Import Spreadsheet and Link
Spreadsheet wizards 149
Getting contacts from Outlook into Access 150
Managing links 151
Cleaning up your imported data 152
Running and scheduling saved imports 153

Getting Data from Another Access Database..153
Getting Data Out of Access..154
Using Access Data in a Word Mail Merge...156

Chapter 5: Avoiding "Garbage In, Garbage Out" 157

Finding the Right Tool to Keep Garbage Out..158
Using Input Masks to Validate and Format Data 159
Using the Input Mask Wizard 160
Creating an input mask manually 162
Creating a Lookup Field 164
Using the Lookup Wizard...165
Knowing when to allow multiple selections...................................168
Modifying the lookup list 170
Validating Data As It's Entered 170

Chapter 6: Relating Your Tables and Protecting Your Data 175

Creating Relationships and Protecting Your Data with
Referential Integrity...177
Deciding on the best path to take...178
Opening the Relationships window...179
Adding tables to the Relationships window...................................179
Setting referential integrity between two tables...........................180
Editing and deleting relationships..181
Creating Referential Integrity with Many-to-Many Relationships 182
Printing the Relationships Window...184

Book III: Queries (Or Getting Information from Your Data).. 187

Chapter 1: Creating Select Queries...........................189

Understanding Types of Queries..190
Creating a Query in Design View 191
Creating a Query with the Simple Query Wizard.................................194
Viewing Your Query 197
Using Query Design View..198
Deciphering Design view..198
Working with tables in Design view..201
Introducing the query design grid..201
Navigating Design view 202
Displaying or hiding table names 202
Taking Tips on Creating a Query 202
Adding tables to the query...203
Inserting fields into a design grid 203

Editing a Query 204
   Sorting a query 205
   Viewing top values..205
   Hiding fields...206
   Changing the format of a query field.......................206
Limiting Records with Criteria Expressions 207
   Querying by example...207
   Using dates, times, text, and values in criteria 208
   Using operators in criteria expressions..................208
   Using multiple criteria..210
   Using lookup fields in criteria 211
   Creating queries with multivalue lookup fields 212
Working with Multiple Related Tables.....................................213
   Joining tables in Design view 214
   Choosing the type of join and setting join properties 215
Working with Query Datasheets...217
   Using the query datasheet to edit data....................217
   Creating AutoLookup queries
      to fill in data automatically 218
Saving Queries 219

Chapter 2: Letting Queries Do the Math **221**
Doing Calculations in Queries...221
Writing Expressions in Access...224
   Using operators in expressions 224
   Using field names in expressions..............................226
   Using functions in expressions 227
Using Expression Builder 228
   Getting help with functions 230
   Entering text in < and > brackets 231
   Nesting functions 232
Going beyond Basic Arithmetic 232
   Formatting calculated numbers in queries 233
   Avoiding problems with null values..........................236
Performing Date and Time Calculations.................................238
   Using literal dates and times in expressions...........239
   Using the Date/Time functions..................................239
Manipulating Text with Expressions.......................................242
   Adding spaces to text expressions............................242
   Using the Access Text functions................................243
Writing Decision-Making Expressions.....................................243
   Making comparisons in IIf().......................................244
   Combining comparisons 245
   To tax or not to tax? 246
Testing for Empty Fields...248
Sorting by Name or Company 248
Creating Flexible Parameter Queries 249
Working with Totals, Subtotals, Averages, and Such 252
   Calculating subtotals in a query 254
   Filtering records based on calculated fields 254

Chapter 3: Doing Neat Things with Action Queries and Query Wizards. 255

Creating Action Queries..255
   Recognizing the dangers of the Run button 256
   Creating action queries safely...257
Changing Data with Update Queries 258
Creating New Tables with Make-Table Queries.......................262
Moving Data from One Table to Another with Append Queries ...265
Deleting Lots of Records with Delete Queries 267
Finding Unmatched Records with a Wizard..............................270
Finding Duplicate Records 272

Chapter 4: Viewing Your Data from All Angles Using Crosstabs . . .277

Aggregating Data in a Crosstab Query.....................................277
Using the Crosstab Query Wizard 278
Creating a Crosstab Query in Design View..............................282
Modifying a Crosstab Query 284
   Using criteria 284
   Using multiple fields for row headings................................284
   Adding aggregate columns 285
   Getting data in order 286

Book IV: Forms for Editing Data 287

Chapter 1: Designing Custom Forms (and Reports) 289

Seeing How Forms and Reports Are Secretly Related 290
Understanding Form Basics 290
Making and Using a Form 293
   Making the easiest possible form with the Form button.............293
   Viewing a form..294
   Editing data in Form view 295
Creating Forms with Wizards..296
   Wizard, make me a form!..296
   More super-speedy forms 299
Modifying Existing Forms and Reports...................................300
Getting Your Fields Lined Up in Layout View 301
   Using a control layout to rearrange fields 302
   Adding and deleting fields 302
   Making a new form from scratch in Layout view......................303
   Adding and deleting rows and columns in the control layout.....304
   Controlling your control layouts 304
   Trying out your new, improved form 305
Configuring the Whole Form or Report 305
   Naming the form 307
   Seeing where records come from..307

Deciding the order of the records 308
Choosing one record or many...308
Using some other cool form properties......................................309
Applying a theme to a form or report 310
Storing Your Forms and Reports..310
Managing forms and reports 311
Importing forms and reports from other databases 311
Printing forms...312

Chapter 2: Jazzing Up Your Forms (and Reports) 313

Creating New Forms Efficiently..313
Making All Kinds of Changes in Design View 314
Changing the layout of an existing form or report 315
Changing the size of a form 317
Taking Control of Your Form or Report 317
Understanding types of form controls.......................................317
Making a new control by dragging a field 320
Making a new control by choosing a control 321
Setting control properties 321
Binding a control to data in the record source.........................322
Making Controls That Display Text, Numbers, and Dates 323
Making and editing labels 323
Adding hyperlink controls 325
Putting Short Text and Long Text fields in text boxes.............325
Displaying Number, Currency, and Date fields 326
Breaking Out of the Control Layout 326
Removing the control layout..327
Moving or resizing a control 327
Neatening your controls 328
Renaming, Resizing, Deleting, and Copying Controls 330
Formatting Numbers and Dates...330
Choosing Fonts, Colors, and Other Decorative Touches 331
Copying your formatting...333
Making bad news red...333
Creating Check Boxes for Yes/No Fields 335
Adding Lines, Boxes, and Backgrounds...335
Controlling Cursor Movement in Your Form 336

Chapter 3: Creating Smarter Forms 339

Creating and Configuring Combo and List Boxes..............................339
Making combo boxes the really easy way 341
Running the Combo Box and List Box wizards...........................341
Changing the properties of a combo or list box 344
Designing Cool Looks for Yes/No Fields...345
Creating Option Groups...345

Creating Command Buttons 348
   Making a Close button 350
   Making a button to display a related form 351
   Making a button to print the current record....................352
   Making other cool buttons 353
   Customizing your command button 353
Making a Find Box 354
Displaying Attachments 355
Adding Form Headers and Footers 357
Creating Tabbed Forms 358
You Can't Type That Here! 360
Making a Main Menu for Your Database 361
   Creating a navigation form 361
   Finding an alternative to navigation forms....................362
   Opening a form automatically when the database opens 363

Chapter 4: Doing Calculations in Forms and Subforms (and Reports) 365
Doing Elementary Calculations..365
   Making a calculated control 366
   Checking your expression 368
   Troubleshooting expressions 368
Calculating and Formatting Numbers 369
Calculating and Formatting Dates 370
Calculating and Formatting Text 370
Displaying Values That Depend on Conditions 371
Formatting Calculated Controls..371
Using a Split Form to Display a Datasheet 372
Using a Subform to Display Detail Records..........................373
   Creating a subform 374
   Viewing the properties of subform controls 378
Adding Subtotals and Totals from Subforms 379
   Using aggregate functions..379
   Referring to a control on a subform 381
   Creating the controls to total a subform 381

Book V: Reporting in Words and Pictures 385

Chapter 1: Creating and Spiffing Up Reports. 387
Knowing Forms Means That You Already Know Reports 388
Creating Reports Automatically 389
   Making the easiest possible report 390
   Running the Report Wizard 391
Editing Reports in Layout and Design View..396

Creating and Managing Report Sections 397
    Setting report and section properties.......................................399
    Adding page headers, footers, and numbers 400
    Grouping your records..402
    Sorting the records in your report 405
    Calculating group subtotals and report totals.......................406
Employing Formatting Tips and Tricks 407
Copying Forms to Reports...409
Adding and Formatting Subreports..409
    Making a subreport...411
    Printing information from a subreport on the main report..........412
Displaying Empty or Long Fields 413
    Displaying long text 413
    Displaying fields that may be empty 413
Viewing Your Reports Onscreen 414

Chapter 2: Printing Beautiful Reports.............................415

Viewing Your Report..415
    Adjusting the view 417
    Looking at lots of pages 417
Formatting the Page...418
    Selecting a printer..418
    Setting margins, paper size, and paper orientation 419
    Controlling page breaks...420
    Avoiding blank pages 421
    Printing only the data..422
Printing the Report...422
    Printing on an actual printer 422
    Creating a PDF, XPS, HTML, or other file of your report 423
Creating Mailing Labels 424
    Running the Label Wizard...425
    Behind the scenes in a mailing-label report 427
    Changing the page setup for labels 428
Sending a Report to Another Application 429
    Exporting your report to Microsoft Excel................................429
    Exporting your report to Microsoft Word 430
    E-mailing your report in Microsoft Outlook 431
    Exporting your report in other formats...................................432
    Automating your exports...432

Chapter 3: Creating Charts and Graphs from Your Data 435

Pulling Up a Seat at the Data Bar...435
Displaying Information with Charts 437
    Creating charts with the Chart Wizard 438
    Making bar charts 443
    Making line and area charts 446
    Making pie and doughnut charts 448
    Making bubble and XY scatter plots 450

Changing Your Charts...451
 Modifying an existing chart 451
 Formatting charts with colors, legends, and titles.....................453
 Changing how data is graphed...454
 Changing which data is charted...455

Book VI: Automation with Macros................... 457

Chapter 1: Making Macros Do the Work 459

Introducing Macros...460
Creating and Editing Stand-Alone Macros.................................460
 Naming, saving, and editing macros..................................461
 Taking action 462
 Specifying arguments to actions.......................................464
 Moving your actions around 464
 Adding comments 465
 Creating subroutines in macros: Submacros 465
Running Stand-Alone Macros and Submacros............................467
 Running a macro when the database opens 467
 Assigning macros to keys 468
Opening Databases That Contain Macros...................................469
 Keeping a macro from turning into a virus.........................470
 Putting your database in a safe place 470
 Signing your database 472
 Knowing which actions you can take.................................474
Telling Access to "Run This Only If I Say So".............................474
 If-Then macros 475
 If-Then-Else macros 476

Chapter 2: Making Macros Smarter 477

Attaching Macros to Tables 478
 Running data macros..478
 Creating a data macro 478
 Trying cool data-macro tricks...481
Running Macros in Forms...482
 Running a macro when a form event happens....................482
 Creating command buttons on forms 484
 Referring to form controls in macros................................485
 Printing matching records from a form 486
Changing the Way Your Form Looks Dynamically.......................487
 Setting the properties of form controls 487
 Hiding unneeded controls on a form.................................488
Setting Up Your Own Main-Menu Form 490
 Creating a form that appears when the database opens.....490
 Creating command buttons for your main-menu form..........491
Using Temporary Variables in Macros 494

Book VII: Database Administration 497

Chapter 1: Database Housekeeping 499
Compacting and Repairing Your Database 499
Making Backups 500
    Backing up a whole database 500
    Backing up part of a database 501
Converting Databases 503
Analyzing and Documenting Your Database 504
    Viewing relationships in the Relationships window 504
    Viewing object dependencies 505
    Analyzing database performance 506
    Documenting your database 508
Loading and Managing Add-Ins 508

Chapter 2: Sharing the Fun: Managing Multiuser Access 511
Putting Your Database Where People Can See It 512
Splitting Your Database into a Front End and a Back End 513
    Why split? 513
    Let's split! 514
    Handing out front ends 516
    Relinking your tables 517
Editing with Multiple Users 518
    Fixing exclusive access 518
    Managing record-locking 519
    Programming locks 521

Chapter 3: Securing Your Data 523
Observing Basic Windows Security 523
Controlling What Happens When You Open the Database 524
Password-Protecting and Encrypting Your Database 528
    Encrypting your database with a password 528
    Opening a password-protected database 529
    Decrypting a database 529
Locking Up Your Database As an .accde File 529
    Creating an .accde file 530
    Making updates later 530
Using the Trust Center 532

Book VIII: Programming in VBA 535

Chapter 1: What the Heck Is VBA? 537
Getting Acquainted with VBA Code 537
    Opening a class module 538
    Creating or opening a standard module 539

Enabling VBA Code..541
    Sub procedures..541
    Function procedures 542
Working with Visual Basic Editor 543
    Using the Code window...544
    Using the Immediate window 546
    Using the Object Browser 548
    Searching the Object Library 549
    Referring to objects and collections 551
    Choosing object libraries..552
    Closing Visual Basic Editor 552
Discovering Code As You Go 553
    Converting macros to VBA code................................553
    Copying and pasting code 555

Chapter 2: Writing Code **557**

Seeing How VBA Works 557
Understanding VBA Syntax 558
    Arguing with VBA..560
    Knowing module level from procedure level 562
    Declaring module options...562
Writing Your Own VBA Procedures 563
    Creating a new standard procedure.........................563
    Creating a new event procedure..............................565
    Passing arguments to procedures............................566
    Returning a value from a function 569
Typing and Editing in the Code Window 570
    Taking shortcuts in the Code window 571
    Typing comments 572
    Breaking lines of code 572
    Dealing with compile errors 574
Testing and Running Your Code..575
    Testing sub procedures 575
    Running sub procedures from Access 576
    Testing function procedures 578
    Using function procedures in Access........................579

Chapter 3: Writing Smarter Code...........................**581**

Creating Variables and Constants 581
    Creating variables...581
    Understanding the scope and lifetime of variables......583
    Defining constants 585
    Organizing variables into arrays...............................585
    Working with multidimensional arrays.....................587
    Following naming conventions for variables 588

Making Decisions in VBA Code..589
   Using If...End If statements 590
   Nesting If...End If statements...592
   Using a Select Case block...592
Executing the Same Code Repeatedly..595
   Using Do...Loop to create a loop.......................................595
   Using While...Wend to create a loop 597
   Using For...Next to create a loop......................................597
   Looping through an array..599
   Analyzing each character in a string.................................600
Using Custom Functions..600

Chapter 4: Controlling Forms with VBA 605

Displaying Custom Messages..605
   Displaying a message box..605
   Responding to what the user clicks 607
Opening Forms with DoCmd...608
   Finding umpteen ways to open a form..............................609
   Closing a form with DoCmd..611
Changing Form Controls with VBA...612
   Some cool control properties 613
   Examples of controlling properties 614
Understanding Objects and Collections....................................619
   Working with properties, methods, and events 620
   Referring to objects and collections 621
   Seeing whether a form is open...623
   Looping through collections 625
   Using With...End With...627

Chapter 5: Using SQL and Recordsets 629

Recordsets and Object Models...629
   Creating quick and easy recordsets.................................630
   Understanding ADO recordset properties and methods..............630
   Looping through a recordset 631
   Defining a recordset's cursor type....................................632
   Using field names in recordsets..633
SQL and Recordsets 633
   Writing SQL statements 634
   Breaking up long SQL statements....................................636
Action Queries in VBA 638
   Creating an action query...638
   Turning off warnings 639
Connection Cleanup...640

Chapter 6: Debugging Your Code.................................641

Recognizing Types of Program Errors......................................641
Fixing Compiler Errors...642

Trapping Runtime Errors...643
    Creating an error handler 643
    Fixing runtime errors..646
    Preventing runtime errors 647
Dealing with Logical Errors 647
    Watching things happen 647
    Slowing procedures 648
    Cleaning up 650

Book IX: Going Beyond Access *651*

Chapter 1: Automation with Other Office Programs..............653

Understanding Automation 653
Working with Object Libraries..654
    Exploring object libraries 655
    Using the Application object 656
Adding Contacts to Outlook...657
    Adding the contact button and code 657
    Examining the contact-form code.....................................659
Merging Data with a Word Document...661
    Creating a Word template...661
    Viewing and inserting bookmarks 661
    Adding the merge button 663
    Entering the merge code..663
    Examining the merge code 664
Exporting Data to Excel 666
    Adding the export button and code 666
    Examining the export code...668

Chapter 2: Using Access As a Front End to SQL Server 671

What Is SQL Server? 671
Using ODBC 672
    Connecting to SQL Server with ODBC.............................672
    Using linked tables in Access 680
    Maintaining linked tables..680
    Using pass-through queries...681
Finding Alternatives to Access Data Projects.............................682

Chapter 3: Using Access with SharePoint........................685

What Is SharePoint? 685
Using a SharePoint List As a Data Source...................................686
    Creating a new SharePoint list 686
    Linking to an existing SharePoint list..............................689
    Moving an existing database to SharePoint 690

Building a Custom Web App 692
    Defining a Custom Web App.. 692
    Meeting the requirements for a Custom Web App....................... 692
    Creating a Custom Web App 693
Designing Custom Web Apps 695
    Adding tables.. 696
    Launching your app... 698
    Entering data in your app 699
    Navigating your app 700
    Editing views 701
    Adding actions 703
    Adding queries 706

Appendix: Installing Microsoft Access 709
Installing Access from a Disc 709
Installing Access from Office 365... 712
Activating Access 713
Repairing, Reinstalling, or Uninstalling Access 715

Index 717

Introduction

Whoa! What happened to menu bars, toolbars, and all that other stuff we used to have? Well, in case you haven't noticed yet, they're all gone. If you've never used Access in your life, you're starting fresh, of course, so never mind. Even if you've never used any version of Microsoft Access before or aren't even sure what a version is, however, you've come to the right book.

The basic idea behind Microsoft Access is to allow individuals and small businesses to manage large amounts of information the way that big corporations do: with relational databases. The difference is that whereas the big boys spend millions for computer hardware, software, and staffs of nerdy database-administrator types, Access allows you to do everything yourself with a run-of-the-mill PC and a realistic software budget.

Microsoft Access 2013 is the latest-and-greatest version of a long line of Access versions, starting (not surprisingly) with version 1. It isn't the 2,013th version, however. Somewhere along the way, Microsoft switched from using sequential numbers for versions to using years — an idea pioneered by the automotive industry, which sells things like 2013 Ford Mustangs as opposed to Mustang Version 9.3s.

Without going into boring detail about what's new in Access 2013, we can tell you that it provides the usual kind of stuff you find in new versions these days, such as more power and more flexibility; that you can do more things with it; and that — along the lines of the Holy Grail of Everything Computerish these days — it lets you take more advantage of everything the Internet has to offer.

About Access 2013 All-in-One For Dummies

If you've ever had the misfortune of trying to read anything written by one of the aforementioned database-administrator types, you know all about facing a decision among the least of *three* evils:

(Option 1) Try to figure out the software by guessing and poking until you break something.

(Option 2) Part with your hard-earned money to hire someone to do the work for you, only to have someone with poor taste in clothing look at you like you're an idiot every time you open your mouth.

(Option 3) Forget computers altogether, and stick with index cards.

Option 1 is the one that most people try first — until they get to the part where they start breaking things, and it starts costing money to get those things fixed. Option 2 is too odious to warrant serious consideration. Option 3 just isn't very realistic nowadays unless you're dealing with a tiny amount of personal information. Which leaves a new Option 4: this book.

The nerds who wrote this book are aware of the fact that *nobody* on the planet was *ever* born knowing what *any* technical term means. In fact, if at all possible, we avoid technical terms the way we do root canals. But because you probably face technical terms outside this book, we do explain what they mean along the way.

As a rule, big fat computer books aren't such great options. For that reason, this book isn't really a big fat computer book. It's several *smaller* computer books combined into one. Each small book represents a single topic that you can pursue — or ignore — as your tastes and immediate needs dictate.

The idea here is definitely *not* to try to read the book cover to cover (unless you're desperately seeking a cure for insomnia). Rather, use the table of contents up front, or the index in back, to look up information when trying to figure something out by guessing just isn't cutting it.

To prevent this book from topping 3,000 pages, we don't explain every possible way to do every possible thing in Access. Instead, we choose what we think are the most important database-management tasks, and we show you the best ways — in our opinions, at least — to do them.

Foolish Assumptions

Despite the fact that the word *Dummies* is clearly emblazoned on this book's cover and elsewhere, we don't presume that you're the junior partner in a ventriloquist act. (The machine you're working with, yes. You, no.) We do assume that you already know how to do some things, such as turn on your computer, and click and double-click things with your mouse. Maybe you can type with at least one finger.

We also assume that you know what those *key+key* references such as Ctrl+Esc mean. (Just in case you don't, though, they always mean "Hold down the first key, tap the second key, and then release the first key.") Also, we always use the term *press* to refer to something you do with the keyboard. The instruction "Press Ctrl+Esc," for example, means "Hold down the Ctrl key on your keyboard, tap the Esc key, and then release the Ctrl key." *Click,* on the other hand, is something you do with the mouse pointer on your computer screen and the buttons on your mouse.

We also assume (perhaps foolishly) that you know how to work menus — not that Access has many menus. When we discuss a menulike sequence, we use the word *choose* followed by the commands to choose separated by an ⇨ symbol. When we say "Choose Start⇨All Programs⇨Microsoft Office 2013⇨Access 2013," for example, that's short for "Click the Start button, click All Programs on the Start menu that appears, click Microsoft Office 2013 on the All Programs menu that appears, and then click Access 2013 on the last menu that appears."

Click, of course, means "Rest the mouse pointer on the item and then tap the left mouse button." When we tell you to *drag* something, we mean for you to move your mouse pointer to the item, click, and then hold down the left mouse button while moving the mouse. To *drop* the item, just release the mouse button after dragging it.

We also show things like website URLs (addresses) — those `www.whatever.com` things you see all over the place. We may even throw in an occasional e-mail address (the `somebody@somewhere.com` things) without explaining how to use them.

We hope that all these assumptions on our part aren't too foolish. But if we had to explain *all* that stuff here, there wouldn't be much space left for talking about Microsoft Access 2013.

How This Book Is Organized

If you've already looked at the "Contents at a Glance" page near the front of this book or the table of contents right after it, you already know how stuff is organized here. In that case, you may skip to the "Where to Go from Here" section. But because showing the contents a third time is customary, we follow suit here without the benefit of page numbers. This book is actually nine little books, organized as follows.

Book I: Getting Started with Access 2013

If you're using Microsoft Access for the first time, and you really don't know where else to go, starting with this minibook is a good idea. This stuff is what you really need to know to get anything done with Access.

Book II: Tables for Storing Your Data

Everything in Access centers on *data* (information) stored in tables (not the coffee kind — the columns-and-rows kind). You can't do much of anything with Access until you have some information stored in tables. This minibook is a good second stop for you *newbies* (beginners).

Book III: Queries (Or Getting Information from Your Data)

Data stored in tables tends to be pretty random and, eventually, plentiful. This minibook shows you how to pick and choose the information you want to see and how to organize that information in a way that's useful to you, such as alphabetically.

Book IV: Forms for Editing Data

You can get away without creating forms in your Access database, but if you get tired of looking at information stored in rows and columns, and you're up for being creative, forms are definitely worth getting into. This minibook shows you how.

Book V: Reporting in Words and Pictures

Whereas forms are a way to get creative with stuff on your screen, reports are a way to get creative with stuff you print on your computer's printer. This minibook shows you how you can do things like print form letters, create mailing labels, and summarize numeric data with totals and subtotals.

Book VI: Automation with Macros

Here's a technical term for you: *macros.* They're nothing to be intimidated by, though. Macros are just a way of writing simple instructions that tell Access how to do something you're sick of doing yourself. They're optional but more fun than the name implies. Find all the details in this minibook.

Book VII: Database Administration

This job sounds like a real yawn, we know. Sometimes, though, you've gotta do some sort-of-tedious things, such as make backup copies of your information or get other people to help you with boring stuff like typing information into your tables. Book VII is the place where we cover those tasks.

Book VIII: Programming in VBA

We didn't let this topic slide, because aspiring meganerds know that über-technogeeks make their money by automating Access with a language rather than macros. If you have no such aspirations, you can skip this minibook.

Book IX: Going Beyond Access

Reading Book IX is kind of like going beyond the final frontier, but with less excitement. The chapters in this minibook show you how to use Access to interact with, and move data to and from, other programs on your computer — or computers all over the world.

Appendix: Installing Microsoft Access

Finally, we present an appendix on how to install Microsoft Access 2013, in case you haven't already gotten that far. If Access is already on your computer, there's nothing noteworthy for you to see here. If you do need to install Access and don't feel like looking at the appendix, though, here's the condensed version: Insert your Microsoft Office or Microsoft Access disc into your computer's disc drive, wait a few seconds, and then follow the instructions that appear onscreen.

What You Don't Have to Read

Because reading the instructions is something everyone does only as a last resort — after guessing and trying to get help on the phone have failed — we try to point out things that you really don't have to read. *Sidebars,* for example (which have a gray background), are little chunks of text with their own titles. If the title looks boring, skip the whole thing.

We also put little *icons* (pictures) in the left margins to point out text that you can skip — or really shouldn't skip. The icons are pretty self-explanatory, so if you want to pass over the next section, that's fine by us.

Icons Used in This Book

As far as those presumably self-explanatory icons go, here are some explanations that you can probably skip (or, at best, glance at).

You probably don't want to ignore stuff that has a Warning icon, because if you do, you may regret it. It's not that you're gonna blow up your computer or the Internet or anything if you ignore a Warning — but the consequences may be inconvenient or unpleasant enough to justify spending a few seconds to read these little notes.

Tips may be worth reading if you're looking for a shortcut or a better way to do things. They're not as important as Warnings but may still be worth a few seconds of your time.

The Remember icon marks stuff that we already told you (and you may have forgotten), as well as things that are worth trying to keep in the back of your mind, even way back there — kinda like where you park your car when you go to the mall.

This book *is* a reference book, and we certainly don't expect you to read it cover to cover. Sometimes, though, you just have to know Subject x before Subject y even comes close to making any sense. So when we're forced to talk about a Subject y kind of thing, we use this icon to point out where Subject x is covered.

Technical Stuff definitely falls into the "insomnia cure" category.

Conventions Used in This Book

Speaking of insomnia, this book (like most books) follows certain conventions to alert you to certain things, as follows:

Boldface: Stuff you actually do while sitting at your computer is shown in boldface, to distinguish it from boring information that you probably don't care about anyway.

Italics: When reality rears its ugly head and we're forced to use a technical term, we always show that term in italics the first time we use it and define that term right there on the spot. You might forget the definition two minutes later, of course, but you can easily flip back a few pages and locate the definition amid all the other words on the page.

`Monofont`: *Monofont text* (text in that typeface right back there) represents *code* — instructions that are written for computers, rather than people, to follow. Computers are so stupid that the term *stupid* is a compliment; unconscious, nonthinking, nonbeings (aka machines) is more like it. Anyway, when you're writing instructions for computers, you *really* have to spell everything out for them, right down to the blank spaces between words. Monofont text makes it easy to see where you have to put the blank spaces so Access won't ask "Huh?" (Actually, it can't even say "Huh?" It's more likely to say something really stupid, like `"Syntax error in something or other."`)

Where to Go from Here

If you patiently read "How This Book Is Organized," earlier in this introduction, you probably know where you need to go next. If not, and if you're a beginner, you should head straight to Book I, Chapter 1 to get your bearings. If you already know some of the basics of Access, just pick whatever book or chapter talks about what you're struggling with right now.

Finally, thanks for buying, begging, borrowing, or stealing (just kidding with that last one) this book. We hope that it serves you well. To those of you who bought an extra copy, thanks for helping us pay down our credit cards a little.

Book I
Getting Started with Access 2013

Contents at a Glance

Chapter 1: Introducing Access 2013 9

Why Use a Database? 10
Plan, Plan, Plan.. 10
The Six Types of Access Objects.. 11
Essential Database Concepts 15

Chapter 2: Getting Started, Getting Around 17

Running Access.. 17
Opening a Database.. 19
Making Friends with the Access Window.................................... 22
Introducing Mission Control: The Navigation Pane 25
Viewing Objects in Your Database... 29
Creating, Deleting, Renaming, Copying, and Printing Objects.............. 31
Introducing Backstage View.. 32
Using Wizards 33
Getting Help.. 34
Saving Time with Keyboard Shortcuts 34

Chapter 3: Designing Your Database the Relational Way 37

What Are Tables, Fields, and Keys? 37
What Are Relationships? 40
Designing a Database 46
Choosing Field Types... 57
Storing Single Facts 60
Creating a Database 61

Chapter 1: Introducing Access 2013

In This Chapter

✔ **Getting a handle on Microsoft Access**

✔ **Listing the six types of Access objects**

✔ **Laying out some essential database concepts**

*A*ccess is the database-management program, part of the Microsoft Office suite, that enables you to maintain *databases* — collections of data arranged according to a fixed structure. Its structure makes the information easy to select, sort, display, and print in a variety of formats. With Access, you can create and maintain as many databases as you need. You can even share them with other people over a local area network or the Internet.

Access works with almost any kind of information. An Access database can be as simple as a list of addresses to replace your card file. Or you can create a wine-cellar database with information about each bottle in your cellar, or a bookstore-inventory database with information about books, publishers, customers, and special orders. Access can also handle complex databases that contain many types of information and lots of customized programming.

An Access database can contain lists of records about almost anything, from sales to sports scores. Unlike a spreadsheet program, Access makes information in lots of formats easy to display — including alphabetical listings, formatted reports, mailing labels, and fill-in-the-blank forms.

Access 2013 comes as part of the Microsoft Office 2013 Professional suite of programs, but it's also available as a separate, stand-alone product. Previous versions of Access have been part of previous Office editions — Access 2010 in Office 2010, Access 2007 in Office 2007, Access 2003 in Office 2003, Access 2002 in Office XP, and so on. Because Access is part of Microsoft Office, sharing information with Word documents and Excel spreadsheets is easy.

In this chapter, we introduce you to the components of an Access database and explain some key concepts related to developing and using Access databases.

Why Use a Database?

Many people use Microsoft Excel, another Office program, to manage their databases. Excel works for storing lists of things — up to a point. Go ahead and start with Excel if you're already comfortable with it, but you'll know that you're ready to move up to Access when

+ **You need to store the same pieces of information in several places.** You can use Excel formulas to duplicate data around a spreadsheet, and you can use the cut-and-paste technique to make copies, but both methods lead to errors.

+ **You don't want to look at your data as columnar tables.** Excel's database features (such as they are) require your data to be laid out in rows and columns. But what if you need a report in some other format? Displaying data in lots of formats is where Access shines.

+ **Your information consists of more than one list of records.** If your database includes information about several types of things — such as customers, orders, and products — you're ready for Access. Excel doesn't give you an easy way to connect and combine information from different columnar tables. Access, however, is a *relational database* that enables you to create forms and reports that include information from related tables.

+ **You want to check your data to ensure that it's correct.** Access allows you to validate data in far more rigorous ways than Excel does. Avoid "garbage in, garbage out"!

Plan, Plan, Plan

Databases are very different from spreadsheets and word processing documents. With spreadsheets and documents, you can just start typing, putting information where you want it to appear when you print the thing.

Databases don't work like that. If you just start typing information into a database, you'll have a total mess. Not to lay a major downer on you, but a database requires planning so that you put the right information in the right place. It's not rocket science, but it's necessary.

The first step is finding out what makes up an Access database, which is what this chapter is about. Chapter 2 of this minibook gets you into the Access program, clicking around and seeing what's there, and Chapter 3 is where you make your plan, designing your own database.

The Six Types of Access Objects

Access databases are made up of *objects* — things you can create, edit, and delete, each with its own name and settings. *Object-oriented* systems allow you to create these things one piece at a time, using pieces that fit together.

These objects can store, display, and print your data, as well as contain programs you write. At first, you'll probably use only a few types of objects, but as you customize your database, you may end up using all six types. You start with *tables* for storing data, *forms* for editing data onscreen, *reports* for printing data, and *queries* for selecting and combining data. Later, you may create *macros* and *modules,* which contain programs that you write.

In this section, we describe the main types of Access objects: tables, queries, forms, reports, macros, and modules.

Tables for storing your data

Tables are where you put your data. A *table* is an Access object that is made up of a series of *records* — the electronic equivalent of the index cards that make up an address list. Each record contains information about one thing, with the same pieces of information. In an address list, each record contains information about one person: name, address, and other facts. Each individual piece of information — such as first name, last name, or street address — is called a *field.*

Your database can contain many tables. A bookstore database, for example, can contain a Books table (with title, publisher, price, and other information about each book), a Vendors table for companies from which you buy books (with company name, address, discount terms, and other information about each vendor), and maybe a Customers table of your regular customers (with name, address, and other information). Figure 1-1 shows a table of names and addresses. Each row is a record, and the fields are shown in columns.

Figure 1-1: A table contains records (rows) and fields (columns).

Con	First Name	Last Name	Company	Address1	Address2	City	Stat	ZIPPostalCo
1	Tori	Pines	Arbor Classics	345 Pacific Coast Hwy	Suite 3232	Del Mar	CA	98765
2	Marilou	Midcalf		500, 999-6th Street SW		Edmonton	AB	T5J 2Z4
3	Wilma	Wannabe	Wilma Whistles	1121 River Road	Suite 121	Cornball	IA	54321-1234
4	Frankly	Unctuous		734 N. Rainbow Dr.		Staten Island	NY	19470
5	Margaret	Angstrom		P.O. Box 1295		Daneville	AK	92067
6	Simpson	Sarah		1370 Washington Lane		Buckingham	PA	19046
7			ABC Productions	Haverston Square	1132 Lincoln Bl	Doylestown	PA	18901
8	Hortense	Higglebotton		P.O. Box 1014	11224 El Secret	Escondido	AK	49384
9	Penny	Lopez		P.O. Box 10		New Hope	PA	18938
10	Matilda	Starbuck		323 Shire Lane		Skeedadle	OK	54321
11	Scott and Nate	Schumack		228 Hollywood Drive		Hollywood	FL	18914
12	Linda	Peterson		823 Paseo Cancun		Redmond	WA	91792
13	Ino	Yasha		1788 Port Carlo Circle		Framington	NM	54321
14			Wiley Widgets	97 Roberts Dr.		Nashua	NH	03063
15	Dominic	Kryzwickl		45 Albany Road		Maritime	RI	08053
16	Rosemary	Stickler		1205 Huntingdon Ct.		Willow Grove	PA	19090-3705

Record: ⏮ ◄ 1 of 37 ► ⏭ 🅺 No Filter   Search   ◄

After you set up tables in your database and type in (or import) information, you can sort the records, select records that match a criterion, and then display and print the records. You can create new tables, or you can link (connect) to existing tables in other Access databases or in databases created with programs like SQL Server and MySQL.

Proper design of your tables — choosing how many tables to create and which fields to store in which table — is key to creating a usable and flexible database. Chapter 3 of this minibook includes a step-by-step procedure for designing your database, and Book II explains how to create tables and fill them with data.

Queries for selecting your data

Queries are operations that slice and dice your data to answer specific data needs. The most commonly used type of query selects data from a table — perhaps the records you want to include in a report. You can create a query that shows you all the people in your address book who live in, say, Vermont, or all those for whom you don't have a phone number. To create this type of query, you enter *criteria* that specify what values you want to match in specific fields in the tables (**VT** in the State field to find Vermonters, an empty Phone Number field to find the phoneless, or both).

You can also use queries to combine information from several tables. A bookstore database may store book author names in the Books table and book-ordering information in the Purchase Orders table. A query can pull information from both these tables — to show, for example, all the Terry Pratchett novels you ordered in the past month. Queries can also create calculated fields, including totals, counts, and averages.

Another type of query is the *action query,* which does something to the records you select — copies records from one table to another, makes a change in all the records you select, deletes records you select, and that sort of thing. *Crosstab queries* help you analyze the information in your tables by summarizing how many records contain specific combinations of values.

Queries are the way you get useful information out of your tables, and you'll probably create zillions of them as you play with your database. Book III explains how to create and use queries of all kinds.

Forms for editing and displaying your data

An easy way to enter data, especially in more than one related table, is to use a *form* — an Access object that displays information from one or more tables onscreen. You can have all kinds of fun with forms:

✦ Edit your data or type new records.

✦ Choose the layout of the table's information on the form.

✦ Specify the order in which your items appear.

✦ Use lines and boxes to group items.

✦ Add drop-down menus, radio buttons, and other types of onscreen controls for entering and editing data.

Figure 1-2 shows a form for entering names and addresses into the Address Book table shown in Figure 1-1.

But why stop there? You can build intelligence into forms, too — program some smart boxes that automatically capitalize what you type, or check your entry against a table of valid values.

After your database goes into production — that is, when you start using it for its intended purpose — forms become your most-used Access objects. As go the forms, so goes the database — so Book IV explains how to design, create, modify, and use forms.

Reports for printing your data

Forms are designed primarily to appear onscreen. *Reports,* on the other hand, are designed to be printed, as shown in Figure 1-3. Like forms, reports display information from tables; you get to choose the layout of the information. Most reports are based on queries; you use a query to choose the information that appears in the report. The *report design* defines the order in which records appear; which fields appear where; and which fonts, font sizes, lines, and spacing are used. (Control freaks, rejoice!)

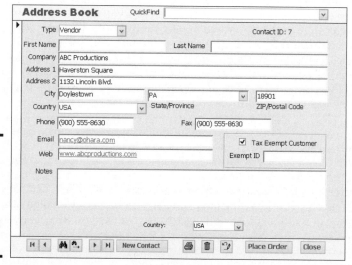

Figure 1-2: A form shows information from one table record at a time.

Figure 1-3:
A report
lets you put
Access data
on paper.

Customers			
Last Name	First Name	Phone	Email
Angstrom	Margaret	(713) 555-3232	margaret@angstrom.com
Bebop	Stacey	(453) 555-2335	stacey@bebop.com
Biasini	Carlos	(184) 555-7493	carlos@biasini.com
Citrus	Michael	(362) 555-2724	michael@citrus.com
Costello	Karen	(600) 555-6069	karen@costello.com
Crusher	Kimerbly	(925) 555-1635	kimerbly@crusher.com
Doerr	Monica	(476) 555-9194	monica@doerr.com
Escovedo	George	(110) 555-5015	george@escovedo.com

In addition to creating reports on normal paper, you can create reports for
printing on envelopes, labels, or other media. Access comes with report
wizards that make creating fancy reports easy. It can also print charts and
cross-tabulations *(crosstabs)* based on the data in your database.

You're not limited to printing reports on paper; you can also save reports as
PDF (Portable Document Format) and XPS (Microsoft's PDF equivalent) files
for e-mailing or posting on the web.

Book V covers how to create and print reports, charts, and crosstabs.

Macros for saving keystrokes

Access includes two separate programming languages: one for macros and
a separate one (Visual Basic for Applications) for larger programs. *Macros*
are programs that automate the commands you give when you use Access.
Every program in Microsoft Office enables you to write macros to work more
efficiently. You could write a macro, for example, that moves the cursor to
the last record in the Orders table whenever you open the Order Entry form.
(What are the chances that you'd want to edit your very first order? Most
of us are likelier to want to edit the *last* order or enter a new order.) Or you
could write a macro that moves the cursor to the next applicable blank in a
form, based on the entries you've made so far.

After you get some practice in creating macros, you can create buttons on
your forms that run the macros when you click them. You can also tell your
form to run a macro automatically whenever you move to a certain field
on the form or enter data in that field. Handy! Access 2013 enables you to
assign a *data macro* to a field in a table, too, so that you can trigger an action
whenever your data changes. You can automatically change other values to
match or validate other data against the values you just changed.

You don't have to be a programmer to create macros; Access helps you
write them by providing menus of commands. Book VI explains how to
create nifty and useful macros to clean up data entry — and other items —
automatically.

Modules for writing your own programs

Okay, now we come to the serious programming stuff: *modules,* which is another term for Visual Basic programs. Visual Basic for Applications (VBA) is a programming language based on the age-old BASIC language; it's specifically geared toward Access and other Office programs. Macros are fine for saving a few keystrokes or cleaning up the data you enter in a field, but when the going gets complex, use VBA.

Programming isn't for the technologically faint of heart, and fortunately, it's rarely necessary. But when everything else is done in your database, take a look at Book VIII for an introduction to VBA programming. Writing small programs isn't all that hard — and if you acquire a taste for programming, who knows what you'll end up creating?

Essential Database Concepts

Here are the Five Commandments of Databases. (Aren't you relieved that there aren't ten?) You'll find lots more important rules and guidelines throughout this book as you discover how to work with various Access objects, but these five rules apply right from the start, no matter what kind of database you're using:

✦ **Store information where it belongs, not where it appears.** Where you store information has nothing to do with where it appears. In a spreadsheet, you type information where you want it to appear when you print the spreadsheet, but databases work differently. In a database, you store information in tables based on the *structure* of the information. (Don't worry — Chapter 3 of this minibook explains how to figure out the structure of your data.) Each piece of information likely appears in lots of reports. In a database for an online bookstore, for example, book titles and author names appear on your invoices, purchase orders, and sales receipts. But the right place to *store* those book titles and author names probably is the Books table, not the Sales table or the Purchase Orders table.

✦ **Store information as it really exists, not as you want it to appear in a specific report.** This rule is a corollary to the first rule. If you want book titles to appear in all uppercase (capital) letters in your purchase orders, Access can capitalize the titles for you. Store the book titles with correct capitalization so you aren't stuck with them in all caps on every report. Access has built-in formatting options that control the way that text, numbers, and dates are formatted, as described in Book II, Chapter 1. Functions are also available for more advanced formatting, as you learn in Book III, Chapter 2.

✦ **Avoid garbage in, garbage out (GIGO).** If you don't bother to create a good, sensible design for your database — and if you aren't careful about entering correct, clean data — your database will end up full of garbage. A well-designed database is easier to maintain than a badly designed one because each piece of information is stored only once, in a clearly named field in a clearly named table, with the proper validation rules in place. Yes, it sounds like a lot of work, but cleaning up a database of 10,000 incorrect records is (pardon the understatement) even more work. See Book II, Chapter 5 for ways to avoid GIGO.

✦ **Separate your data from your programs.** If you create a database to be shared with (or distributed to) other people, store all the tables in one database (the *back end)* and all the other objects in another database (the *front end)*. Then you can link these two databases to make everything work. Separating the tables from everything else streamlines the whole rigmarole of updating queries, forms, reports, or other stuff later without disturbing the data in the tables. See Book VII, Chapter 2 for details on separating a database into a front end and back end.

✦ **Back up early and often.** Make a backup of your database every day. With luck, your office already has a system of regular (probably nightly) backups that includes your database. If not, make a backup copy of your database at regular intervals, and certainly back up before making any major changes. See Book VII, Chapter 1 for information on how to make backups.

Chapter 2: Getting Started, Getting Around

In This Chapter

✔ Starting Access and opening a database

✔ Understanding the Access window

✔ Choosing commands from the Ribbon and the Quick Access toolbar

✔ Getting around via the Navigation Pane

✔ Viewing and working with Access objects

✔ Managing your database in Backstage View

✔ Saving keystrokes with keyboard shortcuts

*B*efore you can do much with Access, you have to get it installed and running. If Access isn't already installed on your computer, see the appendix for directions. Then come back to this chapter for pointers on how to run Access and decipher the stuff you see in the Access window.

Running Access

Access

Windows usually provides more than one way to perform a task; starting Access is no exception. In Windows 7, to run it from the Start button, click Start and choose All Programs⇨Microsoft Access 2013 (unless you've rearranged your Start menu). After you've run it a few times, Access probably will appear on your Start menu, so choosing Start⇨Microsoft Access 2013 will get it going. In Windows 8, just click the Access 2013 tile on the Start screen.

Another way to get the program started is to double-click the name or icon of an Access database in any Windows Explorer window or pretty much anywhere else you see files listed. (This method both starts Access and opens the database you double-click.) Alternatively, double-click the Access icon if it appears on your Windows desktop.

When you start Access without opening a database, the Access 2013 window shows the Welcome screen. On all subsequent launches of Access, what you see looks like Figure 2-1, showing Backstage View. When no database is open, Backstage View shows your choices for opening an existing database or building a new database. We describe opening and creating databases in the rest of this chapter. If you're running Access for the first time, see the nearby sidebar "Choosing whether to update Office automatically."

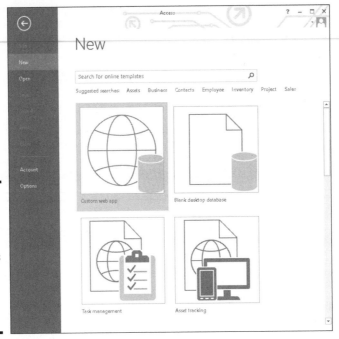

Figure 2-1:
Access's
Backstage
View
displays lots
of options
for creating
a new
database.

Choosing whether to update Office automatically

The first time you run any Office 2013 program, you see the Welcome to Microsoft Office 2013 dialog box.

Like Windows itself, Microsoft Office can download and install updates automatically. Both the Use Recommended Settings and Install Updates Only settings tell Office to receive new updates whenever Microsoft makes them available. The first option also enables these features:

✓ **Online help:** The help system includes information from http://office.microsoft.com, where Microsoft posts updated support information.

✓ **Diagnostic programs:** Office may download and install small program files that help diagnose problems.

✓ **Customer Experience Improvement Program:** You're signed up for Microsoft's Customer Experience Improvement Program, which enables the company to collect anonymous information about how you and millions of other people use Microsoft software so that Microsoft can make new versions even better.

Choose Use Recommended Settings or Install Updates Only, depending how you feel about these three additional features.

Avoid that last setting, however. Don't Make Changes prevents you from getting security updates that you may need to keep your computer virus-free.

When a database is already open, Backstage View displays information about the database as a whole — rather than about specific objects in the database — and the commands that affect the entire database. (See "Introducing Backstage View," near the end of this chapter.)

Opening a Database

Before you can work on a database, you have to open it in Access. If you have an Access database, you can open it by following the instructions in this section. For now, don't worry about which version of Access it was created in; for more details on that topic, see "Opening oldies," later in this chapter.

Okay, but wait a minute: Before you can open a new database, you have to create it! If you want to try Access but don't have a database to work with, skip to "Creating a sample database from a template," later in this chapter, to try Access with a sample database.

Only one database can be open at one time in Access. If a database is already open, Access closes it when you open a new database.

To open a database, follow these steps:

1. **Click the File tab on the Ribbon if you don't already see Backstage View (refer to Figure 2-1).**

People missed having a File command in Office 2007, so Microsoft replaced 2007's Office button with the File tab; it's in the top-left corner of all Office 2010 and 2013 applications.

2. **Click Open on the menu.**

The screen changes, showing databases that have recently been used and giving you a chance to browse for one that isn't listed:

- *Recent:* Choosing Recent takes you to a list of databases you've used recently.

- *SkyDrive:* SkyDrive takes you to your own private place in the cloud where your databases and other Office 2013 files may be stored.

- *Computer:* This option, of course, takes you to the computer you're sitting in front of, as well as any computers that may be connected to it on a network.

- *Add a Place:* Choose this option if the database you want is located somewhere that the preceding three options don't cover.

3. **Choose a place to search and then select the filename in the list that appears.**

You may need to browse to the file by clicking the Browse button that appears.

Access opens the database.

If you see an alarming security message, check out the nearby sidebar "Security warning: Active content disabled."

When you work with a database, panes and tabs appear within the Access window. Exactly what you see depends on the database. A simple database displays the Navigation Pane, described later in this chapter. Some databases display a form and hide the Navigation Pane. You can also program the database to hide the standard Access components (see Book VII, Chapter 3).

Security warning: Active content disabled

If you try to open a database containing any programming (in the form of macros, Visual Basic for Applications [VBA] procedures, or action queries, which we explain in later minibooks), Microsoft wants you to know that you're taking a chance and displays this warning:

Before you panic, consider that unlike viruses in the real world, computer viruses don't just happen. A *virus* is a program that must be intentionally written by a human to do bad things and also to make copies of itself.

So why does Access display a security warning? The warning appears whenever you open *any* document that contains any macros, VBA modules, or action queries. Access doesn't know whether the database contains viruses; it just tells you that programs of some sort — not necessarily viruses — are in the database. To protect you, Access opens the database, turns off the capability to execute code, and displays a warning.

What you do next depends on where the database you're opening came from:

- **If you downloaded the database from an unknown, dubious source,** leave the database content disabled. To be even safer, close the database; create a new blank database; and import the tables, queries, forms, and reports into it (but don't import any macros or VBA code).

- **If the database came from someone within your organization whom you trust,** click the Enable Content button on the message bar.

- **If you created the database,** and that database is *supposed* to contain macros, VBA procedures, or action queries, you can prevent Access from displaying the security message when you open the database. (See Book VI, Chapter 1 for details on security settings for a database that contains macros or VBA modules.)

If you have antivirus software, you'd do well to scan any and all files you download from the Internet for viruses before you actually open such files. These days, most viruses spread through e-mail attachments or files downloaded from the Web. Virtually all antivirus programs automatically scan all incoming e-mail attachments for viruses before allowing you to open them. *The Internet For Dummies*, 13th Edition, by John R. Levine and Margaret Levine Young (John Wiley & Sons, Inc.), describes viruses and spyware, and discusses how to avoid them.

Opening oldies

Access 2007 introduced a new file format for Access, and Access 2013 uses the same format. Access 2013, 2010, and 2007 create .accdb files, whereas Access 2003 and older versions save databases as .mdb files.

Access 2013 can open databases created in Access 2003 and older versions — in addition, of course, to those created in Access 2007, 2010, and 2013. If you create new fields or objects that use new features in Access 2013, those objects won't work if you open the database later in an older version.

Saving in a different version

If you know someone who has Access 2003 or older and needs to use your database, you can save it in Access 2002-2003 format or even in Access 2000 format. Click the File tab on the Ribbon to display Backstage View; then click Save As to see your Database File Types options, which include Access 2002-2003 Database and Access 2000 Database.

You shouldn't use the new-to-2013 features if you know that you need to save the database in an older format.

I have that open already!

Access is a *multiuser database,* which means that more than one person can open an Access database at the same time. The usual way that this works is that several computers on a network (usually, a local area network in an office) run Access, and all the computer users can open the same database at the same time. Access keeps track of who's doing what and prevents the users from (virtually) crashing into one another. If two people are trying to edit the same thing at the same time, the situation can be tricky; Access locks out the second person until the first person is done with the edit.

For more information on multiple people using a database at the same time, see Book VII, Chapter 2.

Creating a sample database from a template

If you want to look around in Access but haven't created your first database yet, you can create a ready-made database from one of the templates that come with the program. Many templates reconfigure the Navigation Pane and make other changes in the way that Access looks, so you need to give a command or two to return Access to its usual appearance. Follow these steps:

1. **Run Access, using one of the many methods described earlier in this chapter.**

    In Windows 7, you might click Start and choose All Programs⇨Microsoft Office⇨Microsoft Access 2013. In Windows 8, just click the Access 2013 tile on the Start screen.

You see Backstage View (refer to Figure 2-1, earlier in this chapter).

2. **Click New, if it's not already selected.**

   Several templates are displayed.

3. **To keep things simple at this point, just select the Blank desktop database.**

   A dialog box appears, asking you to give your database a name.

4. **Fill in the name of your new database and then click the Create button.**

   The Access window appears, with the Fields tab on the Ribbon selected. Access assumes that you want to start by creating a table, so it has conveniently done so, naming it Table1. You can always change the table name later. Now you can add fields to your new table.

Making Friends with the Access Window

After you have a database open, you're ready to have a look around. Figure 2-2 shows the Access window for your newly created database, with the major parts labeled. On the left is the Navigation Pane, which lists objects in the database. (If all you see is a vertical stripe labeled Navigation Pane, click it to see the Navigation Pane.)

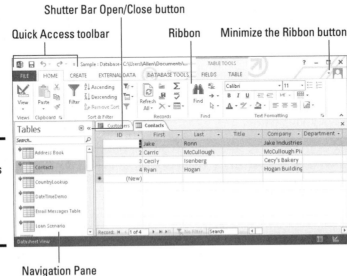

Figure 2-2: The Access window with a database open.

Across the top is the Ribbon, the supermenu that all Microsoft Office programs use. Below the Ribbon and to the right of the Navigation Pane (if any space is left on your screen) is space for you to see and work with the various objects that make up the database: tables, queries, forms, reports, and the rest.

The Ribbon

If you're used to Microsoft Office 2010 or 2007, you're probably not alarmed that Access has no menu bar — no File, Edit, . . . series of commands marching across the top of the window. Instead, you see tabs and a bunch of buttons at the top of the window: the Ribbon, which replaced the menu and toolbars in Office 2007. It's been freshened up for Office 2013 but is essentially the same.

Navigating the tabs

The Ribbon has five tabs that always appear, and additional tabs appear when particular objects are open. The Fields tab, for example, is available when a table is active. These additional tabs are known as *contextual tabs*.

The tabs that always appear are

+ **File:** Clicking the File tab displays Backstage View, described in "Introducing Backstage View," later in this chapter.

+ **Home:** The first button on the Home tab (shown in Figure 2-2) is View, which allows you to change the view of the object displayed. You can view an object in Design view to create and configure it and use other views to actually use the object. The Home tab also contains buttons used for dealing with records: formatting, creating new records, creating totals, and spell checking, as well as sorting, filtering, and finding data. We describe many of the buttons on the Home tab in Book II, Chapters 3 and 4.

+ **Create:** This tab is for — what else? — making new objects in your database. Books II through VI and Book VIII describe how to create the types of Access objects.

+ **External Data:** This tab contains commands for importing and exporting data and objects (see Book II, Chapter 4), collecting data via e-mail using Outlook (see Book II, Chapter 4), and connecting and synchronizing with SharePoint (see Book IX, Chapter 3).

+ **Database Tools:** The Database Tools tab contains commands for running macros (see Book VI), creating VBA modules (see Book VIII), creating relationships between tables (discussed in Book II, Chapter 1), documenting or analyzing your database (see Book VII, Chapter 1), connecting your database to SharePoint or SQL Server (described in Book IX), and performing other advanced tasks.

The Ribbon presents buttons in labeled *groups* separated by vertical lines. The Home tab of the Ribbon shown in Figure 2-2, for example, contains the Views, Clipboard, Sort & Filter, Records, Find, and Text Formatting groups. In this book, we might tell you something like this: "Click the Filter button in the Sort & Filter group on the Home tab of the Ribbon." To find that button, click the Home tab on the Ribbon, find the Sort & Filter group on that tab, and then find the Filter button within that group.

Every button has a descriptive tooltip. If you hover the mouse pointer over a button, you see the tooltip, which displays the name of the button, a keyboard shortcut that you can press instead of clicking the button (press Ctrl+F instead of clicking the Find button, for example), and a brief description of what the button does.

Sometimes, a group contains so many buttons that all the buttons don't fit on the Ribbon. In such a case, the group has a little arrow in its bottom-right corner. (To see an example, take a look at the Clipboard group in Figure 2-2, earlier in this chapter.) Click that arrow to see the rest of the buttons — usually in a dialog box that pops up.

Minimizing the Ribbon

The Ribbon takes up lots of screen space. To minimize it, double-click the active tab, press Ctrl+F1, or click the Minimize the Ribbon button (the upward-pointing caret in the bottom-right corner of the Ribbon). You can change what the Ribbon displays by right-clicking a tab and then choosing Customize the Ribbon from the contextual menu that pops up.

You can use keyboard shortcuts (covered near the end of this chapter) while the Ribbon is minimized.

Hiding and showing the Ribbon

The Ribbon rolls up after you click any button. Click any Ribbon tab to redisplay it.

To redisplay the Ribbon for good, click the Minimize the Ribbon button again, press Ctrl+F1 again, or double-click a Ribbon tab.

The Quick Access toolbar

Toolbars aren't completely gone! Access still displays a small Quick Access toolbar (shown in Figure 2-2, earlier in this chapter) immediately above the left end of the Ribbon.

The Quick Access toolbar includes three of the most commonly used buttons in Access:

✦ **Save:** Saves changes to the current object. (How long will Microsoft continue to use a floppy-disk icon to mean Save, even though most of us haven't touched a floppy disk in years?)

✦ **Undo:** Undoes the last undoable action.

✦ **Redo:** Redoes the last redoable action.

You can easily customize the Quick Access toolbar. Follow these steps:

1. **Click the fourth button from the left: the down arrow.**

A list of buttons that you can add to the Quick Access toolbar appears.

2. **Choose any command (Open, Quick Print, and so on) to add its button to the toolbar.**

If you don't see the command that you want to add, find its button on the Ribbon, right-click it, and choose Add to Quick Access Toolbar from the contextual menu. If you can't find the appropriate button on the Ribbon, add it to the toolbar by choosing More Commands from the Customize Quick Access Toolbar menu. The Customize Quick Access Toolbar menu drops down when you click the down arrow at the right end of the Quick Access toolbar.

Introducing Mission Control: The Navigation Pane

The Navigation Pane — the area on the left edge of the Access window below the heading, which could be All Access Objects, Tables, Queries, or something else (refer to Figure 2-2, earlier in this chapter) — is the table of contents for your database. From it, you can open any table, query, form, report, macro, or VBA module in the database simply by double-clicking the object's name. When you right-click an object in the Navigation Pane, you can choose commands from the contextual menu to open the object in an alternative view; change its name; copy, delete, import, export, hide, or display it; and view the object's properties.

Press F11 to toggle the display of the Navigation Pane, which can roll up into a narrow vertical ribbon. You can also toggle the display by clicking the Shutter Bar Open/Close button (such an egregiously long term for such a tiny button!), which is the double arrow in the top-right corner of the pane (refer to Figure 2-2, earlier in this chapter).

You can make the Navigation Pane narrower or wider by dragging its right edge.

Choosing how database objects are grouped

The Navigation Pane displays the objects in the database in groups. Each group has a heading. To display and hide the group objects, click the double arrow at the right of the group's name.

The familiar way to group database objects is by object type, but you have other choices, too. Click the down arrow on the Navigation Pane's title bar to see the grouping options (see Figure 2-3). The Navigation Pane's menu has two sections: Navigate to Category and Filter by Group. The options in these sections vary, but you can choose one option from the Navigate to Category section at the top of the menu and another from the Filter by Group section at the bottom of the menu.

Figure 2-3:
The
Navigation
Pane's
grouping
options.

You can configure your Navigation Pane by following these steps:

1. **Click the down arrow on the Navigation Pane's title bar.**

You see the Navigation Pane menu. Table 2-1 describes what each option on the menu does.

2. **In the Navigate to Category section, specify how you want objects to be grouped.**

The most popular options are Object Type (which lists tables, queries, forms, reports, macros, and VBA modules, each with its own heading) and Tables and Related Views (which lists all tables and the objects that relate to them).

By default, Access groups database objects by Tables and Related Views.

3. **In the Filter by Group section, specify whether you want to show all objects or only some of them.**

If you usually like to see all objects, choose All Access Objects. When your database gets large, you can change your mind.

The Filter by Group options change when you choose a different Navigate to Category option to list the relevant choices. If you choose to navigate by Object Type, for example, the filter options are different types of objects (tables, queries, forms, and so on). If you choose to navigate by Tables and Related Views, the filter options are the names of the tables in the database.

Table 2-1	Options for Grouping Database Objects
Option	*What It Does*
Custom	Displays objects grouped in the way that you define. See the nearby sidebar "Creating custom groups in the Navigation Pane."
Object Type	Displays objects grouped by object type (Tables, Queries, Forms, Reports, Macros, and Modules), with a heading for each.
Tables and Related Views	Displays objects grouped by table — that is, group names are the same as table names, and the group consists of the table and objects that are related to it in the database. Objects may appear in more than one group.
Created Date	Displays objects grouped by creation date. Groups are Today, Last Week, Two Weeks Ago, Last Month, and Older.
Modified Date	Displays objects grouped by the date when they were last modified. Groups are Today, Last Week, Two Weeks Ago, Last Month, and Older.

Choosing size and details for Navigation Pane objects

You can configure the Navigation Pane to show object names, icons, or more information about each object. Right-click the title bar of the Navigation Pane or the empty space at the bottom of the Navigation Pane, choose View By from the contextual menu, and then choose one of the following options from the submenu:

✦ **Details:** This option displays the name and type of the object, the date it was created, and the date it was last modified.

✦ **Icon:** This option displays a larger icon for each object, leaving more space between listed objects.

✦ **List:** List is the default option — the one that you see in the figures throughout this book. Access displays each object with an icon indicating its type and its name.

Creating custom groups in the Navigation Pane

Rather than use the default categories for Navigation Pane groups, you can create your own custom groups in the Navigation Options dialog box and then drag database objects into the new groups. In a database for a small bookstore, for example, you might want to have one group for the objects that your purchase manager uses and another group for your bookkeeper. Here's how you create those groups:

1. **Right-click the title bar of the Navigation Pane or the empty space at the bottom of the Navigation Pane and choose Navigation Options from the contextual menu.**

   You see the Navigation Options dialog box. The Categories list on the left shows options that appear in the Navigate to Category section of the Navigation Pane's menu. The list on the right, named Groups for Tables and Related Views, shows the options for the selected category.

2. **Select Custom in the Categories list, or create a new category by clicking the Add Item button and then giving your new category a name.**

   The right list shows the options for the selected category.

3. **Create new groups in the right list by clicking the Add Group button and then selecting the groups you want to appear in the Navigation Pane.**

4. **Change the order of the groups, if necessary, by clicking the up and down arrows that appear when a group is selected.**

Be sure to leave the Unassigned Objects category selected until you've assigned objects to their groups.

5. **Click OK to close the Navigation Options dialog box.**

6. **Click the down arrow on the Navigation Pane's title bar and choose Custom or the category you created from the menu.**

   You see the groups you created in Step 3, and the database objects appear in the Unassigned Objects group.

7. **Assign objects to groups by following these steps:**

   a. *Select single objects, or select multiple objects by holding down Ctrl as you click.*

   b. *Drag objects to their new groups, or right-click the object, choose Add to Group from the contextual menu, and choose the group name.*

   When you add an object to a custom group, you create a shortcut to the object. (The shortcut arrow appears with the object's icon.) You can rename a shortcut by right-clicking it and choosing Rename Shortcut from the contextual menu.

8. **When all objects are assigned to groups, deselect the Unassigned Objects group.**

For old hands who grew up with previous editions of Access, custom categories provide a way of organizing objects that replaces some of the functionality of switchboards, which were used in earlier versions of Access.

Sorting objects in the Navigation Pane

You can sort objects within a group in the Navigation Pane by right-clicking the title bar of the Navigation Pane or the empty space at the bottom of the Navigation Pane, choosing Sort By from the contextual menu, and then choosing an option from the submenu. You can select a sort order (ascending or descending) and an attribute to sort by (Name, Type, Created Date, or Modified Date). You can also choose Remove Automatic Sorts (the last choice on the menu).

Searching for an object

If your database contains dozens or even hundreds of objects, they can be hard to find. Luckily, the Navigation Pane includes a Search bar, which appears just below the title of the Navigation Pane. You can type words and press Enter to find objects that contain those words in their titles.

If the Search bar doesn't appear, right-click the Navigation Pane's title bar and choose Search Bar from the contextual menu. Repeat this procedure to make the Search bar go away.

Viewing Objects in Your Database

Chapter 1 of this minibook describes the six kinds of objects that make up an Access database: tables, queries, forms, reports, macros, and VBA modules. (No, you don't have to memorize this list!) When you open an object to work with it, you choose which *view,* or onscreen format, to display it in. You can open a table in Design view to design the fields that make up the table, for example, or you can open it in Datasheet view to enter and edit the data in the table. This entire book describes how to use views to create and configure objects and then use them to manage your data.

When you double-click an object's name in the Navigation Pane, Access opens the object in the default view for that type of object. For tables, for example, the default view is Datasheet, because after you create a table, you're likely to want to type records in it.

To close an open object, click the X to the right of the object tab when the object is active, or right-click the tab and choose Close from the contextual menu.

Viewing lots of objects at the same time

You can open more than one object at the same time. You can open a table in Datasheet view, for example, to look at your data while you're working in Design view to create a form for editing that data.

There are two ways to view multiple objects in Access:

✦ **Overlapping windows:** Access 2003 and earlier versions use this system, in which each object appears in its own window within the Access window, as discussed in "Creating, Deleting, Renaming, Copying, and Printing Objects," later in this chapter. You can resize windows and move them around in whatever arrangement you like. If you like over-lapping windows, and your copy of Access is set to Tabbed documents (described next), you can. Click the File tab to display Backstage View; choose Options; and then, in the Access Options dialog box, choose Current Database. In the Application Options section, set Document Window Options to Overlapping Windows.

✦ **Tabbed documents:** Access 2007 instituted a new way of arranging the objects that you have open. Each object appears with an object tab that bears its name. When you click the object tab, you see that object. Figure 2-2, earlier in this chapter, shows tabbed documents.

If Access is set to Overlapping Windows, and you want to use tabbed documents, you can. Click the File tab to display Backstage View, choose Options, and choose Current Database in the Access Options dialog box. In the Application Options section, set Document Window Options to Tabbed Documents.

Switching views

After you open an object, you can look at it in a different view. Here are several methods:

✦ Click the View button on the Home tab of the Ribbon. (It's the only button in the Views group.) This button switches between the current view and the most recently displayed view.

✦ To choose among all the available views for the object, click the bottom half (the little arrow) of the View button and choose a view from the drop-down menu.

✦ Click one of the View shortcuts (shown in Figure 2-2) at the right end of the status bar, in the bottom-right corner of the Access window. Each view has a button; hover your mouse over a button to see the name of the view.

✦ Right-click the object tab and choose the view you want from the con-textual menu.

Creating, Deleting, Renaming, Copying, and Printing Objects

Throughout this book, we tell you how to create and modify tables, forms, reports, and other Access objects by using the Navigation Pane. Several tasks that work the same way for all Access objects crop up time and time again, so you may as well find out about them right here:

✦ **Creating an object:** Click the appropriate button on the Create tab of the Ribbon (see Figure 2-4). You usually see options to create the object by running a wizard that steps you through the process or by using Design view — a window with settings for designing the object.

Figure 2-4:
The Create
tab of the
Ribbon.

See Book II, Chapter 1 for information about creating tables; Book II, Chapter 2 for more on Design view; Book III for queries; Book IV for forms; Book V for reports; Book VI for macros; and Book VIII for VBA modules.

✦ **Deleting an object:** Select the object in the Navigation Pane, and press the Delete key. Simple enough! Clicking the Delete button on the Home tab of the Ribbon works, too, as does right-clicking the object and then choosing Delete from the contextual menu. Access asks whether you're really, truly sure before blowing the object away. Just remember that when you delete a table, you delete all its data, too.

✦ **Renaming an object:** Click the name of the object and press F2, or right-click the name and choose Rename from the contextual menu. Either way, a box appears around the object's name. Type a new name, and press Enter. Press Esc if you change your mind.

✦ **Copying an object:** Select the object you want to copy, press Ctrl+C, move your cursor to where you want to create the copy, and press Ctrl+V. (The Copy and Paste buttons in the Clipboard group on the Home tab of the Ribbon work too.) Access displays a Paste As dialog box, asking what name to use for the copy. Type a name, and click OK.

When you're creating a form or report, modifying a copy of an existing report is faster than starting a new one from scratch.

✦ **Printing an object:** Select or open the object you want to print and then press Ctrl+P. Alternatively, click the File tab on the Ribbon to display Backstage View, click Print, and choose one of the following options:

Quick Print (to use the existing printer settings), Print (to select printer settings), or Print Preview (to see what you're about to print before wasting paper on it).

You can find lots more about printing in Book V, Chapter 2, which talks about making and printing reports.

✦ **Creating a shortcut to an object:** If you frequently want to start Access, open your database, and immediately open a specific object, you can create a Windows shortcut that performs all three tasks. The object shortcut can live on your Windows desktop, or you can launch Access from the Start screen by right-clicking a blank area and then clicking All Apps on the colored band that appears at the bottom of the screen. Access 2013 is listed in the Microsoft Office 2013 group.

Introducing Backstage View

In Access 2013, as is the case with Access 2010, you click the File tab on the Ribbon to display Backstage View, a page of commands and settings that apply to the entire database or to your Access program. Figure 2-1, at the beginning of this chapter, shows Backstage View when no database is open. Figure 2-5 shows Backstage View with a database open. The Info command is selected by default when you display Backstage View.

Figure 2-5: The Info command in Backstage View shows information about your database.

When the Info command is selected, as in Figure 2-5, you see buttons that allow you to compact or repair a database, or encrypt it with a password. You can also choose the following commands below Info in the left pane:

✦ **New:** Shows you ways to create a new database.

✦ **Open:** Displays several locations that might contain the database you want to open, among them Recent, SkyDrive, and Computer (refer to "Opening a Database," earlier in this chapter).

✦ **Save:** Saves the active database.

✦ **Save As:** Saves the active database or file in any of several file types; also enables you to create an executable-only file or to back up your database.

✦ **Print:** Prints the selected object. *Note:* This command is the only one in Backstage View that affects only the object that was selected when you clicked the File tab.

✦ **Close:** Closes the database.

✦ **Account:** Displays some information about this instance of Access and gives you the option of selecting a background theme.

✦ **Options:** Displays the Access Options dialog box, which enables you to configure the Access program, including customizing the Ribbon and the Quick Access toolbar.

Using Wizards

Years ago, in a land far, far away (Washington state, actually), Microsoft invented *wizards,* programs that step you through the process of executing a commonly used command. Instead of scrolling through a big, hairy-looking dialog box with zillions of options, you step through a wizard, which asks you one or two questions at a time and uses the information you've already provided before asking for more input. All programs in Microsoft Office, including Access, come with wizards.

Wizards appear in windows that pop up in response to a command. All Microsoft wizards ask a series of questions. Answer each question and click the Next button at the bottom of the window to move to the next step. If you want to go back and change the answer you gave in an earlier window, click the Back button. You can bag the whole thing by clicking Cancel. The Finish button is unavailable until you've provided enough information for the wizard to complete its task.

When you're using a wizard, you can select an item in a list by clicking a single arrow pointing to the right or select all items in a list by clicking a double arrow pointing to the right. Deselect an item by clicking an arrow button that points to the left. If you have questions, refer to the section of the book about that particular wizard.

Getting Help

Access offers online help, which can be quite useful, so it's worth learning how to use it. Here's the drill for asking the Access help system a question:

1. **Click the Help button (the question-mark icon in the top-right corner of the Access window), or press F1.**

   The Access Help window appears.

2. **Type some search words in the Search box (labeled Search Online Help) and then press Enter or click the magnifying-glass icon.**

   Access searches its help system for matches and displays any search results.

3. **Click the result that seems to apply to what you're looking for.**

We find the following websites to be helpful for getting answers to questions about Access:

✦ **Access for Developers:** http://msdn.microsoft.com/access

✦ **The Access Web:** http://access.mvps.org/access

✦ **Microsoft Support:** http://support.microsoft.com

✦ **Microsoft TechNet:** http://technet.microsoft.com

Saving Time with Keyboard Shortcuts

Some people like to keep their hands on the keyboard as much as possible. For a fast typist, pressing keys is quicker and more efficient than pointing and clicking with the mouse. For those nimble-fingered folks, Access (like most other Windows programs) includes *keyboard shortcuts* — key combinations that issue the same commands that you normally choose from the Ribbon.

To activate *KeyTips,* which help you navigate the Ribbon without the mouse, follow these steps:

1. **Press the Alt key.**

Letters pop up on the Ribbon. These letters correspond to tabs, sections of the Ribbon, buttons, or drop-down-menu items.

2. **Press the letter for the tab, section, or button you want.**

More letters appear as you type.

3. **Keep typing until you've executed the command.**

Keep the following tips in mind:

- The letters don't change, so you can memorize common keystrokes to get your work done faster.

- Sometimes, more than one character is used for a shortcut, such as *FF* for *font face.* Just type what you see to execute the command.

- If you press the wrong letter, press Esc to back up.

It's possible that old menu commands whose keystrokes you memorized may still work. Give 'em a try before you give up and memorize a new sequence. Table 2-2 shows a list of our favorite shortcuts.

Some of these keystrokes work only in specific situations — when you edit something or work in a particular kind of window, for example. Throughout this book, we tell you which keys do what and when.

Table 2-2	Shortcut Keys in Access
Key or Combination	*What It Does*
F1	Displays the Help window
Ctrl+F1	Hides or displays the Ribbon
F5	Goes to the record with the record number you type
F6	Moves the focus to another area of the window
F7	Checks the spelling in the selected object
F11	Hides or displays the Navigation Pane
Delete	Deletes the selected object
Alt+Enter	Displays the properties of the selected object in Design view
Ctrl+C	Copies the selected text or objects to the clipboard
Ctrl+F	Finds text (with the option to replace it) in the open table, query, or form
Ctrl+N	Starts a new database

(continued)

Table 2-2 *(continued)*

Key or Combination	What It Does
Ctrl+O	Opens a database
Ctrl+P	Prints the selected object
Ctrl+S	Saves the selected object
Ctrl+V	Pastes the contents of the clipboard to the active window
Ctrl+X	Deletes the selected text or object and saves it in the clipboard
Ctrl+Z	Undoes the last action that can be undone (our all-time favorite!)
Ctrl+; (semicolon)	Types today's date
Ctrl+" (quotation marks)	Duplicates the entry in the same field of the preceding record
Esc	Cancels what you're typing

Chapter 3: Designing Your Database the Relational Way

In This Chapter

✔ Designing the tables in which you'll store your data

✔ Streamlining your design to make it truly relational

✔ Linking your tables with joins

✔ Choosing the right data types for your fields

✔ Ensuring compatibility among Access versions

Relational database design? Yikes! It sounds like a serious programming project. But what is it, exactly? Designing a database means figuring out how the information is structured — that is, which information should be stored in each table of the database and how everything connects. Unlike the case when you work with a spreadsheet or word processor, you have to design a database before you use it; you can't just start typing information in it. (Well, sure, you can, but we don't recommend it; the result is usually a mess.) How easy it is later to enter and edit information and to create useful queries, forms, and reports depends on how well your database is designed. A good database design can streamline your work in Access.

This chapter takes you through the process of designing the table(s) you need in your database, including the relationships among them. Book II, Chapter 1 contains instructions for creating the tables in Access.

What Are Tables, Fields, and Keys?

In Access, you store your data in *tables* — lists of records that work like the index cards that make up an address file. Each record contains information in the same format, in *fields* — specified places for individual pieces of information.

If you want to keep track of the customers of a small bookstore, you make a table of customers, with one record per customer. Each record is made up of the same set of fields, including fields that store the following types of data: customer's last name, first name, street address, city, state or province, zip or postal code, country, and phone number (as shown in Figure 3-1).

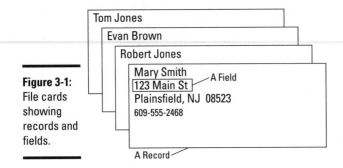

Figure 3-1:
File cards
showing
records and
fields.

After you use Access to create a table, you can *really* get busy — entering, editing, deleting, and sorting the records in various ways, and printing many types of reports (including columnar reports, forms, summaries, mailing labels, and form letters). Access allows you to create as many tables as you need in your database.

Designing a database means deciding (for openers) what tables your database needs to include and what fields are in each table. At the most basic level, it means designing the needed forms and, most likely, reports. This process is the computer equivalent of designing the form or file card on which you write the data, specifying which blanks need to be filled in and which are optional.

Data types

Fields can be different *data types,* depending on what kind of information you want them to store. Some fields contain textual alphanumeric information, such as a last name or street address. Other fields contain numbers, such as someone's age. Others contain logical information — a yes or no regarding some condition. Still others contain dates or times, such as the date when the record was added to the database. Table 3-1 lists the Access data types.

Table 3-1	Commonly Used Data Types for Fields
Data Type	**What It Holds**
Short Text	This data type is for short chunks of text up to 255 characters or special codes that contain non-numeric characters, such as phone numbers (xxx-xxx-xxxx) and zip codes (xxxxx-xxxx) that require parentheses and hyphens, which aren't allowed in numbers.
Long Text	A Long Text field is like a Short Text field, but it allows more characters — up to 65,536 of them. A Long Text field can contain rich text (see the next item), and you can set it to Append Only so that it can accumulate text notes without allowing the user to delete what's already there.

Data Type	What It Holds
Rich Text	The Rich Text data type supports such properties as **bold**, *italic*, and font changes.
Number	The Number data type supports only numbers. You may enter + or – before the number and a decimal point. Number fields come in a bunch of sizes, depending on how large the numbers are and how many decimal places you want to store (see Book II, Chapter 2).
Currency	The Currency data type is for numbers with a currency sign in front of them ($, ¥, and so on). You can do numeric calculations with these fields.
AutoNumber	This data type is for numbers that are unique to each record; it's assigned by Access as you add records, starting at `1`.
Date/Time	These fields calculate (what else?) dates and times.
OLE Object	The OLE (Object Linking and Embedding) Object data type allows you to embed files containing other kinds of data in your database. When you're creating a new database, however, consider using the Attachment data type instead, because it stores data more efficiently than the OLE Object data type does.
Hyperlink	This text string is formatted as a hyperlink. (If you click the link, it takes you to the page.) It's especially useful if there's information on the web (or your organization's intranet) that relates to the data in your table.
Yes/No	This data type indicates whether a particular condition is in effect. It can be used for any two words, such as `True/False`, `On/Off`, and `Male/Female`.
Attachment	Using a system called complex data, you can store one or more entire files — pictures, sound, Microsoft Word documents, and even video — in one Attachment field. You can store a picture of a person, for example, or three Microsoft Excel spreadsheets containing data that relates to a transaction.
Calculated	With this data type, you enter a formula that Access uses to calculate the value of this field based on other fields in the table. A field named `Markup`, for example, could be calculated as `SellingPrice - OurCost`.
Lookup Wizard	This wizard creates a field that enables you to choose a value from another table or from a list of values, such as a combo box or list box. The data type assigned to the field is the same as it was at the source.

Primary key fields for your tables

A *primary key field* (or just *key*) is a field that uniquely identifies each record in a table. If each product in a Products table has a different product code, the `ProductCode` field uniquely identifies a record in this table. If you search the Products table for a specific product code, you come up with — at most — one record.

Not all tables have an obvious key field, however. You may have to combine two or three fields to come up with values that are different for every record in the table. In a Books table, for example, you may have several books with the same title. If you assume that an author never writes more than one book with the same title, a combination of the `Title` and `Author` fields may work as a key field.

For an address list, you may think that the combination of first and last names would do the trick, but it doesn't take long before you realize that you know two Jim Smiths. You could use a combination of first name, last name, and phone number, but you have another, better alternative: Have Access issue each record a unique number, and use that number as the key field. If you can't figure out a good set of keys to use for a table, add an AutoNumber field; Access automatically numbers the records as you add them.

Access doesn't absolutely require every table to have a primary key field (or fields), but if you plan to set up relationships between your tables, some tables definitely need a primary key field. Also, key fields speed a search for records; Access creates an index for each primary key field and can zero in on any record quickly by using those primary key values. When Access offers to add a primary key for you, accept its offer!

What Are Relationships?

No trick question here; some projects (*most* projects) require more than one table. A database for a store, for example, has to handle lists of customers, lists of products, and lists of vendors, just for a start. All those bits of data have to be coordinated in some useful way.

Relational databases fill the bill. A *relational database* contains tables that are related — well, no, not like cousins or sisters-in-law. Two tables are *related* if they contain fields that match. If you have an online store, a relational database system probably includes related Products and Vendors tables:

✦ **The Products table:** This table is a list of the products you sell, containing one record for each product. Each record for a product includes a field that identifies the vendor from which you buy your stock.

✦ **The Vendors table:** This table is a list that includes name, address, and other information about each vendor.

The Products table and the Vendors table are related because the record for each product includes the name or ID code of a vendor, and the record for each vendor, of course, includes the name or ID code of the vendor.

Multiple products may come from one vendor. Figure 3-2 shows how such a *one-to-many* relationship (more about that in a minute) works in a database for a store that sells movies.

Figure 3-2:
A one-
to-many
relationship
links the
Products
and Vendors
tables; three
products
come from
one vendor.

Products

Title	Vendor
Six Stories about Little Heroes	ART
Adventures in Asia-National Geographi	ROU
The Adventures of Curious George	ROU
I've Always Loved Airplanes	CHB
Aladdin and the Magic Lamp	EBA
Aladdin and the Magic Lamp	PV
The Alamo	COL
Amahl and the Night Visitors	MOV
The Amazing Bone and Other Stories	ROU

Vendors

VendorCode	Company	Address1
PV	Palace Video	
REE	Reel.com	1250 45th Street
ROB	Robert's Hard to Find	
ROU	Rounder Kids	1263 Lower Road
SCH	Schunick Productions	2 Winton Court

Well, sure, you *could* store product information and vendor information together, in one big table, but you'd soon be sorry. You may want to add fields to the Products table to contain the address of the vendor from which you bought the product. But here's the problem: Whenever a vendor's address changes, you have to make that change in the record for every item you buy from that vendor. What a pain!

A key principle of database design is this: *Store each piece of information once.* If you store information more than once, you have to update it more than once. (In real life — trust us on this one — if you update it in some places but not in others, you end up with a mess.)

Here's a piece of geekspeak: *Normalizing* a database means figuring out the most efficient way to divide the information into tables so that each piece of information is stored only once and related information is connected. This chapter steps you through the process.

How relationships work

Sorry, we have no advice for the lovelorn here. Luckily, relationships between tables are much simpler than relationships between people. To make two tables related, you specify one or more fields in one table that match the same number of fields in the other table. In Figure 3-2, earlier in this chapter, the Products table relates to the Vendors table because the Vendor field in the Products table contains values that match the VendorCode field in the Vendors table. When you look at a record in the

Products table, you can find out which vendor you buy the product from by finding the record in the Vendors table that has the same value in the matching field.

Relationships come in several flavors:

+ **One-to-many:** One record in one table matches no, one, or many records in the other table. The relationship in Figure 3-2 works this way because one vendor can provide many products.

+ **One-to-one:** One record in one table matches one record (or no record) in the other table.

+ **Many-to-many:** Zero, one, or many records in one table match zero, one, or many records in the other table.

The next three sections explain these three types of relationships.

One-to-many relationships

This type of relationship is the most common among tables. In a one-to-many relationship, many records in one table can match one — and only one — record in another table. Here are some examples of one-to-many relationships:

+ **Items in customer orders:** If you run a store, customers frequently buy several items at the same time. You may have an Orders table with one record for each sale you make, but a sale can include several products. (Maybe someone buys two books and a pair of socks.) One record in the Orders table could match several records in the OrderDetails table.

+ **Vendors and invoices:** If your company buys many items from another company, you end up with a bunch of invoices from (and payments to) that company. The relationship between the Vendors table and the Invoices table in an accounting database is one-to-many.

+ **People living in states or provinces:** The United States and Canada use standard two-letter state and province abbreviations, and if you have an address list, these codes should be correct. (Quick — is Quebec QU or PQ? No peeking.) To make sure that you type the valid state and province codes for the United States and Canada, you can create a StateProvinceCodes table against which you can validate entries in the State field of your Addresses table. One record in the StateProvinceCodes table can match many records in the Addresses table.

You use a one-to-many relationship to avoid storing information from the "one" table multiple times in the "many" table. You don't want to store all the information about each student in the record for every course, for example — unless you want to hear the groan of an overloaded disk drive. Storing each student's information in one place (the Students table) and storing only the student's name and/or student ID in the CourseRegistrations table is more efficient (and easier to maintain).

Many database designers call the "one" table the *master* table and the "many" table the *detail* table. In Access, *primary key* means the matching field(s) in the master table; *foreign key* means the corresponding field(s) in the detail table. In Figure 3-2, the Vendors table is the master table, and the Products table is the detail table. The primary key (in Vendors) is the VendorCode field; the foreign key (in Products) is the Vendor field.

One-to-one relationships

This type of relationship — in which one record in one table matches exactly one record in another table — is much less common in database design. You may have reasons, however (perhaps security reasons), for separating information into two tables. Suppose that you store information about the employees of your company. The Employees table contains the basic information about each employee (name, address, phone, and other personal information). The EmployeeHealth table contains information about each employee's health-insurance policy. (In your company, all employees have insurance.) Each record in the Employees table matches exactly one record in the EmployeeHealth table, and vice versa.

The question is this: If you have exactly the same number of records in the two tables, and those records match exactly, why not just combine them into one table? Most of the time, that's exactly what you should do. In the employee database example, you can just add the health insurance information to the Employees table and do away with the EmployeeHealth table.

Occasionally, however, you have a good reason to separate information into two tables connected by a one-to-one relationship. We came up with three such scenarios:

✦ **Security:** One of the tables contains much more sensitive information than the other, and you want to restrict who can see the information in that table. Store the sensitive information in a separate table.

   See Book VII, Chapter 3 for details on setting up security for a database.

✦ **Subset of records:** Maybe only some of the employees in your company have health insurance. (This is the real world, after all.) Rather than leaving a lot of fields blank in the Employees table, storing insurance data in a separate, related table is more efficient. Not every record in your Employees table may have a record in the EmployeeHealth table.

✦ **Multiple databases:** Some information is stored in a separate database. When you use one database, you can *link* to a table in another database to work with the information in that table as though it were stored in your own database. If someone else's database has information you need, and you link to that database, you can't combine the two tables into one table, but you can set up a relationship between them. (See Book II, Chapter 4 for instructions.)

Don't be surprised if you almost never create one-to-one relationships between database tables; we hardly ever do.

For a one-to-one relationship, you need one or more fields that link the two tables. Make sure that both tables have the same primary key field(s).

Many-to-many relationships

Many-to-many relationships are more complicated than one-to-one and one-to-many relationships because a many-to-many is really two relationships in one. Here are some examples of tables in which zero, one, or many records in one table can match zero, one, or many records in the other:

✦ **Students in courses:** If you create a database to keep track of students in a school, many students are in each class, and each student takes many classes. You have many records in the Students table matching each record in the Courses table — that is, many students are in each course. You also have many records in the Courses table matching each record in the Students table — that is, each student can take many courses.

✦ **Committees:** If you set up a database for a club or religious group, you may want to keep track of who serves on what committee. One person can be on lots of committees, and one committee can have lots of members. The relationship between the People table and the Committees table is many-to-many.

✦ **Books and authors:** One book can be written by a group of authors (such as this book), and one author can write many books. The relationship between the Books table and the Authors table in a bookstore inventory database can be many-to-many.

Figure 3-3 shows a many-to-many relationship between students and courses. Each student is in several classes; each course has its own bunch of students.

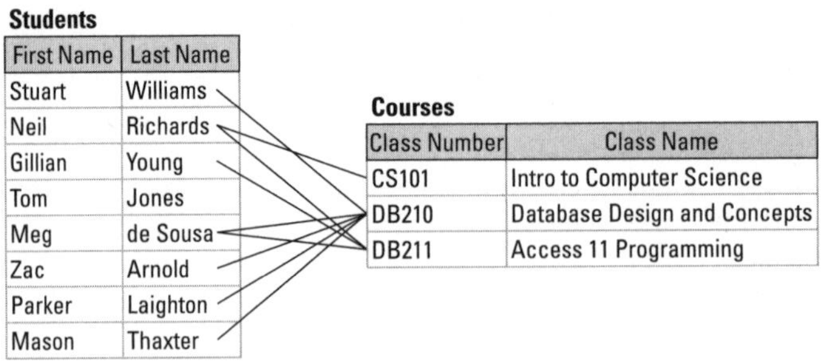

Figure 3-3:
Many
students
can be
in each
course,
and each
student can
take many
courses.

Students

First Name	Last Name
Stuart	Williams
Neil	Richards
Gillian	Young
Tom	Jones
Meg	de Sousa
Zac	Arnold
Parker	Laighton
Mason	Thaxter

Courses

Class Number	Class Name
CS101	Intro to Computer Science
DB210	Database Design and Concepts
DB211	Access 11 Programming

The problem is that Access (and most other relational database programs) can't handle many-to-many relationships. Access refuses to accept that these relationships exist. (Don't we all know people like that?) But don't worry — you can work around this problem. You can create an additional table that saves the day: The new table records the *connections* between the two tables.

In the students-and-courses example, you can make a new table called CourseRegistrations. This new table, called a *junction table,* contains one field that matches the primary key for Courses and one field that matches the primary key for Students; each record in the CourseRegistrations table connects one student to one course. The Students table and the CourseRegistrations table have a one-to-many relationship: The Students table is the master table, and CourseRegistrations is the detail table. The Courses table and the CourseRegistrations table also have a one-to-many relationship: Again, the Courses table is the master table. In fact, you probably want this new table anyway because you need some place to record each student's grade in that course. (We frequently find that the new junction table is useful for storing more than just the relationship.)

Figure 3-4 shows the relationships among the three tables: Students, CourseRegistrations, and Courses. To provide a single primary key field that uniquely identifies each student, we added a `StudentID` field to the Students table. Each record in the CourseRegistrations table connects one student (by student ID) to one course (by class number). In real life, we'd add fields for the student's grade, registration date, payment date, and other information about the student's enrollment in the course.

Figure 3-4:
To store a many-to-many relationship, create a junction table that connects the tables.

Students

Student ID	First Name	Last Name
AR1002	Zac	Arnold
DE0014	Meg	de Sousa
JO4001	Tom	Jones
LA0056	Parker	Laighton
RI0014	Neil	Richards
TH2589	Mason	Thaxter
WI0143	Stuart	Williams
YO1567	Gillian	Young

CourseRegistrations

Student ID	Class Number
DE0014	CS101
TH2589	CS101
JO4001	DB210
RI0014	DB210

Courses

Class Number	Class Name
CS101	Intro to Computer Science
DB210	Database Design and Concepts
DB211	Access 11 Programming

What should you do first?

Creating an Access database and setting up all the objects you need can be a daunting task. Here's the order in which we usually set a new Access database:

1. **Design the database, as described in this chapter.**

2. **Make the tables that you've designed, as described in Book II, Chapter 1.**

3. **If you're moving information from a spreadsheet, another database, or some other source, import data into Access, as described in Book II, Chapter 4.**

4. **Set up the relationships between the tables, as described in Book II, Chapter 6.**

5. **Create the queries that you know you'll need for displaying related data from multiple tables, as described in Book III, Chapter 1.**

6. **Make forms for adding and editing records, as described in Book IV, Chapter 1.**

7. **Set up the reports you want, as described in Book V, Chapter 1.**

You may need to make additional queries to use as the record source for some reports.

Designing a Database

When you feel at ease with the concepts of tables, fields, and relationships, you're ready to design your own relational database. The rest of this chapter walks you through designing your database tables so that your database is easy to use, flexible, and efficient. We use the example of a bookstore as we go through the steps to show you how the design process works.

Identifying your data

Find out what information is available, who maintains it, what it looks like, and how it's used. Make a list of the possible fields. (Don't worry yet about which fields end up in which tables.) A retail store, for example, needs to track product descriptions, prices, purchase dates, customer names, who bought what, shipment dates (for online orders), and other information.

If some of the information you need is already stored in another database — whether it's in Access, SQL Server, MySQL, or another relational database — find out whether the owner of the database will allow you to link to it. Also find out the name of the tables and the names and types of the fields in the tables so that you can see how these tables and fields will connect with the rest of your information.

Eliminating redundant fields

Look over the fields you identified, and make sure they're all actually *needed* for your application. Is each piece of information something that may appear on a form or report later or that may be needed to calculate something? If not, throw it out.

In this case, it's worth repeating: *Don't store the same information in more than one place.* In a database, redundant information makes double the work when you're updating the information. Instead, figure out the right place to store the information, and store it there — once. If you can calculate one field from another field, store only one. Storing both age *and* birth date, for example, is pointless, because a person's age changes, but the birth date doesn't. Store the birth date; you can always get Access to do the math for you.

The same is true of information that you can look up. For codes of all types (state and province codes, product codes, and the like), make a table for the codes that includes a field for each code and a field for the code's meaning. Then all the other tables in your database store only the code, and Access looks up the code's meaning *when you need it to appear* in a form or report. For the online bookstore, you don't need to store the title and author of each item that a customer buys; instead, you can just store the book's ISBN (the unique number assigned to each book).

On the other hand, you can't always avoid redundancy. An item of information may change in one place but not in another, so you may have to store it in more than one place. In the bookstore system, when the price of a book changes, the amount that previous customers paid for the book doesn't change. In addition to storing the book's current selling price, you may want to store the book's price in the record for each sale.

Organizing fields into tables

Okay, you have a bunch of fields. Are they all in one table, or should you set up multiple tables?

One way to tell whether your system needs multiple tables is to check whether you have different numbers of values for different fields. Suppose that the store carries 2,000 products, and you have about 16,000 customers. You have 2,000 different names, prices, and descriptions, while you have 16,000 customer names, addresses, and sets of credit-card information. Guess what? You have two different tables: a Products table with 2,000 records and a Customers table with 16,000 records.

You could start out with a design like this, with two tables called Products and Customers:

Products	*Customers*
Product Code	First Name
Description	Last Name
Price	Street Address
Cover Photo	City
Taxable (Yes/No)	State/Province
Shipping Weight	Zip or Postcode
Vendor Name	Payment Method
Discontinued?	Credit Card Number
Product Type	Credit Card Exp. Date
Product Notes	Check Number
	Tax Exempt (Yes/No)
	Product 1
	Product 2
	Product 3
	Shipping Cost
	Sales Tax
	Total Price
	Purchase Date

When you create the tables and fields in Access, you may not want to use spaces in your table and field names. During the design process, use readable English phrases for your table and field names, and consider removing the spaces or replacing them with underscores later. Access works fine with spaces in table and field names, but most database programs don't. If you end up moving or linking your database with another database program, you'll have trouble. In your forms and reports, you can use more-readable names for your tables and fields. In these examples, we're leaving the spaces in the names to make the examples easier to follow.

As you look at these two tables, you soon realize that one customer can make more than one purchase. What happens when a customer buys something else, perhaps on a different date?

Combining customer information with purchase information won't work. Leave information about the customer in the Customers table (all the facts about the customer that don't change from one purchase to the next), and move information about a specific purchase into a separate Orders table, like this:

Customers	*Orders*
First Name	Customer First Name
Last Name	Customer Last Name
Street Address	Purchase Date
City	Product 1
State/Province	Product 2
Zip or Postcode	Product 3
Phone Number	Shipping Cost
Email Address	Sales Tax
Tax Exempt (Yes/No)	Total Price
	Payment Method
	Credit Card Number
	Credit Card Exp. Date
	Check Number

But wait — what if the customer buys more than three items at a time? (We usually do.) If you own the store, you don't want to put an arbitrary limit on how many items your customers can buy. (Limit your profit for the sake of your database? In a word, nope.) Any time your database design includes a bunch of fields that store essentially the same kind of information (such as `Product 1`, `Product 2`, and `Product 3`), something is wrong. An order can consist of zero, one, or many books. Does that sound familiar? Yes, a one-to-many relationship exists between an order and the items in that order, so you need to make a separate table for the individual items, like this:

Orders	*Order Details*
Customer First Name	ISBN
Customer Last Name	Quantity
Purchase Date	Price Each
Total Product Cost	
Shipping Cost	
Sales Tax	
Total Price	
Payment Method	
Credit Card Number	
Credit Card Exp. Date	
Check Number	

Now each time a customer places an order or comes into your store to make a purchase, you create one record in the Customers table (if this customer hasn't bought from you before), one record in the Orders table, and one record for each item purchased in the Order Details table. The Order Details table has room to store the quantity of the item in case the customer wants more than one of something. You should also store the selling price of the product. Access can calculate the cost of that quantity of each product (price × quantity), so you don't need to store that information.

The following are really good reasons *not* to store multiple fields (such as `Product 1`, `Product 2`, and `Product 3`) in one table and to create a separate table instead:

+ **You can't anticipate the right number of fields.** If someone buys more than three things (as in this example), you have to create a separate order and enter everything twice.

+ **You can't analyze the information later.** What if you sell books, and you want to see a list of everyone who bought the last Honor Harrington book so that you can notify those customers that the next book in the series is coming out? If you have multiple fields for this information, your query needs to look for orders that contain an Honor Harrington book in `Product 1` or `Product 2` or `Product 3`. What a pain.

We don't want to drive this point into the ground, but creating multiple, identical fields is a problem that many first-time database designers make for themselves. Be good to yourself: Don't do it!

Adding tables for codes and abbreviations

Look at your tables to see whether the fields contain any standard codes, such as two-letter state and province codes, zip codes, or other codes. The bookstore's Customers table includes a `State/Province` field and a `Zip/Postcode` field. The Products table contains a `Product Type` field so the store can track sales of books (type `B`) versus other types of stuff (such as `G` for groceries or `D` for DVDs). Determine whether your system needs to do one of these tasks with the codes:

✦ **Validate the codes.** Wrong codes cause trouble later. Validating the codes when you type them is always best. If someone types **VR** for Vermont, the post office may not deliver your package. Later, when you analyze your sales by state, you see that you have some Vermonters with the right code (VT) and some with the wrong code. (See Book II, Chapter 5 for more information on how to set up validation in your database.)

✦ **Look up the meaning of the code.** Codes usually stand for something. Should your system print or display the meaning of the code? If you have a report showing total sales of products by type, printing `Books`, `Groceries`, and `Gifts` rather than `B`, `G`, and `G` is nice.

If you want to either validate or look up the codes you store, create a separate table to hold a list of your codes and their meanings. You could add the following two tables to the bookstore database:

States/Provinces	*Product Types*
State or Province Code	Product Type Code
State or Province Name	Product Type Description
Country	

Although zip codes and postal codes *are* codes (well, yeah), most databases don't include tables that list them. The reason is simple: Pretty soon, your system would be overstuffed with them. (About 100,000 zip codes exist, for openers.) Also, you have to update the table constantly as the post offices issue — and change — zip and postal codes. If you really want to validate your zip codes, you can get a zip-code database from the U.S. Postal Service at `www.usps.com`.

Choosing primary keys for each table

The next step in designing your database is making sure that each table has its own primary key field(s). Each table needs at least one field that uniquely identifies each record in the table. (We find that it's almost always better to use one field as your primary key.) Look for a field in the table that has a different value in each record. If one field is different for every record in the table, you've found your primary key field.

Autonumbering your records

Well, okay, you may not find a unique field. It happens. Tables that list people (such as the Customers table) can pose such a problem. Some people have the same name; family members or roommates can share an address and phone number. Most businesses end up creating and assigning unique numbers to people to prevent this problem.

For privacy reasons, don't even *think* about asking for anyone's Social Security number. Make up your own customer numbers!

Fortunately, assigning each record in a table a unique number is easy in Access: Just add an AutoNumber field to the table. Access numbers the records as you enter them. In your bookstore system, you can add a `Customer Number` field to the Customers table.

The advantage of using an AutoNumber key as the primary key field is that you can't change its values. After you relate two tables by using an AutoNumber field as the primary key, breaking the relationship between the tables later, if you have to edit the value of the AutoNumber field, is impossible.

For the Orders table, you can use `Customer Number` instead of the customer's name to identify who places the order. Because one customer may make several purchases, however, you still don't have a unique key for the Orders table. One solution is to use a combination of fields as the primary key. How about using the `Customer Number` and `Purchase Date` fields together as the primary key? This solution works fine as long as a customer doesn't place two orders on the same day. (Hmm, that may not work either; people sometimes forget to buy everything they need and come back to the store later for one or two more items.) Instead, add an AutoNumber field to this table to provide a unique `Order Number`.

Seeing why two key fields may be better than one

Sometimes, using a combination of fields works fine. In the Order Details table, you'd better add a field for the `Order Number` so that you can get immediate access to whatever order contains these items. You don't need to add a `Customer Number` field in this case; after you identify the `Order Number`, Access can look up the `Customer Number` and other customer information.

The `Order Number` field doesn't uniquely identify records in the Order Details table, because one order can (and a business owner would really love it to) include lots and lots of products. Use a combination of the `Order`

`Number` and the `Product Code` or `ISBN` as the primary key for the table. Then one order includes one entry for each item purchased.

Viewing a sample order-entry database design

Figure 3-5 shows the new, improved table design for a retail-store system, with little key icons by the primary key fields.

Figure 3-5:
Your
database
design
organizes
your data
in related
tables.

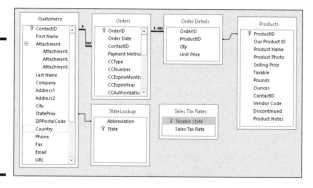

One other thing: We like to include a `Date Last Changed` or `Date Updated` field in every table. This field almost always turns out to be useful. We omitted these fields from Figure 3-5 to save space, but we'd include them in the real database.

Linking your tables

If you end up with only one table, you can skip this step, but that situation is fairly rare. Almost every database ends up with a second table at the very least — to contain those pesky codes.

Look at the tables in your database, and see which tables contain fields that match fields in other tables. Determine whether a one-to-one, one-to-many, or many-to-many relationship exists between the two tables (as described in the "What Are Relationships?" section, earlier in this chapter). For each pair of related tables, you can determine which fields actually relate the tables by following these guidelines:

✦ **One-to-many relationships:** Figure out which is the "one" (master) and which is the "many" (detail) table in this relationship. Make sure that the detail table has a foreign key field (or fields) to match the primary key field(s) in the master table. The Customers and Orders tables have a one-to-many relationship in the bookstore example, because a customer may have no, one, or many orders. (Okay, someone who has no orders technically isn't a customer, but the relationship still counts as one-to-many because she's a potential customer.) The primary key field in the master table (Customers) is `Customer Number`. To relate the tables, you have to give the Orders table a `Customer Number` field to be used as the foreign key.

✦ **One-to-one relationships:** Make sure that both tables have the same primary key field(s). (The example shown in Figure 3-5 doesn't include any one-to-one relationships.)

✦ **Many-to-many relationships:** Access can't store a many-to-many relationship directly. Set up a junction table containing the primary keys of the two tables to connect the tables. In the bookstore example, the Orders and Products tables have a many-to-many relationship: One order can have many products, and one product can occur in many orders. The Order Details table is the junction table that contains the primary key of the Orders table (`OrderID`) and the primary key of the Products table (`ProductID`). This junction table can include additional information. (The Order Details table, for example, includes the quantity of the item that's ordered as well as the price of each item.)

The related fields don't need to have the same name in the two related tables, but the types, lengths, and contents of the fields have to match. (We usually find that giving the two fields the same names is less confusing. Preserving sanity is also good for business.) Figure 3-5, earlier in this chapter, shows the relationships among your tables as lines running between the related fields. For one-to-many relationships, we use 1 at one end of the line and an infinity symbol (∞) at the "many" end.

Refining your links

The relationships among your tables can be a bit more complex. (What relationships aren't?) So you may need to make a few more decisions about how your table relationships work:

✦ **Referential integrity:** This nifty feature means that you can tell Access not to allow a record to exist in a detail table unless it has a matching record in the master record. If you turn on referential integrity checking for the relationship between the Customers and States_Provinces tables, for example, Access won't allow you to enter a record with a `State_Province` code if the code doesn't exist in the `State_Province_Abbreviation` field of the States table. This feature is a "No bogus codes!" rule that doesn't require any programming (as you find out in Book II, Chapter 6).

✦ **Cascading updates:** Another way-cool Access feature updates detail records automatically when you change the matching master record. If you find out that you have the wrong `ProductID` for an item, and you

change it in the `ProductID` field in the Products table, you can configure Access to update the code automatically in the Order Details table.

✦ Cascading deletes: As with cascading updates, this feature deletes detail
records when you delete the master record.

This feature is a bit more dangerous than cascading updates, and you
may not want to use cascading deletes for most related tables. If a
product becomes obsolete, and you stop carrying it, deleting it from
the Products table is a bad idea. Consider: What's supposed to happen
to all those matching records in the Order Details table (assuming that
you sold *some* units of that now-obsolete item)? Don't delete the Order_
Details records, because then the table shows that you never sold those
items. Instead, mark the item as *unavailable* (in the example shown in
Figure 3-5, set the `Discontinued` field in the Products table to `Yes`),
and leave the records in the tables.

Now you have a fully relational database design. The last step is cleaning up
the loose ends.

Seeing what's in a name

Table names should be plural (such as `Products` and `Customers`). Field
names should be singular (such as `City` and `Quantity`). Access doesn't
care, but this system makes things easier for you to read. Don't use all capital letters, either; you'll feel as though Access is yelling at you. We like to
capitalize the first letter of each word.

In this chapter, we use two-word field names with a space between the two
words. Using spaces in names may be a bad idea, however, if you ever want
to link the data from your Access database to a larger database that misin-
terprets the space as an end-of-name flag. Also, it means that when you type
formulas, you have to enclose the name in square brackets to tell Access
where the name starts and ends. Who wants to remember to do that? Decide
in advance whether you're going to use spaces (`Product Code`), underscores (`Product_Code`), or neither (`ProductCode`) in all your names. You
can't use a hyphen, because that means subtraction in Access.

Finally, don't use words that have specialized meanings to Access, including
these words: *Name, Date, Word, Value, Table, Field,* and *Form.* You can actually confuse Access. It's not a pretty sight.

In general, be consistent, to make it easier to remember table and field
names. (Now, was that table name `Product_Code` or `ProductCode`?)

Naming things (for serious database designers)

If you really want to impress your programming friends, consider using prefixes on all your object names to show what kind of object you're naming. Here's a set of commonly used prefixes:

tbl Table

qry Query

frm Form

rpt Report

mcr Macro

bas Module

You might rename the Products table tblProducts, for example.

Fewer programmers use prefixes for fields to show the data type of each field. If you want to, and if you want to read more about the Leszynski naming convention from which these prefixes come, go to http://mvps.org, and search for "Leszynski naming convention."

Cleaning up the design

You have tables, you have fields, and you have relationships. What more could you want in a database design? You're almost done. Look at each field in each of your tables, and decide on the following for each field:

+ **Data types:** The section "Data types," earlier in this chapter, describes the types of information you can store in Access fields. Decide what kind of information each field contains, how large your Text fields need to be, and what kinds of numbers your Number fields hold. (Book II, Chapter 2 explains the sizes of Number fields.) Make sure to use the same data type and length for related fields. If ProductID is a Text field that's 16 characters long in the Products table, make it the same length in the Order Details table.

If you use an AutoNumber field as the primary key in a master table, use a Long Integer Number field for the foreign key in related tables.

+ **Required fields:** You can tell Access not to allow a field to be blank. A record in the Products table should never have a blank ProductID or Price field, for example.

+ **Validation:** You can set up validation (data checking) rules for fields, as described in Book II, Chapter 5. Think about limits on the legal values for the field. You may want to specify that value in the Price field of the Products table can't be more than $1,000 or that the value in the Pounds field must be less than 200. (This rule should work unless you're selling some really heavy stuff.)

✦ **Defaults:** Some fields have the same value for most records. The `Discontinued` field in the Products table will be `No` for most records, especially when you create the record. (How often would you enter an item that's already discontinued?) You can set the default value — the value that the field starts out with — to the most common value; you have to change it only for the records that have a different value.

✦ **Indexes:** If you plan to sort your table or search for records based on the values in a field, tell Access to maintain an index for the field. Like the index of a book, a database index helps you (or Access) find information; Access stores information about the field to speed searches. Access automatically indexes primary key fields and foreign key fields, but you can designate additional fields to be indexed.

That's it. You're done designing your database!

Choosing Field Types

Now that you know the concepts and procedures for designing a relational database, here are a few suggestions on choosing field types for your information.

Choosing between Text and Yes/No fields

Fields that can have only two values (such as `Yes` and `No`, `True` and `False`, or `On` and `Off`) are also called *Boolean* or *logical* values. You can store Boolean information in a one-letter Text field, using `Y` and `N`. But if you use a `Yes/No` field, Access can display the information on forms as a check box, option button, or toggle button.

Another advantage of going the `Yes/No` field route is that you can easily switch between displaying the field as `Yes` and `No`, `True` and `False`, or `On` and `Off` by changing the `Format` property for the field. Using a custom format, you can choose any two text values to display instead of `Yes` and `No`. You can display the values `Discontinued` and `Available` for a `Yes/No` field, for example.

Choosing between Short Text and Long Text fields

Text fields are limited to 255 characters; if you need more, use a Long Text field. An Access Long Text field can contain more than 65,000 characters of textual information, but the extra elbowroom costs you some versatility. You can't index Long Text fields, for one thing, and they can't serve as primary or foreign keys. If you plan to sort or search your records by using the contents of this field — or to use the information in it to relate one table to another — a Short Text field usually is your best bet. So is brevity. On the other hand,

Long Text fields can contain Rich Text — that is, formatted text. If you need boldface, italics, and font changes in your text, you need to use a Long Text field.

Some database designers avoid using the Long Text field because they find that databases with Long Text fields are more likely to get *corrupted* (become unreadable by Access). The same is true of OLE Object fields, which are used for storing pictures, spreadsheets, documents, and other large objects; they may give your database indigestion.

Choosing between Text and Number (or Currency) fields

Access displays and sorts Number and Currency fields differently from Text fields. Here are the differences:

✦ When displaying a Number or Currency field, Access drops any leading zeros. (08540, for example, becomes 8540 or $8,540.)

✦ You can format Number and Currency fields in many ways, giving you control of the number of decimal places, specified currency symbols, and the use of commas. Access can align these fields vertically on the decimal points, which makes columns of numbers easier to read.

✦ Access can calculate totals, subtotals, and averages for Number and Currency fields, as well as do other numeric calculations.

✦ When you sort a Number or Currency field, values sort from smallest to largest — at least, they do when you're sorting in ascending order. But when you sort a Text field, values are sorted alphabetically, starting at the left end of the field. This difference means that in a Text field, Access sorts 55 before 6, because the 5 character comes before the 6 character. The following list shows how Access sorts the same list of numbers in Number and Text fields:

Number Sort	*Text Sort*
1	1
2	11
5	2
11	21
21	44
44	5

Use Number fields for all numbers except numeric codes (such as zip codes or phone numbers), which are described in the next section. Store any number you may want to add to a total in a Number or Currency field. Choose a Currency field for money values.

Storing pictures and other files

Access provides two field types that allow you to store entire files of information, usually pictures. The old type, OLE Object, provides a link to the file, but unless the files are small, doing so turns out to be a bad idea. The database reacts to a large OLE object the way an anaconda reacts to trying to swallow a rhino: Its size balloons. Instead, you can use an Attachment field, which compresses the file before storing it in your database.

You have another option: Don't store the file in your database at all. If your pictures are large, if they change frequently, or if you use them for other purposes and need to store them as separate files anyway, store the pathname that leads to the files containing the pictures. In the retail-store example earlier in this chapter, the Products table includes a `Product Photo` field. Instead of making that field an Attachment field, you can store all the pictures in a separate folder on the hard drive and store filenames for each picture in a Text field or a hyperlink. If the pictures are in various folders, store the entire pathname in the field, as in the following example:

```
D:\Store\Database\Products\teapot.jpg
```

The disadvantage of this method is that if you move your database to another computer, you need to move all these files, too, so that the pathname is the same on the new computer as it was on the old one. You can prevent this problem by storing your photos in the cloud on SkyDrive — a cloud storage facility that's being introduced in Office 2013.

Storing names, money, codes, and other stuff

Here are a few other field-type suggestions:

+ **People's names:** For lists of people, creating a Name field and putting full names in it is tempting. Don't do it! You'll want to sort records by last name, create listings with last name first, or otherwise fool with the format of people's names. Create separate `First Name` and `Last Name` fields. You may even want `Middle Name` and `Salutation` (such as `Mr.` and `The Reverend`) fields.

+ **Phone numbers and postal codes:** Use Text fields rather than Number fields, even if you plan to type only digits in the field. The test to use is this: Is there any chance that you'd ever want to do math with this information? If the answer is no, use a Text field. (If you store a zip code in a Number field, Access feels compelled to drop leading zeros, so the zip code for Middlebury, VT turns from 05753 to 5753 — not good.)

+ **Money:** Use a Currency field rather than a Number field. Calculations made on Currency fields are faster than those made on most Number fields.

✦ **Percentages:** To store percentages, such as discounts, create a Number field, and enter decimal numbers between 0 and 1 (inclusive) for percentages between 0 and 100. When you create the table, you can format the Number field as a percentage. Then, if you enter a value, and habit makes you type **33%**, Access automatically converts the value to 0.33.

✦ **Calculations:** Access 2013 includes a Calculated field type, which stores the results of calculations that use other fields in the same table. Official relational database theory says that fields should contain only raw data; Access can always do the calculations later in your queries, forms, and reports. The space required to store a number is pretty small, however, and if you'll need to use a calculation in lots of forms and reports, it's convenient to enter the formula just once as part of the table definition, so we say go ahead! You may want to enter a Total_Price field in the Order_Details table that multiplies Quantity by Price_Each, because this number is likely to show up on invoices, receipts, and sales reports.

Never create a field in which you enter the result of a calculation yourself. If the numbers on which the calculation was based happen to change, the calculation becomes wrong, which fouls up any calculations or reports based on it. An Access Calculated field updates the result automatically when other fields change.

✦ **Codes:** Decide on the formats to use for phone numbers, invoice numbers, credit-card numbers, purchase order numbers, and other codes. Decide whether to use all capital letters and whether to include or omit dashes and spaces. If you ask Access to search for someone with credit-card number 9999–8888–7777–6666, and the card number is stored as 9999888877776666, the search won't find the record.

Storing Single Facts

Some pieces of information exist all by themselves. They aren't part of a list; there's just one item. The name of your organization is a single piece of information, and so is the pathname to the location of your database. If you want these pieces of information to appear on any reports, forms, or queries, or to use them in calculations or imports, typing them willy-nilly in said reports, queries, or other Access objects is tempting. In practice, doing so turns out to be a lousy idea.

Here's the problem: What happens when one of these facts changes? Suppose that your organization's name or address changes, or you move your database's location to another folder on another computer. You certainly don't want to have to root around your database looking for the places where such information appears.

Secret keys

The primary key field for a table doesn't have to be information that the user sees. In fact, many programmers prefer to use a primary key field that has no use other than to uniquely identify records. If you create an AutoNumber field to act as a primary key field, the user of your database never has to see or type the values of this field.

When you sign in to the Amazon.com website to order a book, for example, you never have to type your customer number. Instead, you sign in with your e-mail address, and Amazon looks up your customer number automatically. Similarly, when you order a book or other merchandise, you never have to type the item number. You just find the item you want and then click a button to add the item to your shopping cart.

Instead, create a table called Constants, Facts, or any name you like *with just one record in it.* Create a field for each piece of information you need to store. Maybe your table contains `Our Name`, `Our Address`, `Our City`, `Our State`, `Our Zip`, and `Our Phone Number` fields. Be sure to include an `Our State Sales Tax` field, too. Wherever you want this information to appear (mainly in reports), Access can look it up in your table. Then, if something changes (such as your telephone area code), you have to update it in only one place!

Creating a Database

Okay, if you've been faithfully reading this book every night before bedtime — doesn't everybody? — you're 60 pages or so in by now. If you still haven't created your database, enough, already! You're armed with your database design, and you're ready to start. (If you haven't been following along, maybe you'd better review those 60 pages *before* you start.)

When you set out to create a new Access database, you have two options: Create it from scratch, or use a template. We discuss both options in the following sections.

Creating a database from scratch

After you have a beautiful database design (allow us to recommend the — ahem! — stellar example in this chapter), you can start with a blank database and create the tables, fields, and relationships, which means running Access without opening an existing database. Follow these steps:

1. **Create a new database by clicking the File tab on the Ribbon and then clicking New (as shown in Figure 3-6).**

You see several choices for creating a new database.

New

Search for online templates

Suggested searches: Assets Business Contacts Employee Inventory Project Sales

Custom web app   Blank desktop database   Task management

Figure 3-6:
Creating a
database.

2. **Click Blank Desktop Database.**

The File Name dialog box appears, offering the option of naming the database file in the File Name box. If you don't choose to name the database on your own, Access will name it Database1.accdb (or another number, depending on how many databases you've created).

Wondering about that Custom Web App button? See Book IX, Chapter 3 for details.

3. **Click the folder icon to the right of the File Name text box to navigate to the folder where you want to store the new database (assuming that you don't want to store it in the default location), and replace the default file name by typing your preferred filename in the File Name box.**

If you're just trying out this procedure, you can use the filename Test. Access automatically adds the extension .accdb to Access database filenames.

4. **Click the Create button.**

Access creates a new, blank database. It assumes that the first thing that you want to do is to create some tables, so it also makes a new, blank table and displays it in Design view.

5. **Create your tables.**

   Book II, Chapter 1 tells you how to create tables. You define each of the fields in the database, including the field name, data type, and field length.

6. **Create relationships among the tables.**

   Making relationships is described in Book II, Chapter 6. Access displays a Relationships window that draws lines between related tables, like the diagram shown in Figure 3-5, earlier in this chapter.

You can always rename the database later. Close the database, and run Windows Explorer. If you have Windows 7 or an older operating system, do this by double-clicking My Computer on the desktop or choosing Start⇨All Programs⇨Accessories⇨Windows Explorer. Navigate to the folder that contains the database, find and select its filename, press F2, and type a new name for the database file. You can't rename an Access database within Access. If you have Windows 8, just navigate to the folder that contains the database and rename it the same way you do in the earlier Windows environments.

If you have Windows 8, click the Folders icon at the bottom of your screen to display Windows Explorer.

When you create a database, Access uses the newer .accdb format that was introduced with Access 2007 unless you tell it to use the older .mdb format. Note that Access 2003 and older versions can't open .accdb-format databases; if you try, you'll just get an error message.

Creating a new database from a template

Access comes with a bunch of *templates* — databases that already include tables and relationships but no data. You also get queries, forms, and reports — very handy! If you're creating a database for a purpose for which Microsoft has designed a template, you can use the template to provide the initial design and then make changes to adapt the objects in the database for your own use. Looking at Microsoft's templates is a good way to get design ideas, too.

To create a database from a template, follow these steps:

1. **Click the File tab on the Ribbon, click New, and look through the templates displayed.**

   You see buttons for several templates.

2. **If you don't see what you want, type a template category** (Assets, Business, Contacts, **and so on) in the Search Online Templates search box, and click the magnifying-glass icon.**

   Access displays a more-targeted set of templates in your chosen category.

3. **Click a template, choose a folder location and a name, and click Create.**

   Choosing the folder and name works the same way as it does for creating a new, blank database as described in the previous section.

4. **If Access protects you from possible malicious code (which it will do if the template contains any active content at all), click the Enable Content button to unleash the full functionality of the database.**

   For some templates, a helpful training video may pop up, compliments of Microsoft. You can decide whether to watch it or go directly to the database.

5. **Prowl around the database, looking at the tables to see whether the design will work for you.**

   Use the Navigation pane, described in Chapter 2 of this minibook, to see the tables. Open each table in Design view to see a list of the fields and their field types.

6. **Change the design as needed.**

   Book II, Chapter 1 describes how to change the design of an existing table. You can rename tables and fields, add fields that the template doesn't include, and delete fields that you don't think you'll need.

If you make a new database from a template, and the template turns out not to be useful for you, you can always delete the database and try another template, or start from scratch.

Analyzing and documenting your table design

Access comes with a wizard that can eyeball your database design, looking at the way that you divide your information into related tables. Specifically, it helps you fix a table that contains repeated values in some fields, splitting the table into two or more related tables. The Table Analyzer Wizard walks you through the process, creating the new tables and moving the fields and values. To run the wizard, click the Analyze Table button in the Analyze group on the Database Tools tab of the Ribbon.

Another Access feature can provide documentation on almost any aspect of your new database, helping you track the changes made in your database and providing information to your users. The Documenter allows you to select the components of your database for which you want to create documentation and then creates that documentation automatically. It even allows you to select the format in which that documentation is stored. To run the Documenter, click the Database Documenter button in the Analyze group on the Database Tools tab of the Ribbon.

Book II
Tables for Storing Your Data

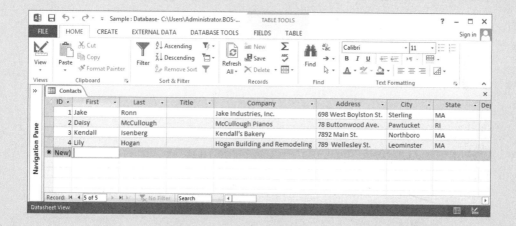

Discover how to filter multiple fields with the flexible Filter by Form feature at www.dummies.com/extras/access2013aio.

Contents at a Glance

Chapter 1: Creating and Modifying Tables 67

Viewing Your Tables 68
Creating the First Table for Your Data.................................... 70
Working with Tables and Fields in Your Database 74
Creating Fields 76
Working with a Datasheet Full of Data.................................. 80
Adding and Editing Records.. 82
Checking Your Spelling... 92
Using AutoCorrect for Faster Data Entry............................... 94
Formatting a Datasheet... 96
Taking Advantage of Subdatasheets 101
Adding a Total Row to the Datasheet 103

Chapter 2: Refining Your Table in Design View 105

Creating Tables in Design View 105
Refining Your Table in Design View..................................... 107
Formatting Fields with Field Properties 113
Defining the Primary Key.. 117
Indexing Fields 118
Printing Table Designs.. 119

Chapter 3: Sorting, Finding, and Filtering Data in a Datasheet 121

Sorting the Rows of a Datasheet... 121
Finding (and Replacing) Data... 123
Filtering a Datasheet 125

Chapter 4: Importing and Exporting Data. 137

Cutting, Copying, and Pasting.. 137
Importing or Linking to Data... 142
Getting Data from Another Access Database........................ 153
Getting Data Out of Access... 154
Using Access Data in a Word Mail Merge........................... 156

Chapter 5: Avoiding "Garbage In, Garbage Out" 157

Finding the Right Tool to Keep Garbage Out 158
Using Input Masks to Validate and Format Data 159
Creating a Lookup Field 164
Validating Data As It's Entered 170

Chapter 6: Relating Your Tables and Protecting Your Data 175

Creating Relationships and Protecting Your Data with
    Referential Integrity 177
Creating Referential Integrity with Many-to-Many Relationships 182
Printing the Relationships Window....................................... 184

Chapter 1: Creating and Modifying Tables

In This Chapter

✔ Making original tables with Datasheet view

✔ Displaying existing tables

✔ Navigating a datasheet

✔ Finding and editing your data

✔ Entering and editing tricky hyperlinks

✔ Spell-checking data

✔ Using AutoCorrect to enter data

✔ Adding formatting to a table

✔ Working with subdatasheets

✔ Totaling the data in a datasheet

*T*ables are the basic building blocks of your database; they hold the data that you need to save and analyze. If you have data and are using Access, this chapter is a great place to start.

Your data may already be in Access, or it may be stored somewhere else, either on paper or in electronic form, and you (or someone you work for) decided that Access is the right tool for storing and analyzing this data. You're probably right!

If you're getting ready to put data into Access, it's important that you first read Book I, Chapter 3. That chapter tells you how to gather all your data and look at it, how to decide how many tables to create to hold your data, and which fields to put in which tables. In that chapter, you also find out all about fields and records (that is, columns and rows in your table). After you've outlined the big picture of your database design, this chapter is the next step. Here, we tell you how to go about creating new tables and putting your data in them.

Creating tables and entering data may not be the most glamorous things you do with your database, but having well-designed tables and correctly entered data makes your database as useful as possible. After you've created a place to store your data in an organized way, you can put Access to work and analyze and view your data in any way you want.

This chapter guides you through creating tables and defining fields in Datasheet view. Chapter 2 of this minibook goes into the details you need to know about creating and editing fields in Design view. The other chapters in this minibook cover all the other important details that keep your tables — and the data in them — in good shape for use in queries, forms, reports, and the other objects in your database, as well as ways to analyze data with the tools available within a datasheet without resorting to the more powerful (and complicated) tools that Access provides.

If you want to look at existing tables, skip to "Working with a Datasheet Full of Data," later in this chapter. When you want to enter new data, change existing data, or refine field definitions, look for the pertinent section headings throughout this minibook.

Viewing Your Tables

Do you already have tables that you want to view? To display an existing table, find the Tables heading at the top of the list in the Navigation Pane, followed by the names of all the tables in the database. Double-click the name of the table you want to display, and the table appears in Datasheet view.

The Navigation Pane appears as a pane on the left side of the Access window or as a white bar along the left side of the window; click the bar to display the pane. (See Book I, Chapter 2 for more information on using the Navigation Pane.)

If you don't see a Tables heading followed by all the tables in the database, here's how to get a look at the tables in your database: Right-click the Navigation Pane title, and choose Category➪Object Type from the contextual menu. Now you should see the objects in the database, sorted by object type — that is, Tables, Queries, Forms, and Reports (see Book I, Chapter 2). You may still need to use the Navigation Pane's drop-down menu to display either Tables or All Access Objects.

You can display tables in two views:

✦ **Datasheet:** This view is similar to a spreadsheet, displaying your data in rows and columns. Rows are the records; columns are the fields. In Figure 1-1, you see a datasheet with all the parts labeled. Use a datasheet to view, enter, edit, and delete data. In Datasheet view, you can also create and delete fields, sort and filter data, check spelling, and find data. This chapter is all about table Datasheet view.

Record   Cell   Field

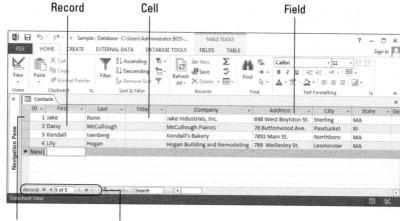

Figure 1-1:
Datasheet
view.

Record selector   Record navigator

Book II
Chapter 1

Creating and
Modifying Tables

View

◆ **Design:** In Design view, you don't see any data. Instead, you see the names of fields in the table. You can edit field names and specify the type of data that each field holds. You can also provide a field description. In addition, Design view contains *field properties* — more advanced ways to define fields and help make sure that data entry is accurate. In Figure 1-2, you see a table in Design view, with its various parts labeled. Chapter 2 of this minibook is all about Table Design view.

Field selector   Data Type drop-down menu   Field description   Fields

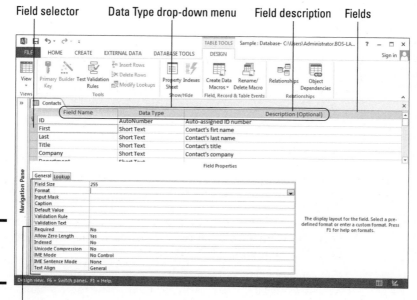

Figure 1-2:
Design
view.

Field properties

After you've displayed a table, you can easily switch between Design and Datasheet view by clicking the View button — the first button on the Home tab of the Ribbon.

Creating the First Table for Your Data

To get you right into the swing of working with Access, we start by showing you how to create a table and enter data in the datasheet.

Before you create a table to hold your data, take some time to consider the design of your database — that is, what fields and tables you need to use so that your data is well organized and easy to analyze. (Book I, Chapter 3 has all the information you need to know before you create your tables.)

After you figure out how to organize your data, you're ready to sit down with Access and create tables. If you're importing data rather than entering it piece by piece, see Chapter 4 of this minibook for more information.

Creating a new table using Datasheet view

The most straightforward way to create a new table is to create a datasheet and begin entering data. A *datasheet* looks like a spreadsheet; if you're familiar with Microsoft Excel or another spreadsheet program, you'll have no trouble entering data in a datasheet. When you have data entered, you can change field names and properties as needed.

In a datasheet, *fields* are columns, and *records* are rows. (If you're confused by this talk of fields and records, refer to Book I, Chapter 3.)

To create a table, first open the database that you want to hold the table. If you've just created a brand-new database, as soon as you name the database, you'll see an empty table in Datasheet view, ready for you to enter your data.

Follow these steps to create a new table in Datasheet view:

1. **Open your database.**

   If you're starting a new, blank database (as opposed to using a template), Access immediately creates a new table in Datasheet view for you. Just skip to Step 3, and start entering your data!

2. **Click the Table button on the Create tab of the Ribbon (the second button on that tab).**

   You see a blank datasheet in Datasheet view, as shown in Figure 1-3. Access names it Table1. (You can change the table's name when you save it.) Access automatically creates an ID field; in Figure 1-3, it's the first field. The ID field automatically gives each record a unique ID number, which is useful as you continue to build your database.

Notice that the Fields tab appears automatically on the Ribbon when you display a datasheet.

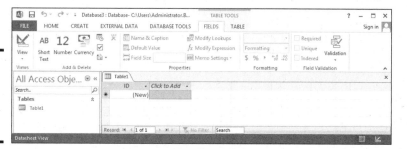

Figure 1-3:
A new, blank table, ready for data.

3. **Save the table by pressing Ctrl+S or by clicking the Save button near the top-left corner of the Access window.**

   Access displays the Save As dialog box, allowing you to name your table.

4. **Type a name for the table in the Table Name field, and press Enter.**

   Use a descriptive name so that you can find the table in the future. For more information on naming database objects, see Book I, Chapter 3.

Entering data and creating fields

When you have a new, blank datasheet, start entering your data. Even if you want to create a form to enter data, it makes sense to enter one record's worth of data and rename the fields to describe the data they hold. Then you'll have the basics of your table defined, and you can use the table to create a form, where you can continue to enter data in a more attractive interface.

As you enter data, Access determines the data type (Number, Date, or Text) and defines the field accordingly. Whenever you're ready, you can rename the fields.

Enter data by clicking the first cell and typing.

To save some time, for the very first piece of data in each field, add the dollar sign for currency numbers or the percent sign for a percentage, and type any dates in a recognized format (**1/10/14** or **January 1, 2014**, for example). Then Access knows the type of data you're putting in the field and automatically defines the data type, which saves you the trouble of changing it later.

After making each entry, press Tab or Enter to move to the next field. You might enter a first name, last name, street address, city, state, and zip code, for example, pressing Tab to move from one entry to the next.

Access uses a yellow highlight on the left border of the row (also called the *record selector*) and in the active field to indicate the location in the table where you're *writing* — that is, entering or editing — data. Access also italicizes the field name of the active cell and shows the cell outlined in pink so that you can easily see where you are on the datasheet. Enter data in as many columns as you think you need in the table.

As you enter data across a row, keep in mind that you're entering one record's worth of related data. Entering someone's first name, last name, and contact information, for example, is a sensible record. Each type of data is stored in a different field (column), and all the data in the row is related (in this case, referring to the same person).

If you want to add more information than can fit in the column width, just go right ahead. Access can store way more information in a cell than it displays in the initial cell widths. You can easily increase the width of your column or use the nifty little Zoom dialog box. Press Shift+F2 to see the contents of the cell in the dialog box (see "Editing the data you have," later in this chapter).

The first time you use Shift+F2 to see a Zoom box, you'll also see a Security Notice. If you are building a database from scratch, or if the database you are using comes from a trusted source, click Open to see the Zoom box. For more information on database security and Access's security warnings, see Book VII, Chapter 3.

Choosing field names

When you have some data in your table, you should name your fields, jettisoning the `Field1` and `Field2` names that Access so helpfully provided and choosing new, descriptive names for your fields.

When you name fields, give at least a couple of seconds' worth of thought to the names you give them. Although you can change a field name, thinking of the name as being permanent is safer. Pick a name that's descriptive and not too long. You often see the name without the description when you're building other objects, so naming fields well now saves you time later.

Starting every name with a number or a letter and keeping it to 64 characters or fewer are good ideas, as is avoiding using words that can confuse Access — notably, the names of functions and Visual Basic for Applications (VBA) commands.

If you're thinking about using your database in a SQL environment, don't use spaces in your field names. SQL doesn't like spaces! You can use capital letters and underscores to make your field names readable instead, as in `LastName` and `Last_Name`.

Changing a field name

In the database-building process, changing field names is easier if you do it sooner rather than later — that is, before you use the names a zillion times in tables, queries, forms, reports, and code.

You can rename a field in a single table, but if you use the field in other places in the database, be sure that the Name AutoCorrect feature is on. To see the Name AutoCorrect options, click the File button near the top-left corner of the Access window; then click the Options button at the bottom of the drop-down menu. Click Current Database in the Navigation Pane of the Access Options dialog box, and scroll down to the Name AutoCorrect Options section, which contains three Name AutoCorrect box check boxes. Make sure that the second check box, titled Perform name AutoCorrect, is selected.

To change a field name in Datasheet view, follow these steps:

1. **Double-click the current name.**

Access displays the name in white letters, highlighted with black. Whatever you type replaces the highlighted name.

2. **Type the new name, and press Enter.**

The field name has been changed. Check it carefully to make sure that it's exactly what you intended.

Alternatively, you can right-click the field name, choose Rename Field from the contextual menu, type a new name, and press Enter.

Saving your table

As soon as you enter data, Access saves it. So why do you need to save your tables? It's not to save the data; it's to save both the structure of the table and its field definitions. What you save when you save a table is the *table definition*, which includes how the table looks in Datasheet view (such as the size and order of the columns) and the information in Design view (the field names, data types, descriptions, and field properties).

Save a table design by using one of these methods:

✦ Click the Save button (which looks like a floppy disk and is on the toolbar above the Ribbon).

✦ Press Ctrl+S.

+ Close Design view, and click the Yes button when Access asks whether you want to save the table.

+ Click the File button in the top-left corner of Access, and choose Save from the drop-down menu.

When the Save As dialog box appears, provide a name that describes the data stored in the datasheet. When you need the data in this table to create other database objects, you'll be grateful that you named the table descriptively.

Working with Tables and Fields in Your Database

Now that you've created a simple table, entered data, changed field names, and saved the table so that your data is well-labeled and easy to find later, you're ready to tackle some of the nitty-gritty details of using Access 2013's Table Datasheet view. We start with other ways to create a table and ways to add preformatted fields to your newly created tables.

Finding other ways to create a table

If you're adding a table to an existing database, the second group of buttons on the Create tab of the Ribbon — the Tables group (see Figure 1-4) — allows you to create new tables.

Figure 1-4:
Click a button in the Tables group to create a new table.

The three buttons in this group are

+ **Table:** Creates a new, blank table displayed in Datasheet view, allowing you to enter data immediately. Clicking this button is the simplest way to create a new, blank table and display it in Datasheet view.

+ **Table Design:** Creates a new, blank table displayed in Design view, allowing you to define fields. See Chapter 2 of this minibook for more information on using Table Design view to refine your table and field definitions.

✦ **SharePoint Lists:** Creates a list on a SharePoint site and a table in the database that links to the newly created SharePoint list. A SharePoint list stored on a SharePoint server allows you to securely share Access data with others who have access to the SharePoint server. See Book IX, Chapter 3 for more information on using SharePoint with Access.

Notice that the Tables group gives you two options for creating tables from scratch: Table and Table Design. If you want help creating your table, Access provides two additional options:

✦ **Table templates:** *Table templates* allow you to choose among available tables with predefined fields (see the next section).

✦ **Field templates:** Another way to get help creating a table is to use *field templates* — predefined fields that you can put in any table. We talk about field templates in the upcoming "Quick-starting your table with field templates" section.

You don't need to stress about whether you want to create a table by defining fields in Design view or entering data in Datasheet view. It's easy to switch back and forth between Datasheet and Design views to define tables and fields exactly the way you want them. If your data fits into a table template, use one. If you have data to enter, and you don't want to use a table template, start by entering data in Datasheet view. If you're defining an entire database and the data is coming later, define the table by using Design view.

Starting with table templates (aka Application Parts)

Microsoft provides some shortcuts for creating common databases. Those tools include database templates, which we cover in Book I, Chapter 2. If your data fits (or almost fits) into a database template, you should use one.

A second option is to use an *Application Part,* which is a portion of one of Microsoft's database templates. To see the available Application Parts, click the Application Parts button on the Create tab of the Ribbon. Some of the Application Parts available are forms, which we cover in Book IV. The Quick Start options at the bottom of the Application Parts list, however, insert part of a database into your database so that you can get your database built faster. These Quick Start Application Parts insert a table into your database, along with supporting queries, forms, and reports that help you enter and analyze the data in the table. They may even prompt you to build new relationships between existing tables and the new table to integrate the new data into your existing database.

To add a table from the Application Parts menu, click the Application Parts button on the Create tab of the Ribbon. The drop-down Application Parts menu lists form templates at the top and then table templates below the Quick Start heading. Access may ask you to create a simple relationship to an existing table in the database but provides an option to create no relationship. You could create a relationship among people stored in a Contacts table and the comments they make stored in a Comments table. If you do create a relationship when adding the Application Part to your database, you see the related field in the new table in addition to the fields listed in the following list. You have five template choices:

✦ **Comments:** This template includes a Comments table with the fields ID, `CommentDate`, and `Comment`.

✦ **Contacts:** This template includes a Contacts table with the fields ID, `Company`, `Last Name`, `First Name`, `E-mail Address`, `Job Title`, `Business Phone`, `Home Phone`, `Mobile Phone`, `Fax Number`, `Address`, `City`, `State/Province`, `Zip`, `Country`, `Web Page`, `Notes`, and `Attachments`, as well as the calculated fields `ContactName` and `FileAs`. Additional database objects included are the `ContactsExtended` query, `ContactDetails` form, `ContactDS` form, `ContactList` form, `ContactAddressBook` report, `ContactList` report, `ContactPhoneBook` report, and `Label report`. This template is a good one to use if you want to store an address book in Access.

✦ **Issues:** This template includes an Issues table with the fields ID, `Summary`, `Status`, `Priority`, `Category`, `Project`, `OpenedDate`, `DueDate`, `Keywords`, `Resolution`, `ResolvedVersion`, and `Attachments`, as well as an `IssueDetail` form and an `IssueNew` form.

✦ **Tasks:** This template includes a Tasks table with the fields ID, `TaskTitle`, `Priority`, `Status`, `Description`, `StartDate`, `DueDate`, `Attachments`, and `Percent Complete`, as well as the calculated field `Active`. Additional database objects are a `TaskDetails` form and a `TaskDS` form. This template can be part of a project-management database.

✦ **Users:** This template includes a Users table with the fields ID, `Email`, `FullName`, and `Login`, as well as `UserDetails` and `UsersMain` forms.

When you've chosen the template you want to use, wait a second while Access creates the table and any other objects. Then you can enter data or change the objects, just as you could if you'd created the objects from scratch.

Creating Fields

In the first part of this chapter, we show you a straightforward and familiar way to enter data in a datasheet, thereby automatically creating fields that you can rename to reflect the data. This method of entering and storing data is familiar to anyone who has used Excel or any other spreadsheet program, and it works well.

In Book I, we emphasize designing your database before you start entering data. If you follow that advice, you may want to define fields and tables before you enter any data at all. This section shows you how to define fields before you enter data while you're in Datasheet view; Chapter 2 of this mini-book tells you how to perform the same task in Table Design view.

You can define fields in four ways:

✦ Enter data in a datasheet, and let Access figure out what kind of data is in each field (see "Entering data and creating fields," earlier in this chapter).

✦ Click the Click to Add heading (the last column in any table datasheet), and choose a field type from the drop-down menu (see "Creating fields by clicking a button," later in this chapter).

✦ Click buttons in the Add & Delete section of the Fields tab of the Ribbon (see "Creating fields by clicking a button," later in this chapter).

✦ Define each field yourself in Table Design view (see Chapter 2 of this minibook).

You may choose to use any combination of these methods as you build your database.

If you want to delete a field, see "Inserting and deleting columns," later in this chapter.

Creating fields by clicking a button

To create fields in a datasheet before you enter data, follow these steps:

1. Open a table in Datasheet view.

Double click a table name, or click the Table button on the Create tab of the Ribbon to create a new table.

2. Click the title of the last column in the table, Click to Add, to see a list of data types.

A drop-down menu opens (see Figure 1-5).

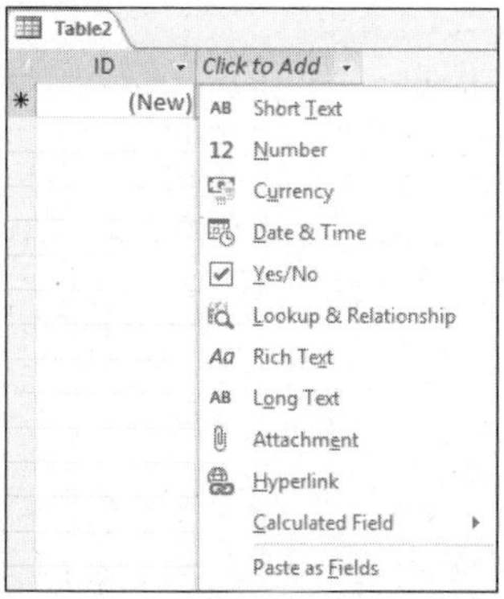

Figure 1-5:
Add a field
to your
datasheet
by choosing
a data type.

Table2		
ID ▾	*Click to Add* ▾	
* (New)	AB	Short Text
	12	Number
		Currency
		Date & Time
	✓	Yes/No
		Lookup & Relationship
	Aa	Rich Text
	AB	Long Text
		Attachment
		Hyperlink
		Calculated Field ▸
		Paste as Fields

3. **Choose the data type that best matches the data for the new field.**

   (We explain field types in detail in Chapter 2 of this minibook.)

   Access creates a field of the correct type, naming it Field1 (or whatever field number is next for this table).

4. **Before you do anything else, type a different name for the field, and press Enter.**

   The name of the new field is selected so that you can rename it, using a name that describes the data that the field will hold.

5. **Repeat steps 2–4 to add all the fields you want.**

If you find your options to be insufficient, instead of clicking Click to Add in Step 2, you may prefer to click the buttons for common field types in the Add & Delete group on the Fields tab of the Ribbon. To see more choices, click the More Fields button to display the More Fields drop-down menu, which lists field types in categories. The first category is Basic Types, which contains options including Number, Date & Time, and Yes/No. In some cases, you may see the type of field you want to create right away. (For details on all these field types, see Chapter 2 of this minibook.) Choose any item to create a new field of the clicked data type.

If you scroll down the list, you see the category Quick Start, which is covered in the next section.

The field type — such as Short Text, Number, or Currency — defines the data type and format (which is how the data is displayed) and may also include field properties (see Chapter 2 of this minibook).

Chapter 2 of this minibook also provides more information about defining fields and performing related tasks in Table Design view.

Quick-starting your table with field templates

If you're adding fields to your table, Access 2013 provides a way for you to quick-start your table. The Quick Start fields (which you access by clicking the More Fields button in the Add & Delete group on the Fields tab of the Ribbon) aren't single fields but groups of fields, and in some cases, selecting a Quick Start field may give you all the fields you need for your table. Each field is defined with the appropriate properties. Figure 1-6 shows the Quick Start field options.

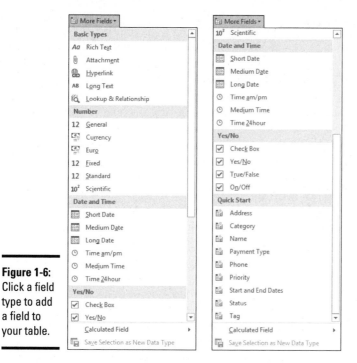

Figure 1-6:
Click a field
type to add
a field to
your table.

Here's a rundown of the Quick Start options:

✦ **Address:** Creates the following fields: `Address`, `City`, `StateProvince`, `ZipPostal`, and `CountryRegion`.

✦ **Category:** Creates a field called `Category`. The input for the field is predefined. When you're inputting data, you can choose `1-Category`, `2-Category`, or `3-Category`. Change the input options that appear on the drop-down menu for this field by switching to Design view and editing the `Row Source` property of the lookup tab.

✦ **Name:** Creates `LastName` and `FirstName` fields.

✦ **Payment Type:** Creates a `PaymentType` field with the options `Cash`, `Credit Card`, `Check`, and `In Kind`. Change these options by switching to Design view and editing the `Row Source` property of the lookup tab.

✦ **Phone:** Creates `BusinessPhone`, `HomePhone`, `MobilePhone`, and `FaxNumber` fields.

✦ **Priority:** Creates a `Priority` field with the options `1-High`, `2-Normal` (the default), and `3-Low`. Change these options by switching to Design view and editing the `Row Source` property of the lookup tab or the `Default Value` property on the General tab.

✦ **Start and End Dates:** Creates `Start Date` and `End Date` fields.

✦ **Status:** Creates a `Status` field with the options `Not Started`, `In Progress`, `Completed`, `Deferred`, and `Waiting`. Change these options by switching to Design view and editing the `Row Source` property of the lookup tab.

✦ **Tag:** Creates a `Tag` field with multiple inputs: `Tag 1`, `Tag 2`, and `Tag 3`. Change these options by switching to Design view and editing the `Row Source` property of the lookup tab.

See Chapter 2 of this minibook for details on changing field properties.

Working with a Datasheet Full of Data

If you've inherited a database full of data, put lots of data into your database, or created queries and displayed the results in datasheets, it's reasonable to expect that you may want to look at the data! You have lots of ways to see your data in Access, which presumably is why you chose Access instead of a spreadsheet program like Excel. Access lets you make your data more approachable, with reports and queries that organize your data or let you look at just part of it. Being able to get around a datasheet is a basic task, and this section gives you a handle on it.

Double-click any table or query name in the Navigation Pane to display the table or query in Datasheet view. (For more information about the Navigation Pane and about opening database objects, see Book I, Chapter 2.)

Looking at a datasheet

A datasheet displays data in a table. It has rows (records), columns (fields), and cells that hold individual pieces of data.

If you're looking at a table in Design view and want to see data, click the View button — the first button on both the Home and Design tabs of the Ribbon — to see the table in Datasheet view. To return to Design view, click the View button again. Also, you can click one of the View buttons in the bottom-right corner of the Access window, if you find them to be more convenient. To see a button's name, let the cursor rest on it.

The important buttons in Datasheet view live on three tabs of the Ribbon:

✦ **Home:** The Home tab contains tools that manage the data displayed in the datasheet. Click those buttons to cut and paste, change the appearance of data (font, color, justification, and so on), check spelling, filter the data displayed, and find the specific data you're looking for.

✦ **Fields:** Fields is the first of the Table Tools tabs, which contain tools for manipulating the database through the datasheet; the other is

Table (discussed next). The Fields tab has buttons that let you add and rename fields, change a field's formatting, and settings to validate data.

✦ **Table:** The second Table Tools tab, Table, has buttons for creating macros and for viewing relationships and object dependencies.

The two Table Tools tabs — Fields and Table — are available only when you have a table open in Datasheet view. If you want to do something to the datasheet that you might otherwise do in Design view, the tool you need probably is on one of these tabs.

Navigating the data

Moving around in a datasheet is pretty straightforward. Use the vertical scroll bar (see Figure 1-7) or the Page Up and Page Down keys to move quickly up and down the datasheet, from record to record. Use the horizontal scroll bar to move from left to right, and press Enter or Tab to move the cursor from field to field.

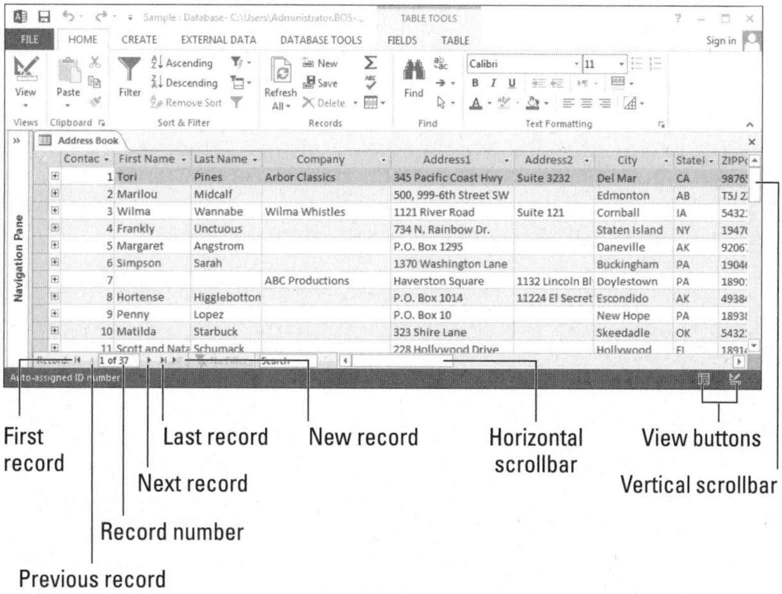

Book II Chapter 1

Creating and Modifying Tables

Figure 1-7: Tools for moving around a datasheet.

First record
Last record
New record
Horizontal scrollbar
View buttons
Next record
Record number
Vertical scrollbar
Previous record

You can use three tools to move around:

✦ **Mouse:** Click a cell, drag the scroll bars, or click the arrows at the ends of each scroll bar.

✦ **Keyboard:** Press Page Up, Page Down, and the other keys listed in Table 1-1.

✦ **Buttons:** Click the record-navigation buttons in the bottom-left corner of the datasheet (refer to Figure 1-7), or click the New Record button on the toolbar to jump to the end of your listings.

Table 1-1	Datasheet Navigation Keystrokes
Keystroke	*Where It Takes You*
Page Down	Down a page
Page Up	Up a page
Tab	Next cell
Shift+Tab	Previous cell
Home	First field of the current record
End	Last field of the current record
Ctrl+↑	First record of the current field
Ctrl+↓	Last record of the current field
Ctrl+Home	First record of the first field (top-left corner of the datasheet)
Alt+F5	Record Number box (type a record number and press Enter to go to that record)

If you know the number of the record you want (such as the fourth record in the table), type the record number in the Record box at the bottom of the datasheet (refer to Figure 1-7) and then press Enter.

Record numbers are relative; Access doesn't assign permanent numbers to records. Sorting the datasheet so that records appear in a different order means that record numbers in the datasheet may change.

Adding and Editing Records

To create a new record, start typing in a blank row. To move to a blank row, click one of the two New Record buttons (one nestled with the record navigation buttons in the bottom-left corner of the datasheet and the other in the Records group on the Home tab of the Ribbon), or press Ctrl++ (hold Ctrl and type a plus sign). Type your data for the field, and press Enter or Tab to move to the next field. When you get to the last field of a record and press Tab or Enter, Access automatically moves you to the first field of a new record.

As you enter data, you may come across fields that are check boxes or drop-down menus. You can easily use the mouse to change a check-box setting or make a choice from a menu, but you can also use the keyboard, as follows:

✦ Press the spacebar to change a check-box setting from selected to deselected, or vice versa.

✦ Press F4 to open a drop-down menu, press the ↓ key to make your
   choice, and then press Enter.

If you change your mind about your entry, press the Esc key to cancel it. If
you've already pressed Enter, you can undo the last entry by clicking the
Undo button (a small button on the toolbar above the Ribbon) or pressing
Ctrl+Z (a shortcut for Undo in many applications). Another useful keystroke
to know is Ctrl+' (apostrophe), which repeats the value in the record immediately above the cursor.

Table 1-2 lists all the keystrokes you'll ever need to enter and edit data.

Table 1-2	Keystrokes in Datasheet View
Keystroke	*What It Does*
Ctrl++ (plus sign)	Moves the cursor to a new record
Enter or Tab	Enters the data and moves to the next cell to the right or to the first field of the next record
Esc	Cancels the current entry
Undo or Ctrl+Z	Undoes the last entry
F4	Displays a drop-down menu (if one is present) in the current cell
Ctrl+C	Copies the selected data
Ctrl+X	Cuts the selected data
Ctrl+V	Pastes data from the clipboard
Delete	Deletes the selected data
Ctrl+Enter	Enters a line break within an entry
Ctrl+—	Deletes the current record
Spacebar	Switches between the values in a check box or option button

Chapter 4 of this minibook covers cutting, copying, and pasting in detail.

Using keystrokes to enter data automatically

Access has a few extremely convenient keystrokes that enter data for you
automatically, and they're listed in Table 1-3.

Table 1-3	Entering Data with Keystrokes
Keystroke	*Data It Enters*
Ctrl+' (apostrophe)	Repeats the entry for the field from the previous record
Ctrl+; (semicolon)	Inserts the current date
Ctrl+Shift+: (colon)	Inserts the current time
Ctrl+Alt+spacebar	Inserts the default value for a field

You can also use the Windows cut-and-paste shortcut keys. Press Ctrl+C to copy the selected information to the clipboard, Ctrl+X to cut the selected information and move it to the clipboard, and Ctrl+V to paste the information from the clipboard at the current cursor location. (See Chapter 4 of this minibook for more information on using the clipboard.)

Editing the data you have

Editing data is pretty straightforward. The only trick is noticing whether you're in *overwrite mode* (the entire contents are selected) or in *edit mode* (a cursor is displayed). To get into edit mode, click where you want to place the cursor, or press F2 to insert the cursor at the end of the data.

To edit data, place your cursor in the cell containing the data you want to change, press the Backspace or Delete key to get rid of unwanted stuff, and then type your replacement stuff.

Use these tricks when selecting text:

✦ To replace the entire value, move the pointer to the left of the field until it changes into a big plus sign and then click to select the whole cell.

✦ Double-click to select a word or value.

✦ Click at the beginning of what you want to select, press the Shift key, and then click at the end of what you want to select.

If you have lots of text in a cell and want to see it all at once, select the cell and press Shift+F2 to see the data in the Zoom dialog box (see Figure 1-8). You can make any changes and then press Enter or click OK to return to the datasheet. Click the Font button in the Zoom dialog box to change the font and the font size. Any changes you make to the font in this dialog box are retained, so the next time you display the Zoom dialog box, you see the data with the new font settings. These settings don't affect how the data is displayed in the datasheet, however.

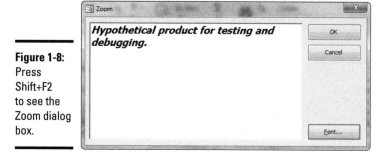

Figure 1-8:
Press
Shift+F2
to see the
Zoom dialog
box.

Table 1-4 lists the keystrokes you can use in editing mode.

Table 1-4	Keystrokes to Use While Editing
Keystroke	*What It Does*
Home	Moves to the beginning of the entry
End	Moves to the end of the entry
← or →	Moves one character to the left or right
Ctrl+← or Ctrl+→	Moves one word to the left or right
Shift+Home	Selects from the insertion point to the beginning of the entry
Shift+End	Selects from the insertion point to the end of the entry
Shift+←	Selects one character to the left
Shift+→	Selects one character to the right
Ctrl+Shift+←	Selects one word to the left
Ctrl+Shift+→	Selects one word to the right

Adding calculated fields to tables

Access 2010 introduced the capability to add calculated fields to tables. In earlier versions of Access, you were forced to create a query if you wanted to calculate a field. Now you can simply name the new field in a table and add an expression to calculate a result. Often, you want your calculated fields to be in queries, but if you need a calculated field in a table, you can define it there.

To add a calculated field, follow these steps:

1. **Display the table in Datasheet view.**

2. **Click the text *Click to Add* in the last column in the table.**

The Click to Add drop-down menu appears, listing types of fields that can be added to the table.

3. **Choose Calculated Field.**

   A submenu of data types is displayed.

4. **Choose the correct data type for your calculated field: Text, Number, Currency, Yes/No, or Date & Time.**

Alternatively, you can click the More Fields button in the Add & Delete group on the Fields tab of the Ribbon, and choose Calculated Field from the drop-down menu to add a calculated field to the table. Access displays the Expression Builder, where you can write your expression. In an Order Details table, for example, you can create a field to calculate quantity × unit price.

The Expression Builder is covered in detail in Book III, Chapter 2.

Rename your field after you define the calculation!

Entering and editing hyperlinks

Working with fields that have the Hyperlink data type can be a little tricky if you want to edit them rather than open the hyperlink, but read on for the solutions.

Creating hyperlinks

Fields are defined as Hyperlink fields in one of two ways:

✦ If you type hyperlink data in a new field in a datasheet, Access may define the field as a Hyperlink field. (Start a web link with http://, https://, or mailto: to have Access recognize it as a hyperlink.)

✦ If you define the field in Design view with the Hyperlink data type or add a hyperlink field in Datasheet view, the field is a Hyperlink field.

The most common types of hyperlinks are links to web pages or to files stored locally. You can enter those kinds of addresses simply by typing the address or path of the page or file you want to link to. An even easier method is to copy and paste a link from your web browser or Windows Explorer.

Editing hyperlinks in the datasheet

When you type in a field defined with the Hyperlink data type, the text instantly turns into a hyperlink — blue, underlined, linked text. You can't click hyperlinks to edit them, however. Clicking a hyperlink always takes you to the linked file, which can prove to be inconvenient. If you want to edit it, you have to take a less-direct route:

✦ Right-click the hyperlink and choose Hyperlink from the contextual menu.

✦ Press the Tab key to move the cursor to the cell that contains the hyperlink; then press F2 to change to edit mode.

✦ Hover the pointer over the top-left corner of the cell until the pointer changes to a plus sign; then click to select the entire contents of the cell and replace the data in it, or press F2 to change to edit mode.

Editing hyperlinks in dialog boxes

Alternatively, you may choose to enter or edit a hyperlink by taking advantage of extra features in the Insert Hyperlink dialog box (shown in Figure 1-9) or the Edit Hyperlink dialog box.

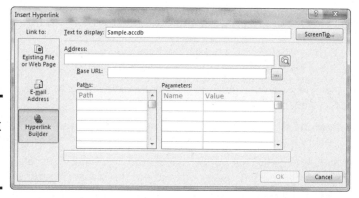

Figure 1-9:
Press Ctrl+K
to enter
or edit a
hyperlink.

To display the Insert Hyperlink or Edit Hyperlink dialog box, do one of the following:

✦ Right-click the `Hyperlink` field and choose Hyperlink➪Edit Hyperlink from the contextual menu.

✦ Press Tab to move the focus to the `Hyperlink` field and then press Ctrl+K.

If the cell already contains hyperlink data, Access displays the Edit Hyperlink dialog box. If the cell is empty but is defined as a `Hyperlink` field, you'll see the Insert Hyperlink dialog box.

Using the Edit Hyperlink dialog box, you can either change the text to display or change the address that the hyperlink points to (near the bottom of the dialog box).

You can also edit a hyperlink by tabbing to it and pressing F2, but what you get onscreen is the multipart hyperlink separated by pound (#) characters — a bit messy to deal with, to be honest — and you can't use the mouse to move the cursor. The dialog-box method is more surefire. (For more information about the parts of hyperlinks, see the nearby sidebar "The official parts of a hyperlink.")

The Insert Hyperlink and Edit Hyperlink dialog boxes provide different options, depending on the type of link you're creating. You can create a link to open any of the following:

✦ An existing file or web page

✦ An e-mail address

Use the buttons on the left side of the dialog box — the ones below the Link To heading — to select the type of link and then enter any additional information about the hyperlink.

The following options always appear in the Insert Hyperlink dialog box:

✦ **Text to Display:** This option lets you specify text that displays as a hyperlink. This text can be, but doesn't have to be, the hyperlink address.

✦ **Address:** Use the Address or E-Mail Address box to specify the URL, file location, or e-mail address.

✦ **ScreenTip:** Click this button to enter text that appears when the cursor hovers over the hyperlink text.

✦ **Remove Link:** This option deletes the hyperlink. You see this button on the Edit Hyperlink dialog box but not the Insert Hyperlink dialog box.

Other options in the dialog box depend on the type of link you're creating.

If you link to an existing file or web page, you see these browsing options for finding the file or web page you want the hyperlink to point to:

✦ **Current Folder:** Displays the current folder on your computer and allows you to enter a path or to browse your computer or local area network.

✦ **Browsed Pages:** Displays pages recently viewed in your browser.

✦ **Recent Files:** Displays the contents of the Windows Recent Documents folder.

✦ **Browse the Web:** Opens your browser.

✦ **Browse for File:** Opens the Link to File dialog box, where you can browse to a file.

✦ **Address:** Displays the URL of the file or page. Access fills in the URL automatically as you type, or you can enter it manually. The drop-down menu displays recently used files and URLs.

If you link to an e-mail address, specify the e-mail address and the subject of the e-mail message to be created when the user clicks the hyperlink.

The official parts of a hyperlink

A hyperlink entry can consist of four parts:

- ✔ The *underlined text* you see in a datasheet or form
- ✔ The *address* that the hyperlink links to (the only required part)
- ✔ The *subaddress* that the hyperlink links to
- ✔ A *screen tip* — text that appears in a small box when the cursor hovers above the hyperlink

If you edit hyperlink data, you'll find that it looks like this: `displaytext#address#subaddress#screentip`. Only the first two parts are required.

Because the full hyperlink entry consists of four parts, separated by # characters, you may find using the Insert Hyperlink and Edit Hyperlink dialog boxes to be an easier way to enter and edit hyperlinks.

Book II Chapter 1

Creating and Modifying Tables

Setting advanced options with the Hyperlink Builder

Clicking the Hyperlink Builder button on the Edit Hyperlink dialog box displays the settings shown in Figure 1-10. The Base URL, Paths, and Parameters options allow you to define a relative hyperlink and also control how the link opens when the hyperlink is clicked.

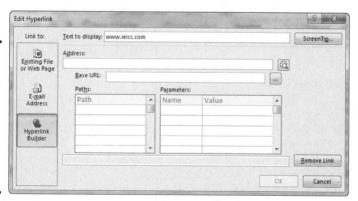

Figure 1-10: Advanced hyperlink settings are available when you choose Hyperlink Builder.

Deleting hyperlinks

You can remove a hyperlink by right-clicking it and choosing Hyperlink⇨Remove Hyperlink from the contextual menu. Both the text and the hyperlink are removed.

Using the Attachment data type

The `Attachment` data type was introduced with Access 2007. When a field is defined with the `Attachment` data type, you can store one or more files for each record in the field, such as a picture of a person or files containing correspondence about an order. Attachments can increase the size of the database dramatically, but because the attached file is stored as part of the database, you're not dependent on network drives being available, as you would be if you had included a hyperlink to the file. As a matter of fact, feel free to delete the original file after you attach it to the database so that you aren't storing it twice or storing multiple versions of the file.

To use the Attachment data type, you must be using Access 2007, 2010, or 2013, and the database must be in the newer .accdb format. Individual files can't be larger than 256MB, and all attached files can't exceed 2GB (the size limit for an Access database).

After you've defined the data type of a field as Attachment, you can't change the field to any other data type.

Normally, a field holds only a single piece of information for each record. In an Attachment field, however, you can store multiple attachments. (Access creates a hidden table to normalize your data.)

You have two ways to create an Attachment field in a table:

✦ Insert a field based on the Attachment data type into your datasheet. (Refer to "Creating Fields," earlier in the chapter, for details.)

✦ Define the field data type as Attachment by clicking the Data Type button in the Formatting group on the Fields tab of the Ribbon, or by choosing Attachment from the Data Type drop-down menu in Table Design view.

In Datasheet view, a paper-clip icon appears in the field-name box to indicate that the field is an Attachment field. An Attachment field can't be renamed in Datasheet view, although the name of the field can be changed in Design view. Each record also contains a paper-clip icon with a number in parentheses indicating how many attachments the record has.

Manage attachments by double-clicking a record's paper-clip icon. The Attachments dialog box opens, as shown in Figure 1-11.

Figure 1-11:
Manage
Attach-
ment fields
by using the
Attachments
dialog box.

Add an attachment by clicking the Add button; then navigate to the file and click Open. Repeat to attach more files.

To view an attached file, open the Attachments dialog box, and double-click the name of the attached file. The file opens in its native application, if that application is available. (An `.xls` or `.xlsx` file opens in Excel, for example.) You can change the file and save it. To save files to the database, be sure to return to Access, click OK in the Attachments dialog box, and click Yes when you're asked whether you want to save your updates to the database.

The Save As and Save All buttons on the Attachments dialog box allow you to save attachments to your hard drive or another location so that they can be opened without opening the database.

Deleting records

It's inevitable that sometimes, you want to delete data. Before you do that, however, here's a word to the wise:

You can't click the Undo button to recover deleted data. Rather than deleting, you may want to consider keeping old data in a new field.

With that caveat firmly in mind, you can delete a record by following these steps:

1. **Select the record you want to delete by clicking the record selector to the left of it.**

   A record is a whole row of data.

2. **Press the Delete key or click the Delete Record button.**

   Access asks you whether you're sure that you want to delete the data.

3. **Click the Yes button to delete.**

   The row you selected is deleted, and the data below the deleted row moves up to fill the space.

Entering special characters

Occasionally, you need to enter characters that aren't on your keyboard. Access doesn't provide an easy way to do that, but if you know how to find the special character in another program, you may want to create it in that program and then cut and paste it into Access. Otherwise, follow these steps:

1. **Choose Start➪All Programs➪Accessories➪System Tools➪Character Map.**

   Alternatively, begin typing **Character Map** in the Start button's Search box and click it when it appears in the list of possibilities. (In Windows 8, just begin typing **Character Map**.)

Character Map appears, displaying a grid of characters. The drop-down menu at the top of the box lists available fonts. The box at the top is where the characters you select in Step 3 appear.

2. **Browse to find the character you need.**

   Each font has a different set of characters, so you may need to browse the fonts to find the character you want. Use the vertical scroll bar to see all the characters within a font.

3. **Double-click the character, or select it and then click the Select button to display it in the Characters to Copy box.**

4. **Repeat Step 3 until you have all the characters you need.**

After you select the character you need, look at the bottom of the Character Map window to see the keystrokes to enter the selected character. Within Access, you can hold down Alt and type the code on the number pad of your keyboard to enter the character.

5. **Click the Copy button.**

   The contents of the Characters to Copy box are copied to the Windows clipboard.

6. **Return to Access, and place the cursor where you want to insert the character.**

7. **Click the Paste button or press Ctrl+V.**

If you don't see the character you copied, you may have to format it with the font you selected in Character Map.

Checking Your Spelling

You can check your spelling in a datasheet or form by clicking the Spelling button in the Records group on the Home tab of the Ribbon. You can easily skip some fields that contain words Access doesn't recognize, especially codes and abbreviations. (To see how, see Table 1-5, later in this section.) You may also find that it makes more sense to spell-check a field or two than to spell-check the whole datasheet. (You can select a field by clicking the field name; select several consecutive fields by selecting the first field and, while holding the Shift key, clicking the last field.)

When you spell-check, Access compares the words in the datasheet with the words in its own dictionary. Access considers anything that it doesn't find in the dictionary to be misspelled. Plenty of words that you use may not be in the Access dictionary, such as technical terms or unique product names, so don't assume that the Spelling dialog box is always right. Checking is a good habit.

Access uses main and custom dictionaries that are shared by all the Microsoft Office applications. You can use Microsoft Word to remove words from a custom dictionary; check Word's online help for details.

To conduct a routine spelling check, follow these steps:

1. **Click the Spelling button in the Records group on the Home tab of the Ribbon to open the Spelling dialog box (shown in Figure 1-12).**

Figure 1-12:
The Spelling dialog box helps you find and correct potentially embarrassing typos.

Access finds the first word that isn't in its dictionary and displays it in the Not in Dictionary box. In the Suggestions list, Access displays possible correct spellings of the word.

2. **Deal with the word, as follows:**

- Double-click a word in the Suggestions list to replace the misspelled word, or select the correctly spelled word and then click the Change button.

- Edit the word by clicking it and making corrections; then click Change or Change All.

- Click the Ignore button to ignore the word and find the next misspelled word.

- Click the Cancel button to exit the spelling check and correct the word in the datasheet manually.

Table 1-5 lists options in the Spelling dialog box that you may want to use while checking spelling.

Table 1-5	Spelling Dialog-Box Options
Options	*What It Does*
Ignore *"Field name"* Field	Tells Access not to check spelling in the field where it has found the latest misspelled word.
Ignore	Skips the current word and finds the next misspelled word.
Ignore All	Skips all instances of the word.
Change	Changes the misspelled word to the word typed in the Not in Dictionary box or selected in the Suggestions list.
Change All	Changes all instances of the misspelled word to the word typed in the Not in Dictionary box or selected in the Suggestions list.
Add	Adds the word to the dictionary. (Use this option carefully, as it's difficult to undo.)
AutoCorrect	Adds the misspelled word *and* the correctly spelled word selected in the Suggestions list to the AutoCorrect list. AutoCorrect automatically replaces words when you enter them (see the next section).
Options	Displays the Access Options window, where you can tell Access whether to suggest words, whether to ignore certain words, and which dictionary to use. (You can specify a foreign language by using the Custom Dictionary option.)
Undo Last	Undoes the last change made by the Spelling dialog box.
Cancel	Closes the Spelling dialog box and retains any changes made.

You can change the way that Access finds and corrects spelling errors by clicking the Options button in the Spelling dialog box or choosing Access Options⇨Proofing.

Using AutoCorrect for Faster Data Entry

AutoCorrect helps you in two distinct ways:

✦ It corrects misspelled words as you type.

✦ It replaces an abbreviation you type with more complete text, saving you time.

To change the way that AutoCorrect works, display the AutoCorrect dialog box, shown in Figure 1-13, by following these steps:

1. **Click the File button (near the top-left corner of the Access window) to display the File menu.**

2. **Choose Options.**

Figure 1-13: The AutoCorrect dialog box helps you set up abbreviations for faster data entry.

The Access Options dialog box appears.

3. **Click Proofing in the navigation section.**

   Spelling and AutoCorrect options appear.

4. **Click the AutoCorrect Options button.**

   The AutoCorrect dialog box appears.

5. **Make sure that the Replace Text As You Type option is selected.**

To add a common abbreviation to the AutoCorrect list, display the AutoCorrect dialog box (repeat steps 1–4 of the preceding list) and then follow these steps:

1. **Enter the abbreviation in the Replace box.**

2. **Enter the full term in the With box.**

3. **Click the Add button.**

4. **Make sure that the Replace Text As You Type option is selected.**

You can delete an AutoCorrect entry by selecting it in the list and then clicking the Delete button.

By default, all the options in the AutoCorrect dialog box are enabled (selected). You may want to disable (deselect) some or all of them if Access is making corrections that you don't want it to make.

The Exceptions button displays the AutoCorrect Exceptions dialog box (shown in Figure 1-14), where you can tell Access not to capitalize after a period that ends an abbreviation (on the First Letter tab) or to leave two or more initial caps the way you enter them (on the INitial CAps tab).

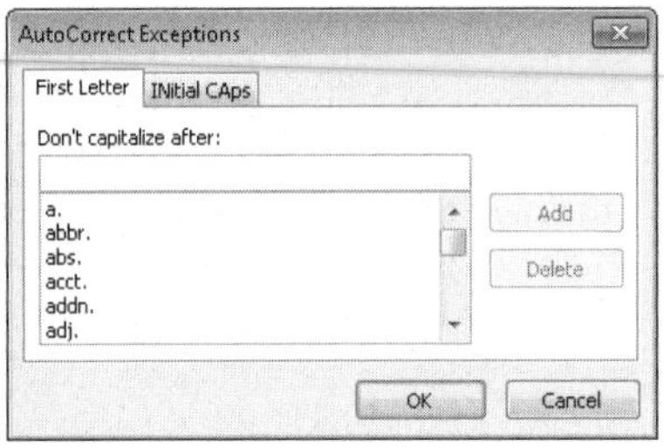

Figure 1-14:
The AutoCorrect Exceptions dialog box makes AutoCorrect more efficient.

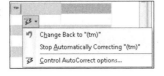

When AutoCorrect is turned on, it checks your typing after you press the spacebar, Tab, or Enter. If you've typed an entry that's in the AutoCorrect list, Access replaces the entry. If you've chosen to display the AutoCorrect Options button (the first check box on the AutoCorrect dialog box), you see the button immediately after AutoCorrect makes a correction. Click the button to see the menu shown in Figure 1-15. The options in this menu allow you to undo the autocorrection in this one instance, to undo all autocorrections, or to display the AutoCorrect dialog box.

Figure 1-15:
The AutoCorrect Options button lets you control each auto-correction.

Formatting a Datasheet

Datasheets can't provide the good-looking output you get with a report or a form, but you can make some changes to make a datasheet more readable and attractive. The formatting options are available on the Home and Fields tabs of the Ribbon.

Usually, you can't undo formatting changes by clicking the Undo button or pressing Ctrl+Z. You can undo changes by closing the table without saving, but of course you lose all the formatting and design changes that you made since the last time you saved the table.

Formatting a field

Field formats are covered in detail in Chapter 2 of this minibook, but you can format fields from the datasheet; you don't have to be in Design view. You can change a number field to show a currency symbol or display data as a percentage, for example. Select any value in a field to format the whole field and then click the Formatting buttons on the Fields tab of the Ribbon. If you can't make the change you want to make, check the field properties in Table Design view.

Be thoughtful about changing the data type. You may want to read the section about data types in Chapter 2 of this minibook, as it's possible to lose data when changing the data type. (Access warns you first, though.)

Use the buttons in the Formatting section on the Fields tab of the Ribbon to change the way that data is displayed. You can change numbers to display with a currency symbol, as percentages, or in comma number format (for instance, 1,000). You can also increase or decrease the number of decimal points displayed by clicking the Increase Decimals or Decrease Decimals button.

Changing the font

In an Access datasheet, the font and font size stay the same for all the data; you can't change the font for just some of the data (except for data in Rich Text fields).

Change the font by using the Text Formatting tools on the Home tab of the Ribbon. Changing the font, font style (bold, italic, or underlined), and font size changes that attribute for the whole datasheet. The Color option changes the color of the data in the datasheet.

Taking advantage of Rich Text

Access 2013 supports Rich Text, which means that you can store formatted text. Rich Text supports several types of formatting: font (including font size, font color, and emphasis [bold, underlined, or italic]), alignment (centered, right-aligned, or left-aligned), indents, numbered and bulleted lists, and fill (left to right or right to left).

In other words, you have just about all the formatting capabilities you need to make pretty text. To take advantage of Rich Text, however, you must create a Rich Text field. Otherwise, you format the whole datasheet rather than just part of one field.

In older versions of Access, formatted text was stored in a field formatted as the `Memo` type, with the `Text Format` property set to `Rich Text`. In Access 2013, Rich Text is stored as `Long Text`, with the `Text Format` property set to `Rich Text`. To add a Rich Text field, click More Fields in the

Add & Delete group on the Fields tab of the Ribbon; choose Rich Text from the drop-down menu, and rename the field. Then you can enter your fancy text in the field.

After you create a Rich Text field, view your data in a datasheet or (even better) on a form and then format away. When you select text in a Rich Text field, a formatting bar pops up with buttons for all the common formatting options. All the formatting options on the Home tab of the Ribbon are available to you. To format text, first select the text you want to format and then select the type of formatting you want to apply.

A Rich Text field can be displayed on a form or report in a text box control. The text box has a `Text Format` property that must be set to `Rich Text` for the text to appear onscreen with its formatting.

Changing gridlines and background color

Gridlines are the gray horizontal and vertical lines that separate cells in a datasheet. You can change the color of the gridlines or choose not to display them at all. You can even choose a special gridline effect other than plain lines.

Access 2013 has a sneaky button that you can click to display the Datasheet Formatting dialog box, shown in Figure 1-16. This button is in the bottom-right corner of the Text Formatting group on the Home tab of the Ribbon. (If you look at the Ribbon, you see a few more of these sneaky buttons that open a dialog box to let you work with all the settings in the Ribbon group.) If you hover the mouse over that button, you see that it's called Datasheet Formatting.

Secret Data Formatting button

Figure 1-16: Use the secret button to display the Datasheet Formatting dialog box.

Click the Datasheet Formatting button to display the Datasheet Formatting dialog box, make any changes (changes are previewed in the Sample box), and click OK. You have the option of making the datasheet work from right to left instead of the usual left to right — not an option that you'll use often, but if you need it, you can find it here.

Rearranging columns in a datasheet

You can rearrange the order of fields in the datasheet in either Datasheet or Design view. Follow these steps to move columns in Datasheet view:

1. **Select the column you want to move by clicking the field name.**

   You may want to select a block of columns by clicking, holding, and then moving the mouse pointer to the last column you want to select or by selecting the first column and then Shift+clicking the last field name in the block.

2. **Release the mouse button, click any selected field name, and drag the column(s) to its new position.**

   As you move the mouse, a dark vertical line shows where the columns will be when you release the mouse button.

 If you can't move a column, it's probably frozen. To unfreeze it, right-click a field name in that column and choose Unfreeze All Fields from the contextual menu. For more information, see the aptly named section "Freezing columns," later in this chapter.

Changing column width

When you initially create a datasheet, all the columns have the same width. Column widths are easy to change, however, and when you save the table, the new column widths are saved too.

To change the width of a column, move the pointer to the bar separating the field names at the top of the column. The mouse pointer changes to a double-headed arrow (shown in the margin). Drag the bar to the appropriate width, or double-click to size the column for the widest data in the column.

You can change the width of several adjacent columns at the same time. Start by selecting them: Click the field name of the first column and drag to the last field name, or click the first field name and then Shift+click the last. Then change the width of one of the selected columns. All the selected columns have the same (new) width.

If you prefer, use the Field Width dialog box to change column width. Right-click a field name and choose the Field Width option from the contextual menu to open the dialog box; then enter the width in number of characters.

You can use the Standard Width check box to reset the column width to the standard or click the Best Fit button to fit the column width to its contents. Click OK to close the dialog box.

Changing row height

You change row height with the mouse or with the Row Height dialog box. When you change the height of one row, all the rest of the rows change to match.

All the rows in a datasheet are the same height; you can't change the height of just one.

Changing row height with the mouse is very similar to changing column width: Move the mouse pointer to the record selector until the pointer turns into a double-headed arrow (shown in the margin). Then drag up to make the row shorter)or down to make the row taller.

Alternatively, right-click a record selector and choose Row Height from the contextual menu to display the Row Height dialog box. Enter the row height in points. (There are 72 points in an inch.) The Standard Height check box formats the row at the standard height for the font size you've chosen: the point size of the font plus cushions for the top and the bottom of the row.

Inserting and deleting columns

Columns are fields, so when you insert a column, you're adding a field, and when you delete a column, you're deleting the field and all its data. You can add and remove fields in Design view, too; see Chapter 2 of this minibook.

To insert a generic field in Datasheet view, follow these steps:

1. **Right-click the field name of the column where you want the new, blank column to appear and choose Insert Field from the contextual menu.**

   Access adds a column with the name Field1 (or some other number). The selected columns and all the columns to the right move to make room.

2. **Rename the field name by double-clicking the name Access gave it or by right-clicking it and choosing Rename Column from the contextual menu.**

3. **Type the new name, and press Enter.**

   The new field also appears in Design view.

To delete a field and all its data (but think really hard about it first), right-click the field name and choose Delete Field from the contextual menu. When Access asks you to confirm that you want to delete the field and its data, click the Yes button.

Hiding columns

If you want to hide a column in a datasheet (perhaps the data is sensitive), select the column or columns, right-click the selected field name(s), and choose Hide Fields from the contextual menu. To display hidden columns, right-click any field name and choose Unhide Fields from the contextual menu. A dialog box appears, allowing you to choose which columns to redisplay. In fact, to hide multiple fields, make the counterintuitive choice and choose Unhide Fields from the contextual menu. The Unhide Columns dialog box allows you to hide several fields at the same time; just deselect the check boxes next to the names of fields that you want to hide.

Freezing columns

When you're working with a wide datasheet, you may want to freeze one or more columns so that they don't scroll off the left side of your screen. To freeze one column, right-click the field name and choose Freeze Fields from the contextual menu. The selected column pops to the left side of the datasheet and stays there. To freeze more than one column, select the columns, right-click a field name, and then choose Freeze Fields from the contextual menu. To unfreeze columns, right-click the field name and choose the Unfreeze All Fields option from the contextual menu.

Changing default formatting for new tables

Access allows you to change default formatting for tables by using the Design tab of the Access Options window. Any changes you make affect only new datasheets, not existing tables and queries.

Display the Options dialog box by clicking the File button (near the top-left corner of the Access window) to display the File menu, and choose File⇨Options. Click Datasheet in the navigation section of the dialog box to display default formatting options for datasheets in the current database. You can change font, gridline, cell-effect options, and default column width. Most of the options in this dialog box (text colors, text font, gridlines, and cell effects) are discussed earlier in this chapter.

Taking Advantage of Subdatasheets

Access has a nifty feature that allows you to display data from related tables in your datasheet. You can also use a form to display related data from different tables.

Access automatically creates subdatasheets in a datasheet if you create a one-to-one relationship with another table or if the datasheet is on the "one" side of a one-to-many relationship with another table. (You need to define a relationship in the Relationship window or use the Lookup Wizard to create a relationship.) If you have a relationship between the Customers and Orders tables, for example, you can display the Customers table and use the subdatasheet feature to see the data from the Orders table showing you when a customer has placed an order. When a relationship is defined with the Order Details table, you can expand the subdatasheet display to another level and see the items that the customer ordered.

Figure 1-17 shows a datasheet with two levels of subdatasheets. The main datasheet shows the names and addresses of customers. The first-level subdatasheet lists order information; the second-level subdatasheet lists order details (items ordered).

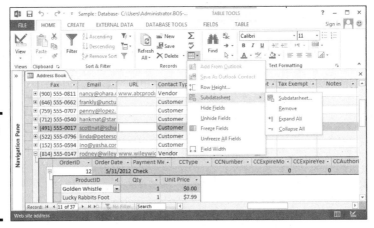

Figure 1-17: This table displays two levels of subdata-sheets.

Queries also may have subdatasheets. See Book I, Chapter 3, and Book II, Chapter 6 for more information on relationships.

When a subdatasheet is available, you see a plus sign (+) in the first column of the table. Click the plus sign to see the subdatasheet. When the subdatasheet opens, the plus sign changes to a minus sign (–). Click the minus sign to remove the subdatasheet. By default, subdatasheets display for a single record in the parent table. To display all data from the related table, click the More button in the Records group on the Home tab of the Ribbon, and choose Subdatasheets⇨Expand All. To hide all subdatasheets, click the More button in the Records group on the Home tab of the Ribbon, and choose Subdatasheets⇨Collapse All.

When a subdatasheet is displayed, you can use it as you would use a table — to view, format, enter, edit, or delete data.

Property
Sheet

Access determines which table to display as a subdatasheet based on the relationships you define in the database. You can select a table or query to be used as a subdatasheet on the Table property sheet. (Display the table in Design view, and click the Property Sheet button on the Design tab of the Ribbon.)

You can use a query as a subdatasheet. Doing so allows you to filter the data displayed in the subdatasheet by using criteria defined in the query.

When you select a subdatasheet manually, you need to know the name of the table or query that you use as the subdatasheet, as well as the names of the two related fields: one in the parent table and the other in the subdatasheet table. The two fields need to meet the requirements of related fields. (See Chapter 6 of this minibook for all the details on related fields.)

To select a table or query to be used as a subdatasheet, follow these steps:

1. **Click the More button in the Records group on the Home tab of the Ribbon.**

2. **Choose Subdatasheet⇨Subdatasheet.**

   The Insert Subdatasheet dialog box (shown in Figure 1-18) appears.

Figure 1-18: Use the Insert Sub-datasheet dialog box when you want to specify the subdata-sheet.

3. **Select the table or query you want to use as a subdatasheet.**

   To view just your tables, click the Tables tab; to view just your queries, click the Queries tab; to view both tables and queries, click the Both tab.

4. **From the Link Child Fields drop-down menu, choose the field in the subdatasheet table that you want to use to link the two tables.**

5. **From the Link Master Fields drop-down menu, choose the field from the parent table that you want to use to link the two tables.**

6. **Click OK.**

Adding a Total Row to the Datasheet

Access has a handy feature that allows you to add a total row to a datasheet. A *total row* can be used to count the number of items in a column, calculate a sum or average, or find the minimum or maximum value. All these options are aggregate functions, which you can use in queries and in a total row on a datasheet.

Follow these steps to create a total row:

1. **Display the datasheet.**

2. **Click the Totals button in the Records group on the Home tab of the Ribbon.**

    Access creates a row titled Total at the bottom of the datasheet.

3. **Click one of the blank cells in the total row to display an arrow; then click the arrow to display a drop-down menu of aggregation options.**

4. **From the drop-down menu, choose the kind of total you want to display.**

    The choices are None, Sum, Average, Count, Maximum, Minimum, Standard Deviation, and Variance. For Text and Rich Text fields, you can choose Count to count the number of entries in the field. For Date fields, your choices are limited to Average, Count, Maximum, and Minimum.

    Access displays the aggregate, as shown in Figure 1-19. To change the kind of aggregation, simply select the cell and choose another option from the drop-down menu.

Totals

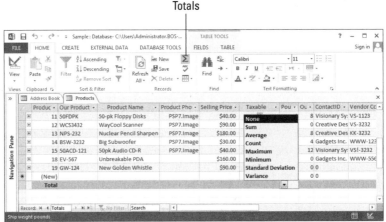

Figure 1-19: Click the Totals button on the Home tab of the Ribbon; then choose the type of aggregation you want for the field.

To clear the total row, simply click the Totals button again. If you change your mind and want your aggregates back, Access remembers the type of aggregation you chose for each field. You may also want to add a total row to queries displayed in Datasheet view (see Chapter 2 of this minibook).

The totals adjust when a filter is applied to the datasheet, as discussed in Chapter 2 of this minibook. Total rows don't appear in subdatasheets.

Chapter 2: Refining Your Table in Design View

In This Chapter

✔ Creating and fine-tuning fields in Design view

✔ Choosing the correct field type

✔ Formatting a field with field properties

✔ Defining a primary key

C hapter 1 of this minibook covers how to create tables and use your data in Datasheet view. This chapter covers creating and refining tables in Table Design view, where you never see any actual data.

In Design view, you can access many settings for all the fields in a table just a little more easily than you can in Datasheet view. If you're creating a table and won't immediately put data in it, Design view is a good place to do that, and if you want to change how your fields work and what data they accept, Design view is a good place to work.

Design view may be a little intimidating to begin with, but it can make your database work better. In Design view, you can work with field definitions without having to look at data. You can even define fields for data to be input later. Datasheets are similar to spreadsheets. Design view takes you into the database realm and allows you to take control of your data by using, for example, the data-integrity tools described in Chapter 5 of this minibook.

Creating Tables in Design View

Design view is a good place to create a table if you know a lot about the type of data that will be in the table and you want to design the fields you create for the data you have to put in them. If you're creating the table but don't yet have any data, Design view is the perfect place to start.

You can always switch to Datasheet view by clicking the View button on the Home or Design tab of the Ribbon or by clicking the Datasheet button near the bottom-right corner of the Access window.

Follow these steps to create a table in Design view:

Table Design

1. **Click the Table Design button in the Tables group on the Create tab of the Ribbon.**

Access opens a blank table in Design view. Notice the blinking cursor in the first row of the Field Name column.

2. **Type the name of the first field, and press Tab or Enter to move to the Data Type column.**

The field you create here will be the first field (the one displayed on the far-left side) in the datasheet. The field properties for the field fill in automatically (at the bottom of the screen in Design view), and the data type is set to the Short Text option, which holds up to 255 characters.

3. **Choose a data type from the Data Type drop-down menu.**

Common choices include Short Text, Long Text, Number, Date/Time, and Currency. Data types are covered in detail in "Choosing a data type," later in this chapter.

4. **(Optional but recommended) Type a description of the field in the Description column.**

The description can be especially useful if many people will use the database or if you don't plan to use the database often. Use the Description column to explain exactly how you intend the field to be used.

5. **Define additional fields in the table by repeating Steps 2–4.**

You can press Tab to move to the next row, where you enter the next field name. Figure 2-1 shows six fields defined.

Figure 2-1:
Defining
fields in
Design
view.

6. **Click the Save button or press Ctrl+S to save the table.**

7. **Type a descriptive name in the Name field, and press Enter.**

8. **When Access asks whether you want to define a primary key, click Yes or No.**

   Don't worry; whatever you choose now, you can change later. If you feel the need to make an informed decision now, skip to "Defining the Primary Key," later in this chapter. If you choose to create a primary key now, Access creates a new, numbered field that gives each record a unique number. (The first field shown in Figure 2-1, for example, is an AutoNumber field, defined as the primary key.) If you want to skip this step, be sure that you define a primary key manually when you know which field(s) you want to use to uniquely identify records.

After you define the fields in Design view, you have the option of displaying the table in Datasheet view and entering data. You also have the option of entering data through a form. (For all the details on forms, see Book IV.)

Refining Your Table in Design View

Design view is the place to go when you want to be really specific about what you want a field to hold. Design view also provides some tools you can use to make sure that the data entered in a field is what you want it to be; we cover this topic in more detail in Chapter 5 of this minibook.

The top part of the Design View window lists the fields in the table and their data types. Descriptions also appear in that part of the window if they've been added.

The bottom part of the Design View window displays *field properties* — configuration information about the current field. If you're a novice Access user, don't worry about field properties; you don't have to do anything with them at all. If you do need them at some point, however, we tell you exactly how to use them.

Many (but not all!) tasks you do in Design view can also be done in Datasheet view. Datasheet view is covered in detail in Chapter 1 of this minibook. The Formatting and Field Validation groups on the Fields tab of the Ribbon (which you can display when a datasheet is active) contain options for changing the format and some field properties (Unique and Required) for a selected field.

Design view has its own Ribbon of tools. To display those tools, click the Design tab that appears at the end of the Ribbon when Design view is displayed.

Table 2-1 lists the Design-view Ribbon tools.

Table 2-1   **Design-View Buttons and Their Functions**

Button	Name	What It Does
Primary Key	Primary Key	Makes the selected field the primary key field for the table.
Builder	Builder	Displays the Expression Builder, which helps you build a field or expression (an equation of some sort). The button is grayed out when creating an expression isn't an option. Builder is available when the cursor is in Field Name, Default Value, Validation Rule, or Smart Tags.
Test Validation Rules	Test Validation Rules	Tests validation rules. See Chapter 5 of this minibook for more information.
Insert Rows	Insert Rows	Adds a row (field) to the table design where the cursor is or inserts as many rows as are selected.
Delete Rows	Delete Rows	Deletes the current row or selected rows in Table Design view.
Modify Lookups	Modify Lookups	Creates a *lookup field* — a field that lists values stored in another field. See Chapter 5 of this minibook for more information.
Property Sheet	Property Sheet	Displays the property sheet for the selected field. A *property sheet* allows you to set even more controls for the field. (Many of the field properties are covered in Chapter 5 of this minibook.)
Indexes	Indexes	Displays the Indexes window, showing the indexed fields in the table and their index properties.
Create Data Macros	Create Data Macros	Creates a macro.
Rename/Delete Macro	Rename/Delete Macro	Displays the Data Macro Manager, where the macros attached to the table are listed.
Relationships	Relationships	Displays the Relationship window, where the relationships in the database are displayed (and can be created and edited).
Object Dependencies	Object Dependencies	Displays the Object Dependencies window, where you can see which database objects depend on the table you're viewing and which objects the table depends on.

Using the Caption property

Access gives you the option of giving a field a caption. A *caption* is text that's used on the datasheet, forms, and reports instead of the field name. The field name must still be used in expressions and in code.

To give a field a caption, use the `Caption` field property in Table Design view.

You can also access the `Caption` property by clicking the Name & Caption button in the Properties section on the Fields tab of the Ribbon in Datasheet view.

Adding a field

If you want to add a field in the middle of a table in Design view, place the cursor where you want the new field to appear (or select the row) and then click the Insert Rows button in the Tools group on the Design tab of the Ribbon. Rows at and below the cursor are pushed down to make room for the new field. Specify the name and data type, and you've created a new field.

Copying a field

You can copy a field definition easily. Be aware, however, that by using this method, you copy only the definition, not the data. You can even copy a field definition from one table to another — an easy way to be sure that related fields have the same definition.

Generally, only one of the matching fields in different tables needs the primary key designation. Be sure to remove the primary key designation from the other field.

To copy a field in Table Design view, follow these steps:

1. **Click the record selector (the gray box to the left of the field name) to select the field.**

2. **Press Ctrl+C, or click the Copy button in the Clipboard group on the Home tab of the Ribbon.**

3. **Move the cursor to an empty row of the table into which you want to copy the field.**

4. **Press Ctrl+V, or click the Paste button in the Clipboard group on the Home tab of the Ribbon.**

5. **Type a new name in the Field Name field, if necessary, and press Enter.**

   The field title is highlighted, so when you type a new name, you replace the old name.

Moving a field

To move a field, select the row by clicking the record selector. (You can select multiple rows by dragging the row selectors.) Then drag the record selector up or down to where you want to drop it. As you move the mouse, a dark horizontal line shows where the row will move when you release the mouse button.

Moving a field in Design view also changes its position in the table datasheet.

Deleting a field

You can delete a field in Design view. Deleting a field deletes the field definition and all the data stored in the field.

Follow these steps to delete a field:

1. **Select the field by clicking the record selector (the gray box to the left of the field name).**
2. **Press the Delete key, or click the Delete Rows button in the Tools group on the Design tab of the Ribbon.**

    If the field has no data, Access deletes it. If the field has data, you see a dialog box that asks you to confirm that you do indeed want to delete the field and its data.

Choosing a data type

Access provides 12 data types for you to choose among. Choose the data type that best describes the data you want to store in the field and that works for the type of analysis you need to use the field. Storing phone numbers in a text field, for example, works fine because you'll never need to add or subtract phone numbers. Prices, however, should be stored in a Number or Currency field so that you can add, subtract, or multiply them by the number of units ordered and create an invoice.

A few fields need data types that may not be obvious — mainly, telephone numbers, zip codes, and other such fields. Generally, even though these fields store numbers, you want to set the data type to Short Text. Doing so allows you to store leading zeros (so that 02138 doesn't appear as 2138) and add characters such as dashes and parentheses. The Input Mask Wizard (covered in Chapter 5 of this minibook) helps you define fields for phone numbers, zip codes, Social Security numbers, and dates. The wizard is also useful for any codes you may use in your database, other types of fields that sometimes appear with spaces or dashes (such as credit-card numbers), or other punctuation so that the data is always entered consistently and you can find it when you need it.

Table 2-2 lists the data types and describes when to choose each type.

Table 2-2	Data Types	
Data Type	*What It Holds*	*When to Use It*
Short Text (formerly Text)	Numbers, letters, punctuation, spaces, and special characters (up to 255 characters).	For all text fields except really long ones; also good for zip codes and phone numbers. You can't do Number-type calculations with a Text field.
Long Text (formerly Memo)	Text, and lots of it — up to 65,536 characters.	When you have lots of text, such as comments. This data type can't be indexed and can't be a key field.
Number	Numbers. When you select the Number type, you may want to change the `Field Size` property to the option that best fits the field. (Field sizes are explained in Table 2-3, later in this chapter.)	For numbers that you want to add, multiply, and do other calculations with. You can also use decimal points and + and – (to designate positive and negative numbers) in a Number field.
Date/Time	Dates and times.	For dates and times. You can do calculations such as finding the number of days between two dates or adding hours to a time to calculate a new time.
Currency	Numbers with a currency sign in front of them.	For storing monetary values, such as prices. Like Number fields, Currency fields can be used in calculations. Calculations with Currency fields are faster than those with Single or Double field sizes (the kinds of numbers that can include fractions for cents). Single and Double field sizes for Number fields are explained in Table 2-3, later in this chapter.
AutoNumber	A unique number generated by Access for each record.	When you want each record to have a unique value that you don't have to type. The value starts at 1 and is incremented for each record.

(continued)

Table 2-2 *(continued)*

Data Type	What It Holds	When to Use It
Yes/No	Binary data such as `Yes/No`, `Male/Female`, and `True/False`.	When you have a field that can have only one of two entries. This data type appears as a check box on the datasheet; it can appear as a check box, option button, or toggle button on forms; it can be either on or off. Use the `Format` field property to define the values, such as `True/False`, `Male/Female`, or `Available/Discontinued`.
Hyperlink	URLs, e-mail addresses, and other types of links.	When you want to link to a web page, e-mail address, or file. We cover hyperlinks in Chapter 1 of this minibook.
Attachment	One or more attachments (files).	When you want to store a file as part of a record. We cover Attachment fields in Chapter 1 of this minibook.
Calculated	Defined by an expression (calculation).	When you want to calculate a result by using other fields in the table. Calculations are covered in short in Chapter 1 of this minibook and in detail in Book III, Chapter 2.
Lookup Wizard	Not really a data type. This option runs the Lookup Wizard.	When you want to select a data from another source to fill a field, such as when you want to select state abbreviations in a list or choose products for an order from that products you actually stock.

AutoNumber fields have one purpose: to act as the primary key field for tables that don't have an existing field to uniquely identify records. Don't use AutoNumber fields for anything else. In fact, most Access database designers use AutoNumber fields to create primary key fields — and then make sure that those key fields never appear on forms and reports.

Here's why the key fields are often hidden: You have no control of the numbers that Access issues when numbering your records. If you start adding a record and then cancel it, Access may decide that particular number is already used and skip it the next time you add a record. You can't change an AutoNumber field's value. If you need a series of numbers to *not* end up with holes (skipped numbers), don't use an AutoNumber field.

Formatting Fields with Field Properties

Field properties generally are used for formatting fields. They can also be used to validate data, which we cover in Chapter 5 of this minibook.

Field properties are defined for each field (not surprisingly!). You can see the field properties for only one field at a time. To see the field properties for a field, select the field in the top half of the Design View window by clicking the field selector (the gray box to the left of the row) or by clicking anywhere in the row. The field selector of the active field is highlighted. Select a new field to see a whole different set of field properties. The field properties you see depend on the data type of the field. You won't see the `Decimal Places` property for a Text field, for example.

Click a field property to see a short description to its right that tells you whether the property is a formatting property and/or a data-validation property. (Some properties can be used in both ways.)

How do you use field properties to format a field? For Number fields, you can define the number of decimal places you want to display. For Text fields, you can tell Access to change the text to all capital letters or all lowercase. You can even use the `Format` property to add extra characters for display purposes to Short Text or Long Text fields. (For most applications, however, the Input Mask Wizard is easier to use than the `Format` property; we discuss input masks in Chapter 5 of this minibook.)

Formatting Number and Currency fields

You can use the `Field Size` and `Format` properties together to define how fields display. The common formats for Number and Currency fields are built right into Access; you can choose among those listed in Table 2-3.

Table 2-3	Number Formats
Number Format	*How It Works*
General Number	Displays numbers without commas and with as many decimal places as the user enters
Currency	Displays numbers with the local currency symbol (determined by the Regional settings in the Windows Control Panel), commas as thousands separators, and two decimal places
Euro	Displays numbers with the euro symbol, commas as thousands separators, and two decimal places

(continued)

Table 2-3 *(continued)*

Number Format	How It Works
Fixed	Displays numbers with the number of decimal places specified in the `Decimal Places` property (immediately after the `Format` property; the default is 2)
Standard	Displays numbers with commas as thousands separators and the number of decimal places specified in the `Decimal Places` property
Percent	Displays numbers as percentages — that is, multiplied by 100 and followed by a percent sign
Scientific	Displays numbers in scientific notation

The `Field Size` property can affect the format. Choose a field size large enough to display your data in the desired format.

You can define your own number format by using the following symbols:

Symbol	What It Does
#	Displays a value if one is entered for that place
0	Displays 0 if no value appears in that place
.	Displays a decimal point
,	Displays a comma
$ (or other currency symbol)	Displays the currency symbol
%	Displays the number in percent format
E+00	Displays the number in scientific notation

To create a number format with comma separators and three decimal places, type the following: **###,##0.000**.

You can define a numeric format so that the format depends on the value. You can define formats for positive and negative numbers, for zero, and for null values (when no value is entered). To use this feature, enter a four-part format in the `Format` property, with the parts separated by commas. The first part is for positive numbers; the second is for negatives; the third is used if the value is 0; and the fourth is used if the value is null (such as `#,##0; (#,##0); "—"; or "none"`). Using this type of format, you can display positive and negative numbers in different colors, if you like, such as positive in green and negative in red. Put the desired color in square brackets in the correct section of the expression. The available colors are black, blue, green, cyan, red, magenta, yellow, and white. In forms, conditional formatting is available, and you can specify an expression to determine format — displaying unshipped status in red, for example.

Setting the field size

Using the `Field Size` property correctly can keep your database efficient; doing so keeps the field size as small as is practical, making for a smaller, more compact database. For Text fields, the `Field Size` property can also help you screen out incorrect data. If you know that you need only four characters in a certain field, set the field size to `4`; anything longer produces an error message. (For more about screening out incorrect data, see Chapter 5 of this minibook.)

Using the `Field Size` property for any of your Number fields is a little more complicated, but again, using the shortest practical field size makes your database more efficient.

Table 2-4 shows your choices for the field size of a Number field, listed from the smallest amount of space required to store each value to the largest.

Table 2-4	Field Sizes for Number Fields	
Setting	*What It Can Hold*	*When to Use It*
Byte	Integers from 0 to 255	When values are small integers less than 256.
Integer	Integers from –32,768 to 32,767	For most fields that need integers unless you need to store values greater than 32,768.
Long Integer	Integers from –2,147,483,648 to 2,147,483,647	When the Integer setting isn't enough.
Single	Numbers from about –3.4E38 to –1.4E–45 for negative numbers and from about 1.4E–45 to 3.4E38 for positive values; decimal precision to 7 places	For numbers with decimal values. This field size holds big numbers and lots of decimal places; Double holds even more. Generally speaking, Single is sufficient, but you can change the setting to Double without losing data.
Double	Numbers from about –1.7E308 to –4.9E324 for negative numbers and from about 4.9E–324 to 1.8E308 for positive values; decimal precision to 15 places	For any values that Single won't hold.

(continued)

Table 2-4 *(continued)*

Setting	What It Can Hold	When to Use It
Decimal	Numbers from −10^28−1 through 10^28−1 in .mdb (Access database) files and numbers from −10^38−1 through 10^38−1 in .adp (Access project) files; decimal precision to 28 places	For values with lots and lots of decimal places.
Replication ID	Globally unique identifier (GUID) used for replication	For an AutoNumber field that is the primary key when you replicate the database and add more than 100 records between replications (not a common choice!).

The default field size for Short Text fields is 255 characters; for Number fields, it's Long Integer. You can change the default size on the Access Options dialog box by clicking the File button in the top-left corner of the Access window and then choosing File⇨Access Options. In the resulting Access Options dialog box, click Object Designers in the Navigation Pane. The default field sizes are the first three settings on the dialog box.

You can change a field size after you enter data, but if you shrink the size, any Text data longer than the new setting is truncated, and any Number data that doesn't meet the requirements is rounded (if you choose an Integer setting) or converted to a null setting (if the value is too large or small for the new setting).

Formatting Date/Time fields

Access provides the most common formats for dates and times; click the down arrow in the Format field property to see the formats. You can also create your own Date/Time format (for online help, press F1 or click the Help button on the toolbar) that provides all the codes you need. Combine the codes in the same way that you combine the text or number codes to define a format.

Formatting Text fields

Use the Field Size and Format properties together to format Text fields. The Field Size property limits each entry to the number of characters you specify. You can change the field size from smaller to larger with no problems. If you change 20 to 10, for example, you lose characters past the 10th character.

You enter symbols in the `Format` property in a kind of code:

For This Format	Type This Format Property
Display text all uppercase	> (greater-than sign).
Display text all lowercase	< (less-than sign).
Display text left-aligned	!.
Specify a color	One of the following colors between [ ] square brackets: **black, blue, green, cyan, magenta, yellow, white**.
Specify a certain number of characters	@ for each required character. (See also Chapter 5 of this minibook.)
Specify that no character is required	**&**.
Display predefined text	**/text**. The `Default Value` property may also be useful. Enter **/NA** to display the text NA, for example. This property appears in all records until another value is entered.

Book II
Chapter 2

Defining the Primary Key

The *primary key* is a field in each table that uniquely identifies each record in the field. (Primary keys are described in Book I, Chapter 3, including how to choose which field or fields to use for your primary key.) The simplest primary key field is a counter with a value of 1 for the first record, 2 for the second record, and so on. You can create a counter field by using an AutoNumber field. If you allow Access to create a primary key for you, it creates an AutoNumber field.

Another example of a primary key is a Social Security number in a table in which each record contains information about a single person and each person is listed only once. Sometimes, each record may be uniquely identified by the combination of two fields, such as an item number and the manufacturer. Note that first names and last names may not always be unique!

After you define a field as a primary key, Access prevents you from entering a new record with the same primary key value. When you're in doubt, an AutoNumber field is a good bet for a primary key, but the AutoNumber field doesn't allow Access to help you avoid repeating important data as using another field, as the primary key does.

Follow these steps to create a primary key:

1. **Display the table in Design view.**

2. **Click the row containing the primary key field or select the row by clicking the record selector.**

To select multiple rows to create a multiple-field primary key, click the first record selector and then Ctrl+click the record selectors you want for any additional fields.

3. **Click the Primary Key button on the Design tab of the Ribbon, or right-click the row selector and choose Primary Key from the contextual menu.**

   Access displays the key symbol in the record selector for the field.

If you already have data in the field, and two records have the same value, you can't make the field the primary key for the table.

The primary key field has to uniquely identify each record.

Indexing Fields

When you index a field, Access sorts and finds records faster by using the Index field. An index can be based on a single field or on multiple fields. The primary key field in a table is indexed automatically, and you can choose other fields to index as well.

Although indexing speeds many operations, it slows some action queries because Access may need to update the indexes as the action is performed.

To index a field, choose one of the Yes values for the field's Indexed property. Three values are available for the Indexed property:

✦ **No:** Doesn't index the field.

✦ **Yes (Duplicates OK):** Indexes the field and allows you to input the same value for multiple records.

✦ **Yes (No Duplicates):** Indexes the field and doesn't allow you to input the same value for more than one record. The primary key automatically gets this value.

You can see details of the indexed fields by clicking the Indexes button on the Design tab of the Ribbon to display the Indexes window, shown in Figure 2-2.

Index Name	Field Name	Sort Order
MessageID	MessageID	Ascending
PrimaryKey	MessageID	Ascending

Indexes: Email Messages Table

Index Properties

Primary	No	
Unique	No	The name for this index. Each index can use up
Ignore Nulls	No	to 10 fields.

Figure 2-2: The Indexes window.

The Indexes window displays all the fields in the table that are indexes, their default sort order (which you can change), and their index properties. The index properties are as follows:

+ **Primary:** Yes when the field is the primary key for the table, No otherwise.

+ **Unique:** Yes when the value of the field for each must be unique, No otherwise.

+ **Ignore Nulls:** Yes when *nulls* (blanks) are excluded from the index, No when nulls are included in the index.

Printing Table Designs

Printing the Design view of your table isn't as easy as clicking the Print button; as you may have noticed already, the Print button isn't available when Design view is displayed. Luckily, Access includes a cool feature called the Documenter dialog box to help you document your database. To print your field definitions with field properties, follow these steps:

1. **Click the Database Documenter button in the Analyze group on the Database Tools tab of the Ribbon.**

Access displays the Documenter dialog box, shown in Figure 2-3. (Your Documenter dialog box will show different objects.)

Figure 2-3:
The Documenter dialog box displays a tab for each type of object in the database.

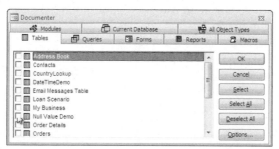

2. **Click the Tables tab to display a list of tables in your database.**

3. **Select the table definition(s) you want to print by clicking the check box in front of the table name.**

Alternatively, click the Select All button to get the whole enchilada — all the tables.

4. **Click the Options button to display the Print Table Definition dialog box, shown in Figure 2-4.**

Figure 2-4:
The Print
Table
Definition
dialog box.

5. **Select the aspects of the table definition that you want to print; then click OK to close the dialog box.**

   The Documenter dialog box makes its return.

6. **Click OK in the Documenter dialog box to display the object-definition report in a form that can be printed.**

   The contents of the report depend on the settings you selected in the Print Table Definition dialog box (Step 5), but the default display shows the following:

   - The properties of the table at the top

   - The name of each field with its properties

   - How the table is related to other tables in the database

   - The table index fields

   - The primary key

7. **Click the Print button on the Print Preview tab of the Ribbon to print the report.**

Chapter 3: Sorting, Finding, and Filtering Data in a Datasheet

In This Chapter

✔ **Sorting data in a datasheet**

✔ **Finding a specific record**

✔ **Using filters to find a subset of a datasheet**

A datasheet is a good place to start analyzing your data, especially if you need to look at the data in only one table. Within a datasheet, you can sort (alphabetize or put in numeric order) by using any field, and you can filter to find matching records or data that meets simple criteria. If you're looking at a datasheet generated by a query, these datasheet tools may be just what you need to find the data you're looking for without redefining the query.

Sorting the Rows of a Datasheet

You may enter records randomly (which isn't necessarily a bad thing), but the data doesn't have to stay that way. Use the Sort buttons to sort the records (rows) into an order that makes sense.

Before you sort, decide which field you want to sort, and place your cursor somewhere in that field. Then click one of the two Sort buttons on the Home tab of the Ribbon to sort the datasheet. Another way to sort the field is to click the down arrow next to the field name; the first two choices on the resulting drop-down menu are Sort Smallest to Largest and Sort Largest to Smallest. (The exact text of the menu options varies depending on the type of data in the field.)

When you sort a Number field in ascending order, Access lists records from the smallest number to the largest. When you sort a Text field in ascending order, records are alphabetized from A to Z. When you sort a Date field in ascending order, records are listed from oldest date to most recent date. Descending order is the opposite in all three cases: largest-to-smallest number, Z to A, or most recent to oldest date.

Sort-order oddities

When you're sorting a Number or Currency field, values sort from smallest to largest (at least, they do when you're sorting in ascending order). But when you sort a Text field, values are sorted alphabetically, starting at the left end of the field. This difference between the two fields means that in a Text field, Access sorts 55 before 6, because the 5 character comes before the 6 character. Access sorts the same list of numbers in Number and Text fields like this:

Number Sort	Text Sort
1	1
2	11
5	2
11	21
21	44
44	5

If you need to sort the numbers in a text field into numerical order, Access has an excellent online help page on the topic. You have to create a new field, using an expression to convert the text to a numerical value, and then you can sort by using that new field. You can find the information in the "Filtering and Sorting" section of the help system.

Sometimes, you need to know exactly how Access sorts blanks and special characters. The sort, in ascending order, looks like this:

- Blanks (null).
- Spaces.
- Special characters such as !, ", #, %, &, (, comma, period, [, ^, `, ~ (in that order).
- Letters. (Access doesn't distinguish between uppercase and lowercase letters when sorting.)
- Numbers.

If you need to know how Access sorts some characters that aren't listed here, make a test table with the characters you need to sort, and sort them!

Sort Button	Sort Order
Ascending	Sorts from smaller to larger and from A to Z
Descending	Sorts from larger to smaller and from Z to A
Remove Sort	Clears all Sorts and returns records to their previous order

When you add a new record to a sorted datasheet, the datasheet doesn't automatically re-sort itself. You have to click the Sort button again to sort the new records with the existing records.

If you want to return records to their unsorted order, click the Remove Sort button on the Home tab of the Ribbon. If you have an order that you want to be able to return to, such as the order in which the records were entered, it's a good idea to have a field that you can sort on when you want to re-create that order.

An AutoNumber field often serves the purpose of re-sorting data into its original order, but if an AutoNumber field won't work for the order you want, consider adding a field that you can sort on to get your data in order. Don't let the order of records be a hidden clue to your data; include the data to sort on explicitly in a field. (You may need a Date or Time Entered field if that information is important, for example.)

Finding (and Replacing) Data

Do you like a quick-and-dirty approach, or do you prefer a more thoughtful and refined strategy? Access accommodates both personalities. To search quickly for data in a datasheet, use the Search box at the bottom of the datasheet; it's located to the right of the Record Navigator and to the left of the scroll bar. Type your search text in the box, and with no further ado, Access takes you to the first instance of the text. You don't even have to press Enter. In fact, as you type, Access is moving the focus in the datasheet to the first instance of the text you're typing. To find the next instance, press Enter. Continue at will!

Book II
Chapter 3

Sorting, Finding, and Filtering Data in a Datasheet

If you want to be more specific about what you're looking for, you may prefer the Find and Replace dialog box. Access even takes the text you typed in the Search box and puts it in the Find and Replace box automatically, so you have it as a starting point. Display the Find and Replace dialog box (shown in Figure 3-1) by pressing Ctrl+F or by clicking the Find button in the Find group on the Home tab of the Ribbon.

Figure 3-1:
Press Ctrl+F to see the Find and Replace dialog box.

Using the Find and Replace dialog box for quick-and-dirty searches is as easy as 1-2-3:

1. **Press Ctrl+F to display the Find and Replace dialog box.**

By default, Access searches the entire table. If you want to search within a single field, put the cursor anywhere in that field's column, click the Find button, and then change the Look In setting on the Find and Replace dialog box to Current Field.

2. **In the Find What box, type what you're looking for.**

3. Press Enter or click the Find Next button.

Access highlights the first instance of the Find What text.

Quick and dirty may work just fine for you, but you need to know about a few refinements of the Find and Replace dialog box, such as telling Access to limit its search to particular places. The default settings tell Access to search the entire table and to match your search term in any part of a field. You may find, however, that other options on the dialog box make it easier to find exactly what you're looking for. Keep reading to find out more!

Exploring the Find and Replace dialog box

If you don't know how to use the options on the Find and Replace dialog box, you won't get much help finding what you're looking for, so a guided tour is in order.

The Find and Replace dialog box has the following options:

✦ **Find What:** Here's where you type the text or value that you're looking for.

✦ **Find Next:** Click this button to find the next instance of the Find What text.

✦ **Look In:** Here's where you tell Access where to look: the field that the cursor is in (Current Field) or the whole table (Current Document). If you select a bunch of fields or records *before* displaying the Find and Replace dialog box, Access searches the selected cells, and you can't change the Look In option. (Select contiguous fields by clicking the first field name and then Shift+clicking the last field name.) If you don't select a particular field, you can choose either the field where the cursor is or the whole table.

✦ **Match:** Choose how the search results match the Find What text. You can choose one of the following options: Any Part of Field, Whole Field, or Start of Field. The Any Part of Field option finds the most instances. If you search for `Flamingo` with the Any Part of Field option, Access finds `Lawn Flamingo`. The Whole Field option finds only cells that match the whole word `Flamingo`; it doesn't find `Lawn Flamingo`. The Start of Field option finds cells that begin with `Flamingo`, such as `Flamingoes`.

✦ **Search:** Choose the direction (from the cursor) to search: Up, Down, or All.

✦ **Match Case:** Match the case of the text. If you want to find `THIS` but not `This`, use the Match Case option.

✦ **Search Fields As Formatted:** This option finds data according to how it looks rather than how it was entered. If you use an input mask on a telephone-number field, for example, you may input ten digits one after another, but they appear with parentheses around the area code and a hyphen after the exchange. If you use the Search Fields as Formatted option, you can search for (508) to find phone numbers in the 508 area code.

The broadest search uses the following options: Look In Current Document (the whole table), Match Any Part of Field, and Search All, with Match Case deselected. Other settings of the Look In, Match, and Search options narrow the search and may miss particular instances of the Find What text. That's not necessarily a bad thing, by the way, especially if you have a clear idea of where you might find what you're looking for.

Replacing the data you find

To replace data with new data, first define what you're looking for, as described in the preceding section, and then select the Replace With option on the Replace tab to define how you want to replace it.

You can replace instances one at a time by clicking the Replace button (to replace) or the Find Next button (to skip). To replace all instances, click the Replace All button.

The Undo button can undo only the last replacement made; it won't undo a whole slew of them. Use the Replace All button carefully.

If the Find and Replace dialog box isn't quite what you need, you may want to filter your datasheet and then make replacements, or you may want to try action queries. For more on filters, see the next section; for more on action queries, check out Book III.

Filtering a Datasheet

Filtering a datasheet is a way to focus on specific records rather than all the records in a table. You can filter out records that aren't relevant to what you're trying to do at the moment and temporarily display only those records that have the data you specify.

When you filter data, you use criteria to tell Access what you want to see. A *criterion* is a test that the data has to pass to be displayed after the filter is applied. You might ask Access to show you the records with an order date of 5/1/12. A more advanced criterion would be orders with a date *on or after* 5/1/12. Then Access shows you only the data that meets your criteria. All other records are hidden until you remove the filter.

In some cases, a filter isn't the best tool for the job. If you're looking for the top or bottom values in a field or for unique or duplicate values, you need to use a query. Also, if you want to use the same filter repeatedly, creating and saving a query is likely to be a better solution for you.

Understanding filtering basics

If you want to get a handle on the whole filtering concept, start by taking a look at the parts of a datasheet that relate to filters. To begin, you can display the filter menu for any field by clicking the arrow next to the field name. To see what common filters are provided, choose the item above all the check boxes (in Figure 3-2, Number Filters). To filter to a particular value, use the check boxes, as we discuss shortly.

You can apply a filter to any datasheet, including a table, of course, but also to subdatasheets and datasheets generated by queries. (When you apply a filter to a subdatasheet, all the data displayed from the subdatasheet table is filtered, not just the record where you apply the filter.) You can enter and edit data in a filtered datasheet as usual. Just be aware that the filter has no effect on any new records until you reapply the filter.

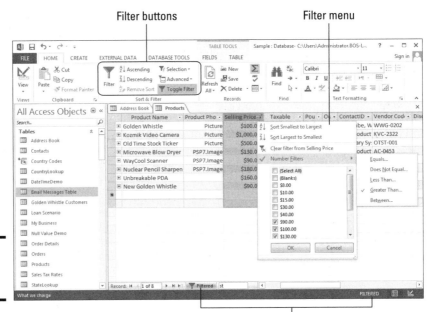

Figure 3-2:
A filtered datasheet.

Filter

To remove a filter, click the Filter button in the Sort & Filter group on the Home tab of the Ribbon. To reapply the last filter you applied, click Filter again. The Filtered/Unfiltered indicator at the bottom of the datasheet is clickable and is another Filter button. To clear the filter so that it isn't applied when you click Filter, choose Advanced⇨Clear All Filters from the Sort & Filter group on the Home tab of the Ribbon.

If you apply a filter to one field and then apply a filter to another field, Access uses both filters to choose the records to display. Only one filter at a time can be used on each field, however; the second filter overrides the first. For that reason, it's a good idea to know how to remove (clear) your filters:

✦ Clear the filters from a single field by clicking the down arrow next to the field name and choosing Clear Filter from *field name* from the resulting drop-down menu.

✦ Clear all filters from the table by clicking Advanced in the Sort & Filter group on the Home tab of the Ribbon and choosing Clear All Filters from the drop-down menu.

TIP

A filter runs a simple query on one table — a good way to start analyzing your data. Filtering can help you warm up to creating more complex queries. If you're confused about queries, creating a filter can help you figure out how to write criteria for a query (and so can Book III!). When you create the filter, click Advanced in the Sort & Filter group on the Home tab of the Ribbon and choose Advanced Filter/Sort from the drop-down menu to see it in the design grid. Look at the Criteria row to see what the criteria look like. To close the design grid, click the Close button.

If you want to use the filter to create forms and reports, save it while you're in the Advanced Filter/Sort window by clicking Advanced in the Sort & Filter group on the Home tab of the Ribbon and choosing Save As Query from the drop-down menu.

TECHNICAL STUFF

Filters appear in the `Filter` property of the property sheet. You can filter a table by entering an expression there, but almost no one does that because the filter stays applied, and some records may be filtered out the moment you open the table.

Using different types of datasheet filters

Now that you've been introduced to filtering, you may wonder how far you can take this new skill. Access has several types of filters, as shown in Table 3-1.

Table 3-1	Types of Datasheet Filters
Filter	*When You Should Use It*
Quick Filter	You want to use one of the many filtering options that Access provides for a given type of data. Quick filters for Text, Number, and Date fields allow you to filter by month, values between values that you specify, or one word within a Text field. These filters are provided in the drop-down menu that appears when the field name is clicked in a datasheet. To access them, choose Text Filters, Date Filters, or Number Filters from the drop-down menu.
Filter by Selection	You have a record with a certain value in a field, and you want to find all the other records that have the same value in that particular field.
Filter by Form	You have more than one criterion. Perhaps you want to find orders placed before 6/1/06 paid for by credit card.
Advanced Filter/Sort	You want to do more than the other filters allow, such as sorting and applying criteria to multiple fields. Advanced Filter/Sort creates a query by using only one table.

Filtering with quick filters

Common filters are built into Access. The available filters depend on the data type of the field that you're filtering. The most interesting choices are for Date/Time fields; you can choose such diverse filter options as year quarters, specific months, yesterday, and last month. Number filters include Equals, Does Not Equal, Less Than, Greater Than, and Between. The available text filters are Equals, Does Not Equal, Begins With, Does Not Begin With, Contains, Does Not Contain, Ends With, and Does Not End With.

Follow these steps to use common filters to filter a field:

1. **To see the filters available for a particular field, click the down arrow next to the field name, or click the Filter button in the Sort & Filter group on the Home tab of the Ribbon when the cursor is in the field.**

   If you want to filter to a specific value, you can deselect all values by clicking the first check box, Select All. Then select the values you want to see when the datasheet is filtered, and click OK to see the filtered datasheet.

2. **To see more filtering options, highlight the menu option immediately above the check boxes.**

   The name of this menu option changes with each data type. You see Date Filters for Date/Time fields, Text Filters for Text data, and Number Filters for Number data.

3. **For Date/Time fields, highlight All Dates in Period to display another level of choices.**

   The options on this submenu let you see data for one quarter or for one month of the year. Figure 3-3 shows all the filtering options available for a Date/Time field.

Filtering by selection

Filtering by selection is the simplest kind of filter; it finds records with matching values in one field. To filter by selection, follow these steps:

1. **Find a record with the value or text you want to match and then place your cursor in that cell to match the whole value.**

   If you want to match part of the value in the cell, select part of the cell, as in these examples:

   - To find all products with a price of $29.99, place the cursor in a `Price` cell with the value `29.99`.

   - To match the beginning of the value, select the first character and as many thereafter as you want to match. To find all entries in the field that start with `La`, for example, highlight the `La` in `Lawn Flamingo` before filtering.

2. **Click the Selection button in the Sort & Filter group on the Home tab of the Ribbon.**

3. **From the drop-down menu, choose the first item, Equals *X*.**

   Access filters the datasheet to display only records that have the same value in that field.

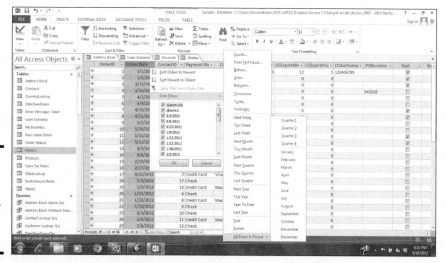

Figure 3-3: Date/Time fields have many, many filtering options.

To see the entire table, click the Filter button in the Sort & Filter group on the Home tab of the Ribbon (which toggles the filter).

When you click the Selection button in the Sort & Filter section on the Home tab of the Ribbon, you can choose among up to four options, which are context-sensitive, depending on data type and whether (and where) data within the cell is selected. Depending on the data type, other options may also be available:

✦ **Number and Date/Time fields:** You can filter to values equal to, greater than, or less than the selected value. The Selection button's drop-down menu also offers a Between option so that you can specify top and bottom limits for the values in the filtered datasheet.

✦ **Text fields:** If you haven't selected text in the cell, you have two options: filter to records that contain the selected text or filter to records that don't contain the selected text. If you choose the first option, further options are available. If you select the word *Magic* for the entry Magic Inkwell and click Selection, for example, you see the following options: Contains *Magic,* Does Not Contain *Magic,* Begins with *Magic,* and Does not Begin with *Magic.* Similar options are available if you select the end of the entry.

Filtering multiple fields

If you want to filter multiple fields, the flexible Filter by Form feature is what you need. Although you can apply the filters to the various fields by using the techniques discussed in this chapter, the Filter by Form feature lets you define all your filters for the table at the same time and then see the results. You can also select multiple criteria for a single field by using the Filter by Form feature. (Don't forget to read about queries in Book III. Queries do all that filters do and more.)

To filter by form, click the Advanced button in the Sort & Filter group on the Home tab of the Ribbon, and choose Filter by Form from the drop-down menu. Access displays a form that looks like a single row of the table you're filtering (see Figure 3-4). Use this form to specify the criteria you want to use to filter your data.

Figure 3-4:
Filtering by form.

When you filter by form, you can use multiple criteria, and you also get to choose how the data filters through the criteria you set up. Do you want a record to meet all the criteria before it shows up onscreen, for example, or is meeting just one criterion enough to display the record in the filtered datasheet? Use the following two operators to tell your criteria how they should act together:

✦ **And:** The criteria act together hand in glove; a record has to pass all criteria to display in the filtered datasheet.

✦ **Or:** A record has to pass only one criterion to display in the filtered datasheet.

You may use more than two criteria with the Or and And operators. The way that you put criteria in the form defines how multiple criteria act together. Use the Look For and Or tabs at the bottom of the form, as follows:

✦ Criteria on a single tab act as though they're joined by the And operator.

✦ Criteria on separate tabs act as though they're joined by the Or operator.

To take advantage of all this versatility, follow these steps to filter a datasheet by form:

Advanced ▾   **1. Click the Advanced button in the Sort & Filter group on the Home tab of the Ribbon, and choose Filter by Form from the drop-down menu.**

Access displays the Filter by Form window (refer to Figure 3-4), which looks like an empty datasheet.

2. Move the cursor to a field for which you have a criterion.

If you want to see only addresses in Pennsylvania, for example, move the cursor to the State field. A down arrow appears in the field.

3. Click the down arrow to see the entries in the field.

You may want to type the first letter or digit of your criterion to move to that point in the drop-down menu.

4. Choose the value that you want the filtered records to match.

Access displays the text that the filter is looking for inside quotation marks.

If you aren't seeking to match the entire field but are looking for a match in part of the field, type **LIKE "*****value that you're looking for*****"** (including the quotation marks). You'd type **LIKE "*new*"** in the City field to find all records with new in the city name, for example. The asterisks are wildcards that stand for anything else that may appear in the cell. You can use more complex criteria, too; for more information, see Book III, Chapter 3.

5. **If you have a criterion for another field that needs to be applied at the same time as the criterion you set in Step 4, repeat Steps 2–4 for the additional field.**

   Setting up criteria to work together illustrates the usefulness of the And operator. If you want to find addresses in San Francisco, set the State field to CA and the City field to San Francisco.

6. **If you have a completely different set of rules to filter records by, click the Or tab in the bottom-left section of the Filter by Form window.**

   Access displays a blank Filter by Form tab. When you set criteria on more than one tab, a record has to meet all the criteria on only one tab to appear in the filtered datasheet.

7. **Create the criteria on the second tab in the same way that you created those on the first — that is, click the field, and choose the value that you want to match.**

   If, in addition to all the addresses in San Francisco, you want to see all the addresses in Boston, set the State field on the Or tab to MA and the City field to Boston.

   When you use an Or tab, another Or tab appears, allowing you to add as many sets of Or criteria as you need.

8. **Click the Filter button in the Sort & Filter group on the Home tab of the Ribbon to see the filtered table.**

Filtering with Advanced Filter/Sort

The Advanced Filter/Sort feature in Access is really a query — the simplest kind of query. It allows you to find and sort information from one table in the database. You can access this option from a datasheet by clicking the Advanced button in the Sort & Filter group on the Home tab of the Ribbon and choosing Advanced Filter/Sort from the drop-down menu.

Use Advanced Filter/Sort when you want to use the more familiar Query by Example (QBE) grid to sort and filter a table. (In fact, you can load filter criteria from an existing query by clicking the Advanced button in the Sort & Filter group on the Datasheet tab of the Ribbon and choosing Load from Query from the drop-down menu.)

Figure 3-5 shows the Advanced Filter/Sort window.

This section gives you the basics of performing an advanced filter-and-sort operation, but because the features of the Advanced Filter/Sort window are nearly identical to the features of queries, you may want to read Book III, Chapter 1 for more details.

Field names   Table name

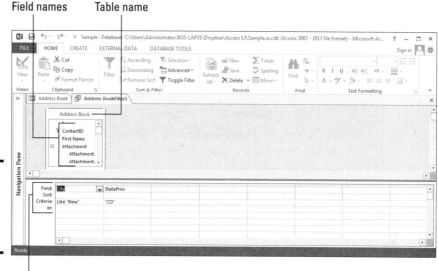

Figure 3-5:
The
Advanced
Filter/Sort
window.

Query by Example (QBE) grid

Follow these steps to sort and filter a table by using the Advanced Filter/Sort feature:

1. **Open the table that you want to filter in Datasheet view.**

2. **Click the Advanced button in the Sort & Filter group on the Home tab of the Ribbon, and choose Advanced Filter/Sort from the drop-down menu.**

    Access displays the Advanced Filter/Sort window, which has two parts, just like Design view for queries. Notice that you now see a tab for the table and a tab for the filter that you're defining. The top half of the window lists the table name and all the fields in the table.

3. **Double-click the first field that you want to use to filter the table.**

    The field appears in the Field row of the first column of the QBE grid in the bottom half of the window.

    Instead of double-clicking a field, you can choose a field from the field list in the QBE grid. Click the Field row of the grid to see the arrow for the field list.

4. **Click the Criteria row in the first column, and type the criteria to limit the records you see.**

    If you want to see only items that cost more than $10, select the `Selling Price` field as the field you want to use as your filter and then type **>10** in the Criteria row of the same column of the QBE grid.

5. **Repeat Steps 3 and 4 to add other fields and criteria to the grid.**

6. **(Optional) Choose a field by which to sort the resulting table and then choose Ascending or Descending order.**

   A drop-down menu appears for the Sort row in the column, containing the field you want to sort. Access sorts the table that results from the advanced filter in ascending or descending order, using the field listed in the same column as the sort key.

7. **When you finish creating all the criteria that you need, click the Filter button to see the resulting table.**

   Access displays all the fields in the original table, but it filters the records and displays only those that meet the criteria.

You can do several things with the resulting filtered table, including the following:

✦ **Filter it again.** Use the filter options to filter the table even more.

✦ **Print it.** Click the Print button.

✦ **Sort it.** The best way to sort is to use the Sort row in the design grid. (Click the tab for the Filter window to display the QBE grid again.) But you can use the Sort Ascending or Sort Descending buttons to sort the table by the field that the cursor is in.

✦ **Fix it.** Click the tab for the Filter window to display the Filter window again to fix the criteria or other information in the grid.

✦ **Add data to it.** Add data to the table by clicking the New Record button and typing the data.

✦ **Edit data.** Edit data the same way that you do in the datasheet. When you look at the unfiltered table, you see any changes you made in the filtered table.

✦ **Delete records.** You can delete entire records, if you want to; click the record you want to delete and then click the Delete Record button.

✦ **Toggle between the filtered table and the full table.** Clicking the Filter button has one of two effects:

   • If you're looking at the full table, clicking the Filter button displays the filtered table (according to the last filter that you applied).

   • If you're looking at the filtered table, clicking the Filter button displays the full table.

If you want to save your advanced filter, return to Design view. After you apply the filter, return to Design view by clicking the tab for the filter. Right-click the Filter tab and choose Save As Query from the contextual menu to save the advanced filter. After the filter is saved, you can find it with the queries in the Navigation Pane.

Creating a report or form with a filter

After you get the hang of filtering a datasheet, you may realize that what you really want to do is create a form or report with the same filter you've just applied to your datasheet. You can do so quite easily by clicking the buttons on the Create tab of the Ribbon. First, filter the datasheet; then select the type of object you want to create. Access prompts you to save the table. Then you can display the new object. Pretty slick.

Chapter 4: Importing and Exporting Data

In This Chapter

✓ Copying and moving data with the clipboard

✓ Importing data from other programs into Access

✓ Linking data from other programs into Access

✓ Cleaning up your imported data

✓ Exporting data from Access

✓ Collecting data though e-mails

*E*ven if you love Access, you may not end up using it for every single data-oriented task you need to do. Because of that, you may need to get data from another format (such as an Excel spreadsheet) into Access. Or you may want to take data from an Access database and use it elsewhere — say, a statistical application, spreadsheet, or word-processing document.

But never fear — you can get data from other applications into Access. Or, if you prefer, you can leave your data in other applications and have Access link to it there (although you should have a really good reason to do that, because it can get tricky).

Access provides several ways to import and export data. The rest of this chapter covers different methods of getting data into and out of Access, starting with the easiest method: cutting and pasting.

 If you're looking for more sophisticated methods of getting Access to share data, such as using SharePoint and using Access as a front end for other databases, check out Book IX.

Cutting, Copying, and Pasting

The most basic way to move information is to cut and paste (or copy and paste) via the Windows clipboard or the Office clipboard. Cutting and pasting is a straightforward and relatively simple way to move or copy information into or out of Access or from one place to another within Access.

You can use the Cut, Copy, and Paste commands in at least two ways: by clicking buttons or by pressing keyboard shortcuts. Figure 4-1 shows the buttons, and Table 4-1 lists keystrokes for cutting, copying, and pasting.

Figure 4-1:
The Cut, Copy, and Paste buttons appear in the Clipboard group on the Home tab of the Ribbon.

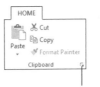

Secret clipboard button

Table 4-1	Cutting, Pasting, and Copying Options
Keystroke	**What It Does**
Ctrl+X	Cuts the selection and stores it on the clipboard
Ctrl+C	Copies the selection to the clipboard
Ctrl+V	Pastes the contents of the clipboard

To copy or cut and paste data, follow these steps:

1. **Select the data or object that you want to cut or copy.**

   You might double-click to select a word, for example.

2. **Choose your favorite method (Ribbon button or hot key) to cut or copy what you selected.**

   You can also right-click the selection and choose Cut or Copy from the contextual menu.

   When you cut something, it disappears from the screen and is stored on the Windows clipboard. When you copy something, it stays where it is, and Access also places a copy on the Windows clipboard.

3. **Move the cursor to the place where you want the item to appear.**

4. **Choose your favorite method (contextual menu, Ribbon button, or keyboard shortcut) to paste the item.**

Using the Office clipboard

Using the Windows clipboard works the same way as using the Office clipboard, except that the Office clipboard has more features; it can store up to 24 clips compared with one clip for the Windows clipboard, for example. You can use the Office clipboard when cutting and pasting within Office applications, and you can use the Windows clipboard for copying and pasting in any Windows application that supports its use. When you cut or copy something to the clipboard, that content is saved on both the Windows and Office clipboards. When you paste from the clipboard by pressing a key or clicking a button, you get the most recent thing you put on the clipboard, which is also the top item on the Office clipboard.

If you always get the most-recently-copied item, what's the point of the Office clipboard storing up to 24 of your recent clips? The Office clipboard stores items from all Office applications: Access, Excel, Word, Outlook, and PowerPoint. If you want to see your clips, click the secret clipboard button on the Home tab of the Ribbon. (Okay, technically it's called the clipboard Dialog Box Launcher, but seriously, what was Microsoft thinking, making those tiny boxes and calling them buttons?) That button is to the right of the word *Clipboard,* below the Paste button, as shown in Figure 4-2.

The clipboard task pane displays the clips that you cut or copy, along with an icon that shows you what type of clip it is (Access, Excel, Word, and so on). Paste any clip — not just the most recent one — at the cursor's position by clicking the clip in the clipboard pane. Delete a clip from the clipboard by right-clicking the icon and choosing Delete from the contextual menu. Clicking the Paste All button pastes all the stored items at the cursor's position.

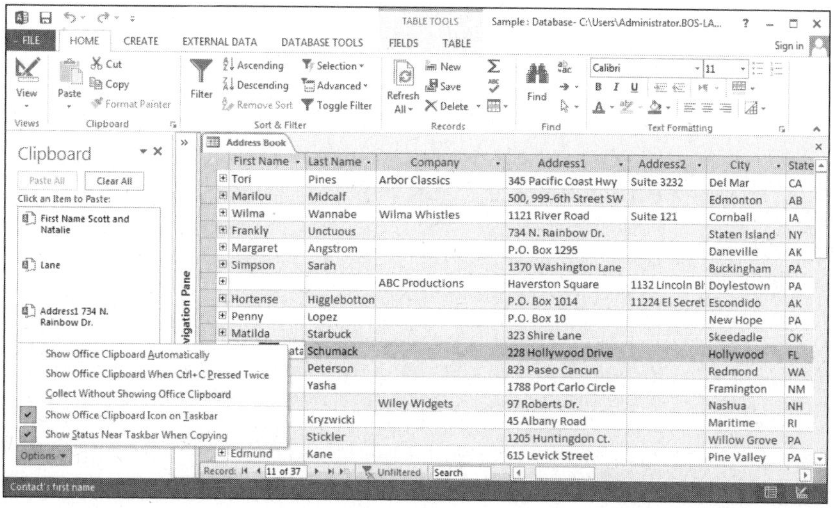

Figure 4-2:
The Office clipboard.

**Book II
Chapter 4**

**Importing and
Exporting Data**

Close the clipboard task pane by clicking the Close button in the pane's top-right corner.

If you want to keep track of what's on the clipboard, you can set it to appear automatically whenever you cut or copy more than one item without pasting. Just click the Options button at the bottom of the clipboard task pane, and choose Options⇨Show Office Clipboard Automatically.

Cutting and pasting small to mediumish amounts of data

Cutting and pasting is most useful for small pieces of data, but you may also use that capability for several fields', or even records', worth of data. If you move lots and lots of data, look at the import and linking options covered later in this chapter. If you're copying small or medium amounts of data, copying and pasting may work just fine. Access gets picky when you paste more than one piece of data into a datasheet. To help make pasting work most effectively, follow these guidelines:

✦ Fields (columns) need to be in the same order in the source document as in Access. You may need to rearrange columns in either Access or the source document.

✦ The data type of the data you're copying needs to match the data type of the field you're pasting into. The exceptions are Text and Memo data types, which can accept any type of data.

✦ You can't paste a duplicate value into the primary key field (just as you can't type a duplicate value in a primary key field).

✦ You can't paste into a hidden field. Unhide all the fields you're pasting data into before you paste that data. To unhide, right-click any field name and choose Unhide Columns from the contextual menu. If you don't have data for one field and want to paste into the fields on either side of it, hiding the field before pasting is a good option.

✦ Data that you paste must meet any validation rules and must work with any input masks. (See Chapter 5 of this minibook for details on those features.)

✦ You can't copy data into an AutoNumber field. Access generates AutoNumber values for copied records.

✦ A good option for pasting multiple cells of data from a spreadsheet program is the Paste Append command. To append entire records (with the exception of any AutoNumber fields) from Excel or another spreadsheet, paste by using Paste Append: Copy the data to the clipboard, display Access, click the arrow below the Paste button on the Home tab of the Ribbon, and choose Paste Append from the drop-down menu.

✦ If you're adding data to a datasheet that already contains data, you may want to paste the new data into a temporary datasheet first to make sure it looks right before you paste it into the permanent datasheet. Another option is to append the table containing the new data to the existing table. Append queries, which do that job, are covered in Book III, Chapter 3.

✦ If you choose not to use the Paste Append command or an append query, you have to select multiple cells (fields, records, or both) if you want to paste content into multiple cells. You don't have to select the exact number of cells that you're copying into. If you don't want to count the exact number of rows or columns that you want to copy data into, just select more than you think the data will fill. To make new records, click the New Record button. You may need to put a piece of data in each record. The dummy data will be overwritten when you copy data into the records.

✦ One easy way to select cells in a worksheet is to click the first cell (in the top-left corner of the range) and then Shift+click the last cell (in the bottom-right corner of the range).

✦ You can't copy into subdatasheets as you copy into the main datasheet. Copy into one table at a time.

Moving data from Excel to Access

Do you want to copy and paste a relatively small amount of data from Excel to Access? If so, these steps are a very convenient way to copy and paste into a brand-new Access table:

1. **In Access, open the database to which you want to copy the data.**

2. **In Excel, open the workbook, and display the worksheet that contains your data.**

   Make sure that the first row of data makes adequate field names. (You can always change them later.)

3. **Select the data in Excel, and press Ctrl+C to copy the data to the clipboard.**

4. **Click any table in the Access Navigation Pane, and press Ctrl+V to paste the data into a new table.**

5. **When Access asks whether the first row of your data contains column headings, click the Yes button.**

   Access creates a new table from the Excel data, giving that table the same name as the Excel worksheet that contained the data. You may need to rename your table, but wasn't that easy?

Alternatively, you can open a new or existing table, arrange your windows so that you can see both the data in Excel and the table where you want to put the data, and then drag the data from Excel to Access.

If you have a large amount of data to move, see the next section, "Importing or Linking to Data," for a better method.

Importing or Linking to Data

If you have large quantities of data that you want to use in your Access database, using the Link Wizard or the Import Wizard may be an easy way to make that data accessible within your Access database.

The wizards (which are very similar) offer some useful features. Using a wizard allows you to do the following:

+ Append records to an existing Access table.

+ Choose a range within the data to import. (The availability of this feature depends on the data's format.)

+ Set Data Type, Name, and some other properties for each field.

+ Skip importing one or more columns of data.

Making data available

You have a several choices about how to make your data available in Access. You must choose whether you want to store the data in Access (import it) or create a link to the data. Here are the differences:

+ **Import:** Make a copy of the data in Access. (Copying from Word, Excel, or wherever your data is and then pasting into Access is the simplest form of importing.)

+ **Link:** Keep the data in another file, and tell Access to get the data each time it's needed.

Following are some factors to consider in deciding whether to import or link:

+ **Storage:** When you import data, you may be doubling the storage required because you're storing the data in Access as well as in its original format.

+ **Customization:** If the data is stored in a format other than an Access database, and you want to define a primary key, enforce referential integrity, change field names, and/or customize field and table properties, you should import the data.

+ **Maintenance:** Does the data get updated, and if so, how? If a system is in place to update data in another format, leaving the data where it is and linking to it makes sense unless you're prepared to create a system to update it in Access. If the data isn't analyzed in its current format, however, moving the data to Access and creating a system for updating it there makes sense.

✦ **Accessibility:** If you're leaning toward linking to the data, will the data always be available when you need it? Is the data likely to move, or will you need it when you're traveling or not on your usual local area network? If the data isn't accessible, Access won't be able to use it for queries, reports, and forms.

If you need the data to get started in Access, and if you'll be using Access exclusively to update and analyze the data, you should import the data. If the data is collected and updated in another format, and if you'll be using the database from a computer that can always access the data source, linking probably is a good option — but scheduled imports may work, too. Evaluate your situation and consider the preceding points to decide whether linking or importing is the better choice.

Understanding what applications are compatible with Access

Here's the scenario: You were lucky enough to find the data you need for your database, and it's even in electronic form. But that data is stored in an ODBC (Open Database Connectivity) database, Excel, Word, another Access database, or some other file format. What do you do?

In most cases, Access knows how to import the data directly or to create a link to the data. If you can't import the file type directly, chances are that you can use the program in which the data was entered to save it in a file format that Access can import. Currently, you can import or link to files as follows (and Access can also export to many of these file types):

✦ Microsoft Access data can be imported, linked to, and exported.

✦ Microsoft Excel spreadsheets can be imported, linked to, and exported.

✦ ODBC data (from SQL Server, for example) can be imported, linked to, and exported.

✦ Text files (delimited or fixed-width) can be imported, linked to, and exported. (Use this option for Microsoft Word files.)

✦ XML documents can be imported and exported but not linked to.

✦ PDF and XPS files can be created by exporting from Access but can't be imported or linked to.

✦ SharePoint lists can be imported, linked to, and exported.

✦ HTML documents can be imported, linked to, and exported.

✦ Outlook folders can be imported and linked to.

If you have data in a format that your version of Access can't use, see whether the application allows you to export the data in one of the accepted formats. (Often, you use the Save As menu command.) Then you can import it into Access.

Getting external data

After you decide whether to import or link to your data, you're ready to take the next step. If you can, look at the external data you want to use. Look for the following factors:

✦ **Are fields stored in columns and records in rows?** This structure is relevant to text and spreadsheet files, which sometimes separate data with commas or other symbols.

✦ **Does the data you need begin at the top of the file?** For text and spreadsheets, Access expects to see one row of names and then the data. If your data isn't set up this way, you need to edit it.

✦ **Is all data within a field of the same type?** If not, the field is imported as a Text field, which can't be used in mathematical equations.

✦ **Is the number of fields in each row the same?** This question is of particular concern in a text file. If necessary, add null values to make your data line up. Two quotation marks with nothing between them (""), for example, represent a null text value.

✦ **Are the field names in the data you're importing identical to the field names in the Access table?** When you append data (that is, add data to an existing Access table), the field names in your source data must be identical to the field names in the Access table you're appending to.

Are you importing the data into a new table, or do you want to append the data to an existing table? Appending can be tricky because the data in the external source and in the Access table have to match in terms of data type and relative location. You may want to import the data into a new table in Access first and then use an append query. (For more on the append query, see Book III, Chapter 3.)

When your data source is cleaned up, you're ready to import or link. Following are general instructions, with some particulars for specific file formats:

1. **Open the database that you want to add external data to.**

2. **Click the button for the kind of data that you're importing on the External Data tab of the Ribbon.**

The External Data tab contains buttons for Excel, Access, ODBC databases, text files, and XML files. The More button's drop-down menu contains the options SharePoint List, Data Service (for web services), HTML Document, and Outlook Folder.

When you've made your choice, Access displays the Get External Data dialog box (shown in Figure 4-3), where you specify the name of the file that contains the data you're importing or linking to.

3. **Click the Browse button to navigate to your data file.**

Navigate through the folders, if necessary, to find the file that contains the data you want to use, and click the filename so that it appears in the File Name box.

If you're linking, and the file that you're linking to is on a local area network or another remote computer, use the universal naming convention (UNC) path for the file rather than a drive letter that's mapped. The UNC path is a more reliable way for Access to locate the data. A UNC path looks like the following:

`\\server\directory\file`

You have to know the server name to type the UNC.

4. **Choose how you want to store the data in the current database.**

You can import the data into a new table in the current database, append the data to an existing table (all the fields must correspond exactly for this option to work), or link to the data outside Access. The advantages and disadvantages of each of these options are discussed in this chapter.

5. **Click OK.**

Depending on the type of file you're working with, you may see a wizard that guides you through the process of choosing the data you want to import or link to.

The windows you see depend on the type of file that contains the data you're importing or linking to. (The following sections guide you through the text and spreadsheet wizards.) Some data types import immediately, ready for use.

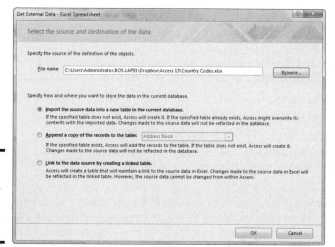

Figure 4-3:
The Get External Data dialog box.

When the import or link is complete, you see a new table listed in the Database window (unless you chose the Append option). Imported tables appear just like other tables, and you use them the way you use any other tables; you can change field names and properties, create relationships, enter data, and edit data. A linked table appears with an arrow and an icon indicating the type of file that the link points to.

You can use linked tables the way you use any other tables in the database, except that you can't enter and edit data. You can't change field properties or enforce referential integrity for linked tables.

The following sections provide details on using import and link wizards for text and spreadsheet files. You may see import wizards for other types of files that are similar to text and spreadsheet files in the information they need. Access wants to know how to get to and use the file, as well as how to break the data into fields.

Importing text or spreadsheet data

If you import or link a text file, the Import Text Wizard or Link Text Wizard starts when you select the appropriate file in the Get External Data dialog box (refer to Figure 4-3, earlier in this chapter). The two wizards are similar, but the Link Text Wizard has fewer steps.

Are you importing a whole worksheet? If not, you may want to create a named range in the spreadsheet to make importing exactly the data that you need easier. Access uses the first eight rows of data to determine the data type. If Access happens to select the wrong data type (based on the first eight rows), format the cells in your spreadsheet to the correct data type. If the first eight zip codes start with a digit other than 0, for example, Access formats the zip codes as numbers. To keep the leading 0, format it in Excel as text.

Follow these steps to complete the text wizards:

1. **In the first wizard window (shown in Figure 4-4), select the Delimited or Fixed Width option to describe how your data is divided; then click the Next button.**

   The Delimited option is for situations in which commas, tabs, or other characters separate fields, whereas the Fixed Width option is for situations in which spaces make the columns line up.

2. **In the second window, further define where one field ends and the next begins; then click the Next button.**

   If you chose the Delimited option in Step 1, you see Figure 4-5, which asks you what character separates your fields. (Choose one of the listed options, or choose Other to specify the character used.) Also specify whether the first row contains field names and whether you're using *text qualifiers* (symbols that surround text, such as double or single quotation marks). Your data is shown with vertical lines separating fields.

Figure 4-4:
The Import (or Link) Text Wizard can turn data like this into fields and records.

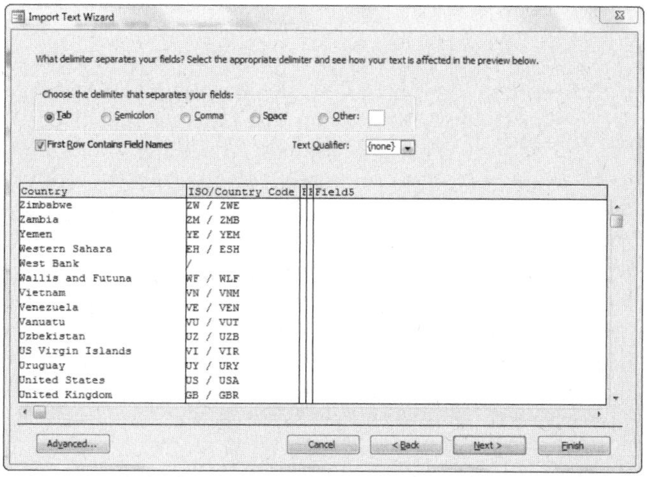

Figure 4-5:
Help Access figure out where each field in your delimited text file begins and ends.

If you chose the Fixed Width option, you see a similar window, which shows you where Access guesses that the field breaks go. If Access is wrong about the field breaks, fix them. Create a break by clicking, delete a break by double-clicking, or move a break by dragging.

3. **In the next window, click a column in the displayed data to change properties for that field; then click the Next button.**

You can further define each field by typing a field name, for example. Choose the data type, specify whether to index the field, and specify whether to skip importing or linking to this particular field.

You don't have to complete this information for each field; you can go with the choices Access makes.

4. **In the next window, select a primary key field, let Access create a new AutoNumber field as the primary key, or specify that the table doesn't have a primary key field; then click the Next button.**

5. **In the last window that appears, name the table by typing a name in the Table Name box; then click the Finish button.**

The last window of the Import Text Wizard contains a check box that runs the Table Analyzer Wizard. If you choose to have a wizard analyze the table, the Table Analyzer Wizard looks for duplicated data and recommends how to create multiple related tables that don't contain repeated data. You may also choose to display the Access help system when the wizard is done.

When you click Finish, Access creates the new table and lists it in the Database window.

Click the Advanced button in the last window of the wizard to display the Import Specification or Link Specification dialog box again. If this operation is an import or link that you may want to repeat, save the specs by clicking the Save As button.

The Import Specification dialog box, shown in Figure 4-6, displays all the specifications for the text-file import. You can edit these specs, save them, or import specs that you created and saved when you did another text-file import. This dialog box has options that you've seen before in the wizard (such as those for file format, field delimiter, and text qualifier), as well as the following options:

Figure 4-6:
The Import Specification dialog box saves the options so that you can import your file faster next time.

✦ **Language:** Select the language for the text in your table.

✦ **Code Page:** Select a code page. Just keep the default selection unless you know for certain that the imported data is using one of the other available options.

✦ **Date Order:** MDY (month/day/year) is standard in the United States, but you can select another option as needed to match your date data.

✦ **Date Delimiter:** Type the character used to separate month, day, and year.

✦ **Time Delimiter:** Type the character used to separate hours and minutes.

✦ **Four Digit Years:** Deselect this option if your data uses only two digits to designate the year.

✦ **Leading Zeros in Dates:** Select this option if your data has zeros before single-digit months (such as 02 for February).

✦ **Decimal Symbol:** Type the character used as a decimal point. In the United States, the decimal symbol is a period, but in many European countries, the decimal is a comma.

✦ **Field Information:** This option lists the field name in the file you're importing or linking (click to edit), the data type that Access has chosen (change by making a new choice from the drop-down menu), and whether the field is indexed (change by making a new choice from the drop-down menu), and it provides a box to check if you want to skip the field.

✦ **Save As:** This option saves the Import Specifications settings (or Link Specifications) for use with a later import or link.

✦ **Specs:** This option lists saved specs that you can select.

When you're done setting your options, click the OK button.

Importing with the Import Spreadsheet and Link Spreadsheet wizards

If you import or link a spreadsheet file, the Import Spreadsheet Wizard or Link Spreadsheet Wizard starts when you select the appropriate file by using the Get External Data dialog box (refer to Figure 4-3, earlier in this chapter). Follow these steps to complete the spreadsheet wizards:

1. **Select the sheet that contains your data in the first window that appears (as shown in Figure 4-7); then click the Next button.**

You can import or link to data on only one sheet at a time. Select the Show Named Ranges option to see named ranges in the spreadsheet if you need to import part of a spreadsheet.

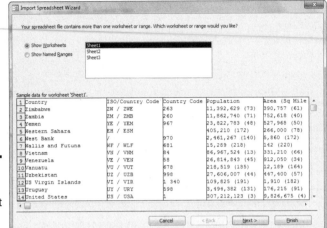

Figure 4-7:
The Import
Spreadsheet
Wizard.

2. **In the second window of the wizard, tell Access whether the first row contains column headings; then click the Next button.**

3. **In the next window, change properties as necessary for each column (click a column in the displayed data and change properties for that field at the top of the window); then click the Next button.**

   This window allows you to further define each field by typing a field name, choosing a data type, choosing whether to index the field, and choosing to skip importing or linking to this particular field. You don't have to complete this information for each field; you can go with the choices Access makes.

4. **In the next window, select a primary key field, let Access create a new AutoNumber field as the primary key, or specify that the table doesn't have a primary key field; then click the Next button.**

5. **In the last window, name the table; then click the Finish button.**

   The last window of the wizard contains a check box that runs the Table Analyzer Wizard. If you choose to have the wizard analyze the table, the Table Analyzer Wizard looks for duplicated data and recommends ways to create multiple related tables that don't contain repeated data. You may also choose to display the Access help system when the wizard is done.

   When the wizard finishes, you see the Database window with your new table listed.

Getting contacts from Outlook into Access

You can import contacts from Outlook into an Access table if you have Outlook, Outlook Express, or Microsoft Exchange Server installed on your computer. If you want to import Outlook data but don't meet these requirements, open Outlook, and export data in Access format or another format that Access can use.

Here's how to link or import Outlook data in its native form:

1. **Click the More button in the Import group on the External Data tab of the Ribbon, and click the Outlook Folder button.**

   Access displays the Get External Data dialog box (refer to Figure 4-3, earlier in this chapter), where you can choose to import the data into a new table, append the data to an existing table, or link to the data (that is, create a new linked table). Then Access asks you to choose a folder or address book to import from.

   The familiar rules apply for appending data to an existing table: The field names and data types must be the same in the imported data as in the existing table. For details, refer to "Importing or Linking to Data," earlier in this chapter.

2. **Choose between importing from your Outlook Address Book and your Contacts folder.**

   If you're not sure which you need, it's easy enough to try one and then switch if you find that you need the other. (Click Next to see the data and then click Back to return and select a different folder.)

3. **After you choose a folder, click Next to see the data.**

   From this point, the import is identical to importing text or spreadsheet data. Access shows you the data and allows you to choose the fields you want. Outlook Contacts creates redundant fields, so make sure that you have the fields that you need; skip any field that you don't need by selecting it and then clicking its Do Not Import Field check box. Empty fields (which are displayed as narrow columns) are created in a new Access table; if you don't want them, select the Do Not Import Field check box. Alternatively, you can delete the empty fields in Access.

Managing links

If you create links to external data sources, you may need to manage those links. When data changes in the source, for example, you can tell Access to get the new data, and if the source file moves, you have to tell Access where to find it. Use the Linked Table Manager to manage your links by following these steps:

1. **Click the Linked Table Manager in the Import & Link section on the External Data tab of the Ribbon, or right-click a linked table in the Navigation Pane (linked tables have an arrow next to them) and choose Linked Table Manager from the contextual menu.**

   Access displays the Linked Table Manager, shown in Figure 4-8.

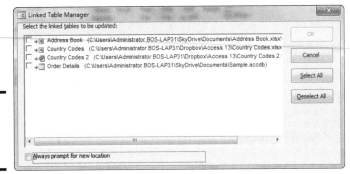

Figure 4-8:
The Linked
Table
Manager.

2. **Select the check box(es) for the table(s) whose links you want to refresh.**

3. **If you want Access always to ask you where the files are, select the Always Prompt for New Location check box.**

4. **Click OK.**

   Access gets the updated data for the selected tables, using the external file listed in the table. If the external file isn't found, you see the Select New Location Of dialog box, where you can specify the new location. If more than one table wasn't found, Access searches the new location for all the missing tables.

Cleaning up your imported data

If you import large amounts of data, you may need to clean it up a bit to make it efficient for use in Access. (If you have any doubt about what clean data looks like, review Book I, Chapter 3.)

One useful tool for cleaning up imported data is the Table Analyzer Wizard. This wizard looks for repeated data to determine whether to break a table into two or more tables. The various import wizards offer to run the Table Analyzer Wizard. You can also run this wizard by clicking the Analyze Table button in the Analyze group on the Database Tools tab of the Ribbon.

If you decide not to use the Table Analyzer Wizard, you may want to inspect your data for duplicate data. The primary key field can't have duplicate data.

Your new table may need relationships defined with other tables in the database. (See Chapter 6 of this minibook for more information on relationships.) You may also want to edit the table name or field names, as well as fine-tune some fields. You can use Design view to edit the data type and properties (as explained in Chapter 2 of this minibook).

Running and scheduling saved imports

If you saved the definition of an import or export operation while using the appropriate wizard, you have the option of running the same import or export again. Click the Saved Exports button in the Export group on the External Data tab of the Ribbon to open the Manage Data Tasks dialog box, where you can see all saved import and export definitions. The dialog box has two tabs: Saved Imports and Saved Exports. From this dialog box, you can run an operation, create an Outlook task, or delete a saved operation. You also have the option of changing the source or destination file; click the filename to change it.

If you create a task in Outlook, you can go to the Outlook task to add a date or define a recurrence. You can run the task straight from Outlook by clicking the Run Export or Run Import button on the Ribbon when the Outlook task is open.

Book II Chapter 4

Importing and Exporting Data

Getting Data from Another Access Database

If the data you need is already in an Access database, decide whether you want to import it or link to it. Refer to "Importing or Linking to Data," earlier in this chapter, if you need help deciding whether to link or import data.

You can also use the following procedure to import another database object (such as a query, form, or report).

If you want to import or link to a table and all its data from another Access database, the process is simple. Follow these steps:

1. **Open the database where you want to use the data.**

2. **Click the Access button in the Import group on the External Data tab of the Ribbon.**

Access displays the Get External Data dialog box (refer to Figure 4-3, earlier in this chapter).

3. **Browse to the database that has the object you need, and click Open.**

4. **Choose Import or Link.**

Either option results in a new database object; no option appends data to an existing table.

If necessary, you can use an append query to combine two tables after you import the data.

5. **Click OK.**

Access displays the Import Objects dialog box, shown in Figure 4-9 (or the similar Link Objects dialog box).

Figure 4-9:
The Import
Objects
dialog box
allows you
to import
database
objects from
another
Access
database.

6. **On the Tables tab, select the table you want.**

To select multiple objects, Ctrl+click and/or Shift+click. Click the Select All button to select all objects displayed on the current tab (all tables, for example). Click the Deselect All button to deselect all objects on the current tab.

Click the Options button and choose the Definition Only option if you don't want to import the data — just the table definition (table properties and field definitions).

7. **Click OK to import the objects or create the link.**

The new objects appear in the Database window. You can view and edit them just as you would any other database objects.

You can use this method to import any database object — not just tables.

Getting Data Out of Access

You can export any object from an Access database to another Access database or to a file that isn't an Access file (an ODBC or Excel file, for example). You can also use this technique to create a static HTML file.

Exporting is a convenient way to go about moving data from one Access database to another. You can export an object without any data, such as when you want to reuse a query definition. Exporting is similar to importing; the difference is which database you have open when you start.

You can even save your export definition if you export data to another application frequently. Notice the Saved button in the Export group on the External Data tab of the Ribbon.

To export an object, follow these steps:

1. **Open the database that contains the object you want to export.**

   You can export a table with or without the data in it. You may also want to export a query with its data, which allows you to get specific information from your database.

2. **Select the object name in the Navigation Pane.**

3. **Click the button for the format you want to export to in the Export group on the External Data tab of the Ribbon.**

   The buttons include Excel, Text File, XML File, PDF or XPS File, Email, Access, Word Merge, and More. The More button displays the export options Word, SharePoint List, ODBC Database, and HTML Document.

4. **Name the file that Access will create with the exported data.**

   You may also need to select a file format, depending on the application you're exporting to. You can export to an existing Access database, but when you export to other file types, you create a new file (which you can then import into an existing file, if necessary).

5. **Click OK.**

   What happens next depends on where the data is going:

   - If you're exporting to a file type other than an Access database, the object is exported.

   - If you're exporting to an existing Access file, you see the Export dialog box, where you can rename the object (if you want to) and tell Access whether you want to export all the data or just the object definition (field names, format, and any expressions).

   - When you save a report to HTML, Access asks you for the name of the HTML template file. You can find out about HTML template files from the Access help system.

   Access quietly completes the export process and asks whether you want to save the export definition.

6. **If you plan to repeat this export, select Save Export Steps to see additional options.**

   You have to name the export. We encourage you to use the Description field to describe the specifics of the export (such as what it does and when it should be used). You also have the option of creating an Outlook task to remind you to repeat the export.

   You can make the Outlook task recur if you go into Outlook, choose the task, and click the Recurrence button.

7. **To see whether the operation worked, open the file to which you exported the object.**

Using Access Data in a Word Mail Merge

If you want to use data from Access in Word, chances are that you need the mail-merge feature, which you generally use to write a letter and personalize it with a person's name and address inserted seamlessly into the letter. We're sure that you can think of other uses for merging your Access data into Word.

Doing a mail merge consists of creating a Word document containing special merge codes that, in the final document, are replaced by data from Access. You can create the document before you begin the merge process or afterward.

To use Access data in a Word document, you should have some knowledge of using Microsoft Word. Creating the Word document is beyond the scope of this book. Word's help system is helpful if you have difficulties.

Follow these steps to export Access data to a Word document:

1. **To begin the merge from Access, select (in the Navigation Pane) the query or table that contains the data you want to use in Word.**

2. **Click the Word Merge button in the Export group on the External Data tab of the Ribbon.**

    The Microsoft Word Mail Merge Wizard starts, asking you whether you want to link your data to an existing Microsoft Word document or to create a new document and then link the data to it.

3. **For this example, choose to create a new Word document and link the data to it; then click OK.**

    If you choose the first option instead, you need to tell Access where the Word document is.

    Microsoft Word opens, with the Mail Merge options displayed. You may need to view Word if it's running in the background.

4. **Proceed to create your Word document.**

5. **At Step 3 of the Word merge process, you see the name of your table (or query) and your database as the recipients of the document; click the Edit Recipient List link to see your data.**

6. **At Step 4 of the Word merge process, insert the codes into your document that coincide with the fields in your database.**

    Word is pretty good at figuring out how to use your data, but if your field names don't match up well with Word's expectations, you can match fields manually. (Look for the Match Fields button as you're choosing the address block and so on.)

That's it for the Access side of the merge. Mail merge can be difficult, but if you have a lot of data that you want to include in letters or similar documents, it's worth the effort.

Chapter 5: Avoiding "Garbage In, Garbage Out"

In This Chapter

✔ Using field properties to get the right data in the right fields

✔ Defining how data in a field looks with input masks

✔ Creating drop-down menus with lookup fields

✔ Filtering data with validation rules

*L*et's face it: If the data that goes into your database through tables and forms is garbage, any output or analysis you do with queries and reports will give you garbage too. Fortunately, Access offers lots of tools to help you make sure that the data that goes in each field is the data that's supposed to go in that field. We're talking about preventing mistakes as data is entered, of course. If someone is purposefully entering erroneous data, these tools may not help much (although we can help you get Access to reject inappropriate data)! Some of the Access features that we discuss in this chapter are described in other chapters, but they deserve a mention here too; the rest are exclusive to this chapter.

Find the tool you need to keep your data clean. The options for each field that you see in Table Design view generally define what you want to be entered. (If you want no more than six characters of text, for example, you can define the field size and the data type.) You can also use Table Design view to format an input mask, which defines a pattern that data in the field must follow, such as two characters followed by a dash and four numbers. The validation rule allows you to specify a rule in the form of an equation that data has to meet. You can even use a validation rule to make sure that, for example, the shipping date comes after the order date. If a field's data should always come from an existing list or table (orders should contain only products you actually sell, or addresses should contain only valid state codes), you can create a lookup field. Read on to figure out what your database needs.

If you don't find the tool you need in this chapter, you may want to check out Books VI and VIII, which cover more-advanced tools: macros and Visual Basic for Applications (VBA) programming.

Finding the Right Tool to Keep Garbage Out

You can find many of the tools you need to keep garbage out in Table Design view. You can use the data type to keep inappropriate data out of a field, and many of the other field properties can work that way too. Field properties, data type, and other field settings can prevent incorrect data from being entered in datasheets and forms. Input masks and validation rules allow you to be even more specific about the data allowed in a certain field.

Field properties appear in the bottom half of Table Design view; make sure that you're viewing the field properties for the field you're working with by clicking the field's name in the top half of Design view. Field properties are also covered in Chapter 2 of this minibook.

As you define a field in Design view, you can use the following field properties to make sure that the right data gets into the right field:

✦ **Data Type:** Use the correct data type to eliminate data of the wrong type. Text (both Long and Short) types accept just about any input, so use the Number, Date/Time, or Currency data type to screen out data of a different type whenever appropriate. (See Chapter 2 of this minibook for details on choosing the right data type.)

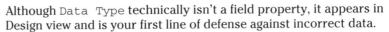

Although Data Type technically isn't a field property, it appears in Design view and is your first line of defense against incorrect data.

✦ **Field Size:** This property limits the number of characters. If you know that a field should never exceed four characters, for example, set Field Size to 4. (See Chapter 2 of this minibook for more on field size.)

✦ **Format:** This property makes the data look right. You can change text to all caps or all lowercase, for example. Input masks, explained later in this chapter, work with the Format field property. (See Chapter 2 of this minibook for details on the Format field property.)

✦ **Input Mask:** An input mask limits the information allowed in a field by specifying what characters you can enter. Use an input mask when you know the form the data should take — such as an order number that has two letters followed by four digits. Phone numbers and zip codes are other examples of fields for which input masks are useful. You find out lots more about input masks later in this chapter.

✦ **Default Value:** This property defines a value that appears by default if no other value is entered. The default value appears in the field until another value is entered.

✦ **Validation Rule:** Data must pass a validation rule before it's entered. This property works with the Validation Text property rule. A Validation Rule property that applies to a whole record is in the property sheet. (You find more on validation rules later in this chapter.) Validation rules are also available from datasheets.

✦ **Required:** This property specifies that the field must have a value for you to save the record. When no value is entered, Access doesn't create a new record when Tab or Enter is pressed, and the New Record button is unavailable. `Required` is also accessible from Datasheet view; it's a check box on the Fields tab of the Ribbon.

✦ **Unique:** This property specifies that each entry in the field must be unique, with no identical values anywhere else in the field.

✦ **Allow Zero Length:** This property specifies whether a zero-length entry, such as " " (quotes without a space between them), is allowed (only for Text and Hyperlink fields). A zero-length field allows you to differentiate between information that doesn't exist and a null value (blank) that is unknown or hasn't been entered. When this option is set, it allows a zero-length string in a required field. When both a zero-length field and a null value are allowed in a single field, you may want to use an input mask to make these elements look different from each other.

✦ **Indexed:** When you choose to index a field, you can specify that no duplicate values are allowed in the field. This property is also accessible from Datasheet view; it's a check box on the Fields tab of the Ribbon.

The rules that keep your data honest and help keep bad data out are sometimes called *data-integrity rules*. You can change a field property that controls data integrity (filters out garbage data) in a field that already has data. Access tells you (when you ask to view the datasheet) that the data-integrity rules have changed and gives you the option of checking existing data against the new rules.

Access tells you only whether existing data violates the new rules; it doesn't flag the offending records in any way.

The rest of this chapter covers input masks; validation rules; and the Lookup Wizard, which allows you to create drop-down menus and choose existing data, eliminating the possibility of misspelling a new entry.

When you use both the `Format` field property and an input mask, Access uses the field property and ignores the input mask.

Using Input Masks to Validate and Format Data

An input mask formats the data and defines the types of characters, as well as the order in which they can be entered. Input masks have two intertwined functions:

✦ **They format data by adding punctuation or changing the look of certain values.** An input mask might display asterisks instead of the text of passwords, for example.

✦ **They block any data that doesn't fit the mold from being entered.** You can't enter 12 characters if the input mask specifies 4, and you can't enter a digit followed by 3 letters if the input mask specifies 2 letters followed by 2 digits.

Use input masks when you know the form the data should take, such as a ten-digit phone number, a nine-digit zip code, or an item number that must be two letters followed by three or more digits.

 A manually entered input mask is even more flexible because you can, say, require two digits and then allow a third, and the same is true with letters. See "Creating an input mask manually," later in this chapter, for more details on defining a custom input mask.

Using the input mask, you can add formatting characters, such as adding parentheses and a hyphen to phone numbers. You can also change the way a value appears, such as choosing to display a date as 27-sep-06 or 9/27/06 or displaying hyphens in a Social Security number. The input mask for the field is in effect when you enter data in the field from a datasheet or a form.

If the data in a field varies or isn't easily described, the field probably isn't a good candidate for an input mask. Street addresses, for example, come in too many formats to describe easily, so making an input mask for an Address field is difficult and could prevent valid entries (and frustrate the person entering data). You can create input masks for Short Text, Number, Date/Time, and Currency field types; other data types don't have the Input Mask field property.

You can use an input mask with a validation rule to protect a field from data that's incorrect or that just doesn't belong there. Validation rules give you more flexibility in limiting the data you can enter, and we discuss them further later in this chapter.

 Input masks are commonly defined in Design view, where they become part of the field definition, and they also apply in forms. You can add input masks to queries and forms in which data may be entered, and the input mask is defined only for that object. In all cases, you have to add an input mask from Design view.

Using the Input Mask Wizard

The easiest way to create an input mask is to use the Input Mask Wizard. The wizard can help you create the input mask for your data, especially if the data in the field is a common type, such as a phone number or a zip code.

 If your data is similar to one of the data types in the Input Mask Wizard, you may want to use the wizard and then edit the input mask in Design view.

To create an input mask with the Input Mask Wizard, follow these steps:

1. **Display the table in Design view.**

   Right-click the table name in the Navigation Pane and choose Design View from the contextual menu.

2. **Select the field to which you want to apply an input mask.**

   Click the record selector, or put the cursor somewhere in the row for that field so that you see its field properties.

3. **Click the `Input Mask` field property on the General tab of the field properties.**

   Access displays the Build button to the right of the Input Mask line.

4. **Click the Build button.**

   Access displays the Input Mask Wizard, shown in Figure 5-1.

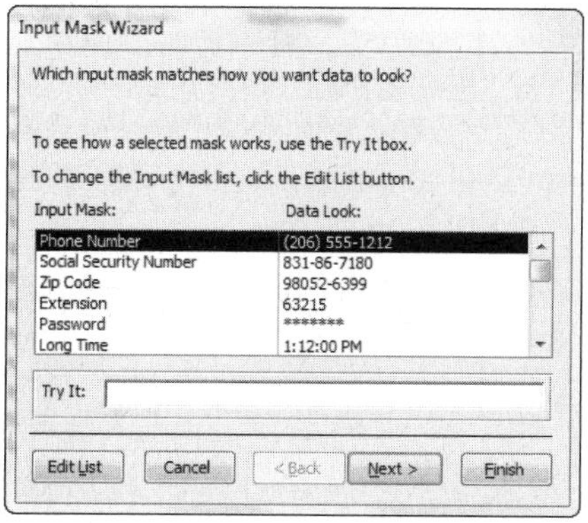

Figure 5-1:
The Input Mask Wizard.

5. **Select the input mask that looks most like the data that you want to allow in the field.**

   You may see an exact match for your field, or you may see a close approximation that you can edit to fit your data.

   You can add an input mask to the list displayed in the wizard by clicking the Edit List button in the first window of the wizard and then filling in the details of the new input mask.

6. **Type some text in the Try It box to see how the field appears with data in it and the input mask applied.**

   Access displays a Try It box on each window so that you can see the effect of any changes you make. Click the Try It box to see what the input mask looks like when you enter data in the field.

7. **Click Next to see more questions about the input mask.**

   The questions you see depend on the type of data you chose in the first window; you may not see all the options in the next three steps.

8. **Edit the input mask, if you want to, using the characters listed in Table 5-1 (later in this chapter).**

   Access displays the input mask it created, and you have the opportunity to edit it.

9. **Choose a placeholder character and then click Next to see the next window of the wizard.**

   A placeholder character holds a place for every character that the user needs to enter so that the user can see that he needs to enter five characters or whatever the input mask defines.

10. **Choose how to store the data and then click Next to display the final window of the wizard.**

    If you include punctuation or other additional characters in your input mask, you can choose how to save the data being entered: the characters entered plus the extra characters, or just the characters entered. Generally, you don't need to save the extra characters.

11. **Click Finish to tell the wizard to put the input mask it created in the Input Mask property for the field.**

    Access displays Design view with the new input mask.

12. **Save the table design by clicking the Save button on the toolbar.**

    Otherwise, you may lose your nifty new input mask!

Creating an input mask manually

To create an input mask manually, enter a series of characters in the Input Mask property of the Field Properties pane to tell Access what kind of data to expect. Data that doesn't match the input mask can't be entered. To block data from a field, first figure out exactly what data you want to allow in a field and then use the characters in Table 5-1 to code the data in the Input Mask field property. A caption explaining the allowed entries can help prevent users from being frustrated in entering data.

If you have trouble formulating an input mask, you may find that a validation rule meets your needs better.

Table 5-1	Creating Input Masks
Input Mask Character	*What It Allows or Requires*
0	Requires a number.
9	Allows a number.
#	Allows a space, converts a blank to a space, and allows + and – .
L	Requires a letter.
?	Allows a letter.
A	Requires a letter or number.
a	Allows a letter or number.
&	Requires any character or a space.
C	Allows any character or a space.
<	Converts the following characters to lowercase.
>	Converts the following characters to uppercase.
!	Fills the field from right to left, allowing characters on the left side to be optional.
\	Displays the character following in the field (\z appears as z).
. ,	Displays the decimal placeholder or thousands separator.
; : – /	Displays the date separator. (The symbol used depends on the setting in the Regional Settings section of the Windows Control Panel.)
Password	Creates a password-entry text box. Any character typed is stored as that character but displayed as an asterisk (*).

Here's how to use characters to create some common input masks:

✦ **AA00999:** This mask requires two letters or numbers followed by two digits and then allows an additional three digits.

✦ **00000\-9999:** This mask, for zip codes, requires five digits, displays a hyphen and provides space for an optional four digits.

✦ **LIL 0L0:** This mask, for Canadian postal codes, requires a letter, a number, and a letter; displays a space; and requires a number, a letter, and a number.

✦ `99:00:00 >LL:` This mask, for long time format, allows two digits; displays a colon; requires two digits; displays a colon; requires two digits; displays a space; and requires two letters, which are displayed in uppercase.

Creating a Lookup Field

You want your database to be as easy to use as possible, right? You also want data to be entered consistently. As orders are entered, for example, you want the name of each product to be entered so that Access can find it in the Products table where you've stored details such as the price. What's the chance that the product name, entered as part of an order, actually matches the exact product name listed in the Products table? Pretty minimal . . . unless you create a lookup field.

A *lookup field* provides users a list of choices rather than requiring them to type a value in the datasheet. You could think of using a lookup field as adding a field from an existing table to your new table. Access uses the field from the other table to create a drop-down menu of your products for users to choose among as orders are entered. Lookup fields enable you to keep your database compact and the data entered accurate and consistent. Lookup fields are very useful and not as complicated as they sound.

The items on the drop-down menu can come from a list you type, or they can be from a field in another table. Storing values for your drop-down menu in a table gives you much more flexibility if you want to modify the list or store additional information about the values later. (If your list contains state abbreviations, for example, you may also decide to include full state names and even state tax rates.) Storing the drop-down-menu data in a table enables you to display one field (such as a customer's full name) and store another (such as a customer number). Working with the logical relationships you set up among tables, you can store less data — thus keeping the database compact — and make entering and manipulating your data easy.

Here's a hint: In almost all cases, it's best to keep the values for your lookup in a table, which gives you much more flexibility in working with your data.

When you have two tables with a one-to-many relationship, the values of the connecting field may be perfect for a lookup field. When you enter records in the detail table (the "many" table in the relationship), the foreign key (related field) needs to match the primary key of the master ("one") table. Consider making the foreign key in the detail table a lookup field, with the primary field in the master table providing the list of possible values. If you have a Products table (the master table) and an Order Detail table (the detail table), make the `Product Code` field a lookup field, using the `Product Code` field from the Products table as the list of values. (You can find more information on relationships in Book I, Chapter 3, and in Chapter 6 of this minibook.)

Using the Lookup Wizard

An easy way to create a lookup field is to use the Lookup Wizard. In this section, we show you how to use the Lookup Wizard to enter the Customer ID number (stored in the Address Book table) in the ContactID field of the Orders table. The Orders table lists information about each order, one record per order. Fields include the order date, the contact ID, payment information, and shipping information. Items ordered are stored in the Order Details table.

Display the table that you want to contain the lookup field in Design view and then follow these steps:

1. **In the top half of Design view, find the field that you want to contain the drop-down menu.**

2. **Click the down arrow to display the Data Type drop-down menu, and choose the Lookup Wizard option.**

3. **For this example, view the Orders table, and change the data type of the ContactID field.**

   Access launches the Lookup Wizard.

4. **Tell the wizard whether the values that you want to appear on the field's drop-down menu come from a field in another table or from a list that you type; then click Next.**

   Storing the values in a table is easier in the long run, even if you have to cancel the wizard and create a new table.

   If you don't want the drop-down menu to display every value in the field in another table, you can base the drop-down menu on a field in a query. (Find out all about queries in Book III.) If you want to retain discontinued products in the Products table but not allow those products to be entered in new orders (that is, the lookup list), you could create a query that displays only products that are currently available.

   If you tell Access that you want to type the values, a table appears in which you can type the lookup list. Click the table in the wizard window (which currently has only one cell), and type the first entry in the list. Press Tab — not Enter — to create new cells for additional entries, and skip to Step 9 when you finish.

5. **Choose the name of the table (or query) that contains the data that you want to appear in the drop-down menu; then click Next.**

   If you want to see queries, click the Queries button. Click the Both button to show the names of both tables and queries.

6. **Tell Access which field(s) you want to display in the drop-down menu by moving field names from the Available Fields list box to the Selected Fields list box; then click Next.**

**Book II
Chapter 5**

Avoiding "Garbage
In, Garbage Out"

Double-click a field to move it from one column to the other. Select multiple fields to display multiple fields on the drop-down menu. You may want to display the Company, First Name, and Last Name fields on the drop-down menu, for example.

Access always adds the primary key of the table that contains the data for the drop-down menu to the list of selected fields, and it always saves the value of the primary key field. Although you may see and select from another field — such as the First Name or Last Name field — the primary key of the Address Book table (which is called ContactID in this example) is the value that's stored. Generally, this value is exactly what you want, even if you don't know it. If you're sure that you don't want the primary key to be stored, you can customize the lookup field after the wizard finishes its business.

7. **If you select more than one field (or only one field that isn't the primary key), select a field to sort by; then click Next.**

   Using this window, you can sort by up to four fields. Click the Ascending button to sort in descending order. (The button toggles between ascending and descending; click it to change from one to the other.) In this example, sort first by last name.

8. **Format your drop-down menu; then click Next.**

   The resulting window, shown in Figure 5-2, shows you a table with the values in the lookup list. You can change the width of the columns by clicking and dragging the border between field names. To automatically fit the widest entry, double-click the right edge of the field name that appears at the top of the column. You can change the order of columns by clicking the field name to select a column and then dragging the column to a new position.

   The window also contains a check box that, when selected, hides the key field. Depending on your application, you may want to display the key field by deselecting the Hide Key Column check box.

Figure 5-2: Change the way your lookup list looks.

Lookup Wizard

How wide would you like the columns in your lookup field?

To adjust the width of a column, drag its right edge to the width you want, or double-click the right edge of the column heading to get the best fit.

☑ Hide key column (recommended)

First Name	Last Name
Frankly	Unctuous
George	Escovedo
Hortense	Higglebottom
Ino	Yasha
James	Neerdowell
Jody	Junket
John	Miller

Cancel   < Back   Next >   Finish

9. **In the final window, change the label (the field name) for the lookup column, if you want to, and choose Enable Data Integrity or Allow Multiple Values (see Figure 5-3); then click Finish.**

If you choose Enable Data Integrity, you're telling Access to make sure that the two (or more) fields linked by the lookup option contain identical data. Data integrity is covered in detail in Chapter 6 of this minibook.

A multiple-value field allows the user to select more than one value for the field in each record when entering data. See the next section for details.

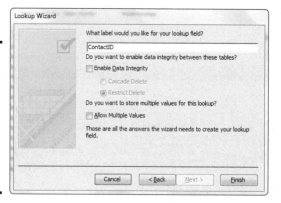

Figure 5-3:
Name the
new field,
and decide
whether
you want
to allow
multiple
values.

10. **If Access tells you that you have to save the table before relationships are created, don't argue; go ahead and save the table.**

A relationship is created automatically between the table with the new field and the table with the field that appears in the drop-down menu when you use the Lookup Wizard.

11. **View your table in Datasheet view to see your new lookup field.**

12. **Click the field's down arrow to display its drop-down menu (see Figure 5-4).**

To make changes in the field by using the Lookup Wizard again, place the cursor on any value in the field (in the datasheet), and click the Modify Lookup button in the Fields & Columns section on the Fields tab of the Ribbon.

The default setting allows users to type a value that doesn't appear in the list. To force users to choose a value from the drop-down menu (or to enter a value that's on the drop-down menu), display the table in Design view, click the Lookup tab in the field properties, and change the Limit to List property from No to Yes. Figure 5-5 shows lookup properties. You may also want to enforce referential integrity, as covered in Chapter 6 of this minibook.

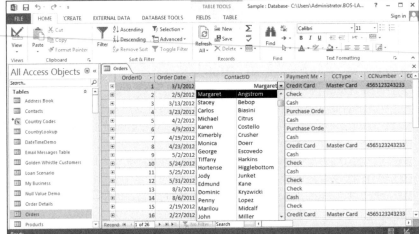

Figure 5-4:
To input
data, click
the arrow to
display the
lookup list,
and choose
the option
you want to
use.

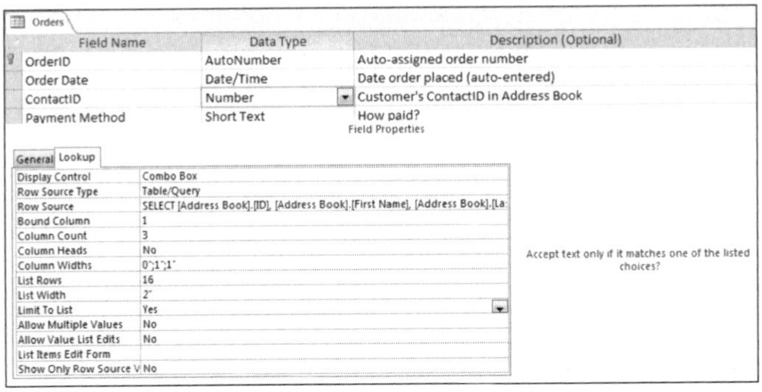

Figure 5-5:
You can
use the
Lookup tab
of the field
properties
to edit the
lookup field.

Using the Lookup Wizard creates a relationship between the table containing the lookup field and the table containing the data shown in the drop-down menu for the lookup field. In this example, the relationship is between the ContactID field in the Orders table and the ContactID field in the Address Book table. If you display the Relationships window (click the Relationships button on the Database Tools tab of the Ribbon), you see the relationship that the Lookup Wizard created. (You can find out more about relationships in Chapter 6 of this minibook.)

Knowing when to allow multiple selections

You may choose to store multiple values within one field and use a lookup list to select them. In a small company, for example, one person may have many roles, and the Employee table can store that information in a single field.

When you select the Allow Multiple Selections check box in the Lookup Wizard, your lookup list looks like Figure 5-6. Access creates a hidden join table to store the many-to-many relationship between the two tables — in this case, the Employee table and the Role table — involved in the lookup. In this case, the multiple-value lookup is used to define multiple employee roles. If Matt is both a manager and a systems administrator, a multiple-value field lets you define him as both. You can run a query to find all managers and see Matt in the list, or to find all systems administrators and see Matt in that list also.

Figure 5-6:
The user can choose multiple options from this drop-down menu.

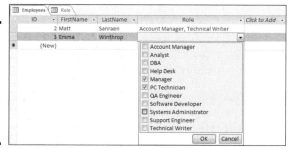

Allowing multiple selections in a lookup field can be a tremendously convenient feature if it's used correctly. You shouldn't use it when you need to add other information about the choice. In the Order Details table, for example, you don't want the item ordered to be a multiple-value field, even though a customer may in fact order multiple items. Instead, you need each item ordered to have its own record so that you can record how many of the items the customer wants and so that you can do calculations with that data down the line (that is, calculate the order total).

Access doesn't really store multiple values in one field, which would break the laws of good database design. Instead, it creates a hidden join table. This intermediate table is the join table in the many-to-many relationship between the two tables. Although it's more work to set up the join table yourself, in many situations, it's the right choice to make. Then you can create a form to make data entry as quick as it would be with a multiple-selection lookup field.

Be aware that if you ever want to upsize your database to SQL Server, the multiple-value feature doesn't convert well, but if you're staying in Access or SharePoint, it's a great feature when used correctly. (We cover using Access with SQL Server and SharePoint in Book IX.)

Modifying the lookup list

Adding values to an existing lookup list is pretty easy. If the lookup list gets its values from a table, just add records to the table to see additional choices in the lookup list. If you typed values for the lookup list yourself, switch to Design view, click the field that contains the lookup, and click the Lookup tab in the field properties (refer to Figure 5-5, earlier in this chapter). You can add options to the `Row Source` property; just be sure to separate the values with semicolons.

Validating Data As It's Entered

Often, you can formulate a rule that data must pass before being entered in a certain field. You may know, for example, that the date is not before 1999, that the price is 0 or greater, or that the entry must be five characters and begin with *P*. The `Validation Rule` field property (in field properties) enables you to specify a rule that data in a single field must pass to be entered in a particular field. Field validation rules are entered in the `Validation Rule` property for the field. Figure 5-7 shows a validation rule for the `Order Date` field.

TIP

If you just want to require that a value be entered, set the `Required` field property to `Yes`.

You can also specify a validation rule for a record rather than a field. Record validation allows you to create a rule to prevent internal inconsistency in a record. You may want to check that the ship date isn't before the order date, for example. You can enter record-validation rules in the `Validation Rule` property, one of the table properties. Display table properties by clicking the Property Sheet button on the Design tab (when the Table Design view is displayed). Figure 5-8 shows a record validation rule.

Figure 5-7:
The `Order Date` field uses a validation rule to make sure that the date is after December 31, 2005.

Orders		
Field Name	Data Type	Description (Optional)
OrderID	AutoNumber	Auto-assigned order number
Order Date	Date/Time	Date order placed (auto-entered)
ContactID	Number	Customer's ContactID in Address Book
Payment Method	Short Text	How paid?

Field Properties

General | Lookup

Format	Short Date
Input Mask	
Caption	
Default Value	=Now()
Validation Rule	>#1/1/2006#
Validation Text	Date must be 2006 or later
Required	No
Indexed	No
IME Mode	No Control
IME Sentence Mode	None
Text Align	General
Show Date Picker	For dates

The error message that appears when you enter a value prohibited by the validation rule. Press F1 for help on validation text.

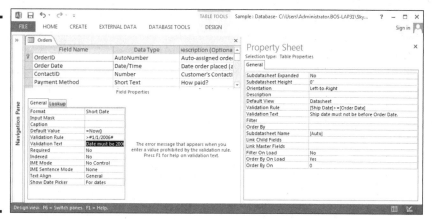

Figure 5-8:
Use the
`Valida-
tion
Rule`
property on
the Table
property
sheet to
establish a
rule for the
record.

Book II
Chapter 5

Avoiding "Garbage
In, Garbage Out"

Table 5-2 shows a few examples of validation rules. If you have a complicated validation rule, read up on creating expressions in Book III. Use expressions in validation rules the same way that you use them in query criteria. If the expression is true, the data can be entered; if the expression is false, the validation text displays, and the data can't be entered.

Criteria are covered in Book III, Chapter 1, and expressions are covered in detail in Book III, Chapter 2. The Build button that appears next to the Validation Rule box when you're entering a rule displays the Expression Builder, which is also covered in Book III, Chapter 2.

Table 5-2	Validation-Rule Examples
Rule for the Field	*Validation Rule*
Date not before 2006	`>#12/31/05#`
Price 0 or greater	`>=0`
Five characters beginning with *P*	`Like P????`
Ship date equal to or later than order date	`[Ship Date]>=[Order Date]`

If a user attempts to enter data that doesn't pass a validation rule, the contents of the `Validation Text` field property pop up to guide the user, using the text you enter. Generally, the validation text guides the user to enter the right data. An exception may occur if you don't want to give away too much information. Maybe Order numbers are always two letters followed by three or more numbers, but you don't want users to guess at an Order number. Your validation text can simply say `Enter a valid Order number`.

The validation text can't be longer than 255 characters.

Use operators to tell Access how to validate your data. *Operators* are symbols, (such as < and >) and words (such as AND, OR, and NOT) that tell Access how to limit your data. (Although +, −, *, and / are also operators, you aren't as likely to use them in validation rules.) You can also use expressions that include functions to create validation rules.

The validation rule can't be longer than 2,048 characters.

To create a validation rule, follow these steps:

1. **Display the table in Design view.**

2. **Select the field to which you want to add a validation rule.**

   Place the cursor anywhere in the row that displays the field and data type, or click the record selector to select the field. When the field is selected, or when the cursor is anywhere in its row, you see the field properties for that field.

   If you want to create a record validation rule, click the Property Sheet button on the Design tab of the Ribbon.

3. **Click the `Validation Rule` property.**

4. **Type your validation rule.**

   Table 5-3 tells you how to create your validation rule.

5. **Enter an explanatory message in the `Validation Text` property.**

   Validation text appears when data entered in the field doesn't meet the validation rule. In most cases, you want this script to help the user to understand why the input wasn't accepted. (In some cases, you may not want someone to make up data that passes the validation rule, so your validation text may be more cryptic.)

Table 5-3	Creating Validation Rules
Validation-Rule Example	*How It Works*
`"Boston" OR "New York"`	Limits input in the field to those two cities
`<10`	Allows values less than 10
`>10`	Allows values greater than 10
`<=10`	Allows values less than or equal to 10
`>=10`	Allows values greater than or equal to 10
`=10`	Allows values equal to 10
`<>0`	Allows values not equal to 0
`In("Boston", "Concord")`	Allows text that is *Boston* or *Concord*
`Between 10 AND 20`	Allows values between 10 and 20

You can test data entered before the validation rule took effect in one of two ways:

✦ Click the Test Validation Rules button in the Tools group on the Design tab of the Ribbon.

✦ Display the datasheet by clicking the View button and then click the Yes button when Access asks whether you want to test existing data.

The Like operator deserves its own explanation. Use the Like operator to test whether an input matches a certain pattern. Use wildcard characters, such as the ones shown in Table 5-4, to help define the pattern.

Table 5-4	Using the Like Operator
Wildcard	*What It Signifies*
?	Any single character
#	Any single number
*	Zero or more characters

You may define a zip-code field to allow only five digits, as follows:

```
Like "#####"
```

You can also define a field to contain only names that start with the letter *S*, as follows:

```
Like "S*"
```

According to the preceding rule, a person can choose not to type any characters after S, because the * wildcard allows zero or more characters. If you always want a certain number of characters to follow S, use the ? wildcard instead. If you want users to type exactly three characters after S, use this validation rule:

```
LIKE "S???"
```

You can use more than one expression in a validation rule by separating the expressions with AND, OR, or NOT. AND and NOT limit the entries that pass the rule. In the case of AND, an entry must pass both rules; in the case of NOT, an entry must pass one rule and fail the other. Using OR increases the likelihood that an entry will pass the rule, because the entry needs to pass only one of the two rules separated by OR.

Chapter 6: Relating Your Tables and Protecting Your Data

In This Chapter

✔ **Creating relationships between tables**

✔ **Protecting your relationships with referential integrity**

✔ **Using cascading updates and deletes to protect data integrity**

✔ **Printing the relationships between tables**

*R*elational database management systems such as Microsoft Access exist because the real world often requires large amounts of data to be stored. One-to-many or many-to-many relationships often exist among pieces of data. Any one customer, for example, may place many orders (a one-to-many relationship). Any one order may be an order for many products. In a school, any one student may enroll in many courses. Any one course has many students enrolled in it.

When information is spread across multiple tables, the data must always link up correctly. If customer Hortense Higglebottom places an order for five lawn flamingoes on April 1, the records from the various tables that record that information must jibe perfectly so that she gets what she ordered and pays the right amount for what she bought, so that her lawn flamingoes are sent to the correct address — and so that she doesn't end up getting 37 golden whistles instead. The technical term for making absolutely sure that all the pieces line up correctly, at all times, is *referential integrity*. Before we get to the specifics of how you enforce referential integrity in your database, we provide a brief review of all the buzzwords and concepts related to the whole idea of storing chunks of data in separate tables.

Book I, Chapter 3 describes relationships among tables from a design perspective.

When two tables are related in a one-to-many relationship, the table on the "one" side of the relationship must have a primary key field that uniquely identifies each record. For this reason, the table on the "one" side is often referred to as the *master table*. For the customers-and-orders example, the Address Book table is on the "one" side of the relationship, and the primary key field, ContactID, has a unique value for each record — that is, each customer listed in the table has a value in the ContactID field that's unique to him. If you want to refer to a customer anywhere else in the database, you can use that unique ContactID value as a shortcut (see Figure 6-1).

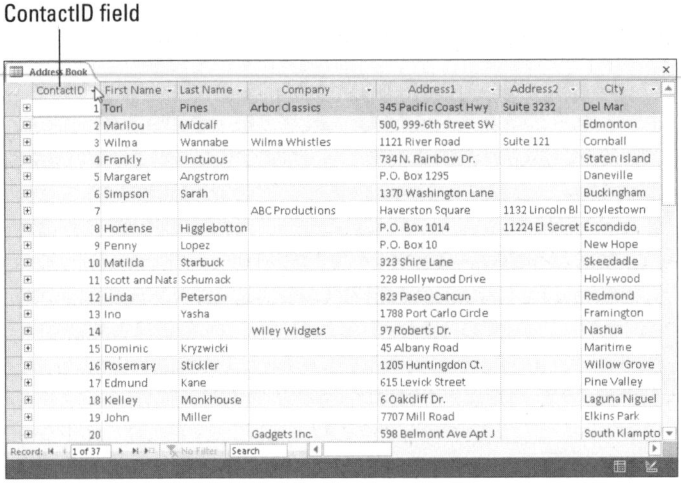

ContactID field

Figure 6-1:
The Address Book table has the Contact ID field as its primary key.

The table on the "many" side of the relationship needs to contain a field that has (preferably) the same name, and (definitely) the same data type and field length as the primary key in the master table. In the table on the "many" side of the relationship, that field is referred to as the *foreign key*. Because that table contains the foreign key, it's often referred to as the *detail table*. In the customers-and-orders example, the Orders table is the detail table. Each order placed is listed in the Orders table, and the customer who placed the order is identified by his ContactID number. Taken together, the primary key and foreign key are often referred to as the *matching keys*. (There's a load of technical jargon for ya.)

You can see how the one-to-many relationship plays out when the two tables contain data. In Figure 6-2, looking up which orders are placed by Margaret Angstrom is easy; the ContactID happens to be 5.

In any given database, one-to-many relationships likely occur among several tables. A *many-to-many* relationship is just two one-to-many relationships among three tables, as we show in the students-and-courses example in Book I, Chapter 3. In the orders example, a many-to-many relationship exists among products and customers. You don't have to do anything special to define a many-to-many relationship. When you link two tables to a common third table, you create a many-to-many relationship.

Figure 6-3 shows relationships defined in an Access database. In the Relationships window, field names with a picture of a key to their left are primary keys. The connecting lines show how the tables relate. In that example, the number 1 on a connection line represents the master table — the table on the "one" side of the relationship. The infinity symbol (∞) represents the detail table — the table on the "many" side.

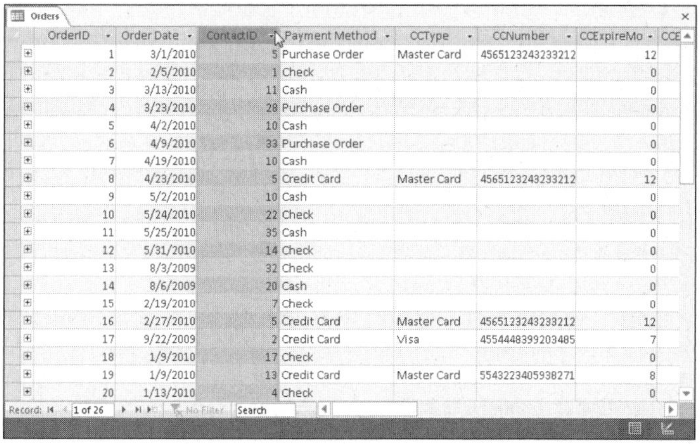

Orders

OrderID	Order Date	ContactID	Payment Method	CCType	CCNumber	CCExpireMo
1	3/1/2010	5	Purchase Order	Master Card	4565123243233212	12
2	2/5/2010	1	Check			0
3	3/13/2010	11	Cash			0
4	3/23/2010	28	Purchase Order			0
5	4/2/2010	10	Cash			0
6	4/9/2010	33	Purchase Order			0
7	4/19/2010	10	Cash			0
8	4/23/2010	5	Credit Card	Master Card	4565123243233212	12
9	5/2/2010	10	Cash			0
10	5/24/2010	22	Check			0
11	5/25/2010	35	Cash			0
12	5/31/2010	14	Check			0
13	8/3/2009	32	Check			0
14	8/6/2009	20	Cash			0
15	2/19/2010	7	Check			0
16	2/27/2010	5	Credit Card	Master Card	4565123243233212	12
17	9/22/2009	2	Credit Card	Visa	4554448399203485	7
18	1/9/2010	17	Check			0
19	1/9/2010	13	Credit Card	Master Card	5543223405938271	8
20	1/13/2010	4	Check			0

Record: 1 of 26

Figure 6-2: The Orders table uses the `Contact ID` field from the Address Book table to identify customers.

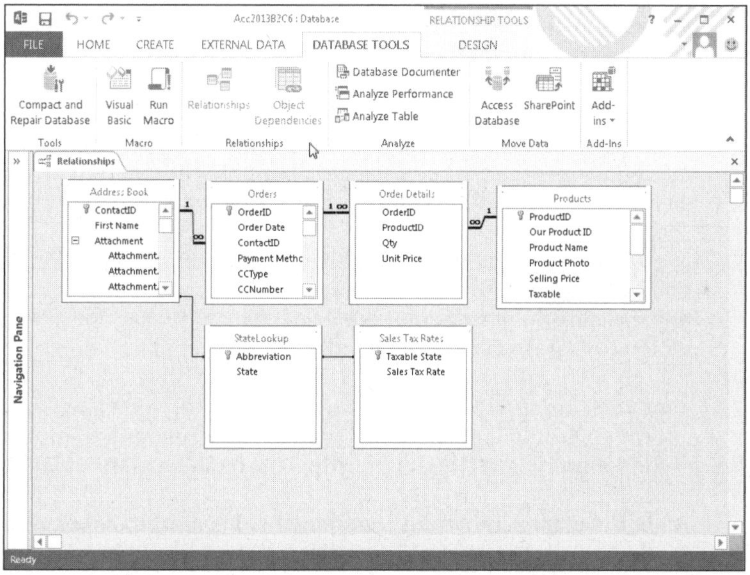

Figure 6-3: Multiple one-to-many relationships exist among the tables in this database.

Creating Relationships and Protecting Your Data with Referential Integrity

We're not referring to your personal relationships. (Well, maybe we are in an abstract sort of way.) Before you join two tables in the Relationships window, think about whether you want Access to enforce referential integrity between those tables. *Referential integrity,* as the name implies, is all about making sure that the relationship between two tables doesn't turn to total garbage.

To see how you convert a one-to-many relationship to garbage, consider the following scenario. Suppose that a table named Products contains a primary key field named `ProductID` that uniquely identifies each record, and say that a hammer in the Products table has a `ProductID` value of 232.

The Order Details table in that same database *also* has a field named `ProductID`, which is the foreign key. Suppose that 100 hammers have been ordered to date, and 100 records in the Order Details table have the value 232 in their `ProductID` fields.

Now someone comes along and decides to change the hammer's `ProductID` code to 98765. Or instead of changing the hammer's `ProductID`, that person just deletes that product from the Products table. Either way, a record in the Products table no longer has a `ProductID` value of 232.

So what becomes of the 100 records in the Order Details table that still have 232 in their `ProductID` fields? Do you leave them referring to the now-nonexistent record 232? If you do that, you destroy the referential integrity of the relationship between the tables.

How, you may ask, did you manage to do that? Well, a bunch of records in the Order Details table now point to absolutely nothing; there's no way to tell what products the customers bought. The referential relationship between the Products and Order Details tables has lost its integrity.

Enforcing referential integrity prevents these bad things from happening. When you enforce referential integrity, you prevent yourself from accidentally messing up your relationships. (Well, okay, that doesn't apply to your personal relationships, even abstractly, but you get the point.)

Some rules exist to help you determine whether you can even choose to enforce referential integrity. You can enforce referential integrity only when all the following statements are true of the tables in the relationship:

✦ In the master table, the matching field is a primary key or a field with its `Indexed` property set to `Yes (No Duplicates)`.

✦ In the detail table, the foreign key is of the same data type as the primary key, or if the primary key is an AutoNumber field, the foreign key is a `Number` field with its `Field Size` property set to the `Long Integer` width.

✦ Both tables are stored in the same Access database.

Deciding on the best path to take

Assuming that all the rules for enforcing referential integrity are met (see the preceding section for a refresher), you're ready to get started. Just keep in mind that you can enforce either of two distinct types of referential integrity:

✦ **Cascade Update Related Fields:** This option ensures that if the value of the primary key field changes in the master table, the same change cascades to all records in the detail table. (This option doesn't apply if the primary key is an AutoNumber field.)

After an AutoNumber field receives a value, that value never changes.

✦ **Cascade Deleting Related Records:** This option ensures that if a record in the master table is deleted, all corresponding records in the detail table are also deleted.

We describe both options in "Setting referential integrity between two tables," later in this chapter.

You can choose to enable referential integrity as soon as you join two tables in the Relationships window, which we discuss later in this chapter. You can change or disable referential integrity options at any time, so you're not making a lifelong commitment or anything.

Opening the Relationships window

The place where you actually join tables and enforce referential integrity between them is called the *Relationships window* — the same window we show in Figure 6-3, earlier in this chapter. Clearly, if you want to be able to set up referential integrity between two tables, you're going to need some hints on how to open the Relationships window. How about some explicit instructions, such as the following?

1. **If any tables are open, close them.**

Access can't create a relationship if one of the tables involved is open.

2. **Click the Relationships button in the Relationships group on the Database Tools tab of the Ribbon.**

Access opens the Relationships window.

The Relationships window may be empty when you first open it, but if we know you, it won't be that way for long; you can (and probably will) add tables to the window at any time, as the next section makes clear. It's also possible that some relationships may have already been created, even if you don't remember creating them. There are ways to define relationships that don't use the Relationships window, such as using the Lookup Wizard.

Book II, Chapter 5 describes relationships created with the Lookup Wizard.

Adding tables to the Relationships window

When the Relationships window is open, you can add tables to it by following these steps:

Show
Table

1. **Click the Show Table button in the Relationships group on the (Relationship Tools) Design tab of the Ribbon.**

   The Show Table dialog box appears.

2. **Click the name of any table you want to add to the Relationships window and then click the Add button.**

3. **Repeat Step 2 as many times as you want to add multiple tables to the Relationships window.**

   You can select multiple tables by holding down the Ctrl key as you select table names.

4. **Click the Close button in the Show Table dialog box.**

   The Show Table dialog box closes, and voilà — the tables you chose are visible in the Relationships window. The window doesn't display the entire table, of course; that would be too big. Only a *field list,* which shows the names of all the fields in the table, appears for each table you select. You can move those field lists around by dragging their title bars and size them by dragging any corner or edge.

Setting referential integrity between two tables

When you have two or more tables in the Relationships window, you can define their relationships and referential integrity. Here's how:

1. **Click the matching key in either table to select that field name.**

   If you're joining the Address Book and Orders tables shown in Figure 6-3, earlier in this chapter, you click the `ContactID` field in either table.

2. **Drag the selected field name to the corresponding field name in the other table, and drop it there.**

   The Edit Relationships dialog box opens (see Figure 6-4).

3. **If you want to turn on referential integrity, select the Enforce Referential Integrity check box.**

   The Cascade options (below the Enforce Referential Integrity check box) are enabled.

Figure 6-4:
The Edit
Relationships
dialog box.

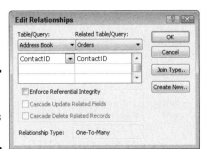

4. **If you want matching records in the detail table to update automatically when the value of a primary key field changes, select the Cascade Update Related Fields check box.**

5. **If you want matching records from the detail table to be deleted automatically after you delete a record in the master table, select the Cascade Delete Related Records check box.**

6. **Click the Create or OK button to save your changes and close the Edit Relationships dialog box.**

   The OK button replaces the Create button when you edit an existing relationship, as opposed to creating a new one.

If you join two tables without enforcing referential integrity, the connecting line (the *join* line) in the Relationships window is just a thin black line, as shown in the top two tables in Figure 6-5. If you enforce referential integrity, the connecting line displays 1 near the master table, and an infinity symbol (∞) appears for the detail table, as shown at the bottom of Figure 6-5.

Figure 6-5:
Joined
tables
without (top)
and with
(bottom)
referential
integrity
enforced.

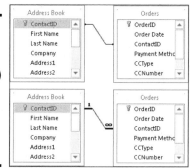

The relationships that you define aren't etched in stone. You can change the relationship between two tables at any time.

Editing and deleting relationships

Before you change or delete the relationship between two tables in the Relationships window, you need to select the relationship you want to change. Selecting a relationship is trickier than you think. Follow these steps to select the join line that represents the relationship you want to change:

1. **In the Relationships window, right-click the join line that you want to change or delete.**

   A contextual menu displays the options shown in Figure 6-6.

   If you see different options, you right-clicked too close to a table. Clicking the line itself can be tricky: Try right-clicking nearer the center of the join line that you want to change.

Figure 6-6:
Right-click a
connecting
line to
delete or
change it.

2. **Choose one of the following options from the contextual menu:**

   - *Delete:* If you want to delete the line (which deletes the relationship and turns off referential integrity), choose the Delete option.

   - *Edit Relationship:* If you want to change something about the relationship, choose the Edit Relationship option.

     If you choose the Edit Relationship option, the Edit Relationships dialog box opens, allowing you to change or disable referential integrity. Make your changes and then click OK.

The Join Type button in the Edit Relationships dialog box allows you to set a default join type to be used in queries. Join types have no bearing on referential integrity.

See Book III, Chapter 1 for more information on join types.

Creating Referential Integrity with Many-to-Many Relationships

As we discuss in Book I, Chapter 3, a many-to-many relationship often exists among chunks of data. Think of a school, which has many students enrolled in many courses. To design a database that contains information about students, courses, and enrollment, you need three tables:

+ One table, perhaps named Students, contains a record for each student, with a primary key field named `StudentID` that uniquely identifies each student.

+ A second table, perhaps named Courses, contains one record for each course, with a primary key named `CourseID` that uniquely identifies each course.

+ To keep track of which students are enrolled in which courses, you need a third table (called a *junction table*) containing a record that pairs a `StudentID` with a `CourseID`.

For the sake of the example, suppose that the junction table is named Enrollments, as in Figure 6-7. When looking at data in the tables, you see how each record in the Enrollments table links a student to his or her courses.

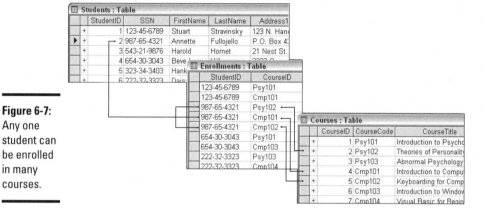

Figure 6-7:
Any one student can be enrolled in many courses.

The same tables and same relationships link any given course to the students who are enrolled in it, as shown in Figure 6-8.

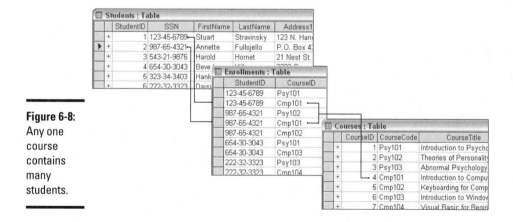

Figure 6-8:
Any one course contains many students.

Although a many-to-many relationship is conceptually its own beast, Access recognizes only one-to-many relationships. To set up referential integrity among the tables, you don't create a special many-to-many join. Rather, you just connect the fields and enforce referential integrity on each join line, as shown in Figure 6-9.

Figure 6-9:
The relationships among the Students, Courses, and Enrollments tables are set to enforce referential integrity, as indicated by the *1* and ∞ symbols.

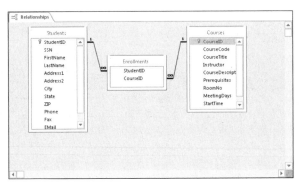

Printing the Relationships Window

You can print a copy of your Relationships window at any time. Doing so isn't necessary, but if you'd like to have a printed copy to refer to in the future, just follow these steps:

1. **Make sure that the Relationships window is open and looks just the way you want the printed copy to look.**

2. **Click the Relationship Report button in the Tools group on the (Relationship Tools) Design tab.**

The printer won't start churning right away. Instead, a preview of what the printer will print appears in a new tab.

Print

3. **Click the Print button in the Print group on the Print Preview tab.**

Now the printer actually prints the relationships.

Close Print Preview

4. **Click the Close Print Preview button in the Close Preview group on the Print Preview tab.**

A Report Design screen suddenly opens, but don't be alarmed: It appears in case you want to save a copy of the Relationships window as an Access report. If you haven't gotten into reports yet and don't know what we're talking about here, don't worry; just continue with the next step.

5. **Click the Close (X) button in the top-right corner of the Report Design window.**

6. **When you're asked whether you want to save the changes made in the report, click the No button.**

You return to the Relationships window.

7. **To close the Relationships window, click the Close (X) button in its top-right corner.**

As we say in Step 4, you don't need to concern yourself with this business of reports right now, so don't worry about the weird stuff that happens when you print your Relationships window.

Just so you know, Access reports are covered in Book V.

Book III

Queries (Or Getting Information from Your Data)

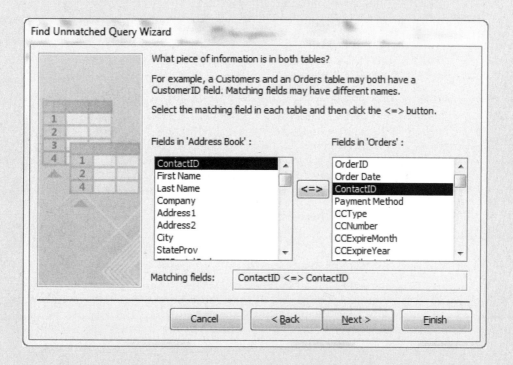

Contents at a Glance

Chapter 1: Creating Select Queries.........................189

Understanding Types of Queries......................... 190
Creating a Query in Design View 191
Creating a Query with the Simple Query Wizard.................. 194
Viewing Your Query 197
Using Query Design View 198
Taking Tips on Creating a Query 202
Editing a Query 204
Limiting Records with Criteria Expressions 207
Working with Multiple Related Tables 213
Working with Query Datasheets 217
Saving Queries 219

Chapter 2: Letting Queries Do the Math.....................221

Doing Calculations in Queries........................ 221
Writing Expressions in Access....................... 224
Using Expression Builder 228
Going beyond Basic Arithmetic 232
Performing Date and Time Calculations 238
Manipulating Text with Expressions 242
Writing Decision-Making Expressions 243
Testing for Empty Fields 248
Sorting by Name or Company 248
Creating Flexible Parameter Queries 249
Working with Totals, Subtotals, Averages, and Such 252

**Chapter 3: Doing Neat Things with Action Queries
and Query Wizards...........................255**

Creating Action Queries........................... 255
Changing Data with Update Queries 258
Creating New Tables with Make-Table Queries 262
Moving Data from One Table to Another with Append Queries 265
Deleting Lots of Records with Delete Queries 267
Finding Unmatched Records with a Wizard............... 270
Finding Duplicate Records 272

Chapter 4: Viewing Your Data from All Angles Using Crosstabs . . .277

Aggregating Data in a Crosstab Query.................. 277
Using the Crosstab Query Wizard 278
Creating a Crosstab Query in Design View............... 282
Modifying a Crosstab Query 284

Chapter 1: Creating Select Queries

In This Chapter

✔ Seeing what queries do and what kind of queries you can make

✔ Creating a select query with a wizard

✔ Creating and editing a select query in Design view

✔ Using criteria and sorting to get the data in your queries

✔ Using query datasheets to enter and edit data

✔ Saving your queries

*Q*ueries are a way to ask questions of your data. Do you want to know who ordered a lawn flamingo? Which customers live in California? Which orders contain items that have been discontinued? What your ten best-selling items are? Queries can tell you all that and more.

Like tables, which we cover in Book II, queries have two views: Design and Datasheet. In Design view, you define your query, telling Access which fields you want to see, which tables they come from, and the criteria that any record has to meet to appear on the resulting datasheet. In Datasheet view, you see the fields and records Access finds that meet your criteria.

You can use queries to do the following:

✦ Look at data from related tables.

✦ Look at *subsets* of your data — selective slices that meet certain criteria that you specify.

✦ Sort and alphabetize data.

✦ Create new calculated fields.

You can make as many queries as you want to. Usually, some queries are made on the fly and not saved; others are saved and used as the basis for forms and reports.

To create a query, you need to know what data — more specifically, which fields — you want to see and which tables those fields are in. As you define the query, you may have criteria that limit the data. After you define the query, you can view the data in a datasheet (or in a form or report to see the data in a different format). The datasheet created by a query is *dynamic* — that is, you see the data that meets the query definition each time you view the datasheet. If data has been added, edited, or deleted, the query data-sheet may display different data.

To create a query, you use a wizard or Design view (or both) to tell Access which data you want to see. The easiest way for a beginner to create a query is to use the Simple Query Wizard, but after you understand queries, you may prefer to go right to Design view.

We start this chapter by telling you about the different types of queries that Access offers; then we introduce you to Design view. This chapter concentrates on select queries, which are the most common type, and the skills you use to create select queries. Next, we guide you through creating a query with the Simple Query Wizard. The wizard provides some features that are difficult for beginners to add in Design view, such as summary fields. Because the Simple Query Wizard doesn't allow you to define criteria (such as limiting records to those ordered this month or viewing only products that cost more than $20), you probably want to move quickly to the next sections on using Design view and criteria. At the end of the chapter, you find all the details on working with your query data in a datasheet. Use the two views together to get the data you want.

If you want to send a query through Access to an SQL database, you need to create a pass-through query. See Book IX, Chapter 2 for more information.

Understanding Types of Queries

The many types of queries that Access provides give you many ways to select and view specific data in your database. You choose the type of query, choose the fields you want to see, and define criteria to limit the data shown as necessary.

These types of queries are available in Access:

- ✦ **Advanced Filter/Sort:** The simplest kind of query, Advanced Filter/Sort allows you to find and sort information from a single table in the data-base. You can access this option in any datasheet by clicking Advanced in the Sort & Filter group on the Home tab of the Ribbon and then choosing Advanced Filter/Sort. Advanced Filter/Sort is covered Book II, Chapter 3.

- ✦ **Select:** A select query selects the data you want from one or more tables and displays the data in the order in which you want it displayed. A select query can include criteria that tell Access to filter records and display only some of them. Select queries that display individual records are detail queries; those that summarize records are totals or summary queries (see the next item).

✦ **Totals or Summary:** These queries are subsets of select queries, but they allow you to calculate a sum or some other aggregate (such as an average) rather than display each individual record. (Totals queries are covered in Chapter 2 of this minibook.)

✦ **Parameter:** A parameter query asks you for one or more pieces of information that Access then uses to filter the data before displaying the datasheet.

✦ **AutoLookup:** An AutoLookup query fills in information for you. (AutoLookup queries are covered later in this chapter.)

✦ **Action:** Action queries change your data based on some set of criteria. Action queries can delete records, update data, append data from one or more tables to another table, and make a new table. (We describe action queries in Chapter 3 of this minibook.)

✦ **Crosstab:** Most tables in Access, including ones generated by queries, have field names across the top, with each row containing a record of data. Crosstab queries produce tables with the values from one field down the side and values from another field across the top of the table. A crosstab query performs a calculation; it sums, averages, or counts data that is categorized in two ways, as defined by the row and column labels. (Crosstab queries are covered in Chapter 4 of this minibook.) You could use a crosstab query to show states across the top and products down the side, for example, so that you can see how sales differ by state.

Select queries are the most common type of queries used in Access. In fact, select queries are the most general type; all the other query types add features to select queries. When you define a select query, you use the design grid to select which fields and records to display in the new datasheet. The skills you use to define select queries also apply to the other types of queries.

Creating a Query in Design View

If you're completely new to queries, this section is for you. Here, we create a simple select query so you can see exactly what a query does.

Just follow these steps to create a simple query:

1. **Click the Query Design button in the Queries group on the Create tab of the Ribbon.**

Access displays Design view and the Show Table dialog box, as shown in Figure 1-1.

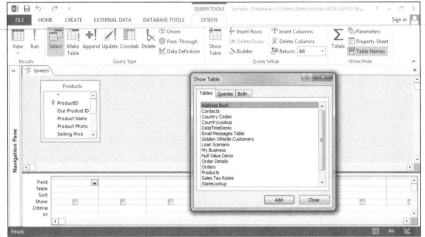

Figure 1-1:
Start your
query by
selecting
the table
that has the
data you
need.

2. In the Show Table dialog box, select the table that contains the fields you want to display in the query datasheet; then click the Add button.

Queries can show data from more than one table, but for this example, we're showing you a simple query that shows data from only one table.

3. Click the Close button in the Show Table dialog box.

Design view displays the table you selected in the top pane and the empty design grid in the bottom pane.

Notice the new tab that's available when you're working on a query design: Design. It contains many options to help you refine your query.

You can close the Query property sheet if it's displayed; you don't need it right now. Redisplay it at any time by clicking Property Sheet in the Show/Hide group on the Design tab of the Ribbon.

4. Double-click a field name in the top pane to display that field name in the bottom pane (the design grid).

5. Repeat Step 4 as often as necessary to include any additional fields.

The fields you put in the grid are the fields that will be used by the query.

You can drag a field name to the design grid or double-click a field name to move it to the grid. You can also choose the fields that you want to use from the drop-down field and table menus. To select multiple field names in the field list, use the standard Ctrl+click or Shift+click selection technique and then drag all selected field names to the design grid.

Figure 1-2 shows a query asking to view three fields from the Products table: ProductID, Product Name, and Selling Price.

Table used in query

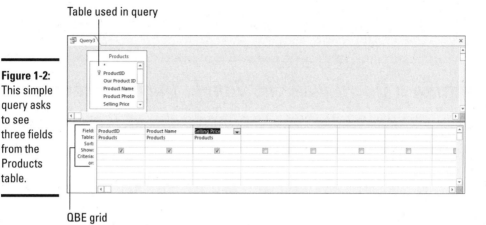

Figure 1-2:
This simple
query asks
to see
three fields
from the
Products
table.

QBE grid

6. **Click the View button (the first button on the Design and Home tabs)
to see the datasheet with the data selected by your query.**

The datasheet shown in Figure 1-3 shows the three fields we put in the
design grid.

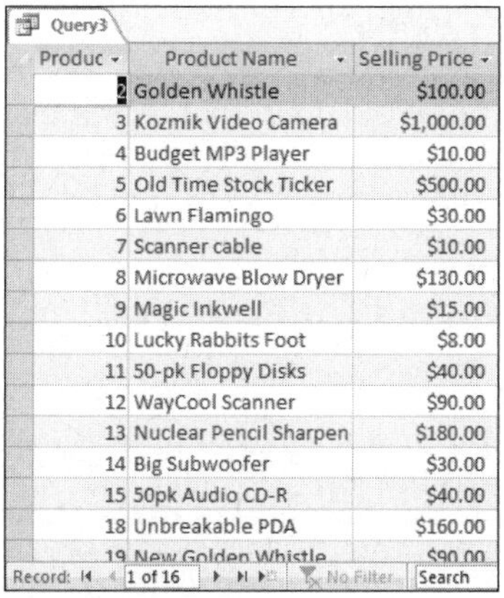

Figure 1-3:
The
datasheet
shows the
data asked
for in Query
Design
view.

If you want to save the query, click the Save button on the toolbar. Give the
query a name that indicates the data it selects. Remember that the next time
you open the query in Datasheet view, you'll see updated data; if any
records have been added, deleted, or modified, the query reflects those
changes. You may choose not to save the query if you won't need it again.
Just close it and then click the No button when Access asks whether you
want to save it.

Now that you have the hang of what a query is, you're probably ready for more: getting summary data out of a query, sorting the results, limiting results with criteria, and so on. Read on!

Creating a Query with the Simple Query Wizard

The Simple Query Wizard does a great deal of the work of creating a query for you. It's most useful when you want to use fields from different tables and when you want a query that summarizes your data by calculating totals.

The Simple Query Wizard gives you the option of creating a summary query or a detail query. A *detail query* lists every record that meets your criteria. A *summary query* (also called a *totals query)* performs calculations on your data to summarize it. You can create a summary query if the fields you choose for the query include both of the following:

✦ A field with values

✦ A field with repetitions or a field with dates, used to group the values

A summary query gives you the option of totaling (summing), averaging, or counting the number of values in a field, or finding the minimum or maximum value in a field. A summary query creates new calculated fields that you can use in other queries or in reports.

Need an example? Here's one: If you have a field that lists the amount spent and a field that lists the dates on which the money was spent, the Simple Query Wizard creates a summary query for you that sums the amount spent by date. Pretty neat, huh?

Ready to give the Simple Query Wizard a spin? Just follow these steps to use the wizard to create a query:

1. **Click the Query Wizard button on the Create tab of the Ribbon.**

2. **Select Simple Query Wizard in the New Query dialog box and then click OK.**

Access displays the first window of the Simple Query Wizard, shown in Figure 1-4.

3. **From the Tables/Queries drop-down menu, choose the first table or query that contains fields you want to use in this query.**

Many queries are based on tables, but you also have the option of basing a query on another query. Maybe you've already created a query to select sales data only from 2013. Now, without modifying the original query, you want to create a query that lists 2013 sales by state or limits the analysis to just a few salespeople.

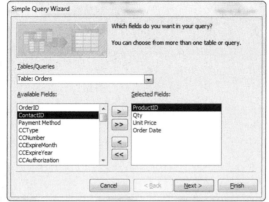

Figure 1-4:
Choose
fields for the
query; they
can come
from more
than one
table.

When you select a table or query, fields from that object appear in the Available Fields list box.

4. **Move the fields you want to use in the query from the Available Fields list to the Selected Fields list by double-clicking a field name (or selecting the field name and then clicking the > button).**

5. **If you're using fields from more than one table or query, repeat Steps 2 and 3 to add fields from other tables or queries to the Selected Fields list; then click Next.**

   From this point on, the windows you see depend on the types of fields and the type of query (detail or summary) you choose.

6. **Choose the type of query you want: Detail or Summary.**

7. **Depending on your selection in Step 6, do one of the following:**

   • *If you chose a summary query,* click the Summary Options button.

   • *If you chose a detail query,* click Next, and jump to Step 11.

   The Summary Options window appears, as shown in Figure 1-5, allowing you to tell the wizard how to summarize each field. Choose these summary calculations carefully. In some cases, you may need to write a calculation in the query to get the data that you need; the summary options may not be sufficient.

8. **Choose how to summarize your data, click OK to close the Summary Options dialog box, and click Next to see the next window of the wizard.**

9. **Select check boxes to indicate the new fields that you want Access to create.**

   If you want to add all the values in the Qty field, for example, to calculate how many items have been sold, select the Sum check box in the row for the Qty field.

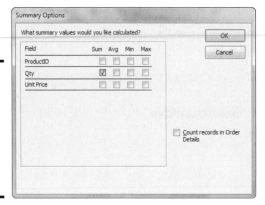

Figure 1-5:
Choose
how to
summarize
your data
by setting
these
options.

Don't overlook the Count check box(es) that may appear in this window. Selecting a Count check box tells the wizard to create a field that counts the records within each grouping.

10. **If the fields being summarized can be grouped by a Time/Date field, you see a window where you can choose to group data by date; choose the time interval the records should be grouped by and then click Next.**

You won't see this window if your data doesn't contain a Time/Date field.

If you choose to include the Order Date field in the query and to sum the Qty field, for example, you can group by month to see how many units of each item you sold in each month. You can choose to display totals by the following date grouping options: Day, Month, Quarter, and Year. The Unique Day/Time option groups records by each unique date and time; if your data includes times, all records with the same date and time are grouped together. If your data includes only a date without the time, all records from the same day are grouped together (the same as the Day option).

11. **Type a name for the query in the box at the top of the window.**

12. **Choose one of these options:**

- *Open the Query to View Information:* This option shows you the query in Datasheet view.

- *Modify the Query Design:* This option shows you the query in Design view.

13. **Click Finish to view the query.**

If you chose the Open the Query to View Information option in Step 12, you see the query in Datasheet view, shown in Figure 1-6. If you chose the Modify the Query Design option, you see your resulting query in Design view.

Order Details Query1			
ProductID ▾	Unit Price ▾	Order Date I ▾	Sum Of Qty ▾
Golden Whistle ▾	$0.00	March 2012	1
Golden Whistle	$0.00	April 2012	5
Golden Whistle	$0.00	May 2012	6
Golden Whistle	$100.00	February 2012	2
Kozmik Video Camera	$0.00	January 2012	1
Kozmik Video Camera	$0.00	February 2012	1
Kozmik Video Camera	$1,000.00	August 2011	1
Kozmik Video Camera	$1,000.00	March 2012	1
Budget MP3 Player	$0.00	September 201	1
Budget MP3 Player	$0.00	January 2012	3
Budget MP3 Player	$0.00	February 2012	2
Budget MP3 Player	$0.00	April 2012	2

Figure 1-6:
The datasheet shows data summarized by product and date.

You can edit the query created by the Simple Query Wizard in Design view, about which we say lots more in the rest of this chapter.

The Simple Query Wizard doesn't allow you to include criteria to choose which records you want to include in the query datasheet. If you want to include criteria in your query, open the query created by the wizard in Design view and then add the criteria. (Details on Design view appear throughout this chapter.)

Viewing Your Query

After you create a query, you can look at it in any of these views:

+ **Design view** displays the query definition, where you can select tables and fields, create criteria and expressions, define sort order, and do all the other things you need to do to define a query.

+ **Datasheet view** displays the data from the query in a datasheet, just as though you were looking at a table datasheet.

+ **SQL view** displays the query definition as a statement in SQL (Structured Query Language).

The quickest way to view a query is to double-click the query name in the Navigation pane. When the query is open in Datasheet view, switch between Design and Datasheet views by clicking the View button (the leftmost button on the Home tab of the Ribbon). Alternatively, click one of the three buttons in the bottom-right corner of the Access window — Datasheet View, SQL View, and Design View — or click the down arrow on the View button to open the drop-down menu of View options and then choose the correct view.

Using Query Design View

If you've followed this chapter from the beginning, you've created a simple, one-table query and used the Simple Query Wizard to create another query. Queries can do so much more, though, so dive into Design view and figure out what's what.

Deciphering Design view

Design view is where you tell Access about the data you're looking for. In Design view, you specify the tables (or other queries) where Access finds the data you want, the fields from those tables that you want to see, and any criteria that the data must pass to appear in the datasheet. You also use Design view to choose the type of query, specify calculations, and define the sort order of the resulting data.

The top half of Design view is the Table pane, where you view the tables (or queries) containing the fields to be used in the query. The bottom half is the Query by Example (QBE) grid, where you define the fields you want to see and any criteria to limit the data you want to see. Queries can do even more than that, as you see in the remainder of this minibook.

Here are our two favorite ways to display a query in Design view (shown in Figure 1-7):

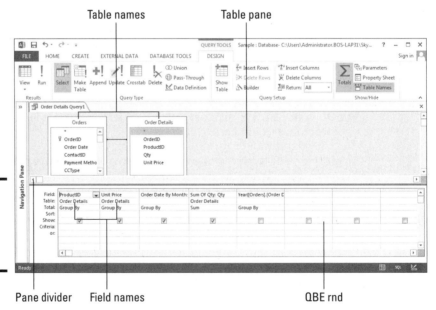

Figure 1-7:
A query displayed in Design view.

✦ Click Queries in the Navigation pane, right-click the query name, and choose Design View from the contextual menu.

✦ Click the View button on the Home tab of the Ribbon when the query is displayed in Datasheet view.

Table 1-1 explains what the most useful buttons on the Query Tools Design tab on the Ribbon do (see Figure 1-8).

Figure 1-8:
The buttons of the Query Tools Design Ribbon.

Book III
Chapter 1

Creating Select Queries

Table 1-1	Buttons in Design View	
Button	*Button Name*	*What It Does*
View	View	Displays Datasheet view — the data set defined by the query.
Run	Run	Runs the query. (For a select query, clicking the Run button does the same thing as clicking the View button. When the query is an action query, the Run button performs the action. Use this button carefully.)
Make Table	Query Type group	Chooses a query type: Select Query, Crosstab Query, Make-Table Query, Update Query, Append Query, or Delete Query. Union, Pass-Through, and Data Definition queries are covered in Book IX, Chapter 3.
Show Table	Show Table	Displays the Show Table dialog box so that you can add tables to the query.
Builder	Builder	Displays the Expression Builder dialog box. (This button can be clicked only when the cursor is in the Field or Criteria row.) See more about building expressions in Chapter 2 of this minibook.

(continued)

Table 1-1 *(continued)*

Button	Button Name	What It Does
⁼⁼ Insert Rows	Insert Rows	Inserts a row into the QBE grid (when you run out of rows for criteria).
▧✕ Delete Rows	Delete Rows	Deletes a row in the QBE grid. The row deleted is the one containing the cursor.
ᵘᵗᵘ Insert Columns	Insert Columns	Inserts a column into the QBE grid to the left of the column containing the cursor (to add a field to the query).
✕ Delete Columns	Delete Columns	Deletes the column of the QBE grid (and its contents) that contains the cursor.
Return: All ▾	Return (Top Values)	Limits the result of the query displayed in the datasheet to the number of records or the percentage of records displayed in this option (All, 5, or 25, for example). You can choose values from the drop-down menu or type values. You can choose to display the top 5 values or the top 25 percent of values, for example.
Σ Totals	Totals	Displays the Totals row in the design grid. (Use the Totals row to create calculations that summarize your data.)
[?] Parameters	Parameters	Displays the Query Parameters box.
▤ Property Sheet	Property Sheet	Displays properties for the selected field or field list.
ˣʸᶻ Table Names	Table Names	Hides and displays the Table row in the QBE grid.

You can change the size of the panes in Design view by dragging the pane divider. Just move the mouse pointer to the divider, where it changes shape; then click, hold, and drag to move the divider.

Working with tables in Design view

The tables in the Table pane (the top pane of the Design View window) are really just little field-list windows that you can move and size the same way you move and size windows. Change the size of a table window by moving the mouse pointer to the border of the window; when the pointer turns into a double-headed arrow, drag the border to change the size of the window. To move a table in the Table pane, drag its title bar. This technique may come in handy when you work with related tables and want a clear look at the relationships among them.

If your query contains tables that have existing relationships that were defined with lookup fields (or created in the Relationships window), you see those relationships as lines between the related tables. (You can see more about relationships in Book II, Chapter 6.)

Introducing the query design grid

The bottom pane of Design view is technically the Query by Example (QBE) grid but is often simply called the *query design grid.* It's your handy visual aid for defining the data you want to select with your query. Each row in the design grid has a specific purpose. Table 1-2 lists how to use them.

Table 1-2	Rows in the Query Design Grid
Row	*What It Does*
Field	Displays the name of a field that you want to include in a query.
Table	Displays the name of the table that the field comes from. (Hide or display this row by clicking the Table Names button in the Show/Hide group on the Design tab of the Ribbon.)
Total	Performs calculations in your query. (This row isn't always visible; click the Totals button in the Show/Hide group on the Design tab of the Ribbon to display or hide it.)
Sort	Determines the sort order of the datasheet produced by the query.
Show	Shows or hides a field. (If you want to use a field to determine which records to display on the datasheet but not actually display the field, deselect the check box in the field's Show column.)
Criteria	Tells Access the criteria — such as records with values less than 10 or records with dates after 12/3/2005 — for the field in the same column.
Or	Contains additional criteria.

Each of these query features gets detailed coverage later in this chapter.

Navigating Design view

You can work in Design view by using the mouse (to click the pane that you want) and the scroll bars (to see parts of the view that don't fit onscreen). If you prefer, you can use the keyboard to move around.

The keys listed in Table 1-3 move you around Design view.

Table 1-3	Shortcut Keys in Design View	
Key	*What It Does in the Table Pane*	*What It Does in the Design Grid*
Tab	Moves to the next table	Moves to the next row to the right
Shift+Tab	Moves to the previous table	Moves to the next row to the left
Alt+↓ or F4	Nothing	Displays the drop-down menu (if the row has one)
Page Down	Displays more field names in the active table	Displays more OR criteria
Home	Moves to the top of field names	Moves to the first column in the grid

Displaying or hiding table names

You can view table names for each field in the query design in the Table row, or you can choose not to see the Table row.

To make the Table row appear or disappear, use one of these methods:

✦ Right-click the design grid and choose Table Names from the contextual menu.

✦ Click the Table Names button in the Show/Hide group on the Design tab of the Ribbon.

Taking Tips on Creating a Query

The "Creating a Query in Design View" section, earlier in this chapter, includes the basics on creating a query in Design view, but you can do much more. This section delves into a few more aspects of the query-creation story.

Adding tables to the query

To use a table's fields in a query, you have to add the table name to the top pane of the Design view. To do that, you need to view all table names by opening the Show Table dialog box in either of the following ways:

+ Right-click the Table pane of Design view and then choose Show Table from the contextual menu.

+ Click the Show Table button in the Query Setup group on the Design tab of the Ribbon.

After the Show Table dialog box opens, add a table to the query by using whichever of the following methods is more convenient:

+ Double-click the table name in the Show Table dialog box.

+ Select the table and then click the Add button.

After you add all the tables that you need, click the Close button in the Show Table dialog box to get back to work in Design view.

To remove a table from a query, just press Delete (on your keyboard) when the table in the Table pane is selected (that is, when any field in the table is highlighted). When a table is deleted from Design view, all the fields in the design grid from that table are deleted too. Because deleting a table from a query is so absurdly easy — and can have damaging consequences for your query — take care when your fingers get close to the Delete key. Also, save your query design often so that you can easily restore a saved version if you accidentally delete something important.

If you want to include a field generated by another query, you can add queries to a query by clicking the Queries tab or the Both tab of the Show Table dialog box and then double-clicking the query name.

Inserting fields into a design grid

You can move a single field from the Table pane to the design grid in any of three easy ways:

+ **Double-click the field name.** Access moves the field to the first open column in the grid.

+ **Drag the field name from the Table pane to the Field row of an unused column in the design grid.** This option is popular among dragging fans and for putting a field in a specific location in the grid.

+ **From the drop-down menu in the Field row of the design grid, choose the field you want.** If you use this method with a multiple-table query, you may find it easier to choose the table name from the Table drop-down menu before selecting the field name. If you don't have the Table row in your design grid, see "Displaying or hiding table names," earlier in this chapter.

You can place all the field names from one table in the design grid in either of two ways:

✦ **Put one field name in each column of the grid.** If you have criteria for all the fields, you can put one field name in each column of the design grid in just two steps. Double-click the table name in the Table pane of Design view to select all the fields in the table; then drag the selected names to the design grid. When you release the mouse button, Access puts one name in each column.

✦ **Put all the field names in one column.** This method is useful if you want to find something that can be in any field, you have one criterion for all the fields in the table, or you want to include all the fields in a table without criteria. To tell Access to include all field names in one column, drag the asterisk (above the first field name in each table window) to the grid. The asterisk is also available as the first choice in the Field drop-down menu in the design grid; it appears as `TableName.*`.

Editing a Query

You can do some major reconstruction to your query in the design grid, such as moving columns, deleting columns, or deleting all the entries in the grid.

Before you can do any of those things, though, you have to select the column in the grid by clicking the *column selector* — the narrow block at the top of each column in the grid.

Table 1-4 lists some of the things you can do to make changes in the design grid.

Table 1-4	Editing Your Query
When You Want To . . .	*Do This*
Move a column	Click the column selector to select the column, click a second time, and then drag the column to its new position.
Delete a column	Click the column selector to select the column; then press Delete or click the Delete Rows button on the Design tab of the Ribbon to delete the column.
Insert a column	Drag a field from the Table pane in Design view to the column in the design grid where you want to insert it. Access inserts an extra column for the new field, moving all other columns to the right to make space for the new column. Or click the Insert Columns button to insert a column to the left of the cursor. Select multiple columns before clicking to insert the same number of columns.
Change the displayed name	Use a colon between the display name and the actual name of the field in the Field row (display name: field name).

Sorting a query

You can sort or alphabetize the results of a query in several ways. The first way is to use the Sort row in the design grid. Use the Sort row to tell Access which field to use to sort the datasheet. The second way is to click the Sort Ascending and Sort Descending buttons on the Home tab of the Ribbon when a datasheet is displayed. (For more on sorting in a datasheet, see Book II, Chapter 3.)

If you summarize a query by month, Access alphabetizes the months — which usually isn't what you want. Reports, on the other hand, know how to put months in chronological order. If you have monthly data that you want to sort, a report is a better object to use than a query.

To sort by a field, display your query in Design view and then follow these steps:

1. **Move the cursor to the Sort row in the column that contains the field by which you want to sort the records that the query selects.**

2. **Display the drop-down menu for the Sort row.**

   Access displays the options for sorting: Ascending, Descending, and (not sorted).

3. **Choose to sort in ascending order or descending order.**

Book III
Chapter 1

You can use the Sort row in the design grid to sort by more than one field. Suppose that you want to sort the records in the datasheet by last name, but several people have the same last name. You can specify another field (perhaps First Name) as the second sort key.

When you sort by using more than one field, Access always works from left to right, first sorting the records by the first field (the *primary sort key)* that has Ascending order or Descending order in the Sort row and then using the second sort key to sort any records that have the same primary sort key value.

You can't sort by the following field types: OLE Object, Attachment, and multivalue fields.

Viewing top values

Return: All

If all you care about are the top values produced by a query, you can tell Access to find and display only those records. Use the Return (Top Values) box on the Design View toolbar to see the top records produced by the query. A value in the Return (Top Values) box specifies exactly how many records in the datasheet you want to display; a percentage shows you the percentage of those records that the query finds.

Note that using a percentage doesn't show values that fall in the top *x* percent; it shows you the top *x* percent of the values. Suppose that you're looking at the test scores of 20 students. The test scores fall between 0 and 100 but are mostly in the 80s and 90s. If you ask to see the top 20 percent, Access shows you the top 4 scores (20 percent of 20 records) — *not* the scores that are 80 or higher. To see the scores that are 80 or higher, type the criterion **>=80** in the Test Score column of the design grid.

To display the top values found by a query, follow these steps:

1. **Create your query with all the fields and criteria that you need.**

2. **Choose the field you want to sort by.**

3. **Set the field's Sort row to ascending or descending order.**

   Access uses this setting to figure out which top values you're looking for. If you sort products by using the `Selling Price` field and sort in ascending order, the cheapest products are at the top of the datasheet. When you ask for the top five prices, you get the five cheapest products. To get the most expensive products, sort in descending order so that the most expensive products appear at the top of the datasheet.

4. **Change the** Return (Top Values) **option by typing a value or a value followed by a percent sign.**

   You can also choose a value from the drop-down menu. To see the top three values, type **3**. To see the top 3 percent of the values, type **3%**.

5. **Click the View button to see only the top values in the datasheet.**

Hiding fields

You can use fields to sort data — or use criteria for the fields to filter data — without having to display the field in the query datasheet. Deselect the Show check box in the design grid when you don't want to display the column in the datasheet. The next time you open the query in Design view, you find that Access has moved the hidden field(s) to the right side of the grid. If the field is hidden and not used for sort order or criteria, Access removes it from the grid.

Changing the format of a query field

The format of fields displayed in a query is determined by the field's properties in its native table. If the field is defined as having a currency format in its table, that's what you see in the query. Note, however, that you can change the format of any field for the query.

To change the format of a field, follow these steps:

1. **In Design view, right-click anywhere in the column that contains the field you want to format and then choose Properties from the contextual menu.**

If a property sheet is displayed already, just clicking the field displays the properties for that field.

2. **Click the `Format` property and then click the arrow to display a drop-down menu of format options.**

3. **Choose a format option.**

The format options in the property sheet are exactly the same as the options for the `Format` property in the field properties for a table, and you can use them exactly the same way. When you format a field in a query, however, you affect how that field appears only in the query datasheet. (Formatting fields is covered in detail in Book II, Chapter 2.)

Limiting Records with Criteria Expressions

In addition to using queries to select only a few fields to show, you may use queries to display a limited selection of records. Criteria enable you to limit the records that the query displays. You use the Criteria and Or rows in the design grid to tell Access exactly which records you want to see.

Querying by example

Querying by example makes defining criteria easy: If you tell Access what you're looking for, Access goes out and finds it. If you want to find values equal to 10, the criterion is simply `10`. Access finds records that match — that are equal to 10.

The most common type of criterion is a logical expression, which gives a `Yes` or `No` answer. Access shows you the record if the answer is `Yes` but doesn't show the record if the answer is `No`. The operators commonly used in logical expressions include <, >, AND, OR, and NOT.

Although uppercase is used to distinguish operators and functions, case doesn't matter when you type in the design grid.

If you want to find all the addresses in California, the criterion for the `State` field is simply the following:

```
CA
```

You may want to add another criterion in the next line (`OR`) to take care of different spellings, as follows:

```
California
```

Access puts the text in quotes for you. The result of the query is all records that have either `CA` or `California` in the `State` field.

> You can find records with null values by using the `Is Null` criterion. If you want all records except those with null values, use the `Is Not Null` criterion.

Using dates, times, text, and values in criteria

Access does its best to recognize the types of data you use in criteria; it relies on its best guess when providing characters to enclose the elements of the criteria expressions you come up with. You, however, are less likely to create criteria that Access doesn't understand if you use those characters yourself.

Table 1-5 lists the types of elements you may include in a criteria expression, as well as the character to use to make sure that Access knows the element is text, a date, a time, a number, or a field name.

Table 1-5	Dates, Time, and Text in Criteria
Use This Type of Data . . .	*In an Expression Like This*
Text	`"text"`
Date	`#1-Feb-13#`
Time	`#12:00am#`
Number	`10`
Field name	`[field name]`

You can refer to dates or times by using any allowed format. `December 25, 2013`, `12/25/13`, and `25-Dec-13` are all formats that Access recognizes. You can use 12-hour (a.m./p.m.) or 24-hour time.

Year numbers between 0 and 29 are prefixed with `20`. (If you enter the year as **20**, Access completes the year as `2020`.) Year numbers between 30 and 99 are prefixed with `19`. (If you enter **45** as the year number, Access completes the year as `1945`.) You have the option of entering all four digits of the year, of course, to make sure that you enter the year you want.

Using operators in criteria expressions

Don't be surprised if your criteria are frequently more complicated than "all records with `California` in the `State` field." Use operators in your criteria expressions to tell Access about more-complex criteria.

Table 1-6 lists the operators that you're likely to use in an expression that specifies criteria.

Table 1-6	Using Operators in Criteria
Relational Operator	*What It Does*
=	Finds values equal to text, a number, or date/time. (*Equal to* is understood when you type a criterion without an operator; you don't need to type it.)
<>	Finds values not equal to text, a number, or date/time.
<	Finds values less than a given value.
<=	Finds values less than or equal to a given value.
>	Finds values greater than a given value.
>=	Finds values greater than or equal to a given value.
BETWEEN	Finds values between or equal to two values.
IN	Finds values or text included in a list.
LIKE	Finds matches for a pattern.

When you type your criterion, you don't have to tell Access the field name. Just put your criterion in the same column as the field, and Access applies the criterion to the field that appears in the same column.

Table 1-7 explains how different criteria affect the records that appear onscreen in the query datasheet.

Table 1-7	Examples of Criteria with Operators
When Field1 Has This Criterion . . .	*You See These Records*
<15	Displays records in which Field1 is less than 15.
<#9/1/03#	Finds records in which Field1 contains a date before September 1, 2003.
>15	Finds records in which Field1 is greater than 15.
>#12:00am#	Finds records in which Field1 is a time value after 12 a.m.
>[Max Price]	Finds records in which Field1 is more than the value in the Max Price field.

(continued)

Table 1-7 *(continued)*

When Field1 Has This Criterion . . .	You See These Records
`<>15`	Finds records in which `Field1` is not equal to 15.
`>10 AND <20`	Finds records in which `Field1` is between 11 and 19.
`>=10 AND <=20`	Finds records in which `Field1` is 10 to 20, inclusive.
`BETWEEN 10 AND 20`	Displays the same as `>=10 AND <=20`.
`IN ("Virginia", "VA")`	Finds records in which `Field1` contains either `Virginia` or VA.
`LIKE "A*"`	Finds records in which `Field1` begins with A. You can use `LIKE` with wildcards, such as `*`, to tell Access in general terms what you're looking for. For more information on the wildcards that Access recognizes, see Book II, Chapter 5.

Using multiple criteria

Often, one criterion isn't enough. You may want to prune the records displayed by using multiple criteria for a single field or multiple criteria for different fields. To get the data you want, however, you do need to know how Access combines your criteria.

When you have criteria for only one field, decide whether you want to see records that meet all criteria (in which case you join the criteria with AND) or whether you want records that meet only one criterion (in which case you join the criteria with OR). You may have three or more criteria, and you can join them with both AND and OR.

To join criteria for a single field with AND, type them in the Criteria line of the grid with AND between them, like this:

```
<5 And >65
```

This entry shows you records with values less than 5 as well as those with values greater than 65.

To join multiple criteria for one field with OR, use one of these methods:

✦ Type your expressions in the Criteria row, separating them with OR.

✦ Type the first expression in the Criteria row, and type subsequent expressions by using the Or rows in the design grid.

Whichever approach you take, the result is the same: Access displays records that satisfy one or more of the criteria expressions.

When you have criteria for different fields, you join them with the OR or AND operator. The operator is implied in the way you put the criteria in the design grid. Here's how that works:

✦ **Criteria on the same row are implicitly joined by AND.** Access assumes that you want to find records that meet all the criteria. If you type criteria on the same row for two fields, a record has to meet both criteria to be displayed in the datasheet.

✦ **Criteria on different rows are joined by OR.** Access assumes that you want to find records that meet at least one criterion. If you type criteria on different rows for two fields, a record has to meet only one criterion to be displayed in the datasheet.

✦ **When you use multiple rows for criteria, the expressions within each row are treated as though they're joined by AND, but each row's worth of criteria are joined by OR.** Access first looks at one row of criteria and finds all the records that meet all the criteria on that row. Then it starts over with the next row of criteria — the Or row — and finds all the records that meet all the criteria on that row. The datasheet displays all the records that are found. A record has to meet all the criteria in only one row to display in the datasheet.

Using lookup fields in criteria

When you define a criterion for a query, tell Access what you're looking for by entering a value or using a logical expression. If you use a criterion to limit the number of records displayed from a lookup field, however, you have to figure out exactly what value you want to find — which may not be the value you see in the table. See Book II, Chapter 5 for details on creating a lookup field.

Suppose that you want to find orders for the Budget MP3 Player. The Order Details table stores this data, as shown in Figure 1-9. Notice that the ProductID field is a lookup field; it displays values from the Product Name field of the Products table but stores the values from the Products table's primary key field, which is ProductID. The Products table is shown in Figure 1-10.

Because the ProductID field in the Order Detail table is a lookup field, the criteria need to refer to the value that is stored in the field, not the value that displays. The value stored is the primary key field from the Products table. The value that displays is the product name. If you enter **Budget MP3 Player** as the ProductID criterion and then try to view the datasheet, you get a Data type Mismatch in Criteria Expression error message.

You need to go back to the Products table and find the `ProductID` number for the Budget MP3 Player.

A lookup field always stores the primary key field.

The `ProductID` for the Budget MP3 Player is 4 (see the third line of Figure 1-10). With that information, you can create the query criterion: 4.

Figure 1-9:
The `Product ID` field in the Order Details table is a lookup field.

Order Details				
OrderID	ProductID	Qty	Unit Price	
18	50pk Audio CD-R	1	$0.00	
4	50pk Audio CD-R	23	$39.99	
11	50-pk Floppy Disks	1	$39.99	
1	Big Subwoofer	1	$39.99	
21	Budget MP3 Player	1	$0.00	
1	Golden Whistle	1	$39.99	
4	Kozmik Video Camera	25	$39.99	
24	Lawn Flamingo	1	$0.00	
5	Lucky Rabbits Foot	1	$0.00	
11	Magic Inkwell	1	$29.99	
18	Microwave Blow Dryer	1	$0.00	
26	New Golden Whistle	1	$0.00	
24	Nuclear Pencil Sharpei	1	$0.00	
8	Old Time Stock Ticker	1	$0.00	
25	Scanner cable	1	$0.00	
	Unbreakable PDA			
	WayCool Scanner			

Record: 1 of 81   Search

Figure 1-10:
The Products table holds the data shown in the Order Details table drop-down menu.

	Produc	Our Product	Product Name	Product Pho	Selling Price
+	2	GW-123	Golden Whistle	Picture	$100.0
+	3	KVC-2322	Kozmik Video Camera	Picture	$1,000.0
+	4	BMP3-01	Budget MP3 Player	Picture	$10.0
+	5	OTST-001	Old Time Stock Ticker	Picture	$500.0
+	6	FF-232	Lawn Flamingo	PSP7.Image	$30.0
+	7	SC001	Scanner cable	PSP7.Image	$10.0
+	8	TBD001	Microwave Blow Dryer	PSP7.Image	$130.0
+	9	IW-2322	Magic Inkwell	PSP7.Image	$15.0
+	10	RF-3322	Lucky Rabbits Foot	PSP7.Image	$8.0
+	11	50FDPK	50-pk Floppy Disks	PSP7.Image	$40.0
+	12	WCS3432	WayCool Scanner	PSP7.Image	$90.0
+	13	NPS-232	Nuclear Pencil Sharpen	PSP7.Image	$180.0
+	14	BSW-3232	Big Subwoofer	PSP7.Image	$30.0
+	15	50ACD-121	50pk Audio CD-R	PSP7.Image	$40.0

Record: 1 of 16   No Filter   Search

Creating queries with multivalue lookup fields

Multivalue lookup fields make queries a little more complicated. The question is whether you want to display the complete multivalue field with the values separated by commas or put each value on its own line in the query datasheet. If you want to do complicated analysis with multivalue fields, you may want to reconsider your database design and add tables and fields to save the same data without the multivalue field.

Although a multivalue lookup field seems to be cumbersome, it can still give you the results that you want if you simply have your query display the multiple values separated by commas. If you want to deconstruct your data some — and ensure that each value in a multivalue field has its own line — add the `Value` property to the field name. Here's how: Instead of entering just *multivalue field name* in the query grid, enter *multivalue field name. Value*.

In addition to the special instructions about multivalue fields, be aware of the caveat about lookup fields: The value you see may not be the value that's actually stored. (Fortunately, the preceding section offers tips on using lookup fields in your criteria.)

Working with Multiple Related Tables

One powerful feature of queries allows you to view related fields from different tables together in a query datasheet. Using your database, you can create a query to list customer name and contact information with order dates and numbers, even though two different tables store the data. The relationship between the two tables is the `ContactID` field, which is the primary key of the Address Book table. The same field, `ContactID`, is in the Orders table; it identifies the customers who placed each order. (For more information about relating tables, see Book I, Chapter 3, and Book II, Chapter 6.)

To have Access display data from different tables, you must define a relationship between the tables. A relationship between tables is created in one of these ways:

+ A lookup field exists, creating a relationship between two tables. (For more on lookup fields, see Book II, Chapter 5.)

+ A relationship was defined in the Relationships window, as described in Book II, Chapter 6. (Creating a lookup field automatically creates a corresponding relationship in the Relationships window.)

+ Access automatically creates a relationship when it finds related fields in two tables — that is, if the two fields have the same name and data type, and one of the matching fields is the primary key of its table.

+ You create a relationship in Query Design view.

When a relationship exists between two tables displayed in Design view, the tables are joined by a line, as shown in Figure 1-11.

If you use data from two tables that aren't directly related, you have to make sure that any other tables related to the fields you want to display in the query datasheet appear in Query Design view.

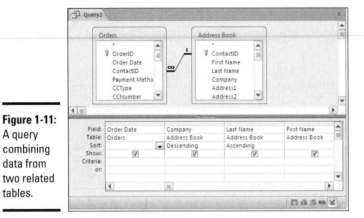

Figure 1-11:
A query combining data from two related tables.

If referential integrity is enforced, the 1 and infinity (∞) symbols appear on the relationship line to denote the "one" and "many" sides of the relationship. If referential integrity isn't enforced, those symbols don't appear on the line. (See Book II, Chapter 6 for more on referential integrity.)

Figure 1-12 shows the result of the query shown in Figure 1-11. Each order is listed once, with the name of the customer. Many customers have multiple orders, so they appear more than once in the datasheet.

OrderID	Order Date	Company	Last Name	First Name
2	2/5/2012	Arbor Classics	Pines	Tori
17	9/22/2011		Midcalf	Marilou
20	1/13/2012		Unctuous	Frankly
26	2/12/2012		Unctuous	Frankly
1	3/1/2012		Angstrom	Margaret
8	4/23/2012		Angstrom	Margaret
16	2/27/2012		Angstrom	Margaret
15	2/19/2012	ABC Productions		
21	1/22/2012		Higglebotton	Hortense
22	1/28/2012		Lopez	Penny
5	4/2/2012		Starbuck	Matilda
7	4/19/2012		Starbuck	Matilda
9	5/2/2012		Starbuck	Matilda
23	2/3/2012		Starbuck	Matilda
3	3/13/2012		Schumack	Scott and Nata
24	2/6/2012		Schumack	Scott and Nata
19	1/9/2012		Yasha	Ino
25	2/8/2012		Yasha	Ino

Record: 1 of 26   No Filter   Search

Figure 1-12:
This datasheet shows the results of the query from Figure 1-11.

Joining tables in Design view

Although you can create or edit a relationship between two tables in Design view, the relationship defined in Design view is used only for the query; it's not used in any other part of the database. You can use a type of join that you may not want to use in the database as a whole but that you may find useful for a single query (which you may then use as the source data for a form or report). You can also delete a relationship in Design view without deleting the same relationship in the Relationships window. (To delete the join, click the line and then press Delete.)

To create a join, use the Table pane of Design view, and follow the same procedure you use for creating a relationship in the Relationship window. First, identify the two related fields (each in a different table) you want to join; then drag the field from one table to the related field in the other table. Voilà — a join!

Choosing the type of join and setting join properties

You can edit the join properties of a relationship for the query in Design view. To do so, double-click the relationship line to display the Join Properties dialog box, shown in Figure 1-13.

Figure 1-13: The Join Properties dialog box.

If you have trouble double-clicking the relationship line, keep trying! The tip of the pointer needs to be right on the line.

The new properties apply only in the current query and not in any other objects in the database except those based on this query.

The Join Properties dialog box's options are largely self-explanatory, but using the dialog box effectively requires knowledge of a few buzzwords that describe particular types of relationships but don't appear in the dialog box. The buzzwords *inner join, left outer join,* and *right outer join* are included in the descriptions of the following three options:

✦ **Option 1 (inner join):** A query displaying records from both tables displays only those records that have counterparts in the related table. Records that don't have matching partners in the opposite table are hidden, as though they didn't even exist. This setting is the default, meaning that if you don't set a join type, this type is what you get.

✦ **Option 2 (left outer join):** A query displaying records from both tables displays all records from the table on the left. From the table on the right, only records that have matching partners in the table on the left appear.

✦ **Option 3 (right outer join):** A query displaying records from both tables displays all records from the table on the right. From the table on the left, only records that have matching partners in the table on the right appear.

The line that connects two tables in the Relationships view (and in Design view as well) reflects information about how the tables are joined, as shown in Figure 1-14. The arrow points to the table that contributes matching records; all records from the other table display in the query datasheet.

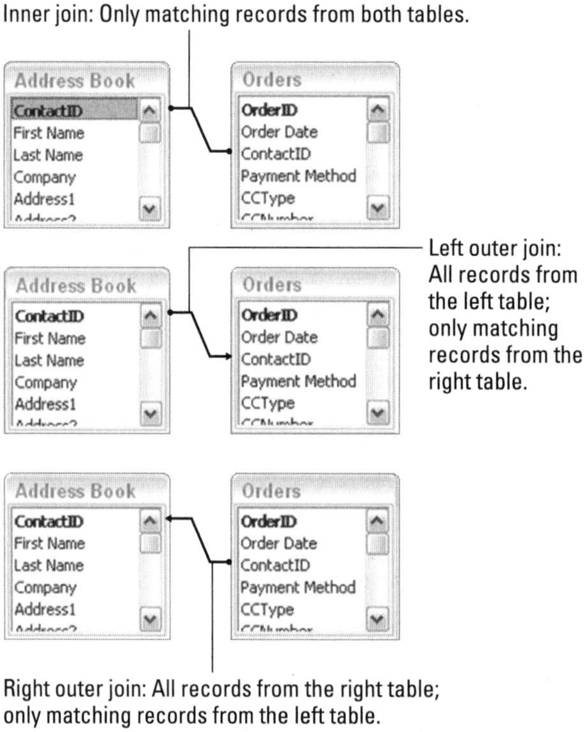

Inner join: Only matching records from both tables.

Left outer join: All records from the left table; only matching records from the right table.

Figure 1-14: Join lines and outer joins.

Right outer join: All records from the right table; only matching records from the left table.

When would you use an outer join? Suppose that you create a sales report and want to see products that haven't sold at all. You want an outer join that shows all the products from the Products table, regardless of whether they appear in the Order Details table.

If you create a query with fields from two tables that don't have a relationship defined, Access doesn't know how to relate records, so *every* combination of records between the two tables displays in the datasheet. Generally (as you might expect), these queries won't give you meaningful results.

Working with Query Datasheets

A query datasheet looks a great deal like a table datasheet. You can sort, filter, navigate, and (in many circumstances) enter data in a query datasheet. The data displayed in the query datasheet is sometimes referred to as a *dynaset* — a *dyna*mic sub*set* of your data.

The query result reflects changes in the data in your tables. The actual records displayed in a dynaset aren't stored in the database; only the design of the query is stored. Each time you open the query in Datasheet view, Access runs the query definition against the contents of the tables used in the query, and the result determines which records appear in the datasheet.

Because working with queries in Datasheet view is similar to working with tables in Datasheet view, turn to Book II for specific instructions on working in Datasheet view.

To toggle between Datasheet and Design view, click the View button, which is the first button on the Home and Design/Datasheet tabs of the Ribbon.

Using the query datasheet to edit data

In many cases, you can edit the data in the query datasheet and use the datasheet to add new records. Any changes you make are reflected in the table that holds the data you changed; edits are permanent and apply to the underlying tables, not just to the query.

When your query includes fields from multiple tables, you may see some funky things onscreen when you edit data. Not to worry. They're all features!

When you're editing datasheet data that results from a query on multiple related tables, you may see the following:

✦ Other data in the datasheet changes when you make an edit. If your query includes related tables, you may see repeated data, such as the repeated names in Figure 1-12. If you make edits, all the repetitions of the name change when you change one instance. Because you're changing a single record repeated in the datasheet, the other instances change to reflect the change in the underlying table. When this happens, you have an AutoLookup query (see the next section).

✦ If your query meets the qualifications of an AutoLookup query, Access fills in fields after you enter a single value.

If you work with a query datasheet that shows data from multiple related tables, you may not be able to modify data. The rules get complicated, but generally, all data on the "many" side of a one-to-many relationship can be updated. Data on the one side usually can be updated if you're not editing the primary key field.

**Book III
Chapter 1**

Creating Select Queries

Creating AutoLookup queries to fill in data automatically

AutoLookup queries can be terrific tools when you want to enter one value (such as a customer number) and see other data from the same table (such as the customer's name, address, and phone number). You may want to use this feature while you enter a new order: You can enter a customer number and see the contact information, and then enter the particulars of the order, such as the date and payment method. You can even create an AutoLookup query and use it as the basis of a form, in which it may be more convenient to enter data. AutoLookup queries may sound complicated, but in fact, they're pretty simple.

The AutoLookup feature also works in forms.

The key to creating an AutoLookup query is including the `Join` field from the "many" side of the one-to-many relationship (also known as the *foreign key).* Then, when you enter a value for that field, Access fills in other fields from the "one" side of the relationship automatically.

The query shown in Figure 1-15 displays fields from the Orders and Address Book tables. The `ContactID` field comes from the Orders table (the key field on the "one" side but displayed from the "many" table).

When new orders are entered in the query datasheet, only the customer number needs to be entered. Access automatically fills in the first name, the last name, and other contact information from the Address Book table. Then you can add the rest of the order information.

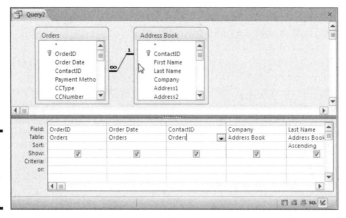

Figure 1-15:
An
AutoLookup
query.

Saving Queries

A query doesn't store data; it just pulls data from tables and puts it in query datasheets for you to look at. A query is *dynamic;* as you add to or change your data, the result of the query also changes. When you save your query, you're not saving the table that the query produces; you're just saving the query *design* so that you can ask the same question again.

You don't have to save a query. Often, you create queries on the fly to answer a question. There's no need to clutter your database with queries you're unlikely to need again.

That said, you can certainly save a query design when you need to. Use one of the following methods:

 + **In Design or Datasheet view, click the Save button or press Ctrl+S.** If you haven't saved the query yet, Access asks you for a name for the query. Type the name in the Save As dialog box and then click OK.

 + **Close the query.** (Clicking the Close button is a popular method.) If you've never saved the query, or if you've changed the query design since you last saved it, Access asks whether you want to save the query. Click the Yes button to save the query. If you've never saved the query, give it a name in the Save As dialog box and then click OK.

Give your new query a name that tells you what the query does. That way, you won't have to open one query after another to find the one you're looking for.

If you want to create a query similar to one you already have in your database, select or open the query, and choose File⇨Save As to save the query with a new name. You keep the original query and make changes in the new copy.

If you want to save the query dynaset, export the data to its own file, using one or more buttons in the Export group on the External Data tab of the Ribbon. For more information about exporting data, see Book II, Chapter 4.

If the query you need is in another Access database, or if you create a query that you want to use in another database, simply import or export it. For information on importing and exporting objects, see Book II, Chapter 4.

Book III
Chapter 1

Creating Select Queries

Chapter 2: Letting Queries Do the Math

In This Chapter

✔ Performing math in queries

✔ Writing expressions

✔ Working with Expression Builder

✔ Performing nonbasic math

✔ Calculating dates and times

✔ Using expressions to manipulate text

✔ Writing expressions that make decisions

✔ Looking for blank fields

✔ Using flexible parameter queries

✔ Calculating totals, subtotals, averages, and the like

*I*f you ever find yourself doing math to figure out what to put in a field, you made a mistake when designing your table. A table needs only the raw data — the factual information that can't be calculated from known data. A table may contain Qty and Unit Price fields to indicate how many items of some product were ordered and at what price. Having an Extended Price or Subtotal field in the table is pointless, though, because Access is smart enough to determine totals on its own by multiplying the Qty field by the Unit Price field for you.

Letting Access do the math for you has advantages beyond just saving you the time of doing the calculation yourself. For one thing, Access can do any mathematical calculation, no matter how complex, in less time than you take to blink your eye — and its calculations are always correct. You don't need to worry about typing a wrong value in an Extended Price field or forgetting to change a field storing calculated data after you change the Qty or Unit Price field. Just let Access do all the math.

Doing Calculations in Queries

Access can do the math for you in queries, forms, reports, and macros. In many cases, you should do the math in a query. When you do, any forms, reports, or macros that use the query automatically have access to the calculated value. To do the math in a query, you create a *calculated field* within the query. Unlike the name of a regular field in a query, a calculated field's name doesn't match any of the field names in the tables; in fact, its value doesn't come directly from any field in any table. The calculated field exists only in the query.

A calculated field starts with a field name, followed by a colon and then an expression that defines the field's contents, in this order:

```
fieldname: expression
```

fieldname is any name you want to use (provided that it doesn't match the name of another field in a table), and *expression* is a formula that tells the query how to do the math.

Take a look at Figure 2-1, which shows a query in Design view. The first four field names in the Query by Example (QBE) grid at the bottom of the window — OrderID, Product Name, Qty, and Unit Price — are regular fields that get their values from the Order Details or Products table in the top pane of the window.

Figure 2-1:
ExtPrice
is an
example of
a calculated
field in a
query.

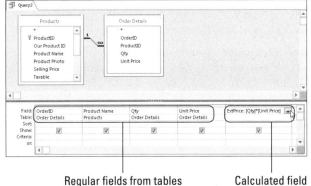

Regular fields from tables   Calculated field

The last field is a calculated field:

```
ExtPrice: [Qty]*[Unit Price]
```

The field name is ExtPrice (short for *extended price*). The expression is [Qty] * [Unit Price], which means "the Qty (quantity) field times the Unit Price field."

Figure 2-2 shows the same query as Figure 2-1, but in Datasheet view.

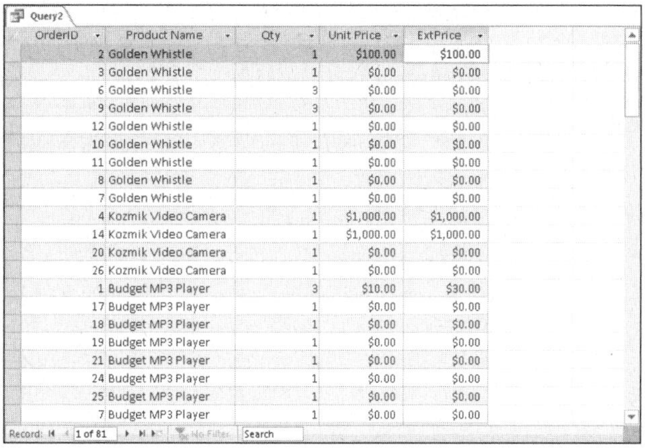

Query2

OrderID	Product Name	Qty	Unit Price	ExtPrice
2	Golden Whistle	1	$100.00	$100.00
3	Golden Whistle	1	$0.00	$0.00
6	Golden Whistle	3	$0.00	$0.00
9	Golden Whistle	3	$0.00	$0.00
12	Golden Whistle	1	$0.00	$0.00
10	Golden Whistle	1	$0.00	$0.00
11	Golden Whistle	1	$0.00	$0.00
8	Golden Whistle	1	$0.00	$0.00
7	Golden Whistle	1	$0.00	$0.00
4	Kozmik Video Camera	1	$1,000.00	$1,000.00
14	Kozmik Video Camera	1	$1,000.00	$1,000.00
20	Kozmik Video Camera	1	$0.00	$0.00
26	Kozmik Video Camera	1	$0.00	$0.00
1	Budget MP3 Player	3	$10.00	$30.00
17	Budget MP3 Player	1	$0.00	$0.00
18	Budget MP3 Player	1	$0.00	$0.00
19	Budget MP3 Player	1	$0.00	$0.00
21	Budget MP3 Player	1	$0.00	$0.00
24	Budget MP3 Player	1	$0.00	$0.00
25	Budget MP3 Player	1	$0.00	$0.00
7	Budget MP3 Player	1	$0.00	$0.00

Record: 1 of 81 No Filter Search

Figure 2-2: The query from Figure 2-1 in Datasheet view.

Notice two things about this Datasheet view:

- The `ExtPrice` field looks just like any other field.
- The value shown in the `ExtPrice` column is equal to the value of the `Qty` field times the `Unit Price` field in each column.

Even though the `ExtPrice` column in Datasheet view looks like a regular field, it doesn't behave exactly like a regular field. If you try to change the contents of the `ExtPrice` field, Access won't let you. The contents of the `ExtPrice` field in this query *always* show the quantity times the unit price and can't possibly show anything else, because `ExtPrice` is a calculated field.

If you change the `Qty` or `Unit Price` field in any record, however, the `ExtPrice` field instantly — and automatically — changes to show the correct result based on the change you make. If you change the `Qty` field in the first record in Figure 2-2 from `1` to `2`, the `ExtPrice` field for that record also changes to show `$200.00`.

Follow these steps to create calculated fields in queries:

1. **Create a normal select query, like any of those shown in Book III, Chapter 1.**
2. **To the `Field` row of the QBE grid, add any fields that you want the query to display.**
3. **To add a calculated field, pick any empty column, and type a unique new field name in the `Field` row, followed by a colon (:) and an expression that performs the calculation.**

   What you get looks a lot like the `ExtPrice` calculated field shown in Figure 2-1, earlier in this chapter.

Zooming in on expressions

The tiny space provided in the `Field` row of the QBE grid doesn't exactly make typing lengthy expressions easy. In fact, the text may be so small that you have difficulty seeing even when you're typing a short expression.

To see what you're typing, press Shift+F2 while the cursor is in the calculated field, or right-click the calculated field and choose the Zoom option from the contextual menu. The Zoom dialog box opens, showing what you've already typed in the field (if anything). You can use all the standard Windows text-editing keys and techniques to type your expression. Press the End key to move the cursor quickly to the end of the expression, for example.

To make the text easier to read, click the Font button. In the Font dialog box that opens, choose a larger font size and then click OK to accept the change. Type your expression and then click OK in the Zoom dialog box to copy the expression into your calculated field in the QBE grid.

Your query can contain any number of calculated fields; you're not limited to having just one or two. The big trick, of course, is knowing how to write the expression. When you write expressions, the possibilities are almost endless, although some basic tools and rules exist that help you create any expression, as we discuss next.

Writing Expressions in Access

An *expression* tells Access how to perform some calculation. An expression can contain operators, field names, literal text, or all of those — and can also use any of the Access built-in functions. Built-in functions can be mind-boggling, but if you take them one step at a time, you'll soon create them like a pro.

Literal text, in Access jargon, means text that isn't the name of some field or other object. Whereas `LastName` may be the name of a field in a table, `Smith`, `Jones`, and `123 Oak Tree Lane` are all examples of literal text. Always put your literal text in quotes (`"Smith"`). For a classic example of how to use literals, flip ahead in this chapter to the "Using literal dates and times in expressions" section.

Using operators in expressions

An *operator* is a character that operates on data. Table 2-1 presents some of the most commonly used operators, listed in *order of precedence* — the order in which Access performs the calculations when an expression contains two or more operators.

Table 2-1	Operators in Order of Precedence	
Operator	*Purpose*	*Example*
( )	Grouping	(2+2)*5 returns 20.
^	Exponentiation (raising a number to a specified power)	5^2 returns 25.
* /	Multiplication, division	5*6/3 returns 10.
+ –	Addition, subtraction	6+6−2 returns 10.
&	String concatenation (connecting chunks of text)	"Hello" & "There" returns HelloThere.

The order or precedence that operators follow can be a real gotcha if you're not careful. Take a look at the following simple expression, which includes an addition operator (+) and a multiplication operator (*):

5+3*2

When you do the math, do you get 16 — or do you get 11? If you do the addition first (5 + 3 = 8) and then the multiplication (2 * 8), you end up with 16. But if you do the multiplication first (3 * 2 = 6) and then the addition (6 + 5), you end up with 11. So which is the correct answer: 11 or 16?

Give up? The correct answer (and the one Access comes up with) is 11, because the order-of-precedence rules state that multiplication and division are always performed before addition or subtraction.

Multiplication and division are performed in order of precedence. If an expression involves both of those operations, they're executed in left-to-right order. In the following expression, the division operation takes place first because it's to the left of the multiplication operation:

10/5*3

The result of the preceding expression is 6, because 10 divided by 5 is 2, and 2 times 3 equals 6.

Addition and subtraction work the same way. If an expression includes both addition and subtraction, the calculations take place in left-to-right order.

You can control the order of precedence by using parentheses. Access always works from the innermost parentheses to the outermost, as in the following example expression:

5^2+((5−1)*3)

When it's faced with this expression, Access goes inside the innermost parentheses first (5-1) and does that calculation. So the expression (for an instant) becomes

```
5^2+(4*3)
```

Next, Access calculates the remaining pair of parentheses in the expression (4*3). For a moment, the expression becomes

```
5^2+12
```

Because no more parentheses are left, Access uses the regular order of precedence to do the rest of the calculation. Exponentiation has a higher order of precedence than addition, so for an instant, the expression becomes

```
25+12
```

Then Access does the final math and returns the result: 37.

If you're a real math-head, you'll appreciate the fact that two more operators have the same order of precedence as multiplication and division. The \ operator returns only the integer portion of a quotient, and the MOD (for *modulo*) operator returns only the remainder after division. Although 16/3 (normal division) returns 5.3333, 16\3 returns 5, and 16 MOD 3 returns 1.

Using field names in expressions

If you're thinking, "Big deal — I could have done those preceding calculations on my $2 calculator," that's certainly true. Access expressions aren't limited to numbers and operators, however. You can use field names in expressions to perform math on data stored in fields. The sample query shown at the start of this chapter uses the field names [Qty]*[Unit Price] to multiply the value in the Unit Price field by the value in the Qty field.

Technically, you need to enclose field names in square brackets only when the field name contains a blank space, as in [Unit Price]. But you can put square brackets around any field name, just in case (so to speak). For the sake of consistency — and to make the field names in expressions stand out — we always put them in square brackets throughout this book.

The sample expression shown in the query at the start of this chapter, [Qty]*[Unit Price], is a prime example of using field names in expressions. The expression, in English, simply means "the contents of the Qty field in this record times the contents of the Unit Price field in this same record."

Using functions in expressions

Wait — there's more. An Access expression can also contain any number of functions. A *function* is sort of like an operator in that it performs some calculation and then *returns* some value. The way that you use a function is different, though: Every function includes a name followed by a pair of parentheses. The Date() function, for example, always returns the current date.

Many functions accept *arguments,* which are enclosed within the parentheses. To calculate the square root of a number, you use the Sqr() function. The Sqr() function accepts one parameter: a number, the name of a field, or an expression that contains a number. The Sqr() function returns the square root of whatever value passes to it as an argument.

The following expression returns 9 because the square root of 81 is 9 (because 9 times 9 is 81). In this example, we use a number as the argument to the Sqr() function:

```
Sqr(81)
```

Note that in the example, we use 81 as the argument to the Sqr() function. Another way to state this is to say that we *pass* the number 81 to the function. In other words, the term *pass* in this context means "to use as an argument in a function."

The following Sqr() function uses an expression (5*20) as its argument:

```
Sqr(5*20)
```

Because the expression, 5*20, is inside the parentheses, the multiplication happens first. For an instant, the function contains Sqr(100). Then Sqr(100) returns 10 because 10 is the square root of 100.

You can use field names in functions as well. Suppose that you have a table that contains a number field named bigNumber. The following Sqr() function returns the square root of whatever value is stored in the bigNumber field:

```
Sqr([bigNumber])
```

Dozens of functions are built into Access. In fact, memorizing all the functions is nearly impossible. We recommend looking up functions as you need them, using Expression Builder as your guide. What's Expression Builder? Read on to find out.

Using Expression Builder

Expression Builder is a tool that helps you write meaningful expressions by using any combination of operators, field names, and functions. To use Expression Builder while creating a calculated field in a query, follow these steps:

1. **If you haven't saved the current query yet, do so now, and name it.**

Press Ctrl+S, type a name for your query in the Save As dialog box, and then click OK.

2. **Type a new field name, followed by a colon (:), in the `Field` row of an empty column in the QBE grid.**

The QBE grid is in the bottom pane of the Design View window. For more on this grid (and its lovely home, the Design View window), see Book II, Chapter 2.

3. **Right-click the empty space to the right of the colon you just typed and choose Build from the contextual menu, or click the Builder button in the Query Setup group on the (Query Tools) Design tab of the Ribbon.**

Expression Builder opens, looking like Figure 2-3. Any text that you've already typed in the QBE grid is already in Expression Builder.

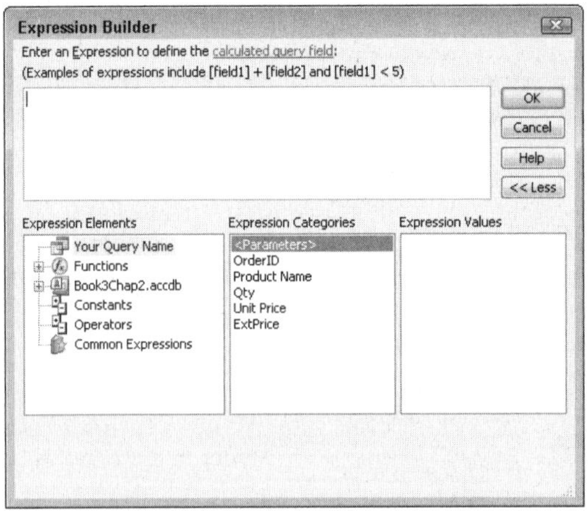

Figure 2-3:
Expression
Builder.

The large white area at the top is where you compose your expression, as shown in Figure 2-4. You can type and edit in that large area, using the keyboard and all the standard Windows editing techniques.

Query name folder   Expression

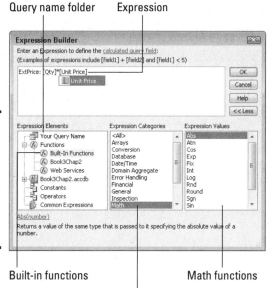

Figure 2-4:
Main
options for
creating
expressions
in a query's
calculated
fields.

Built-in functions   Math functions

Function categories (Math selected)

Not everything in Expression Builder is geared to creating expressions for queries; some features of Expression Builder are better suited to creating expressions in forms and reports. When you're working with a query, the main things you want to focus on are the following:

✦ **Expression:** This box at the top of the Expression Builder is where operators, fields, and functions appear when you select them in the bottom portion of the screen.

✦ **Query name:** The first item in the Expression Elements list shows the name of the query that's open (refer to Figure 2-4). When you click your query name, fields from that query appear in the Expression Categories column. Clicking a field name in that center column adds the name to the expression.

If you don't save the query before opening Expression Builder, clicking the Your Query Name folder in Expression Builder won't display anything!

✦ **Built-In Functions folder:** If you click the plus (+) sign next to the Functions folder, a couple of options appear. Click the Built-In Functions folder to see the categories and names of available functions in the center column. Click a category name in the middle column to display the names of functions within that category in the right column.

Whatever you insert into your expression is inserted at the position of the blinking cursor or (if no blinking cursor is visible) at the end of whatever text is currently in the expression. If you need to move the cursor before inserting something into an expression, just click the spot where you want to position the cursor. You can also press the ←, →, Home, and End keys to position the cursor. Press the Backspace and Delete (Del) keys to delete text in the expression. To undo your most recent change in an expression, press Ctrl+Z.

Getting help with functions

Just seeing the name of a built-in function in the third column of Expression Builder doesn't tell you much. You don't know what the function does or how you use it, but you can get instant information by clicking the Help button. Follow these steps to access a help window:

1. **In the left column of Expression Builder (refer to Figure 2-4), if the Functions folder has a plus sign (+) next to it, click that sign to expand the list.**

2. **Click the Built-In Functions folder in the first column.**

   The category names appear in the center column.

3. **Click a category name in the middle column to see functions within that category listed in the third column, or click <All> in the middle column to see all functions in the third column.**

   The functions for that category appear in the third column.

4. **In the third column, click the name of the function that you want to find out more about.**

5. **Click the Help button in the top-right corner of Expression Builder.**

   The help window for that function opens.

6. **If you don't see specific help for the function, type the function name in the Access Help search box.**

   Functions are listed by type in the help system, so if you need to find a function in the help system, you'll be able to find it quicker if you know that it's a Financial function, for example.

To see how this works, select the Financial category of functions in the center column, click the PV function in the third column, and then click the Help button. The help page that opens not only describes what the PV function does, but also describes the syntax required for using the function. The *syntax* of a function describes what information you need to pass (provide) to the function for the function to do its calculation and return a result.

The syntax for a function usually looks something like the following:

```
functionName(arg1,arg2,[arg3])
```

functionName is the name of the function, and *arg1, arg2,* and *arg3* represent arguments that the function accepts. The number of arguments that a function accepts varies. Some functions take no arguments; others take many. If a function accepts two or more arguments, the arguments must be separated by commas.

Any argument name in square brackets is optional, meaning that you can omit the entire argument.

A function name is always followed by parentheses — even if the function accepts no arguments. `Now()`, `Sqr(81)`, and `PV(apr,TotPmts,Income)` are all examples of valid function syntax. Note as well that when typing an argument, you can use a literal value (like the name `"Smith"` or the number `10`), a field name, or an expression as an argument. The following three expressions all pass literal values to their functions:

```
Sqr(100)
PV(.035,120,250)
UCase("howdy")
```

Book III
Chapter 2

The next three expressions all pass data from fields to the function (provided that `Hypot`, `Apr`, `Months`, `Amount`, and `Company` are the names of fields in the current query):

```
Sqr([Hypot])
PV([Apr],[Months],[Amount])
UCase([Company])
```

Letting Queries Do
the Math

In the next examples, we use expressions as arguments:

```
Sqr(227*[Hypot])
PV([Apr]/12,[Months]*12,-1*[Amount])
UCase([First Name] & " " & [Last Name])
```

We know that these examples look weird, but we do have a reason for the madness. The ability to pass literal data, field names, and/or expressions to functions gives you a lot of flexibility.

Entering text in < and > brackets

When you use the buttons in the bottom half of Expression Builder to insert text into your expression, that text often includes *placeholders* — text in angle brackets (< >). You may see placeholders such as *<expr>*, *<interval>*, *<npers>*, or something equally bizarre in Expression Builder. Each of these bracket things is a placeholder for an argument that you need to type.

If a placeholder represents an optional argument, and you don't plan to use that argument, you can just delete the placeholder. If the placeholder represents a required argument, though, you need to replace the placeholder with valid data.

Using the help feature often when working with functions is very important. We doubt that anybody has ever managed to memorize all the functions because of the sheer number of them, all supporting so many different arguments.

Nesting functions

You can *nest* functions, meaning that you can put a function inside another function. Because Access always works from the innermost parentheses outward, the inside function is always calculated first. The Date() function, for example, always returns the current date. It requires no arguments. The WeekDay() function accepts any date as an argument, meaning that its syntax looks like the following:

```
WeekDay(date)
```

Because the Date() function always returns a date, you can use it as the argument to the WeekDay() function. The expression turns out to be

```
WeekDay(Date())
```

Access returns a number from 1 to 7, indicating which day of the week today is. (Day 1 is Sunday, Day 2 is Monday, and so on.) If the current date is the 23rd, for example, and that day is a Tuesday, the WeekDay() function returns 3.

Going beyond Basic Arithmetic

Near the start of this chapter, we talk about how you can use the +, –, *, and / operators in expressions to perform simple arithmetic. As you know, not all math is quite that simple. Some calculations require more than just addition, subtraction, multiplication, and division.

Access offers many mathematical and financial functions to help with more-complex math. All these functions operate on numbers. The math functions include Cos() (cosine), Tan() (tangent), and Atn() (arctangent), in case you need to do a little trigonometry in your queries. The financial functions include things such as IRR() (internal rate of return), Fv() (future value), and Ddb() (double-declining balance depreciation). You're unlikely to need financial functions unless your work specifically requires those sorts of calculations.

Rather than list all the functions that allow you to do complex math, we provide a few examples in Table 2-2 to give you a sense of how these functions work.

Table 2-2   Examples of Built-In Math and Financial Functions

Function and Syntax	*Returns*	*Example*
`Abs(number)`	Absolute value (negative numbers convert to positive numbers)	`Abs(-1)` returns 1.
`Int(number)`	Integer portion of a number	`Int(99.9)` returns 99.
`Round(number [,decimals])`	Numerical value number rounded to a specified number of decimal places (decimals)	`Round(1.56789,2)` returns 1.57.
`Pmt(rate, nper, po[, fv[, type]])`	Monthly payment on a loan or annuity	`Pmt(.058/12, 30*12, -50000)` returns 293.3765 (payment on a $50,000 30-year loan at 5.8 percent).

If you need help with any function in Expression Builder, you can find all the gory details that you need to make the function work for you in the help system.

Formatting calculated numbers in queries

When you create a table and define a field as the Number data type, you can choose a format, such as Currency, for displaying that number. In a query, you don't predefine a field's data type. The number that appears as the result of a calculation is often displayed as a *General number* — no dollar sign and no fixed number of decimal places.

Figure 2-5 shows a query based on a hypothetical table named Loan Scenarios. Within the Loan Scenarios table, the APR (annual percentage rate) is a Number field with its `Format` property set to `Percent`. The `LoanAmount` field is a Number field with its `Format` property set to `Currency`. Those formats carry over to the results of the query (the query's Datasheet view). The result of the calculated `MonthlyPayment` field displays as a General number with no currency sign, no commas, and a lot of numbers to the right of the decimal point, as you see in the bottom half of Figure 2-5.

Percent format in table

Currency format in table

Calculated field

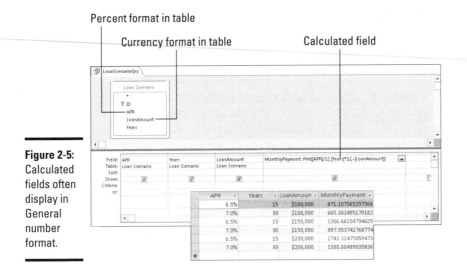

Figure 2-5:
Calculated
fields often
display in
General
number
format.

You can format a calculated field so that the result appears in Currency format in a couple of ways. If you intend to build any forms or reports based on this query, you can just save the query and forget about formatting the field. Later, when you're designing a form or report based on the query, create a control for the calculated field, the way you do for any other field in the query; then set that control's Format property in the form or report to Currency. The data looks the way you want in the form or report, and you don't have to mess around with the query at all.

 See Book IV, Chapter 1 for the goods on creating forms and reports. For the specifics on formatting controls, see the section on setting control properties in Book IV, Chapter 2.

Optionally, if you have no intention of creating any forms or reports based on the query, you can use one of the conversion functions to format the data. Table 2-3 lists some of the conversion functions, all of which are accessible via the Conversion category of the Built-In Functions folder in Expression Builder. As usual, you can click a conversion function name in the third column of Expression Builder and then click the Help button for more information on the function.

 Think of the starting letter *C* in each conversion function's name as standing for "Convert to." CCur, for example, means "Convert to Currency."

 Be careful when you use a conversion function, because you're defining the data type, as well as the appearance, of the calculated field. Setting the format of a calculated field in a form or report, rather than directly in the query, is often easier.

Table 2-3	Main Built-In Conversion Functions	
Function	*Acceptable Expression Type*	*Return Type*
CBool(expression)	String or number	Boolean
CByte(expression)	Number from 0 to 255	Byte
CCur(expression)	Number	Currency
CDate(expression)	Date/time	Date
CDbl(expression)	Number	Double
CDec(expression)	Number	Decimal
CInt(expression)	Whole number from –32,768 to 32,767	Integer
CLng(expression)	Whole number	Long
CSng(expression)	Number	Single
CStr(expression)	Any	String
CVar(expression)	Any	Variant

The big trick is to enclose the entire expression (everything to the right of the field name and colon) within the conversion function's parentheses in the QBE grid. To display the MonthlyPayment field from the sample Loan Scenarios query as Currency data, for example, you must contain the entire expression within the CCur() parentheses, as in the following expression:

```
MonthlyPayment: CCur( Pmt([APR]/12,[Years]*12,-[LoanAmount]) )
```

Figure 2-6 shows the result of using CCur() in the MonthlyPayment calculated control to display the results of the expression in Currency format.

Book III
Chapter 2

Letting Queries Do the Math

What's with the 12s in the expression?

If you're wondering why the sample expression contains things like /12 and *12, the answer has to do with how the Pmt() function works. The APR value is the annual percentage rate, and the term of the loan is expressed in years. When you want the Pmt() function to return a monthly payment, you need to divide the annual percentage rate by 12: [APR]/12. You also need to multiply the number of years by 12 to get the number of monthly payments: [Years]*12.

Typically, Pmt() returns a negative number as the result, because each payment is a debit (expense). By placing a minus sign in front of the LoanAmount field name (that is, -[LoanAmount]), you convert that LoanAmount to a negative number (a debit), which in turn converts the calculated monthly payment to a credit (a positive number).

Calculated field

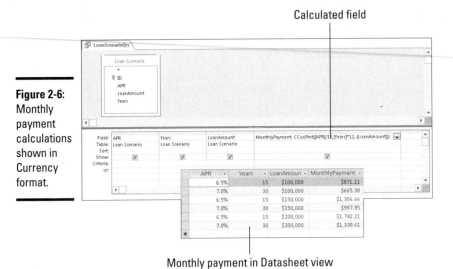

Figure 2-6:
Monthly
payment
calculations
shown in
Currency
format.

Monthly payment in Datasheet view

Avoiding problems with null values

Sometimes, a field in a record may be empty because nobody ever typed any
information in that field. The official name used to describe the value of an
empty field is *null*. If a field contains nothing, we say that it contains a *null value*.

Mathematical calculations don't automatically treat a null value as being
the same thing as zero. If any field that's used in a calculated field contains
a null, the expression itself also returns null. In Figure 2-7, the SubTotal
calculated field multiplies the contents of the HowMany field by the Price
field. In the query results, shown at the bottom of Figure 2-7, any field that
has a null in the HowMany or Price field ends up with a null value in the
SubTotal field as well.

Use the Nz() function to convert a null to a zero. What Nz() really means
is this: "If this field contains a null, make that into a zero, and do the math
using that zero." To use the Nz() function, put the entire field name within
the function's parentheses. In Figure 2-8, the modified calculated field uses
the following expression:

```
SubTotal: Nz( [HowMany], 0 ) * Nz( [Price], 0 )
```

In the Datasheet view of that same query, shown at the bottom of Figure
2-8, records that contain a null HowMany or Price field yield a zero result,
rather than null, in the SubTotal field. That's because the modified calculated control tells Access to use a zero rather than nothing (a null) to do the
math when a field is null.

Calculated field

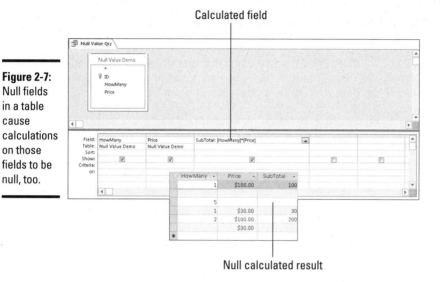

Figure 2-7:
Null fields
in a table
cause
calculations
on those
fields to be
null, too.

Null calculated result

Modified calculated field

Figure 2-8:
The Nz()
function
in the
calculated
control
forces
Access to
use zeroes,
rather than
nulls, to
calculate a
result.

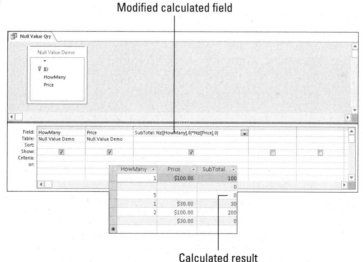

Calculated result

If you want the third column in Figure 2-8 to show results in Currency
format ($100.00, $0.00, $0.00, and so on), enclose the entire expres-
sion in a CCur() function, such as SubTotal: CCur(Nz([HowMany],
0)*Nz([Price], 0)).

You can also use the IsNull() function to test for a null field. (See "Testing
for Empty Fields," later in this chapter, for more information.)

Performing Date and Time Calculations

The built-in Date and Time functions operate on data stored in Date/Time fields. You can perform some basic calculations — called *date arithmetic calculations* — on dates by using simple + (addition) and − (subtraction) operators. Date arithmetic calculations follow a few simple rules:

+ **If you subtract one date from another, you get a number indicating the number of days between those dates.** 1/15/2013–1/1/2013 returns 14 because there are 14 days between January 15 and January 1.

+ **If you add a number to, or subtract a number from, a date, you get a new date rather than a number.** That new date is the date that's *n* days away from the original date (where *n* stands for the number of days you add or subtract). 1/1/2013+30 returns 1/31/2013 because January 31 is 30 days after January 1. The result of 12/31/2000−999 is 4/7/1998 because April 7, 1998, is 999 days before 12/31/2000.

Figure 2-9 shows a sample query that uses some basic arithmetic in query calculated fields. In the underlying table, both the StartDate and EndDate fields are defined as the Date/Time data type (with the Short Date format).

Design view

Figure 2-9: Sample calculated fields with Date functions in a query in Design view and Datasheet view.

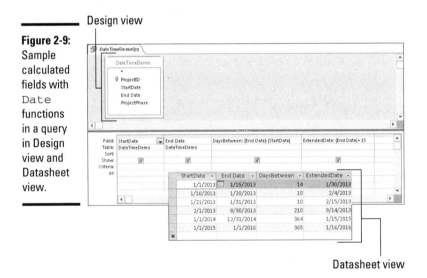

Datasheet view

The first calculated field is the following expression:

```
DaysBetween: [EndDate]-[StartDate]
```

This field calculates and displays the number of days between the StartDate value and the EndDate value in each record.

The `ExtendedDate` calculated field

`ExtendedDate: [EndDate]+15`

adds 15 days to whatever date is stored in the `EndDate` field.

The bottom half of Figure 2-9 shows the query results in Datasheet view. The `DaysBetween` column shows the number of days between the `StartDate` value and the `EndDate` value. The `ExtendedDate` column shows the date 15 days after the `EndDate` value, as specified by the expression in the calculated fields.

Using literal dates and times in expressions

When writing expressions that include dates, you can use a literal date, as opposed to the name of a field that contains a Date/Time value. A *literal date* is one that isn't stored in some field; it's just a specific date you want to use in the expression. You can't just type the date in an everyday format like 12/31/2012, however, because Access interprets that entry as "12 divided by 31, divided by 2012." Also, you can't use quotation marks, which define literal text. Instead, you have to use the awkward # character to *delimit* (surround) a literal date.

`#01/01/2013#` is literally the date January 1, 2013. The expression `#01/01/2013#` + `14` returns 1/15/2013, the date that's 14 days after January 1, 2013. The expression `#3/31/2013#` − `#1/1/2013#` returns 89 because March 31, 2013, is 89 days after January 1, 2013.

To express a literal time, use colons (`:`) to separate the hours, minutes, and seconds between the # delimiters. You can also tack on a blank space followed by AM or PM. `#7:30:00#` is literally 7:30 AM, as is `#7:30:00 AM#`. The literal time `#7:30:00 PM#` refers to 7:30 at night. You can use military time as well: The literal time `#19:30:00#` is also 7:30 PM.

Using the Date/Time functions

You're not limited to basic date arithmetic in Access. Quite a few built-in Date/Time functions exist in Access, and you can use them to manipulate dates and times in other ways. Like all built-in functions, the Date/Time functions are available in Expression Builder. Again, if the Functions folder in the left column has a + next to it, click that + to expand the list. Next, click the Built-In Functions subfolder in the left column and the Date/Time category in the center column. Then click any function's name in the right column, and click the Help button for details on the function.

We spare you the details of every available Date/Time function. Chances are that you'll never need to use the most obscure of these functions. Table 2-4 lists some of the most commonly used Date/Time functions and provides examples of their use.

Table 2-4

Examples of Access Date/Time Functions

Function and Syntax	Returns	Example
`Date()`	The current date	Returns the current date according to your computer's clock.
`Time()`	The current time	Returns the current time according to your computer's clock.
`Now()`	The current date and time	Returns the current date and time according to your computer's clock.
`CDate(expression)`	The date from an *expression*, which can be any string that looks like a date	`CDate("Mar 31, 2013")` returns `3/31/2013`.
`DateAdd(interval, number, date)`	The date that is *number* of days, weeks, months (*interval*) from *date*	`DateAdd("m", 14, #1/1/2013#)` returns `3/1/2014`, the date that's 14 months after January 1, 2013.
`DateDiff(interval, date1, date2[, firstdayofweek[, firstweekofyear]])`	The number of hours, days, weeks, (*interval*) between two dates	`DateDiff("w", #1/1/2013#, #1/1/2014#)` returns 52 because there are 52 weeks between the two dates.
`Day(date)`	The day of the month expressed as a number between 1 and 31	`Day(#1/15/2013#)` returns 15 because 1/15/2013 falls on the 15th day of the month.
`Hour(time)`	The hour of a time	`Hour(Now())` returns a number representing the current hour of the day.
`MonthName(monthNumber[, abbreviate])`	The month of a date, spelled out (if *abbreviate* is False) or abbreviated (if *abbreviate* is True)	`MonthName(12, False)` returns `December`; `MonthName(12, True)` returns `Dec` because December is the 12th month of the year.

As you can see in Table 2-4, the DateAdd() and DateDiff() functions allow you to specify an *interval* argument. That argument defines the time interval used for the calculation.

If you just use plain date arithmetic to subtract two dates, for example, the difference between the dates automatically displays as the number of *days* between those dates. By using the DateAdd() or DateDiff() function, you can tell Access to express the difference between the dates in seconds, minutes, hours, weeks, months, or years — whichever interval provides the accuracy you need.

To specify a time interval argument in a DateAdd() or DateDiff() function, you use one of the settings (enclosed in quotation marks) listed in the left column of Table 2-5.

Table 2-5	Settings for the Interval Argument in Date/Time Functions
Setting	*Description*
"d"	Day
"h"	Hour
"m"	Month
"n"	Minute
"q"	Quarter
"s"	Second
"w"	Weekday
"ww"	Week
"y"	Day of year
"yyyy"	Year

Book III
Chapter 2

Letting Queries Do the Math

Take a look at an example of using an interval in a DateDiff() function. If you don't use the DateDiff() function at all, the expression #12/25/2013# - #12/24/2013# returns 1, because there is one day between those dates, and "day" is the default interval for subtracting dates. On the other hand, the expression DateDiff ("h",#12/24/2013#,#12/25/2013#) returns 24, because the "h" interval specifies hours, and there are 24 hours between those two dates.

Manipulating Text with Expressions

You can use the contents of Text fields (also called *strings,* which is short for "a string of characters") in expressions as well, but adding, subtracting, multiplying, and dividing with strings doesn't make sense. After all, Smith times Jones or Smith divided by Jones makes no sense at all. Instead, you can use the ampersand (&) operator to *concatenate* (join) strings.

The expression [First Name] & [Last Name], for example, joins the contents of the Last Name and First Name fields. If the Last Name field contains Pines, and the First Name field contains Tori, the expression [First Name] & [Last Name] returns ToriPines.

Adding spaces to text expressions

"But wait," you say. "Shouldn't that be *Tori Pines,* with a space in between?" To you and me, it should be — but that's not what the expression says. The expression says, "Stick the First Name value and Last Name value together." It doesn't add, "And put a space between them." Computers are literal-minded, so you can fix the problem easily by using literal text.

Literal text is any text that doesn't refer to a field name, a function, or anything else that has special meaning to Access. To use literal text in a calculated field expression, enclose the text in quotation marks. A blank space is a character — a chunk of literal text. Watch what happens if you rewrite the previous example expression like this:

```
[First Name] & " " & [Last Name]
```

The result is Tori Pines with a space in between. The expression says, "Display the contents of the First Name field, followed by a blank space, followed by the contents of the Last Name field."

Two quotation marks right next to each other, with no blank space between them, is a *zero-length string,* which is basically nothing at all. [First Name] & " " & [Last Name] returns something like Tori Pines, and the expression [First Name] & "" & [Last Name] returns something like ToriPines (the first and last names with nothing in between).

Suppose that a table contains City, State, and ZIP fields. The following expression displays the city name followed by a comma and a blank space, followed by the state name, followed by two blank spaces, followed by the zip code:

```
[City] & ", " & [State] & "  " & [ZIP]
```

An example of the preceding expression might look something like this:

```
Los Angeles, CA  91234
```

Using the Access Text functions

Access provides several functions for working with text. You find them in the Text category in the middle column of Expression Builder. In this section, we focus on some of the most commonly used functions and show examples of their use. (For information on more Text functions and additional details, click the Help button in Expression Builder.)

Table 2-6 lists common Text functions.

Table 2-6	Examples of Built-In Text Functions	
Function and Syntax	*Returns*	*Example*
LCase(*string*)	*string* converted to lowercase	LCase("AbCdEfG") returns abcdefg.
UCase(*string*)	*string* converted to uppercase	UCase("AbCdEfG") returns ABCDEFG.
Left(*string*,*n*)	Leftmost *n* characters of *string*	Left("abcdefg",3) returns abc.
Right(*string*,*n*)	Rightmost *n* characters of *string*	Right("abcdefg",2) returns fg.
Mid(*string*, *start*[, *length*])	Middle *length* characters of string starting at *start*	Mid("abcmnyz",4,2) returns mn.
Len(*string*)	Length of *string*	Len("Howdy") returns 5.
Trim(*string*)	*string* with any leading and trailing spaces trimmed off	Trim(" abc ") returns abc.
InStr([*start*,] *string1*, *string2*)	Position of *string2* in *string1* starting at *start*	InStr("abcxdef","x") returns 4 (because x is the fourth character in *string1*).

Book III
Chapter 2

Letting Queries Do the Math

Writing Decision-Making Expressions

One of the most useful functions in Access is the Immediate If function, IIf(), which accepts three arguments:

```
IIf(conditionalExpression, doThis, elseDoThis)
```

In this function,

✦ *conditionalExpression* is an expression that results in a True or False value.

✦ *doThis* is what the function returns if the *conditionalExpression* proves to be True.

✦ *elseDoThis* is what the function returns if the *conditionalExpression* proves to be False.

The value of the IIf() function lies in its capability to make a decision about what to return based on the current situation. Suppose that your business requires charging 7.25 percent sales tax to New York residents and no sales tax to everyone else. The State field in the underlying table contains the state to which the order is shipped. The following expression says, "If the State field contains NY, return 7.25%; otherwise, return 0":

```
IIf([State]="NY",0.0725,0)
```

Note: In the preceding expression, 0.0725 is just a way of expressing 7.25 percent as a regular decimal number (remove the % sign and shift the decimal point two places to the left).

Another example of an IIf() function occurs when a Paid field in a table is a Yes/No field. A Yes/No field can contain only either a True or False value. The field name alone is a sufficient conditional expression for an IIf() function, as in the following sample expression:

```
IIf([Paid],"Receipt","Invoice")
```

In English, the expression says, "If the Paid field contains True (or Yes), return the word Receipt. Otherwise, (if the Paid field contains False) return the word Invoice."

Making comparisons in IIf()

Access offers several comparison operators that you can use to define expressions that result in the True or False values. Selections for these operators appear in Expression Builder when you choose Operators⇨ Comparison. Table 2-7 describes the Access comparison operators.

The following example IIf() function uses the >= comparison operator to make a decision based on the contents of a field named Qty:

```
IIf([Qty]>=10,"Discount","No Discount")
```

In English, the expression says, "If the Qty field contains a value greater than or equal to 10, return Discount. Otherwise, return No Discount."

Table 2-7	Built-In Comparison Operators	
Comparison Operator	*Name*	*Meaning*
=	Equals	Is equal to
>	Greater than	Is greater than
>=	Greater than or equal to	Is greater than or equal to
<	Less than	Is less than
<=	Less than or equal to	Is less than or equal to
<>	Not equal to	Is not equal to
Between	Between	Is within the range of
In	In	Is one of a list of values
Like	Like	Is similar to (for string expressions)

Combining comparisons

You can use the Access built-in *logical operators* to combine several comparisons into a single expression that results in a True or False value. Table 2-8 lists the logical operators.

Table 2-8	Built-In Logical Operators
Logical Operator	*Meaning*
And	Both conditions are True.
Or	One condition is True, or both conditions are True.
Xor	Exclusive "or" — one condition is True, but both conditions aren't True.
Not	The condition is not True.
Eqv	Both expressions are True, or both expressions are False.
Imp	This operator performs a bitwise comparison of identically positioned bits in two numeric expressions. Refer to Access help for assistance with the Imp operator.

Take a look at the following example IIf() function, which uses the And operator:

```
IIf([Last Name]="Pines" And [First Name]="Tori","No Charge","Charge")
```

The conditional expression, `[Last Name]="Pines" And [First Name]="Tori"` means "if the `Last Name` field contains `Pines` and the `First Name` field contains `Tori`." One condition is that the `Last Name` field contain `Pines`; the other condition is that the `First Name` field contain `Tori`. If both those conditions are `True`, the expression returns `No Charge`. If either condition is `False`, or if both conditions are `False`, the expression returns `Charge`.

Another example of the `Or` operator is the following expression:

```
IIf([State]="NY" Or [State]="NJ","Tax","No Tax")
```

In the preceding example, the first condition is that the `State` field contains `NY`. The second condition is that the `State` field contains `NJ`. The `Or` operator says that either or both of the conditions must be met for the whole conditional expression to return `True`. If the `State` field contains `NY` or `NJ`, the expression returns `Tax`. If the `State` field contains anything other than `NY` or `NJ`, the expression returns `No Tax`.

To tax or not to tax?

A practical example of using an `IIf()` function in calculated field expressions is whether to tax. Suppose that you have a query like the one shown in Figure 2-10. Your business requires that you charge 7.25 percent tax to all orders shipped within the state of New York. You charge no sales tax on orders shipped outside New York. The `StateProv` field in the query contains the state to which the order is shipped.

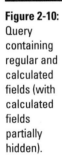

Figure 2-10: Query containing regular and calculated fields (with calculated fields partially hidden).

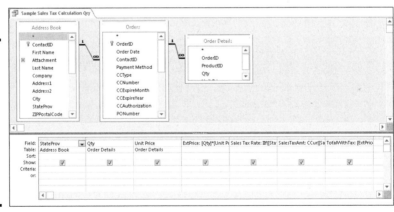

Obviously, you can't see all the expressions in the query; the QBE grid isn't wide enough on many monitors to show them. You can expand the width of individual columns to see that column's full expression. Following is a quick summary of what the fields in the query represent:

✦ **StateProv:** A regular Text field from the underlying Address Book table, representing the state to which the order is being shipped.

✦ **Qty:** A regular Number field from the Order Details table, representing the quantity of items ordered.

✦ **Unit Price:** A regular Currency field from the Order Details table, representing the unit price of the item ordered.

✦ **ExtPrice:** A calculated field, ExtPrice: [Qty]*[Unit Price], that multiplies the contents of the Qty field by the contents of the Unit Price field.

✦ **Sales Tax Rate:** A calculated field, SalesTaxRate: IIf([StateProv]="NY",0.0725,0), meaning "If the StateProv field contains NY, put 0.0725 in this field. Otherwise, put 0 in this field."

✦ **SalesTaxAmt:** A calculated field, SalesTaxAmt: CCur([SalesTaxRate]*[ExtPrice]), that multiplies the extended price by the sales tax rate. The CCur() function makes the result appear in Currency format rather than as a General number.

✦ **TotalWithTax:** A calculated field, TotalWithTax: [ExtPrice]+[SalesTaxAmt], that adds the extended price to the sales tax amount.

Figure 2-11 shows the result of the query. Records that have NY in the StateProv field show a sales tax rate of 7.25 percent (0.0725). Records that don't have NY in the StateProv field show 0 as the sales tax rate. The SalesTaxAmt and TotalWithTax fields show the results of adding sales tax. (Because the SalesTaxRate value is 0 outside NY, those records end up getting no sales tax added to them.)

StateProv	Qty	Unit Price	ExtPrice	Sales Tax Rate	SalesTaxAmt	TotalWithTax
AK	1	$39.99	$39.99	0	$0.00	$39.99
AK	1	$39.99	$39.99	0	$0.00	$39.99
AK	3	$10.00	$30.00	0	$0.00	$30.00
AK	1	$9.98	$9.98	0	$0.00	$9.98
AK	1	$89.99	$89.99	0	$0.00	$89.99
CA	1	$100.00	$100.00	0	$0.00	$100.00
CA	1	$29.99	$29.99	0	$0.00	$29.99
CA	10	$7.99	$79.90	0	$0.00	$79.90
FL	1	$500.00	$500.00	0	$0.00	$500.00
FL	1	$0.00	$0.00	0	$0.00	$0.00
NY	23	$39.99	$919.77	0.0725	$66.68	$986.45
NY	25	$39.99	$999.75	0.0725	$72.48	$1,072.23
NY	1	$1,000.00	$1,000.00	0.0725	$72.50	$1,072.50
NY	5	$179.99	$899.95	0.0725	$65.25	$965.20
OK	1	$0.00	$0.00	0	$0.00	$0.00
OK	1	$0.00	$0.00	0	$0.00	$0.00
OK	1	$0.00	$0.00	0	$0.00	$0.00
NM	3	$0.00	$0.00	0	$0.00	$0.00
NM	1	$0.00	$0.00	0	$0.00	$0.00
NM	1	$0.00	$0.00	0	$0.00	$0.00

Figure 2-11: Result (Datasheet view) of the query shown in Figure 2-10.

Testing for Empty Fields

Sometimes, having an expression know whether a field is empty, or null, is useful. Access includes an `IsNull()` function that you can use to test whether a field is empty. The syntax of the function is pretty straightforward:

```
IsNull([fieldname])
```

fieldname is the name of the field you want to test.

If the specified field is empty, `IsNull()` returns a `True` value. If the specified field isn't empty, `IsNull()` returns a `False` value. The next section provides an example of using `IsNull()` in an expression.

To treat a null field as a zero in mathematical expressions, use the `Nz()` function, described in the section "Avoiding problems with null values," earlier in this chapter.

Sorting by Name or Company

A fairly common problem comes up in tables that store names and addresses. Some records in such a table may list a person's name but no company name; other records may contain a company name but no person's name. If you sort records in such a table by the `Last Name`, `First Name`, and `Company` fields, as in Figure 2-12, the records with empty `Last Name` and `First Name` fields are listed first.

Sort by Last Name, First Name, Company fields.

In query results (Datasheet view), records with null Last Name fields are listed first.

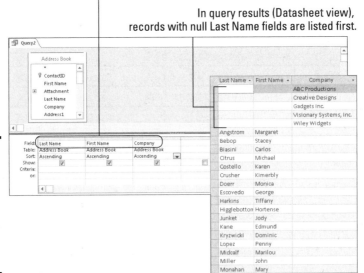

Figure 2-12: Sorting by name and company fields puts empty name fields at the top.

Suppose that you prefer to see names listed in alphabetical order by person name — or by company name, if there is no person name. In that case, create a calculated field in Design view. You can name this field anything you want; in Figure 2-13, we named the field `CustLookup`. The expression for that field reads

```
CustLookup: IIf(IsNull([Last Name]),[Company],[Last Name] & ", " & [First Name])
```

The `IIf()` expression says, "If the `Last Name` field is null, put the company name in this field. Otherwise, put the person's last name in the field, followed by a comma, a space, and the person's first name (`Pines, Tori`, for example)." Setting the `Sort` row for that calculated field to Ascending order puts records in alphabetical order by last name or company (if there is no last name), as shown in Figure 2-13.

Calculated field

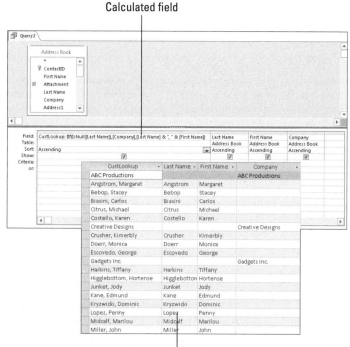

Book III
Chapter 2

Letting Queries Do
the Math

Figure 2-13:
Sorting by
calculated
field sorts
by name or
by company
if the `Last
Name` field
is blank.

Alphabetized by name or company

Creating Flexible Parameter Queries

A *parameter query* is a query that intentionally omits a piece of needed information so that you can enter the information on the fly when you open the query in Datasheet view. Suppose that you create a query that shows orders from all records in a table (or tables) from all records in your database. You also like to have queries that show orders from each month.

Rather than create 12 different queries (one for each month), you can create a parameter query that asks for the month number. Then, as soon as you enter a month number, the query shows orders for just the month you specified. In other words, the month number that you're interested in becomes a parameter that you define and pass (provide) to the query just before the query opens.

To create a parameter query, start by creating a normal select query (as detailed in Book III, Chapter 1). You can add tables and field names just as you would in any other query. Then follow these steps to make your query a parameter query:

1. **In the Design View window, click Parameters in the Show/Hide group of the (Query Tools) Design tab on the Ribbon.**

   The Query Parameters dialog box appears.

2. **Enter a parameter name and its data type in the appropriate columns.**

   The parameter name can be any name you like, as long as it doesn't match the name of a regular or calculated field that's already included in the table. The data type matches the type of data that the parameter will ask for, such as Text for text, Currency for a dollar value, or Date/Time for a date or time. You can repeat this step to create as many parameters as you want.

3. **Click OK to close the Query Parameters dialog box.**

In the QBE grid, you can treat the parameter name the way you do a value from a field. In fact, you enclose the parameter's name in square brackets just as you do a field name.

In Figure 2-14, we created a `Month Number` parameter that contains an integer. In the `Criteria` row for the `Order Date` field in the QBE grid, we used the parameter name in the following expression, as shown in Figure 2-14. The criterion tells the query to show only those records in which the month of the order date is equal to whatever we type as the `Month Number` parameter, as follows:

```
Month([Order Date]) = [Month Number]
```

After defining your parameter and using it in the QBE grid, you can save the query as you do any other query. The parameter doesn't come into play until you open the query in Datasheet view. When you do, an Enter Parameter Value dialog box opens, like the one shown near the top of Figure 2-15. Type a value for the parameter, and click OK. For the sake of this example, suppose that you type **9** to view September orders only. Then, when you click OK in the Enter Parameter Value dialog box, the query opens in Datasheet view, using the parameter value you specified. In this example, the query shows only records that have 9 as the month number in the Order Date field, as shown in the bottom half of Figure 2-15.

Month Number parameter defined

Figure 2-14: Defining and using a query parameter.

Month Number listed in criteria

Book III
Chapter 2

Letting Queries Do the Math

Before a query opens, you provide a parameter value (9).

Figure 2-15: The result of opening a parameter query and specifying 9 as the month number.

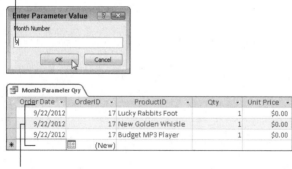

The opened query shows orders only for September (month 9).

You also see the Enter Parameter Value dialog box if you enter a typo or another error and Access doesn't recognize a field name in your query design.

Working with Totals, Subtotals, Averages, and Such

So far, all the calculations in the queries we've discussed operate on individual fields within records. Suppose that you want a different sort of total, such as the total dollar amount of all sales in all records. You can perform such a calculation in two ways:

✦ **Report:** The better — and perhaps easier — way is to use a report rather than a query. Reports provide more flexibility and allow you to display the information in more meaningful ways than queries do.

   For the goods on creating reports with totals and subtotals, see Book V, Chapter 1.

✦ **Totals query:** The other approach is to use a totals query. A totals query doesn't give you the flexibility or pretty output that a report does, but it's useful when you want to perform some quick calculations on the fly without formatting a fancy report.

If you just want to do some quick subtotals, totals, or other multirecord calculations, and you really don't care how the data looks onscreen or in print, you can use a query to do the math. As for the other multirecord calculations we just mentioned, Table 2-9 lists all the calculations you can do in a totals query.

Table 2-9	Operations Available in a Totals Query
Choice	*Returns*
Avg	Average of records in field
Count	How many records
First	Value stored in first record
Group by	Nothing (used only for grouping)
Last	Value stored in last record
Max	Highest value in all records
Min	Lowest value in all records
StDev	Standard deviation
Sum	Sum of records in field
Var	Variance

To create a query that performs calculations on multiple records, start with a normal select query that contains the table (or tables) on which you want to perform calculations. Then do either of the following:

Totals

✦ Click the Totals button in the Show/Hide group of the Design tab on the Ribbon.

✦ Right-click the query grid and choose Totals from the contextual menu.

The only change you see is a new row, titled `Total`, in the QBE grid. The next step is to drag any field name on which you want to perform math down to the `Field` row of the grid. Optionally, you can create a calculated field and then perform a calculation on that value.

When the field is in place, click the `Total` row and then choose an option from the drop-down menu, as shown in Figure 2-16. Repeat this process for each field on which you want to perform a calculation.

When you switch to Datasheet view to see the results of the query, don't be shocked if your large table, which consists of many records, is suddenly reduced to many fewer records. No, you didn't make an error; totals queries work this way. The query shown in Figure 2-17 results in a datasheet that has one record for each product sold. The `SumOfQty` field is created automatically by the totals query (using the `Qty` field that you included in the query). The `ExtPrice` field lists the net income for each product.

TIP

To see a single value — the total income for all products — delete the `ProductID` field from the query design.

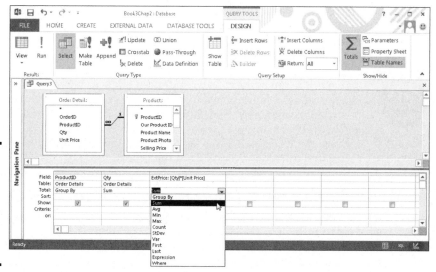

Figure 2-16: The `Total` row in a totals query allows you to pick a calculation.

Figure 2-17:
The query
design in
Figure 2-16
produces
this
datasheet,
with one
line for each
`Product`
`ID` (the
`Group`
`By` field).

ProductID	SumOfQty	ExtPrice
Golden Whistle	13	$100.00
Kozmik Video Camera	4	$2,000.00
Budget MP3 Player	11	$30.00
Old Time Stock Ticker	4	$1,500.00
Lawn Flamingo	13	$149.95
Scanner cable	4	$29.94
Microwave Blow Dryer	2	$129.99
Magic Inkwell	3	$0.00
Lucky Rabbits Foot	14	$87.89
50-pk Floppy Disks	28	$1,039.74
WayCool Scanner	7	$269.97
Nuclear Pencil Sharper	8	$1,079.94
Big Subwoofer	3	$29.99
50pk Audio CD-R	27	$999.75
Unbreakable PDA	10	$0.00
New Golden Whistle	7	$0.00

Record: 1 of 16 No Filter Search

Calculating subtotals in a query

To calculate subtotals, use another field in the query that identifies the field
on which the subtotals should be based. Set the `Total` row for that field to
a `Group By` value. In the top half of Figure 2-16, earlier in this chapter, we
added the `ProductID` field from the Order Details table to the QBE grid and
set its `Total` row to a `Group By` value.

The bottom half of Figure 2-17 shows the result of that query in Datasheet
view. The query returns the total extended price of orders for each individual product. The figure shows sales of $100 worth of Golden Whistles, $2,000
worth of Kozmik Video Cameras, and so on.

The results of a totals query aren't always easy to interpret. Alas, the small
amount of detail in the query results can make it difficult to see what the calculated values are based on. In fact, the lack of detail in queries is the most
important reason why reports are so much better than queries for totals
and subtotals. In a report, you can include all the details you want — and
arrange things in such a way that you can easily grasp the meaning of every
calculated total just by looking at the report.

Filtering records based on calculated fields

You can filter records based on the results of a calculated field. Suppose
that you want to do a query like the one in Figure 2-16, but you want to see
only those records in which the total extended price is greater than or equal
to $1,000. In that case, just set the `Criteria` row for the calculated field
to `>=1000`. In Datasheet view, only those products with sales totals results
greater than or equal to $1,000 show up.

Chapter 3: Doing Neat Things with Action Queries and Query Wizards

In This Chapter

✔ **Making systematic changes to your data**

✔ **Using action queries safely**

✔ **Using update queries to change data into tables**

✔ **Creating new tables with make-table queries**

✔ **Adding data from one table to another table with append queries**

✔ **Gathering stray sheep with the Find Unmatched Wizard**

✔ **Getting the hang of the Find Duplicates Wizard**

Chapter 1 of this minibook concentrates on creating select queries, which are the most common type of queries created by Access users. You may not realize that Access has other types of queries. Action queries can make systematic changes to your data. You can set up a query to make a change to all the records that match a criterion, for example. And two query wizards — the Find Duplicates Query Wizard and the Find Unmatched Query Wizard — can help you clean up the data in your database.

Creating Action Queries

Action queries let you make global corrections in your database. They're very powerful; they can be tremendously useful and save you a lot of time. They can also make an enormous mess of your database if used incorrectly, however.

Action queries differ significantly from select queries. A select query shows you data that meet your criteria, whereas an action query looks for the data that meets your criteria and then does something with it, such as making changes to the data or moving records to a new table.

Four kinds of action queries exist, corresponding to four very specific tasks. You may find that creating an action query saves you tons of time if you want to do any of the following things:

✦ Delete records that meet certain criteria *(delete query).*

✦ Copy data from one table to another table *(append query).*

✦ Update (change) information in some records *(update query).*

✦ Create a new table from data stored in other tables *(make-table query).*

Make a backup *before* you run an action query. Action queries can make huge changes in your database, and even if you're careful, you may make a mistake. Making a backup doesn't take much time, especially compared with the time it takes to recover from an action query's unintended effects. You may want to back up the whole database or just make copies of the tables and the data in them that is affected by the query. (To find out about making copies of a database object, see Book I, Chapter 2; to find out about backing up a database, see Book VII, Chapter 1.)

The usual way to create a query is to click the Query Wizard or Query Design button on the Create tab of the Ribbon. When you click either button, Access automatically creates a select query. You can change the type of any query, whether it's new or well used. To change the query type, click the Query Type buttons available in Query Design view on the Design tab of the Ribbon. Make Table, Append, Update, and Delete are all types of action queries.

Recognizing the dangers of the Run button

As you may realize by now, action queries make changes; they don't just display data. You need to know how to create an action query safely without running it before you finish defining exactly how you want it to work. The key is in when you use the View and Run buttons and how you open the query:

✦ When you work with a *select query,* the View and Run buttons do the same thing.

✦ When you work with an *action query,* the View and Run buttons do completely different jobs:

View

- *View:* The View button displays Datasheet view with all the records that match your selection criteria, which is a good way to preview what records will change when you run the action query. The View button is a safe way to look at the datasheet of an action query to see whether the query will work the way you want.

Run

- *Run:* The Run button executes the action — deletes or changes data in your database. You can't undo the action after you click the Run button in an action query, so be very sure that you set up the query correctly before you run it — and be sure to have backups of the affected tables just in case disaster strikes. (To find out about making copies of a table, see Book I, Chapter 2.)

You also need to be careful about how you open an action query. Action queries are always rarin' to go. When you open an action query from the Navigation Pane by double-clicking the query name or by selecting it and clicking the Open button, you tell Access to *run* the query, not just to show it. Access does at least warn you that you're about to run an action query by telling you `You are about to run a query that will modify data in your table.` If you don't want to run the action query, click No to cancel it. If all you want to do is work on the design, be sure to right-click the query name in the Navigation Pane and choose Design view from the contextual menu.

Action queries have exclamation points next to their names in the Navigation Pane, making them easy to spot.

You may see an error message when you try to run an action query. By default, Access disables all action queries unless your database resides in a trusted location or unless the database itself is signed and trusted.

Settings for action queries are in the Trust Center, which you access by clicking the File tab on the Ribbon and choosing File⇨Options⇨Trust Center. Click the Trust Center Settings button to display the Trust Center options. Action queries are affected by the ActiveX options. The Trust Center is covered more extensively in Book VII, Chapter 3.

Try storing the database in a trusted location (such as your hard drive) to enable action queries.

Creating action queries safely

You need to perfect an action query before you run it so that you don't wreck your data. (If you make a mistake, you have a backup, right?) Make the action query, look at it, maybe test it on a few records in a test table, and then finally run it.

The process for creating an action query is as follows:

1. **Back up your database or make copies of the tables that the action query will change.**

   Because action queries can do so much work (good or bad), make a backup before you run the query.

2. **Create a select query to show the data needed for the action query.**

   Click the Query Design or Query Wizard button on the Create tab of the Ribbon. Add tables (or queries) and fields to the design grid. Define criteria and sort order as needed.

   The point is to create a query that displays the records that the action query acts on.

View

3. View the records that the query will act on by clicking the View button.

Check the datasheet displaying the records that the query will act on. Make sure that you see all the records you want to change and none that you don't want to change.

4. Click one of the Query Type buttons — Make Table, Update, Append, or Delete — to choose the type of action query you need.

You see the Query Type buttons when you view a query; they're on the Query Tools Design tab.

5. Add the information about what you want the query to do (update data, append data, make a table, or delete data).

The details are covered in the following sections on each type of query.

View

6. Double-check that you're asking Access to act on the correct data by clicking the View button again.

!
Run

7. Click the Run button to run the query.

Access warns you that you're about to make changes that you can't undo.

If you see a message that the action has been blocked, refer to the steps at the end of the preceding section.

8. Click the Yes button to run the query.

Access runs the query. Keep breathing!

9. Check your results.

View the affected tables to make sure that the results are as desired. Viewing the action query's datasheet isn't enough. If the action query acts on a field that you use in a criterion, you may not see the records that change after the query has run; you may have to look at the table that holds the raw data or create a new query to view the results.

The make-table query creates a new table. View those results in the affected tables, not in the query datasheet.

10. If you won't be using the action query again, delete it.

Action queries are dangerous things to have lying around!

Changing Data with Update Queries

You can use an *update query* to change a pile of data at the same time — to raise prices by 10 percent, for example, or to replace a product number with a new product number.

You may create a query to find orders that haven't yet been shipped, including orders for Golden Whistle, a discontinued item for which you have a substitute. Then you can use the update query to change the item number in records that meet those criteria to New Golden Whistle, the replacement item.

Using the update query when you work on lots and lots of data or when you want to update multiple fields makes sense. But before you delve in to the complexities of an action query, consider whether you can use the much simpler Find and Replace dialog box to find and replace data instead. (See Book II, Chapter 3 for more information on the Find and Replace dialog box.) You can use the Find and Replace dialog box in a datasheet created by a query; if you change the data in the query, the table holding the underlying data reflects the change.

To create an update query, follow these steps:

1. Back up the database, or make copies of the tables and/or fields that will be affected by the update.

Update queries can be hard to get right, so play it safe in case you need to get your data back the way it was before you ran the update query.

2. Create a new select query in Design view.

See Chapter 1 of this minibook for more information on creating a query.

Include tables that you plan to update or that you need fields from to establish the update criteria.

3. Put fields in the design grid.

Add the fields you want to see in the datasheet, the fields you want to use with criteria to tell Access exactly what to update, and the fields you want to change by using the update query.

See Chapter 1 of this minibook for more information on using the design grid.

4. Add the criteria to tell Access how to choose the records you want to update.

Figure 3-1 shows the select query that finds all unshipped orders for the Golden Whistle. You see two fields included in the query: Shipped, to look for orders that haven't been shipped (this is a Yes/No field; No finds unshipped orders), and Product ID, to look for orders that contain the Golden Whistle product.

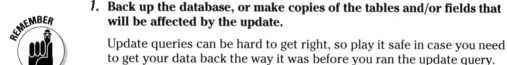

5. Click the View button to view the datasheet to make sure that all the records you want to update, and none that you don't, are included.

Edit the query as needed until you see only the records you want to update. Figure 3-2 shows the datasheet for the query shown in Figure 3-1.

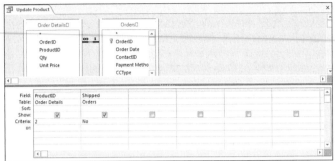

Figure 3-1:
This select
query finds
all orders for
the Golden
Whistle
that haven't
shipped.

Figure 3-2:
The
datasheet
for the
query in
Figure 3-1,
showing
the Golden
Whistle
orders that
haven't
shipped.

TIP

If you use an expression to define how a record is updated, you may want to create a test field now to try your expression and make sure that it works the way you want in a select query before you use it in an update query. If you want to increase prices by 10 percent, for example, you can create a new field: `[New Price]: [Selling Price]*1.10`. The test field appears in the datasheet when you view it, and you can check it for accuracy. Then change the query type and move the tested expression to the Update To row. For more information about writing expressions, see Chapter 2 of this minibook.

6. **Return to Design view, and click the Update Query button in the Query Type group on the Design tab of the Ribbon to change the query to an update query.**

    Access adds an Update To row to the design grid.

7. **Use the Update To row to tell Access how to update the field.**

    The easiest update is to change one value to another simply by typing the new value in the Update To box for the appropriate field.

More-complex updates include expressions that tell Access exactly how to update the field. To increase the `Selling Price` field in a table by 10 percent, for example, you use the expression `[Selling Price]*1.10`. You can use the Expression Builder to help build an expression for the Update To row; just click the box and then click the Build button. (See Chapter 2 of this minibook for more information on using Expression Builder to create expressions.)

If you created a test field in Step 5, move the expression to the Update To row for the field that will be updated, and delete the field you created to test the expression. Note that you move the expression that appears after the colon in the test field. You don't need to include a field name and a colon in the Update To row.

Figure 3-3 shows the update query that finds all orders for the Golden Whistle and changes them to orders for the New Golden Whistle (which has a `ProductID` of 19).

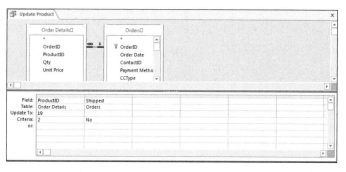

Figure 3-3: This query finds all orders with a `Product ID` of 2 (Golden Whistles) that haven't shipped and changes their `Product ID` to 19 (New Golden Whistle).

8. Click the View button.

Access displays the datasheet with the records that the query changes when you run it. If the records aren't the ones that you want updated, return to Design view to correct the fields and criteria. This data is the same data that you displayed in Step 5; display it again to make sure you're making the changes you want to make. Check Design view carefully to make sure that the Update To row is correct.

If you want to get a fuller picture of the records you're updating (see the data for all the fields, for example), you can change the query back to a select query, add fields, and view the datasheet that your criteria produces. When you change the query back to an update query, the Update To options that you added are still there. Remove any additional fields from the query grid before you run the update.

Only fields that are updated or used for criteria are allowed in update queries.

Be aware that the datasheet shows the data that will be changed. You can't see the actual changes until you run the query. If you use an expression in the Update To row, testing that your expression produces the desired result by using a calculated field in a select query is important (see Step 5).

9. Click the Run button to run the update.

Run

Access warns you that after the records update, you can't undo the changes, as shown in Figure 3-4.

Figure 3-4:
When you click the Run button to run an update query, you see a warning like this one.

10. Click Yes to update the data.

11. Check the tables with affected fields to see whether the update query worked correctly.

12. Delete the query if you won't be using it again; press Ctrl+S to save it if you'll need it again.

Creating New Tables with Make-Table Queries

A *make-table query* is useful if you need to make a new table to export or to serve as a backup. You can use a make-table query to create a new table that contains a copy of the data in a table or query. The new table can contain some or all of the fields and records from an existing table, or it can combine the fields from two or more tables, similar to the result of a select query.

You can use a make-table query to create a table of customers who bought Golden Whistles, for example. Maybe you decided to share their addresses with a school that offers whistle lessons.

To create a table with a make-table query, follow these steps:

1. Create a select query that produces the records you want in a new table.

See Chapter 1 of this minibook for more information on creating a select query.

Figure 3-5 shows a select query that finds the contact info for all customers who ever ordered Golden Whistles. Notice that although you need only fields from the Address Book and Order Details tables, the Orders table is also included in the query to define the relationship between the Order Details and Address Book tables.

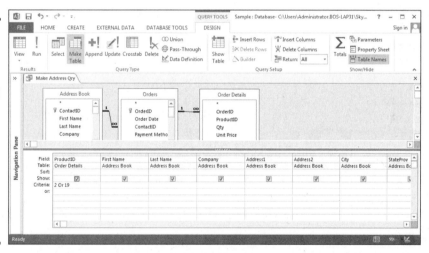

Figure 3-5: The select query finds customers who ordered Golden Whistles (item numbers 2 and 19), and lists their names and addresses.

Book III Chapter 3

Doing Neat Things with Action Queries and Query Wizards

2. Click the View button on the toolbar to view the results.

Figure 3-6 shows the datasheet for the query.

3. Click the View button on the toolbar to display Design view.

You don't want to include the `ProductID` field in the table that the make-table query creates, so return to Design view and deselect the check box in the Show row for the `ProductID` field.

4. Change the query type to a make-table query by clicking the Make Table button in the Query Type group on the Design tab of the Ribbon.

Access immediately displays the Make Table dialog box, shown in Figure 3-7.

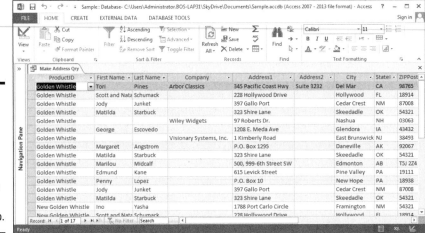

Figure 3-6:
The datasheet shows Golden Whistle purchasers and their contact info.

Figure 3-7:
The Make Table dialog box.

5. **In the Table Name field, type the name of the table you're creating.**

   Although you're offered a drop-down menu, you'll probably want to create a new table with a new name, so type a name for the table that isn't the name of any table currently in your database.

6. **Choose whether to create the new table in the current database or in another database.**

   If you choose the Another Database option, you can browse for an existing database.

   You can't use a make-table query to create a new database — only a new table in an existing database.

7. **Click OK to close the dialog box.**

   If you need to change the settings in the Make Table dialog box, click the Make Table button again to display the dialog box again.

8. **Click the View button to see the records that will be in the new table.**

   You may need to return to Design view to edit the query until all the records you want in the new table appear in the datasheet when you click the View button.

9. **Click the Run button to create the new table.**

Run

Access asks whether you're sure, because you won't be able to undo your changes.

10. **Click Yes to create the new table.**

Access quietly creates the new table.

11. **Check the new and old tables to make sure that you got what you need in the new table.**

You may want to edit the table design because the new table doesn't inherit the field properties or the primary key setting from the original table. (See Book II, Chapter 1 for more information on table design.)

Moving Data from One Table to Another with Append Queries

An *append query* copies data from one or more tables or queries in your database and adds the data selected by the query to an existing table as new records. As with other queries, you can use criteria to tell Access exactly which data to append.

Append queries are useful for archiving information, moving data between databases, and performing other useful housecleaning chores.

Cutting and pasting may be an easier way to append records from one table to another if you're appending only a few records. See Book II, Chapter 4 for more information.

Access gets a little picky about data that you append with an append query, especially primary key field data. You must follow these rules when appending records to another table:

✦ **Data that you want to append must have unique values in the primary key field.** Each value in the primary key field must be unique in the table to which the data is being added, because by definition, no value can repeat in a primary key field. If the field is blank, or if the same value already exists in the table, Access doesn't append the records.

✦ **If an AutoNumber field is in the table to which the data is being appended, don't append data in that field.** Access automatically generates new numbers in the AutoNumber field for the new records; AutoNumber values previously generated can't be appended.

✦ **The data type of each field you're appending must match the data type of fields in the table to which they're being added.**

To create an append query, follow these steps:

1. **Create a select query that produces the records that you want to add to another table, and display the query in Design view.**

   See Chapter 1 of this minibook for details on creating a select query.

   You can check the criteria by viewing the datasheet to see whether the query is selecting the data you want to append. Click the View button on the toolbar to display the datasheet, and click the View button again to return to Design view.

2. **Change the query type to an append query by clicking the Append button in the Query Type group on the Design tab of the Ribbon.**

   Access immediately displays the Append dialog box, shown in Figure 3-8.

Figure 3-8: The Append dialog box tells Access where you want to append data.

3. **From the Table Name drop-down menu, choose the table to which you want to append the records.**

   You can add the records to a table in another database. Find the database by clicking the Browse button.

4. **Click OK.**

   Access adds an extra row to the design grid: the Append To row. If the field names match the names of the fields you're appending, Access automatically fills in the Append To row with the names of the fields in the table to which you're appending records.

5. **Carefully check the Append To row of the query grid, and make any necessary changes.**

   The Field and Table rows show where the field comes from, and the Append To row shows where the data will be appended.

   If some of the fields don't have field names in the Append To row, display the drop-down menu in the Append row, and choose the name of the field you want to append to. When you're finished, check each column to ensure that

- The Field row contains the name of the field that contains data that you want to append to another table.

- The Table row contains the name of the table that contains the data.

- The Append To row contains the name of the field that the data will be appended to.

- No field appears more than once in the Append To row.

6. **Click the Run button to run the append query.**

   Access tells you that you're about to append rows and that you won't be able to undo the changes.

   Be careful about running this query. If you run it twice, you append the records twice!

7. **Click the Yes button to run the query.**

   Access adds the records to the table you specified. Now you have the same information in two tables.

8. **Save the query by pressing Ctrl+S if you think you'll use it again; otherwise, close it without saving.**

   Consider changing it back to a select query if you want to save it so that it doesn't get run accidentally.

9. **Check your results.**

   Check the table you appended to as well as the table you appended from to make sure that Access copied all the records you wanted to copy.

Deleting Lots of Records with Delete Queries

A *delete query* deletes whole records from tables, usually based on criteria you provide (although you can also use delete queries to delete all records in a table while keeping the field and table properties intact). Delete queries are dangerous because they permanently delete data from the tables in your database. Obviously, delete queries are powerful and should be treated with respect!

Always make sure that you have a backup before you run a delete query. You may want to back up the whole database or just the tables affected by the delete query.

Because delete queries can wreak such havoc with your database, you may want to consider deleting records manually. You can delete a record by selecting it (click the record selector, which is the gray box to the left of the record) and pressing Delete or by clicking the Delete Record button on the toolbar. You can select a group of records by clicking the first record selector and dragging to the last in the group, or by selecting the first record and then Shift+clicking the last in the group. You can use this procedure in a table or some queries.

Before you run a delete query, you need to be aware of how the table you're deleting data from is related to other tables in the database. In some cases, running a delete query can delete records in related tables. If the table you're deleting data from is on the "one" side of a one-to-many relationship, and cascading deletes are enabled for the relationship, Access looks for related data to delete. The Products table, which holds information for all the sold products, is related to the Order Details table, where ordered items are listed. The relationship is one-to-many, with Products on the "one" side. When you created the relationship between the two tables by using the Edit Relationships dialog box (displayed in the Relationships window), if you selected Enforce Referential Integrity and Cascade Delete Related Records, deleting records from the Products table results in deleting records from the Order Details table. Customers may not get the products they ordered, and no record of their orders for those items will exist in the database. In this case, adding a `Discontinued` field to the Products table may be a better solution than deleting the records! (For more information on one-to-many relationships, see Book I, Chapter 3. For more information on referential integrity, see Book II, Chapter 6.)

When you tell Access to create a delete query, the Sort and Show rows in the QBE grid (the grid in the bottom pane of Design view) are removed, and the Delete row is added. The Delete row has a drop-down menu with two options that you see only with delete queries: Where and From. Use these two options to define the fields you want to see and the fields that you're using to define criteria to select the fields that will be deleted by the query:

✦ **Where:** Tells Access to use the criteria for the field to determine which records to delete.

✦ **From:** Displays the field when you view the datasheet for the query. You can choose the From option only when you use the * choice in the `Field` row to include all fields from a table. The asterisk appears as the first field for each table shown in the top half of Design view; when the asterisk is dragged to the design grid, Access displays all fields from the table in the query datasheet. Viewing all fields from a table in the datasheet gives you a more-complete picture of the data you're deleting; otherwise, all you see in the datasheet are the values from the fields included in the design grid with criteria — rather than the entire record that the delete query will actually delete when you run it.

Follow these steps to create a delete query:

1. **In Design view, create a select query that includes all the tables with records you want to delete.**

See Chapter 1 of this minibook for details on creating a select query. Make sure that you add to the query all tables containing records you want to delete.

2. Drag the * option from each field list in the top half of Design view to the design grid to display all fields from the table(s) containing records you want to delete.

Using the * option allows you to view all fields in the table. When you change the query to a delete query, only the * allows you to display fields that aren't being used for criteria.

3. Add fields that you have criteria for to the design grid and then define those criteria.

4. Click the View button on the toolbar to view the datasheet.

The records you see should be the records that you want the delete query to delete. If you see records that shouldn't be deleted, or if you don't see records that you do want to delete, refine your query definition, and repeat until the query produces the correct records.

5. Change the query type to a delete query by clicking the Delete button in the Query Type group on the Query Tools Design tab of the Ribbon.

When you change the query type from select to delete, Access changes the rows in the design grid. The Sort and Show rows are removed, and the Delete row is added.

6. Choose a value for the Delete row (if it's not set automatically) from the drop-down menu:

a. Set the fields that you want to view to the From option.

b. Set the fields that define criteria to the Where option.

Figure 3-9 shows an example of a delete query that deletes records with the `ProductID` value of `35` from the Order Details and Products tables. Note that when you view the datasheet, you're seeing data from two different tables. All that data will be deleted, so data will be deleted from both tables.

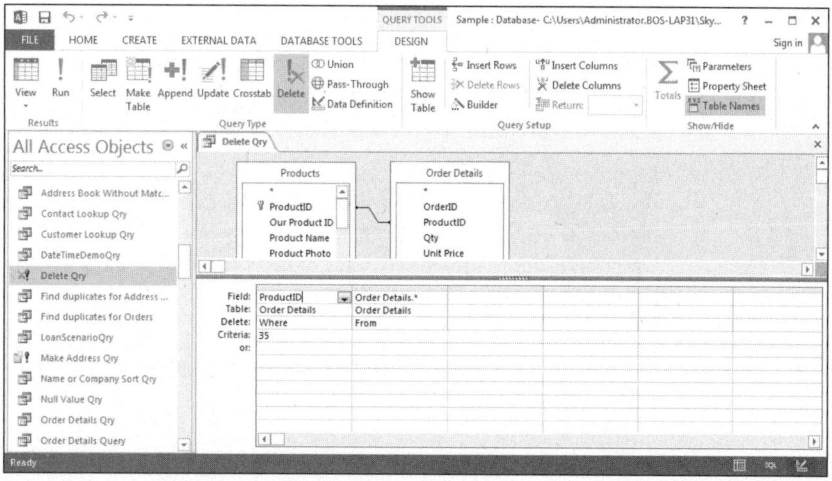

Book III
Chapter 3

Doing Neat Things with Action Queries and Query Wizards

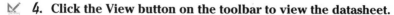

Figure 3-9:
This delete query deletes records with the `Product ID` value `35` from the Order Details and Products tables.

7. **Click the View button to view the datasheet again.**

   Check to make sure that you see only the records that the delete query should delete. If you see data in the datasheet that shouldn't be deleted — or if data that you want to delete is missing — correct the design of the query before you run it.

   A delete query deletes entire records.

8. **Return to Design view by clicking the View button.**

9. **Click the Run button to run the query.**

   Run

   Access deletes the data that you saw in Datasheet view. It's gone for good!

Finding Unmatched Records with a Wizard

Access has two categories of Neat Things You Can Do with Queries: action queries and the two query wizards covered in this section. The Find Unmatched Query Wizard finds records in one table that have no matching records in another, related table. You may store orders in one table and details about customers in another table, for example. If the tables are linked by, say, a `Customer Number` field, the Unmatched Query Wizard can tell you whether you have any customers listed in the Orders table who aren't listed in the Customers table.

Use the Find Unmatched Query Wizard to find unmatched records in the following way:

1. **Click the Query Wizard button in the Queries group on the Create tab of the Ribbon.**

   The New Query dialog box opens.

2. **Select the Find Unmatched Query Wizard option and then click OK.**

   The first window of the wizard appears.

3. **Select the table (or query) that may have unmatched records in a second table and then click Next.**

   If you're looking for customers with no orders, select the table that holds the names of customers in this window. If you're looking for orders for which you don't have the customer address, select the Orders table in this step. The final result of the query lists records from the table that you select in this step that don't have matching records in the table you select in the next step.

   If you want to choose a query, select the Queries or Both radio button.

4. Select the table (or query) that should contain the matching records for the data in the table you selected in Step 3 and then click Next.

If you're looking for customers with no orders, select the table that holds the order information. If you're looking for orders that don't have the customer address, select the table that holds customer addresses when you do this step.

5. Check to make sure that Access correctly guessed the related fields in the two tables you selected in the third window of the wizard (shown in Figure 3-10); if it did, click Next.

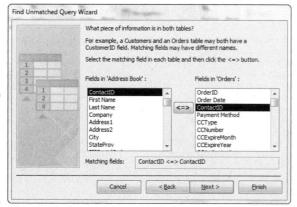

Figure 3-10: Select related fields to find unmatched records.

The window shows field names in the two tables you selected. The names of the related fields probably are highlighted. Click the related field in each table if Access hasn't selected the correct related fields. The two fields that you select should contain the same information and be of the same data type.

6. Select the fields you want to see in the query results in the next window of the wizard and then click Next.

To select all fields, click the double arrow pointing to the right.

7. Accept the name that Access gives the query, or name the query yourself in the final window of the Find Unmatched Query Wizard.

Access is good at naming the results of this query descriptively. Notice whether the name reflects the query you thought you were creating. If not, click the Back button to redefine the query.

8. Choose whether you want to view the results or modify the design and then click Finish.

Access displays the query in Design or Datasheet view, as you requested.

Note that you don't have to use a wizard to create this kind of query. The query shown in Figure 3-11 finds unmatched records in the Address Book table by using an inner join between the tables and the `Is Null` criteria for the related field in the table where matching records are stored. (For more about inner joins, see Chapter 1 of this minibook.)

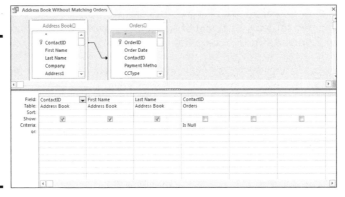

Figure 3-11:
Find unmatched records by using an inner join and the `Is Null` criterion.

If you need to avoid unmatched records, define the relationship between the tables to enforce referential integrity. Define referential integrity to avoid creating orders for customers in the Orders table when you don't have contact information for them in the Address Book table. You may still find the Find Unmatched Query Wizard to be useful, though. You may want to find customers who haven't placed any orders, for example, or products that haven't been ordered. (For more information on referential integrity, see Book II, Chapter 6.)

Finding Duplicate Records

When a table contains hundreds or thousands of records, spotting duplicates isn't always easy, but the Find Duplicates Query Wizard can find them in an instant. Before you use the wizard, though, you need to really think about which combination of fields in a record constitutes a duplicate. In a table of names and addresses, you wouldn't necessarily consider two records with the name `Jones` in the `Last Name` field to be duplicates, because two different people in your table may have the last name `Jones`.

Not even the `First Name` and `Last Name` fields combined necessarily pinpoint duplicate records, because more than one `Joe Jones` or `Sarah Jones` can be in your table. On the other hand, if two or more records in your table contain the same information in the `Last Name`, `First Name`, `Address1`, and `Zip Code` fields, there's a good chance that those records are duplicates. You can use loose criteria to find duplicates, though, because you can decide later whether to delete them. Perhaps looking at repeated addresses is a good start. If you do mass mailings, you may be sending two or more of every item to the customers whose records are duplicated.

Before you go looking for duplicate records, think about which combination of fields in your table will indicate records that are likely duplicates; then use the Find Duplicates Query Wizard to locate those records. Because the Find Duplicate Query Wizard finds only duplicates, you can use your judgment to decide whether to delete records that look like duplicates. Follow these steps to run the wizard:

1. **Click the Query Wizard button in the Queries group on the Create tab of the Ribbon.**

   The New Query dialog box opens.

2. **Select the Find Duplicates Query Wizard option and then click OK.**

   The Find Duplicates Query Wizard starts.

3. **Click the name of the table that you want to search in the first window of the wizard and then click Next.**

   Optionally, you can click the Queries option and choose a query to use as the basis for the search.

4. **Click the > button to copy fields from the Available Fields list to the Duplicate-Value Fields list in the second window of the wizard and then click Next.**

   Be sure to include all fields that contain the data needed to define duplicate records. The query in Figure 3-12, for example, is about to find records that have identical information in the First Name and Address 1 fields.

**Book III
Chapter 3**

Doing Neat Things
with Action Queries
and Query Wizards

Figure 3-12:
Specify
fields to
compare in
the second
window
of the Find
Duplicates
Query
Wizard.

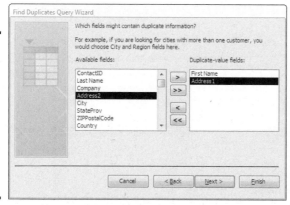

5. **Choose the fields to be shown for additional information in the third window of the wizard and then click Next.**

   The fields you specify aren't used for comparing records, but they appear in the query results to help you better identify any duplicate records. If your table has a primary key and/or `Date Entered` field, both are good candidates for this third field.

6. **Give the query a name.**

   Change the suggested name for the query, if you want, or select the suggested name in the last window of the wizard.

7. **Choose the View the Results option.**

8. **Click the Finish button.**

The results of the query appear in Datasheet view. If no records appear, no records have identical values in the fields you specified in the wizard. You have nothing to worry about.

On the other hand, if records do appear, you know that you have duplicates. In Figure 3-13, for example, two records for Frankly Unctuous appear. Note the identical `First Name`, `Last Name`, and `Address1` fields. The `ContactID` field allows you to see that two records for this customer are indeed in the table.

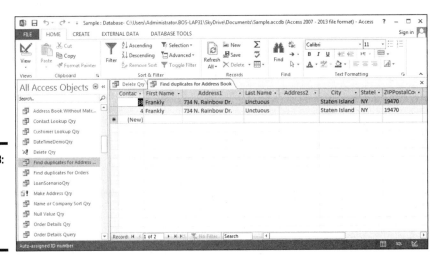

Figure 3-13:
Frankly
Unctuous
has two
records in
the table.

The handy Unique Values and Unique Records properties

Sometimes, rather than finding duplicates and deleting them, you just want to hide them. You may need to see only a list of states that your customers come from; you don't need to see Massachusetts 56 times (if you have 56 customers in Massachusetts).

The property sheet has two properties that allow you to hide duplicate values:

✔ **Unique Values:** Set this property to Yes when you want to see only unique values for the fields displayed in the query. The Unique Values property omits duplicate data for the fields selected in the query. Every row displayed in the query datasheet is different.

✔ **Unique Records:** Set this property to Yes when you want to see only unique records based on all fields in the underlying tables. The Unique Records property affects only fields from more than one table. A record is considered to be unique if a value in at least one field is different from a value in the same field in another record. Note that the primary key fields are included when records are compared.

To display the property sheet, right-click an empty part of the Table pane in Query Design view (the top half of the design grid) and choose the Properties option from the contextual menu, or click the Properties button on the toolbar.

The Unique Values and Unique Records properties apply only to select, append, and make-table queries. Note that when both are set to the No value (which is the default), the query returns all records.

Chapter 4: Viewing Your Data from All Angles Using Crosstabs

In This Chapter

✔ Understanding Crosstab queries

✔ Running the Crosstab Query Wizard

✔ Creating Crosstab queries in Design view

Sometimes, instead of viewing your data in records, you want to see it organized and categorized. (What a concept.) You may want to see sales of each product by month, and you may want to see that information in a compact table, with months as the column titles, product names as the row titles, and the sum of sales in the body of the table. Access creates that kind of table with a Crosstab query. Crosstab queries organize data and create totals by using the aggregate function of your choice, Sum, Avg (average), and Count being the most popular. You create Crosstab queries in Design view.

Aggregating Data in a Crosstab Query

A *Crosstab query* is a specialized query for summarizing data. Instead of creating a table with rows showing record data and columns showing fields, you can choose a field and group its data by using two other fields as row and column labels. Access groups the data the way you tell it and aggregates the grouped field in the body of the table. You can choose among the usual aggregate functions, such as Sum, Avg, Min (minimum), Max (maximum), and Count.

It's far easier to show you than to explain. Figure 4-1 uses the ProductName field for the row labels, the Order Date Month field for the column labels, and the field that contains the sales subtotal for the product (price × quantity) as the information to put in the body of the table, and tells Access to sum the result. The resulting Crosstab query is shown in Figure 4-1, with sales of each product displayed by quarter. (You can choose the time period, too.) The result is a compact, spreadsheetlike presentation of your data.

ProductID	Total Of ExtPrice	Qtr 1	Qtr 2	Qtr 3
Golden Whistle	2100	700	1300	100
Kozmik Video Camera	4000	3000		1000
Budget MP3 Player	110	80	20	10
Old Time Stock Ticker	2000	1000	500	500
Lawn Flamingo	390	240	30	120
Scanner cable	40	40		
Microwave Blow Dryer	260	130	130	
Magic Inkwell	45	30	15	
Lucky Rabbits Foot	112	96	8	8
50-pk Floppy Disks	1120	1080	40	
WayCool Scanner	630	450	90	90
Nuclear Pencil Sharper	1440	1260		180
Big Subwoofer	90	60	30	

Product Sales_Crosstab

Record: 1 of 16 — No Filter — Search

Figure 4-1:
This
Crosstab
query
shows sales
by product
and quarter.

If you want to aggregate data without using a Crosstab query, see Chapter 2 of this minibook, as well as the forms and reports chapters in Books IV and V.

Using the Crosstab Query Wizard

The Crosstab Query Wizard provides an automated way to create a Crosstab query. The wizard works only with one table or query. If the fields you want to use in the Crosstab query aren't in one table, you have to create a query that combines those fields before you use the Crosstab Query Wizard. Although the wizard gives you the option of aggregating date data (taking a Date/Time field and combining the data into months), you don't have to write an expression to aggregate data yourself. The Orders table, for example, saves the time and day when an order is submitted. The Crosstab Query Wizard takes that date field and converts it to just the month (or year, quarter, or day). For the option to aggregate data by date (such as day, month, quarter, year), you must use the date field as a column heading.

Start the Crosstab Query Wizard by following these steps:

1. **Click the Query Wizard button in the Queries group on the Create tab of the Ribbon.**

   The New Query dialog box opens.

2. **Select the Crosstab Query Wizard option and then click OK.**

   Access starts the Crosstab Query Wizard, shown in Figure 4-2.

3. **Select the table or query that contains all the fields you need for your Crosstab query and then click Next.**

   If you create a query to hold the fields you need, select the Queries or Both radio button to see the query name.

   All your fields for the Crosstab query must be in a single table or query.

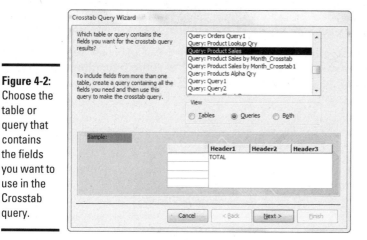

Figure 4-2:
Choose the table or query that contains the fields you want to use in the Crosstab query.

4. **In the new window that appears, shown in Figure 4-3, select the field(s) whose values you want to use as row headings and then click Next.**

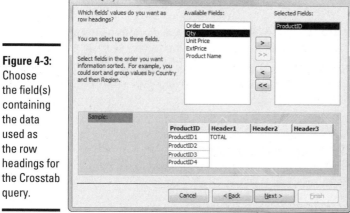

Figure 4-3:
Choose the field(s) containing the data used as the row headings for the Crosstab query.

You can select up to three fields to fine-tune the breakdown of your data. As you select fields, the sample at the bottom changes to reflect how your finished query will look.

Generally, the fields you select as row and column headings contain repeated data that is grouped in the Crosstab query. The ProductID field, for example, comes from the Order Details table and identifies products in each order. The Crosstab query can show you how many times a product is ordered or how many units of each product are sold.

If you want the option of grouping date values, don't pick a Date/Time field here; use it for column headings instead.

5. **In the new window that appears, shown in Figure 4-4, select the field(s) whose values you want to use as column headings and then click Next.**

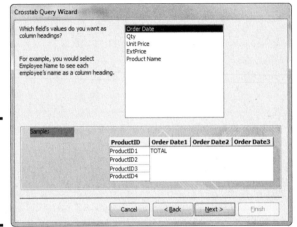

Figure 4-4:
Choose the field(s) you want to use as column headings.

You can select only one field to use as the column headings. You may want to use a field containing dates and tell Access to group date values.

6. **If you select a date field as the column headings, you see the window shown in Figure 4-5; choose how to group dates and then click Next.**

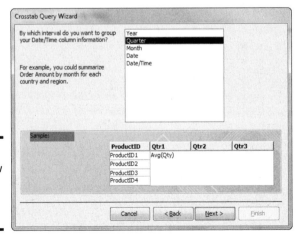

Figure 4-5:
Choose how to group date and time data.

Choose one of the options listed. The Date/Time option shows data by unique date and time. Data isn't grouped at all when you pick this option unless you have data with exactly the same time and date.

7. **In the new window that appears, shown in Figure 4-6, choose the field whose values you want to see grouped by the row and column headings that you selected.**

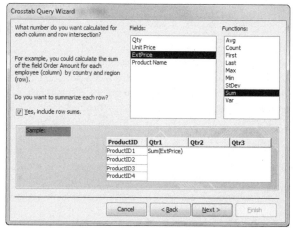

The field you select usually contains numerical data that can be aggregated in some way (added, averaged, and so on). An exception occurs if you want to count instances; in that case, the field doesn't need to contain numbers.

Figure 4-6 uses the `ExtPrice` field, which is price × quantity — the dollar amount of sales for each product.

8. **Select a grouping method in the Functions list.**

You can find out more about these functions in Chapter 2 of this minibook. You can easily change this function in Design view if you change your mind after you view the Crosstab query.

9. **Choose whether to include row sums by selecting the check box on the same page as the function choices and then click Next.**

If you choose to include row sums, Access creates an extra column that contains the sum of the row — in this example, the total sales for the product.

10. **Name the query (or use the name that Access suggests), choose how you want to view the query (viewing the query datasheet or viewing the query in Design view), and then click Finish to see the Crosstab query.**

Figure 4-7 shows how the sample Crosstab query turned out.

Figure 4-7:
This
Crosstab
query
shows sales
of each
product by
quarter.

ProductID	Total Of ExtPrice	Qtr 1	Qtr 2	Qtr 3
Golden Whistle	2100	700	1300	100
Kozmik Video Camera	4000	3000		1000
Budget MP3 Player	110	80	20	10
Old Time Stock Ticker	2000	1000	500	500
Lawn Flamingo	390	240	30	120
Scanner cable	40	40		
Microwave Blow Dryer	260	130	130	
Magic Inkwell	45	30	15	
Lucky Rabbits Foot	112	96	8	8
50-pk Floppy Disks	1120	1080	40	
WayCool Scanner	630	450	90	90
Nuclear Pencil Sharper	1440	1260		180
Big Subwoofer	90	60	30	

Record: 1 of 16   No Filter   Search

TIP

Look at the results of the Crosstab Query Wizard in Design view to get ideas about how to create a Crosstab query from scratch. You can get your Crosstab query started with the Crosstab Query Wizard and then put the finishing touches on the query in Design view, which is covered in the next section.

You can format your crosstab query data in Design view by right-clicking the column that defines the value in the table, choosing Properties from the contextual menu, and changing the format on the property sheet.

Creating a Crosstab Query in Design View

A simple Crosstab query has three fields:

✦ One used for row headings (Date, for example).

✦ One used for column headings (Product, for example).

✦ The Value field, which contains the data that you want to appear in the cells of the table (such as an item subtotal). Tell Access how to summarize your data in the Crosstab query by choosing Sum, Avg, Min, Max, Count, StDev, Var, First, or Last.

TIP

You also have the option of using an expression for any fields in the Crosstab query design. See Chapter 2 of this minibook for more information on creating a field with an expression.

Follow these steps to create a simple Crosstab query:

1. Create a new select query in Design view with the tables or queries that contain the fields you want to use in the Crosstab query.

Chapter 1 of this minibook covers creating select queries.

2. **Change the query to a Crosstab query by clicking the Crosstab button in the Query Type group on the Design tab of the Ribbon.**

Access displays a Crosstab row in the design grid (the grid in the bottom half of the Design window). You use the Crosstab row to tell Access how to build the Crosstab query. Access also displays the Total row in the design grid, which allows you to choose one of the aggregate functions or the Group By option.

In the next steps, you double-click fields in the Table pane of Design view to move them to the design grid and then make choices from the Crosstab row's drop-down menu to specify the way each field is used to create the crosstab.

3. **Double-click the field you want to use for row labels in the Table pane in the top half of Design view.**

When you double-click the field name, Access moves it to the design grid.

4. **Click the Crosstab row, click the down arrow, and choose Row Heading from the drop-down menu.**

5. **Set the Total row to the Group By option for this column in the grid.**

6. **Double-click the field you want to use for column labels in the Table pane.**

Access places the field in the design grid.

7. **Click the Crosstab row for the new field, click the down arrow, and choose Column Heading from the drop-down menu.**

8. **Set the Total row to the Group By option for this column in the grid.**

Click the Total row to display the arrow for the drop-down menu. (Chances are that you won't have to make this change.)

9. **In the Table pane, double-click the field containing the values that you want to aggregate in your Crosstab query to put that field in the grid.**

This field — the `Value` field — provides the values that fill the Crosstab query.

10. **Click the Crosstab row for the new field in the grid, click the down arrow, and choose the Value option from the drop-down menu.**

11. **Choose the option to summarize the data from the drop-down menu in the Total row of the `Value` field's column.**

Sum and average are common, but one of the other options may be the one you need. See Chapter 2 of this minibook for more information on aggregate options.

Figure 4-8 shows Design view for a Crosstab query that creates a query similar to the one created by the Crosstab Query Wizard in the preceding section.

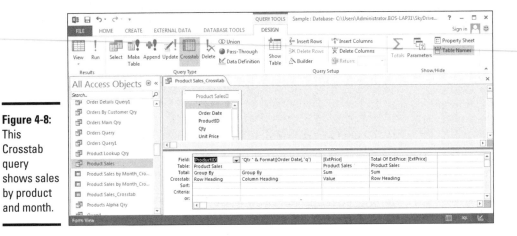

Figure 4-8:
This
Crosstab
query
shows sales
by product
and month.

12. **Click the View button to view your new Crosstab query.**

You may want to edit your query design or make some of the modifications described in the next section.

Modifying a Crosstab Query

After you figure out the basics of creating a Crosstab query — choosing fields for the row headings, column headings, and the `Value` field, and then specifying how the data is aggregated — you may want to do any of the following to add more to the query design.

Using criteria

You can include criteria to narrow the data aggregated in a Crosstab query. You add criteria in the design grid to the fields used for row headings and column headings, but not to the field used for values. If you want to specify a criterion for the value field, you can put the field in the query a second time, set its Total row to the Group By option, leave the Crosstab row option blank, and define the criteria. Using the same method, you can add any field to the design grid and define criteria; just leave the Crosstab row blank.

Using multiple fields for row headings

You can use more than one field for row headings. The resulting Crosstab query groups rows by using both fields. Figure 4-9 shows hours grouped by company and project.

Figure 4-9:
This Crosstab query uses two fields, `Company` and `Project Description`, to categorize hours worked.

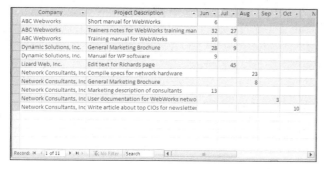

To use multiple fields to group data by row, specify more than one field as a row heading in the design grid. Access figures out the order in which to use the fields. The field on the "one" side of a one-to-many relationship displays first. Figure 4-10 shows the design grid for the same query.

Figure 4-10:
Specifying two fields as row labels to group hours worked.

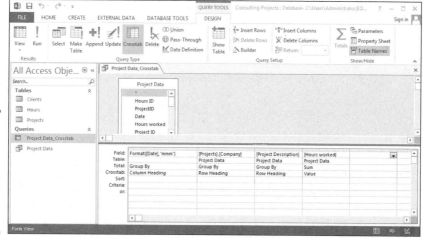

Adding aggregate columns

An *aggregate* column is an additional column in the query that totals rows displayed in the query. You may add a column that calculated the total number of the product sold to a query that displays sales by month and product.

You can add aggregate columns to a Crosstab query. These columns are added as row headings and appear by default as the first columns after the actual row headings. If you include row sums in a Crosstab query, a calculated column is automatically created as a row heading that uses the Sum option in the Total row. You may want to calculate other values by using other aggregate functions.

Getting data in order

By default, Access sorts column and row headings in alphabetical or numerical order, but you can fix your Crosstab query to appear in any specified order in one of two ways:

✦ **Move columns manually in Datasheet view.**

  a. *Click the column heading to select the column.*

  b. *Drag the column heading to its new position.*

✦ **Specify the sort order in the property sheet for the query.**

  a. *Click anywhere in the column in Design view, which contains the column heading.*

  b. *Display the property sheet by clicking the Property Sheet button on the Design tab of the Ribbon.*

Property Sheet

  c. *Type the headings in order in the* Column Headings *property, using quotes around the headings and separating headings with commas, as shown in Figure 4-11.*

  Be sure to use the data as it appears on the datasheet.

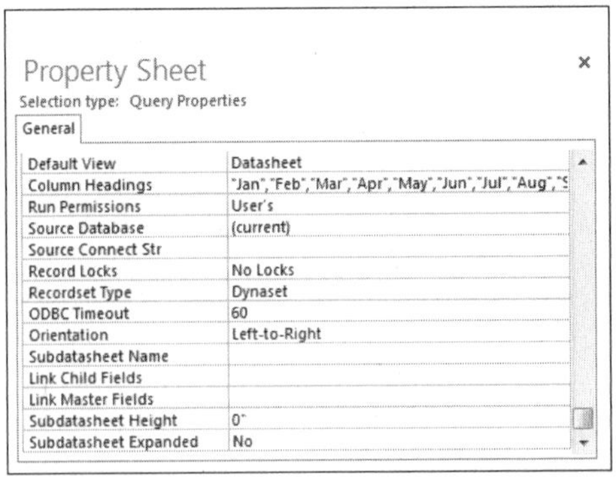

Figure 4-11: Use the Column Headings property to list column headings in order.

Property Sheet	
Selection type: Query Properties	
General	
Default View	Datasheet
Column Headings	"Jan","Feb","Mar","Apr","May","Jun","Jul","Aug","S
Run Permissions	User's
Source Database	(current)
Source Connect Str	
Record Locks	No Locks
Recordset Type	Dynaset
ODBC Timeout	60
Orientation	Left-to-Right
Subdatasheet Name	
Link Child Fields	
Link Master Fields	
Subdatasheet Height	0"
Subdatasheet Expanded	No

Book IV

Forms for Editing Data

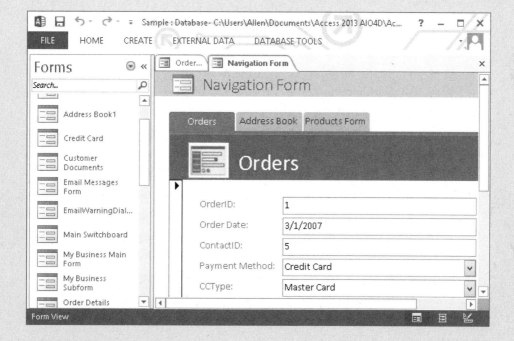

See how to efficiently create new forms at www.dummies.com/extras/access2013aio.

Contents at a Glance

Chapter 1: Designing Custom Forms (and Reports) 289

Seeing How Forms and Reports Are Secretly Related 290
Understanding Form Basics 290
Making and Using a Form 293
Creating Forms with Wizards..296
Modifying Existing Forms and Reports..300
Getting Your Fields Lined Up in Layout View 301
Configuring the Whole Form or Report 305
Storing Your Forms and Reports...310

Chapter 2: Jazzing Up Your Forms (and Reports) 313

Creating New Forms Efficiently...313
Making All Kinds of Changes in Design View 314
Taking Control of Your Form or Report 317
Making Controls That Display Text, Numbers, and Dates 323
Breaking Out of the Control Layout 326
Renaming, Resizing, Deleting, and Copying Controls 330
Formatting Numbers and Dates..330
Choosing Fonts, Colors, and Other Decorative Touches 331
Creating Check Boxes for Yes/No Fields 335
Adding Lines, Boxes, and Backgrounds..335
Controlling Cursor Movement in Your Form 336

Chapter 3: Creating Smarter Forms 339

Creating and Configuring Combo and List Boxes...............................339
Designing Cool Looks for Yes/No Fields 345
Creating Option Groups..345
Creating Command Buttons 348
Making a Find Box 354
Displaying Attachments..355
Adding Form Headers and Footers 357
Creating Tabbed Forms 358
You Can't Type That Here! 360
Making a Main Menu for Your Database..361

Chapter 4: Doing Calculations in Forms and Subforms
(and Reports) 365

Doing Elementary Calculations...365
Calculating and Formatting Numbers 369
Calculating and Formatting Dates 370
Calculating and Formatting Text 370
Displaying Values That Depend on Conditions 371
Formatting Calculated Controls..371
Using a Split Form to Display a Datasheet 372
Using a Subform to Display Detail Records...373
Adding Subtotals and Totals from Subforms......................................379

Chapter 1: Designing Custom Forms (and Reports)

In This Chapter

✔ Understanding and using forms

✔ Creating a form with a wizard (the easy way)

✔ Using your new form to enter and edit records

✔ Creating or modifying a form in Layout view

✔ Changing the properties of a form

✔ Saving, copying, printing, importing, and renaming your forms

A lthough datasheets are convenient for looking at, entering, and edit-ing the information in tables and queries, there's a lot to dislike about them as well. Datasheets show records one per row, and if your table or query has a lot of fields, you need to scroll left and right to see all the fields. Also, datasheets rarely look anything like the paper forms that your informa-tion may be coming from. Finally, datasheets display information from only one table or query at a time, even though when you enter or edit data, you may need to make changes in related tables at the same time.

Forms to the rescue! When you design your own forms to display infor-mation onscreen, you choose where fields appear, what explanatory text appears, and what lines and boxes to add. Your forms can include calcula-tions, such as the total number of items that a customer is ordering. You can also include *subforms,* which are small forms that display information (usually, more than one record's worth) from a related table or query. You can also make forms that contain buttons that run programs (Visual Basic for Applications [VBA] modules), open other forms, print reports, or exit Access — your own Mission Control.

After you design a form (a first draft, anyway), you can save the form design as part of your database and use it any time to view the table or query with which the form is associated. You can always change the design of a form later; no one makes a perfect form the first time.

This chapter describes how to make simple forms (by using a wizard or by creating them from scratch) and how to rearrange the fields on a form in Layout view.

Chapter 2 of this minibook explains how to modify the design of a form after you create it in Design view. Chapters 3 and 4 of this minibook cover fancier forms, including forms with calculations, totals, and subforms.

Seeing How Forms and Reports Are Secretly Related

This chapter describes how to make and edit forms, but it secretly also describes how to make and edit reports. Forms and reports are very similar. You create them with many of the same commands, tools, and properties to make stuff look good onscreen and on paper. How you use forms and reports, however, is different. Forms are for interacting with data onscreen, whereas reports are for printing data on paper.

 This chapter describes how to create a form, but creating a report works the same way. To make a report, skim the instructions in this chapter and then skip to Book V, which is about the aspects of reports that differ from forms, such as how they print.

Understanding Form Basics

A form doesn't store any data: It displays data from a table or query, called its *record source.* When you create a form, you tell Access what the record source will be for the form.

The things that appear on a form or report are called *controls,* and they include text boxes that display data from the database; text labels that explain how to use the form; buttons you can click to save, navigate, or perform other operations; and check boxes. Chapter 2 of this minibook explains the available controls. You don't have to know much about controls when you get started making and using forms and reports, because Access can make entire forms and reports, including their controls, for you.

Many controls display the data from fields in the record source. Your form or report doesn't have to include all the fields in the record source. You can omit irrelevant fields that the user never needs to know about, such as the AutoNumber ID field. Also, the fields on a form don't need to appear in the same order in which they occur in the table or query.

Usually, a form displays the fields from a single record — either one record in a table or one record from a query result datasheet. You can also make a *continuous form,* which displays several records one below another. You can even make a *split form,* which is a single record form with a datasheet below it. When you click a record in the datasheet, that record is displayed in the single-record form. In this section, we show you how to make all these types of forms. (Book V describes how to make and print various types of reports.)

Access provides several ways to create forms. The method you use depends on whether you want Access to do the work, whether you want complete control of what you see, or whether you want some combination of laziness and control.

Take a look at the Forms group on the Create tab of the Ribbon to see the ways that you can create forms. Table 1-1 explains what each button does.

Table 1-1		Creating Forms with the Forms Group Buttons	
Button	*Name*	*What It Does*	*Where to Find More Info*
Form	Form button	Creates a quick and easy form for the table, query, or report you have open or selected. You enter information in this kind of form one record at a time.	"Making the easiest possible form with the Form button," later in this chapter
Form Design	Form Design button	Allows you to design your own form from scratch, in Design view	Chapter 2 of this minibook
Blank Form	Blank Form button	Allows you to design your own form from scratch, in Layout view	"Making a new form from scratch in Layout view," later in this chapter
Form Wizard	Form Wizard button	Walks you through the creation of a form, helping you choose fields from multiple tables and queries and to add summary calculations. The results are bland and standard, but you can use Design or Layout view later to make changes.	"Wizard, make me a form!" later in this chapter

(continued)

Table 1-1 *(continued)*

Button	Name	What It Does	Where to Find More Info
Navigation ▾	Navigation button	Creates switch-boardlike forms with buttons that display any form or report you want.	Chapter 3 of this minibook
More Forms ▾	More Forms button; then choose Multiple Items	Creates a datasheet-like columnar form.	"More super-speedy forms," later in this chapter
More Forms ▾	More Forms button; then choose Datasheet	Creates a form designed to be viewed in Datasheet view rather than Form view.	"More super-speedy forms," later in this chapter
More Forms ▾	More Forms button; then choose Split Form	Creates a form that includes a regular form at the top and a datasheet below it.	"More super-speedy forms," later in this chapter
More Forms ▾	More Forms button; then choose Modal Dialog	Creates a form that keeps the focus. You must close this form to return where you came from. The form is often confused with a dialog box.	"More super-speedy forms," later in this chapter

Whoa! Wait a minute. The Forms group used to have two additional buttons: PivotChart and PivotTable. What happened to them? As it turns out, those two form types were very rarely used. With Access 2013, Microsoft has addressed one of the major criticisms of its products: Each succeeding version of a product contains more and more functions, which are often hard to learn, take up space in memory and on disk, and slow load times. To move away from the unglamorous description of its products as bloatware, Microsoft decided to trim unnecessary features in a bid to improve performance. You see other examples of this slimming-down process here and there throughout the book as we discuss the various parts of Access 2013.

Making and Using a Form

The easiest way to create a form is to let Access create it for you. (Why work when a program can do the work instead?) In this section, we show you how to make a form so that you can see how it looks in Layout view, how to save it, and how to display a record in a form.

Before you can create a form, of course, you must have a database open that contains at least one table. To illustrate the making and using of a form, we use the database described in Book II.

Making the easiest possible form with the Form button

Follow these steps to make and save a new form:

1. **In the Navigation Pane, select the table or query that contains the records that you want to view or edit in the form.**

    If you want to work with the records in your Address Book table, for example, select it in the list of tables in the Navigation Pane.

2. **Click the Form button in the Forms group on the Create tab of the Ribbon.**

    You don't have a lot of options — none, actually — but you get a usable form with no waiting. You see a form that displays all the fields in one record of your table or query, as shown in Figure 1-1. Access gives the form the same name as the table or query that you selected in Step 1 (unless you already have a form with that name).

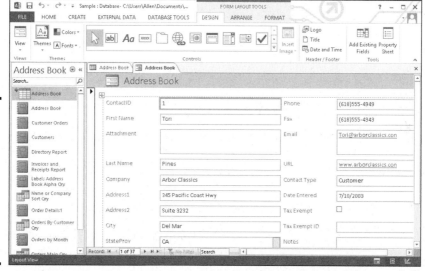

Figure 1-1:
Access whips up a form that displays one record at a time and shows the form in Layout view.

Access displays your new form in Layout view — a view that allows you to move the fields and labels around if you don't like where Access put them.

3. **Make whatever changes you see fit.**

We describe how to use Layout view in "Getting Your Fields Lined Up in Layout View," later in this chapter.

4. **Save the form that so you can use it later by right-clicking the object tab for the form and choosing Save from the contextual menu.**

In Figure 1-1, you would right-click the AddressBook tab.

5. **When Access asks for a name for the form, accept its suggestion or type a different name; then click OK.**

That's it — you're done. You can close the form by clicking the X button at the right end of the form's object tab or by right-clicking the object tab for the form and choosing Close from the contextual menu.

Viewing a form

After you create a form, you can open it in any of these views:

✦ **Layout view** displays the form with some sample data, ready for you to move the form elements into a more pleasing arrangement. You usually use this view right after you create a form, to fix layout problems. You can find out how to use Layout view in "Getting Your Fields Lined Up in Layout View," later in this chapter.

✦ **Design view** displays the form elements with no data so that you can customize the form layout and behavior. You usually use this view after Layout view, when the form elements are in the right places, to tweak your design. See Chapter 2 of this minibook for details on using Design view.

✦ **Form view** displays the form as you (or the Form Wizard or AutoForm) designed it, as described in the next section. When you finish creating and customizing your form, you'll use this view on an ongoing basis to maintain the data in your database.

✦ **Datasheet view** displays the fields on the form as a datasheet and ignores the layout of the form. Most forms have Datasheet view disabled. See "Using some other cool form properties," later in this chapter, for details on enabling Datasheet view.

To open a form in Form view, just double-click it in the Navigation Pane, where it appears in the Forms section. To open a form in any view, right-click the form name in the Forms section of the Navigation Pane and choose the view you want from the contextual menu. (If the Navigation Pane has no Forms section, right-click the Navigation Pane's heading and choose

Category⇨Object Type from the contextual menu.) Now you see the objects in the database, sorted by object type, such as Tables, Queries, Forms, and Reports.

When the form is open, you can switch views by clicking the View button in the Views group on the Home tab of the Ribbon. The View button changes depending on which view you're in. When you're in Layout view, the default View button is Form view, and when you're in Form view, the default is Layout view. To get into Design view with the View button, click the bottom part of the button and choose Design View from the drop-down menu.

You can also switch among views by right-clicking the object tab or title of the form and choosing the view you want from the contextual menu.

The View button provides possible views depending on what type of object you're working on. The views available for tables and queries can be different from those for forms.

Editing data in Form view

After you design and create your form, you can enter, edit, and display records. To open a form in Form view, double-click its name in the Forms section of the Navigation Pane. The Contacts form in Form view looks very much like Figure 1-1, earlier in this chapter, except that now you can edit and add data.

The form itself doesn't store data. The data that a form displays comes from tables in the database (the record source), and any changes you make are stored in the tables. When you add a record via a form, Access stores the record in the table(s). If your form displays information from a query, the changes are stored in the tables that provide the records for the query. If your form has subforms, as described in Chapter 4 of this minibook, you can edit records from several tables at the same time.

In general, you use all the same keystrokes that you use when editing records in Datasheet view, as described in Book II, Chapter 1. You can press Tab or Enter to move from one field to another. You can also click the navigation buttons at the bottom of the form to move to different records. A Search box at the bottom of the form allows you to search for the text in whatever field your cursor is in.

If you prefer to use the keyboard to move around a form, check out Table 1-2 for a list of keys to use.

Table 1-2	Using the Keyboard to Move in a Form
To Move Here in a Form . . .	*Press This Key or Key Combination*
Following field	Tab, Enter, or →
Previous field	Shift+Tab or ←
First field of current record	Home
Last field of current record	End
Subform	Ctrl+Tab
Main form	Ctrl+Shift+Tab
New record	Ctrl++ (plus sign)

You can cut and paste, search, and filter your records just as though you were working in Datasheet view, as described in Book II, Chapter 3. To select an entire record, click the record selector (the vertical strip at the left edge of the window). You can cut and paste a record from another table into your form as long as the field names match. For all the fields with matching names, Access pastes the data into the correct field on the form.

Access saves the current record when you move on to another record. You can also save what you've typed so far by pressing Ctrl+S or by clicking the File button on the Ribbon and choosing Save. Even easier, just click the Save button on the Quick Access toolbar; the button looks like a vintage floppy disk.

Creating Forms with Wizards

The Form button made you a form, but it may not be the kind of form you want. You have lots of ways to arrange fields on a form, and the form that Access made may not be what you had in mind. Before you give up and make a form from scratch in Design or Layout view, give the Form Wizard and the More Forms button a try.

Wizard, make me a form!

The Form Wizard lets you choose which fields to include and the order in which the fields are placed. This wizard is especially useful if you want to create a form that includes data from more than one table or query. The wizard can create subforms for you and even apply formatting to make the form look a little less vanilla. The Form Wizard can be a great way to get started with a complex form; you may not like the exact appearance of the finished form, but it works and has all the fields you want. When the wizard finishes, you can make all the changes you want in Layout or Design view.

Follow these steps to create a form with the Form Wizard:

Form Wizard

1. **In the Navigation Pane, click the Form Wizard button in the Forms group on the Create tab of the Ribbon.**

   You see the Form Wizard dialog box, which looks like Figure 1-2.

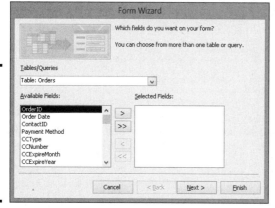

Figure 1-2: The Form Wizard steps you through the process of creating a new form.

2. **From the Tables/Queries drop-down menu, choose the first table or query for which you want to include fields.**

   Choose the table or query from which the form gets the data to display or edit.

3. **In the Available Fields list, select the fields that you want to appear on the form, and move them to the Selected Fields list by double-clicking them or by selecting them and then clicking the right-arrow button (>).**

   The order doesn't matter. If you decide that you don't want a field after all, double-click it in the Selected Fields list — or select the field and click the left-arrow button (<) — to move it back to the Available Fields list.

4. **Repeat Steps 2 and 3 to choose fields from other tables or queries.**

   The additional tables or queries have to be related to the first table or queries. Otherwise, Access asks you to use the Relationships window to create relationships, and you have to start the wizard over. See Book II, Chapter 6 for information on creating relationships between tables.

5. **When all the fields that you want to display in the form appear in the Selected Fields list, click the Next button.**

   The next Form Wizard window appears.

   If you selected fields from only one table or query, skip to Step 9. Otherwise, the Form Wizard asks how you want to view your data, as shown in Figure 1-3.

**Book IV
Chapter 1**

**Designing Custom
Forms (and Reports)**

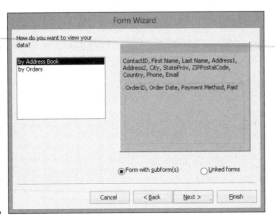

Figure 1-3:
The Form
Wizard can
create a
form with a
subform for
information
from a
related table
or query.

6. **Choose an organization scheme for your form by clicking the table or query by which you want to group records.**

   In Figure 1-3, the form includes fields from the Customers table (which contains a record for each customer) and the Orders table (with one record for each order) from a business database. Do you want the form to display one customer, with all the orders for that customer, or do you want to display one order, with all its customers? (The second option makes no sense, because each order is placed by only one customer.) You decide by clicking an option in the list on the left side of the window.

7. **Choose whether to include the second table or query as a subform or as a second form.**

   If you choose the Form with Subforms option, you end up with one form, with the records from the second table or query in a box (subform) on the form. If you choose the Linked Forms option, you get two separate forms, each in its own window, with a button on the first form that displays the second form. When in doubt, try subforms. (See Chapter 4 of this minibook for details on how subforms work.)

8. **Click Next.**

   Access displays a window that asks you to choose the layout for the subform, if you're creating one; otherwise, skip to Step 10.

9. **Choose the layout, and click Next.**

   You can click a layout option to see what it looks like. If you're not sure which option to use, stick with the Tabular layout; using and editing the layout is easy.

10. **Give the form a name, and if you created a subform or second form, give it a name too.**

    This name is what Access uses when saving the form. The name doesn't have to appear on the form.

11. **Choose whether to open the form now (in Form view) or to make changes in the form design (in Design view).**

Why not open it first, to see how it looks? You can always edit the design later.

12. **Click Finish to create the form.**

13. **When you finish admiring your new form, close it by clicking the Close button.**

A form made by the Form Wizard is rarely totally usable right off the bat, but it's a good start. For information on changing its design, see Chapter 2 of this minibook.

More super-speedy forms

One of a few other predefined form choices may give you just what you want, or maybe not — but you get a usable form with no waiting. Try this:

1. **In either the Tables section or the Queries section of the Navigation Pane, select the table or query you want to use as the source of the records displayed on the form.**

📠 More Forms ▾　***2.*** **Click the More Forms button in the Forms section on the Create tab of the Ribbon.**

You see these options:

* **Multiple Items:** You get a form that displays more than one record. (It's called a *continuous form,* as described in "Choosing one record or many," later in this chapter.) The fields are arranged in a column, like a datasheet, as shown in Figure 1-4. Unless your table or query includes only a few fields, the form is likely to be way too wide to be useful.

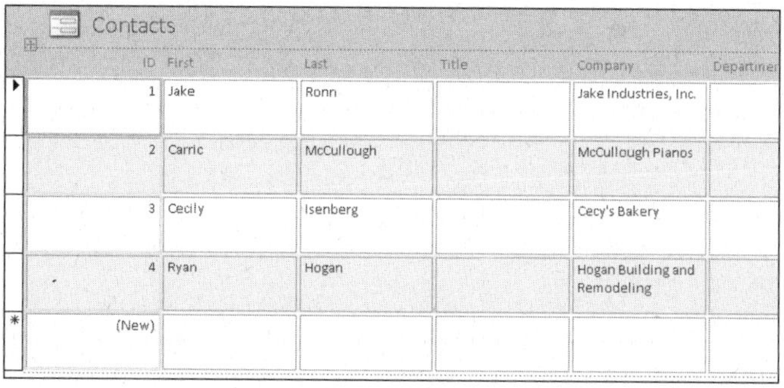

Figure 1-4: Choosing Multiple Items creates a form that looks like a dressed-up datasheet. You can customize the field sizes later.

	ID	First	Last	Title	Company	Departmer
▸	1	Jake	Ronn		Jake Industries, Inc.	
	2	Carrie	McCullough		McCullough Pianos	
	3	Cecily	Isenberg		Cecy's Bakery	
	4	Ryan	Hogan		Hogan Building and Remodeling	
*	(New)					

Contacts

- **Datasheet:** Access creates a form to be viewed in Datasheet view. You can view it only in Design view (to choose which fields to include, as described in Chapter 2 of this minibook) or Datasheet view (to add and edit records).

- **Split Form:** A *split form* displays some information in a regular form and some in Datasheet view, as shown in Figure 1-5.

- **Modal Dialog:** Access creates a blank form for you that's configured to look like a dialog box, containing an OK button and not much else. This type of form is useful when you want a form that the user must deal with before proceeding to other work.

3. **Select a More Forms option.**

   Voilà — you have a form! Exactly what you see depends on which option you choose.

4. **If you like the form, save it when you close it; if you don't like it, just close it and decline to save it when Access asks.**

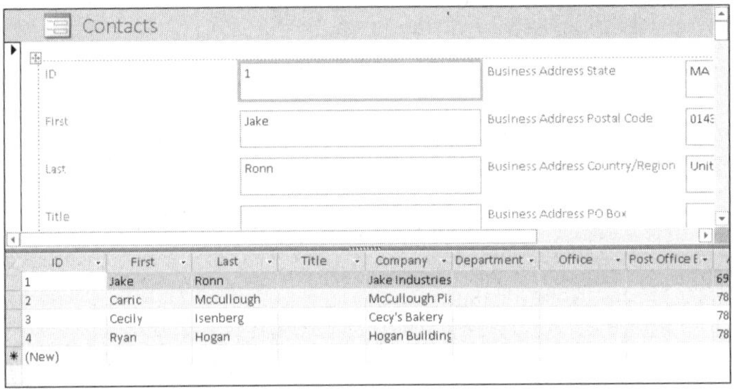

Figure 1-5:
In a split form, you can select a record from the datasheet at the bottom, and the data is displayed in the form at the top.

Modifying Existing Forms and Reports

Neither the Form Wizard nor the More Forms button creates perfect forms. These computer-generated forms are good places to start, but you usually want to make further refinements before a form is really usable.

Two views are useful for this purpose: Layout and Design. You can use these views to create new forms from scratch, too.

Layout view, which was new in Access 2007, shows you your form with data in it but allows you to make some changes in the form itself. The form looks almost exactly as it will look in Form view, with the addition of some lines and icons you can use to make changes. In Layout view, you can mess with your controls (text boxes, check boxes, labels, and so on), including moving them around, resizing them, and adding and removing field controls. Layout view makes it easy to arrange your controls tastefully because it provides a layout (hence, the name) with rows and columns so that your controls line up nicely.

Layout view is limited, however. If you want to make other changes, such as adding validation rules to fields, you need to use *Design view.* Design view doesn't look much like your form; no data appears, but you can see the controls on your form and configure the properties of each one.

In either Layout or Design view, you can display the *property sheet,* which shows the properties of the entire form, sections of the form, or individual controls. Both views also work with the *field list,* which lists the fields in the record source.

Read on to try rearranging your fields in Layout view. Chapter 2 of this mini-book explains making all kinds of changes in Design view, setting the properties of controls and forms with the property sheet, and adding controls by dragging fields from the field list.

Getting Your Fields Lined Up in Layout View

Layout view enables you to impose a *control layout* on your form, which restricts where controls can appear on the form. When form controls are in a control layout, it's easy to get them to line up neatly, because Access does the work for you.

Access provides two control layouts:

✦ **Stacked:** The label for the control is to the left of the control, as shown in Figure 1-1, earlier in this chapter. This control layout is useful for single-record forms.

✦ **Tabular:** The label for the control is at the top of a column of controls, as shown in Figure 1-4, earlier in this chapter. This control layout is useful for continuous forms, which can display the data from multiple records in columns.

The Tabular control layout is useful only for continuous forms, which are described in "Choosing one record or many," later in this chapter.

A form can have one or more control layouts, each occupying a rectangular part of the form, and each with rows and columns containing controls that display labels, fields, and other things. Each control layout appears in Layout view as a dotted rectangle. In Figure 1-1, earlier in this chapter, a control layout encloses a column of controls and their labels. Your form may have a second control layout to the right of the first one if it has a second column of controls. Control layouts are invisible in Form view; you, the form designer, can see them in Layout and Design view.

If you can't see Layout view — if it just doesn't appear as an option in your menus and buttons — it may be disabled for this database. Click the File tab of the Ribbon, choose Options to see the Access Options dialog box, and click Current Database to see the options for this database. Make sure that the Enable Layout View check box is selected.

Using a control layout to rearrange fields

Suppose that you followed the steps in "Making the easiest possible form with the Form button," earlier in this chapter, to create the form shown in Figure 1-1, but you don't like the arrangement of fields on the form. Well, we have good news for you: You can use Layout view to make some changes.

To open a form in Layout view, right-click the form name in the Navigation Pane and choose Layout View from the contextual menu. The form appears, as shown in Figure 1-1, with the controls (text boxes and check boxes) and labels (the names to the left of each control) lined up neatly in a grid. The arrangement looks very much like a table in a word-processing document or spreadsheet. Faint dotted lines separate the rows and columns in the grid. When your form is in Layout view, three tabs of the Ribbon contain useful buttons: Design, Arrange, and Format.

You can move a field to another spot on the form by clicking and dragging its control. Access forces the field into a row and column in the control layout; if there isn't space for the field, Access inserts a row to make space. The control's label may not come along with it, so you may need to drag it to the spot to the left of the relocated field.

Adding and deleting fields

The easiest way to add fields to an existing form is to use the field list. Display the field list by clicking the Add Existing Fields button in the Tools group on the Design tab of the Ribbon. Click the plus sign to the left of the table that contains the fields you want to display on the form, so that you see the field names. Then drag the field name from the field list to where you want it on the form. (Another way is to click the buttons in the Controls group on the Design tab of the Ribbon. We describe this method in Chapter 2 of this minibook.)

You can get rid of a field that you don't want to appear on the form. (Removing the field from the form doesn't delete it from the table where it's stored; Access just doesn't display the field on this form.) Right-click the field control and choose Delete from the contextual menu. You may need to delete the label or explanatory text about the field in the same way.

Making a new form from scratch in Layout view

You can add a control for a field that doesn't appear on your form. In fact, you may want to create a new form by starting with a blank form in Layout view and then adding the fields you want. Here's how:

1. Click the Blank Form button in the Forms group on the Create tab of the Ribbon.

Access creates a new form (tentatively named something like Form1) and displays it in Layout view. It also displays a Field List pane to the right of the form, as shown in Figure 1-6. (Click the Shutter Bar Open/Close button in the top-right corner of the Navigation Pane to shrink this list out of your way.)

Figure 1-6: You can create a form from scratch in Layout view by dragging the fields from the field list to the form.

2. In the Field List pane, click the plus sign to the left of the table that contains the fields you want to display on the form.

You see the list of fields in that table. (If you want the form to display fields from the results of a query, skip to "Seeing where records come from," later in this chapter, for details on changing the record source for the form.)

3. Drag each field that you want to appear on the form from the Field List pane to the form.

Access creates a control (usually, a text box) and a label (text to the left of the text box) for the field.

4. Keep adding fields, rearranging them as needed.

5. Close the form.

6. **Click Yes when Access asks whether you want to save it.**

7. **Type a name for the form, and click OK.**

Don't worry if you can't get your form to look right in Layout view. Design view, which we describe in Chapter 2 of this minibook, gives you much finer control of your form. Layout view is great for getting the overall arrangement right, but you can't use it for everything.

Adding and deleting rows and columns in the control layout

You can open some rows and columns in the control layout in Layout view to make space for your new controls. Here's how:

1. **Click a control on your form that you want to change.**

2. **Click one of these buttons in the Rows & Columns group on the Arrange tab of the Ribbon:**

   - *Insert Above:* Adds a row above the control

   - *Insert Below:* Adds a row below the control

   - *Insert Left:* Adds a column to the control's left

   - *Insert Right:* Adds a column to the control's right

3. **Drag fields into the blank rows and columns in the control layout.**

If you end up with an empty row or column in your control layout, you can get rid of it. Right-click the empty row or column and choose Delete Row or Delete Column from the contextual menu.

Controlling your control layouts

What if you *don't* want your controls to line up neatly in rows and columns? You may want the text boxes for the City, State, and Zip Code fields to appear right next to one another, the way they look on an addressed envelope. You need to remove the control layout that forces these text box controls into line.

To see exactly what's in a control layout, click somewhere in the control layout and then click the Select Layout button in the Rows & Columns group on the Arrange tab of the Ribbon. Orange lines appear around the control layout, separating its rows and columns. Here are some things to do with your control layout:

✦ **Change the spacing between the rows and columns.** You can adjust the padding (space) by selecting the control layout and then clicking the

Control Padding button in the Position group on the Arrange tab of the Ribbon.

✦ **Move the control layout.** When you select a control layout, a little four-arrows icon appears in its top-left corner. You can drag this icon around to move the entire control layout, including the controls that it contains.

✦ **Remove the control layout.** To remove a control layout so that the fields, labels, and other controls in that area of the form can roam free instead of being constrained into rows and columns, select the control layout, right-click it, and choose Layout/Remove Layout from the contextual menu. The orange lines are still there, but when you click somewhere in that area to deselect it, the dotted lines that represented the control layout are gone.

If you have some controls that aren't in a control layout but you wish that they were so that they'd line up, you can put them into a control layout like this:

1. **Select all the controls that you want to enclose in the layout.**

Select the first control and hold down the Shift key while clicking each of the other controls.

2. **Click the Stacked or Tabular button in the Table group on the Arrange tab of the Ribbon.**

Access moves all the controls into neat rows and columns, and you see the control-layout dotted line around them all.

Trying out your new, improved form

After you make some changes in your form, switch to Form view to see how it works. To do so, right-click the object tab (the tab with the form's name at the top of the form) and choose Form View from the contextual menu, or click the View button in the Views group on the Design tab of the Ribbon. You can switch back and forth between Layout and Form view, making changes until you like the result.

From time to time (maybe each time you sit back to admire your work), save your form by right-clicking the object tab and choosing Save from the contextual menu or by pressing Ctrl+S.

Configuring the Whole Form or Report

Some properties apply to an entire form, such as what records appear in the form or report, how many records appear at the same time, and what scroll bars and buttons appear around the edges. You can view and edit the properties of any object in Access by using the property sheet. This section explains how to set these form and report properties, and why you'd want to.

Reports have additional properties and sections, which are described in Book V, Chapter 1.

Follow these steps to display the properties that apply to the whole form or report:

1. **Open the form (or report) in Layout or Design view.**

2. **If the property sheet isn't already open, open it.**

Property Sheet

To do so, click the Property Sheet button in the Tools group on the Design tab of the Ribbon, or right-click anywhere in the form and choose Form Properties from the contextual menu.

You see the properties of whatever object is selected: the entire form, a section of the form, or an individual control. Figure 1-7 shows what a property sheet looks like when the entire form is selected.

Figure 1-7:
A property sheet can show the properties of an entire form or report (as shown here), a section of a form or report, or a single control.

Property Sheet	✕
Selection type: Form	
Form	⌄
Format	Data	Event	Other	All
Caption	
Default View	Single Form
Allow Form View	Yes
Allow Datasheet View	No
Allow Layout View	Yes
Picture Type	Embedded
Picture	(none)
Picture Tiling	No
Picture Alignment	Center
Picture Size Mode	Clip
Width	6.1694"
Auto Center	No
Auto Resize	Yes
Fit to Screen	Yes
Border Style	Sizable
Record Selectors	Yes

3. **To see the properties for the entire form or report, make sure that the Selection Type drop-down menu at the top of the property sheet is set to Form.**

If you're looking at Design view, you can click the small box in the top-left corner of the form, where the two rulers intersect.

The property sheet lists the properties in several categories (Format, Data, Event, and Other), each on its own tab, or you can click the All tab to see all the properties.

In addition to showing you the form properties, the property sheet enables you to change their settings. The next few sections of this chapter describe properties that you may want to change.

If the properties in the property sheet look strange, you're probably looking at the properties for part of the form or maybe just one control on the form. The property sheet displays the properties of whatever part of the form is selected. To see the properties of the entire form, set the Selection Type drop-down menu to Form. Chapter 2 of this minibook describes setting properties for individual controls.

Naming the form

Every form has a name, and that name usually appears on the object tab for the form when the form is open. You can provide a different name to appear on the object tab, however. This feature is useful when your form name isn't very user-friendly. To change the caption — the name on the tab — change the `Caption` property, which is on the Format tab of the property sheet. When the `Caption` property is blank, Access uses the form name, but you can type something else.

Seeing where records come from

When you created your form or report, you (or an Access wizard) chose the record source — the table or query that provides the records to display. You rarely want to change the record source; if you want to use different data, you may as well start with a new form or report.

To see or change the record source, follow these steps:

1. **Open the form or report in Layout or Design view.**

2. **Display the property sheet with the properties for the forms.**

3. **Click the Data or All tab of the property sheet.**

Whichever tab you click, the first property listed is `Record Source`, which shows the name of the table or query from which the form or report displays records.

4. **To change the record source, click the down arrow at the right end of the `Record Source` property and choose a different table or query from the drop-down menu.**

5. **If the form or report is based on a query, and you want to modify that query, click the Expression Builder button — the ellipsis (...) button to the right of the `Record Source` property.**

See Book III for details on how queries work.

If you're going to change the record source, do it *before* you spend a lot of time working on the design of the form. Having the correct record source makes creating and editing your form or report much easier, because Access already knows what fields may appear on it.

If you use the new Application Part feature to create a blank form, as described in the nearby sidebar, you need to set the `Record Source` property before you can add field controls to the form.

Deciding the order of the records

You can also control the order in which records appear. You may want to browse through an Address Book table by last name or by city, for example, or through an Orders table by date. Normally, Access displays the records in the same order as they appear in the record source. If the record source is a table, records appear in primary key order from that table. If the record source is a query, records are in the sort order specified in the query.

You can change the order of the records by changing the `Order By` property of the form or report, which appears on the Data tab of the property sheet for the form. Type the field name for the `Order By` property. If you want the records to appear in reverse order, type a space and **DESC** after the field name (for descending order).

Choosing one record or many

You usually want your form to show only one record at a time, like a paper form. Most forms display one record at a time. The Address Book form in Figure 1-1, earlier in this chapter, displays one record from an Address Book table. Sometimes, though, you want to see more than one record at a time, as in the form shown in Figure 1-8. (Reports use a different system to determine whether one or many records appear in the report, as described in Book V, Chapter 1.)

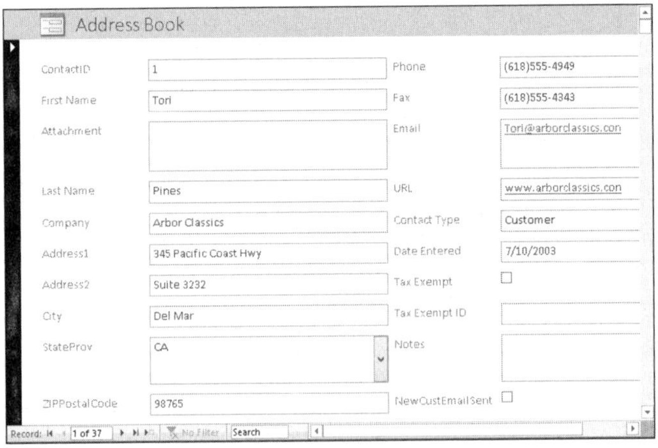

Figure 1-8:
A continuous form displays many records, one below another.

	Address Book			
ContactID	1	Phone	(618)555-4949	
First Name	Tori	Fax	(618)555-4343	
Attachment		Email	Tori@arborclassics.com	
Last Name	Pines	URL	www.arborclassics.com	
Company	Arbor Classics	Contact Type	Customer	
Address1	345 Pacific Coast Hwy	Date Entered	7/10/2003	
Address2	Suite 3232	Tax Exempt	☐	
City	Del Mar	Tax Exempt ID		
StateProv	CA	Notes		
ZPPostalCode	98765	NewCustEmailSent	☐	

Record: 1 of 37 ▶ ▶ No Filter Search

Application Parts forms

A new Access feature called Application Parts enables you to add preformatted (or even preprogrammed) objects to your database. To add a form from the library of Application Parts, click the Application Parts button in the Templates group on the Create tab of the Ribbon. You see a menu of precooked parts, starting with some blank forms:

When you click a blank form, Access adds a copy of the form to your database.

When you open the new form in Layout or Design view, the first thing you need to do is to set its Record Source property, as described in "Seeing where records come from." Then you can drag fields to the form in Layout view and fine-tune the design in Design view.

To display more than one record at a time, change the form's Default View property. (It's on the Format tab of the property sheet for the form.) To display one record at a time, set this property to Single Form; to display multiple records, change the property to Continuous Forms.

Continuous forms are useful when what you want is a glorified datasheet with more than one row of fields for each record, more control of the layout of the fields, or other form features that aren't available for datasheets.

Using some other cool form properties

A few other useful form properties appear on the property sheet for the form. Here's what they do:

✦ **Datasheet view:** You can enable Datasheet view so that you can view the same set of fields that are on the form, but in a datasheet. Set the Allow Datasheet View property to Yes on the Format tab of the property sheet.

✦ **Read-only forms:** You can make the information in a form *read-only* — that is, not editable (look, but don't touch!) — by setting the Allow

`Edits` property, which appears on the Data tab. This property is normally set to `Yes`, but you can change it to `No`. You can prevent the addition of new records by setting the `Allow Additions` property to `No`, and you can prevent deletions by setting the `Allow Deletions` property to `No`.

✦ **Record selectors:** A gray box — the record selector — appears to the right of the information for one record. When you're editing records in your form, you can delete or copy a record by clicking its record selector and pressing the Delete key or Ctrl+C.

For a form that displays a single record rather than a continuous form with lots of records, the record selector may not get much use, though, and you may not want to display it. You can control whether the record selectors appear on the form by setting the form's `Record Selectors` property, which appears on the Format tab.

✦ **Scroll bars and navigation buttons:** Normally, forms include horizontal and vertical scroll bars if the entire form is too large to fit in the window. You also see navigation buttons that take you to the first, previous, next, and last records. You can turn the scroll bars and navigation buttons on and off by setting the `Scroll Bars` and `Navigation Buttons` properties, both of which appear on the Format tab.

Applying a theme to a form or report

Access comes with some predesigned themes, which set a color scheme and font choices. When you apply a theme to a form or report, Access sets the colors and fonts for the whole form (or for most of the controls on the form).

To apply a theme in Layout view, click the Themes button in the Themes group on the Design tab of the Ribbon, and choose a theme. As you hover your mouse over a choice, Access changes the open form to use that theme, even before you make your choice. (Try before you buy!) Alternatively, you can apply just the color scheme to your form by clicking Fonts in the Themes group on the Design tab of the Ribbon.

Storing Your Forms and Reports

You spend oodles of time and energy getting your form or report looking just right. You don't want to lose all that hard work, do you? Save your form or report by pressing Ctrl+S or by right-clicking the form's object tab and choosing Save from the contextual menu. If Access displays the Save As dialog box (as it does if you haven't given this form or report a name yet), type a name. This name usually appears in the title bar of the form, although you can change this setting.

When you finish designing your form or report, close it by clicking its Close button (the X in the top-right corner). If you haven't saved it, Access asks whether you want to do so.

You can display the form or report at any time; click its name in the Forms or Reports list in the Navigation Pane. If you want to change the design some more, right-click the name and choose Layout View from the contextual menu.

Managing forms and reports

You can rename, delete, and copy forms and reports from the Navigation Pane, too. To rename one, click its name, press F2, edit the name in the little box that appears, and press Enter. To delete it, select the name, and press the Delete key. To make a copy of the form or report design, click its name, press Ctrl+C, press Ctrl+V, and type a name for the new form or report.

Importing forms and reports from other databases

What if you create a terrific form or report in one database and want to use the same one in another database? You can import a form or report from another Access database by following these steps:

Access

1. **Click the Access button in the Import & Link group on the External Data tab of the Ribbon.**

   You see the Get External Data – Access Database dialog box, shown in Figure 1-9.

2. **Browse for or type the filename of the Access database.**

3. **Select the radio button labeled Import Tables, Queries, Forms, Reports, Macros, and Modules into the Current Database.**

4. **Click OK.**

   You see the Import Objects dialog box, shown in Figure 1-10.

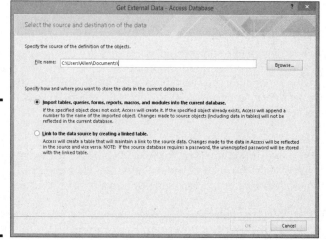

Figure 1-9:
You can import a form or report from another Access database.

Figure 1-10:
The Import
Objects
dialog box.

5. **Click the Forms tab or the Reports tab, depending on what you want to import.**

6. **Choose the form(s) or report(s) you want to import.**

   You can select a group of items by clicking the first one and Shift+clicking the last. You can add a form or report to the ones you've already selected by Ctrl+clicking it.

7. **Click OK.**

   Access copies the forms or reports from the other database into the current database. If you already have an object of the same type with the same name, Access adds 1 to the end of the name.

Printing forms

Forms aren't designed to be printed — reports are the Access objects that give you the most printing and formatting options — but you can print them anyway. Don't just click the File tab on the Ribbon and choose Print when you're using a form in Form view, however. If you do, Access prints the form for every single record in the table or query, not just the record you're viewing!

One method of printing the form for just the current record is to apply a filter to select only the current record and then click the Print button. Be sure to remove the filter before trying to move to any other records.

Book II, Chapter 3 explains how to create, apply, and remove a filter. Chapter 3 of this minibook describes how to create a command button on your form that prints just the current record.

Chapter 2: Jazzing Up Your Forms (and Reports)

In This Chapter

✓ Creating new controls on your form or report

✓ Adding controls to display text, numbers, dates, and Yes/No fields

✓ Arranging and formatting the controls on your form

✓ Spiffing up your form with lines and boxes

✓ Controlling how the cursor moves from field to field when you use the form

Chapter 1 of this minibook explains how to make a form or report by using either a wizard or your bare hands. It also describes using Layout view to rearrange the fields on a form. In this chapter, you find out how to use Design view to create and configure *controls* — the objects on the form or report that actually display information. You use controls to add lines, boxes, and pictures to forms, too. You use Design view to fool around with your form or report and make it as clear and easy to use as possible.

The information in most of this chapter works for creating and editing reports, too. Just substitute the word *report* for *form,* and give it a try!

Creating New Forms Efficiently

Here's how we usually make a new form:

1. **Create the form by using a wizard, adding an Application Part, or making a blank form.**

Decide among these options based on what you want your form to look like. You may want to run a few wizards and add a few Application Parts forms to see whether any of them looks like a good starting point for the form you want to create. You can always close the wizards without saving if they aren't useful. These methods of creating a form are described in Chapter 1 of this minibook.

2. **Open the form in Layout view, and drag the fields around where you want them.**

See Chapter 1 of this minibook for instructions.

3. **Open the form in Design view by right-clicking its name in the Navigation Pane and choosing Design View from the contextual menu.**

   See Chapter 1 of this minibook for details on opening forms from the Navigation Pane. If your form is already open in Layout view, click the bottom of the View button in the View group on the Design or Home tab of the Ribbon and then choose Design View from the drop-down menu. You see your form in Design view, as described in the next section.

4. **Make a change (add a control, change an existing control, turn the background purple, or whatever).**

   Read on to find out how to make all kinds of specific changes.

5. **To see how your form looks with the change, switch to Form view by clicking the View button in the View group on the Design or Home tab of the Ribbon.**

   View

   When either the Home tab or the Design tab is selected on the Ribbon, the View button shows a tiny form; it defaults to Form view. Clicking the View button when it's in tiny-form-mode tells Access to display your form in Form view — including a record from the table or query that the form is based on — so you can see whether you made the form better or worse. (See Chapter 1 of this minibook for the views available for forms.)

   For reports, you often want to preview what the report will look like when it's printed. See Book V, Chapter 2 for details on previewing and printing reports.

6. **Switch back to Design view by clicking the bottom part of the View button and choosing Design View from the drop-down menu.**

   When you're in Form view, the View button defaults to Layout view, so you need to specifically choose Design view.

7. **Repeat Steps 4–6 until your form is gorgeous and works perfectly.**

   Be smart: Press Ctrl+S every few minutes to save your work, even before you're completely finished.

8. **Close the form's window.**

   It doesn't matter whether you're in Design view, Layout view, Form view, or Print Preview.

9. **If you haven't saved the form recently, click the Yes button when Access asks whether you want to do so now.**

Making All Kinds of Changes in Design View

If you're a glutton for punishment, you can create a form in Design view by clicking the Form Design button in the Forms group on the Create tab of the Ribbon. We find it a lot easier to create a form as described in the preceding section, however; we reserve Design view for improving the appearance and behavior of an existing form.

Changing the layout of an existing form or report

To change the layout of an existing form or report, open it in Design view by right-clicking its name in the Navigation Pane and choosing Design View from the contextual menu. Your form looks like Figure 2-1.

Design view shows the controls that make up your form or report and enables you to create, move, and delete the controls. You can also set the properties of your controls to change the way they look and act.

We can hear you asking, "What's a control?" A *control* is an object on a form or report that displays some information. Some controls display text, whereas others display check boxes, command buttons, drop-down menus, or pictures. You choose what information appears on your form by making controls to display that information. The most popular controls of all time are a text box (to show text, usually from a field in your table), a label (to show explanatory text), a combo box (to show a drop-down menu), and a command button (to run a little program, such as a macro or a Visual Basic for Applications [VBA] module). For information about other types of controls, see "Understanding types of form controls," later in this chapter.

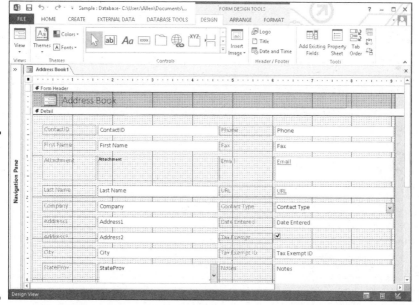

Figure 2-1:
In Design view, you can configure the controls individually, including text boxes and labels.

Other things that you may see in Design view include the following:

✦ **Grid:** Access displays a grid of lines and dots in the background of the Design View window to help you align objects neatly, as well as rulers at the top and left sides of the window. Figure 2-1, earlier in this chapter, shows the grid.

✦ **Design tab:** The Controls group on the Design tab of the Ribbon (viewable when a form is open in Design or Layout view) contains a button for each type of control you may want to create, as well as buttons for creating a header or footer for your form.

✦ **Format tab:** This Ribbon tab offers buttons for formatting text and numbers, setting a background image, and doing other kinds of formatting.

✦ **Field List pane:** This pane lists the fields in the table or query on which this form is based, as shown in Figure 2-2. It also lists fields in other tables that are related to the table or query on which the form is based. You use the Field List pane when creating a new control to display a field from your table or query or from one of the other tables. Display the Field List pane by clicking the Add Existing Fields button in the Tools group on the Design tab of the Ribbon.

✦ **Property sheet:** The property sheet (refer to Chapter 1 of this minibook) displays the properties of the selected object, which can be the whole form, a section of the form, or an individual control. Tabs display the different types of properties. The properties listed depend on the type of object that you select. Click the All tab to see all the properties of the selected item in one long list.

Field List ✕

☐ Show only fields in the current record source

Fields available for this view:

⊟ Address Book   Edit Table
    ContactID
    First Name
    ⊟ Attachment
        Attachment.FileData
        Attachment.FileName
        Attachment.FileType
    Last Name

Fields available in related tables:

⊞ Orders   Edit Table
⊞ StateLookup   Edit Table

Fields available in other tables:

⊞ MSysACEs   Edit Table
⊞ MSysComplexColumns   Edit Table
⊞ MSysDataCollection   Edit Table
⊞ MSysIMEXColumns   Edit Table
⊞ MSysIMEXSpecs   Edit Table
⊞ MSysObjects   Edit Table
⊞ MSysQueries   Edit Table

Figure 2-2:
The Field List pane appears to the right of the Design view of a form.

Property Sheet

Display the property sheet by clicking the Property Sheet button in the Tools group on the Design tab of the Ribbon. To change which control's properties display, choose another control name from the Selection Type drop-down menu at the top of the property sheet or just click a control in Design view.

When you're in Layout or Design view, you can display the properties of a control on your form by double-clicking the control.

Changing the size of a form

If you use tabbed documents (described in Book I, Chapter 2), when you open a form in Form view, the form uses the entire space in the Access window except for the space that the Navigation Pane takes up. With tabbed documents, the size of a form is defined as the size of the Access window. If the form is smaller, the right and bottom parts of the form appear to be blank in Form view, and if the form is larger, scroll bars appear so that you can scroll to see the rest of the form. Overlapping Windows is the default setting, so to display tabbed documents instead, you must click the File tab of the Ribbon, select Options in the list on the left edge of the window, and then select Tabbed Documents in the dialog box that appears.

In Design view, you can set the size of the form by dragging the bottom edge of the grid up or down or by dragging the right edge of the grid left or right.

Taking Control of Your Form or Report

The heart of form design is the *controls* — the objects that appear on forms and reports. Controls on forms include boxes that display text and numeric data from fields, check boxes for Yes/No fields, drop-down menus for lookup fields, buttons that you click to run a macro or VBA procedure, and other stuff you're used to seeing on computer screens. (For reports, all controls just sit there on the paper.)

To display or edit a field, you have to create a *bound control* — a control that's connected to a field in your table or query — so that Access knows what information to display in the control. You can also display *unbound controls,* which contain information that's not stored in your table or query, such as the form's title or explanatory text.

Designing a form or report, or changing the design of an existing one, consists mainly of adding controls where you want them to appear, getting rid of controls you don't like, and moving or configuring existing controls.

Understanding types of form controls

Table 2-1 lists the types of controls that can appear on forms and reports when the report is open in Design view, along with the buttons that create each type of control. The buttons are in the Controls group on the Design tab of the Ribbon. As with any button, hover the mouse pointer over a button to see the button's name. If your Access window isn't wide enough to display all the buttons, you see a single Controls button (refer to Figure 2-1, earlier in this chapter) that you click to see all the control buttons in a bunch, as shown in Figure 2-3.

TIP

Form and report design tips

Keep the following design tips in mind so that you can create perfect (or at least tasteful) forms:

✔ **Make sure that the Snap to Grid feature is turned on.** This feature tells Access to make all the edges of your controls line up with the grid that appears in Design view, which makes your form or report look neater. To turn this feature on, open the report in Design view, click the Size/Space button in the Sizing & Ordering group on the Arrange tab of the Ribbon, and see whether the Snap to Grid button appears to be selected in the Control Layout group. If its icon doesn't have an orange box around it, it's not selected, and the feature is turned off. Click Snap to Grid to turn the feature on.

✔ **Before you make any big changes to your form or report, save it (by clicking Save on the File tab of the Ribbon or pressing Ctrl+S).** If you want to be double-sure, click Save As on the File tab of the Ribbon to save it with a different name (such as Members Test), and fool around with the big change you're planning to make on the copy. Either way, if you don't like the results, close the modified version without saving it.

✔ **If you make a change and are instantly sorry, press Ctrl+Z or click Undo (the button with the curvy backward arrow) on the Quick Access toolbar to reverse your change.** Whew!

TECHNICAL STUFF

If you used an earlier version of Access, this menu of buttons is what the Toolbox window turned into.

Figure 2-3:
If your Ribbon isn't long enough (and whose is?), click the Controls button on the Design tab to see the buttons for creating controls.

Table 2-1	Types of Controls on Forms	
Control Button	*Control Type*	*Description*
ab|	Text box	Contents of a field.
Aa	Label	Text, not editable. Hyperlinks are special types of labels (see "Adding hyperlink controls," later in this chapter).
xxxx	Button	Button that performs an action when clicked.
	Tab control	Tab for displaying different controls, like the tabs at the top of many dialog boxes.
	Hyperlink	Clickable link to a web page or other object.
	Web browser control	Web browser window displaying the web page you specify in the properties of the control.
	Navigation	Tab for displaying forms or reports from your database (see Chapter 3 of this minibook).
XYZ	Option group	Group of option (radio) buttons, check boxes, or toggle buttons.
	Insert page break	Division between one form page and the next.
	Combo box	Drop-down menu that allows you to choose an option or type a new one.
/	Line	Straight line, for visual effect.
	Toggle button	Button that's either on (pressed) or off (not pressed).
	List box	Drop-down menu from which you can choose an option; you can't type a new value.
	Rectangle	Rectangle, for visual effect.

(continued)

Table 2-1 (continued)

Control Button	Control Type	Description
✓	Check box	Box that contains or doesn't contain a check mark.
	Unbound object frame	Object Linking and Embedding (OLE) or embedded object (graph, picture, sound file, or video) that isn't stored in a field in a table.
◉	Option button	Option (radio) button that's part of an option group.
	Subform/subreport	Control that adds a subform or subreport to the form,
XYZ	Bound object frame	OLE or embedded object (graph, picture, sound file, or video) that's stored in a field in a table.
	Image	Bitmap picture.

Many of these controls are bound controls, displaying values from a field, such as the text box (for text fields), check box (for Yes/No fields), and attachment (for Attachment fields) controls. Others are unbound controls, like the image (for displaying an icon or picture not stored in a database table), line, or page break. This chapter shows you how to use many of these types of controls.

Making a new control by dragging a field

Making most forms and reports consists mainly of setting up the bound controls to display the fields from the record source. Access makes the job easy with a quick drag-and-drop procedure:

1. **Open your form in Design view.**

2. **Display the field list, if it isn't already displayed, by clicking the Add Existing Fields button in the Tools group on the Design tab of the Ribbon.**

3. **If the fields for the table you've chosen aren't displayed, click the plus sign to the left of the table name to display them.**

   Figure 2-2, earlier in this chapter, shows the field list, with a list of the fields in your table or query. If your form doesn't have a record source, or if the fields look like the wrong ones, see Chapter 1 of this minibook.

4. **To make a control for a field, drag the field from the field list to the form, dropping it where you want the control to appear.**

   Access creates a control (usually, a text box) that's bound to the field you dragged. It also creates a label control containing the name of the field, followed by a colon. The text box (or other control) is where the contents of the field will appear.

Making a new control by choosing a control

The field list helps you create a control for your field, but you don't get to decide what kind of control to make. If you don't like what the field list provides, or if you want to create an unbound control (one that doesn't display a field at all), you have another way to create controls.

To make any kind of control, open your form in Design view and then follow these steps:

1. **Click the button for the type of control you want in the Controls group on the Design tab of the Ribbon.**

   A Controls button has a colored box around it when it's selected.

2. **Click the place on the form where you want the control to appear.**

   Access creates a new control and, for some control types, runs a wizard to help you configure it.

Whether you use the field list or a Controls buttons to create a control, you usually need to configure it by setting its properties on the property sheet, as described in the next section. You can change the text of a label control; change the field that a text box control displays; make text bold, huge, or a different color; and make other changes. The rest of this chapter describes how to configure your controls. You can change the properties of any of the components of the form, from text box properties to the background color of the form itself.

This chapter tells you everything you need to know about making and configuring text boxes, labels, and check boxes, along with drawing lines and boxes on your form. Chapter 3 of this minibook describes how to create and configure more-advanced controls, including combo boxes, list boxes, toggle buttons, option groups (groups of radio buttons), and command buttons.

Setting control properties

After you create a control on a form or report, you can change what information the control displays, how the control looks, and how the control acts by changing its properties. To see or change a control's properties, open the form in Design view, and follow these steps:

Property
Sheet

1. **If the property sheet isn't already visible, display it by clicking the Property Sheet button in the Tools group on the Design tab of the Ribbon.**

You see the property sheet, as shown in Figure 2-4.

Figure 2-4:
The
properties
of a text box
control.

2. **On the form, click the control whose properties you want to change.**

The property sheet shows the properties for that control.

3. **Find and change the appropriate property.**

Finding the property is the hardest part. You can guess which tab it's on, or you can click the All tab and scan the whole list. Wouldn't it be nice if Access listed the properties in alphabetical order to make them easier to find?

Advanced form designers can make macros or VBA modules run when users move the cursor in or out of the controls on the form. To connect a VBA module or macro to a form (or to a control on the form, like a button), you set a property on the Events tab of the property sheet. It's not hard! See Book VI for details on creating macros and connecting them to form events. Book VIII discusses creating VBA modules for forms.

Binding a control to data in the record source

The most important property of most controls is `Control Source`, which tells Access what information to display in the control. The `Control Source` property usually is a field in a table or query that's the record source for the form. If a form's record source is the Customer List table in the database for a business, one text box may have the ID field as its control source; the text box displays the contents of the ID field in the current record of the Customer List table.

A control's name usually is the same as its control source, but not always. You can have a text box named TextBox123 for which the control source is the Selling Price field in the Products table, for example. Giving your controls the same names as the fields that they display is good practice, though, and cuts down on confusion. When you drag a field from the field list to the form, Access usually names the new control after the field that it displays.

Making Controls That Display Text, Numbers, and Dates

Face it: The most important information on most forms and reports is text. Pictures are interesting, but text (including numbers and dates, which can be displayed as text) usually is the heart of the matter. Access has several types of controls that display text on forms and reports, including the following:

✦ **Label controls:** Display fixed text — text that isn't based on the record that you're displaying on the form

✦ **Text box controls:** Display information from fields in the record source of the form, or calculated information

✦ **List box and combo box controls:** Display drop-down menus of values, usually for a field in the record source

This section describes how to create and format labels and text boxes. For a discussion of combo boxes, list boxes, and option buttons (radio buttons), see Chapter 3 of this minibook.

Making and editing labels

Every form has a title on its object tab, which you can set by editing the Caption property of the form (as described in Chapter 1 of this minibook). But you may want some other titles on the form, including explanations of how to use the forms, headings for different sections of the form, and labels that apply to the controls for specific fields. (Labels are unbound fields; they don't take their information from a table.)

For reports, you use labels wherever you want to display text that doesn't come from the record source, such as the report title, the date, instructions, or any other text that's not stored in a table. (For more formatting options that are available for reports, see Book V, Chapter 1.)

To make a label, follow these steps:

1. **Click the Label button in the Controls group on the Design tab of the Ribbon.**

2. **Click the form to create a tiny text box for your label.**

   Don't worry — you can always move and resize it later.

3. **In the property sheet for the Label control, in the space to the right of the `Caption` property, type the text that you want to appear in the label; then press Enter to tell Access that you're done typing.**

   Your form looks something like Figure 2-5. When you place the cursor on the right edge of the box that forms the border of the control, it turns into a double-headed arrow. Hold down the mouse button and drag the right border so that it shows the entire text of the label. If you want more than one line of text to appear in the label box, press Ctrl+Enter to start a new line.

4. **To edit any text that you entered, click the label control once to select it; then click it again or press F2 to edit the text.**

5. **Press Enter when your edits are complete, or press the Esc key to cancel editing.**

To change the font, size, or color of the label, see "Choosing Fonts, Colors, and Other Decorative Touches," later in this chapter.

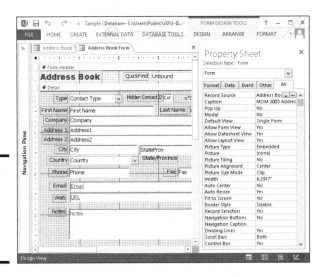

Figure 2-5:
Creating label, text box, and hyperlink controls.

Adding hyperlink controls

You can make a special kind of label that consists of a web address (hyperlink) that you click to display a web page. This kind of label may be nice if you want to provide helpful information about using the form on a website.

Instead of clicking the Label button, click the Hyperlink button in the Controls group on the Design tab of the Ribbon; then click the form in the location where you want to place the Hyperlink control. The Insert Hyperlink dialog box appears, as shown in Figure 2-6. Type the text that you want to appear on your form in the Text to Display box, type the web address in the Address box, and click OK. (You don't have to type the `http://` part; Access adds it for you.) You get a *hyperlink control* — a clickable label that displays the text you specified, as shown in Figure 2-5, earlier in this chapter. In Form view, clicking the label switches to your browser (or runs it, if it's not already running) and displays the web page you specified.

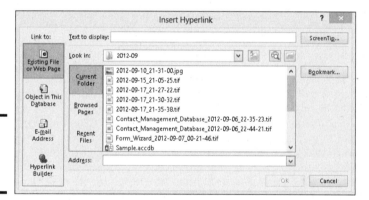

Figure 2-6:
Creating a
hyperlink
control.

You can turn an existing label into a hyperlink label by changing its `Hyperlink Address` property. In the property sheet for the label control, click the Format tab, and type a web address in the Hyperlink Address box.

Putting Short Text and Long Text fields in text boxes

To make a text box for a Short Text or Long Text field, drag the field name from the field list to the place in the form or report where you want the text box to appear. Alternatively, click the Text Box button in the Controls group on the Design tab of the Ribbon, and draw an outline where you want the text box to appear. Access makes a text box the size you indicated, along with a label control displaying the name of the field (refer to Figure 2-5, earlier in this chapter). Yes, you get two controls for the price of one!

You can format the contents of Short Text, Long Text, and Hyperlink fields a bit, mainly by controlling capitalization. Book II, Chapter 1 lets you in on how to display text in uppercase or lowercase, limit what you type to a certain number of characters, and add preset characters to a field (such as dashes or parentheses in phone numbers); you find out what magic characters to type in the Format property of your text box. For other types of formatting, such as fonts and colors, see "Choosing Fonts, Colors, and Other Decorative Touches," later in this chapter. Chapter 3 of this minibook explains ways to make your text boxes smarter, starting with understanding preset default values and validating the information that people type.

Displaying Number, Currency, and Date fields

Number, Currency, and Date fields appear in text boxes, too, just like Short Text and Long Text fields. You create text box controls to display Number, Currency, and Date fields the same way you create them for Text fields, using the field list or button in the Controls group on the Design tab of the Ribbon.

Breaking Out of the Control Layout

In Chapter 1 of this minibook, we talk about using Layout view to arrange your controls. In Layout view, you can use a control layout to move your controls into neat rows and columns. Control layouts, however, insist that your controls appear in rows and columns, which isn't always where you want them. For forms that include fields for an address, for example, we like to use one label (something like City, State Zip) followed by three text boxes for the fields that contain the city, state/province, and zip code or postcode. You may want to tighten the design in lots of little ways, as shown in Figure 2-7. That's not possible in a control layout.

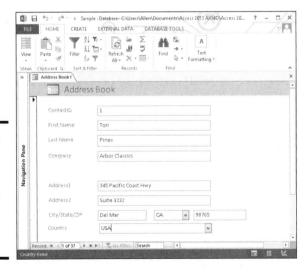

Figure 2-7: What if you don't want your controls to appear in rows and columns?

Removing the control layout

Even in Design view, control layouts restrict the positions of your controls. You can see the outline of a control layout in Design view as a dashed line, as shown in Figure 2-8. You can remove the control layout (without removing the controls *from* the control layout) by clicking within the layout to select it. Next, click the Remove Layout button in the Table group on the Arrange tab in the Form Design Tools area of the Ribbon. The dashed line indicating a control layout disappears.

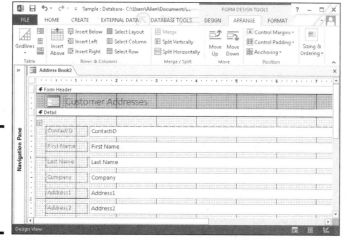

Figure 2-8:
Control layouts work in Design view, too.

Remove the control layout only if you want to move your controls out of a strict row-and-column arrangement. You can leave the control layout in place when you make other kinds of changes, such as changing the color or numeric format of a text box control.

Moving or resizing a control

Now you're ready to move your controls anywhere on the form. First, select the control by clicking it. You can tell when the control is selected, because Access draws an orange box around the control. Little boxes called *handles* appear at the corners and the centers of the sides, as shown in Figure 2-9. You can click and drag the handles to resize the control. You see a gray box at the top-left corner of the control; click and drag this box to move the control. If the control has a label associated with it, a gray box appears in its top-left corner, too, so you can move the label independently of the control.

To move a control, click the control to select it. When your cursor is over the control, it becomes a four-arrow icon; click and drag to move both the control and its associated label, if any. You can click the gray box in the top-left corner to drag just the control. If the control has a label that moves

**Book IV
Chapter 2**

Jazzing Up Your
Forms (and Reports)

along with it (an *associated label*), you can move the label separately by clicking the gray box in *its* top-left corner and dragging it.

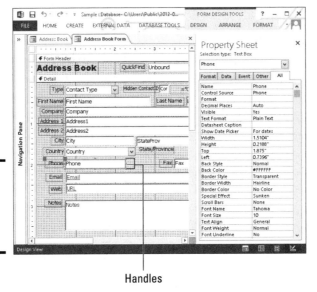

Figure 2-9:
Drag a control's handles to resize it.

Handles

Now that you're free of the tyranny of the control layout, you can move the control anywhere you want. On the other hand, getting the control in exactly the right place can be very tricky. See the next section for help.

You can select the label associated with a control separately from the control itself. To select only the control and not the label, click the gray box in the top-left corner of the control. To select only the label, click the gray box in the label's top-left corner. This method enables you to move the label closer to or farther from its control.

To change the size of a control, drag one of the handles to move that edge of the control. Exactly what happens depends on the control. Some controls, such as option buttons, can't be resized. Labels, text boxes, and many other controls stretch or shrink as you drag their edges.

Neatening your controls

You can spend hours fooling with the formatting of your forms and reports, moving controls around, getting all the labels to match, and choosing fonts and colors. (We certainly have!) One important aspect of design is neatness. Forms are easier to use and reports are easier to read if they look neat and organized. People can find the information they're looking for — or the entries that they need to make — more easily if everything lines up nicely.

Luckily, Access has features that make it easy to line up your controls, so you don't have to squint at the screen and drag each control left or right by microscopic amounts. Instead, you can select a bunch of controls and deal with them all at the same time. To select more than one control, click one control and Shift+click the rest of the controls, or drag your mouse around the group of controls. Access selects all the controls that are within that area, even if only part of a control is in the area.

After you select a bunch of controls, you can do the following things with them:

✦ **Move groups of controls.** If you want to move a bunch of controls together, select them all and then drag them to a new location. Access leaves the spacing among the controls unchanged.

✦ **Make controls the same size.** You can tell Access to make all the selected controls the same height or width. To make the widths of the selected controls the same, click the Size/Space button in the Sizing & Ordering group on the Arrange tab of the Ribbon, and choose To Widest to make all the controls as wide as the widest control you selected or To Narrowest to match the narrowest (left to right). To make the heights of the controls the same, choose To Tallest or To Shortest.

✦ **Line up your controls.** You can adjust the edges of your controls to line up with the gridlines that appear in Design view. With the controls selected, click the Align button in the Sizing & Ordering group on the Arrange tab of the Ribbon, and choose To Grid. Access moves the edge of each control to the nearest gridline.

You can also get Access to move all the selected controls so that they're left-aligned (that is, the left edges line up) or right-aligned. Click the Align button in the Sizing & Ordering group on the Arrange tab of the Ribbon, and choose Left or Right. We like to see labels right-aligned next to text boxes that are left-aligned, but it's a matter of taste!

You can turn on Snap to Grid for the whole form so that when you move or resize controls, Access aligns their sides with the grid. Click the Size/Space button in the Sizing & Ordering group on the Arrange tab of the Ribbon to see whether Snap to Grid is selected (outlined in orange). If it isn't, click it!

✦ **Space controls evenly.** Controls look better if a consistent amount of vertical space appears between one control and the next — one gridline or two gridlines, for example. You don't have to move controls up and down by hand; Access can perform this task for you. Select the controls you want to space, click the Size/Space button in the Sizing & Ordering group on the Arrange tab of the Ribbon, and choose Equal Vertical. You can move all the controls together or apart by choosing Decrease Vertical or Increase Vertical.

Renaming, Resizing, Deleting, and Copying Controls

Here are other things you can do after selecting a control:

+ **Rename a control.** Change the Name property of the control, which appears on the Other tab of the control's property sheet. (The name doesn't affect what data appears in the control. The Control Source property on the Data tab determines that.)

+ **Delete a control.** Press the Del key. (Oops! If you didn't mean to delete it, press Ctrl+Z or click the Undo button in the top-left corner of the page.)

+ **Copy a control.** Press Ctrl+C to copy the control to the Windows clipboard. Press Ctrl+V to paste a copy from the clipboard back into the Design View window. Then drag the copy where you want it to be. Cleverly, if you press Ctrl+V *again* to paste another copy of the control, Access tries to figure out where you want the new one to be based on where you dragged the last copy (a nice feature, we think). After you copy and paste the control, you can modify it as you like.

You can also change the type of a control. If you make a text box and later wish that it were a combo box (see Chapter 3 of this minibook), you don't have to delete the control and start over. Instead, right-click the control, choose Change To from the contextual menu, and choose the new control type.

If you want to change a property for a bunch of controls, you can select all the controls and change the property for the whole group. First, select the group of controls by clicking the first one and then Shift+clicking each of the rest or by drawing a rectangle with your mouse to select all the controls in that rectangle. The message Selection Type: Multiple Selection appears at the top of the property sheet. If you change the settings of any properties, Access changes all the selected controls accordingly. Similarly, you can click buttons on the Formatting toolbar to format all the controls at the same time.

Formatting Numbers and Dates

Numbers and dates appear in text boxes, but Access can display them in a lot of formats. You can set a text box to display a currency sign (such as a dollar sign), control the number of decimal places that appear, and display thousands separators. (In the United States and Canada, we use commas for this purpose.)

For dates in a text box, you can control the order of the month, day, and year; whether to omit the day or year; how many digits to show for the year; and whether to display the name or number of the month.

On the Format tab of the property sheet for the text box, click the down arrow at the right end of the `Format` property, as shown in Figure 2-10. You see a drop-down menu of numeric or date formats. To control the number of decimal places that appear, set the `Decimal Places` property. (The `Auto` setting means that Access decides how many places to display.)

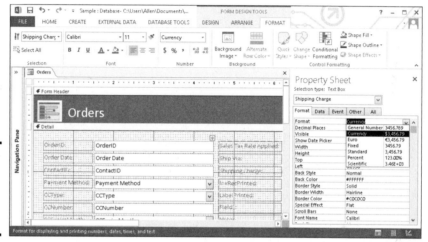

Figure 2-10:
Setting the format for a number in a text box.

For a Date field, you can display a little calendar icon that the user can click to choose a date from a calendar. Set the `Show Date Picker` property to `For dates`.

If you want to make fancier numeric or date formats, see Book II, Chapter 1. Forms and reports can include calculated numbers and dates, too. An order form can display the sales tax based on the total amount of the order, for example. See Chapter 4 of this minibook for details on how to get Access to do the arithmetic for you.

Choosing Fonts, Colors, and Other Decorative Touches

You can format label and text box controls in lots of ways, almost as though you were using a word processor. When you select a text box, label, or other control with text, numbers, or dates in it, you can use the tools in the Font group on the Format tab on the Ribbon, as shown in Figure 2-11, or set properties on the Format tab of the property sheet. The choice is yours.

Figure 2-11:
Changing
the font,
background
and
foreground
colors, and
number
formats on
the Format
tab of the
Ribbon.

Here are some of the properties of labels, text boxes, and some other controls that you may want to set:

✦ **Font:** You can control the typeface by clicking the Font box in the Font group on the Format tab of the Ribbon or by changing the Font Name property. Don't choose anything really fancy; if you do, your text will be unreadable. (For most of the figures in this chapter, we use a font named Calibri.) Adjust the size of the text by clicking the Font Size box or setting the Font Size property. The Font group on the Format tab of the Ribbon also has buttons for boldface, italics, and underlining (or you can set the Font Weight, Font Italics, or Font Underline properties).

✦ **Color:** Text doesn't have to be boring black on ho-hum gray. With the control selected, click the down arrow on the Font Color button in the Font group on the Format tab of the Ribbon; from the drop-down menu, choose the color that you want to use as the text color. (If you don't see the color you want, choose More Colors.) To set another control to the same color, select the control and click the same Font button. (The current color is the color of the bar below the *A* on the button.) You can set the background color the same way by clicking the Background Color button.

These buttons set the Fore Color and Back Color properties of the control, which are on the Format tab of the property sheet. These properties appear as horrendous-looking seven-character codes — the same color-naming system used in the HTML formatting codes for web pages. The first character is always #, followed by three pairs of two characters that represent the amounts of red, green, and blue in the color.

✦ **Alignment:** To left-align, right-align, or center the text within the edges of the control, click the Align Text Left, Center, or Align Text Right button in the Font group on the Format tab of the Ribbon, or set the Text Align property on the Format tab of the property sheet. If you want to get really weird, you can display the text sideways within the box by setting the `Vertical` setting on the Other tab of the property sheet to `Yes`.

Copying your formatting

After you go to the effort of prettifying one control, why reinvent the wheel to make another control to match it? You can simply copy the formatting from one control to another by using the Format Painter. The Format Painter copies all formatting — colors, fonts, font sizes, border sizes, alignment, and anything else that you can think of. Select the beautifully formatted control, and click the Format Painter button in the Font group on the Format tab of the Ribbon. Your mouse pointer now has a paintbrush attached to it, so you know that the tool is active. Click the control that you want to format like the original control.

Making bad news red

Access has a cool feature called *conditional formatting* that lets you make a control look one way normally and a different way — maybe boldface and red — under special circumstances. The total amount of an order for an online store, for example, ought to be a positive number unless the customer is due a refund. Wouldn't it be great if the form reached out and grabbed you when the total order amount is negative? Well, Access can't reach out of the screen, but it can make the control appear in bright red, boldface, or both.

To set up conditional formatting, you create rules based on two specifications:

+ What **condition** must be true for the format to apply? You can check whether a date is in the past (that is, it's < today) or whether a number is less than zero.

+ What **formatting** applies? You can make the control a bright color (text or background), boldface, italic, or underlined.

You can create more than one rule. If the order amount is more than $100, for example, display it in green; if it's less than zero, display it in red.

Follow these steps to set up conditional formatting:

1. **Select the control in Design view.**

2. **Click the Conditional Formatting button in the Control Formatting group on the Format tab of the Ribbon.**

You see the Conditional Formatting Rules Manager dialog box, shown in Figure 2-12. You can use this dialog box to create rules that set the formatting based on the value of the field or on values in other fields or records.

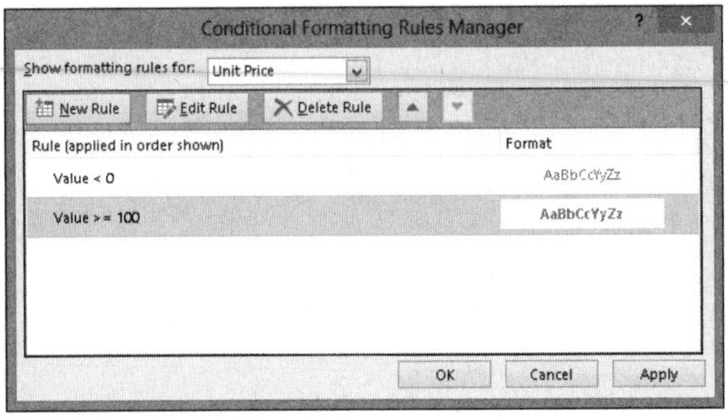

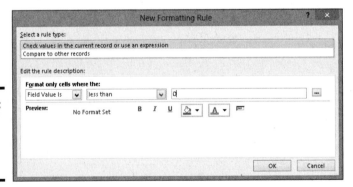

Figure 2-12:
The
Conditional
Formatting
Rules
Manager
dialog box.

3. **Click the New Rule button.**

You see the New Formatting Rule dialog box, shown in Figure 2-13.

4. **Specify whether the condition is based on information in the current record or other records.**

5. **In the Edit the Rule Description section, set the drop-down menus to display the condition.**

In Figure 2-13, the condition is that the value of the field is less than 0.

6. **Click OK.**

You return to the Conditional Formatting Rules Manager dialog box, where the rule you just defined appears.

Figure 2-13:
Creating a
conditional
formatting
rule.

7. **Repeat Steps 3–6 to create other rules as needed.**

In Figure 2-12, earlier in this chapter, one rule turns negative amounts red, and another rule turns amounts $100 and over green and boldface. (You'll just have to imagine that these figures are in color!)

8. **Click OK.**

Creating Check Boxes for Yes/No Fields

When you drag a Yes/No field from the field list to a form or report in Design view, Access assumes that you want to display the field as a check box: A `Yes` value appears as a checked box, and a `No` value appears as a blank box. You can't change the size of a check box. Dragging its edges expands the box around it, but the check box just sits there.

 Another way to create a check box is to click the Check Box button in the Controls group on the Design tab of the Ribbon and then click the form where you want a check box to appear. If you use this method, you need to set the check box's `Control Source` property on the Data tab of the property sheet to the name of the Yes/No field.

 Alternatively, you can display different information depending on whether the value of the Yes/No field is `Yes` or `No`. For tax-exempt companies, for example, your order form can display a Tax Exempt ID box that appears only if the `Tax Exempt` field is set to `Yes`. See Chapter 3 of this minibook for information on displaying information that depends on other fields in this way.

Adding Lines, Boxes, and Backgrounds

Some forms and reports have several sections, and they're easier to use if you separate the sections with lines or boxes. An order form might have one section with information about the customer, another section showing what items were ordered, and a third section with payment information.

To draw a line, click the Line button in the Controls group on the Design tab of the Ribbon, and draw the line on the form with your mouse.

Drawing a box works the same way. Click the Rectangle button in the Controls group on the Design tab of the Ribbon and draw the box, starting at one corner and dragging the mouse to the opposite corner.

You can set the colors and thickness of a line or box by clicking the Shape Outline button in the Control Formatting group on the Format tab of the Ribbon and choosing a color, line thickness, or line type.

You can specify a picture to display in the background of the form or report. Picture backgrounds seem like demented ideas to us; we hate forms and reports that have clouds or sunsets in the background because they make the forms look busier and more confusing. But if you want to jazz up your form or report, click the Background Image button in the Background group on the Format tab of the Ribbon; then choose an image from their gallery or click Browse to choose a picture of your own. Select the image and click OK to set the `Picture` property on the Format tab of the property sheet to the filename of a picture.

Controlling Cursor Movement in Your Form

You made a bunch of controls and formatted them nicely, and your form looks pretty spiffy. But here's a question you may not have thought about: When you (or other people) are using the form to enter or edit data, how does the cursor move from control to control? That is, when you press Enter or Tab to leave a text box or other control that allows you to edit information, which control does your cursor move to? Access calls the sequence that the cursor goes through the *tab order* of the form.

Access stores the tab order for each form — a list of the editable controls on the form (that is, controls that allow data entry or editing in Form view). When you press Enter or Tab in Form view, your cursor moves from control to control in the same order as the Access list. Here's the problem: When you create a new control, Access adds it to the bottom of the list even if the control is at the top of the form. As a result, your cursor skips around when you try to use the form.

The solution is to adjust the tab order of the form. To see the tab-order list, follow these steps:

1. **With the form in Design view, click Tab Order in the Tools group on the Design tab of the Ribbon.**

You see the aptly named Tab Order dialog box, shown in Figure 2-14.

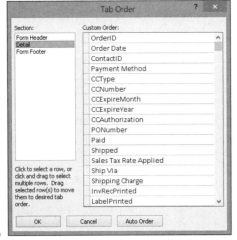

Figure 2-14:
Controlling
the order
in which
your cursor
moves from
field to field
on a form.

2. **Change the order of the controls by clicking the gray box to the left of a field name and dragging it up or down the list.**

Alternatively, click the Auto Order button to tell Access to put the controls in order based on their positions — from top to bottom and left to right — on the form.

Access reorders the controls, and you can look at the new order to see whether Access got it right.

3. **Click OK when the controls are in the right order.**

You've probably already guessed this, but this whole tab-order discussion doesn't apply to reports.

Chapter 3: Creating Smarter Forms

In This Chapter

✔ Making drop-down menus and list boxes

✔ Displaying Yes/No fields as option or toggle buttons

✔ Grouping radio buttons

✔ Adding cool command buttons

✔ Making a Find box for searching records

✔ Adding headers and footers to your forms

✔ Displaying form data on multiple tabs

✔ Validating what people type

✔ Creating a main-menu form for your database

✔ Setting a form to run automatically when you open the database

*I*n Chapters 1 and 2 of this minibook, we explain how to make forms and reports, as well as how to add labels, text boxes, check boxes, lines, and rectangles to them. You can go a long way with just those controls, but you'll miss a lot of the power of Access. Combo boxes and list boxes enable you (or your users) to choose values from lists instead of typing them, and these lists can come from related tables in the database. If a field contains a small number of possible values, you may want to present them as radio buttons. Best of all, forms can display records from more than one table through subforms. This chapter explains all this — and more.

This chapter doesn't apply to reports. Because you can't use reports for entering and editing data, the interactive features discussed in this chapter just don't work for reports (at least, not unless you have much fancier paper than we do!).

Creating and Configuring Combo and List Boxes

Combo boxes and *list boxes* are two controls that work like the drop-down menus that you see in Windows programs. Each box displays a list of values from which you can choose one value. The difference between the controls is how many values they display. A combo box shows only the currently selected value; you click the down arrow on its right side to get the list to drop down so you can select a different value. A list box shows all the possible values (or as many as fit in the control, with a scroll bar you can use to see the rest of the values), of which one is selected. Figure 3-1 shows a combo box and a list box.

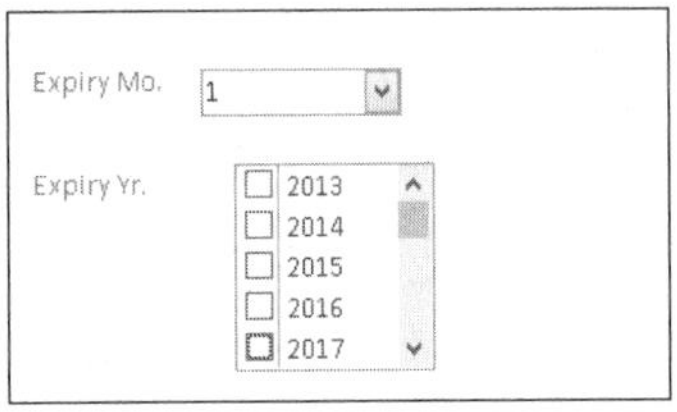

Figure 3-1:
You can use
a combo
box (top) or
a list box
to choose
values from
a list.

List boxes take up more room on forms than combo boxes do, so they're used far less often. On the other hand, they allow you to see more values at the same time. We explain in this chapter how to create both list and combo boxes (the process is almost the same), but our examples concentrate on combo boxes.

Before you create a combo or list box, consider the following questions:

✦ **Where will the values come from?** The combo or list box displays a list of values. Are the values stored in a table, or will you type them in the control's property sheet? If you use this list of values in any other control on another form anywhere in your entire database, put the values in a table — just a plain old table, with one field for the value and additional fields if you store other facts about each value. Make sure that the table has a primary key to uniquely identify each record. If your bookstore sells three types of products, for example, these product codes need to be in a table, because you're sure to use them in lots of different forms and reports. Don't type them in the combo or list box's property sheet.

✦ **If the values are stored in a table, which field (or fields) of the table do you want to appear in the control?** You can choose one or more fields, but don't choose too many; if you do, the list gets enormous. A combo or list box for a `StateOrProvince` field, for example, can display the two-letter state or province abbreviation, the full state or province name, or both.

✦ **When the user of the form makes a choice from this control, what happens to the selected information?** Most forms are used for editing the records in a table or query (the record source for the form). If the purpose of the combo box or list box is to help the user enter a value in a field, make a note of the field name. On the other hand, you may want to use the combo or list box for another purpose, such as allowing the user to find a record (as described in "Making a Find Box," later in this chapter).

For an order-entry database, for example, you may want a combo box that lists the states and provinces in the United States and Canada. You have a table called StateLookup with a field for the two-letter abbreviations, a field for the full names of the states and provinces, and a field for the sales-tax rate you need to charge for orders from that state. You can have your combo box or list box display only the state or province name on the form, but have the control store only the abbreviation for the selected state or province in the order-entry table that you're editing.

Making combo boxes the really easy way

In the table that's the record source for the form, you can set up a field as a *lookup field* — a field that must match the primary key field in a table of codes. If you do this, Access creates a combo box when you drag it from the field list to the Design View window of the form. Easy enough! By configuring the field as a lookup field, you've already told Access what table and field to use for the list of values. In the order-entry database example, when you set up the Customers table, you'd configure the `StateOrProvince` field as a lookup field that must match values in the StateLookup table.

To find out how to make a lookup field, see Book II, Chapter 5.

Running the Combo Box and List Box wizards

To make a combo box or list box when you didn't designate the field as a lookup field, a wizard steps you through the process. Before you start, determine where the list of values comes from, as described in "Creating and Configuring Combo and List Boxes," earlier in this chapter. The Combo Box and List Box wizards ask the same questions that we pose, so you'd better have the answers. In this section, we describe the Combo Box Wizard, because combo boxes outnumber list boxes 10 zillion to one in actual use, but the List Box Wizard is similar.

To create a combo box with the Combo Box Wizard, follow these steps:

1. **Open the form in Layout or Design view.**

If either Layout or Design view is new to you, jump back to Chapter 1 of this minibook for an overview.

2. **Click the Combo Box button in the Controls group on the Design tab of the Ribbon.**

If you don't see the Combo Box button, click the Controls button and choose the Combo Box button from the drop-down menu.

3. **Click the place in the form where you'd like the top-left corner of the combo box to appear.**

A plus sign appears on the form with a little combo box icon beside it, marking the spot. Don't worry if the combo box isn't in exactly the right spot; you can always move the edges later.

4. **Drag the cursor down and to the right to outline the border of the combo box, and release the mouse button when the outline is the size you want.**

Access displays the Combo Box Wizard, shown in Figure 3-2.

Figure 3-2:
The Combo Box Wizard steps you through creating a combo box (drop-down menu) on your form.

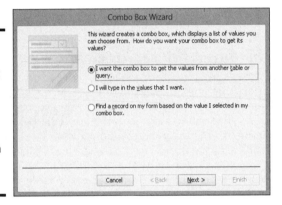

5. **Specify where the list of values comes from, and click Next.**

If the list comes from an existing table or query, choose the first option, and go to Step 6. If the list of options doesn't exist in a table, choose the second option, and go to Step 9. The third option creates a combo box that lets you jump to a specific record in your table (see "Making a Find Box," later in this chapter).

The wizard displays all the tables, all the queries, or both so that you can choose the table or query you want. If the table doesn't have a primary key field, you can't choose it.

6. **When the wizard shows you a list of the fields in the table or query, choose the fields to display in the combo box and then click Next.**

You can choose more than one field if you want more than one to appear in the combo box. Double-click a field in the Available Fields list to move it to the Selected Fields list (and vice versa). In Figure 3-3, two fields are selected.

7. **Choose the field you want to display and the order in which you want the records to appear in the combo box, and then click Next.**

The wizard allows you to choose Ascending or Descending order for up to four fields.

Be sure that the field on which you're sorting also appears in the combo box; otherwise, the order can be confusing. If you sort states and provinces by their two-letter codes, for example, the names don't appear in order, which looks weird if the codes don't also appear.

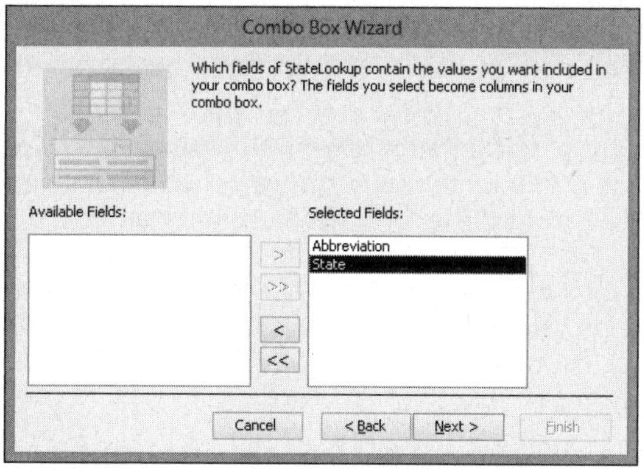

Figure 3-3:
Choose
which field
will appear
when the
user clicks
the combo
box and
the drop-
down menu
appears.

Combo Box Wizard

Which fields of StateLookup contain the values you want included in your combo box? The fields you select become columns in your combo box.

Available Fields:

Selected Fields:

Abbreviation
State

Cancel   < Back   Next >   Finish

8. **Adjust the widths of the columns by dragging the column divider left or right, click Next, and skip to Step 10 unless you're typing values instead of using a table.**

   Depending on the fields you've chosen, Access may display a check box titled Hide Key Column (Recommended). If this box is checked, the key column that you selected won't be displayed.

9. **If you chose to type the list of values, type them in the datasheet, one per row, and then click Next.**

   The wizard displays a datasheet in which you can type the list. You can create multiple columns (for a code and its meaning, for example), one of which will be stored in the record source of the form.

10. **Choose the field that identifies each row of the combo box, and click Next.**

    The wizard asks which field uniquely identifies each row in the combo box — the equivalent of the primary key field in a stored table. (Aren't you beginning to wish that you'd just stored the list in the table? Hint, hint!) This value is what gets saved as the value of the combo box in the next step.

11. **Choose whether to remember the value for later use or store it in a field, and click Next.**

    The wizard asks what you want to do with the value of the field when the user chooses it from the combo box: remember the value for later use (refer to it in a query parameter, macro, or Visual Basic for Applications [VBA] module), or store it in a field of the table or query that's the record source for the form. Most of the time, you want to store the value in a field, so choose the field name from the list.

12. **Type a label for the combo box, and click Finish.**

    The wizard creates your combo box.

13. **Adjust the edges of the control to resize the combo box, and drag its label to the right place.**

We never get the size and position of a combo or list box right the first time, and Access never puts its label in the right place. Good thing Access gives us a chance to touch things up a bit! You can drag the control and its label around the form to the right positions.

When the wizard finishes, you end up with a combo or list box. The next section describes the properties you may want to change if you don't like the way your combo or list box turns out.

Changing the properties of a combo or list box

Property
Sheet

You're never stuck with what a wizard creates: You can change the way that a combo or list box works by editing its properties. Click the Property Sheet button in the Tools group on the Design tab of the Ribbon to display the property sheet. The properties you're most likely to change are shown in Table 3-1.

Table 3-1	Properties of Combo Boxes and List Boxes
Property	*Description*
Control Source	Field in the record source in which Access stores the value that you choose from the combo or list box.
Row Source Type	Where the items on the list come from: Table/Query, Value List, or Field List. (That last option displays a list of the fields in a table or query.)
Row Source	Source of the current row's data. If you choose the Table/Query or Field List option for the Row Source Type property, enter the name of a table or query (or a SQL statement). If you choose the Value List setting, type a list of values separated by semicolons (;).
Column Count	Number of columns to display in the combo or list box.
Column Heads	Whether to display headings for the columns of values.
Column Widths	Widths of the column(s) for the list. If you've got more than one column, separate the widths with semicolons.
Bound Column	Column number in the combo or list box of the column that gets stored in the control source.
List Rows	Number of rows that appear in the drop-down menu of a combo box. If the list has more values than this number, a scroll bar appears so that the user can display more values. (This property isn't used for list boxes because the size of the list box control on the form determines how many rows appear.)

Property	Description
Limit to List	Whether entries in the combo box are limited to values on the drop-down menu. Choose the No setting if you want to be able to type other values in the control. (This property isn't used for list boxes, which are always limited to the values listed.)

Designing Cool Looks for Yes/No Fields

Chapter 2 of this minibook describes how to create a check box for a Yes/No field, which looks pretty spiffy. But you have other options for Yes/No fields: *option buttons* (little round radio buttons) and *toggle buttons* (rectangular buttons that appear to be pressed in when they're selected). You can display a Yes/No field in a text box, too, but the Yes value appears as –1 and the No value appears as 0, which may not be what you want. Figure 3-4 shows a check box, option button, and toggle button.

Figure 3-4: Ways to display a Yes/No field.

One of the easiest ways to make a toggle or option button for a Yes/No field is to create a check box for it and then change it into a toggle or option button. Drag the field from the field list to the desired location on your form, and Access makes a check box for the field. Right-click the field and choose Change To⇨Option Button or Change To⇨Toggle Button from the contextual menu that appears. Adjust the sizes and positions of the control and its label, and you're done!

Creating Option Groups

If a field is set to one of a small number of numeric, integer values — such as 1 to 10 — you can display the values in a box, with an option button next to each value. When you're editing records by using the form, you click the option for the value to which you want to set the field. Only one option can be selected at a time; clicking one option deselects the other options.

Making a group of option buttons for a field requires creating an *option group* — a rectangle within which you put an option button for each possible value of the field. Figure 3-5 shows option buttons in an option group. Luckily, Access comes with the Option Group Wizard, which you can use to create the option group and all the option buttons.

Figure 3-5:
An option group contains an option button for each value that the field can take.

Before you run the Option Group Wizard, make a note of the values that the field takes. After the wizard is running, you can't open another table to see the values to which the field is limited. You may want to keep the table that lists the possible values open and visible in the corner of the Access window while you run the wizard.

Note that option groups work only with integer, numeric values. You can show any label you want next to each option button, but the value that Access stores for the option group has to be a whole number. In the option group shown in Figure 3-5, the actual category codes may be the numbers 1 to 7.

An option group can contain option (radio) buttons, check boxes, or toggle buttons, but most people expect check boxes and toggle buttons to stand by themselves, not to be in a group of mutually exclusive options. We recommend sticking with option buttons in option groups.

To make an option group and option buttons for a field, display your form in Design view and then follow these steps:

1. **Click the Option Group button in the Controls group on the Design tab of the Ribbon.**

2. **Click the place on the form where you want the option group to appear.**

   A plus sign appears at the point that you click, with a small Option Group icon beside it.

3. **Click again to instantiate the option group.**

Access draws a box for the option group and then runs the Option Group Wizard. Don't worry if the rectangle for the option group is the wrong size; you can resize it later.

4. **When the wizard prompts you for a list of the labels for the individual option buttons, type the labels, one per line, and then click Next.**

Don't press Enter after typing a value; if you do, the wizard thinks that you're clicking Next and takes you to the next window. Instead, press Tab or the down arrow to move to the next row in the datasheet. (If you accidentally press Enter, click the Back button to get back to this window.)

5. **In the next window, choose the default value for the field or choose the No I Don't Want a Default option, and then click Next.**

This answer determines whether one of the choices that you just typed starts out as selected when you create a new record in the table.

When you click Next, you see a list of the labels that you typed in Step 4.

6. **In the Values column on the right side, type the number to store for each value, as shown in Figure 3-6, and then click Next.**

Each label must have a different value, and all the values have to be whole numbers. Access will fill in autoincrementing default values, but you can change them if you want to.

Figure 3-6:
When you create an option group, you specify a label and a value for each option button in the group.

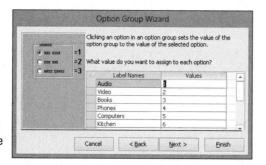

7. **Choose to save the value for later use or to store it in a field (and specify the field), and click Next.**

If you're creating a form for editing a table, choose the Store the Value in This Field option. If the form is *unbound* (not connected to a record source), and the options are for use as input to a query, macro, or VBA module, choose the Save the Value for Later Use option. (See Book VI, Chapter 1 for details on running macros from a form, possibly using inputs from the form.)

8. **Specify whether the options should appear as option buttons, check boxes, or toggle buttons; choose the style for the option group box; and then click Next.**

   We strongly recommend choosing option buttons (the default), because most people expect option buttons to be in groups of mutually exclusive options, and they expect check boxes and toggle buttons to work independently of one another.

   The style for the option group controls the box that Access draws around the group of option buttons; it's an aesthetic decision.

9. **Type a caption (label) for the option group, and click Finish.**

   The caption appears at the top of the option group. When you click Finish, the wizard creates your option group and an option button (or check box or toggle button, if you callously disregarded our advice) for each value you specified.

When the wizard finishes, you can resize the option group box and move the option buttons around inside it.

If you change the list of possible values later, the option buttons on your form don't change automatically. If a set of option buttons shows all the categories of products that your store sells, and you add a new product category, you need to remember to edit the form and add a new option button to the option group. For this reason, combo boxes are used more frequently to provide lists of possible values, because when you update a table from which the combo box gets its list of values, the combo box updates automatically the next time you open the form.

You can create a new option button to add to an option group by clicking the Option Button button in the Controls group on the Design tab of the Ribbon.

Creating Command Buttons

Dialog boxes contain command buttons, such as Save and Cancel, and your forms can, too. To create a command button, display your form in Design view and click the Button control in the Controls group on the Design tab of the Ribbon. When you create a command button, you tell Access what program the button should run.

Programs can take two forms: macros (described in Book VI) and VBA modules (described in Book VIII).

Luckily, wizards can do a lot of the work for you. You don't need to know how to create either macros or VBA modules to make nifty command buttons on your forms.

This section covers how to run the Command Button Wizard to make command buttons that do useful stuff. The wizard creates a macro for the form to contain the programs for the buttons on the form. The wizard makes buttons with actions that it divides into categories. When you place a command button on a form, the Command Button Wizard appears, showing two lists: Categories and Actions.

Different actions apply to the different categories. The names of the actions are pretty self-explanatory.

The items in the Categories list are

+ **Record Navigation:** These commands are for moving from record to record. Most of them duplicate the navigation controls that appear at the bottom of most forms (Go to First Record, Go to Previous Record, Go to Next Record, and Go to Last Record), but you can also make a Find Record button that displays the Find and Replace dialog box or a Find Next button that repeats the preceding search. If you want to make a box right on the form in which you can type a value, as well a Find button that searches for that value, see "Making a Find Box," later in this chapter.

+ **Record Operations:** This category includes buttons for adding, deleting, duplicating, printing, saving, and undoing the edits to a record (the current record, in most cases). The Duplicate Record button adds a new record that's a duplicate of the current record. The Print Record button prints the form with the data for the current record.

+ **Form Operations:** These commands apply or edit filters (described in Book II, Chapter 3), close this form, open another form, or print another form.

    If you print another form, you get *all* the records in that form, so you may want to come up with another method.

    You can also make a button that reloads the data on the form, in case it has changed since you loaded the form.

+ **Report Operations:** You can make command buttons that preview, print, mail, or save a report to a file. You can't restrict the report to a specific record without editing the code behind the form, however.

+ **Application:** Quit Application is the only command in this category.

+ **Miscellaneous:** This last group of commands includes commands that dial a phone number (assuming that your computer is connected to a dial-up modem and a phone), print a table in Datasheet view, run a macro, or run a query and display the resulting datasheet.

Making a Close button

Who needs a Close button when forms already have a big X button in the top-right corner? Some people like to have a Close button anyway, though, and it's easy enough to make. Here's how:

1. **With your form open in Design view, click the Button icon in the Controls group on the Design tab of the Ribbon.**

2. **Click the place on the form where you want the button to appear.**

   Don't worry about the exact location; you can always move it later. Access starts the Command Button Wizard, shown in Figure 3-7.

Figure 3-7: The Command Button Wizard includes lots of prepro-grammed commands for your button to run.

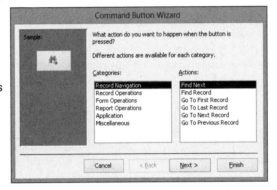

3. **Select the Form Operations category and the Close Form action, and then click Next.**

4. **Choose whether you'd like to have text or a picture on the button, specify what text or which picture, and then click Next.**

   If you choose the Text option, you can edit the text in the box. (Access suggests Close Form for the text, which sounds pretty good to us.) If you choose the Picture option, you can choose a suggested icon from a list or click the Browse button to look at the full set of icons that Access provides. When you select an icon, it appears on the left side of the dialog box. You can use any bitmap (.bmp) file as an icon.

5. **Type a name for your new control.**

   The suggested name is something like Command7, so change it to something meaningful, such as CloseButton.

6. **Click Finish.**

   The wizard creates a command-button control where you originally clicked the form. Now you can drag the edges of the button to resize it or drag the whole button to another location.

After creating a command button with the wizard, you can edit its properties, as described in "Customizing your command button," later in this chapter.

Making a button to display a related form

You can make a command button that displays another form. You can display any old form in the database, but this kind of command button is most powerful when you use it to display a form that shows the records of a table that relate to the records in your original form. Suppose that you're working on an Order form that displays information about each order from your online store. You can add a command button that opens the Address Book form to show the record for the customer who placed the current order, including the customer's address, phone number, and other information.

Here's how to add a button that displays another form:

1. **With the form open in Design view, click the Button control icon in the Controls group on the Design tab of the Ribbon.**

2. **Click the form where you want the button to appear.**

   The Command Button Wizard fires up to create your button (refer to Figure 3-7, earlier in this chapter).

3. **Select the Form Operations category and the Open Form action, and then click Next.**

   Access displays a list of the forms in your database.

4. **Choose the name of the form you want the button to open, and click Next.**

   The wizard asks whether to display the form with all records available or to display a specific record. In this example, it would be nice to display the Address Book record for the customer whose order you're editing.

5. **Choose the option titled Open the Form and Find Specific Data to Display, and click Next.**

   You see two lists of fields, as shown in Figure 3-8. The left list shows the fields in the record source of the current form. The right list shows the fields in the record source of the form that you want the button to open.

6. **Select the fields from the two forms that match (click a field in the left list and a field in the right list); click the <-> button; and then click Next.**

   If you're adding a button to open the Address Book1 form with the record of the customer who placed the order displayed on the Orders form, the ContactID field on the Orders form should match the ContactID field on the Address Book1 form.

7. **Choose the text or picture to appear on the form, and click Next.**

Figure 3-8:
The
Command
Button
Wizard
asks which
fields to
use to find
a matching
record.

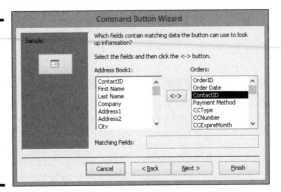

8. **Type a name for the control.**

   How about using `OpenAddressBookForm` for the control name? We don't mind using long names when they provide clarity.

9. **Click Finish.**

   The wizard makes the command button.

10. **Switch to Form view (by clicking the View button on the toolbar) to try out your new button!**

    When you click the button, Access opens the new form in a separate tab (or in a separate window, if you've configured Access to use multiple windows).

Making a button to print the current record

The Command Button Wizard offers several print actions, but most of them don't work the way you may want them to. The Print a Form action prints a form once for every single record in the form's record source, for example, so you need to come up with a way to restrict the records to the one(s) you want. If you want to print the current record in the current form, run the Command Button Wizard, and select the Record Operations category and the Print Record action. These categories and actions are among those you can choose, as shown in Figure 3-8, earlier in this chapter.

If you want to print a report — rather than the current form — for just the current record, you need to do some extra work. Specifically, you need to create a macro or VBA module that the button runs, and you need to set up the macro or VBA to print the report with the records limited to those records that match the record currently displayed on the form.

Luckily, this macro is short and easy to make. See Book VI, Chapter 1 for specific directions.

Making other cool buttons

You can run the Command Button Wizard to make lots of other useful buttons. Command buttons, for example, do some of our favorite things. Following are a few of the available actions:

✦ **Add a new record that's a duplicate of the current record.** Choose the Record Operations category and the Duplicate Record action.

✦ **Save the current record.** Choose the Record Operations category and the Save Record action.

✦ **Display the results of a query in Datasheet view.** Choose the Miscellaneous category and the Run Query action. You could display all the other orders by the same customer or all the recent orders for the same product, for example.

✦ **Run a macro.** Choose the Miscellaneous category and the Run Macro action. (Book VI describes how to make macros that do all kinds of things.)

Customizing your command button

You can change the properties of a command button after you create it. To do so, display the button's property sheet by right-clicking the command button in Design view and choosing Properties from the contextual menu.

The following table lists some of the most useful properties and describes what they do.

Property	*Description*
`Caption` (Format tab)	Text that appears on the button unless it displays a picture. (If the `Picture` property specifies a picture, the button shows the picture, not the caption.)
`Picture` (Format tab)	Picture (icon) that appears on the button. The term `(image)` indicates that you selected a picture. Click the Build button to the right of the property to select a different picture. If the picture is blank, Access displays the Caption text.
`On Click` (Events tab)	Program (macro or VBA module) that Access runs when you click the button.

You can tell Access to run programs when you click, double-click, move into, or move away from the button (and at other times, too) by setting the Events properties of the command button — or almost any other kinds of controls, for that matter. See Book VI, Chapter 1 for information about how events work on a form.

Making a Find Box

When you're using a form, you can select a control, press Ctrl+F to display the Find and Replace dialog box, and jump directly to a record that matches the value you entered for the selected control. But wouldn't it be nice to have a combo box right on the form with the Find button next to it so that you can locate a record without bringing up a separate dialog box? Access makes this setup surprisingly easy.

On an Address Book form, for example, you could create a combo box that lists all the customers in your Address Book. When you choose a customer, the macro takes you right to that customer's record.

Follow these steps to create a Find box:

1. **With your form open in Design view, click the Combo Box button in the Controls group on the Design tab of the Ribbon.**

2. **Click your form where you want the Find box to appear.**

   The Combo Box Wizard runs, as described in "Running the Combo Box and List Box wizards," earlier in this chapter.

3. **Choose the option labeled Find a Record on My Form Based on the Value I Selected in My Combo Box, and click Next.**

   Access displays a list of the fields in the record source of the form.

4. **Choose the field(s) containing the values that the user can choose to finding a record, and click Next.**

   If you choose a field that's unique for each record (such as the OrderID field for a form that displays orders), the combo box provides a list of the values for the field, and choosing a value takes you right to the order. If you choose a field that's not unique, the combo box displays a list with duplicate values and finds records unpredictably. You can choose more than one field — Last Name and First Name, for example.

5. **Adjust the width of the column(s) that will appear in the drop-down menu by dragging the column divider(s), and click Next.**

6. **Type a name for the combo box control, and click Finish.**

   The wizard creates the combo box.

7. **Switch to Form view by clicking the View button on the toolbar, and test the control.**

   It looks something like Figure 3-9.

Figure 3-9:
You can
display
a form
with the
record that
matches
the current
record of
the current
form.

You can change the text of the label that Access creates for the combo box to something like Find or Find by Name — whatever you think will be clear to the user.

Displaying Attachments

Attachments are files that can be imported into an Attachment-type field in a table. You can display attachments on a form by dragging the field from the field list to the form in Design view. In the field list, an attachment appears as a group of fields: the field itself followed by `FileData`, `FileName`, and `FileType`. In Figure 3-10, `CustomerDocuments` is an Attachment field.

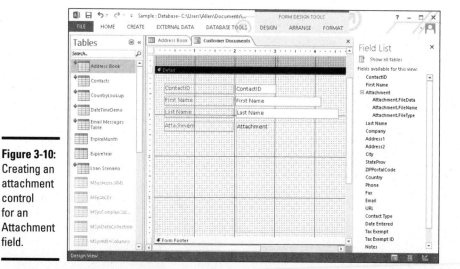

Figure 3-10:
Creating an
attachment
control
for an
Attachment
field.

To create a control to display an Attachment field, click the field name in the field list to select the entire Attachment field. When you drag it to the form, Access creates an attachment control.

In Form view, the attachment control looks like an empty rectangle for records, with no attachments stored in the field. If one or more pictures are stored in the Attachment field for a record, the first picture appears in the rectangle, as shown in Figure 3-11. If you click the Attachment field, three buttons appear: Back (to see the preceding attachment for this record, if any); Next (to see the next attachment for this record, if any); and Manage Attachments, which displays the Attachments dialog box, shown in Figure 3-12. (Double-clicking the attachment control displays the dialog box too.)

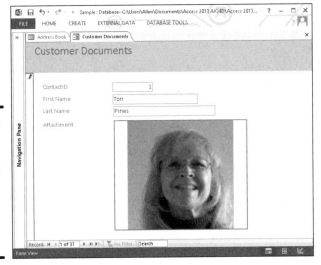

Figure 3-11: In Form view, you can see the attached files for the current record one at a time.

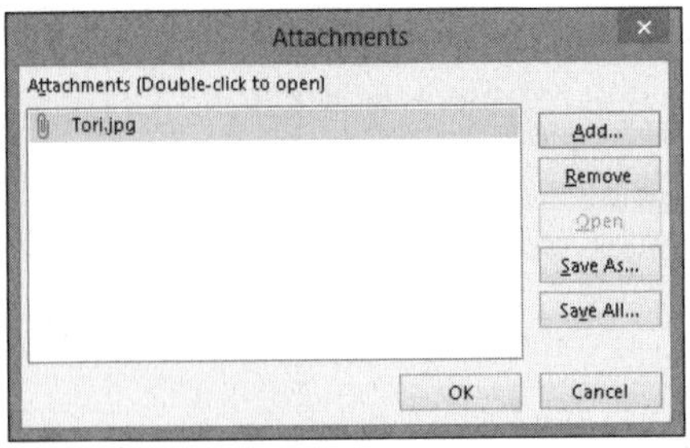

Figure 3-12: Managing the files stored for one record in an Attachment field.

You can use the Next and Previous buttons to flip through the files stored in the Attachment field for the current record. The files that aren't pictures appear as the icons for the program that can open them (Word for word-processing documents, Excel for spreadsheets, and so on). The Attachments dialog box is where you can

+ Add new files to the record.

+ Remove a file from the record.

+ Open the file by using the default program for the type of file.

+ Save the file with the name you specify.

+ Save all the files attached to the current record.

Adding Form Headers and Footers

The part of the form that you've been working with so far is the Detail section. In Design view, a Detail divider bar runs along the top of the form (refer to Figure 3-10, earlier in this chapter).

You may want to display information at the top and bottom of your form, however. Yes, you can just put controls at the top and bottom of the Detail section of your form, and most people do just that. If the window displaying the form is too small for the whole form to fit in it, however, the information may not always be visible.

Access's Form Wizard creates forms that include header and footer sections. Figure 3-13 shows the Header section that the Form Wizard creates, gussied up a little bit by options available on the contextual menu that pops up when you right-click anywhere within the form. When you switch to Form view by clicking the View button, the controls in the header and footer sections are always visible, no matter what the size of your Form window is.

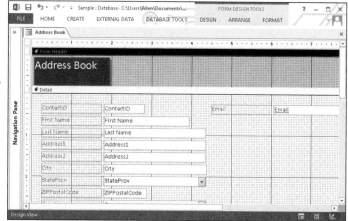

Figure 3-13:
Forms can have headers and footers that always appear onscreen.

You can add Form Header and Form Footer sections to your form by opening the form in Design view, right-clicking anywhere in the form, and choosing Form Header/Footer from the contextual menu. (You can get rid of the sections by repeating the process.) Access creates a new, blank Form Header section at the top of the form and a new, blank Form Footer at the bottom.

You can add controls to these sections by clicking the buttons in the Controls group on the Design tab of the Ribbon:

✦ **Logo:** Adds a picture (which doesn't have to be a logo) in the Header section

✦ **Title:** Adds a label in the Header section

✦ **Date and Time:** Adds a text box with the current date, time, or both to the Header section

You'll find that the buttons in the Header/Footer group on the Design tab of the Ribbon are useful, too.

To control the vertical size of the Header section, drag the top of the Detail divider bar up or down to make the Header section larger or smaller. Similarly, at the bottom of the form, you can drag the bottom edge of the Footer section up or down.

Creating Tabbed Forms

Sometimes, you need to fit tons of information on a form, and you can see that the form is getting to be the size of Nebraska. In addition to not fitting on the screen, large forms are confusing: Where is the right box in which to type this information?

One way to fit lots of information on a form while keeping the window size down and making the form less confusing is to divide the form into tabs. We're talking about the kind of tabs that stick up from the tops of folders, like those on the property sheet. Your forms can have tabs, too, with different controls on each one. The entire form can be on the tabs, or the tabs can occupy part of the form, with controls that remain visible regardless of which tab you're looking at. (We recommend the latter approach.)

To create tabs, first create a tab control on the form and then create controls on the tab. Before you start, decide how many tabs you want and what controls go on each tab. Then follow these steps:

1. **With your form open in Design view, make some space on your form where you want the tabs to go.**

   If your form is already crowded, just expand the form outrageously by dragging its bottom edge down or its right edge right, and drag groups of controls out of the way of your new tabs.

2. Click the Tab Control button in the Controls group on the Design tab of the Ribbon.

3. Click the form where you want the top-left corner of the tabs to appear.

Access creates a tab control and two tabs (also called *pages*), usually named Page1 and Page2 but perhaps named Page9 and Page10, as shown in Figure 3-14.

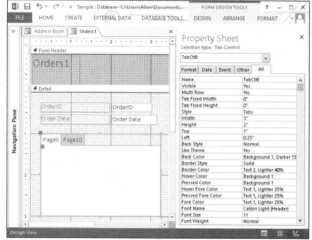

Figure 3-14: Creating tabs on your form.

4. Drag the edges of the tab control to fix the size of the control.

If you want to move the whole tab control, click the first page (usually, Page1) so that it's selected, and drag the black handle that appears in its top-left corner. You can also drag the handles on the top, bottom, and sides of the control to resize it.

You can fix up your new tab control as follows:

✦ **Rename the pages.** Page9 and Page10 probably aren't what you want to call your tabs. Click the tab to select the page, display the property sheet by clicking the Property Sheet button on the Ribbon, and change the Name property on the property sheet.

✦ **Add, delete, or reorder the pages.** If you want to have more than two pages, right-click the tab control (or any of its pages) and choose the Insert Page option from the contextual menu. To delete a page, select it, right-click it, and choose the Delete Page option from the contextual menu. To switch the order of the pages, right-click any of the pages and choose the Page Order option from the contextual menu; in the Page Order dialog box that appears, click the Move Up and Move Down buttons to reorganize the list of pages.

✦ **Put controls on the pages.** This part is the good part: You can drag existing controls from the rest of the form, or you can create new controls on the form in the same way that you create controls for the rest of the form. Click the page on which you want to put the controls so that the page appears "on top." Then move or create the controls you want.

Figure 3-15 shows a form with three tabs in Design view.

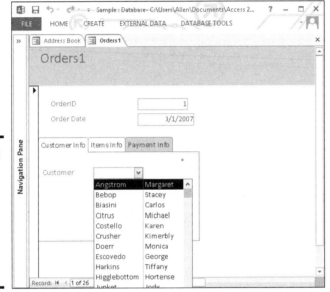

Figure 3-15:
This tab control contains three pages, and each page contains controls.

You Can't Type That Here!

The main purpose of forms is to provide easy-to-use onscreen display and editing for your records. Most people use forms rather than datasheets for entering and editing data.

Book II, Chapter 5 describes how to create defaults and validation rules for your tables to prevent the dreaded "garbage in, garbage out" syndrome that so many databases suffer from. You can add validation to your form controls, too.

Use validation in your tables when you want data to follow rules all the time, no matter how it's entered. Use validation in form controls when you want to validate one field against another or to do validation that applies only at certain times (such as when someone is using the form). You may want to make sure, for example, that the Ship Date can't be earlier than the Order Date, which you can't enforce using field validation in the table design.

Form controls that display data have properties with which you can validate and format that data. In fact, they're the very same properties that you can set as part of your table design:

+ **Default Value:** The starting value for this field when you add a new record

+ **Input Mask:** A pattern for field data to follow, including where letters, numbers, and punctuation appear and how letters are capitalized

+ **Validation Rule:** A rule Access applies to values entered in this field

+ **Validation Text:** An error message you see if you try to enter data that breaks the validation rule

These settings appear on the Data tab of the property sheet for controls. For help with creating input masks and validation rules (which can be a little complicated, frankly), click the setting on the property sheet and then click the Build button to the right of the setting. For input masks, you see the Input Mask Wizard, and for validation rules, you see the Expression Builder. (For details about using these settings, see Book II, Chapter 5.)

Making a Main Menu for Your Database

As you set up your database, you end up with various forms and reports that you (or the users for whom you're creating the database) will use regularly. The database would be easier to use with a main menu from which these frequently used objects can be chosen. Older versions of Access used *switchboards* to create menus from which you could open forms and reports. Navigation forms replace switchboards, although switchboards in databases created in earlier versions of Access continue to work.

Creating a navigation form

A *navigation form* is a form that includes a navigation control that can display one or more forms and reports. The navigation control has tabs — which can appear down the left side of the form, along the top, or in other places — that you can click to choose the form or report to display. Very nice!

You can create a navigation form by running a wizard or by making it with your bare hands. Here are some suggestions for using both:

+ **By wizard:** Click the Navigation button in the Forms group on the Create tab of the Ribbon. Choose one of the options that the button displays to create a form with one or two levels of horizontal or vertical tabs (that is, form-name tabs that run horizontally along the top of the form or vertically down the left or right side of the form).

✦ **By hand:** Create the form in Layout view by clicking the Blank Form button in the Forms group on the Create tab of the Ribbon. You can create a navigation form in Design view, but Layout view makes it easier by positioning the forms nicely. Click the Navigation Control button in the Controls group on the Design tab of the Ribbon; then click the form to create the control.

Either way, you see a form with a navigation control: a box with an Add New tab near the top-left corner of the form. For each form for which you want a tab, drag the form from the Navigation Pane onto the navigation control. Access creates a tab with the name of the form and displays the form in the main part of the navigation control, as shown in Figure 3-16.

Figure 3-16:
A navigation form can serve as Mission Control for your database.

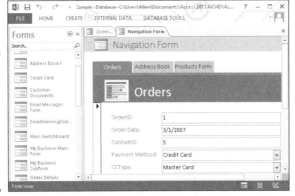

A navigation form doesn't have to be the main menu for your whole database. You can make one for a specific function, such as end-of-the-month reporting, or for things that the bookkeeper does. You can even include one navigation form in another: You might make a Main Menu navigation form that has a tab that opens a Bookkeeping Menu navigation form.

Finding an alternative to navigation forms

You don't have to use a navigation control to make a main-menu form for your database. You can use a regular old form with command buttons on it instead.

To make a main-menu form, create an unbound form — that is, a form for which the `Record Source` property for the form is blank. (See Chapter 1 of this minibook for details on setting the record source of a form, and see Book VI, Chapter 2, for more information about making a main menu.) Use labels to give the form a title (such as Main Menu), and create a command button for each command you want to be available on the form. When the Command Button Wizard (discussed earlier in this chapter) runs for each button, select Form Operations and Open Form to open a form, or select Report Operations and Preview Report to display a report that can be printed. The result could be something that looks like Figure 3-17.

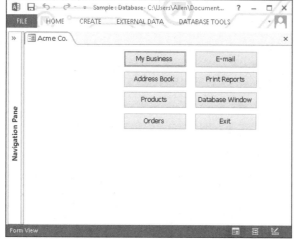

Figure 3-17:
You can use a regular form with lots of command buttons as a main menu too.

Opening a form automatically when the database opens

Now that you have a main menu, wouldn't it be nice to have it open automatically when the database opens? It's easy:

1. **Click the File tab on the Ribbon to see Backstage View.**

2. **Click Options to see the Access Options dialog box.**

3. **Click the Current Database button on the left side of the dialog box.**

4. **Set the Display Form option to the name of the form you want to open.**

5. **Click OK.**

Access warns you that you need to close and open the database for this change to take effect. Good enough!

Chapter 4: Doing Calculations in Forms and Subforms (and Reports)

In This Chapter

✔ Including calculated results on your forms and reports

✔ Using numbers in calculations

✔ Using dates in calculations

✔ Using strings — that is, text — in calculations

✔ Using split forms to display a datasheet on a form

✔ Adding subforms to a form

✔ Totaling and counting information from subforms and subreports

The first three chapters of Book IV explain how to make forms with all kinds of controls, showing information in all kinds of ways. In the process, you find out how to create reports, because creating and editing reports is so similar to working with forms. Up to this point, all the information you've dealt with is sitting there waiting for you, nicely contained in tables and queries. How about calculating data that isn't stored anywhere? Your forms and reports can calculate and display information that you can also store in the record source for the form (that is, store the results so you can use them in other objects). You may want the Order form for an online store, for example, to calculate the total price of all items ordered, the sales tax, and the grand total for the order.

In addition to calculating numbers, you can perform text, date, and logical calculations, giving Access instructions such as "If `Tax Exempt` is `True`, `Sales Tax` is 0; otherwise, it's `Tax Rate` times `Product Total`." Text calculations include things such as keeping only the first five digits of a zip code or capitalizing a text entry.

Doing Elementary Calculations

The title of this section sounds like algebra class, doesn't it? Don't worry; creating calculated values for your forms won't cause you to scream in terror, the way your high school algebra teacher did. You'll recognize some arithmetic signs (especially the equal sign), but all the calculations are easy.

A *calculated value* is a value that Access creates by doing a calculation based on other information, usually by using fields from your tables. Access can add the product total to the shipping cost for an order to come up with the total cost, for example.

To include a calculated value on a form or report when the calculation isn't already stored in a calculated column in a table, create a text box and then enter an expression in the Control Source property of the text box. An *expression* is a formula that tells Access how to calculate an answer from field values and other values. Expressions start with an equal sign (=). If field names include spaces, enclose them in square brackets. (Actually, we enclose *all* field names in square brackets, just so we don't forget.) Following is an example expression:

```
= [Product Total] + [Shipping Cost]
```

Here's another one:

```
= "Your total will be " & [GrandTotal] & "."
```

The expressions you use on forms and reports are the same as the expressions you use to create calculated columns in tables and calculated fields in queries. Turn to Book II, Chapter 1 for information on using calculated columns in tables, and see Book III, Chapter 2 to find out how expressions work in queries, including the operators and functions they can include.

Making a calculated control

A *calculated control* is a control that uses an expression rather than a field name as its Control Source property (as explained in Chapter 2 of this minibook). Usually, it's a text box control. To create a calculated control, follow these steps:

1. **With the form or report open in Design or Layout view, click the Text Box button in the Controls group on the Design tab of the Ribbon.**

   For an introduction to the tools in the Controls group, see Chapter 2 of this minibook. You have to use buttons in the Controls group, rather than the field list, to create a control with a blank control source. (A control with no control source is called an *unbound control*.)

2. **Click the form where you want the text box to appear, and drag to the right and down to form a rectangle.**

   The rectangle becomes a text box when you release the mouse button. In Design view, the text box displays Unbound; in Layout view, it's blank. The control has no control source; Access doesn't know what to display in the text box.

3. **If it isn't already visible, display the property sheet for the control by right-clicking the new text box and choosing Properties from the contextual menu.**

4. **Click the Data tab of the property sheet to display the data properties.**

The `Control Source` property is the first property on the Data tab — and lo! It's blank.

5. **Type an expression, starting with an equal sign, directly in the text box.**

Enter your expression as shown in Figure 4-1. You could also type the expression in the `Control Source` property on the Data tab of the property sheet. As an alternative to typing, you can use the Expression Builder to build your expression. Click the Build button, which looks like an ellipsis (...), at the right end of the `Control Source` property in the property sheet. The Expression Builder appears. (See Book III, Chapter 2 for details on how the Expression Builder works.)

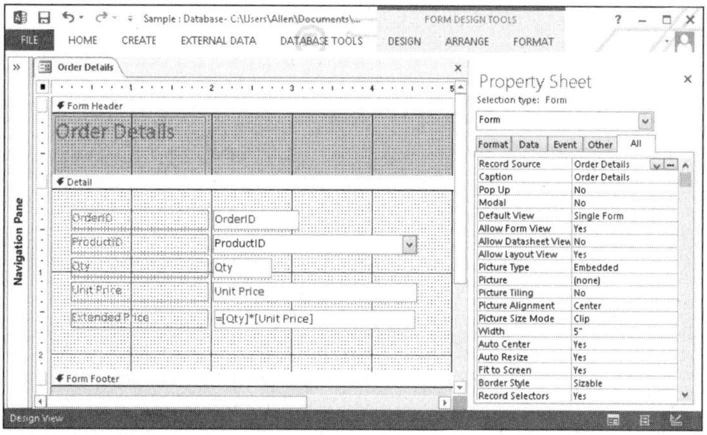

Figure 4-1:
When you type an expression with or without the Expression Builder, be sure to start it with an equal sign.

6. **Click the Other or the All tab of the property sheet, and change the Name property to something descriptive.**

Don't leave it named something like `Text17`, which won't give you much of a hint about what you had in mind when you look at this control later.

If you want to edit the expression later, you can change the `Control Source` entry on the property sheet.

TIP

Expressions can get long, and it can be hard to see them. When you're editing a long expression, you can press Shift+F2 to display it in the Zoom dialog box, as shown in Figure 4-2, or you can click the ellipsis (...) button again to display the Expression Builder.

**Book IV
Chapter 4**

Doing Calculations in Forms and Subforms

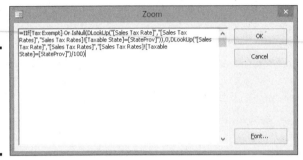

Figure 4-2:
The Zoom dialog box displays a long, scary expression.

Don't give the text box control the same name as a field in the record source for the form or report! If the table or query that provides the records has a field called `Full Name`, for example, don't create a calculated text box with that name. Two objects with the same name confuse Access; if you refer to that name, Access won't know whether you want the field or the control.

Checking your expression

After you type an expression in the `Control Source` property of a text box (or use the Expression Builder to create it), you see the expression itself in the text box. What about the answer?

To check whether the expression works, switch to Form view by clicking the View button on the Design or Home tab of the Ribbon. (For reports, switch to Print Preview.) Check the answer in several records to see whether the expression works as you expect.

Troubleshooting expressions

If you make a mistake in your expression, you may see one of three things in Form view or Print Preview: a wrong answer, `#Name?`, or another error message that starts with #. If you find an error, check out these ideas for fixing your calculated text box and its expression:

✦ `#Name?` indicates that Access can't understand a field name in your expression. The most likely reason is that you forgot the equal sign (=) at the beginning of the expression. Alternatively, you may have misspelled a field name or forgotten to enclose it in square brackets. If your text box control has the same name as a field, Access can't tell which one you're referring to, so check the name of the text box too. (It's the `Name` property on the All tab of the property sheet.)

✦ `#Div/0!` means that you're dividing something by zero, which is impossible in standard arithmetic. Check the fields in your expression to see whether 1 in the denominator might be 0 for some records.

✦ `#Error` indicates some other problem; check the expression carefully.

Where should you put your calculations?

When you want to include a calculated value on a form or report, you can do it in one of three ways:

- **In a calculated column in a table** that contains the fields on which the calculation is based. (This feature of Access 2013 is described in Book II, Chapter 1.) Choose this method if the calculation uses fields from only one table and will be used in more than one query, form, or report. If you need to change the way that the calculation works, it's more efficient if you have to update it in only one place.

- **In a query** that you use as the record source for the form or report. Use this method if

You plan to use the calculated value to select the records to include in the form or report so that you can set the Sort row of the query to ascending or descending for the calculated field.

You use the calculation in more than one form or report that has this query as its record source, or the calculation is based on fields from more than one table. See Book III, Chapter 2 for details on creating calculated fields in queries.

- **In a text box control on the form or report.** Use this method in all other cases.

Calculating and Formatting Numbers

To display a numeric calculation on a form or report, you can use the arithmetic operators that we describe in Book III, Chapter 2. Access also has numeric functions, which we describe in the same chapter.

Some sample numeric expressions (you can guess what the fields contain from their names) are included in the following table.

Numeric Expression	*Purpose*
`=[TaxableTotal]*[SalesTaxRate]`	Sales tax on an order
`=3.50 + ([ItemCount] * 2)`	Shipping cost ($3.50 plus $2 per item)
`=[OrderSubtotal] + [SalesTax] + [Shipping]`	Grand total for an order

After you type an expression in the `Control Source` property of a text box and switch to Form view or Print Preview to make sure that it works, you usually want to format the number. You may not like the number of decimal places, the use of commas, or the lack of a currency symbol in your calculated text box, for example.

To format a number, display the properties of the text box, and click the All or Format tab of the property sheet, as shown in Figure 4-1, earlier in this chapter. For a text box with numeric values, you can click the down arrow at the right end of the `Format` property to display a menu of numeric formats. See Book II, Chapter 1 for details about numeric formats, which are the same formats that you can use to format the fields in your tables.

Calculating and Formatting Dates

Access includes operators and functions that work on dates, including finding the number of days between two dates, separating a date into its components (day, month, year, hour, minute, and second), and adding days to a date. Book III, Chapter 2 describes the operators and functions you can use. A few examples are in the following table.

Date Expression	Purpose
`=DateDiff("w", [OrderDate], [ShipDate])`	Number of weeks between ordering and shipping
`=[InvoiceDate] + 30`	30 days after the invoice date
`=Date() + 10`	10 days after today
`=DatePart("q", [OrderDate])`	Quarter in which order was placed

Access gives you lots of date formats to choose among, as listed in Book II, Chapter 1. You set them in the `Format` property on the Format (or All) tab of the property sheet.

Calculating and Formatting Text

For forms and reports, you want things to look just right, and text expressions allow you to do all kinds of things to slice and dice the text that appears in your text boxes. Book III, Chapter 2 describes the operators and functions you can use with text values. A few examples are in the following table.

Text Expression	Purpose
`=[FirstName] & " " & [LastName]`	First and last names, with a space in between
`=[LastName] & ", " & [FirstName]`	Last name first, with a comma and space in between
`=UCase([LastName])`	Last name, in all capital letters
`=Left([ProductCode], 2)`	First two characters of the product code

You can create a so-called *input mask* that determines the formatting of a calculated text box, as we describe in Book II, Chapter 5. An input mask can add parentheses and dashes to a phone number or dashes to a Social Security number, for example.

Displaying Values That Depend on Conditions

Some calculations have an *if-then* component, which essentially says, "*If* this is true, *then* do this." If the order is from your home state, for example, charge sales tax; otherwise, don't. If the order is for more than $100, shipping is free. Access handles these types of if-then calculations by using its IIf() (immediate-if) function, which we describe in Book III, Chapter 2.

If you charge sales tax only for Vermont orders, for example, you use this expression:

```
= IIf([State]="VT", [TaxableTotal]*.06, 0)
```

The condition ([State]="VT") is either True or False. If the condition is True, the expression is [TaxableTotal]*.06 (6 percent of the taxable total); if it's False, the expression is 0.

The condition can be a Yes/No field: If the field is Yes (true), the function returns the first value, and if it's No (false), you get the second value. The following expression looks at the Yes/No field TaxExempt to determine whether this customer is exempt from sales taxes. For taxable customers, the function returns the value of the TaxableTotal field. For tax-exempt customers, it returns 0.

```
= IIf([TaxExempt], 0, [TaxableTotal])
```

Here's the mind-boggling part: You can *nest* functions, including the IIf() function. That is, you can use a function inside another function. The following example expression combines the last two examples to calculate sales tax based on both the customer's tax-exempt status and the customer's state:

```
= IIf([State]="VT", IIf([TaxExempt], 0, [TaxableTotal]*.06), 0)
```

Formatting Calculated Controls

When you display calculated values on a form, the value isn't editable in Form view; you can't type a different value in its place or delete it. The expression controls what appears in the text box.

To make it clear which text boxes are editable, we like to make calculated text boxes look different from the text boxes we type in. We recommend that you display the Format tab of the property sheet for each calculated control and make the following changes:

✦ Set the `Back Style` property to `Transparent` so that the background of the calculated value matches the background of the form itself.

✦ Set the `Special Effect` property to `Flat` so that the value doesn't appear in a box at all.

Using a Split Form to Display a Datasheet

A *split form* is a form that displays a datasheet of the records from the record source, usually at the bottom of the form. A split form enables you to browse through the records in datasheet format and at the same time have a detailed view of each record as you browse.

The easiest way to create a split form is to follow these steps:

1. **Select the table or query that you want to be the record source of the main form by clicking it in the Navigation Pane.**

   For this example, click the Orders table. (The Order Details table will be the record source of the datasheet, but that step comes later.)

2. **Click the More Forms button in the Forms group on the Create tab of the Ribbon and then choose Split Form from the menu that appears.**

   Access creates a new split form in Layout view. A regular-looking form appears at the top, with a control for each field in the record source, and a datasheet appears at the bottom, as shown in Figure 4-3.

Figure 4-3:
A split form shows a datasheet of the record source plus a form showing one record.

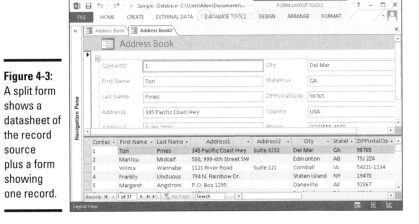

Property
Sheet

3. **To adjust the properties of the form, display the property sheet (if it's not already visible) by clicking the Property Sheet button in the Tools group on the Design tab of the Ribbon.**

   Make sure that the Selection Type menu is set to Form so that you see the properties of the whole form.

4. **Click the Format tab of the property sheet, and scroll down to the Split Form properties.**

   The properties that control split forms are listed in Table 4-1.

Table 4-1	Properties of Split Forms
Property	*Description*
Split Form Size	Specifies the height (usually, in inches) of the part of the form that is *not* occupied by the datasheet. The default setting is Auto, which tells Access to use a height that displays the whole form.
Split Form Orientation	Specifies where the datasheet appears on the form: Left, Right, Top, or Bottom. Bottom is the default.
Split Form Splitter Bar	Specifies whether a splitter bar appears in Form view. The user can drag the splitter bar up and down to change how much of the form appears.
Split Form Datasheet	Specifies what the user can do in the datasheet: Allow Edits or Read Only.
Split Form Printing	Specifies what is printed if you print the form: Form Only or Datasheet Only.

Using a Subform to Display Detail Records

Sometimes, you need to display information from two different tables or queries on the same form. For an online store, if you have a form that shows information about one order from your Orders table, it would be nice if you could also see a list of the items that were included in the order, which may be stored in the related Order Details table.

Figure 4-4 shows an example. The main part of the form displays records from the "one" side of a one-to-many relationship — the Orders table — and the subform displays records from the "many" side — the Order Details table. As a result, the subform displays many records that relate to the "one" record on the main form.

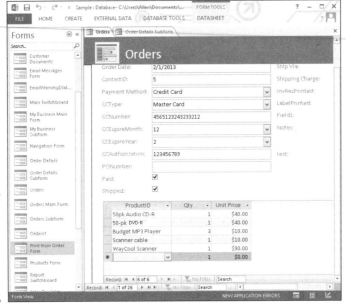

Figure 4-4:
A subform shows the list of products for one order.

Before you create a subform, make sure that the table containing the data to be displayed by the proposed subform is on the "many" end of a one-to-many relationship with the table that is the source of data for the main form. Book II, Chapter 6 shows you how to tell Access about the relationships among tables by using the Relationships window.

A subform can have its own form layout and navigation buttons for moving around the records within the subform. One form can have more than one subform if data from more than one table on the "many" end of a one-to-many relationship with the primary table is displayed in the main form.

Each subform is stored as a separate form in Access. You see the subform's name in the Navigation Pane. You create a subform the same way that you do a regular form because it *is* a regular form. To display it as a subform, you create a subform control on the main form, showing Access how and where you want the subform to appear on the main form.

Creating a subform

The easiest way to create a form is to use a wizard (surprise, surprise!). You can always edit and improve the subform later. (If you're creating a report, see the section on subreports in Book V, Chapter 1.)

To add a subform to a form, follow these steps:

1. **Display the main form in Design view.**

2. **If the form doesn't have enough room for the subform, make some space by dragging the bottom edge of the form down.**

   You don't know yet exactly how much space your subform will occupy, of course, but make a space a few inches high.

3. **Click the Subform/Subreport button in the Controls group on the Design tab of the Ribbon.**

4. **Click the form where you want the top-left corner of the subform to appear.**

   Access creates a subform control and runs the SubForm Wizard to lead you through the process of configuring the control. (If the wizard isn't installed on your system, Access offers to install it.)

5. **Do one of the following and then click Next:**

   - If you already have a form that you'd like to display as a subform, choose the Use an Existing Form option, select the form in the list, and skip to Step 8.

   - Otherwise, choose the Use Existing Tables and Queries option, and proceed to Step 6.

     The wizard asks which fields you want to include in the subform and what table or query the fields come from (that is, the record source of the subform), as shown in Figure 4-5.

6. **From the Tables/Queries drop-down menu, choose the table or query that you want to use as the record source of the subform.**

   The table or query that you choose must contain a unique field that can act as the primary field in a one-to-many relationship with the records on the main form. If you're adding a subform with order details (that is, the specific items that were purchased) to an order form, the Order Details and Orders tables may be related by an `OrderID` field.

7. **Choose the fields you want to display on the subform by selecting fields and clicking the > button; then click Next.**

   Alternatively, you can double-click a field name to move it from one list to the other. If you want to display all the fields, click the >> button. As you select fields, they move from the Available Fields list to the Selected Fields list. Don't choose too many fields; you have to fit them all into the subform!

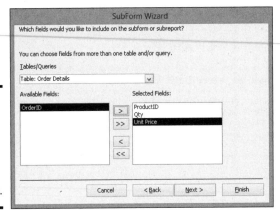

Figure 4-5:
You specify
the record
source and
the fields to
display on
the subform.

Don't include the primary key, which relates to the record in the main form. If you're adding an order-details subform to an order form, the main form displays one order at a time, including its order number. The subform displays all the order-details records that have the same order number. If you include the order number on the subform, you just see the same order number over and over — once for each record in the subform. What a waste of screen space!

8. **Select a relationship in the list, or choose the Define My Own option and select the matching fields on the form and subform; then click Next.**

   The wizard needs to know how the records in the subform relate to the records in the main form. It displays a list of the relationships you've already defined, and this list usually contains the right relationship. In Figure 4-6, the wizard suggests Show Order Details for Each Record in Orders Using OrderID — that is, it uses the `OrderID` field in the Order Details table to match the `OrderID` field in the Orders table (the record source of the main form).

   If you choose the Define My Own option, the wizard's window changes to allow you to choose the matching fields of the form (the "one" side of the relationship) and the subform (the "many" side).

9. **Type a name for the subform or accept the wizard's suggestion; then click Finish.**

   The wizard creates the subform as a separate form in your database. It also creates a subform control on the main form, as shown in Figure 4-7. You can adjust the edges of the subform control by dragging them. You can delete the label for the subform if its function is obvious.

Figure 4-6:
Tell the
SubForm
Wizard
how the
records in
the subform
relate to
the records
in the main
form.

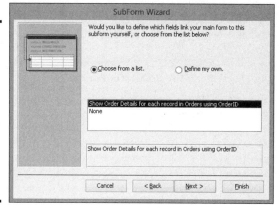

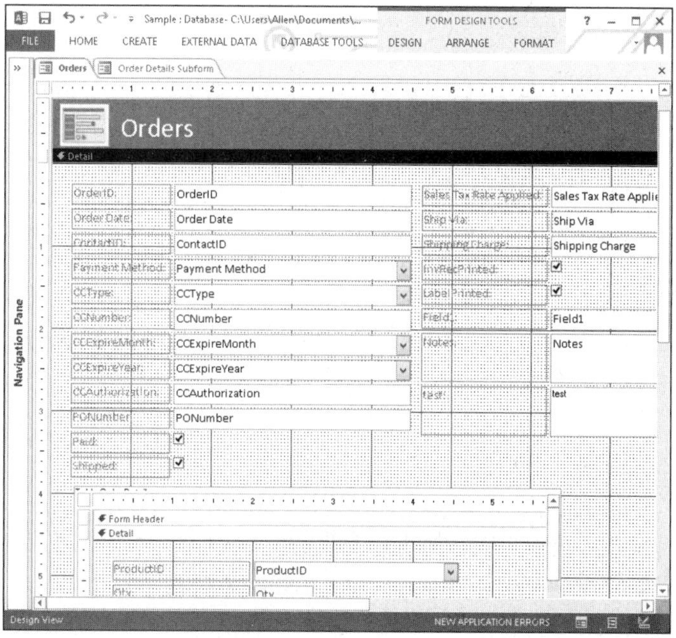

Figure 4-7:
In Design
view, the
subform
looks
terrible,
but it looks
better
in Form
view as a
datasheet.

**Book IV
Chapter 4**

Doing Calculations
in Forms and
Subforms

The subform may look totally wrong in Design view but fine in Form view.
The subform appears in Datasheet view when the main form is in Form view,
so the exact placement of the controls, the background color, and other features don't matter.

To adjust the column widths of the subform, which usually is in Datasheet
view, just drag the column dividers left or right in Form view. After you have
nice-looking columns, switch the main form back to Design view and adjust
the width of the subform control until it's the right size to fit your columns.

Viewing the properties of subform controls

After you create the subform, you can edit it in either of two ways:

+ Open the subform by right-clicking its name in the Navigation Pane and choosing Design View from the contextual menu.

+ Open the main form in Design view and double-click the subform control to start editing the subform that appears in the control.

Either way, Access saves the changes to the subform separately from the changes to the main form. When you save your main form, Access saves changes to your subform, too.

While you're fooling with the fields on the subform, you may want to change the properties of the subform control that displays the subform on the main form. To see the properties of the subform control, display the main form in Design view, display the property sheet, and then click the subform.

Don't click the gray box in the top-left corner of the subform. If you do, you end up seeing the properties of the form that you're using as a subform rather than the properties of the subform control.

When you're viewing the properties of the subform control, the Selection Type drop-down menu at the top of the property sheet shows the name of the subform control; if it doesn't, choose the subform control name from the menu.

Here are some useful entries that you can change on the Data tab of the property sheet for the subform control:

+ **Source Object:** The name of the form to display in this subform control.

+ **Link Child Fields:** The field name in the record source of the subform. This field must match the `Link Master Fields` field.

+ **Link Master Fields:** The field name in the record source of the main form. This field must match the `Link Child Fields` field.

Other properties have to be changed in the subform itself. Open the subform in Design view, and display the property sheet for the form. Alternatively, with the main form open in Design view, click the subform control to select it and then click the gray box in the top-left corner of the subform to select the form properties.

If you're editing the properties of a subform in Design view of the main form, click elsewhere on the main form to tell Access to update the subform properties. Otherwise, your changes won't appear to have taken effect when you switch to Form view.

Adding Subtotals and Totals from Subforms

If your form includes a subform (or if your report includes a subreport), and the information shown in the subform includes quantities, you may want to display a total on the main form. On an Orders form that contains an Order Details subform, the main form can include the total cost of all the items in the subform and maybe a count of the records in the subform. Figure 4-7, earlier in this chapter, shows an Orders form with a subform listing the items that the customer is buying.

Unfortunately, you can't make a control on the main form that calculates a total for the records on the subform. You can, however, make a control on the subform that calculates the total and then make a control on the main form that displays the value of this control. This process seems like an extra step to us, but it works. The following sections cover what you need to know to create totals and counts of subform records.

Using aggregate functions

An *aggregate function* is a function that combines a bunch of values. The Sum() function, for example, adds a bunch of numbers together. (Simple enough!) When doing calculations based on a bunch of records, you can use the aggregate functions outlined in the following table.

Function	Description
Sum()	Totals the values.
Count()	Counts the values.
Avg()	Averages the values (sum divided by count).
Min()	Calculates the smallest value (for numeric values), the earliest date (for date values), or the first value in alphabetical order (for text values).
Max()	Calculates the largest value (for numeric values), the latest date (for date values), or the last value in alphabetical order (for text values).
First()	Uses the value from the first record.
Last()	Uses the value from the last record.

Aggregate functions work only when Access knows what set of records you want to work with. On forms, they work in the form footer of a subform. (See Chapter 3 of this minibook for a description of a form footer unless you've already guessed that a *form footer* is a section that appears at the bottom of a form.)

Summarizing lots of records

In addition to the functions that work with the field values in the current record, Access has *domain aggregate functions* — functions that work with field values in some or all the records in a table or query. (*Domain* is a fancy name for *table* or *query*.) You may want a form to display the grand total of all the orders so far this year or the amount of the largest order placed, for example. To total the value of a field for a bunch of records, you use the DSum function, which has this syntax:

```
DSum(expression, domain,
    criterion)
```

Replace *expression* with the field name that you want to total (or an expression such as [Price] * [Qty]), in quotes. Replace *domain* with the table or query name, in quotes. Optionally, you can include a *criterion* that limits which records to include.

The following example expression totals the extended price (Price × Qty) for all the records in the Order Details table:

```
DSum("[Price] * [Qty]", "Order
    Details")
```

Following are some of the other domain aggregate functions you can use (all of which have the same syntax as DSum):

- ✔ **DAvg:** Averages the values.

- ✔ **DCount:** Counts the values.

- ✔ **DFirst:** Displays the value of the first record.

- ✔ **DLast:** Displays the value of the last record.

- ✔ **DMin:** Displays the minimum value. (For numbers, this value is the smallest; for text, it's the first in alphabetical order; for dates, it's the earliest.)

- ✔ **DMax:** Displays the maximum value. (For numbers, this value is the largest; for text, it's the last in alphabetical order; for dates, it's the latest.)

One other useful domain aggregate function is DLookup, which returns the value of a specific field for a specific record in a table or query. The following expression returns the date OrderID 5000 from the Orders table:

```
DLookup("[Order Date]",
    "Orders", "[OrderID] =
    5000")
```

In this DLookup function, the expression is "[Order Date]" — the date of the order. The domain is the Orders table. The criterion — "[OrderID] = 5000" — limits the records to include only the record with that specific ID.

Suppose that you have an Orders form and an Order Details form that lists the items included in the order. The total of the Qty field in the Order Details subform would be useful to tell the shipping clerk how many items need to be shipped for this order. The expression is

```
= Sum([Qty])
```

If a field name contains spaces, you have to enclose it in square brackets. We enclose all field names in square brackets just to be safe.

You can also total a calculation. To come up with the total cost of the items ordered, use this expression:

```
= Sum([Qty] * [Unit Price])
```

If you want to total, average, or count all the records in an entire table or query, or the selected records in a table or query, use the functions described in the nearby sidebar "Summarizing lots of records."

Referring to a control on a subform

To create a control on the main form that shows information from the subform, you need to know how to refer to a control on the subform. Use this format for an expression that displays a value from a subform:

```
= [subform control name].Form![control name]
```

This syntax looks hideous, but hold on! Replace *subform control name* with the name of the subform control on the main form that displays the subform, and replace *control name* with the name of the text box on the subform that displays the value you want to see.

If your main form is the Orders form shown in Figure 4-7, its subform control is called `Order Details subform`. If you want to display the information from that subform's Order Subtotal text box, the expression would look like this:

```
= [Order Details subform].Form![Order Subtotal]
```

Creating the controls to total a subform

To calculate a total (or a count) of the values of a control on the subform and to display it on the main form, you create two controls: one in the form footer of the subform and one on the main form, wherever you want the total to appear.

Be careful when entering the expressions for calculating and displaying the total. In some cases, you type the name of the field; in other cases, you type the name of the control that displays the field. It can get confusing!

Follow these steps to display the subform total on the main form:

1. **Open the subform in Design view, and display its property sheet by clicking the Property Sheet button in the Tools group on the Design tab of the Ribbon.**

If you already have the main form open in Design view, you can right-click the subform control and choose Subform in New Window from the contextual menu.

2. Add a Form Footer section (assuming that the subform doesn't already have one) by right-clicking the location where you want to add a footer and then choosing Form Header/Form Footer from the contextual menu.

If you see a Form Footer divider bar and space below it, you already have a footer. Click the bottom edge of the bar and drag down to expand the footer and make space for a text box or two. (See Chapter 3 of this minibook for more information about form headers and footers.)

3. Note the name of the field in the record source (not the control on the form) that contains the values you want to count or total, or note the expression you want to total.

Frequently, the control that displays a field has the same name as the field itself, but not always. Be sure to use the field name, not the name of any control on the form that displays the field. For this example, you want to total the expression [Unit Price] * [Qty].

4. Make a text box by clicking the Text Box button in the Controls group on the Design tab of the Ribbon and then clicking the Form Footer section on the form.

Access creates an unbound text box.

5. On the Data tab of the property sheet for the text box, type the expression that you want to calculate in the Control Source property.

For this example, type = **Sum([Qty]*[Unit Price])** in the Control Source property, as shown in Figure 4-8. Access displays hints just below where you're typing, such as the names of fields and functions.

6. Enter a descriptive name for the control in the Name property on the Other tab of the property sheet.

Make a note of the control name (such as OrderSubtotal), because you need it to display the value on the main form. You may want to change some other properties later, such as switching to Currency format for the new field in the footer, if appropriate.

7. Switch to Form view by clicking the View button on the Ribbon to make sure that the new text box works.

Because you're looking at the subform as an independent form, the subform shows all the records in its record source, and the calculation totals all the records, not just those for one order. Don't be surprised if you see a very large number. When this form is used as a subform, the linkage between the subform and the main form restricts the records in the subform to one order at a time, and the control totals the records for only the current order.

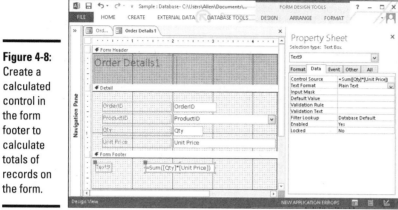

Figure 4-8:
Create a
calculated
control in
the form
footer to
calculate
totals of
records on
the form.

8. **If you plan to display the subform in Form view, not just in Datasheet view, hide the Form Footer section by setting its `Visible` property to `No`.**

   Otherwise, you display the subtotal once on the subform and once on the main form, which looks odd. Most subforms appear in Datasheet view, which doesn't display form headers and footers. If you do need to hide the footer, click the Form Footer divider bar, find the `Visible` property on the Format tab of the property sheet, and set the `Visible` property to `No`.

9. **Save and close the subform.**

   Press Ctrl+S to save your changes. Then go ahead and close the Design View window; you're done with it.

10. **Open the main form in Design view, and display its property sheet by clicking the Property Sheet button in the Tools group on the Design tab of the Ribbon.**

11. **Create a text box to control the total by clicking the Text Box button in the Controls group on the Design tab of the Ribbon and then clicking the form where you want the calculated control to appear.**

    You get a new unbound control that's ready to display your calculated total.

12. **Set the text box's `Control Source` property to an expression that refers to the calculated control on the subform.**

    Here's the expression that refers to the calculated control shown in Figure 4-8, earlier in this chapter:

    ```
    = [Order Details subform].Form![Order Subtotal]
    ```
    `Order Details subform` is the name of the subform control.

13. **Format the new control with the numeric format you want, and edit its label to a sensible name (such as Total Products or Order Subtotal).**

    If you don't format the text box, Access usually displays way too many decimal places for calculated values. On the Format tab of the property sheet, set the Format property to Currency (or whatever format you prefer). Set Decimal Places to 2.

14. **Switch to Form view to test the control.**

    If all goes well, you see a text box like the one shown in Figure 4-9.

    If you see #Name or #Error instead of the subtotal, check the expression for the control on the main form carefully, and make sure that you correctly entered the expression, the name of the control on the subform, and the name of the subform control — the control you put on the main form. (What a zoo!)

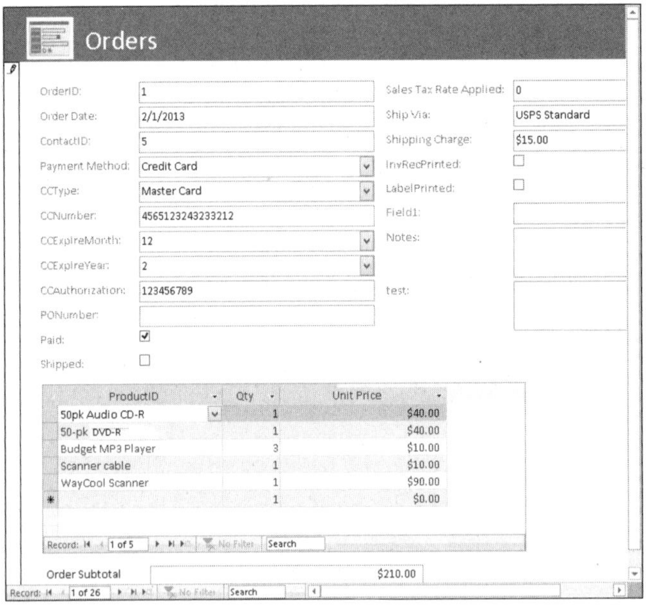

Figure 4-9:
You can display the total from the subform in the main form, along with other calculations based on that total.

Orders	
OrderID: 1	Sales Tax Rate Applied: 0
Order Date: 2/1/2013	Ship Via: USPS Standard
ContactID: 5	Shipping Charge: $15.00
Payment Method: Credit Card	InvRecPrinted: ☐
CCType: Master Card	LabelPrinted: ☐
CCNumber: 4565123243233212	Field1:
CCExpireMonth: 12	Notes:
CCExpireYear: 2	
CCAuthorization: 123456789	test:
PONumber:	
Paid: ☑	
Shipped: ☐	

ProductID	Qty	Unit Price
50pk Audio CD-R	1	$40.00
50-pk DVD-R	1	$40.00
Budget MP3 Player	3	$10.00
Scanner cable	1	$10.00
WayCool Scanner	1	$90.00
*	1	$0.00

Record: 1 of 5   No Filter   Search

Order Subtotal $210.00

Record: 1 of 26   No Filter   Search

Book V
Reporting in Words and Pictures

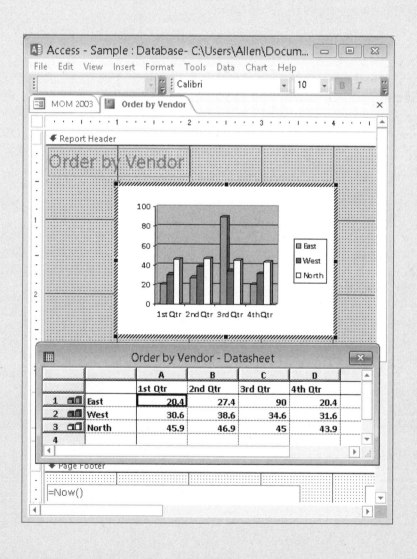

Understand how to avoid blank pages appearing in reports at www.dummies.com/extras/
access2013aio.

Contents at a Glance

Chapter 1: Creating and Spiffing Up Reports 387

Knowing Forms Means That You Already Know Reports 388
Creating Reports Automatically 389
Editing Reports in Layout and Design View 396
Creating and Managing Report Sections 397
Employing Formatting Tips and Tricks 407
Copying Forms to Reports 409
Adding and Formatting Subreports 409
Displaying Empty or Long Fields 413
Viewing Your Reports Onscreen 414

Chapter 2: Printing Beautiful Reports 415

Viewing Your Report 415
Formatting the Page 418
Printing the Report 422
Creating Mailing Labels 424
Sending a Report to Another Application 429

Chapter 3: Creating Charts and Graphs from Your Data 435

Pulling Up a Seat at the Data Bar 435
Displaying Information with Charts 437
Changing Your Charts 451

Chapter 1: Creating and Spiffing Up Reports

In This Chapter

✔ **Getting a handle on how reports are like forms**

✔ **Creating reports by running wizards**

✔ **Editing reports in Design view**

✔ **Adding page headers and footers**

✔ **Creating groupings and subtotals**

✔ **Printing information from related tables**

✔ **Viewing reports onscreen**

Reports are the best ways to put information from your database on paper and in PDF files and other formats. In a report, you can choose how to display your data, including which information to include (tables and fields); where to print each field on the page; which text fonts, font sizes, and spacing to use; and how to print lines, boxes, and pictures.

Reports can include information from different tables. You can display the customer information, followed by all the items that the customer has bought from all orders, for example. The Report Wizard simplifies creating reports that list, summarize, and total your data. You can also use calculations in reports to create totals, subtotals, and other results. You can create invoices, packing slips, student rosters, and all kinds of other reports. Thanks to the trusty Label Wizard, reports are also the best ways to create mailing labels from addresses in your database.

This chapter explains how to create and modify reports so that they're ready to print. Chapter 2 of this minibook talks about previewing and printing reports, and Chapter 3 of this minibook describes graphical reports: graphs and charts.

Knowing Forms Means That You Already Know Reports

Reports and forms are used very differently, but you create them in similar ways. You can create both forms and reports by running wizards. You can create or modify both forms and reports in Layout view, where you can create and rearrange controls, and in Design view, where you can customize the controls and sections of a report, along with their properties.

To see a list of the reports in your database — and, eventually, to open or modify a report — scroll down in the Navigation Pane until you get to the Reports section. If you don't see the Reports section in the Navigation Pane, click the down arrow on the title bar of the Navigation Pane and choose Object Type from the drop-down menu. The items displayed in the Navigation Pane change. Now click the down arrow again. Reports is one of the options on the drop-down menu.

You can look at a report in four views:

✦ **Layout view:** Allows you to rearrange the controls on your report and create new ones. It works like Layout view for forms, as described in Book IV, Chapter 1.

✦ **Design view:** Gives you a behind-the-scenes look at what fields the report displays where. It works like Design view for forms, as described in Book IV, Chapter 2.

✦ **Report view:** Displays the report formatted with real data, as described in "Viewing Your Reports Onscreen," at the end of this chapter.

✦ **Print Preview:** Shows how the report will look when you print it, including page breaks, headers, and footers. Chapter 2 of this minibook describes how to check how your report will look before you waste paper printing it.

To open a report, right-click its name in the Navigation Pane and choose a view from the contextual menu. You can switch between views by clicking the View button in the Views group on the Home tab of the Ribbon. You can switch to any view by clicking the down arrow on the View button and choosing the view you want from the drop-down menu.

This chapter describes how to make reports by running wizards, as well as how to customize reports in ways that don't work for forms. For information about how to create and customize reports in Layout view and Design view, including adding controls and setting properties, applying themes and other formatting (such as conditional formatting), and creating calculated fields, see Book IV, Chapters 1, 2, and 4.

What view opens when you open a report?

Now that Access has four (count 'em) views in which to open a report, it can be hard to guess which view you'll see when you double-click a report in the Navigation Pane to open it: Report view or Print Preview. To clear up this confusion, you can set the Default View property of the report.

 With a report open in Design or Layout view, display the property sheet for the form. (Double-click the top-left corner of the form in Design view, or click the Property Sheet button in the Tools group on the Design tab of the Ribbon in either

Design or Layout view and then choose Report from the Selection Type drop-down menu.) Then, on the Format tab of the property sheet, set the Default View property to Report View or Print Preview.

Be sure that you're looking at the property sheet for the report, not for one of the elements of the report. While you're at it, set the Allow Report View and Allow Layout View properties to No if you don't want to enable those views.

Reports can include features that don't appear on forms, including these:

✦ **Grouping and sections:** When you design a report, you frequently want to group certain information. A monthly sales report, for example, may list sales by product, with subtotals for each product; a mailing-label report may start a new page for each new zip code and print the total number of labels for each zip code. You can have up to four grouping levels. You can add grouping levels by adding section headers to your report in Design view, as described in "Grouping your records," later in this chapter.

✦ **Page headers, footers, and numbers:** Most reports have page numbers and many need other information printed at the top or bottom of every page. For details, see "Adding page headers, footers, and numbers," later in this chapter.

✦ **Margins, paper size, and paper orientation:** Reports usually end up on paper, and you can configure your report to fit, as described in Chapter 2 of this minibook.

First, we cover how to create some reports the easy way: by using a wizard.

Creating Reports Automatically

You create a report the same way that you create other objects in your database. Take a look at the Reports group on the Create tab of the Ribbon to see some ways to make a report. The buttons are listed in Table 1-1.

Table 1-1	**Creating Reports with Reports-Group Buttons**		
Button	*Name*	*What It Does*	*Where to Find More Info*
Report	Report	Creates a quick and easy report for the table, query, or form you have open or selected. You can customize the report later.	Book IV, Chapter 1
Report Design	Report Design	Allows you to design your own report from scratch, in Design view.	Book IV, Chapter 2
Blank Report	Blank Report	Allows you to design your own report from scratch, in Layout view.	Book IV, Chapter 1
Report Wizard	Report Wizard	Walks you through the creation of a report, helping you choose fields from multiple tables and queries. You can use Design or Layout view later to make changes.	"Running the Report Wizard," later in this chapter
Labels	Labels	Creates a report to print data from one table or query on labels.	Book V, Chapter 2

Making the easiest possible report

You can click the Report button to create a report by using the data from a single table or query. This button doesn't give you any options, but it makes a report in just a second or two.

To create a report based on a table or query, follow these steps:

1. **In the Navigation Pane, choose the table, query, or form from which you want the data to come.**

   The report will include all the fields in this table, query, or form. (After you create the report, you can delete the controls for the fields that you don't want to appear on the report.)

2. Click the Report button in the Reports group on the Create tab of the Ribbon.

Report

Access creates a report in tabular format and displays it in Layout view, as shown in Figure 1-1.

| Orders | | | | Monday, November 12, 2012 |
| | | | | 11:05:20 AM |

OrderID	Order Date	ContactID	Payment Method	CCType
13	8/3/2006	32	Check	
14	8/6/2006	20	Cash	
17	9/22/2006	2	Credit Card	Visa
18	1/9/2007	17	Check	
19	1/9/2007	13	Credit Card	Master Card

Figure 1-1:
The Report button makes a columnar report.

3. Customize the report as you would any other report.

Use Layout view or Design view to get rid of the unwanted fields, widen the controls for the fields and field names you want to keep, or switch to landscape printing (or all three).

Running the Report Wizard

Running the Report Wizard usually is a better way to start making a report, especially if you want to create a report that groups data from one or more fields, with headings or subtotals for each group. When the wizard finishes, you can add your own formatting touches in Layout or Design view.

One big advantage of using the Report Wizard is that you can choose fields for the report from more than one table or query; you don't have to gather all the data you want into one query. If you have an online store, for example, you may want to create a report that lists all the orders for each customer. The information for this report comes from several tables: Address Book (which stores one record for each customer, including name and address), Orders (with one record for each order, including the order date), and Order Details (with one record for each item in an order, including the quantity ordered and the price per item).

The Report Wizard asks different questions depending on the data in the record source and on options you select, so don't be surprised if you don't see every window each time you run it.

Follow these steps to create a report:

1. Click the Report Wizard button in the Reports group on the Create tab of the Ribbon.

Access displays the first Report Wizard window, shown in Figure 1-2.

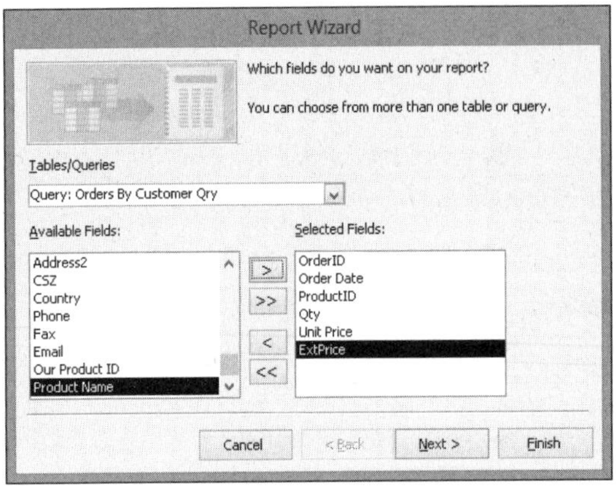

Figure 1-2:
The Report
Wizard
can build a
report from
one or more
tables and
queries.

2. **From the Tables/Queries drop-down menu, choose the table or query that stores the records you want to include in the report.**

   If you plan to use information from several tables or queries, choose one of them. The Available Fields box lists the fields in the selected table or query.

3. **Select the fields you want to display in the report in the Available Fields box and add them to the Selected Fields list by clicking the > button.**

   Double-clicking a field name also adds it to the Selected Fields list. Click the >> button to add all the fields.

4. **Repeat Steps 2 and 3 for fields in other tables or queries until all the fields you want to include in the report appear in the Selected Fields list.**

   You can use some fields from tables and other fields from queries. For a customer-order listing, for example, you might select fields from the Address Book table, the Orders table, and the Order Details Qry query (which includes the Ext Price field, a calculated field that equals Price × Qty).

5. **Click Next to see the wizard's next question: How do you want to view your data?**

   You may want to show the information from the first table on top or per-haps in some other order.

6. **Select the table that you want to organize by and then click Next.**

7. **Specify any grouping levels that you want to add.**

Access gives you a chance to choose how you want to group the data. For a customer-order report, grouping by customer is a good idea because it keeps all the information about one customer together. Within the section for each customer, the secondary grouping is by order so that all the items in each order are listed together, as shown in Figure 1-3.

As you decide how to group your data, if you realize that you forgot to include any fields you need, click Back to return to Step 2 and then add them.

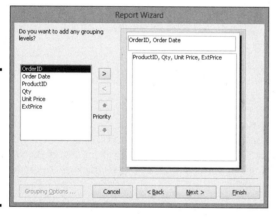

Figure 1-3:
The Report
Wizard
enables you
to group the
information
in the
report.

To add another level of grouping, select a field in the list and click the > button. (You can remove a field by selecting it and clicking the < button.) After you add a field, you can change the importance (grouping level) of a field by selecting the field and then clicking the Priority buttons (up arrow and down arrow).

8. Click the Grouping Options button to customize how records are grouped.

Clicking the Grouping Options button (which isn't always available, depending on your groupings) displays the Grouping Intervals dialog box, shown in Figure 1-4, where you can specify exactly how to group records by using the fields you choose:

- For Date fields, you can group by day, month, or year.

- For Number fields, you can group by 10s, 50s, 100s, 500s, 1,000s, 5,000s, and 10,000s so that you can categorize values by magnitude.

- For Text fields, you can group on the first 1, 2, 3, 4, or 5 characters.

9. Click OK to exit the Grouping Intervals dialog box and return to the wizard.

10. **Click Next to see the next wizard window, which asks how you want to sort your records.**

Access automatically sorts by the fields on which you're grouping records. If you're grouping records by customer and then by order, the customers appear in alphabetical order by name or in numerical order by customer number. Within the lowest level of grouping, you can choose what order the records appear in and specify up to four fields on which to sort. If you aren't grouping your records at all, you can also sort them here. In the customer-orders-report example, you've already grouped by customer and order, but you can sort the products by product ID in each order.

11. **Choose how you want to sort the records within the lowest-level grouping.**

Click in the 1 box (shown in Figure 1-5), choose a field, and click the adjacent Ascending button if you want to switch to a descending sort. Additional sort fields are used only when the 1 sort field is identical in two or more records, in which case, the 2 field is used. If the 1 and 2 fields are identical in two records, Access sorts by the 3 field and then the 4 field.

12. **If you want to print counts, averages, or totals, click the Summary Options button to display the Summary Options dialog box, shown in Figure 1-6.**

Access displays a list of the numeric fields in your report, with check boxes for Sum (total), Avg (average), Min (minimum or smallest value), and Max (maximum or largest value).

13. **Set the options as desired.**

You can set any of the following options:

- Select the appropriate check boxes for each field in your report: Sum, Avg, Min, and Max.

- If you want to use only the summary values, without information for individual records, select the Summary Only radio button.

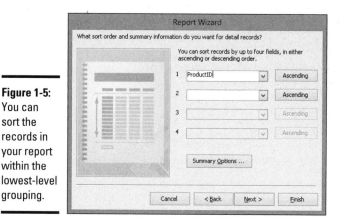

Figure 1-5:
You can
sort the
records in
your report
within the
lowest-level
grouping.

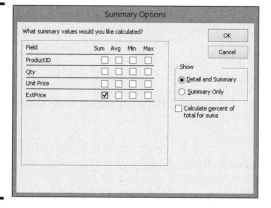

Figure 1-6:
The Report
Wizard can
add totals,
subtotals,
averages,
percent-
ages,
and other
summary
statistics to
your report.

- If you want Access to calculate the percentage of the total that each grouping represents (such as the percentage of orders that each customer represents), click the Calculate Percent of Total for Sums check box.

In the customer-order report you're cooking up here, you'd click the Sum check box for the Ext Price field to get a total of the items in each order and for each customer.

14. **Click OK to close the dialog box and return to the Report Wizard.**

15. **Set the layout options for your report (see Figure 1-7), and click Next.**

You can preview the layout options by clicking one of the Layout radio buttons. The sample box on the left changes to show what your chosen layout looks like. If you want to print your report sideways on the paper, click the Landscape radio button. We can more or less guarantee that none of these layouts will be exactly what you want and that you'll end up adjusting them in Layout or Design view.

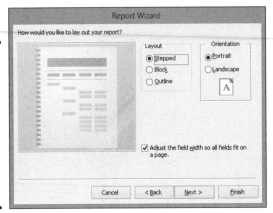

Figure 1-7:
Choose a
Stepped,
Block, or
Outline
layout, as
well as
Portrait or
Landscape
orientation.

16. **Type a title for the report.**

17. **Choose whether to display the report in Print Preview or go to Design view to modify the report.**

18. **Click Finish.**

The title appears at the top of the report. The Report Wizard takes a moment to create the report and then displays it in the view you chose in Step 17.

The report may look close to perfect, or it may look like a complete wreck. The customer-order report as created by the Report Wizard contains some of the right information, but it may look lousy. Luckily, you can switch to Layout or Design view to fix it, as we discuss in the next section.

Editing Reports in Layout and Design View

Access provides two views for creating and modifying the design of reports, just as it does for forms:

+ **Layout view** shows your report with data in it. You can use it to move information around and to add or remove information. See Book IV, Chapter 1 for information on editing reports in Layout view, including how control layouts keep information neatly in rows and columns.

+ **Design view** is the traditional Access tool that enables you to make all kinds of changes in your report. Book IV, Chapter 2 describes how to use Design view. Figure 1-8 shows a report in Design view.

You can modify your report in many ways, some of which work just as they do when you modify a form. Check out the following list for some of the ways:

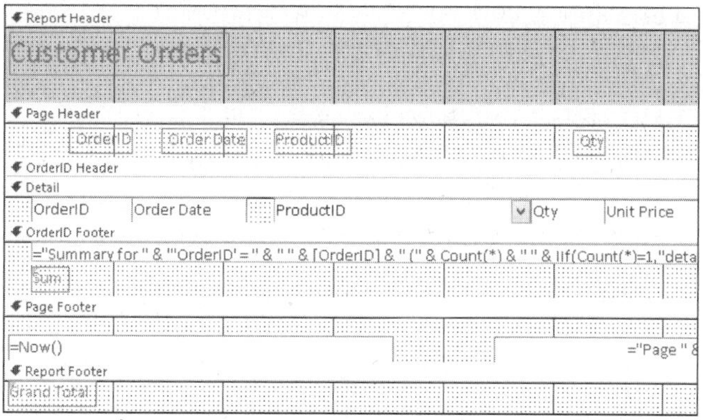

Figure 1-8:
A report
in Design
view.

✦ **Creating, editing, moving, and deleting controls:** Controls are the boxes on the Design grid that display labels, data from fields, and other information. The easiest way to move them around is in Layout view, which is described in Book IV, Chapter 1.

✦ **Editing controls:** If you need to set the properties for a control, set fonts and columns, use conditional formatting, or make other fine adjustments, use Design view, as described in Book IV, Chapter 2.

✦ **Creating calculated controls:** To make a control that displays a calculated value, see Book IV, Chapter 4.

✦ **Drawing lines and boxes:** Book IV, Chapter 2 has a section devoted to this topic.

✦ **Setting report properties:** See Book IV, Chapter 1 for details.

✦ **Saving, importing, copying, and renaming reports:** See Book IV, Chapter 1 for details.

Some things work differently for forms and reports, however. For one thing, reports don't have command buttons and drop-down menus (because they wouldn't work on paper). Also, reports have to fit correctly on the printed page, and they need page headers, footers, and headings for subsections.

The rest of this chapter describes report-specific features. Chapter 2 of this minibook describes controlling the way that reports print.

Creating and Managing Report Sections

In Design view, your report is broken into parts called *sections,* as shown in Figure 1-8, earlier in this chapter. The main part of the report is the *Detail section,* which shows information from fields in the table or query that's the record source for the report. The other sections come in pairs around the Detail section, with a header section above and a footer section below.

Sections provide headers and footers for your pages and allow you to group data by using a particular field. If you have several reports with the same value in a field, you can display those records together in the report. If your record source has a Date/Time field, for example, you can create a section for that field and group records that have the same date, with subtotals by date.

Table 1-2 lists the sections that a report can include, with tips for using the section.

Table 1-2	Sections of Reports
Report Sections	*Where the Sections Appear and How to Use Them*
Report Header and Footer	Appear at the beginning and end of the report. These sections are for summary information about the entire report. The report header can include a title page, and the report footer can include totals for all the records in the report.
Page Header and Footer	Appear at the top and bottom of each page. These sections usually include the report name, the date, and the page number.
Grouping Header and Footer	Appear at the top and bottom of each grouping (before the first record and after the last record) in a group that has the same value for a specific field. Your report may have more than one grouping header and footer (one pair for each grouping). The footer may include subtotals. Format your grouping headers and footers to make the hierarchy of the report obvious (using larger fonts for first-level groups and smaller fonts for second-level groups, for example).
Detail	Displays values for each record.

In Design view, the white bar names the section, and the controls below the bar appear every time that section of the report prints. In the report shown in Figure 1-8, earlier in this chapter, the report header prints only once: at the beginning of the report. The Page Header contains only one line. Records are grouped by order number. The Detail section prints information about each product in the order. The Order ID Footer section contains the total number of items in each order. The Page Footer section includes the current date and time, the page number, and the total number of pages in the report. The Report Footer section has a grand total of the extended price for all records in the report.

Figure 1-9 shows the top of the first page of the report when printed. Group headers are printed at the top of each group. In the example in Figure 1-8, earlier in this chapter, the OrderID group header is empty, so nothing is printed for it. The Detail section prints once for each product ordered in each order. The Page Header and Page Footer sections print once each per page.

Customer Orders

OrderID	Order Date	ProductID	Qty
1	3/1/2007	Budget MP3 Player	3
		Scanner cable	1
		50-pk DVD-R	1
		WayCool Scanner	1
		50pk Audio CD-R	1

Summary for 'OrderID' = 1 (5 detail records)
Sum

2	2/5/2007	Golden Whistle	2
		Lawn Flamingo	1
		Lucky Rabbits Foot	10

Summary for 'OrderID' = 2 (3 detail records)
Sum

3	3/13/2007	Golden Whistle	1
		Old Time Stock Ticker	1

1   ▶ ▶ ▶   No Filter

Figure 1-9:
The printed report includes product information grouped by customer and order.

When you use the Report Wizard to create, you get a section for each field on which you grouped the records. When you create a report from scratch in Design view, Access gives you just the Page Header, Detail, and Page Footer sections. You can add or delete sections in Design view, as described in the following section titled Adding page headers, footers, and numbers. You can also adjust the sizes of sections by dragging the section dividers up and down.

You can't delete the Detail section, but you can leave it blank if you want a summary report with subtotals and totals but no data for individual records. Drag its bottom edge (the top of the next section divider) up to shrink the section to nothing. (In Figure 1-8, earlier in this chapter, for example, the Page Header section is reduced to almost nothing.)

Setting report and section properties

Like most Access objects, each section and control in your report has properties — and so does the entire report itself. You can display and change the properties on the property sheet (see Figure 1-10).

You have two ways to display the property sheet for the whole report:

✦ Click the report selector (the white box in the top-left corner of the Design View window).

✦ Click the Property Sheet button in the Tools group on the Design tab of the Ribbon to display the property sheet, and choose Report from the Selection Type drop-down menu.

Click the tabs to see the different categories of properties, or click the All tab to see all of them. Click a property to change it.

Property Sheet ×

Selection type: Section

GroupHeader0

| Format | Data | Event | Other | All |

Name	GroupHeader0
Visible	Yes
Height	0"
Back Color	Background 1
Alternate Back Color	Background 1, Darker 5
Special Effect	Flat
Auto Height	Yes
Can Grow	No
Can Shrink	No
Display When	Always
Keep Together	Yes
Repeat Section	No
Force New Page	None
New Row Or Col	None
On Click	
On Format	
On Dbl Click	
On Mouse Down	
On Mouse Up	
On Mouse Move	
On Paint	
On Print	
On Retreat	
Tag	

Figure 1-10:
You can set the properties of the entire report or of individual sections or controls.

To see or change the properties of a particular section, double-click the section header, or select the section header and click the Property Sheet button in the Tools group on the Design tab of the Ribbon. When the property sheet is visible, you can click a section header or control to see its properties.

You can display or hide the property sheet quickly by pressing Alt+Enter.

Adding page headers, footers, and numbers

To add Report or Page Header or Footer sections, right-click anywhere in the report in Design view and choose Report Header/Footer or Page Header/Footer from the contextual menu. Access adds these sections in pairs: If you have a page header, you have a page footer. You can leave one or the other section blank, though. To delete a Report or Page Header or Footer section, choose the same command again: Access deletes the Header/Footer pair and all the controls in the sections (after warning you that it's about to do so).

If you want just a header or just a footer, change the height of the section that you *don't* want to appear by dragging the bottom border of the section up to the top border. The header or footer is still there, but you've shrunk it to nothing, so nothing prints.

You can't do this, of course, if you have something in the section, such as a control. Be sure that a section is empty before you try to hide it by dragging the bottom border up to the top border.

Adding page numbers

Page Numbers

When you have a Page Header or Footer section to put controls in, you can create controls in that section or drag the controls there from other sections. The easiest way to add page numbers — probably among the most common controls that you'll find on reports — is to click the Page Numbers button in the Header/Footer group on the Design tab of the Ribbon. When you see the Page Numbers dialog box (shown in Figure 1-11), choose the format of the numbering, the position, and the alignment (Left, Center, Right, Inside, or Outside). Inside and Outside page numbering refer to alternating left and right positions on odd and even pages. You can omit the page number on the first page by deselecting the Show Number on First Page check box. Click OK to save your changes.

Figure 1-11:
Adding page
numbers to
your report.

If you'd rather make your own page-numbering controls, you can create your own text box control by following these steps:

1. **Open the report in Design view.**

2. **Create a text box control in the Page Header or Footer section by clicking the Text Box button in the Controls group on the Design tab of the Ribbon and then clicking the Header or Footer section.**

   Don't worry if the text box doesn't appear in exactly the right place; you can drag it there later.

3. **If Access created a label to go with the text box, delete the label by clicking the label and then pressing the Delete key.**

   Your page number doesn't need a label!

Property
Sheet

4. **Click the Property Sheet button in the Tools group on the Design tab of the Ribbon to display the property sheet, if it's not already onscreen.**

   You see the property sheet with the properties of the text box you just created.

5. **Click the Data tab on the property sheet, click the** `Control Source` **property, and type the following expression:**

   ```
   = Page
   ```

To display the word `Page` as well as the number, type

```
= "Page " & Page
```

Adding the date and time

If you want to include the current date or time on your report, follow the same steps as in the preceding section, but type the following expression in the `Control Source` property of another text box:

```
= Now()
```

The `Now()` function returns both the date and time (`11/25/12 1:55:48 PM`). If you want to print only the current date, format the box as a date by setting the `Format` property accordingly. (In the property sheet for the text box, click the Format tab and set the `Format` property to one of the date formats, all of which omit the time.)

Controlling which pages get page headers and footers

You can choose whether the Page Header and Footer sections print on all pages, all but the Report Header page (so that your cover page isn't numbered), all but the Report Footer page, or all but the Report Header and Footer pages.

To change the Page Header and Footer sections' properties, follow these steps:

1. **With the report open in Design view, display the property sheet for the report.**

2. **Click the Format tab of the property sheet.**

3. **Set the `Page Header` and `Page Footer` properties.**

   Your options are `All Pages`, `Not With Rpt Hdr`, `Not With Rpt Ftr`, and `Not With Rpt Hdr/Ftr`.

 Displaying the first value of a field in the Page Header section to make a telephone-book–style header is easy. Just create a text box in the Page Header section that displays the field. When you print the report, the text box shows the value for the first record on the page. You can also print the value of the last record on the page in the Page Footer section.

Grouping your records

To create *grouping sections,* you tell Access to group the records in your report by the value of one or more fields. For each field, you get a Grouping Header and Footer section for that field (as listed in Table 1-2, earlier in this chapter). The report shown in Figure 1-8, earlier in this chapter, lists customer orders, with records grouped by customer (identified by `ContactID`) and within customer by order (`OrderID`). If you choose to add both a header and footer section for each group, you end up with ContactID

Header, OrderID Header, OrderID Footer, and ContactID Footer sections (in that order).

🗐 Group & Sort   To see and change your grouping sections, open the report in Design or Layout view, and click the Group & Sort button in the Grouping & Totals group on the Design tab of the Ribbon. Access displays the Group, Sort, and Total pane, shown in Figure 1-12. You see any fields that are currently used for sorting or grouping the records on your report. If more than one field appears, the topmost field is the major grouping, and the other fields are subgroups.

Figure 1-12:
The Group, Sort, and Total pane defines how the records in your report are grouped for subtotals.

Adding a group

To add a group, follow these steps:

1. **Display the Group, Sort, and Total pane as described in the preceding section.**

2. **Click the Add a Group button.**

3. **Choose a field from the Field/Expression drop-down menu to add a section (grouping).**

   You see a list of the fields in the record source for your report. After you select a field, Access automatically uses an ascending sort (with *A* at the top) for the new field. You can choose expression if you want to group on a calculated value.

   When you choose a field, Access adds a Group on line to the Group, Sort, and Total pane for this grouping, and it adds a Grouping Header to the report design. The Group on line includes drop-down menus of settings you can use to customize the grouping. The exact settings depend on the type of data in the field; different settings are available for Text, Number, and Date fields.

4. **Customize the group as described in the next section.**

   You can sort in ascending or descending order, group by ranges of values rather than individual values, and make other changes.

5. **Close the Group, Sort, and Total pane by clicking the X button in its top-right corner.**

Customizing your groups

You can customize how each group works in various ways by using the Group, Sort, and Total pane (refer to Figure 1-12, earlier in this chapter). Click the More button to the right of the field name to see your additional options (see Figure 1-13), which vary depending on the data type of the field. (When the additional options are shown, you can click the Less button to hide them again.)

Figure 1-13: In the Group, Sort, and Total pane, you can customize your groups.

Here are some changes that you can make for each group:

✦ **Sort the field in descending order.** Click the down arrow next to `from smallest to largest` (which appears for Number fields), `from oldest to newest` (which appears for Date fields), or `with A on top` (which appears for Text fields). Then choose `from largest to smallest`, `from newest to oldest`, or `with Z on top`.

✦ **Group on each individual value of the field or ranges of values.** Click the down arrow next to `by entire value`, and choose the range you want. You see different options for Text, Number, and Date fields.

✦ **Display subtotals and totals.** Click the down arrow next to `with no totals`, and choose whether you want to use summary statistics, which can include totals, averages, minimum, maximum, or counts for each group or for the whole report. See "Calculating group subtotals and report totals," later in this chapter, for more information.

✦ **Add a title.** Click the `click to add` link next to `with title`, and enter a title.

✦ **Hide or display headers and footers for the group.** Click the down arrows next to `with(out) a header section` and `with(out) a footer section`, and make your choices.

✦ **Control page breaks.** Click the down arrow next to `do not keep group together on one page`, and make your choice.

As soon as you choose to hide or display a group footer or header or to add or remove a subtotal or total field, Access reflects your changes in Design or Layout view.

To change what's displayed in a Grouping Header or Footer section, just create or remove controls in that section of the report in Design or Layout view.

Changes in the Group, Sort, and Total pane cause changes in the sections and controls of the report or the properties of the grouping section. You can look at the properties of a section by double-clicking the section's title bar in Design view.

Removing a group

To remove a group, click the X button at the right end of its line in the Group, Sort, and Total pane. If you want to remove the header or footer for a group, you can also delete all the controls in that section of the report and drag the divider below the section up to shrink the section to nothing.

Sorting the records in your report

You can sort a report by sorting the record source — the table or query that provides the records for the report — before you print. A more foolproof method, however, is to use the Group, Sort, and Total pane to make a sort or a group for the field(s) by which you want to sort. When you tell Access to group by a field, you get sorting thrown in for free, so click either Add a Group or Add a Sort in the Group, Sort, and Total pane (refer to Figure 1-12, earlier in this chapter). If you make a group, selecting without a header section and without a footer section in the Group, Sort, and Total pane tells Access to sort by the field but not to print any grouping sections.

To sort the records in a report by two fields, decide which field is the primary sort field and which is the secondary one. The secondary sort field works like a tiebreaker, used only when two or more records have the same value for the primary sort field. To sort order records by customer name, for example, you usually sort by last name (primary sort field) and first name (secondary sort field). If you have a large number of records, you may want additional sort fields. You could sort a mailing list by zip code, next by last name, and then by first name.

When you add a group to your report, Access automatically sorts the group in ascending order based on the field on which you grouped the report. In the Group, Sort, and Total pane (refer to Figure 1-12, earlier in this chapter), click the down arrow next to `from smallest to largest`, `from oldest to newest`, or `with A on top`, and then choose `from largest to smallest`, `from newest to oldest`, or `with Z on top`.

You can sort by a calculated value that isn't one of the fields in the record source of the report. Choose `expression` in the Sort By section of the Group, Sort, and Total pane, and enter an expression. (See Book III, Chapter 2 for an introduction to expressions.) If you print a list of products, you may want to sort them by profit margin — by `[Selling Price]` – `[Purchase Price]`.

Calculating group subtotals and report totals

If you use the Report Wizard to create a report, and you click the Summary Options button to request sums, averages, minimum values, or maximum values for each group, you already have subtotals and totals on your report. Alternatively, you can make them yourself in Design view.

In the Group, Sort, and Total pane (refer to Figure 1-12, earlier in this chapter), you can display subtotals and totals in your report for the group. On the line for the grouping, click the down arrow next to `with no totals`, and choose whether you want to use summary statistics, which can include totals, averages, minimum, maximum, or counts for each group or for the whole report. Set these options:

✦ **Total On:** This field is the one that you want to summarize on (total count and so on), and usually, it isn't the same field that you're grouping on. If you're grouping on `Contact ID` (customer), you may want to total the `ExtPrice` field (price × quantity of each item ordered).

✦ **Type:** Choose what calculation you want Access to do. Your options are Sum, Average, Count Records (all records), Count Values (different values of this field), Maximum, Minimum, Standard Deviation, and Variance. (The last two are statistical analyses.)

✦ **Show Grand Total:** Choose this option to include a total at the bottom or top of the report.

✦ **Show Group Subtotal As % of Grand Total:** Choose this option to include a calculated field for each group, showing the percentage of all records in the report that the group represents.

✦ **Show Subtotal in Group Header:** Choose this option to include a calculated field in the header for each group, using the total, average or whatever type calculation you chose.

✦ **Show Subtotal in Group Footer:** This option is the same as Show Subtotal in Group Header, but it affects the footer for each group (where totals usually appear).

In the group footer section, Access creates a text box control for each sum, count, or other summary information that you want to print. Alternatively, you can make these controls yourself. To print totals and counts for the entire report, make a text box in the Report Header or Report Footer section; then type an expression in the `Control Source` property for the text box, using aggregate functions such as Sum(), Avg(), and Count(). (See Book IV, Chapter 4 for the scoop.)

When you use aggregate functions in a group header or footer section, Access automatically restricts the records to those in the current group. The Sum() function, for example, totals the values of a field for all the records in the group. To subtotal the amount paid for each product in the current group, you use the following expression in a text box control:

```
= Sum([Price])
```

To print the number of records in the report, type the following expression in the Control Source property (located on the Data tab of the property sheet) for a text box in the Report Header or Report Footer section:

```
= Count(*)
```

Don't use aggregate functions in the Page Header or Page Footer sections of a report. If you do, you get an #Error message.

Figure 1-8, earlier in this chapter, shows a report in Design view with Sum() functions in both the OrderID and ContactID footers (for groupings) and in the Report Footer section (for the entire report). The Sum() function in the OrderID Footer section prints a subtotal of the cost for each order, the Sum() function in the ContactID Footer section prints a subtotal of the cost for all the orders for each customer, and the Sum() function in the Report Footer section prints the total cost for all the records in the whole report.

Employing Formatting Tips and Tricks

Following are a few tricks for making nicely formatted controls for your reports, most of which involve setting report, section, or control properties on the property sheet:

✦ **Printing calculations:** Print a *calculated field* — a field whose contents are decided by an expression — the same way that you display one on a form. Create a text box, and enter an expression in the Control Source property. Be sure to set the control's Format property, too. (Book IV, Chapter 4 provides the excruciating details on displaying calculations on forms; the same methods work for reports.)

✦ **Prompting for information to print:** Just as Access can prompt for information when running a query (as described in Book III, Chapter 2), you can use parameters when printing a report. Parameters allow you to specify information — usually, in the Report or Page Header or Footer section — that you want to print. Create a text box control where you want the information to print. For the Control Source property of the text box, enter the parameter prompt in square brackets so that it looks something like the following:

```
[Enter title line]
```

✦ **Preventing spaces between fields:** When you display several fields in a row, you may not want to leave gaps between them. In a mailing label or form letter, you may want to print fields containing first names and last names with only one space between them. To eliminate extra spaces between fields, regardless of the length of the values in the fields, *concatenate* the fields (glue them together) by using the & operator. (We describe calculated fields and the & operator in Book III, Chapter 2.) Create a text box control, and type an expression in its Control Source property, such as the following:

```
= [First Name] & " " & [Last Name]
```

This expression glues together the first name, a space, and the last name. If the first name is Elvis and the last name is Presley, you end up with Elvis Presley (the name, anyway).

✦ **Using conditional calculations:** You can print one thing in some circumstances and another thing in others by using the IIf() function. (For more on the IIf() function, see Book III, Chapter 2.) You may make a report that can print either an invoice or a receipt, depending on whether the customer has paid. At the top, you include a text box with an expression in the Control Source property that specifies that Access should print an invoice or a receipt, depending on the value of the Paid field. That expression looks something like the following:

```
= IIf([Paid], "Receipt", "Invoice")
```

✦ **Calculating a running sum:** You can tell Access to sum the values of a numeric field showing the total of the current record (a *running sum*). Set the Running Sum property of the text box control displaying that field to Yes. You may want to include two text box controls for the numeric field: one to show the value for the current record (with the Running Sum property set to No) and one to show the running sum (with the Running Sum property set to Yes).

✦ **Hiding duplicate values:** If all the records in a group have the same value for a control, and you want the value to print only the first time it appears, you can set the Hide Duplicates property of the field to Yes. This setting is especially useful in tabular reports, in which each field appears in a separate column.

Don't use a field name as the control name for a calculated control. When you create controls, Access names them automatically, although you can change the names later. If you rename a calculated control, make sure that the name you assign isn't the same as that of any field mentioned in the expression (or any field in the record source of the report). Access gets confused about whether references to that name are to the field or to the control, and the report displays an error message.

Copying Forms to Reports

If you have a form that you want to print, you can certainly print it as is, but you have a lot more control of the format if you turn the form into a report first. Then you can change the design of the report so that it prints nicely without changing the format of the original form.

To save a form as a report, select the form in the Navigation Pane, click the File tab on the Ribbon, choose File⇨Save As, and choose Save Object As. In the Save the Current Database Object panel, select the Save Object As rectangle, and click the Save As button (a vintage floppy-disk icon). When you see the Save As dialog box, type a name for the new report, and choose Report from the Save As drop-down menu. When you click OK, Access creates a new report based on the design of the form.

Most forms have colored backgrounds. After saving a form as a report, be sure to change the background of your new report to white before printing the report. Otherwise, you'll waste a lot of ink (or toner). Just right-click the background of each section, choose the Fill/Back Color option from the contextual menu, and select the white box in the palette of colors.

Adding and Formatting Subreports

A *subreport* provides detail information from other tables. You can create a *subreport control* to print another report as part of your report. If you have a report about customers, for example, a subreport can list the orders for each customer.

Figure 1-14 shows a report with two subreports in Design view, and Figure 1-15 shows the same report in Report view.

An *unbound subreport* isn't connected to the records in the main report: No relationship exists between the record source of the main report and the subreport. The unbound subreport in Figure 1-14 displays information from the My Business table, which contains one record with the business's name, address, and other information. (We like to create a My Business table to store this information in one place, for use in all the forms and reports in the database. If your phone number changes, for example, you change it in the My Business table, and all your forms and reports are updated automatically.)

With an unbound subreport, Access prints the same information for each record in the main report. In Figures 1-14 and 1-15, the business information from the My Business table is printed at the top of each invoice or receipt.

A *bound subreport* provides detail from other tables. In Figures 1-14 and 1-15, the bound subreport lists the items in the current order, pulling the information from the Order Details table. Bound subreports help you print information from a one-to-many relationship: The main report displays records from the master ("one") table, and the subreport displays records from the detail ("many") table.

TIP

If you always print two or more reports at the same time, include them in a new, unbound report as unbound subreports. When you print the new report, Access prints each of the subreports. Just make sure that all the reports require the same kind of paper!

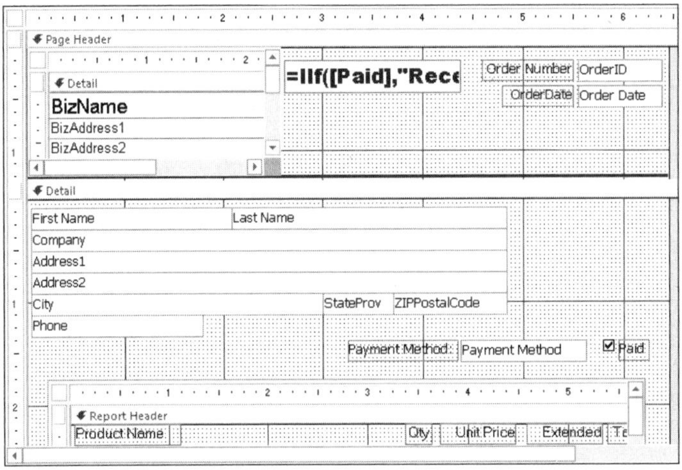

Figure 1-14:
A subreport can be bound to or unbound from the main report.

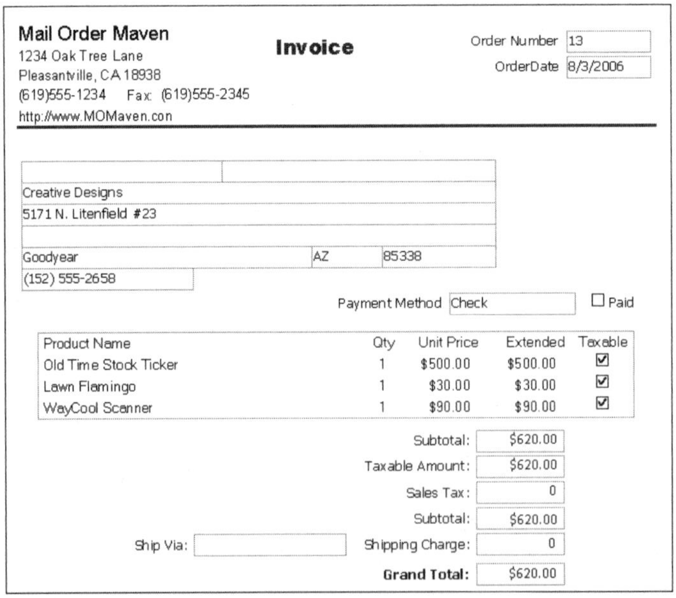

Page Header		
Detail		=IIf([Paid],"Rece — Order Number OrderID — OrderDate Order Date
BizName		
BizAddress1		
BizAddress2		

Detail	
First Name	Last Name
Company	
Address1	
Address2	
City	StateProv ZIPPostalCode
Phone	
	Payment Method: Payment Method ☑Paid

Report Header				
Product Name	Qty	Unit Price	Extended	Ta

Figure 1-15:
A report with subreports, in Report view.

Mail Order Maven
1234 Oak Tree Lane
Pleasantville, CA 18938
(619)555-1234   Fax (619)555-2345
http://www.MOMaven.con

Invoice

Order Number 13
OrderDate 8/3/2006

Creative Designs
5171 N. Litenfield #23

Goodyear	AZ	85338

(152) 555-2658

Payment Method Check   ☐ Paid

Product Name	Qty	Unit Price	Extended	Taxable
Old Time Stock Ticker	1	$500.00	$500.00	☑
Lawn Flamingo	1	$30.00	$30.00	☑
WayCool Scanner	1	$90.00	$90.00	☑

	Subtotal:	$620.00
	Taxable Amount:	$620.00
	Sales Tax:	0
	Subtotal:	$620.00
Ship Via:	Shipping Charge:	0
	Grand Total:	$620.00

Making a subreport

Subreports work just like subforms do (see Book IV, Chapter 4). To create a subreport, whether bound or unbound, follow these steps:

1. **Create and save the report that you plan to use as a subreport.**

   To make the report shown in Figures 1-14 and 1-15, earlier in this chapter, you make one report appear as the unbound subreport, with the My Business table as its record source. You create another report as the bound subreport, with the Order Details table as its record source. When you preview the report by itself, Access displays all the records in the record source. When a report serves as a subreport, however, Access restricts the records whenever the subreport prints, printing only the records that match the current record in the main report.

   When you create this report, nothing about it says "subreport." Any report can be used as a subreport. We like to use the word *subreport* in the names of reports that never print on their own; they exist only as subreports of other reports.

2. **Open the main report in Design view.**

3. **Make space for the subreport control (also called a *Subreport/ Subform control*) in the Detail section of the report.**

   Drag your other controls out of the way.

4. **In the Navigation Pane, scroll down to the Reports section.**

   This step gets you ready to drag the subreport to the Design View window.

5. **Select the subreport-to-be in the Reports list in the Navigation Pane, and drag it to the place in the report where you want it to appear.**

   Access creates a subreport control on the main report containing the report you selected. The `Source Object` property for the subreport control contains the name of the report that you dragged.

6. **Delete the label that Access created for the subreport if you don't like it.**

   Access creates a label for the subreport with the name of the report, but you can select and delete it if you want to.

7. **Move and size the subreport control.**

   Drag the control to the location where you want it, and drag its edges to adjust its size.

8. **Click the subreport control and then click the Property Sheet button in the Tools group on the Design tab of the Ribbon to display the property sheet for the subreport control.**

Figure 1-16 shows the property sheet for a subreport control with the Data tab selected. (While you've got the property sheet displayed, you can adjust the format properties, too.) The Source Object property contains the name of the subreport that the control displays.

9. **Check the Link Child Fields and Link Master Fields properties on the Data tab of the property sheet.**

   These properties contain the names of the fields that relate the main and subreports. The Link Master Fields property should contain the name of the field in the record source of the main report that relates to a field in the subreport. The Link Child Fields property contains the name of the matching field in the record source of the subreport.

Figure 1-16:
The
properties of
a subreport
control link
the records
in the
subreport
with those
in the main
report.

Printing information from a subreport on the main report

Just as you can display totals from a subform on a main form, you can print totals from a subreport on the main report. (See Book IV, Chapter 4 for details on creating a control on the main report to display a total from a subreport.)

When you enter the expression in the text box control on the main report, use this format:

```
= [subreport control name].Report![total control]
```

Replace *subreport control name* with the name of the subreport control. Replace *total control* with the name of the text box control in the subreport that displays the total. The following example expression may display the total extended price (price × quantity) for the records in the report that display in the Order Detail Subreport subreport control:

```
= [Order Detail Subreport].Report![Total Ext Price]
```

Displaying Empty or Long Fields

Short Text and Long Text fields can pose problems in reports because they can contain one character or hundreds of characters. Anticipating how much space to leave for them is hard. Luckily, Access has some features that help you deal with long fields.

Displaying long text

If a Short Text or Long Text field in your report contains more than a few words, you may want the field to wrap onto additional lines. The Description field in a Products table may contain a whole paragraph about the product. You could display the field in a very large text box control that can fit the largest description in the table, but Access would leave a large empty space in the report after short descriptions. Instead, each text box can expand or shrink vertically to fit the amount of text in the field for each record.

Property
Sheet

To make a text box grow, start by making it big enough to fit just one line of text. (See Book IV, Chapter 2 for details on making a text box control.) Display its property sheet by clicking the Property Sheet button in the Tools group on the Design tab of the Ribbon. Then set its Can Grow property (which is on the Format tab, a long way down the list of properties) to Yes. When Access prints each record, the text box control expands until the entire value of the field fits. The remaining controls move down the page.

When you set a control's Can Grow property to Yes, Access sets the Can Grow property for the section that contains the property, too. When Access prints the report, the section expands as well as the control, so nothing gets cut off. If you don't want the section to expand, you can change its Can Grow property back to No to omit information that doesn't fit in the section. Set the Can Grow property to No when you're printing forms of a predetermined size, such as mailing labels. (In Chapter 2 of this minibook, we show you how to set up a report that prints mailing labels.)

Displaying fields that may be empty

To avoid leaving blank lines when a field is blank, set the Can Shrink property for the text box to Yes. (This setting is on the Format tab of the property sheet, just below the Can Grow property.) Many address lists, for example, are stored in tables that have two lines for the street address. If the second line is empty, the mailing label looks better if the City/State/Zip line prints right below the first address line with no gap.

To make a text box control that shrinks when the value is blank, make the text box big enough to fit the longest value in the table; then set its Can Shrink property to Yes. When printing the report, Access omits the control if the field's value is blank.

When you set the `Can Shrink` property of a control to `Yes`, Access doesn't automatically change the `Can Shrink` property of the section that contains the control. Leave the `Can Shrink` properties of the Detail section set to `No` if the Detail section must always be the same size, as with mailing labels or other preprinted forms. Otherwise, set these properties to `Yes`.

Viewing Your Reports Onscreen

Report view displays your report on the screen as it will appear on paper, except without page breaks, headers, and footers, as shown in Figure 1-17. You can't edit the data in the report (that's what forms are for), but you can use the report to find information that you're looking for. The Home tab of the Ribbon includes most of the same Sort & Filter, Records, and Find groups of buttons that you can use when you're viewing records in Datasheet view (see Book II, Chapter 3).

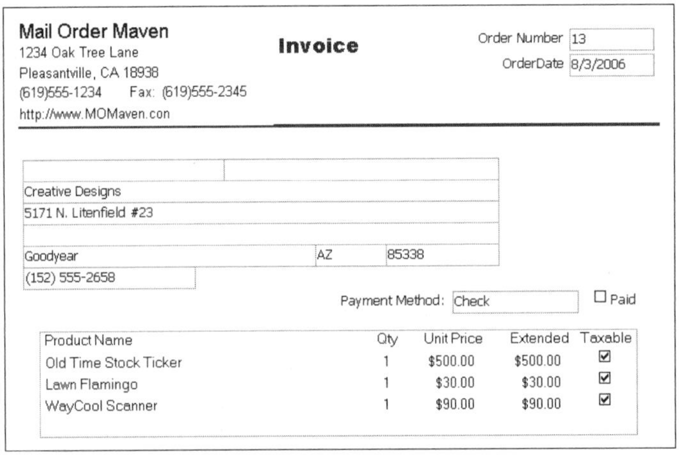

Figure 1-17:
Your report will look just like this on paper.

Chapter 2: Printing Beautiful Reports

In This Chapter

✔ Previewing your report onscreen

✔ Choosing which printer to print on

✔ Controlling report margins and page orientation

✔ Making reports that print mailing labels

✔ Saving Access reports in other Office formats

✔ E-mailing reports with Outlook

After you create a good-looking report onscreen, the next step is seeing whether it looks good on paper or in a PDF file that simulates paper. To make it perfect (okay, close to perfect), you have to be able to control how the printer prints the report. This chapter describes page formats, margins, and other printer settings, as well as how to print mailing labels and export your reports to other Office programs.

Viewing Your Report

You can see how the printed report will look *before* you spend the time, paper, and ink or toner to print it. You can use Report view to see your report (as described in Chapter 1 of this minibook), but that view doesn't include page breaks, page headers, or page footers, so you don't get a true idea of how the report will look on paper. Using Print Preview, you can see onscreen whether your controls are positioned as you want them, whether the right information appears in each control, and whether your headers and footers appear correctly.

To see how your report looks in Print Preview, try any of the following methods:

✦ Double-click the report name in the Navigation Pane to open it. If its default view is Print Preview, there you are!

✦ With the report open in any other view, right-click the report's tab and choose Print Preview from the contextual menu.

✦ With the report open in any other view, click the small Print Preview icon in the bottom-right section of the Access status bar.

✦ With the report open in any other view, click the bottom of the View button in the Views group on the Home tab of the Ribbon, and choose Print Preview from the drop-down menu. (If the View button shows the Print Preview icon, you can just click the button.)

✦ Click the File tab on the Ribbon to see Backstage View, and choose Print⇨Print Preview.

The report appears in Print Preview, showing you the top of the first page of your report (see Figure 2-1).

You can display almost any Access object in Print Preview and then print it. When you're looking at a table in Datasheet view or a form in Form view, you can access Print Preview by clicking the File tab on the Ribbon and choosing Print⇨Print Preview. Reports have more formatting options than any other type of objects in Access, but sometimes datasheets and forms are worth printing too.

You can also set page and print options in Design view by clicking buttons on the Page Setup tab of the Ribbon, as shown in Figure 2-2.

Print Preview is different from most other views in that it takes over Access. Only the File and Print Preview tabs are visible on the Ribbon. When you're done previewing (and possibly printing) the report, you can click the Close Print Preview button at the right end of the Print tab of the Ribbon to close the report.

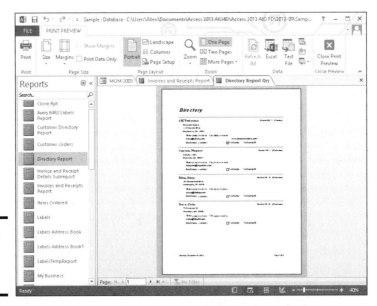

Figure 2-1:
A report
in Print
Preview.

Figure 2-2:
The Page
Setup tab
in Design
view.

Adjusting the view

When you're in Print Preview mode, your cursor changes to a magnifying glass, and your report shrinks to display an entire page on the screen. Click anywhere on the report to zoom in. Click the report a second time to shrink it back to fit on the screen. Alternatively, you can use the Zoom control, located in the bottom-right portion of the Access window. This control is a slider that runs between a minus (–) button and a plus (+) button. Click the minus button to reduce the size by 10 percent. Click the plus button to increase the size by 10 percent. Drag the slider control to change the size in other increments.

Use the vertical scroll bar to scroll the report up and down within the Print Preview window. Use the horizontal scroll bar to pan sideways. To see other pages of the report, click the navigation buttons in the bottom-left corner of the Print Preview window.

Looking at lots of pages

You can zoom *way* out by displaying two or more pages at the same time. Click the Two Pages button on the Zoom tab in Print Preview mode to display two pages at a time, side by side. Though this view doesn't support editing, it shows you where section breaks occur and how full the pages are. To see more than two pages, click the More Pages button in the Zoom group on the Print Preview tab of the Ribbon, and choose an arrangement of pages. Your choices are 4 pages (as shown in Figure 2-3), 8 pages, and 12 pages. Click the Zoom button to zoom in and out on Two Pages view and More Pages views.

To change the size of the display of a report, right-click it and choose a zoom value of 10 percent to 1,000 percent from the contextual menu, or type your own value.

To display different ways of displaying multiple pages, right-click the report, choose Multiple Pages from the contextual menu, and choose one of the following options: 1×1, 1×2, 1×3, 2×1, 2×2, or 2×3.

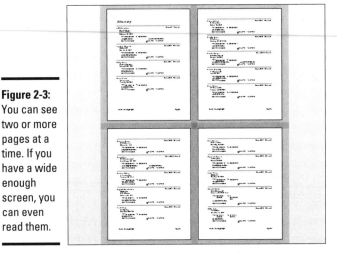

Figure 2-3:
You can see two or more pages at a time. If you have a wide enough screen, you can even read them.

Formatting the Page

Access stores print-setup information with each report, so you can design reports to be used with specific printers or paper.

Selecting a printer

When you format your report in Print Preview, Access takes into account the size and shape of the paper you plan to use. (Okay, most paper is rectangular, but you know what we mean.) Before you're ready to print, specifying what printer you plan to use is important.

If you plan to use the Windows default printer, you don't have to do anything. If you want to print to a different printer, choose the printer when you're ready to print. Click the Print button in the Print group (it's the only button in the Print group) on the Print Preview tab of the Ribbon to display the usual Windows Print dialog box, shown in Figure 2-4. Choose your printer from the Name drop-down menu.

To see what printers your computer is configured to use, just open the Name drop-down menu in the Print dialog box. Choose the printer you want, and print away.

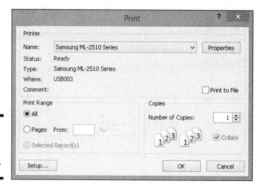

Figure 2-4:
Selecting
your printer.

Setting margins, paper size, and paper orientation

Following are other print settings that you can configure from the Print
Preview tab of the Ribbon:

✦ **Margins:** Click the Margins button in the Page Size group, and choose
Normal, Wide, or Narrow from the drop-down menu. If you've set the
margins in the Page Setup dialog box, Custom Setting will be selected.

✦ **Paper orientation:** Click the Portrait button in the Page Layout group
to print normally on the page, or click the Landscape button to print
sideways.

✦ **Paper size:** Click the Size button in the Page Size group, and choose your
paper size from the drop-down menu.

✦ **Columns:** Most people use columns only for printing mailing labels,
but you can set any report to print in two or more columns. Click the
Columns button to display the Page Setup dialog box with the Columns
tab selected. Then choose the number of columns, the spacing, and the
orientation of records (whether records print across the columns and
then down to a next row, or down the page and then up to the
next column).

If you end up wanting to change the margins for almost every report you
create, you can change the default margins for all new reports. Click the
File tab of the Ribbon, choose Options➪Client Settings, scroll down to the
Printing section, and change the default margin settings shown in Figure 2-5.

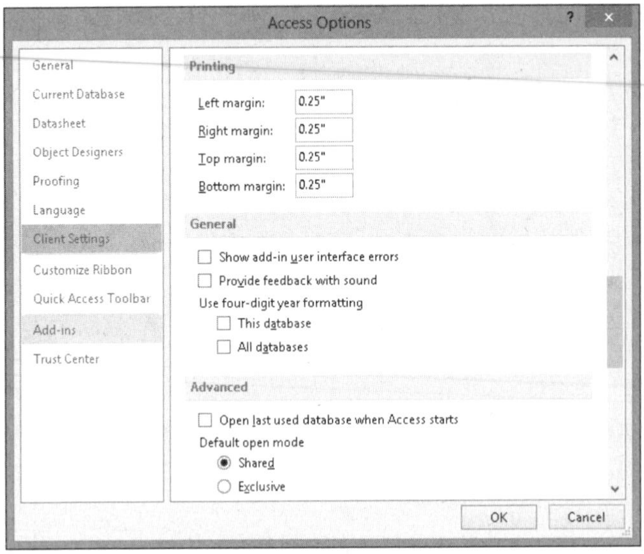

Figure 2-5:
Checking
(and setting)
the default
margins for
all reports
in your
database.

Controlling page breaks

Normally, Access fills each page from top to bottom, starting a new page only when the preceding one is full. You can insert a page break (start a new page) wherever you want, however. You can add page breaks to a report in several ways:

+ **After each record (print one page per record):** Set the Force New Page property of the Detail section to Before Section or After Section. If you choose the Before & After setting for this property, Access makes sure that only one record is printed on each page. With the report in Design view, double-click the section name bar at the top of the Detail section to display the property sheet for the section and then click the Format tab to see the Force New Page property.

+ **After each group of records:** See Chapter 1 of this minibook for details on grouping records. Set the Force New Page property for the Group Footer to After Section. Access prints the Group Header section, the Detail section for each record in the group, and the Group Footer section; then it starts a new page for the next group of records.

+ **Within a section of your report:** Use a page-break control. The Detail section of the report, for example, may print a packing slip and an invoice for each order on separate pages. To add a page-break control to the Detail section of the report, click the Insert Page Break icon in the Controls group on the Design tab of the Ribbon and then click where you want the page break to occur. Access puts the page-break control in the left margin of the report.

Don't place page-break controls in the Page Header or Page Footer section. Doing so starts a new page at the top or bottom of every page, which just creates confusion (and an error). You can put a page break in the Report Header or Report Footer, though, if you have multipage cover sheets.

Avoiding blank pages

Almost every Access user winds up with blank pages in a report. The blank pages appear in Print Preview, but what causes them?

Access knows the width of your paper and how much space to leave for the left and right margins because these sizes are specified in the report's property sheet. Access adds the width of your report to the left and right margins to come up with the total width of the printed report. If the total is wider than your paper, Access splits the report into vertical bands and prints the left and right halves of the report on separate pieces of paper, so you can tape them together to create a very wide report.

If the report is just a little bit too wide to fit across one piece of paper, all the text of the report is printed on the left half, leaving the right half blank. These blank right halves are the blank pages that Access prints. If the right part of the report has no controls in it, Access alerts you to this fact with this message:

```
The section width is greater than the page width, and there are no items
                in the additional space, so some pages may be blank.
```

To get rid of the blank pages, follow these steps:

1. **Click the File tab on the Ribbon, and choose Options⇨Client Settings to display the Access Options dialog box.**

2. **Scroll down to the Printing section.**

   You see something that looks like Figure 2-5, earlier in this chapter.

3. **Subtract the left and right margin settings from the width of your paper to get the maximum width of the report.**

   Standard U.S. paper is 8½ inches wide. If the left and right margins are too wide, make them smaller in this dialog box and then use the new values in your calculation. If your paper is 8½ inches wide, and you have half-inch left and right margins, your report can't be more than 7½ inches wide.

   You can change the margins if you want to use different defaults.

4. **Click OK to exit the Access Options dialog box.**

5. **With the report open in Design view, note the report's width — the location along the ruler of the right edge of the grid area.**

Alternatively, look at the Width property of the report in the property sheet. (Double-click the gray box in the top-left corner of the report in Design view, where the rulers meet, to display the property sheet for the form.) This property is on the Format tab of the property sheet.

6. **If the report is too wide to fit on the page, drag the right edge of the report leftward.**

If the edge won't move, a control extends to the right of where you want the page to end. Move or shrink any control that extends too far to the right, and move the right edge of the report to the left. Alternatively, change the Width property of the report. If you can't find the control that's in the way, use your mouse to select the apparently empty area of the report grid. An orange border appears, showing what has been selected — frequently (in our experience) a horizontal line.

Another possible reason for blank pages is an incorrect setting for the Force New Page property of one of the sections of the report. See "Controlling page breaks," earlier in this chapter, for information on controlling page breaks before or after groups.

Printing only the data

If you're printing on a form rather than on blank sheets of paper, you can design a report that looks like the form, including labels and lines that match the form. When you print the report, you can skip printing the labels and lines, and print only the data. In Print Preview, select the Print Data Only check box in the Page Size group on the Print Preview tab of the Ribbon. Access updates Print Preview to show only your report data.

Printing the Report

After you have your page and margin options set, you're ready to risk wasting paper to print your report. You can print your report when it's open in Print Preview, open in Design view, or not open at all.

Printing on an actual printer

Open the report in Print Preview. Then click the Print button on the Print Preview tab of the Ribbon, click the File tab of the Ribbon, and choose Print⇔Print. Alternatively, you can simply press Ctrl+P. Access displays the Print dialog box, shown in Figure 2-4, earlier in this chapter (the same Print dialog box that most Microsoft programs display). Click the Setup button if you want to take a look at the Page Setup dialog box. Click the printer name if you want to choose a different printer. Otherwise, click OK to send your report to the printer.

To send your report directly to the printer without displaying the Print dialog box, click the File tab of the Ribbon, and choose Print➪Quick Print. Make sure that you're really ready to print before you click!

You may want to print only part of a report — say, just the first page to see how the margins look — or to reprint a specific page. In the Print Range section of the Print dialog box (refer to Figure 2-4), click the Pages radio button, and enter the starting and ending page numbers in the From and To boxes.

Creating a PDF, XPS, HTML, or other file of your report

PDF (Portable Document Format) files have become standard ways to distribute print-ready documents. Heck, even the Internal Revenue Service uses them for tax forms (at www.irs.gov). PDF format enables you to distribute reports on the web or by e-mail in a format that most people can open, read, and print; nobody has to have Access to see your reports.

You can download a free program (Adobe Reader) that displays and prints PDF files. Get this program at http://get.adobe.com/reader.

Office 2013 comes with PDF-creation software and allows you to export reports in several other formats. When you export a report (or another Access object), Access asks whether you want to save the steps that you followed to perform the export, as shown in Figure 2-6. To see how this process works, see "Automating your exports," later in this chapter.

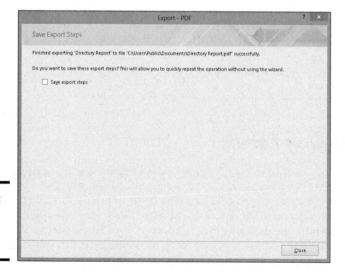

Figure 2-6:
Saving export steps.

Here's how to create a file containing your report in one of these formats when you have the report open in Print Preview:

✦ **PDF file:** Click the PDF or XPS button in the Data group on the Print Preview tab of the Ribbon. You see the Publish As PDF or XPS dialog box, shown in Figure 2-7. Make sure that the Save As Type setting is PDF, and choose where you'd like to save the PDF file. Access automatically adds `.pdf` to the end of the filename. When you click the Publish button, Access exports the report in PDF format and then opens it in the default PDF reader program on your computer (if any).

✦ **XPS file:** The XML Paper Specification (XPS, or OpenXPS) format is Microsoft's version of PDF. You can create XPS files the same way that you create PDF files: by clicking the PDF or XPS button. Just change the Save As Type setting to XPS Document.

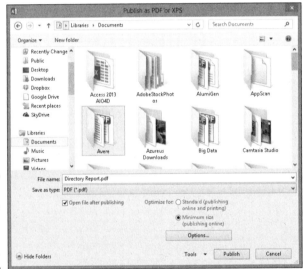

Figure 2-7: Access now comes with a built-in PDF creator.

Creating Mailing Labels

A perennial database task is printing mailing labels from lists of names and addresses. The easiest way to create a report that prints on labels is to use the Label Wizard, which contains a long list of preset formats for all standard Avery-brand and compatible labels. (Most boxes of label sheets include an Avery number that specifies the size of your labels.) After you create a report with the wizard, you can make further changes in Design view.

Running the Label Wizard

To run the Label Wizard, follow these steps:

1. **In the Navigation Pane, select the table or query that contains the information you want to print on your labels.**

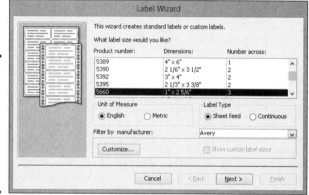 Labels

2. **Click the Labels button in the Reports group on the Create tab of the Ribbon.**

   You see the Label Wizard, as shown in Figure 2-8.

Book V
Chapter 2

Printing Beautiful
Reports

Figure 2-8: The Label Wizard knows the sizes and shapes of most sheets of labels.

3. **Select the type of label in the Product Number list.**

4. **(Optional) To see nondefault labels, make a different choice from the Filter by Manufacturer drop-down menu.**

   Access normally shows the labels according to the numbers assigned by Avery, a major manufacturer of labels.

5. **Select a label type.**

   If you plan to print continuous-feed labels (the sheets are connected) rather than individual sheets of labels, select the Continuous radio button instead of Sheet Feed.

6. **(Optional) If you're printing on custom-printed labels, click the Customize button to open the New Label Size dialog box, click the New button in that dialog box, and tell Access about your labels.**

7. **Click Next to move to the next wizard window.**

8. **Choose the font, font size, weight (light, normal, or bold, among others), and color; then click Next.**

   Access uses these settings for the text boxes in the report.

For mailing labels, do your letter carrier a favor: Choose a readable size, such as 12 points.

9. **Choose the fields that you want to include on the label, as shown in Figure 2-9; then click Next.**

Figure 2-9:
You tell the Label Wizard what fields you want on your label, and the wizard creates the text box controls.

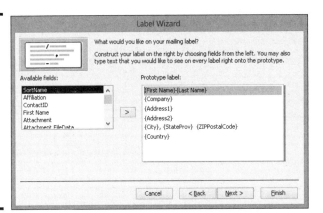

The Prototype Label list shows the layout of fields on the label, including spaces, punctuation, and text that prints on every label (such as `First Class` or your return address). You arrange the fields and other information in the Prototype Label list. Dotted lines show where the lines of text can go. One line in the Prototype Label box is selected (it's gray), showing that new fields are added to this line. You can press the ↑ and ↓ keys to move to a different line.

To print a field on your mailing labels, click the field in the Available Fields list and then click the > button to add it to the current line of the Prototype Label list. (Double-clicking a field does the same thing.) To add text, such as a space, comma, other punctuation, or words, just move your cursor to the location in the Prototype Label box where you want the text to appear, and type it.

The first line of a mailing label, for example, usually consists of the first name, a space, and the last name. With the first line of the Prototype Label list selected, double-click the `First Name` field (or whatever it's called in your table), type a space, and then double-click the `Last Name` field. To move to the next line, press Enter or ↓.

If you put a field in the wrong place, click it in the Prototype Label list and then press the Delete key to remove it.

Be sure to type a comma and a space between `City` and `StateProv` fields in the Prototype Label list, and type a space between `StateProv` and `ZIPPostalCode` fields too.

10. **Choose the field(s) by which you want to sort the records; then click Next.**

    To sort by last name within zip code, for example, choose the ZIPPostalCode field and then the Last Name field.

11. **Type a name for the report.**

12. **Click Finish.**

    The wizard creates the report for you. Figure 2-10 shows a report created by the wizard — just a regular report, but the layout will fit on the type of labels you specified.

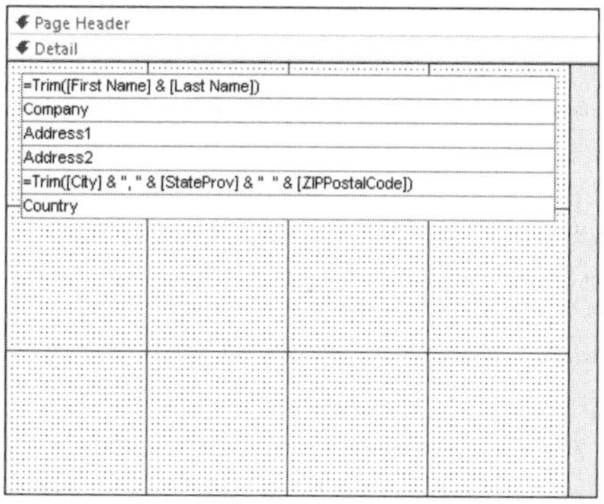

Figure 2-10:
The Label Wizard creates a report that will print on the labels you chose.

```
◀ Page Header
◀ Detail
=Trim([First Name] & [Last Name])
Company
Address1
Address2
=Trim([City] & ", " & [StateProv] & " " & [ZIPPostalCode])
Country
```

If the label report looks good in Report view, print it on a blank piece of paper before you start printing sheets of labels. Hold the printed sheet up to a blank sheet of labels, and see whether the names and addresses line up with the labels. This method prevents you from wasting sheets of expensive labels while you refine your label report. Chapter 1 of this minibook discusses how to print reports.

Behind the scenes in a mailing-label report

The Label Wizard makes a report that looks like Figure 2-10 in Design view. You see the fields and text that you told the wizard to include, followed by enough blank space to reach down to where the text should start on the next label. When more than one field (or text) appears on a line, the Label Wizard cleverly writes expressions (starting with =) that use the & operator to *concatenate* (glue together) the information. In expressions, the wizard encloses each field name in square brackets [ ] because, for field names that contain spaces, these brackets prevent the spaces from confusing Access. The wizard also uses the Trim() function to eliminate any extra spaces at the ends of fields.

The first line of the label in Figure 2-10 contains a text box with this expression as its `Control Source` property:

```
=Trim([First Name] & [Last Name])
```

This scary-looking expression glues the first name, a space, and the last name together and then discards any spaces at the right end.

If you don't like the way that information appears on your mailing labels, you can delete the text boxes, add new ones, alter the expressions in the existing text boxes, and change the formatting of the text boxes — the same kinds of changes you can make in the controls of any report.

Changing the page setup for labels

Unexpectedly, the report is only the size of a single label. You don't see a whole page full of labels. How does Access know how many labels to print across a row? The Page Setup tab of the Ribbon contains this information. If you specified the wrong Avery number in the Label Wizard (or if you have labels that don't have Avery numbers), you can change these settings.

With the report open in Design view, click the Columns button in the Page Layout group on the Page Setup tab of the Ribbon to display the Page Setup dialog box, with its Columns tab selected (as shown in Figure 2-11).

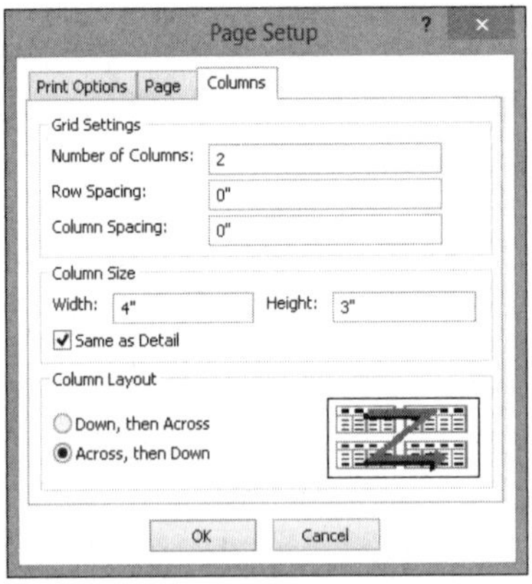

Figure 2-11:
The Columns tab of the Page Setup dialog box defines how your report prints on sheets of labels.

You see the following settings:

✦ **Number of Columns:** How many columns of labels to print per page.

✦ **Row Spacing:** How much blank space to leave between one row of labels and the next (usually zero, because Access includes this space in the report design).

+ **Column Spacing:** How much blank space to leave between one column and the next (that is, between one label and the next across each row).

+ **Column Width and Column Height:** The size of the labels. If you leave the Same As Detail check box selected, Access adjusts these settings to be the same size as the Detail section of the report.

+ **Down, Then Across and Across, Then Down:** The order in which the labels print on each page.

You can use the settings on the Columns tab of the Page Setup dialog box to create newspaper-style "snaking" columns for any report, not just mailing labels. Make the Detail section of the report narrower than half the width of the paper, specify two columns, and set the `Column Layout` property to `Down Then Across`.

Sending a Report to Another Application

The nice thing about Microsoft Office is that all the programs are designed to work together. Sometimes, they even *do* work together.

What if you want to include a report from your Access database in an Excel spreadsheet? You can export reports, tables, and queries in file formats that other Office programs can understand. If you export the same report regularly, saving it in the same folder with the same name, you create a *data task* that you can run again and again.

Exporting your report to Microsoft Excel

To export a report in Excel format, follow these steps:

1. **In the Navigation Pane, click the report that you want to export to Microsoft Excel.**

2. **Click the Excel button in the Export group on the External Data tab of the Ribbon.**

The Export – Excel Spreadsheet dialog box opens, as shown in Figure 2-12.

Another way to open this dialog box is to open the report in Print Preview and then click the Excel button in the Data group on the Print Preview tab of the Ribbon.

3. **Click the Browse button to choose the folder where you want to store the exported file, and type a name for the file in the File Name text box.**

If you want to open the exported report automatically in Excel, select the check box labeled Open the Destination File After the Export Operation Is Complete. You can check that box only if the Export Data with Formatting and Layout check box is already selected.

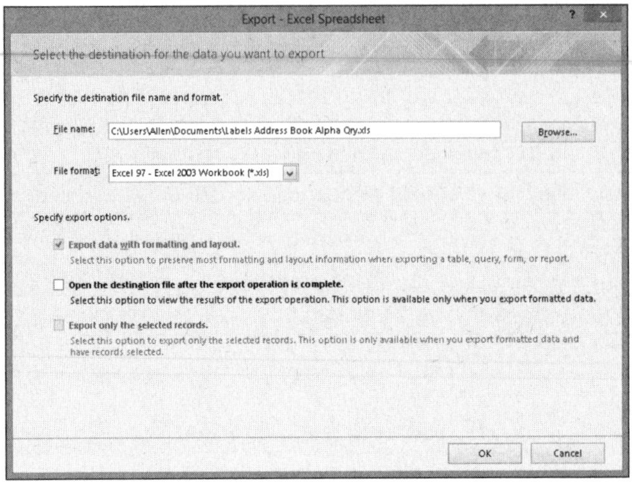

Export - Excel Spreadsheet

Select the destination for the data you want to export

Specify the destination file name and format.

File name: C:\Users\Allen\Documents\Labels Address Book Alpha Qry.xls   Browse...

File format: Excel 97 - Excel 2003 Workbook (*.xls)

Specify export options.

☑ Export data with formatting and layout.
   Select this option to preserve most formatting and layout information when exporting a table, query, form, or report.

☐ Open the destination file after the export operation is complete.
   Select this option to view the results of the export operation. This option is available only when you export formatted data.

☐ Export only the selected records.
   Select this option to export only the selected records. This option is only available when you export formatted data and have records selected.

OK   Cancel

Figure 2-12:
The Export –
Excel
Spreadsheet
dialog box.

If you just want to export the data without any associated formatting, don't select any of the check boxes.

4. **Click OK.**

   Access creates an Excel spreadsheet with a column for each field and a row for each record on the report.

   Another Export dialog box appears, asking whether you want to save the steps you took to perform this export operation.

5. **Decline the offer.**

   Usually, it isn't worthwhile to save these steps.

6. **Click the Close button.**

   Exporting is just that easy!

If your report contains a subreport, Access creates a set of rows for the subreport below the row for the record in the main report, with the columns for the subreport fields off to the right. This format makes sense because it keeps the data organized, with a column for each field, but it's hard to read.

Exporting your report to Microsoft Word

You can export an Access report as a Word document in a similar way. Actually, the exported file is an RTF (Rich Text Format) file that can be opened in Word or any other program that supports RTF.

Exporting to an RTF file is almost identical to exporting to an Excel file. To export to RTF, follow the steps in the preceding section for exporting an Excel spreadsheet, but click the More button in the Export group on the

External Data tab of the Ribbon or in the Data group on the Print Preview tab of the Ribbon. Either way, you see a list of export formats that the Access folks couldn't shoehorn onto the Ribbon. Click Word. Access creates an RTF file in Word that looks just about identical to the report in Access.

If you want to use a table or query with the Microsoft Word merge feature, you can. Select the table or query in the Navigation Pane; click the Word Merge button in the Export group on the External Data tab of the Ribbon; and follow the prompts of the Microsoft Word Mail Merge Wizard, shown in Figure 2-13. When you open the document in the Word document into which you want to merge your data, click Insert Word Field to include a field from your table or query in the document.

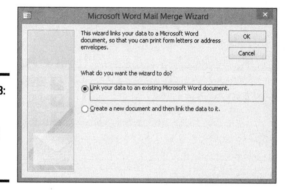

Figure 2-13:
The
Microsoft
Word Mail
Merge
Wizard.

E-mailing your report in Microsoft Outlook

If you use Microsoft Outlook, the e-mail program that comes with Microsoft Office, you can e-mail a report directly from Access. With the report selected in the Navigation Pane, click the E-Mail button in the Export group on the External Data tab of the Ribbon. You see the Send Object As dialog box, shown in Figure 2-14. Select a format, and click OK. Access fires up Outlook and creates a message that includes your report as an attachment.

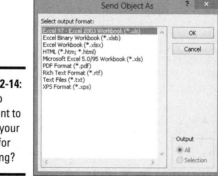

Figure 2-14:
How do
you want to
export your
report for
e-mailing?

If you don't use Outlook, you see an error message telling you to set up Outlook to use this feature.

Exporting your report in other formats

Access can export to a few other formats when you click certain buttons in the Export group on the External Data tab of the Ribbon. Here are some of them:

✦ **Text file (click the Text File button):** You can choose to preserve formatting, which tells Access to add spaces to approximate the layout of the report. Then Access runs the Export Text Wizard, which helps you create a text file containing one line per record.

✦ **XML file (click the XML File button):** XML (Extensible Markup Language) is a standard data transfer format. It doesn't include any formatting — only data.

✦ **HTML file (click the More button and choose HTML Document):** You can save your report as a web page. Not all formatting is preserved, but the results usually are pretty good.

See Book IX, Chapter 3 for details on using SharePoint to put your whole database on the web.

Automating your exports

If you plan to export any report regularly and want Access to remember the directory and filename you specified, you can create a data task for the export. Select the Save Export Steps check box when you see the second Export – *Whatever* dialog box mentioned in Step 4 of "Exporting your report to Microsoft Excel," earlier in this chapter, regarding export to an Excel spreadsheet. The dialog box expands to ask some additional questions, as shown in Figure 2-15.

Type a name for the export in the Save As box and, if you feel like it, a description in the Description box. If you use Outlook as your e-mail program and want to make a task in Outlook, you can select the Create Outlook Task check box. When you click Save Export, Access creates a data task with the name you specified.

To run the export again, click the Saved Exports button in the Exports group on the External Data tab of the Ribbon. Select the data task, and click the Run button (see Figure 2-16).

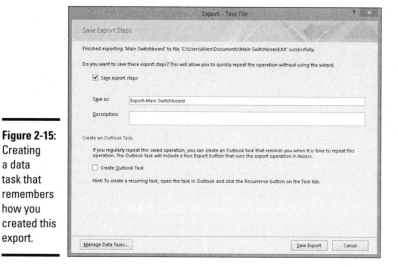

Figure 2-15:
Creating
a data
task that
remembers
how you
created this
export.

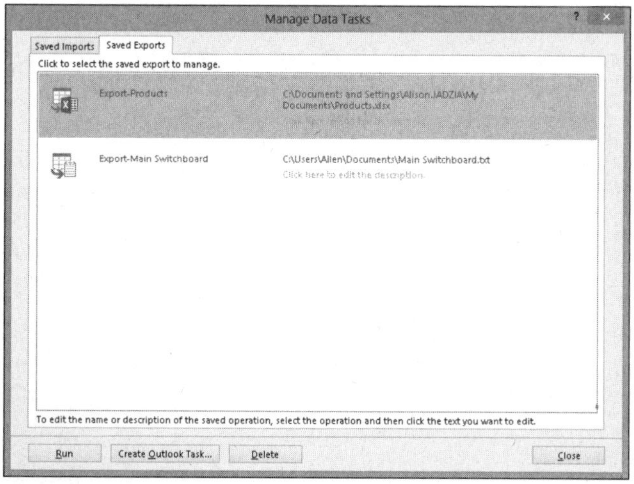

Figure 2-16:
Re-export
an export by
running the
data task
you created.

Chapter 3: Creating Charts and Graphs from Your Data

In This Chapter

✔ Adding data bars to your reports

✔ Making charts and graphs with the Chart Wizard

✔ Drawing bar charts

✔ Crafting line and area charts

✔ Displaying pie and doughnut charts

✔ Doing XY scatter and bubble charts

✔ Changing the format of your chart

Charts and graphs often communicate the meaning of your data better than columns of names and numbers do. (What's the difference between a *chart* and a *graph?* Actually, the two words mean the same thing, so we'll call them both *charts* from now on to save ink.) You can add a chart to any report by using the chart control. Access 2013 has a feature called *data bars,* which are little bar charts that can appear as part of any report.

Pulling Up a Seat at the Data Bar

You've probably heard of a bar chart, but who ever heard of a *data bar?* Microsoft coined this term to describe little horizontal bars that you can display on a report. If you display a bunch of data bars one below another, you make a bar chart. Figure 3-1 shows a report with data bars showing the number of each product sold. The data bar displays both a horizontal bar and the quantity as a number.

Figure 3-1:
Data bars
are text
boxes that
contain
numbers
and are
formatted as
horizontal
bars.

The data bar is actually a text box that contains a numeric value. To make the text box look like a horizontal bar, Access strangely uses conditional formatting to apply the format. Here's how:

1. **Create a new report, or open an existing report in Design or Layout view.**

   Report
   Design

   To make a new report, click the Report Design button in the Reports group on the Create tab of the Ribbon. To open an existing report in Design view, right-click the report and choose Design View from the contextual menu. (See Book V, Chapter 1 for details on editing reports in Design and Layout views.) For this example, we created a new report based on the Product Sales by Month_Crosstab query. The report opens in Layout view.

2. **In the new report, select a value in the Total of ExtPrice column.**

   Access encloses the selected value in an orange box.

3. **Click the Conditional Formatting button in the Control Formatting group on the Format tab of the Ribbon.**

   The Conditional Formatting Rules Manager dialog box opens, with Total of ExtPrice selected after the Show Formatting Rules For prompt.

4. **Click the New Rule button to display the New Formatting Rule dialog box, shown in Figure 3-2.**

5. **Set the Select a Rule Type drop-down menu to Compare to Other Records.**

   Now the dialog box shows settings for data bars, and it looks a lot more like Figure 3-2.

6. **Configure your data bars.**

Figure 3-2:
To format a
text box to
appear as
data bars,
set the
control's
conditional
formatting.

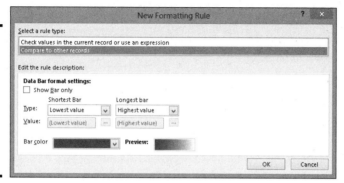

Your options are as follows:

- If you don't want a value to appear at the right end of the control, click the Show Bar Only check box.

- Set the number that will be represented by the shortest bar. The default is for it to represent the lowest value in the field to be graphed. You can set Shortest Bar to Number and enter a specific number for the shortest bar to represent (0 may be a good choice for many charts), or you can set Shortest Bar to Percent and enter a percentage (.5 for 50 percent, for example).

- Set the number that will be represented by the longest bar. The default value is for it to represent the highest value. In Figure 3-2, the default settings are selected.

7. **Click OK to save your new formatting rule and close the New Formatting Rule dialog box.**

   You return to the Conditional Formatting Rules Manager dialog box.

8. **Click OK to dismiss the Conditional Formatting Rules Manager dialog box.**

In Layout view, you see your data bars right away. If you're using Design view, switch to Layout view or Print Preview to see them. (Right-click the tab for the report and choose Layout View or Print Preview from the contextual menu.)

Displaying Information with Charts

Access databases contain different types of objects: tables, queries, forms, reports, and the rest. But what about charts? Where are they stored?

Access stores charts as controls on forms or reports because they're meant to be viewed (such as forms) or printed (such as reports). Before you make a chart, you create a new form or report — or open an existing one — and then add a chart control. In this chapter, we describe storing your chart controls in reports, but you can include them in forms if you prefer.

We recommend running the Chart Wizard and customizing the chart afterward. Heck, why not make the wizard do most of the work? If you insist on making a chart control manually, see the sidebar "Making charts the old-fashioned way," later in this chapter, but don't say we didn't warn you.

The Access Chart Wizard is very limited; Microsoft Graph can draw more types of charts. If you want to create a stacked bar chart, radar chart, or multiple-ring doughnut chart, the wizard can't help you. You can make a similar chart with the wizard and modify the chart afterward in Design view. Another method of making better charts is to export your data to Excel 2013 — yet another component of Microsoft Office 2013 — and use its more powerful Chart Wizard. See Book II, Chapter 4 for information on exporting records from Access to Excel.

Creating charts with the Chart Wizard

If you want to create charts in Access, the Chart Wizard is the only good way to start. You may want to add a chart to an existing report or create a chart that stands alone (meaning that no other controls are on the report). The Chart Wizard allows you to do either thing.

Whether you create a new report for your chart or add a chart to an existing report, you start with the Reports list in the Navigation Pane. If the Navigation Pane isn't visible, click the Shutter Bar Open/Close button (>>). Then scroll to see the list of your existing reports.

You can add a chart to a report that you've already created by adding a chart control to your report. Follow these steps:

1. **Determine which table or query contains the data you want to chart (the *record source*).**

    To make a chart, you need at least one numeric field. Find a table or query (or make a query) that contains the fields you want on your chart. You don't have to use all the fields; the Chart Wizard enables you to select just those that you want.

    If you're charting values by date, make sure that your record source includes the date field. If you want to chart sales per week for each week of the year, the record source needs to include both the sales-number field and the sale-date field. The fields don't have to be weekly totals: The Chart Wizard can total your fields for you.

2. **Create a new report, or open an existing report in Design or Layout view.**

3. **Click the Chart button in the Controls group on the Design tab of the Ribbon.**

   Now when you move your mouse pointer back to the Design View window, it appears as a teeny graph.

4. **Click the section of the report where you want the chart to appear.**

   A box appears on your report, and the Chart Wizard starts. This wizard starts just like the Report Wizard described in Chapter 1 of this minibook, asking what table or query contains the data that you'd like to graph.

5. **Click the Tables, Queries, or Both radio button to display the list from which to make your choice; make your selection; and click Next.**

   The wizard asks what fields you want to use on your chart. It still looks just like the Report Wizard.

6. **Choose the fields you want to chart by moving them from the Available Fields list to the Fields for Chart list; then click Next.**

   To move a field from one list to the other, select the field and click the arrow button between the two lists, or double-click a field to move it to the other list.

   Later, you tell the wizard how to represent each field, and you don't have to represent all the fields you choose here. Go ahead and include any field that you *may* want to include on the chart.

7. **Select the type of chart that you want to create from the screen shown in Figure 3-3; then click Next.**

   When you select a chart type, the wizard displays the name of that type of chart as well as some information about that type of chart and the kind of data that it displays best. Click around to see what looks good and what will display your data clearly.

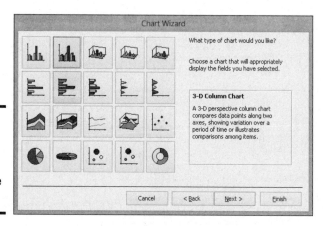

Figure 3-3:
You're not limited to boring old bar and line charts!

When you click Next, the wizard displays a small version of the chart, as shown in Figure 3-4. The chart shows three labels: the Axis (the horizontal x-axis on most types of graphs), the Data (usually, the vertical y-axis), and the Series (usually, fields displayed in the chart as bars, lines, or other shapes).

The wizard guesses which field is on the x-axis, which is on the y-axis, and which fields are the series. Sometimes, its guess makes sense; at other times, it produces a chart that doesn't make sense or just doesn't show what you had in mind.

8. **Drag fields to the chart on the left side of the wizard window, and tell the wizard how to use the fields you've selected (refer to Figure 3-4).**

The fields that you choose appear as buttons on the right side of the window. Unused fields are parked over there. Fields that appear on the chart have only a shadowy box in that parking area, and their buttons appear on the chart as follows:

- The field that defines the x-axis appears below the x-axis.

- The field that defines the y-axis appears above the y-axis.

- The field(s) that appears in the graph appears to the right of the chart.

You specify how to use each field by dragging its field name to the parking area or to one of these three locations on the sample chart. If Access guessed wrong about how to use the fields, drag the field names around to more sensible locations. Don't worry about how the field names appear; you can fix the legends on the chart later.

How the Axis, Data, and Series settings work depends on the type of chart you're creating. The next four sections describe how to specify fields for bar, line, area, and other types of charts.

You don't have to use all the fields; you can leave some languishing in the parking area.

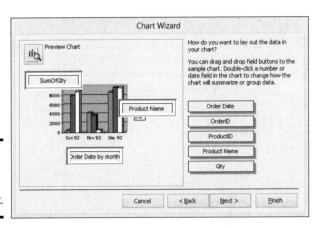

Figure 3-4:
Laying out
your fields
on the chart.

***9.* Double-click a field's box to open the Group or Summarize dialog box, and specify how the data is to be grouped or totaled.**

For date fields, the Group dialog box (shown on the left side of Figure 3-5) shows your options. The Summarize dialog box (shown on the right side of Figure 3-5) shows how you can combine values for a numeric field.

Figure 3-5:
Choosing
how a date
field is
grouped or
a numeric
field is
summarized.

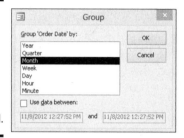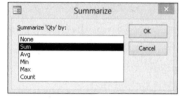

***10.* Click the Preview Chart button in the top-left corner of the window to see how your chart looks so far, and click the Close button to return to the Chart Wizard window.**

The Sample Preview window helps you figure out whether you chose the right fields for the X-Axis, Y-Axis, and Series settings.

***11.* Repeat Steps 8–10 until the chart looks right.**

If you omitted fields that you need, you can click the Back button to return to earlier questions that the wizard asked.

***12.* When everything looks the way you want it, click Next.**

In the next window, Chart Wizard asks whether you want the chart to change from record to record (see Figure 3-6). Typically, you do.

Figure 3-6:
The Chart
Wizard asks
whether
you want to
change from
record to
record.

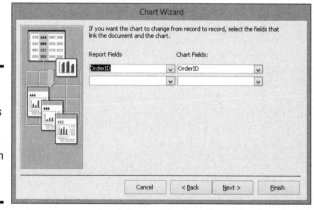

13. **Link the chart to the report by specifying a common field to link them; then click Next.**

In the example in Figure 3-6, we formed the link with the `OrderID` field. You may have to try more than one field before you find the one that works best.

14. **Enter a title.**

The title appears at the top of the report. The wizard suggests the name of the table or query you chose as the record source.

15. **Specify whether to display legends.**

Legends show what the colors of the bars, lines, or pie sections mean. Usually, including them is a good idea.

16. **Click Finish.**

The wizard creates a new chart control in your new or existing report.

In Design view, Access shows a sample chart, not the actual chart. The chart is of the type that you select, but with sample data. Don't worry; your real chart is on the report. Switch to Print Preview to see the actual chart, as shown in Figure 3-7.

Figure 3-7:
Your actual chart doesn't appear in Design view, but you can see it in Print Preview.

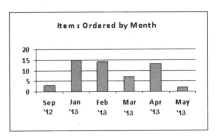

17. **Drag and resize the chart control as needed.**

After the Chart Wizard creates your chart control, you can move the control around your report by dragging it. You can also resize the chart by selecting the control and then dragging the black handles on the edges of the control. (If you double-click the chart control, you find yourself in a strange new editing mode, described in "Formatting charts with colors, legends, and titles," later in this chapter.)

A report can contain more than one chart control. You may want to make a report that contains three chart controls that display three different charts. Just make the additional controls in Design view by clicking the Chart button in the Controls group on the Design tab of the Ribbon and specifying where you want the new control to appear.

Farewell to pivot charts

Earlier versions of Microsoft Access included an additional chart type: pivot charts. This capability has been removed from Access 2013. Pivot charts are still available in Excel 2013.

Now you know how to use the Chart Wizard to create a chart. The next few sections describe popular types of charts.

Making bar charts

The Chart Wizard can make a bunch of kinds of bar charts, some with vertical bars and some with horizontal bars. The types of bar charts in which the bars run vertically appear in the first row of buttons shown in Figure 3-3, earlier in the chapter. Here's some information on what you can create with those buttons:

✦ **Column Chart:** Flat vertical bars.

✦ **3-D Column Chart:** Three-dimensional–looking vertical bars.

✦ **Cylinder Column Chart:** Same thing as a column chart, but the bars are cylindrical.

✦ **Cone Column Chart:** Another column chart, but with cones instead of bars.

✦ **Pyramid Column Chart:** Same as the preceding two charts, but with pyramids instead of cones or bards.

You can also make the same charts run horizontally. The following buttons appear in the second row of buttons in Figure 3-3:

✦ **Bar Chart:** Flat horizontal bars.

✦ **3-D Bar Chart:** Three-dimensional–looking horizontal bars.

✦ **3-D Cylinder Bar Chart:** Same thing as a bar chart, but the bars are cylindrical.

✦ **3-D Cone Bar Chart:** Another bar chart, but with horizontal cones. (They look rather odd, we think.)

✦ **3-D Pyramid Bar Chart:** Same as the preceding two charts, with horizontal pyramids (which look even odder).

Unfortunately, the Chart Wizard can't draw stacked bar charts. To make them, you have to choose another type of bar chart in the Chart Wizard and then change the chart type to a stacked bar chart later (see "Changing Your Charts," later in this chapter).

The key to creating bar charts with the Chart Wizard is specifying the right fields for the Axis, Data, and Series settings — the field selections discussed in "Creating charts with the Chart Wizard," earlier in this chapter. Keep reading to find out how the X-Axis, Y-Axis, Data, and Series settings work.

The X-Axis setting

For graphs with vertical bars (or other vertical shapes), set X-Axis to the field that determines the labels that run along the bottom of the graph. For horizontal bar graphs, the x-axis runs up the left side of the graph. This setting also determines what bars sprout up from the x-axis. A bar graph has one bar (or group of bars) for each value (or range of values) of the X-Axis setting.

Figure 3-8 shows two bar charts: one vertical (select Column Chart to get this particular chart type) and one horizontal (select Bar Chart for this one). The X-Axis setting in Figure 3-8 is the Order Date field, and the Y-Axis setting is the Qty field.

Figure 3-8:
Vertical and horizontal bar charts, with Order Date as the X-Axis setting.

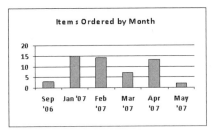

If you use a Date/Time field for the X-Axis setting, you can choose to group the dates in time periods such as a month or year. The X-Axis setting in the Chart Wizard window tells you how Access plans to group the information by date. An Order Date field may appear as "Order Date by month" (refer to Figure 3-4, earlier in this chapter). To change the grouping, double-click the X-Axis field to display the Group dialog box, shown in the dialog box on the left side of Figure 3-5, earlier in this chapter. You can choose to group your data by year, quarter, month, and so on. The Group dialog box also allows you to choose to limit the values plotted on your graph to values within a specified date range. Just select the Use Data Between check box and enter the beginning and end dates you want for your chart. Access ignores records with dates outside that range.

You can't control how numeric or text values are grouped or limit their ranges on the graph.

The Y-Axis setting

For vertical bar charts, drag the fields that determine the heights of the bars — along with the values that appear up the left side of the chart — to the Y-Axis setting. On horizontal bar charts, the Y-Axis fields control the lengths of the bars and the values that run along the bottom of the chart. In Figure 3-8, earlier in this chapter, the Y-Axis field contains the number of items sold; it runs up the left side of the vertical bar chart and across the bottom of the horizontal bar chart.

If you group dates together along the x-axis, you can specify how the values are combined in the bars. If you want to graph sales by month, and your record source has one record for each order, you may set the Y-Axis field to be the `Grand Total` field of each order. Then you can specify how to combine the values of the orders into months. You may want the total value of all the orders for the month, or you may want the average value. The Y-Axis setting in the Chart Wizard window indicates how the values are combined. In Figure 3-4, earlier in this chapter, the Y-Axis setting contains the variable `SumOfQty`, so Access sums up the `Qty` field for the orders in each month.

To change how Access combines the values of a Y-Axis field, double-click the Y-Axis field to display the Summarize dialog box, as shown on the right side of Figure 3-5, earlier in this chapter. Then specify how you want the values for each time period to be combined — Sum, Avg (average), Min (minimum value), Max (maximum value), or Count (number of records) — and click OK.

Unlike the X-Axis setting in the Chart Wizard, the Y-Axis setting can be more than one field. If you drag more than one field to the Y-Axis setting, you see a listing of the Y-Axis fields, as shown in Figure 3-9. For each Y-Axis setting, you get a separate bar.

You can drag the same field to the Y-Axis setting twice. You may want to see the count and the total of the same field, for example.

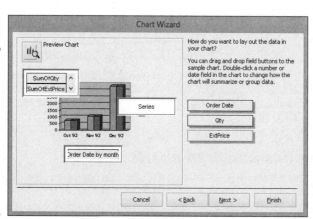

Figure 3-9: This chart has two bars for each month: one for quantity and one for extended price.

The Series setting

Unlike the X-Axis and Y-Axis settings, the Series setting in the Chart Wizard is optional; most charts leave this setting blank. The field used for the Series setting tells Access how to break down the bars (or columns, cones, or pyramids) into a group of smaller bars.

If you graph sales by month, each bar normally shows the total of the sales records for that month. If you drag a field to the Series setting, Access divides the bar for each month into several bars according to the value of the Series field. If you set Series to a field that represents which vendor sold you the product, you get a group of bars for each month, with one bar for each vendor.

Figure 3-10 shows the Chart Wizard settings for a graph that separates sales by Vendor Code, and Figure 3-11 shows the resulting chart. (There are four different vendors.)

Figure 3-10:
The Vendor Code field is used as the Series setting, which splits each month's sales into separate bars for each vendor.

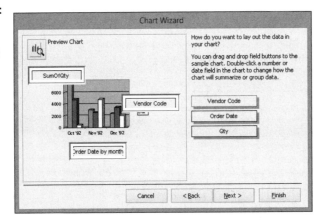

If you choose three or more fields to use in your chart, the Chart Wizard usually guesses that you want to use one of the fields as the Series setting. But for most charts, you use only the X-Axis and Y-Axis settings; just leave the Series setting blank. If the wizard puts a field there, drag it back over to the parking-area list of fields on the right side of the wizard's window.

Making line and area charts

Line and area charts work similarly to bar charts. A bar chart draws a bar (or other shape) for each value of the X-Axis series, with its height determined by the Y-Axis series. A *line chart* works the same way, but instead of drawing a bar, Access draws a dot where the top of the bar would be and then connects the dots. An *area chart* is basically the same thing, but Access colors the area below the line, as shown in Figure 3-12. Line and area charts appear on the third row of buttons in Figure 3-3, earlier in the chapter. (All the buttons in that row except the last one create line and area charts.)

Figure 3-11:
The Axis field contains sales dates grouped by month, the Data field contains the values of the products sold, and the Series field contains the `Vendor Code`.

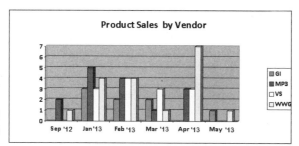

Figure 3-12:
Line and area charts work the same way that bar charts do.

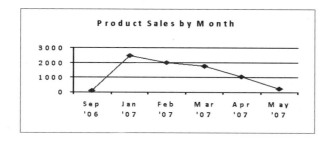

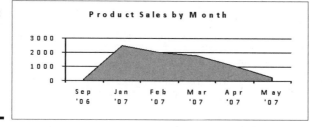

In a line or area chart, the X-Axis series defines the labels that run along the bottom of the graph, and the Y-Axis series defines the distance from the bottom of the chart up to each dot that the lines connect. If you have two or more Y-Axis series, a line chart shows a line for each series, as shown in the chart on the left side of Figure 3-13. An area chart colors the area between one line and the next. A 3-D area chart shows the area below each line as a color slab, as shown in the chart on the right side of Figure 3-13.

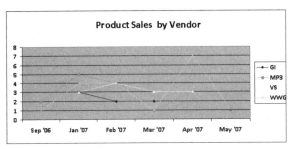

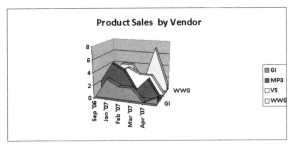

Figure 3-13: An area chart with two Series fields shows one area in front of the other (bottom). The quantity of the Series field is split into several lines or areas (top).

As with bar charts, Access uses the Series field to split the amounts for each line into several lower lines. The charts shown in Figure 3-13 use `Vendor ID` as the Series field.

Making pie and doughnut charts

A *pie chart* shows how a total amount is split up by percentages. Access needs to know what field contains the numbers you want to sum to make the total amount, as well as what field contains the information that you want to use to split this total into pie slices. A *doughnut chart* is a pie chart with a hole in the middle, but you can specify more than one field, and you get a concentric ring for each field. Pie and doughnut charts appear on the fourth row of buttons in Figure 3-3, earlier in the chapter.

When you run the Chart Wizard, choose just two fields to include in the chart, as shown in Figure 3-14:

✦ The field below the sample pie chart is the one that contains the numbers Access will sum to create the total pie. For a doughnut chart, you should be able to specify more than one field and get a concentric ring for each field. If you can't specify all the fields in the Chart Wizard, you can add them later; see "Changing which data is charted," later in this chapter.

◆ The field above and to the right of the sample pie chart can be a numeric or text field, a Yes/No field, or a Date/Time field. Access makes a separate pie slice for each value of this field.

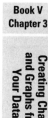

Figure 3-14:
Creating a
pie chart
with the
Chart
Wizard.

Figure 3-15 charts total sales by vendor as a pie chart and as a doughnut chart.

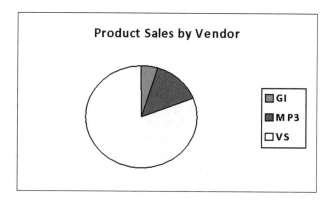

Figure 3-15:
A pie chart
(top) and a
doughnut
chart
(bottom).

Making bubble and XY scatter plots

An *XY scatter plot* needs two numeric fields because it plots one field against the other. For each record, you see a point with the horizontal and vertical positions determined by the numbers in the fields. A *bubble chart* works the same way, except that Access draws a circle instead of a point, and the numeric value of a third field determines the size of the circle.

You can try making these graphs in the Chart Wizard, but we haven't had much luck. (Consider exporting the data to Microsoft Excel and charting it there.) If you want to try the Chart Wizard, drag the numeric field you want to graph along the horizontal (X) axis to the Series setting, and drag the field you want to graph along the vertical (Y) axis to the Data setting. If the wizard decides to aggregate either of the fields (in which case you see `"Sum Of"` — *the field name*), double-click the field name, and change the aggregation setting to `None`.

Making charts the old-fashioned way

By far the easiest way to create a chart is to use the Chart Wizard. If you want to create one without a wizard, however, here's how to do it. Follow these steps:

1. **Open a report or form in Design view.**

 2. **Click the Unbound Object Frame button in the Controls group on the Design tab of the Ribbon.**

3. **Click the place in the Design View window where you want your chart to appear.**

   You see the Microsoft Access dialog box (which really ought to be called something like the Insert Object dialog box).

4. **Do one of the following:**

   ✔ If you've created a graph in some other program (perhaps in Excel or Word),

   choose the Create from File option, click the Browse button, and choose the file.

   ✔ If you're making a new chart, choose the Create New option, choose Microsoft Graph Chart in the Object Type list, and click OK.

   Yes, *Microsoft Graph Chart* sounds redundant, but you're creating a chart by using the Microsoft Graph program. Makes sense!

   Access creates a sample bar chart based on sample data that appears in a Datasheet window. To replace the data with your own data, type your own headings and numbers in the Datasheet window. To change the type of chart, see the nearby section "Changing Your Charts."

Changing Your Charts

The Chart Wizard can't make all the types of charts that Microsoft Graph can draw. It can't even make all the charts that the Excel Chart Wizard can make. Wouldn't you think that these two wizards would get together sometime and compare notes? Luckily, you can change the settings of a chart after the wizard creates it. You can fix charts that don't look quite right, as well as create charts that the Chart Wizard doesn't know about.

To modify a chart, you change the properties of the chart control on the report that contains the chart. This section gives you a general idea of how to modify a chart after you make it; the next three sections provide more details.

Modifying an existing chart

To modify an existing chart, follow these steps:

1. Open the report that contains the chart in Design view.

To do so, right-click the report in the Navigation Pane and choose Design View from the contextual menu.

If the report is open in Print Preview, click the down arrow on the View button and choose Design view from the drop-down menu.

You see the report in Design view, including the chart control that defines the chart.

In Design view, the chart control displays sample data, not the actual data. Don't worry — Access hasn't forgotten the actual data that you want to plot. Just switch to Print Preview to see the real chart.

2. Click the chart control to select it.

Now you can drag it to a different location in the report or resize it.

You can tell when the chart control is selected because a selected control sprouts *handles* — little squares in the corners and on the sides. Drag anywhere in the middle of the chart control to move the chart. Drag a handle to resize the chart control. The handles are the little black squares at the four corners and the midpoints of the four edges.

Property
Sheet

When the chart control is selected, click the Property Sheet button on the toolbar to display the property sheet, which is shown in Figure 3-16. In the property sheet, you can change configuration settings for the graph, as described in the next three sections.

The chart control appears as an Unbound Object Frame because the chart frame contains information that comes from another program: Microsoft Graph. The chart control is unbound because it's not connected to the records in a table or query.

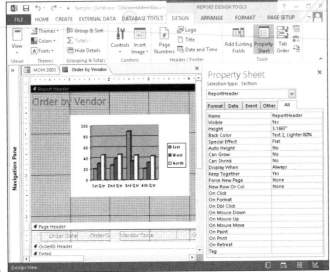

3. Double-click the chart control to start the Microsoft Graph program.

When Microsoft Graph is running, the chart control appears with a hashed line around it, as shown in Figure 3-17. Your Microsoft Access Ribbon goes away and is replaced by the Microsoft Graph menus and toolbars. The next three sections describe what some of the buttons on these toolbars do.

Microsoft Graph also displays a datasheet containing the sample data that it uses to make the graph that appears in Design view. Editing this sample data changes the chart in Design view. It's important to remember, however, that editing the sample data has absolutely no effect on the real chart that appears in Print Preview (or on the data in the database).

Click the View Datasheet button to get rid of the datasheet, or drag it out of the way.

4. Make changes in your chart, as described in the next three sections.

5. Exit Microsoft Graph by clicking the report in Design view, outside the chart control.

The extra toolbars disappear, the funny border around the control disappears, and you return to Access.

6. Click the View button to see how your graph looks in Print Preview.

7. Repeat Steps 4–6 until you have the chart the way you want it.

8. Save the report.

When you save the report that contains the chart control, you also save the changes you made in the control.

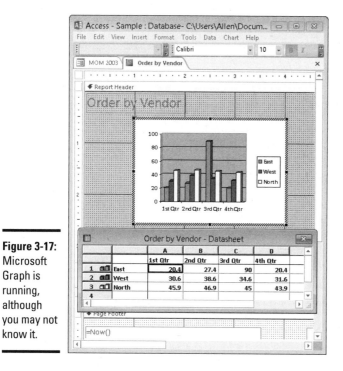

Figure 3-17:
Microsoft
Graph is
running,
although
you may not
know it.

The next three sections describe changes you can make in your chart. You make some of these changes in the property sheet for the chart control; you make others by clicking buttons on the various Microsoft Graph toolbars; and you make still others by giving commands while Microsoft Graph is running. (Don't worry — we let you know when to do what.)

Formatting charts with colors, legends, and titles

The Chart Options dialog box, shown in Figure 3-18, enables you to change the titles, axis labels, gridlines, legends, data labels (which appear on the graph itself), and data table placement. To display it, first double-click the chart control in the Design View window to get Microsoft Graph up and running; then choose Chart⇨Chart Options.

Here are some other ways that you can format your graph when Microsoft Graph is running (that is, when the chart control has a hatched border):

✦ **Background color:** Click part of the graph, click the down arrow on the Fill Color button on the standard toolbar, and choose a color from the drop-down menu. Alternatively, you can right-click the plot area (the graph itself) or a blank part of the chart and choose Format Chart/Plot Area from the contextual menu.

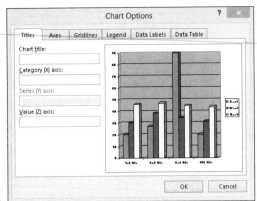

Figure 3-18:
The Chart
Options
dialog box
contains
lots of
formatting
settings for
your graph.

✦ **Gridlines:** To add or remove gridlines, click the Category Axis Gridlines and Value Axis Gridlines buttons on the standard toolbar.

✦ **Title:** To change the title that appears on the graph, click the title to select it; then click it again to edit the text. Move the title by selecting it and dragging. You can also change the font by double-clicking it or by right-clicking it and choosing Format Chart Title from the contextual menu.

✦ **Legend:** To display or remove the legend — the table that explains the meanings of the colors or symbols in the graph — click the Legend button on the standard toolbar. Move the legend by dragging it to a new location within the chart control. Change the fonts by double-clicking the legend to display the Format Legend Entry dialog box.

✦ **Data table:** Click the Data Table button on the standard toolbar to add a table to the chart showing the data used in the table. You need to make the control that contains your chart on your report bigger to make room for the data table.

You can change other formatting options by making choices from the Chart Objects drop-down menu, which is the leftmost item on the standard toolbar. Choose Chart Area, Chart Title, Legend, or any of the other parts of the chart; then click the Properties button on the same toolbar. (Actually, this button looks just like the Properties button in Access, but its name changes based on what object is selected. Anyway, just click it.) You see the dialog box with the settings for that object.

Changing how data is graphed

When Microsoft Graph is up and running, you can also change the chart itself.

Just double-click the chart control in Design view to call up Microsoft Graph, and follow these guidelines to change the chart:

✦ **Type of chart:** If you want to switch from a bar chart to a line chart or from one kind of bar chart to another kind of bar chart, or if you want to make one of the types of charts that the Chart Wizard doesn't even know about, click the down arrow on the Chart Type button and choose a different type of chart from the drop-down menu. For more options, choose Chart➪Chart Type, or right-click the chart control and choose a Chart Type option from the contextual menu.

✦ **Axes:** Because Microsoft Graph treats your data as though it were stored in a spreadsheet — graphing the data row by row or column by column — switching which field is represented along which axis of the chart is pretty easy. To see other ways of representing your data on the same type of graph, just click the By Row and By Column buttons on the standard toolbar.

Save your chart first, in case you don't like the results. Switching your chart back to its original format isn't always easy.

✦ **Trendline:** If your graph shows information over time (a Date/Time field is shown along one axis), you can add a *trendline,* which shows the general direction of growth or decline in the numbers. To add a trendline, choose Chart➪Add Trendline.

✦ **3-D View:** Choose 3-D View on the Chart tab of Microsoft Graph, and use it to rotate a 3-D view around an axis or change the scale. Figure 3-19 shows the 3-D View dialog box that you can use to perform these operations.

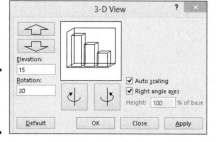

Figure 3-19:
3-D View
dialog box.

Changing which data is charted

If you want to change the fields included in the chart, you can change the Row Source setting of the chart control. Display the property sheet for the chart control by single-clicking (not double-clicking) the chart control in Design view and then clicking the Property Sheet button in the Tools group on the Design tab of the Ribbon. (Microsoft Graph can't be running at the time. To exit Microsoft Graph, click the report outside the chart control.)

The Row Source setting (on the property sheet's Data tab) may contain a SQL statement that describes the fields to be graphed. (See Book VIII, Chapter 5 for information about SQL.) You can change the statement by clicking the Row Source setting and then clicking the Build button to its right. Set Row Source Type to Table/Query; click the Row Source setting; and then click the Build button (an ellipsis [...] button). You see a Query Builder tab, which looks just like Design view for queries. Each column in the Query by Example (QBE) grid corresponds to a field in the graph, although the exact number and use of the columns depend on the type of the chart. Book III describes how to create queries with QBE.

If you make changes in the query, Access asks whether you want to save your changes when you close the window. (To save before closing the window, press Ctrl+S or click the Save button on the Quick Access toolbar.) When you switch the report containing the chart control to Print Preview, you see the results of your changes.

Book VI
Automation with Macros

Find out how to create a form that will appear when a database is opened at www.dummies.com/extras/access2013aio.

Contents at a Glance

Chapter 1: Making Macros Do the Work 459

Introducing Macros 460
Creating and Editing Stand-Alone Macros.............................. 460
Running Stand-Alone Macros and Submacros.......................... 467
Opening Databases That Contain Macros 469
Telling Access to "Run This Only If I Say So" 474

Chapter 2: Making Macros Smarter 477

Attaching Macros to Tables 478
Running Macros in Forms.. 482
Changing the Way Your Form Looks Dynamically 487
Setting Up Your Own Main-Menu Form 490
Using Temporary Variables in Macros 494

Chapter 1: Making Macros Do the Work

In This Chapter

✔ Seeing what macros do

✔ Creating a macro

✔ Understanding macro actions and arguments

✔ Running macros

✔ Telling Access to trust the macros in your databases

✔ Making macros run conditionally

*A*ccess is a pretty smart program. Throughout the program are thousands of nice little features that make Access intelligent, such as validation rules and formats that help you keep your data neat and tidy. Sometimes, however, you want Access to be even smarter. You may want to format a field in a way that Access doesn't allow, for example, or you may want your form to include a command button that the Command Button Wizard doesn't make. No problem — you can make Access even smarter by writing your own programs within Access.

Strangely, Access includes two (count 'em) ways of putting a program together: macros and Visual Basic for Applications (VBA). The differences between the two are

✦ **Macros** are the original Access do-it-yourself program makers, dating back to the Dawn of Access (1991). The macro language is limited, however, and Microsoft suggests that you not use macros for any major programming tasks.

✦ **VBA** is the standard programming language for Microsoft Office and other applications. VBA is a version of Visual Basic that's similar to VBScript, which works on the web. Microsoft recommends that you use VBA for all significant programs. We describe VBA in detail in Book VIII.

So why use macros at all? Here's why: If you want to do something small and simple, making a little macro is a piece of cake (as you find out in this chapter). Also, you can always convert the macro to VBA later with the Access conversion command. This chapter explains how to make standalone, general-purpose macros, whereas Chapter 2 of this minibook covers *data macros* (macros that are stored as part of a table) and macros that are embedded in forms and reports.

Introducing Macros

A *macro* is a list of actions that happen when you run the macro. (That general definition works for almost any programming language, actually.) You may have a macro that performs these actions when you click a button on a form:

1. Saves the current record.
2. Prompts you to put a blank mailing label in the printer.
3. Prints a report, filtering the records to include only those that match the record currently displayed on the form.

Most macros are short and sweet, like this example. For more complex programs, you need VBA.

Macros can live as independent, stand-alone objects, or they can be embedded in tables, forms, or reports, as follows:

+ **Stand-alone macros** are among the types of objects that Access displays in the Navigation Pane. (If the Navigation Pane doesn't appear in your Access window, press F11 to expand it.) If you don't have any stand-alone macros, the Navigation Pane doesn't display a section for macros, even when you display objects by type (by right-clicking the Navigation Pane and choosing Category➪Object Type from the contextual menu). When you have at least one macro, the macros section appears.

+ **Data macros** are stored as part of a table. You can configure your table to run macros before or after a record is added, edited, or deleted. These macros are great for validating data or setting values automatically. See Chapter 2 of this minibook for directions on setting them up.

+ **Embedded macros** are stored as part of a form or report. These macros are run only when events are triggered by the form or report, or by objects on the form or report. Chapter 2 of this minibook describes how to create embedded macros that run when you use a form or report.

Creating and Editing Stand-Alone Macros

Creating a stand-alone macro (a macro that's not embedded in a table, form, or report) is easy. Follow these steps:

Macro

1. **Click the Macro button in the Macros & Code group on the Create tab of the Ribbon, opening the Macro Builder.**

   Access displays a tab with a new, blank macro, where you enter the actions that make up the macro. Figure 1-1 shows a macro with one action already entered. Macros in Access 2013 contain a list of actions along with *arguments* (additional information) for each action.

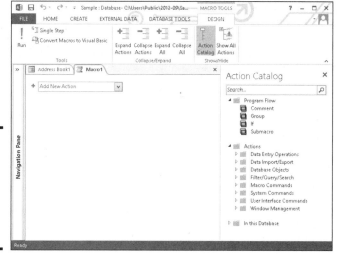

Figure 1-1:
A macro with one action entered, waiting for more.

You see the list of actions in the macro. The Action Catalog on the right side of the window shows a list of the actions that you can add to the macro, grouped by type. The Design tab of the Ribbon displays macro-related buttons.

2. **Enter the action that you want the macro to take, as described in "Taking action," later in this chapter.**

3. **For each action, specify the arguments for that action in the form that appears.**

   Click each box in turn and set the value of the argument. For some arguments, you type a value; for others, you choose a value from a list. If a down arrow appears at the right end of the box, click it to see a drop-down menu of your options.

4. **Repeat Steps 2 and 3 for each action you want the macro to take.**

   When you run the macro, Access executes the actions you specified, starting on the first row of the macro and proceeding until it reaches a blank row.

When you edit a macro, you open it in Design view, which opens the Macro Builder.

Naming, saving, and editing macros

Before you run a macro, you need to save it with a name. Press Ctrl+S, click the Save button on the Quick Access toolbar, or click the Close button and then click the Yes button in the Save As dialog box to save the macro. (The Save As dialog box appears the first time you save a macro. Name the macro, and click OK.)

You can edit your macro by right-clicking the macro name in the Navigation Pane and choosing the Design View option from the contextual menu. You see the macro again in its own tab or window. When the macro is open in Design view, you can change actions and arguments as described in the following sections.

Taking action

To tell Access what to do when running the macro, you specify actions and arguments. Access provides dozens of actions that you can use in your macros. Table 1-1 lists some common macro actions.

Table 1-1	Macro Actions
Action	*Comments*
Apply Filter	Applies a filter to the records in a datasheet, form, or report. Set the Filter Name argument to the name of an existing query, or type an SQL WHERE statement as the Where Condition argument.
Beep	Beeps. (You were perhaps expecting it to do something else?)
CloseWindow	Closes an Access object.
FindNextRecord	Repeats the last search you performed (perfect for a Find Next button on a form!).
FindRecord	Searches the current datasheet or form for the record you specify.
GoToControl	Moves the focus (cursor) to the control you specify. This action is useful on forms.
MessageBox	Displays a message box with the text you specify.
OpenForm	Opens a form in Form or Design view or in Print Preview.
OpenQuery	Opens a query in Datasheet or Design view or in Print Preview.
OpenReport	Opens a report in Design view or Print Preview or just prints the report, depending on what you specify for the View argument.
OpenTable	Opens a table in Datasheet or Design view or in Print Preview.
PrintPreview	Displays the object that you specify in Print Preview. From there, the user can choose whether and what to print.
Requery	Recalculates the value of the current control or reruns the record source query.
RunCode	Runs a VBA function (see Book VIII).

Action	Comments
RunMenuCommand	Runs an Access menu command.
RunMacro	Runs another macro. When the other macro finishes running, the first macro continues with the next action.
SaveRecord	Saves the current record.
SelectObject	Selects the object that you specify.
SetProperty	Sets the property of a control, field, or other object to the value you specify (which can be an expression).
ShowAllRecords	Removes any filter from the current table, query, or form.

You have at least three ways to add an action to a macro in Design view:

✦ Click the Add New Action box at the bottom of the macro, and select an action in the alphabetical list of actions.

✦ Double-click an action in the Action Catalog.

✦ Click an action in the Action Catalog, and drag it where you want to add it in the list of actions in your macro.

Either way, Access adds this new action to your macro and displays a form with space for information about the action (see Figure 1-2).

Book VI
Chapter 1

Making Macros
Do the Work

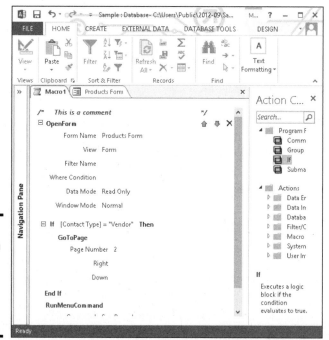

Figure 1-2:
Macros can
have lots
of actions.
Click one
to enter its
arguments.

Action
Catalog

The Action Catalog lists a *lot* of actions. We can never find the one we want. The solution? Type part of the action name in the Search box at the top of the Action Catalog to display only actions that contain what you type. To return to seeing all actions, click the Stop Filtering icon to the right of the Search box.

Specifying arguments to actions

After you select an action, Access displays its arguments — additional information that Access needs to perform the action (refer to Figure 1-2, earlier in this chapter). Click an argument's box to set it.

Some arguments start out blank, whereas others start with a default value. The `OpenForm` action, for example, has a `View` argument that specifies which view you want the form to appear in. The default value for the `View` argument is `Form view`. (You usually want forms to open in Form view.)

These arguments appear in many macro actions:

✦ **View:** View that Access opens the object in. The `OpenForm` action, for example, includes the `View` argument, and you can choose the `Form`, `Design`, `Print Preview`, `Datasheet`, or `Layout` argument from a drop-down menu. These arguments are all the possible views for a form.

✦ **Object Name:** Name of the object (table, query, form, report, macro, modules, or data access page) that the action affects. Access provides a drop-down menu of the objects of that type in your database.

✦ **Filter Name:** Name of a query (or filter saved as a query) that specifies which records to include in the action.

✦ **Where Condition:** Expression that specifies which records to include, written in SQL (Structured Query Language). Click the Build button to the right of the argument to display the Expression Builder. Book VIII, Chapter 5 explains how to use SQL.

When you've specified the arguments for an action, you may not want the action to occupy so much screen space. You can collapse the action by clicking the minus (–) button to the left of the action so that the arguments are listed on the same line as the action. You can expand the action again at any time by clicking the plus (+) button.

Moving your actions around

You can change the order of the actions in a macro by clicking an action to select it and then clicking the up or down arrow near the right end of the action (refer to Figure 1-2, earlier in this chapter), or by dragging the action up or down. You can delete the selected action by clicking the X at the right end of the action.

You can copy an action, too, which can be useful after you've created an action and entered all the appropriate arguments for it. To copy an action, hold down the Ctrl key while you drag it to a new location. Access leaves the action where it is and creates a copy where you tried to drag it.

Adding comments

Earlier versions of Access had a Comment column in the Macro window where you could type descriptions and explanations to make the macro more readable. In Access 2013, you add comments between actions, which is the way that most programming languages work. To add a comment, drag the Comment action from the Action Catalog to any location in your macro, or choose Comment from the Add New Action drop-down menu and then move the comment up to the spot where you want it. The first line of the macro in Figure 1-2, earlier in this chapter, is a comment, shown as text surrounded by /* and */ characters. (These characters may seem like odd choices, but several programming languages use them to mark where comments start and end.)

Adding comments to your macros is a great idea. Add a comment at the beginning of the macro that says what the macro is supposed to do. If people other than you use the Access database, also add your name and the date.

Creating subroutines in macros: Submacros

Programs, even macros, can get long and confusing. Programs also can get repetitive; you may find yourself using the same series of actions in different macros. Programmers the world over use *subroutines* to store a set of actions (or commands) with a name. Instead of duplicating this set of actions in all the places you want the actions to run, you *call the subroutine* by using its name. Later, if you think of a better way to perform that series of actions, you can change the subroutine, and all the programs that call it get the new, improved version. Very efficient.

Starting in Access 2013, macros now have subroutines, called *submacros.* Put any actions you want in a submacro (even another submacro!), and give the submacro a name. When you run a macro, it does *not* run the actions inside a submacro unless you specifically call the submacro by name.

To create a submacro in a macro, follow these steps:

1. **Display the Action Catalog, if it's not already displayed, by clicking the Action Catalog button in the Show/Hide group on the Design tab of the Ribbon.**

2. **If the Program Flow group of actions isn't expanded (that is, doesn't have a list of actions below it), click the plus box to its left.**

   The Program Flow group is already expanded in Figure 1-2, earlier in this chapter.

3. **Drag the Submacro action to your macro.**

TIP

Access puts all submacros at the bottom of your macro and creates a group, with a name and actions, as shown in Figure 1-3.

Another way to make a submacro is to right-click anywhere in your macro and choose Make Submacro Block from the contextual menu.

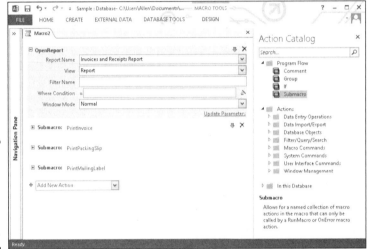

Figure 1-3:
A macro
can contain
as many
submacros
as you want.

4. **Type a name for the submacro in the Submacro box.**

5. **Enter the macro's actions and arguments inside the submacro area by making choices from the Add New Action drop-down menu or by dragging actions into the submacro area from the Action Catalog.**

When you run a submacro, you specify the name of the macro followed by a dot and the submacro name. If you're working on a set of macros for use on your Orders form, you could call the macro OrderForm. One submacro might be the actions required to print an invoice; if you name that submacro PrintInvoice, the submacro's full name is [OrderForm]. [PrintInvoice]. (The square brackets are required for names that include spaces, and using them isn't a bad idea anyway.)

Refer again to Figure 1-3, which shows a macro with three submacros. The first one is expanded so that you can see its actions, whereas the other three are collapsed so that only their names appear. To expand a collapsed submacro (which sounds like a medical condition, doesn't it?), click the plus box to the left of the submacro's name.

You can also create groups in macros, which allows you to enclose a set of actions in a box with a name. We're not sure what the point is, however. Stick with submacros, which are very useful!

Running Stand-Alone Macros and Submacros

You can run a stand-alone macro directly by double-clicking the macro in the Navigation Pane, or you can right-click it and choose Run from the contextual menu. If the macro contains only groups, Access runs just the first macro in the group.

The most common way to run a macro or submacro, however, is to assign it to an event on a form, such as the On Click event of a command button. You specify the name of the macro or the full name of the submacro (macro name, a dot, and submacro name) in one of the properties of a command button. We cover using macros on forms in Chapter 2 of this minibook. In this section, however, we cover two other cool ways to run macros: autoexecution when the database opens and execution when certain keystrokes are used.

Running a macro when the database opens

We like our databases to automatically display a main-menu form, or some other commonly used form, as soon as the database opens. If the first thing you usually do after opening the database is open the Order Entry form, why not tell Access to open it for you? You may have other actions that you'd like Access to take when your database opens. Perhaps you want to prompt the user for his or her name or to display a list of reports.

To tell Access to do something automatically when the database opens, you can write a macro with the actions you want Access to take and then tell Access to run the macro on startup.

Running a macro when the database opens is a snap: Just name the macro AutoExec. That's the whole thing. When you open a database, Access looks in the database for a macro named AutoExec, and if it finds one, it runs the macro. Enter the actions and arguments for the AutoExec macro in the usual way.

If you *don't* want the AutoExec macro to run when you open the database, hold down the Shift key while the database is loading.

Another way to make something happen when your database opens is to tell Access to open a form. Click the File tab on the Ribbon, click Options to display the Access Options dialog box, click Current Database, and set the Display Form option to the name of the form you want to open.

Assigning macros to keys

Your database can contain a *key-assignment macro* — a macro that assigns keys on the keyboard to run macros. If you create a macro group named `AutoKeys`, and it contains submacros with the names of keys (or key combinations) on the keyboard, Access runs the appropriate submacro when you press the key. Figure 1-4 shows the submacro code for an `AutoKeys` macro with a submacro assigned to function key F3.

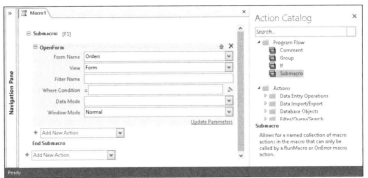

Figure 1-4: An `AutoKeys` macro assigns submacros to keystrokes.

To name a key-assignment macro, use ^ for the Ctrl key, + for the Shift key, and { } around key names that are more than one letter long. Table 1-2 shows the names of the keys you can use. You're restricted to letters; numbers; and the Insert, Delete, and function keys, used in conjunction with the Shift and Ctrl keys. Here are a few examples of key-assignment macros:

+ **^G:** Means Ctrl+G

+ **+{F2}:** Means Shift+F2

+ **{INS}:** Means the Insert key

All the submacros in the `AutoKeys` macro must be key assignments with names of key combinations; otherwise, Access will complain when you save your macro.

Table 1-2	Key Names in AutoKeys
Key Name	*Key*
A	A letter key (ditto for the rest of the letter and number keys)
{F1}	F1 function key (ditto for the rest of the function keys)
{INS}	Insert or Ins key
{DEL}	Delete or Del key

If you assign a submacro to a key that normally does something else (such as Ctrl+F, which usually summons the Find and Replace dialog box), your submacro overrides the Access command.

Opening Databases That Contain Macros

A feature in Access 2013 guards against databases that contain viruses in the form of macros. Unfortunately, this feature also guards against normal databases that contain macros, action queries, and VBA procedures. When you open a database that contains one of these types of objects, you may see a message asking whether you really want to take a chance on running the macros in the database, as shown in Figure 1-5. You can choose whether to open the database with the macros enabled (see Book I, Chapter 2 for details). If you or someone you trust created the database, click the Enable Content button in the message; otherwise, click the Close icon to dismiss the message, leaving some macros disabled.

Book VI
Chapter 1

Making Macros Do the Work

Figure 1-5:
Access has detected that your database contains macros.

When Access has disabled macros, you can read about it by clicking the File tab on the Ribbon, clicking Info, and noticing the big fat warning message. If the security warning shown in Figure 1-6 doesn't appear, macros are enabled.

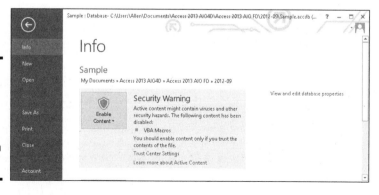

Figure 1-6:
If macros are disabled, you can enable them later.

Keeping a macro from turning into a virus

Writing a virus is no small feat; it requires pretty advanced programming skills. To qualify as a virus, a macro has to be intentionally written to do bad things to your computer and to replicate itself. Writing code that makes copies of itself in other files on other computers isn't easy. If you're concerned that you may accidentally create a virus, you can stop worrying about that. Creating a virus by accident is about as likely as writing an entire book, or driving across the country, by accident.

If the database is something that you created yourself, it's absolutely, positively, 100 percent safe to enable the macros. You have several options:

✦ **Put up with the annoying security warning message every time you open the database, and click the Enable Content button each time.** Actually, Access may not show you this message when you reopen the database if nothing significant has changed in the database. This method works, but it's annoying.

✦ **Store the database in a folder you've indicated that Access can trust — a *trusted location*.** (We envision this folder's looking like a CIA safe house in a spy movie.) We describe this folder in the next section, "Putting your database in a safe place."

✦ **Digitally sign your database by adding security code.** This code — a digital signature — tells Access, "It's okay. This is my own database, and I can vouch for its safety." This digital signature works only when you open the database on your own computer. "Signing your database," later in this chapter, describes how to sign your database.

✦ **Enable all macros in all databases and just wait for a virus to come along.** We don't recommend this option. Access's security features may be annoying, but they were created because computers get infected by viruses. We'll bet that you don't want your computer to be one of them. If you do decide to change the security settings for Access, click the File tab on the Ribbon, click Options, click Trust Center, click Trust Center Settings, and click Macro Settings to see your options.

We recommend storing your databases in a trusted location or signing them digitally. You don't have to put up with annoying messages, and you don't open your Access program to viruses from other people.

Putting your database in a safe place

You can tell Access that a folder is a trusted location — that is, a place where only you and your trusted associates can store databases. To tell Access that the databases in a specific folder are safe, follow these steps:

1. **Click the File tab on the Ribbon, and click Options on the menu that runs down the left edge of the screen.**

You see the Access Options dialog box.

2. **Select Trust Center in the left column, and click the Trust Center Settings button.**

At last, the Trust Center dialog box appears.

3. **Click Trusted Locations in the left column.**

The Trust Center dialog box looks like Figure 1-7. Microsoft recommends that trusted locations be on your own hard disk, not on network drives, so the Allow Trusted Locations on My Network check box normally isn't selected. If you share files with other people at your office (or in your home, for that matter), you may need to store your database on a network drive.

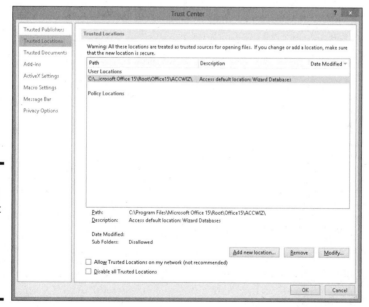

Figure 1-7:
You can tell Access that a specific folder is safe — a trusted location.

4. **If you plan to store your database on a network drive, select the Allow Trusted Locations on My Network check box.**

5. **Click the Add New Location button.**

You see the Microsoft Office Trusted Location dialog box, shown in Figure 1-8.

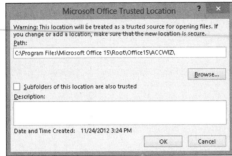

Figure 1-8:
Do you want
subfolders
to be
trusted, too?

6. **Browse to the folder where you plan to store your Access databases, and click OK.**

If you might store databases in subfolders, too, click the Subfolders of This Location Are Also Trusted check box. You return to the Trust Center dialog box, whether you can modify and remove folders from the list of trusted locations.

7. **Click OK to return to the Access Options dialog box.**

8. **Click OK in the Access Options dialog box to return to your database.**

Now when you open databases in the specified folder, Access won't display any alarming messages, or disable macros or VBA code in the databases.

Signing your database

Another way to turn off Access's security measures is to sign your databases. Signing a database for your own use is easy: You create your own digital signature and then use it to sign your databases. This signature works only on your own computer: When other people open your database, they still see the security warning message. If you want to create a digital signature that works everywhere, you need to contact a certification authority and buy one.

Follow these steps to create a digital signature for use on your own computer:

1. **Depending on your operating system, do one of the following:**

- In Windows 7, choose Start⇨All Programs⇨Microsoft Office⇨ Microsoft Office 2013 Tools⇨Digital Certificate for VBA Projects.

- In Windows 8, click the Digital Certificate for VBA Projects tile on the Start screen.

Windows System 7 may prompt you to install this program unless you've used it before. If so, follow its prompts. You see the dialog box shown in Figure 1-9.

Figure 1-9:
Creating
a digital
signature
for use with
your own
databases.

2. **Type a name for your certificate (such as your own name), and click OK.**

   The program reports that it created a certificate, or digital signature.

3. **Click OK.**

If you plan to distribute your database to other people, and you need a certificate that works on computers other than yours, you need to buy a digital certificate. For information, see the Symantec website at https://www. symantec.com/products-solutions/families/?fid=code-signing.

When you have a digital certificate, sign your database by following these steps:

1. **With your database open, click the File tab on the Ribbon, and choose Save As.**

   You see two options: Save Database As and Save Object As.

2. **Below Save Database As, in the Advanced section, double-click Package and Sign.**

   You see the Windows Security dialog box, shown in Figure 1-10.

3. **If you have more than one certificate, click the Choose button, and choose one of the digital signature certificates stored on your computer.**

   Your certificate name appears in the Windows Security dialog box.

4. **Click OK.**

   Access displays the Create Microsoft Access Signed Package dialog box, which looks just like a Save As dialog box.

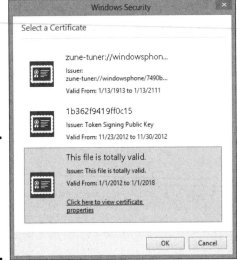

Figure 1-10:
You can
add your
own digital
signature
to your
database.

5. **Specify where to store the signed copy of the database and what file-name to use.**

6. **Click Create.**

Now when you open this database, Access doesn't complain. Whew!

Knowing which actions you can take

Show All
Actions

Normally, when you edit a macro in Design view, Access shows you only the actions that it considers to be safe, such as actions that don't allow you to change data outside the database. If you want to see all possible macro actions, click the Show All Actions button in the Show/Hide group on the Design tab of the Ribbon. More actions appear on the Add New Action drop-down menu and in the Action Catalog.

Telling Access to "Run This Only If I Say So"

Every programming language worth its salt has an if-then feature, which ensures that a command is carried out only under specific circumstances. You may want Access to print a report for the current order only if the order number isn't blank, for example. If the order number *is* blank, don't print the report, and if the order number *isn't* blank, print the report. The technical term for an if-then situation is *conditional execution.* The *condition* is a value or expression that can be either true or false — in geek speak, a *Boolean.*

If-Then macros

You add conditional execution to a macro action by adding an If-Then block to the macro window and then typing a condition. Suppose that you want to print an invoice for the current order (using the OpenReport action), but you don't want to print it if the total amount of the order is zero. You use the [Orders]![Total Product Cost] > 0 condition to tell Access to perform the action only if the order contains products that cost money. To do so, follow these steps:

1. **Open your macro in Design view by right-clicking it in the Navigation Pane and choosing Design View from the contextual menu.**

   You see your macro, ready to edit.

2. **If the Action Catalog isn't already visible, click the Action Catalog button on the Show/Hide group on the Design tab of the Ribbon.**

   The Action Catalog appears to the right of the macro.

3. **Drag the If item from the Program Flow group of the Action Catalog to your macro, or double-click the If item.**

   Either way, you end up with an If block in your macro (see Figure 1-11).

Figure 1-11: The If block is where you type a condition that controls whether Access performs a set of actions.

4. **Enter a condition in the Conditional Expression box, or click the Expression Builder to its right to help you write the condition.**

   For the condition, you can use any expression that comes out to be True (Yes) or False (No). Conditions work just like the criteria that you use when creating queries, as described in Book III, Chapter 1. You can compare values by using comparison operators such as =, <, and >, and you can use Is Null and Is Not Null to spot blank and non-blank values, respectively.

5. **Enter actions and arguments in the `If-Then` block, using the Add New Action box, or add actions from the Action Catalog.**

   If the `If` command is selected in the Action Catalog, double-clicking another action adds the action inside the `If` block. You can move an action into or out of an `If` block by dragging it or by clicking the up and down arrows at the right end of the action.

   Any actions that are inside the `If` block's box are executed only if the condition is `True`. If the condition is `False`, Access skips the `If` block and continues executing the macro with the action following the `If` block.

If-Then-Else macros

If you want an if-then-else condition — you want to run one set of actions if the condition is `True` and another set if the condition is `False` — you can add an `Else` or `ElseIf` section to your `If` block. An `Else` section gives you a place to add actions to your macro that will be executed only if the `If` condition is `False`. An `ElseIf` section enables you to enter a second condition for Access to check.

To add an `Else` or `ElseIf` section to your `If` block, click the Add Else or Add ElseIf link in the bottom-right corner of the `If` block's box.

The example macro shown in Figure 1-12 prints a receipt if the order has been paid for, and it prints an invoice if the order hasn't been paid for. The `OpenReport` actions have been collapsed (shrunk) so that their arguments appear on the same line as the action, which saves screen space (and paper).

Figure 1-12:
An `If-Then-Else` macro executes one set of actions if a condition is `True` and another set if the condition is `False`.

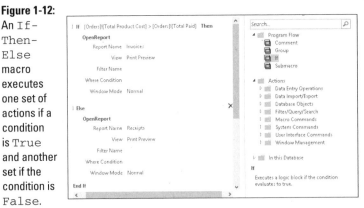

Chapter 2: Making Macros Smarter

In This Chapter

✔ **Validating and setting fields in your tables by using data macros**

✔ **Making your forms smarter with macros**

✔ **Changing form control properties with a macro**

✔ **Creating your own main-menu form**

✔ **Using temporary variables in macros**

*T*he macros we describe in this chapter are fired off automatically by *events* — that is, by things that happen (usually, things that the database user does) to tables or forms. Examples of events are a form opening, a record in a table being added, or the value of a field in a table changing. You can tell Access that when one of these events happens, it should run a specific macro. This setup makes your macros *event-driven.* The events that can trigger data macros, which are attached to tables, are events that happen to records in tables. The events that trigger form macros are events that happen to forms and the objects they contain.

Event-driven macros can be very powerful. You can use them to validate values in your tables or to set the values of fields based on changes in other fields. You can also use the `On Click` event of buttons on a form to run any macro you want.

Although macros are simple and powerful, they aren't the full-featured programming language that Visual Basic for Applications (VBA) is. If you create a macro and later wish that you'd written a VBA procedure to do the job, Access can convert the macro to VBA. See Book VIII, Chapter 1 for details on converting a macro to a VBA program. If you want to use navigation forms rather than regular forms, see Book IV, Chapter 3.

This chapter describes some nifty ways to use macros with tables and forms, including setting up your own main-menu form.

Attaching Macros to Tables

When you create a table, you can specify validation rules that control what values can be stored in each field and defaults that set field values when adding records. These validation rules, however, are limited to looking at values in the same record in the same table. Defaults have to be constants. Wouldn't it be cool if you could define smarter validations and defaults that could look at values in any record in any table and use if-then-else logic? Now you can by defining *data macros* that are attached to your table.

The Orders table in an order-entry database, for example, might contain information about each order placed at an online store, including how much sales tax the customer owes. If the customer's address is in the same state as your store, the sales tax rate is your state's tax rate; otherwise, it's zero. Also, if the customer is tax exempt, the sales tax for the order is zero. You could make `Sales Tax Rate Applied` a calculated field, but you may need to override it. Instead, you can have a data macro set the field whenever the customer's state and tax-exempt status change.

Running data macros

You don't actually run a data macro. Instead, the data macro runs whenever the triggering event happens — when someone adds or deletes a record or edits a field. Access automatically runs the data macro whether the data was changed in Datasheet view or in a form, or by another macro or VBA module. Data macros can't include actions that require user input; the macros must be triggered by another program rather than by a human being.

Creating a data macro

You create data macros as part of a table. Here's how:

1. **Open the table in Design view by right-clicking the table name in the Navigation Pane and choosing Design View from the contextual menu.**

   The Access window looks something like Figure 2-1, and the Design tab of the Ribbon shows tools for designing tables.

Figure 2-1:
A table
in Design
view, ready
for data
macros.

2. Click the Create Data Macros button in the Field, Record & Table Events group on the Design tab of the Ribbon.

You see a list of the events that can trigger a data macro, as listed in Table 2-1. When a user, a macro, or a VBA module performs one of these actions on this field, the macro runs.

Table 2-1	Data Macro Events
Event	**Description**
After Insert	After a new record has been added to this table
After Update	After any field in a record in this table has been updated
After Delete	After a record in this table has been deleted
Before Delete	When a record in this table is about to be deleted
Before Change	When a record in this table is about to be updated
Create Named Macro	When you create a new macro and give it a name
Edit Named Macro	When you edit a named macro

3. **Choose an event from the list of triggering events.**

   The most common choices are `After Insert` and `After Update`, for checking information that has been entered. Access creates a macro that's attached to the table; this macro is named `table name : event` (`Orders : After Update`, for example). When you make your choice, the Macro Builder appears.

4. **Add actions to the macro based on what you want Access to do when the triggering event occurs.**

   In the Macro Builder, when you click the Add New Action check box or look at the Action Catalog, the available actions aren't the same as those that are available when you're making regular actions. The actions that you can use center on editing a record in the table.

   Figure 2-2 shows a data macro that sets the `Sales Tax Rate Applied` field:

   - The `EditRecord` action tells Access to make and save changes to the current record.

   - The `SetField` action sets the value of a field (specified with the `Name` argument) in that record to the value in the `Value` argument.

Figure 2-2:
This data macro sets the sales tax based on the state and tax-exempt status.

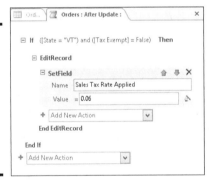

5. **Close the macro tab to return to your table in Design view.**

6. **Close the table in Design view, or switch to Datasheet view.**

   When you save changes to the table design, Access saves changes to the data macros for the table too.

Now when you edit records in the table, Access runs the data macro after each update. If Access makes a change, a red box appears briefly around the field that it's changing.

To edit a data macro for a table, open the table in Design view; click the Create Data Macros button in the Field, Record & Table Events group on the Design tab of the Ribbon; and choose the same event you chose before — that is, follow the same steps you used to create the macro. Access displays the macro that's saved for that event. (We think that the button should be called Create or Edit Data Macros, but a name that long would never fit on the Ribbon!)

The one feature to which this dual functionality doesn't apply is named macros. You create a named macro with the Create Named Macro option, and you edit a named macro with the Edit Named Macro option. Named macros give you added flexibility. You can invoke them by name, as well as have them execute when a triggering event occurs. You might create a named macro called `SendEmail` to send an e-mail message to an operator whenever a certain error condition occurs, for example.

Book VI
Chapter 2

Making Macros Smarter

You have just one data macro for each triggering event for the table, not a separate macro for each field. If you want to update two different fields in a record, your macro can have two `SetField` actions. While a data macro is open in Design view, you can't view any other Access objects until you close the macro; we're not sure why. This limitation is inconvenient, and we hope that Microsoft considers it to be a bug and fixes it.

Data macros don't show up on the Navigation Pane; they aren't considered to be separate objects. They're stored as part of the table to which they're attached.

Trying cool data-macro tricks

Here are a couple of questions that show the kind of things you can find out, using functions and properties in data macros:

✦ **Did the value of this field even change?** When you write a data macro triggered by an `AfterUpdate` or `BeforeChange` event — by an edit of the record — how can you tell whether the value of a specific field changed? Maybe the record was edited, but who knows which fields actually changed? You can find out by using the `Updated("`*fieldname*`")` function. The following condition, for example, is `True` only if the `ProductCount` field in the Orders table changed and the value of that field is less than 6:

```
If Updated("ProductCount") And ProductCount < 6
```

✦ **What did the value used to be?** If the value of a field changed, you may want to know what the previous value was. If the `ProductCount` went up, for example, you may want to do something about recalculating the shipping charge. You can use the `Old.[`*fieldname*`]` property for a value that the field had before the edit. (Note that you don't use quotation marks around the field name.)

Running Macros in Forms

Most macros are used with forms to make form controls smarter or to power command buttons. Every control in a form has events connected to it — things that happen when the user clicks the control, changes its value, or opens or closes the form itself.

You can run two kinds of macros from a form:

✦ **Regular old stand-alone macros,** like the ones described in Chapter 1 of this minibook. You can make a macro for the form, and in the macro, you can create a submacro for each event for which you want a macro to run.

✦ **Embedded macros,** which Access creates when a wizard makes a command button on a form. These macros are attached to the form in the same way that data macros are attached to tables. You can get to them when you have the form open in Design view.

The rest of this section describes how to run both types of macros from your forms.

Running a macro when a form event happens

To tell Access to run a macro when an event happens, you enter the macro name in the event property for the control (or for the whole form). Follow these steps:

1. **Create and save the macro you want to run.**

You can store the macro by itself or as a submacro in a macro for the form. (We usually create one macro for each form and make a submacro for each event for which we want something to happen.) Save the macro before continuing.

You can keep the macro open in Design view if you plan to make further changes in your macro.

2. **Open the form in Design view.**

See Book IV, Chapter 2 for information about editing a form in Design view.

3. **Display the property sheet by clicking the Property Sheet button in the Tools group on the Design tab of the Ribbon, and click the Event tab.**

Property Sheet

See Book IV, Chapter 1 for information about the property sheet. The Event tab displays all the events for the selected object.

4. **If you're attaching a macro to a control (such as a command button), click that control.**

5. **To attach the macro to the form itself, click the box where the rulers intersect in the top-left corner of the form.**

   Now the property sheet shows the available events for the control or for the form itself.

6. **Click the event property that you want to use.**

   If you're attaching a macro to a command button, for example, click the On Click property to run the macro when the user clicks the command button. If you want the macro to run whenever you insert a record by using the form, click the Before Insert property.

7. **Click the down arrow at the right end of the property, and choose the name of the macro from the drop-down menu.**

   Access lists all the macros and submacros in alphabetical order. If the Order Form macro contains a macro named AddRecord, for example, choose Order Form.AddRecord. If none of the existing macros is appropriate for your purpose, you can create an event procedure instead, writing it in the form of a VBA subroutine.

   See Book VIII, Chapter 1 for a detailed description of VBA.

Most controls have several events to which you can assign a macro, including when your cursor enters and exits the control, when you click or double-click it, or when its value changes. Figure 2-3 shows the Event tab of the property sheet for a command-button control, with a macro name in the On Click event property.

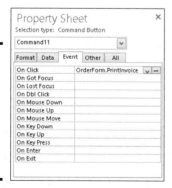

Figure 2-3:
The Event properties of a command-button control on a form.

Table 2-2 shows the events that most commonly occur for controls on a form.

Table 2-2	Some Form-Control Events
Event	**Description**
Before Update	When the control or record is about to be updated
After Update	Immediately after the control or record is updated
On Not in List	When a user tries to enter a value in combo and list boxes that's not in the list of values
On Enter	When focus (the cursor) moves to the control
On Exit	When focus (the cursor) leaves the control
On Click	When you click the control
On Dbl Click	When you double-click the control

You can make a macro for an order form that automatically moves you to the last record in the table, for example. (You rarely want to edit the first, oldest order in the table, but you may well want to edit the newest order.) The macro runs when you open the form. The macro, which you might name GoToLastRecord and store in your Order Form macro, looks like Figure 2-4. It uses the GoToRecord action, with the Record argument set to Last.

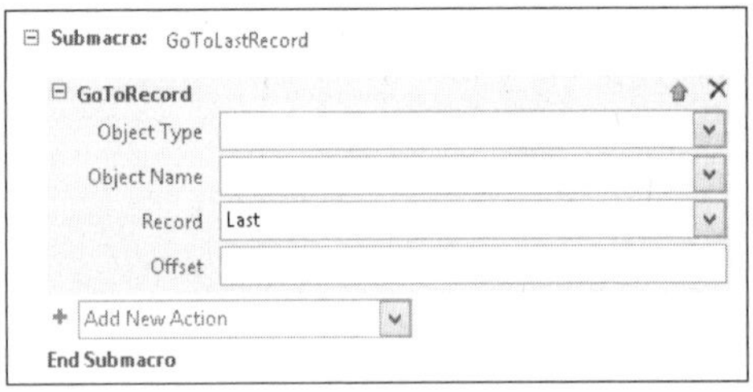

Figure 2-4:
A single-action macro moves the cursor to the last record in the record source of the form.

```
⊟ Submacro:  GoToLastRecord

   ⊟ GoToRecord                                    ⬆ ✕
         Object Type  [              ] ⌄
         Object Name  [              ] ⌄
              Record  [Last          ] ⌄
              Offset  [              ]
   ✛ | Add New Action | ⌄
   End Submacro
```

To make the macro run each time you open the form, set the form's OnOpen event property to the name of the macro: Order Form.GoToLastRecord.

Creating command buttons on forms

Book IV, Chapter 3 describes how to make command buttons on a form. The Command Button Wizard can write macros for many tasks that you may want a button to carry out, such as going to the first or last record, applying a filter, or finding a record. The wizard writes a macro that's attached to the form — an *embedded macro*.

Keyboard shortcuts for command buttons

Some people would rather use the keyboard than the mouse. You can give your command buttons keyboard shortcuts, in the form of the Alt key combined with a letter or number.

To assign a shortcut to a command button, include an ampersand (&) in the Name property

of the control. The keyboard shortcut is the Alt key combined with the letter or digit that follows the ampersand. If you name a command button &Print, for example, its keyboard shortcut is Alt+P.

To look at or edit an embedded macro, open the form in Design view, display the Events tab of the property sheet, and click the control to which the macro is attached. The On Click event of the control says Embedded, and you can click the Macro Builder (...) button to open the macro in Design view. While you're editing an embedded macro, you can't view any other objects in the database until you close the macro. Embedded macros don't show up in the Navigation Pane; they aren't considered to be separate objects. Those macros are stored as part of the form to which they're attached.

Referring to form controls in macros

When you write a macro that runs from a form — whether it's an embedded macro or a stand-alone macro that runs from an event on the form — the macro has to refer frequently to the current value of a control on the form. In the arguments you use to specify macro actions, you can just type the name of the control that displays the field or the field name. To set the shipping charge to $3 per item when the handling charge is $3.75, for example, you can use the SetValue action with these arguments:

```
Name: [Shipping & Handling]
Value: ([Total Qty] * 3) + 3.75
```

If you're referring to a control on a form other than the form from which the macro was called, however, you need to specify which form the control is on, as follows:

```
[Forms]![formname]![controlname]
```

Replace *formname* with the name of your form and *controlname* with the name of the control on the form.

The OpenReport action, for example, displays or prints a report. You can use its Where argument to restrict the records that appear in the report. If you want the report to include only records with the same OrderID value as the order displayed on the Orders form, you type this value in the Where Condition argument of the OpenReport action:

```
[OrderID] = [Forms]![Orders]![OrderID]
```

The first OrderID field is the one in the record source of the report; the second one is the OrderID field on the form.

The next section, "Printing matching records from a form," shows you how to make a button on your form that uses this condition to print a report containing only records that match the record displayed on the form.

In the Where Condition argument of many actions (an argument that you use to filter records), you must always use this longer version of the name of the control that you want to refer to. If you don't, Access won't know what to do and will display an annoying error message.

Printing matching records from a form

Now you know everything that you need to know to create a useful command button: a button that prints a report for the record displayed in the form. An order form may have a button to print a mailing label, a button to print a packing slip, and a button to print an invoice (if not paid) or receipt (if paid), all filtered to include only the order that's currently displayed on the form. Store these button macros as submacros in a macro for the form (such as the Order Form macro).

The PrintInvoiceOrReceipt submacro, shown in Figure 2-5, saves any changes made in the current record on the form and then prints the invoice for the current record. For each macro, you create a button that calls the macro via the button's On Click property. Figure 2-6 shows a form in Design view, with the property sheet for the Print Invoice/Receipt command button.

Figure 2-5:
A macro that prints a report containing only records for the order currently displayed on the form.

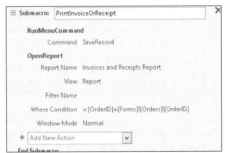

Figure 2-6:
You set
the `On`
`Click`
property
for your
button to the
submacro
you want
the button to
run.

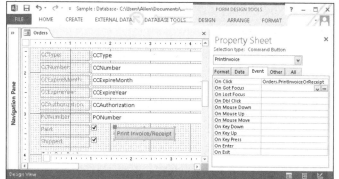

Changing the Way Your Form Looks Dynamically

A *really* smart form changes in response to the information you type in it. Making smart forms isn't hard: You need only know how to make a macro display, hide, enable, or disable controls on the form in response to what you enter.

Setting the properties of form controls

Macros have no problem changing the *values* of controls; a macro can copy a value from one control to another, for example, or store a calculation in a control by using the `SetValue` action. But that's not all. Macros can also change the properties of controls, in essence changing how controls look or act onscreen. The following properties, for example, are all eminently changeable when a macro gets its hands on them:

✦ **Fore Color:** We're guessing that `Fore Color` is short for *Foreground Color*. In any event, `Fore Color` refers to the text-color property of a label. Changing this property makes the text appear in a different color. Why is this property neat? A macro can change the color of a label to, say, bright red if an order isn't paid for, which makes tracking down deadbeats much easier for you. `Back Color` works the same way for the background color.

✦ **Visible:** If the `Visible` property is set to No, the control is hidden. You can have a macro make controls invisible based on the values of other controls. If an order is paid by check, for example, the credit-card controls aren't needed and can be hidden.

✦ **Enabled:** If the `Enabled` property is set to No, the cursor won't move to it, and you can't change the control's value. You can make a macro that sets the value of some controls and then disables them so that the value can't be changed.

Hiding unneeded controls on a form

On an order form, if the payment method isn't purchase order, what's the point of displaying a place to type a purchase order number? How cool would the form be if it could hide the PO Number control if the Payment Method control didn't contain the value Purchase Order?

Follow these steps to make a submacro that changes the properties of a form control:

1. **Open your macro in Design view.**

   To do this, right-click the macro in the Navigation Pane and choose Design View from the contextual menu.

2. **Make a submacro named something like ShowHidePONumber.**

   Double-click Submacro in the Action Catalog, or drag a Submacro from the Action Catalog to your macro.

   The order of the submacros in a macro doesn't matter; each submacro runs only when it's called or triggered.

3. **Add an If action to your macro.**

   You can choose If from the Add an Action drop-down menu in the sub-macro box or drag If from the Action Catalog into your submacro.

4. **In the If box, type the condition under which you want to change the property of the control.**

   In Figure 2-7, the condition is [Payment Method] = "Purchase Order". The submacro displays the PO Number control if this condition is True and hides it otherwise.

Figure 2-7: Don't display the PO Number control if the customer isn't paying by purchase order.

In Figure 2-7, the macro hides a text box control if a control is blank (null) and displays the text box if the control isn't blank. You'd probably want to display or hide the text box's label, too, but we're keeping this example macro short.

5. **Add a `SetValue` action in the `If` block.**

    The `SetValue` action works for setting properties, too.

6. **In the `Item` argument of the `SetValue` action, type the name of the control whose property you want to set, followed by a dot and the name of the property.**

    If the control name includes spaces, enclose it in square brackets. (If the name has no spaces, using square brackets can't hurt.) Access adds brackets around the property name for you. In Figure 2-7, the `Item` argument is `[PO Number].Visible` — the `Visible` property of the `PO Number` text box.

7. **In the Expression argument box, type the value to which you want to set the property.**

    To display the `PO Number` text box, set its `Visible` property to `Yes` or `True`.

8. **To hide the `PO Number` text box, add an `Else` action by clicking the Add Else link in the `If` block.**

9. **Add a `SetValue` action to the `Else` action.**

10. **Set the `Item` argument to the same property as in Step 6.**

    You're still setting the properties of the same control: the `PO Number` text box.

11. **Set Expression to `No` or `False`.**

12. **Save the macro by pressing Ctrl+S.**

13. **Open the form in Design view.**

14. **Set the `After Update` event property for the `Payment Method` control to the name of the submacro you just created.**

    You may want to set the control's `On Exit` event, too, so that the sub-macro runs whenever the user's cursor leaves the control.

 When you set the Item argument of the `SetValue` action to the property you want to change, you can click the Build button to the right of the Item box to use Expression Builder.

 By default, Access displays only the actions that are allowed in databases that haven't been trusted. Click the Show All Actions button in the Show/Hide group on the Design tab of the Ribbon, below the Macro Tools heading, to see the complete list of actions in the Action drop-down menu.

Setting Up Your Own Main-Menu Form

You can make your own main-menu form by creating an *unbound form* (a form with no record source) with command buttons that run macros (see Figure 2-8). For some commands, you can use the Command Button Wizard to create an embedded macro instead of writing the macro yourself.

Here's the sequence:

1. **Create the main-menu form.**

2. **Create a macro to contain submacros run by buttons on the main-menu form.**

3. **Create a macro named `AutoExec` that contains an `OpenForm` action to open your main-menu form so that Access displays the form automatically when you open the database.**

4. **Create each command button that you want to use on the main-menu form.**

5. **For a command button that does something that the Command Button Wizard doesn't offer, write a submacro for the command button to run, and set the button's `On Click` event property to run the submacro.**

Creating a form that appears when the database opens

To create an unbound form that appears when you open the database, follow these steps:

1. **Create a new form by clicking the Form Design button in the Forms group on the Create tab of the Ribbon.**

   Access opens a form in Design view.

2. **Save the blank form by clicking the Save button on the Quick Access toolbar or by pressing Ctrl+S.**

3. **In the Save As dialog box, type a name for the form, and click OK.**

   Call the form something like `Main Menu`. Leave the form open; you make buttons for it later.

   Now you're ready to make the `AutoExec` macro that opens the form automatically.

4. **Create a new macro.**

   A blank macro appears.

5. **Add an `OpenForm` action to the macro.**

6. **Set the `Form Name` argument to the name of the form you just created (Main Menu).**

   To do so, click the `Form Name` argument, click its down arrow, and choose the form from the drop-down menu that appears.

7. **Close the macro, click the Yes button to save it, and name it `AutoExec`.**

   You have to name your macro `AutoExec` if you want the macro to run automatically each time you open the database.

8. **Create another macro by clicking the Macro button in the Macros & Code group on the Create tab of the Ribbon.**

   Your main-menu form needs a macro to contain the submacros your buttons will run. You could make all your buttons by using the Command Buttons Wizard, which stores its submacros as embedded macros, but if you want to make your own submacros for your buttons, you can store them in the macro you create here.

9. **Click the Save button or press Ctrl+S to save the new macro.**

10. **Type a name for the macro, and click OK.**

    You don't *have* to give the macro the same name as the main-menu form — but you'll find yourself less confused if you do! If you took our advice in Step 3, name the macro `Main Menu` or `Main Menu Form`.

11. **Click the tab for the Main Menu form so that you can start adding buttons.**

    Now you're ready to return to your main-menu form (the one you created back in Step 1 — remember?) and add command buttons.

The form is ready and appears when you open the database; all it needs is buttons!

Creating command buttons for your main-menu form

For each button you want to use on the main-menu form, create a command button and (if necessary) a macro for it to run. When you create a command button, the Command Button Wizard writes embedded macros to open forms, print reports, and run queries. The most useful Command Button Wizard choices for buttons on a main-menu form are

✦ **Open Form** (in the Form Operations category): Opens any other form.

✦ **Preview Report** (in the Report Operations category): Opens a report in Print Preview.

✦ **Print Report** (in the Report Operations category): Prints a report without previewing it.

✦ **Run Query** (in the Miscellaneous category): Runs an action query or opens a select query in Datasheet view.

✦ **Run Macro** (in the Miscellaneous category): Runs a macro. The macro needs to exist before you create the command button.

If you want to do something else, you need to create a submacro in your macro and then tell the command button to run it. The next two sections describe both ways to make a command button: letting the Command Button Wizard write an embedded macro for your button and writing your own macro for the button.

Letting the wizard make your command button

If the Command Button Wizard knows how to write the embedded macro for your button, use the wizard. Book IV, Chapter 3 describes how to tell the Command Button Wizard what you want the button to do.

Open your main-menu form in Design view, and follow these steps:

XXXX

1. **Click the Button button in the Controls group on the Design tab of the Ribbon and then click the form where you want the button to appear.**

Access starts the Command Button Wizard. (See Book IV, Chapter 3 for the details.)

2. **Select the category and action for what you want the button to do, and click Next.**

Depending on which action you choose, the wizard asks for specific information about what you want to do. If you choose Open Form as the action, for example, the wizard asks which form you want to open and whether you want it to display all or specific records.

3. **Answer the wizard's questions about what form you want to display, what report you want to preview or print, and what query you want to open or run; then click Next.**

4. **When the wizard asks what the button should look like, click Text or Picture, specify the text or icon to appear on the button, and then click Next.**

5. **Type a short name for the command button, and click Finish.**

    Choose a name that has something to do with what the button does.

    The wizard creates the command button and sets the button's `On Click` property to execute the embedded macro it just wrote. This property causes Access to run the embedded macro when someone clicks the command button.

6. **Move or resize the command button as you like, and create a label to go next to it.**

    If the button displays text, it may not need a label.

The Command Button Wizard sets the `On Click` property of each command button to an embedded macro that it writes. In the property sheet, you see `Embedded macro` in the property; click the property and then click the Macro Builder (...) button to see the submacro in Design view.

If you want to change the button to run a different macro, click the `On Click` property on the Event tab of the property sheet, click the down arrow for the property, and choose your macro from the drop-down menu.

TIP

If you're not sure whether the Command Button Wizard can write an embedded macro for the task you want the button to perform, run the wizard according to the preceding steps to find out. In Step 2, browse the various programs that the wizard knows how to write. If you don't see the program you need, cancel the wizard, and try the steps in the next section of this chapter.

Making command buttons that run your macros

There's a chance that you ran the Command Button Wizard but couldn't find the option you need. The wizard just doesn't do everything. In that case, you can create a button and then write a macro for the button to run.

If you followed the steps in "Creating a form that appears when the database opens," earlier in this chapter, you've already created a macro for the macros run by command buttons on your main-menu form. Follow these steps for each command button that runs a macro:

1. **Open the macro in Design view by right-clicking the macro name in the Navigation Pane and choosing Design View from the contextual menu.**

    If you've already created macros for this form, this macro already contains submacros. No problem! Just add another submacro.

2. **Create a submacro by double-clicking Submacro in the Action Catalog; then add actions and enter arguments for each action.**

    Chapter 1 of this minibook describes how to choose the actions and arguments for a macro.

3. **Save the macro by pressing Ctrl+S or clicking the Save button on the Quick Access toolbar.**

   You can't assign the macro name to the command button's `On Click` property if the macro isn't saved.

4. **Switch to the form in Design View by clicking the form's tab.**

   If your main-menu form isn't open in Design view, open it now. (In the Navigation Pane, right-click the form name and choose Design View from the contextual menu.)

5. **Click the Button button in the Controls group on the Design tab of the Ribbon and then click the form where you want the button to appear.**

   Access starts the Command Button Wizard. The wizard creates a command button and starts asking questions.

6. **Click Cancel to dismiss the wizard.**

7. **Move or resize the command button as you like, and create a label to go next to it.**

8. **Set the button's properties to display the text or picture you want.**

   Book IV, Chapter 3 describes how to configure a command button.

9. **Set the button's On Click event property to run the macro you created in Steps 2 and 3.**

10. **Save the macro and the form.**

11. **Try out your new button!**

Using Temporary Variables in Macros

Now that Microsoft has decided that macros are here to stay, it has decided to beef up the features of macros. One fairly new feature is *temporary variables* — variables that are like fields that belong to no table. You can use a temporary variable to store a value that you'll need later in the macro's execution. You can make as many temporary variables as you like — well, up to 255, but that's a lot! — and they stick around even after your macro stops running. You can set a temporary variable in one macro and read its value in another macro, or when the same macro runs again later.

Each temporary variable has a name that you choose. To create a temporary variable or change the name of an existing one, use the `SetTempVar` action in your macro. It has two arguments:

✦ **Name:** A name that you create, such as `RecordID`

✦ **Expression:** The value to assign to (or store in) this temporary variable, which can be any expression

To refer to the temporary variable later so that you can use the value it contains, type an expression like this:

```
[Tempvars]![varname]
```

Replace *varname* with the name of the temporary variable.

If the temporary variable doesn't exist, Access doesn't complain. Instead, you get the value `Null` as the value of the nonexistent temporary variable. To delete a temporary variable, you can use the `RemoveTempVar` action.

Nobody's perfect: Dealing with errors

Originally, when a macro ran into a problem (like a reference to a record or control that didn't exist, or an expression that divided a number by zero), it just died, displaying a message for the user to see. Error handling allows the macro to detect an error and do something about it.

If you want macros to try to handle any errors that may arise, you can use the `On Error` action to tell Access what to do if it runs into an error. Set the action's `Go To` argument to one of these options:

✔ **Next:** Just ignore the error and go on to the next action in the macro.

✔ `Macro Name`: Run a macro. Set the `Macro Name` argument to the macro you want it to run.

✔ `Fail`: Give up and display an error message.

If you choose `Next` or `Macro Name`, your macro can find out what the error was by looking at `[Macro Error].[Number]` to see the error number or `[Macro Error].[Description]` to see a description of the error. You can use an `If` action to determine what to do, depending on the type of error.

Book VII

Database Administration

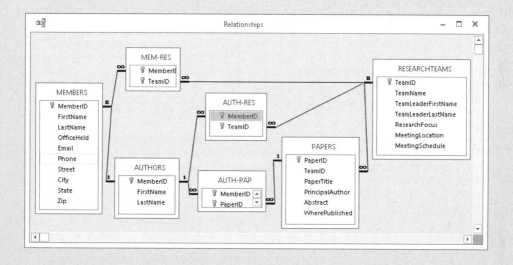

Contents at a Glance

Chapter 1: Database Housekeeping 499

Compacting and Repairing Your Database 499
Making Backups 500
Converting Databases 503
Analyzing and Documenting Your Database.. 504
Loading and Managing Add-Ins... 508

Chapter 2: Sharing the Fun: Managing Multiuser Access 511

Putting Your Database Where People Can See It 512
Splitting Your Database into a Front End and a Back End 513
Editing with Multiple Users 518

Chapter 3: Securing Your Data. 523

Observing Basic Windows Security 523
Controlling What Happens When You Open the Database.................... 524
Password-Protecting and Encrypting Your Database............................ 528
Locking Up Your Database As an .accde File.. 529
Using the Trust Center... 532

Chapter 1: Database Housekeeping

In This Chapter

✔ Taking out the garbage (compacting your database)

✔ Backing up part or all of the database

✔ Analyzing how the objects in your database work together

✔ Loading Access add-ins

An Access database can get big and complicated, with dozens or even hundreds of objects — tables, queries, forms, reports, macros, and other stuff that you find out about in other parts of the book. You need to keep your database neat and tidy; otherwise, it becomes just plain confusing to use, and the file size balloons. This chapter describes how to compact, repair, back up, analyze, and configure your database.

Compacting and Repairing Your Database

When you make changes to your database, Access stores new information in the database file and marks the old information for deletion. The old information isn't actually removed from your database file right away, however. In fact, most database files have a tendency to get larger and larger because Access (like most other programs) isn't very good at taking out the garbage. To shrink your database, you have to compact the database file.

The process of compacting a database also repairs errors that crop up in the file. Occasional Access bugs, Windows bugs, or cosmic rays from a black hole in another galaxy can cause objects in the database to become corrupted — or broken, if you prefer a more straightforward term. Compacting the database repairs these corrupted objects.

To compact and repair your database when the database is open, follow these steps:

1. **Close all tables, queries, forms, reports, and other database objects, including the Visual Basic Editor.**

   Access can't compact the database if objects are open.

2. **Click the File tab of the Ribbon to see Backstage View.**

3. **Click Info (if it isn't selected already) and then click Compact & Repair Database.**

   Access compacts the database. When the status indicator at the bottom of the Access window hits 100 percent, and the mouse pointer no longer looks like an hourglass, the compacting is complete. If you don't see any error messages, the compacting worked perfectly and needs no repairs.

If your computer is on a network, and you suspect that other people are using your database, make sure that no one else has your database open before compacting it.

Making Backups

Backing up your database is vital. If you're not sure, think about the amount of effort it took to create the database. Think about how furious your boss would be if the database vanished from your hard disk. Think about the killing boredom of typing all that information again. Okay, you get the idea: Backups are good things.

Ideally, you should back up your entire hard drive — at least, the files that you create or edit. (Backing up program files usually is pointless: You should have all the CDs or downloaded executable installation files to reinstall your programs, if need be.) A good backup system creates regular backup copies of all your files — perhaps all the files in your Documents or My Documents folder — on tapes, writeable CDs, writeable DVDs, or another hard disk (such as your organization's file server).

Backing up a whole database

Follow these steps to back up your whole database:

1. **Click the File tab of the Ribbon, and choose Save As.**

2. **In the File Types section of the screen, make sure that Save Database As is selected.**

3. **In the Advanced heading, select Back Up Database.**

4. **Click the Save As button.**

   The Save As dialog box appears, displaying your database name (with today's date appended) in the File Name field.

   Clicking the Save button at this point saves the database in the default location. If you want to save it somewhere else, you can change the folder in the folder drop-down menu at the top of the dialog box.

5. **If you want to save the database somewhere other than the default location, navigate to the folder where you want to store the backup.**

6. **Click Save.**

TIP

If you use Access at work, consult your system administrator. If you store your Access databases on a network drive, the databases may be backed up for you automatically on a regular basis.

Backing up part of a database

You may want to back up only part of your database, such as a few tables containing data that changes frequently. You can export objects to another Access database for backup. The first order of business is creating a blank database to which you can export objects; then, when the objects have someplace to go, you can export them.

Creating a blank database

Follow these steps to create a new, blank database:

1. **Click the File tab of the Ribbon, and choose Close to close the database you're working with (if any).**

   Don't close the Access window. Stay in Backstage View. You still need to use Access for this task.

2. **Click the Blank Desktop Database button.**

   A dialog box appears, with a suggested filename, a folder icon, and a Create button.

3. **Click the folder icon to the right of the File Name box, and browse to the folder where you want to place the database.**

4. **Give the database a meaningful name (ideally, one related to the database that you're backing up, such as MyDBbackup).**

5. **Click the Create button.**

   Access displays a new, blank database and opens a new, blank table to encourage you to start.

6. **Close your new backup database.**

   Now, with no database open, Access looks pretty empty. The next section, "Exporting database objects," shows you how to populate the new database.

Exporting database objects

Follow these steps each time you want to back up an object in your Access database:

1. **Open the database that contains the object that you want to export.**

2. **In the Navigation Pane, select the object that you want to export.**

Access

3. **Click the Access button in the Export group on the External Data tab of the Ribbon.**

   You see the Export – Access Database dialog box.

4. **Click the Browse button, and locate and select the backup database you created.**

   Refer to the preceding section, "Creating a blank database."

5. **Click Save to return to the Export – Access Database dialog box and then click OK.**

   You see the Export dialog box, shown in Figure 1-1.

Figure 1-1:
You can
export a
single table,
form, or
other object
from one
Access
database to
another.

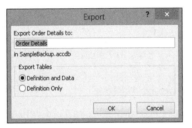

6. **Choose whether to export only the structure or the data, too, if you're exporting a table.**

   Select the Definition and Data option if you want to include all the records in the table, or select the Definition Only option if you want a blank table with no records. For backup purposes, go with Definition and Data.

7. **Click OK.**

   Access creates a duplicate object in the backup database with the same information stored in the current database. Then it asks whether you want to save these export states so that you can back up in the same manner later.

8. **If you plan to back up this object regularly, click the Save Export Steps check box; if not, leave the check box deselected.**

9. **Click Close.**

   If you chose in Step 8 to save your steps, one more dialog box appears, asking for a name and description for the saved task (see Figure 1-2).

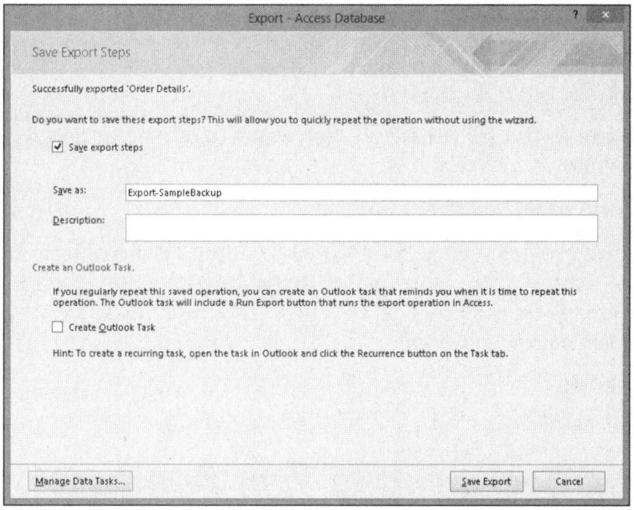

Figure 1-2:
Save the steps that you used to create a backup copy of a database object.

> **10.** **Enter a name (or accept the suggested name), and click Save Export.**
>
> To export the same object to the same database later, click the Saved Exports button in the Export group on the External Data tab of the Ribbon, and choose one of your saved export tasks from the list that appears.

Converting Databases

Access 2013 uses the same file format as Access 2007 and Access 2010 for storing its databases, but previous versions of Access use a different format. Book I, Chapter 2 describes how to choose among older file formats. It also describes what happens when you open older Access databases in Access 2013.

You can tell what version a database is by opening it in Access and looking at the title bar. The title bar may display (Access 2000 file format) or (Access 2002-2003 file format) for an old format, or nothing or (Access 2007 - 2013) for the new format.

To convert a database from an older file format to the Access 2013/2010/2007 format, follow these steps:

> **1.** **Open the database.**
>
> **2.** **Close any open objects.**
>
> **3.** **Click the File tab of the Ribbon to enter Backstage View, and choose Save As.**

4. **In the Save As dialog box, below the Save Database As heading, select Access Database (*.accdb).**

5. **Click the Save As button.**

6. **Browse to the folder where you want to store the new version of your database.**

7. **Enter a name for the database.**

   Access creates a new database containing all the objects in the old database, stored in the new format, with the extension `.accdb`. Additionally, a message warns you that this new database can't be opened in Access 2003 or earlier versions.

8. **Click OK.**

Analyzing and Documenting Your Database

Access includes several commands that help you analyze your database, especially how the objects in your database connect. The following sections detail some of these commands.

Viewing relationships in the Relationships window

Relationships

Keeping the relationships among tables straight can be tricky. For help, click the Relationships button in the Relationships group on the Database Tools tab of the Ribbon to display the Relationships window (shown in Figure 1-3), which shows you how your tables connect. In an order-entry database, for example, your Customers table has a one-to-many relationship with your Orders table because one customer may place many orders, but each order is placed by one — and only one — customer. (See Book II, Chapter 6 for information on using this window, including moving items around.)

Figure 1-3:
The Relationships window can get complicated if your database has a lot of tables.

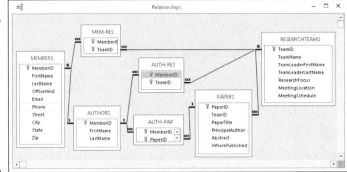

Viewing object dependencies

Access can show you a list of the tables, queries, forms, and reports that depend on an object. Suppose that your database contains a query that you never use, but you're not sure you can delete the query, because it may very well be the record source for a form or report. Access can ease your worried mind on this subject.

To display a list of object dependencies, select an object in the Navigation Pane, and click the Object Dependencies button in the Relationships group on the Database Tools tab of the Ribbon. You may see several message boxes, saying that dependency information needs to be updated and that various steps may take a few minutes; click OK in each message box. In the end, the Object Dependencies pane appears on the right side of the Access window, as shown in Figure 1-4.

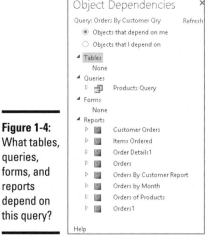

Figure 1-4: What tables, queries, forms, and reports depend on this query?

At the top of the Object Dependencies pane is the name of the object that you're analyzing. In Figure 1-4, the object in question is the Orders By Customer Qry query. (The object has to be a table, query, form, or report; Access can't show the dependencies of macros or Visual Basic for Applications [VBA] modules.) Two options follow the object's name:

✦ **Objects That Depend on Me:** Choosing this option lists the tables, queries, forms, and reports that use this object as a data source. The objects that depend on a table include the queries based on the table and the forms and reports that use the table as a record source. The objects that depend on a form include forms of which this one is a subform.

✦ **Objects That I Depend On:** Choosing this option lists the tables, queries, forms, and reports that directly provide input for this object. The objects that a report depends on include the query or table that makes up its record source and any reports used as subreports of this report.

After the Object Dependencies pane displays information about one object, you can't simply switch to another object. To see the dependencies for another object, click the object in the Navigation Pane and then click the Refresh link in the Object Dependencies pane. When you finish looking at object dependencies, click the X button in the top-right corner of the pane.

Analyzing database performance

The Performance Analyzer examines and improves the speed and efficiency of your database and suggests changes, such as shrinking unnecessarily large fields and adding indexes. Creating indexes for fields in your tables speeds sorting and searching. (See Book II, Chapter 2 for details on creating an index for a field in a table.)

To improve your database's performance, follow these steps:

1. **Open the database.**

2. **Close any open objects.**

The Performance Analyzer can't analyze an open object.

3. **Click the Analyze Performance button in the Analyze group on the Database Tools tab of the Ribbon.**

You see the Performance Analyzer dialog box, shown in Figure 1-5.

Figure 1-5:
The Performance Analyzer improves your database's performance — in this case, the relationships among tables.

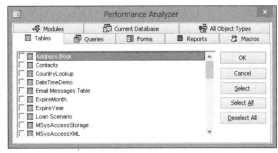

4. **Select the objects you want to analyze.**

Select the object types you want (on the Tables, Queries, Forms, Reports, Macros, and Modules tabs) and then click the check boxes next to the specific objects you want to include in the analysis. To select all the objects of an object type, click the tab for the type and then click the Select All button. On the Current Database tab, click the Relationships check box to ask Access to look at the relationships among your tables. If you want Access to analyze all the object types, click the All Object Types tab and then click the Select All button.

5. **Click OK to begin the analysis.**

   Analysis may take a few minutes. When the analysis is complete, a new Performance Analyzer dialog box appears, as shown in Figure 1-6. Each result in the list is classified as a recommendation (a change that Access recommends and can make for you), a suggestion (a change that Access can make for you that may have some drawbacks), or an idea (a change that Access can't make but you can make yourself). When you click a result, more information about the result appears at the bottom of the Performance Analyzer dialog box.

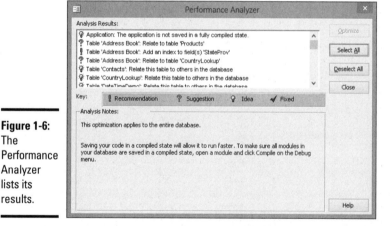

Figure 1-6:
The Performance Analyzer lists its results.

Book VII
Chapter 1

Database
Housekeeping

6. **For each recommendation or suggestion that you want Access to fix, select the result and then click the Optimize button.**

   Access tries to make the recommended or suggested change and displays a message about its success.

7. **Make a note of the ideas that you may want to try.**

   Write down any of the ideas that you want to look into, because you can't print the ideas, and you can't give any commands until you close the Access windows.

8. **Click the Close button to close the Performance Analyzer dialog box.**

The Performance Analyzer does a good job of spotting fields that should be indexed to speed searches and sorts.

Documenting your database

You can create reports that describe the design and properties of the objects in your database. With the database open and all objects closed, click the Database Documenter button in the Analyze group on the Database Tools tab of the Ribbon to open the Documenter dialog box.

The Documenter dialog box looks and works just like the Performance Analyzer dialog box (refer to Figure 1-5, earlier in this chapter). You click tabs and select check boxes to specify which objects in your database you want to document. When you click OK, Access creates a report showing details on the properties of the object. If you select a table, the report looks similar to Figure 1-7, including information about the table and each field (column) in the table. The report for a form or report includes the properties of all the controls in the form or report design.

C:\Users\Allen\Documents\Access 2013 AIO4D\Access 2013 AIO FD\2012-09\Sample.accdb			Sunday, November 25, 2012
Form: Address Book			Page: 1

Figure 1-7: The Documenter's report includes the gory details about a form.

Properties

AllowAdditions:	True	AllowDatasheetView:	False
AllowDeletions:	True	AllowDesignChanges:	True
AllowEditing:	True	AllowEdits:	True
AllowFilters:	True	AllowFormView:	True
AllowLayoutView:	True	AllowPivotChartView:	False
AllowPivotTableView:	False	AllowUpdating:	No
AlternateBackShade:	95	AlternateBackThemeColorIn	1
AlternateBackTint:	100	AutoCenter:	True
AutoResize:	True	BackShade:	100
BackThemeColorIndex:	1	BackTint:	100
BorderShade:	100	BorderStyle:	Edited Record
BorderThemeColorIndex:	3	BorderTint:	100
Caption:	Address Book	CloseButton:	True
Container:	Forms	ControlBox:	True
Count:	25	CurrentView:	0
Cycle:	Transparent	DataEntry:	False
DatasheetAlternateBackColo	15921906	DatasheetBackColor:	16777215
DatasheetBackShade:	100	DatasheetBackThemeColorI	1
DatasheetBackTint:	100	DatasheetBorderLineStyle:	1
DatasheetCellsEffect:	Flat	DatasheetColumnHeaderUn	1
DatasheetFontHeight:	11	DatasheetFontItalic:	False
DatasheetFontName:	Calibri	DatasheetFontUnderline:	False
DatasheetFontWeight:	Normal	DatasheetForeColor:	0
DatasheetForeShade:	100	DatasheetForeThemeColorIn	0
DatasheetForeTint:	100	DatasheetGridlinesBehavior:	Both
DatasheetGridlinesColor:	15132391	DatasheetGridlinesShade:	100

Choose just one object to document at a time; the report can be many pages long!

Loading and Managing Add-Ins

Like all the programs in Microsoft Office, Access allows you to extend its functionality with *add-ins* — custom components, usually created by professional programmers. If you work in a large corporation that has an information technology (IT) department, programmers may create an add-in to make Access easier to use with your company's data.

To use an add-in, first you must copy it to your computer's hard drive. To do that, you need the name and location of the add-in. If your company's IT department created the add-in, it can tell you the name and location of that add-in. After you copy the add-in to your hard drive, using the add-in is simple. Just follow these steps:

1. **Click the Add-Ins button in the Add-Ins group on the Database Tools tab of the Ribbon.**

2. **From the drop-down menu that appears, choose Add-In Manager.**

   The Add-In Manager dialog box appears, listing the add-ins you've already installed.

3. **To install an add-in, click the Add New button.**

   The Open dialog box appears.

4. **Navigate to the folder in which the add-in is stored, and click the Open button.**

5. **Repeat Steps 3 and 4 to add as many add-ins as you want.**

6. **When you finish, click the Close button in the Add-In Manager dialog box.**

To remove an add-in, open the Add-In Manager dialog box, select the name of the add-in you want to remove, and click the Uninstall button.

**Book VII
Chapter 1**

**Database
Housekeeping**

Chapter 2: Sharing the Fun: Managing Multiuser Access

In This Chapter

✔ Sharing an Access database over a LAN

✔ Dividing your database into front and back ends

✔ Editing data when someone else may be editing the same record

*Y*our database probably contains such terrific information that lots of people in your organization want to use it. If the database stores customer names and addresses, for example, your colleagues may want to use this information. Also, wouldn't it be great if only one person had to enter an address correction in a shared address book instead of everyone having to maintain a separate one?

Well, Access has been a multiuser database right from the beginning. Many people can get at the information in your database. Here's how:

✦ **Everyone can use Access to open the database.** If your computer is on a local area network (LAN), you can store your Access database on a shared network drive, and other people can run Access and open your database. This option works for only a small number of users, however.

✦ **People can see the database information via web-based forms.** You can allow anyone on your LAN (anyone who has access to the database file, that is) to see or edit database information by using a web browser. Book IX, Chapter 3 describes how to use Access with SharePoint to create web-based forms.

✦ **You can store your data in a big, industrial-strength database server application.** If your database gets really large, or if you want a lot of people (more than, say, 15 or 20 people) to be able to see and maintain it simultaneously, Access may not be able to handle the load. This isn't a big problem. Move the tables to a database server program, such as Oracle or SQL Server, and continue to use your Access queries, forms, or reports to work with it. You just link your Access database to the tables in the database server. Because this situation is increasingly common, Access 2013 comes with an option to migrate the data to a SQL Server database, which we describe in Book IX, Chapter 2.

This chapter describes the first method: setting up a database so that more than one person can open it at the same time, using computers that connect to a LAN.

Putting Your Database Where People Can See It

For other people on a LAN to be able to open your Access database, you need to store it in a shared folder — a *share,* for short. The shared folder can be on your computer or on a file server — a computer whose primary job is storing files for use over the LAN. If you work in an organization, check with your LAN administrator to find out the best place to store your database.

If you decide to store the database on your own computer, you need to share the folder with other people. On the Start screen, type **explorer** in the Search box and then choose File Explorer from the menu that appears. Next, find or create the folder where you plan to store the database. Here's how to share a folder on your LAN, depending on which version of Windows you use:

✦ **Windows XP:** Put the database in a folder inside the Shared Documents folder.

Alternatively, to configure any folder as shared, right-click the folder in Windows Explorer and choose Sharing and Security from the contextual menu. On the Sharing tab of the Properties dialog box that appears, click the Share This Folder option, and give the folder a name, which will appear on other users' computers. Click the Permissions button to set whether other people can only read files in the folder or also edit them. Then click OK in both dialog boxes to close them.

✦ **Windows Vista:** Put the database in a folder inside the Public folder.

✦ **Windows 7:** In Windows Explorer, click the folder name. Choose Share With from the menu that appears; then choose Homegroup (Read), Homegroup (Read/Write), or Specific People.

✦ **Windows 8:** In File Explorer, right-click the folder name and choose Share With from the contextual menu; then choose Homegroup (View), Homegroup (Read/Write), ASP.NET Machine Account, or specific people.

You can tell whether a folder is shared by right-clicking it and choosing Properties from the contextual menu. Click the Sharing tab of the Properties dialog box to see the sharing status of the folder.

If you store a shared database on your computer, everyone else depends on the stability and speed of your computer. If you restart Windows after installing the latest update to your favorite game of solitaire, everyone else loses the edits they make to the database. If you decide to run a big, hairy application that slows your computer to a crawl, the other computers that are using the database on your computer crawl too. If your database is important, consider storing it on a network server or at least on a little-used or lightly used PC.

For more information on sharing files on a LAN, read *Windows 8 For Dummies, Windows 7 For Dummies, Windows Vista For Dummies,* or *Windows XP For Dummies,* all by Andy Rathbone (John Wiley & Sons, Inc).

Splitting Your Database into a Front End and a Back End

If you create a multiuser database, consider splitting your database into two pieces: the data (the tables and the relationships among them) and everything else. The database with the data is the *back end,* and the database with everything else — the queries, forms, reports, macros, and Visual Basic for Applications (VBA) procedures — is the *front end.* You and other database users open the front-end database, which contains links to the tables in the back-end database.

Why split?

Splitting your database has some advantages. Here are two scenarios that have nothing to do with multiuser databases:

✦ You don't need to back up the front end nearly as often as the back end because the front end rarely changes. By splitting your database into two files, you can back up just the back end, where the constantly updated data lives. (You *do* back up your data every day, right? See Chapter 1 of this minibook to find out how.)

✦ You improve the front-end database and replace everyone's old front-end database with your new one without messing up each person's data, which is stored safely in the back end. You may create a database that tracks church members, committees, and donations, for example, and then sell the database to zillions of congregations. By splitting the database, you can provide updates to the front end later (with improved forms, reports, and programming) without disturbing each congregation's data in the back-end database.

Splitting your database is even more important if you create a multiuser database in which everyone opens the same forms and edits the same data, possibly at the same time. Here's why:

✦ **Each person has his or her own front-end database with user-specific forms and reports.** All the front ends can connect to the shared back-end database. Each user is free to make new queries, forms, and reports in the front-end database without affecting any other user.

If you have queries, forms, reports, or macros that you want to make available for use after the split, be sure to export them to files so that they can be imported back into all the new front ends that people will be using.

✦ **You can protect the front-end database by saving it as an .accde file.** (See Chapter 3 of this minibook for instructions.) People can't change the VBA code, macros, forms, or reports in an .accde file.

✦ **Performance is better.** Your database will run faster if the front-end objects — queries, forms, and reports — are stored on the local computer instead of transmitted across the LAN.

✦ **Security is better.** In an organizational setting, if you store the back-end database on a file server, it can be backed up with the rest of the files on the server. Also, security on a server usually is better than security on a local PC.

✦ **You can move back-end data without changing the front end.** If the database grows into a huge project, you can move the data from the back-end Access database to a larger database system (such as MySQL or SQL Server) without changing the Access front end. Your Access front end can link to large corporate databases as well as to an Access back-end database.

A few disadvantages exist, of course:

✦ **You need to keep track of both files.** You can't get far with only one of the two databases. If you need to move your database to another computer, be sure to move both files. Back up both files regularly, too.

✦ **If you want to change the design of the tables in your database, remember to make your changes in the back-end database.** Make sure that the links still work from the front end.

Let's split!

Access comes with a Database Splitter Wizard that splits a database into front and back ends and also creates the links between the two databases.

To split your database into front-end and back-end databases, follow these steps:

1. **Make a backup copy of your database.**

   You never know what could go wrong, and you certainly don't want your entire database to get trashed. (See Chapter 1 of this minibook for info on backing up your database.)

2. **Open the database.**

   Close all tables and anything that may refer to a table, because the wizard can't run if any objects are open.

What if some people have older versions of Access?

Be aware of which Access version you use for your database files. Access 2013, 2010, and 2007 use a different file format from earlier versions of Access. If anyone uses older versions of Access, you have two options: Upgrade this person to Access 2007 or later, or make your database readable by earlier versions. You can choose to create your database in Access 2000 format, Access 2002–2003 format, or Access 2007–2013 format. (If people are using versions of Access earlier than Access 2000, make them upgrade: Too much has changed since Access 95 and Access 97!)

If you have to support older Access users, your back-end database must be stored in the appropriate format. In Access 2013, choose the appropriate file format when you're creating your database: Click the File tab on the Ribbon, click New, click Blank Database, browse to the folder where you want to store the database, and set the Save As Type option in the File New Database dialog box to the appropriate

version of Access. Put this older-format database in the shared folder that everyone links to. Fortunately, because of the differences in the file extensions, these older versions can have the same name and reside in the same location as your Access 2013 versions.

You also need to create a front end in the same version of Access as the back end that you just created. Usually, the best idea is to maintain as many front ends as you have database users: one version in Access 2013, one in Access 2003 (for your version 2002 and 2003 users), and one in Access 2000 (for your version 2000 users). Tell your users to copy the appropriate version to their computers for their own use.

Having said that, maintaining multiple versions of the same database is a really bad idea. Persuade management to upgrade everybody to the latest version, which will save you immense grief.

Access
Database

3. **Click Access Database in the Move Data group on the Database Tools tab of the Ribbon.**

The Database Splitter Wizard appears, as shown in Figure 2-1, explaining its plans.

4. **Click the Split Database button.**

You see the Create Back-End Database dialog box, which looks just like a Save As dialog box.

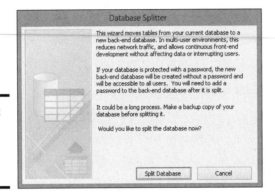

Database Splitter

This wizard moves tables from your current database to a new back-end database. In multi-user environments, this reduces network traffic, and allows continuous front-end development without affecting data or interrupting users.

If your database is protected with a password, the new back-end database will be created without a password and will be accessible to all users. You will need to add a password to the back-end database after it is split.

It could be a long process. Make a backup copy of your database before splitting it.

Would you like to split the database now?

Split Database   Cancel

Figure 2-1:
The
Database
Splitter
Wizard.

5. **Type a name for the back-end database, and click the Split button.**

   The wizard suggests the name of your original database, followed by -be (for *back end*). You may want to use the original name plus Data.

   Access creates a new, empty database with the name you specify. It exports every table from your original database to this new database, including the relationships among the tables, and then creates links from the original database to the tables in the new back-end database. The original database becomes the front-end database.

   The wizard displays a message when it finishes, indicating whether the split was successful.

6. **Click OK to close the wizard.**

If you open the back-end database directly in Access, you find only tables — no queries, forms, reports, macros, or VBA modules. If you open the original database (which is now the front end), the tables are replaced by links to the tables in the back end.

Handing out front ends

Each person who uses your shared database needs a copy of the front-end database on his or her computer. (You can open a front-end database from a shared folder, but it loads and runs much more slowly.) You can copy the front end to each person's computer, or copy the front end to a shared folder and tell everyone to copy the file.

Before you pass out the front-end database, consider saving it as an .accde file so that people can't accidentally mess up the forms, reports, or VBA code. (See Chapter 3 of this minibook for details on saving a database file as an .accde file.) If you do, save a copy of the .accdb file, too, so that you have a way to make updates.

The Navigation Pane lists every object in an Access database, but having to click and scroll around the list to find the forms and reports that you use most can be annoying. Wouldn't it be nice to have a list of just the objects you usually use? Better yet, if several people use the database, each person might like to have a list of favorite objects in daily use. You can create a group on the Navigation Pane for each user; see Book I, Chapter 2 for instructions.

Relinking your tables

The links between the front-end and back-end databases work only as long as the files are in the same positions relative to each other. If you create the back-end database in the same folder as the original database, the two databases need to be in the same folder to work. If you need to move one of the files, you have to relink the tables. (You may decide to move the back-end database to a network drive where you can share it with other users on a LAN and give copies of the front-end to people in your office.)

To relink tables, follow these steps:

1. Put the front-end and back-end databases in their new locations.

The two databases need to be in their new positions to ensure that everything works.

2. Open the front-end database, and view the list of tables in the Navigation Pane.

Now you're ready to relink the tables.

3. Do one of the following:

- Right-click any table name and choose the Linked Table Manager option from the contextual menu.

- Click the Linked Table Manager button in the Import & Link group on the External Data tab of the Ribbon.

The Linked Table Manager opens, showing a list of your linked tables along with the name of the database that each table links to. (Not all linked tables have to link to the same database!)

4. Click the Select All button, check the Always Prompt for New Location box, and then click OK.

The Select New Location Of dialog box appears.

5. Navigate to the folder in which you put the back-end database, and click its icon.

6. Click the Open button in the Select New Location Of dialog box.

The Linked Table Manager displays a dialog box saying that all selected linked tables were successfully refreshed.

7. **Click OK to close the Select New Location Of dialog box.**

   You return to the Linked Table Manager dialog box.

8. **Click the Close button in the Linked Table Manager dialog box.**

   Now Access knows the correct locations of your linked tables.

See Book II, Chapter 4 for information about creating a link in one database to a table in another database.

Editing with Multiple Users

To set up Access so that more than one person can open your database at the same time, you don't have to do a thing other than store the database file in a shared folder. Access has multiuser features built in! Just open the database one time on your computer and again on a second computer. Poof! Both computers are using the database!

Everything works fine if multiple people use front-end and back-end databases, too. One back-end database lives in a shared folder, and multiple people have copies of the front-end database running on their computers. When several people open the front end at the same time, they all link to tables in the back end. No problem!

Multiuser access works great as long as everyone looks at the data without making any changes. Two people can look at the same table — even the same record — at the same time. People can open forms and print reports. Peachy.

Fixing exclusive access

Okay, you may have to do one thing: If the second person who tries to open your database gets an error message saying that the database is already in use, it means that the database is in exclusive mode and can be opened by only one person at a time. (How very exclusive!) If this happens, the person who has the database open must follow these steps:

1. **Click the File tab of the Ribbon, and select Options in the list on the left side of Backstage View.**

2. **Select Client Settings in the pane on the left.**

3. **Scroll down to the Advanced section, and set Default Open Mode to Shared (see Figure 2-2).**

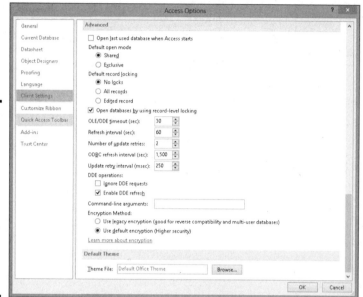

4. **Click OK.**

5. **Close the database and then reopen it.**

Access opens the database in shared mode.

Managing record-locking

Everyone can look at the information in the database. But what happens when two people want to edit a table at the same time — or, worse, two people want to edit the same record at the same time? The Access record-locking feature handles this situation.

To turn on the record-locking feature, click the File tab of the Ribbon, choose Options, select Client Settings, scroll down to the Advanced section, and look at the Default Record Locking section (refer to Figure 2-2, earlier in this chapter). You have three options: No Locks, All Records, and Edited Record. The following sections detail how these options work.

No Locks (Doesn't lock records)

Multiuser editing works as follows without record-locking (when you check the No Locks check box in the Access Options dialog box):

1. Person A opens a table or query (or a form based on a table or query) and begins editing a record.

2. Person B opens the same table or query, or a form or other query based on the same table that Person A is editing. Person B starts making changes in the same record that Person A is editing.

3. When Person A or Person B tries to save the record, Access displays the Write Conflict dialog box, shown in Figure 2-3.

   If one person clicks the Save Record button, his or her changes write over whatever changes the other person made in the record. Not good. If that person clicks the Drop Changes button, he or she loses the changes in process. Also not good. Clicking the Copy to Clipboard button allows a user to compare the two people's changes and then choose between them or combine them. (This process usually is a pain; you have to check with the other person, compare changes, and decide which changes to keep.)

Figure 2-3:
Two people
are trying
to change
this record
at the same
time.

The No Locks option usually is a bad choice, because people can end up losing changes to records. Why not let Access prevent this situation from happening? Sometimes, the computer really does know best.

The solution is for Access to lock the information that someone is editing. While the user is editing the information, no one else can make any changes. When the first person saves the changes, the next person can start editing. Each person takes a turn, which is simple enough.

All Records (Locks the whole table)

If you choose the All Records option, when someone starts editing a record, Access locks the entire table that contains the record. When someone else tries to edit any record in the table, Access just beeps and refuses to allow changes. This option means that two people can't change different records at the same time. Some databases require this option, especially if each record contains information based on the records before it. In most databases, however, each record stands on its own, so you can allow simultaneous editing of separate records.

Records versus pages

Sometimes, Access locks more than just the record being edited. Like most programs, Access stores information in chunks called *disk pages* or *pages.* It retrieves information from your hard drive a page at a time, and it can lock an entire page's worth of information much more easily than it can lock a single record, which usually is smaller than a page. (How many records fit in a page depends on how big each record is. If your table has large records with lots of fields, a record may even be larger than a single page of storage.)

Access uses a system called *page-level locking* rather than real record-level locking.

Page-locking is faster and easier for Access than real record-locking, but in some applications, page-locking just isn't good enough. If you have several people entering and editing orders in an order-entry database at the same time, they may end up continually locking one another out of records, which is very annoying.

You can control whether Access does true record-level locking or just page-level locking. In the Advanced section of the Client Settings pane of the Access Options dialog box (refer to Figure 2-2, earlier in this chapter), check the Open Databases by Using Record-Level Locking check box to use record-level locking.

Edited Record (Locks one record)

Our favorite record-locking setting is Edited Record, which locks only the record that's being edited. Leave the rest of the records available for other people to edit.

If you try to edit a record that someone else is editing, Access beeps and doesn't allow you to make changes. The international "don't even think about it" symbol (a red circle with a diagonal line through it) appears in the record selector when a record is locked. Within a few seconds after the other person saves his or her changes, Access displays the changes onscreen. Then you can make your own changes.

Programming locks

Property Sheet

If you use forms to edit your tables (as most people do), you can control how each form locks records when someone uses the form to edit a record. Open the form in Design view by right-clicking the form in the Navigation Pane and choosing Design View from the contextual menu. Display the Properties sheet for the form by clicking the Property Sheet button in the Tools group on the Design tab of the Ribbon. Click the Data tab on the property sheet, and look at the Record Locks property of the form. You can set it to No Locks, All Records, or Edited Record.

What's happening behind the scenes?

Whenever anyone opens an Access database, Access creates a *locking information file* that contains information about who's doing what with the information in the database. Even if only one person opens the database, Access makes the file in the same folder and with the same filename as the database, but with the extension `.laccdb`. (People usually refer to this file as the *LDB file*.) When you close the database, Access deletes the file. If more than one person has the database open, Access doesn't delete the file until the last person closes the database.

You can also write VBA code to control the way that tables and records are locked. See Book VIII, Chapter 5 for details on writing VBA code that edits records.

If you want different people to have permission to see or change different information, you need to find out about the Access security features, which we describe in Chapter 3 of this minibook.

Chapter 3: Securing Your Data

In This Chapter

✔ **Surveying the types of Access security**

✔ **Configuring your startup options to secure the database**

✔ **Setting a database password**

✔ **Creating an .accde file**

✔ **Setting other options in the Access Trust Center**

A fter you create a database, you may want to control who can open the database and change the data. If you're creating a database in which many people link to a shared back-end database, you should design security from the beginning; otherwise, your data is sure to deteriorate as different people use the database in different ways. Foolish consistency may be the hobgoblin of little minds, but consistency is vital for clean data. You owe the users of your database protection against accidentally doing something dumb.

Be sure to use validation in your tables and forms, too. Read all about it in Book II, Chapter 5.

Access has several mechanisms for adding security to your database:

✦ Startup options that you use to display your own forms or run other code when the database opens. See "Controlling What Happens When You Open the Database" in this chapter.

✦ Password-protecting your database. See "Password-Protecting and Encrypting Your Database" in this chapter.

✦ Converting your database to an .accde file to prevent anyone from editing forms, reports, and Visual Basic for Applications (VBA) modules. See "Locking Up Your Database As an .accde File" in this chapter.

Observing Basic Windows Security

No matter what Access security options you choose, your first line of defense for your Access database is securing the computer where you store the database.

Be sure that you set a Windows password. If the database lives in a shared folder on a local area network (LAN), check with your LAN administrator to make sure that only the right people have access to the shared folder. Part of security is making sure that no one walks off with your database — such as copying it and taking it offsite — or deletes it! That's why Windows-level and LAN-level security are important.

For information about networking and Windows security, see *Networking For Dummies,* 9th Edition, by Doug Lowe; or see *Windows 7 For Dummies, Windows Vista For Dummies,* or *Windows XP For Dummies,* all by Andy Rathbone (John Wiley & Sons, Inc.).

Controlling What Happens When You Open the Database

If you don't want users entering data (except in the forms you create); modifying your tables, queries, forms, and other database objects; and generally screwing up your lovely Access system, you can prevent them from using — or even seeing — Design view and Layout view in Access. You can set the startup options to control what the database user can see and do.

Click the File tab on the Ribbon, choose Options to display the Access Options dialog box, and select Current Database (see Figure 3-1). The settings in the dialog box apply to the current database. If you change them, many don't take effect until you exit and reopen the database.

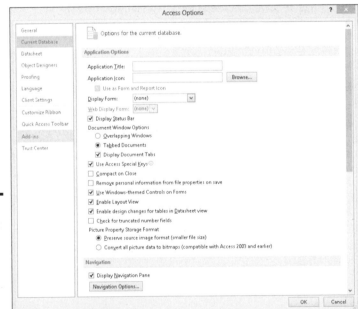

Figure 3-1:
The Current
Database
page of the
Access
Options
dialog box.

Table 3-1 lists some settings that control what users can see and do when they open your application.

Table 3-1	Access Settings for the Current Database
Setting	*What It Does*
Application Options	
Application Title	Sets the title of the application in the title bar.
Application Icon	Associates a unique icon with the application. This icon overrides the default Access icon.
Display Form	Designates the form that opens automatically when the database opens.
Web Display Form	Designates the form that opens automatically in a browser when a web database opens.
Display Status Bar	Specifies whether the status bar appears at the bottom of the Access window.
Document Window Options	*Overlapping Windows:* Specifies that you want the default action of windows opening one at a time and overlapping one another, as used in older versions of Access.
	Tabbed Documents: Specifies that you want new windows to open as one document with tabs rather than as individual windows.
	Display Document Tabs: Determines whether the tabs appear if you choose Tabbed Documents. (We recommend that you keep this check box checked if you're using tabbed documents.)
Use Access Special Keys	Sets the database to allow the use of Show Navigation Pane, Show Immediate Window, Show VB Window, and Pause Execution key combinations.
Compact on Close	Sets the database to compact automatically each time a database closes, rather than only when you compact it manually.
Remove Personal Information from File Properties on Save	Surprise — removes personal information from the database file's properties when you close it.
Use Windows-Themed Controls on Forms	Allows form controls to inherit the theme of the Windows operating system.
Enable Layout View	Allows users to view (and usually alter) forms and reports in Layout view.

(continued)

Table 3-1 *(continued)*

Setting	What It Does
Application Options	
Enable Design Changes for Tables in Datasheet View	Allows users to make design changes to tables in the database when they view them in Datasheet view.
Check for Truncated Number Fields	Makes sure that you aren't losing significant digits in numbers. If users are entering numbers that are 10 digits, and your field is defined as only 8 digits, you'd lose information unless you check for truncated number fields.
Picture Property Storage Format	*Preserve Source Image Format (Smaller File Size):* Allows you to store TIFF, JPG, or GIF images as in their original formats rather than converting them to bitmap images. *Convert All Picture Data to Bitmaps (Compatible with Access 2003 and Earlier):* Converts all images to bitmaps (the default in older versions of the database).
Navigation	
Display Navigation Pane	Allows all users to see the Navigation Pane. Clicking the Navigation Options button opens a dialog box with additional options for grouping objects.
Ribbon and Toolbar Options	
Ribbon Name	Specifies a custom Ribbon for the application. You can create your own Ribbon and even define your own buttons.
Shortcut Menu Bar	Specifies a custom shortcut menu bar (the menu of keyboard shortcuts that you see when you press Alt).
Allow Full Menus	Allows users to see the full menu options for all menus.
Allow Default Shortcut Menus	Allows users to use the default shortcut menus and any new custom ones.
Name AutoCorrect Options	
Track Name AutoCorrect Info	Tells Access to track name changes to your objects.
Perform AutoCorrect	Renames an object If name-change tracking is on. Access automatically changes the object name wherever it appears. (If you change a field name in a table, for example, Access updates the field name in all queries and forms that refer to the table.)
Log Name AutoCorrect Changes	Logs any object-name changes made by the Perform AutoCorrect feature.

Setting	What It Does
Filter Lookup Options for Sample Database	
Show List Values In:	
Local Indexed Fields	Shows list values only in indexed fields.
Local Non-Indexed Fields	Shows list values only in nonindexed fields.
ODBC Fields	Shows list values for Open Database Connectivity (ODBC) fields.
Don't Display Lists When More Than This Number of Records Is Read	Sets maximum number of records to be read.
Caching Web Service and SharePoint Tables	
Use the Cache Format That Is Compatible with Microsoft Access 2010 and Later	Specifies caching format.
Clear Cache on Close	Applies only to Microsoft Access 2010 and later cache format.
Never Cache	Applies only to Microsoft Access 2010 and later cache format.

Consider changing these settings:

✦ Do you want people to be able to use Layout view to change your forms and reports? If not, deselect the Enable Layout View check box.

✦ Do you want a form to open automatically when the database opens? Set the Display Form option to the form of your choice.

✦ Do you want a macro to run automatically when the database opens? After you customize a database by using the Access Options dialog box, when anyone opens this database, Access performs the startup actions you specify. Then Access runs the AutoExec macro, if any, which performs additional actions. (See Book VI, Chapter 2 for details on creating an AutoExec macro.)

✦ Do you want to create any keyboard shortcuts? You can define them by using an AutoKeys macro, which we describe in Book VI, Chapter 1.

Sometimes, you need to bypass the settings in the Current Database section of the Access Options dialog box. No problem! Hold down the Shift key while the database opens.

Password-Protecting and Encrypting Your Database

Halt — who goes there? You can tell Access not to allow anyone to open your database until he or she enters the right password. This system is all-or-nothing, which is a problem. After you allow someone to open the database, he or she can do anything to the database unless you take additional security measures. When you add a password to your database, Access takes the additional precaution of encrypting the database too.

The database may work a little more slowly, however, because Access has to encrypt and decrypt the information every time it reads or writes the database file.

Encrypting your database with a password

Follow these steps to encrypt your database with a password:

1. **Make a backup copy of the database, and store it somewhere safe.**

   This backup copy doesn't have a password. If you lose the password to the database, at least you have this backup. You may want to burn it on a CD and store the CD in something heavy that's locked.

2. **Close the database.**

3. **Make sure that you're in Backstage View and that no one else has the database open.**

   You need sole access to the database to assign a password. In fact, you need exclusive access, with everyone else being locked out temporarily.

4. **Click Computer rather than selecting the database from the Recent list.**

5. **Browse to the appropriate folder, and select the database you want.**

6. **From the Open Control drop-down menu in the bottom-right corner of the Open dialog box, choose Open Exclusive.**

   Access opens the database with exclusive access.

7. **Click the File tab of the Ribbon, choose Info, and click the Encrypt with Password button.**

   You see the Set Database Password dialog box, shown in Figure 3-2.

Figure 3-2:
Setting a password for a database.

Set Database Password	?	✕
Password:		
Verify:		
	OK	Cancel

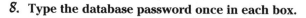

8. **Type the database password once in each box.**

   If you don't type the password the same way in both boxes, Access complains, and you have to type them again.

   Capitalization counts in passwords. A password can contain up to 20 characters and can include letters, numbers, and some punctuation.

9. **Click OK.**

   Encryption may take a few minutes. You may see a message if your database uses any features that are incompatible with encryption.

Opening a password-protected database

After you set a password, whenever you try to open the database (or when anyone else does), the Password Required dialog box appears.

If you forget your database password, you're hosed. No command, service, or secret incantation can get your password back.

What happens if another database (one with no password) links to your password-protected database? Answer: When you create a link to a password-protected database, Access asks you for the password. If you don't know it, you can't create the link. After you create the link, however, Access saves the password, so you can see the linked table without entering a password. Therefore, you have an unguarded back door into your password-protected database (to the linked tables in your database, at least). Keep this fact in mind when you split databases into a front end and a back end. Password-protecting the back-end database does no good if the front-end databases that link to it aren't protected too.

Decrypting a database

You can change your mind about encrypting a database. Click the File tab of the Ribbon, choose Info, and click the Decrypt Database button.

Locking Up Your Database As an .accde File

If you make an Access database for other people — especially people who may be a teeny bit clueless about Access — you may want to lock your database to prevent other users from making changes that may break it. One option is to convert your database from an `.accdb` file to an `.accde` file.

We hear you asking, "What's an `.accde` file?" An `.accde` file is the same as a regular Access `.accdb` database file, with the following changes:

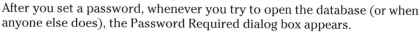

Book VII
Chapter 3

Securing Your Data

+ All VBA procedures are *compiled* — converted from human-readable code (more or less readable, anyway) to a format that only the computer understands. This change prevents a database user from reading or changing your VBA code. (See Book VIII for information on writing VBA procedures.)

+ No one can create forms or reports or modify the existing ones, or even open them in Design or Layout view. No one can import any forms or reports, either.

Be sure to keep a copy of your original .accdb file! If you need to make changes in your VBA code, forms, or reports (or create new ones), you need to use the .accdb file, not the .accde file. Most commonly, .accde files are used for the front-end database when you split an application into two databases (front end and back end), as we describe in Chapter 2 of this minibook.

Creating an .accde file

Saving your .accdb file as an .accde file is easy. Follow these steps:

1. **Make sure that your database is in Access 2007–2013 file format by opening the database.**

   Look at the title bar of the Access window. If the title bar says anything but (Access 2007-2013 file format), you need to convert it to the latest file format. (See Chapter 1 of this minibook for directions.)

2. **Click the File tab on the Ribbon, choose Save As, click Save Database As, and double-click Make ACCDE.**

   Access closes the database to do the conversion. Then you see the Save As dialog box.

3. **Specify the folder and filename for the file.**

4. **Click the Save button.**

   Access creates the new .accde file while leaving the original .accdb file untouched. Then the new .accde file opens.

If Access runs into a problem while making the .accde file, a message box appears, with a Show Help button. Click the button to find out what's wrong.

Making updates later

Eventually, you're going to want to make a new report or fix an annoying typo in a form. You have to go back to your .accdb file to make these kinds of changes because you can't make changes in an .accde file.

If the .accde file is a front-end file, with no data stored in it, you can just make your changes in the original .accdb file and resave it as an .accde file. Because all your data lives in the back-end database, you're all set. (If you're wondering what we're talking about, see Chapter 2 of this minibook.)

If your .accde file contains tables full of valuable information, however, you can't just abandon it. If you use the .accde file for data entry and editing, that file contains your up-to-date tables. The original .accdb file has editable forms, reports, and VBA code, but it doesn't have the latest version of the data stored in your tables.

No problem. Follow these steps:

1. **Rename your .accde file as a backup file.**

   You could add today's date to the end of the filename (right before the .accde part). You're about to create a new .accde file, but you don't want to lose the data in this file.

2. **Open the original .accdb file.**

3. **Make any changes you want in the forms, reports, and VBA code.**

   If you plan to make drastic changes, make a backup copy of the .accdb file first.

4. **Save this database as an .accde file with the name that your .accde file originally had.**

5. **Click the File tab of the Ribbon, choose Save As, click Save Database As, and double-click Make ACCDE.**

   Now you have an updated .accde file with new, improved forms, reports, and VBA procedures with old data. You also have an updated .accdb file with your new, improved forms, reports, and VBA code with out-of-date tables.

6. **Delete all the tables from this new .accde file.**

   Deleting tables sounds dangerous, but you have all these tables stored safely in your original .accde file.

7. **Import the tables from the old .accde file to the new one.**

   Click Access in the Import & Link group on the External Data tab of the Ribbon, and choose the name you gave your old .accde file in Step 1.

   You see the Import Objects dialog box, with tabs for tables, queries, forms, reports, and other objects.

8. **On the Tables tab, click the Select All button and then click OK.**

   Access imports your tables from the original .accde file to the new .accde file, replacing the obsolete data in the tables with the current data.

9. **Import any queries or macros from the old .accde database that you created or changed.**

   Repeat Steps 7 and 8, but use the Queries and Macros tabs on the Import Objects dialog box to import whatever changed.

Granting database access to specific users

Access 2003 and earlier versions had a system of user-level security in which you could create users and groups of users and then grant them specific permissions. When each user opened the database, he or she typed a username and password, so Access always knew who was using the database and allowed or disallowed commands accordingly. This system still works with old-format (.mdb) database files.

This system was confusing, hard to set up, and not hard to break into, however, so Microsoft abandoned it in Access 2007. Access 2013 can still open an .mdb file that has user-level security, if you have the necessary permissions and password, but you can't set up or change this type of security for use with .accdb files.

If you want to apply different security settings to different users, you should use a more secure back-end database (such as SQL Server or MySQL) to store your tables and give each user an account on that database with appropriate permissions. When you link to each table from Access, you enter the user's username and password, which prevents that user from viewing or editing tables for which he or she doesn't have permission. (Book IX, Chapter 2 describes how to use Access to link to SQL Server.)

For a detailed, if slightly out-of-date, write-up on Access user-level security, see http://office.microsoft.com/en-us/assistance/HA011381161033.aspx.

If you're going to perform this procedure often, consider splitting your table into a front end and a back end, as described in Chapter 2 of this minibook. With a split database, you don't have to import your updated tables again; you can just leave them in the unchanged back-end database.

Using the Trust Center

Access 2013 handles many of its security settings in one dialog box: the Trust Center. One feature is that Access wants to know whether you *trust* the database because you trust the folder where it's stored, you trust the publisher who created and signed the database, or you just trust this specific database. If you trust a database, you can use the macros and VBA modules in the database. Book VI, Chapter 1 describes the settings that determine how to tell Access that you trust a database.

The Trust Center has a few other settings that affect the security of the database and your computer. To see the Trust Center dialog box, click the File tab on the Ribbon, choose Options to open the Access Options dialog box, select Trust Center in the left pane, and then click the Trust Center Settings button. Figure 3-3 shows one page of the Trust Center dialog box.

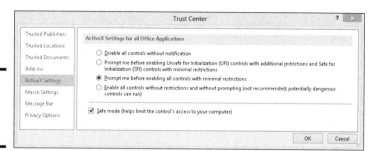

Figure 3-3:
The Trust
Center
dialog box.

Here are some settings to consider:

✦ **Add-Ins:** Add-in programs could be malicious, so you may want to select the check box titled Require Application Add-Ins to Be Signed by Trusted Publisher on the Add-Ins page of the Trust Center.

✦ **ActiveX Settings:** *ActiveX controls* are tiny programs that can be included in web pages and various Office applications. They can carry viruses, so you should be aware when an ActiveX control is installed on your computer. The default setting on the ActiveX page of the Trust Center is a prudent one: Prompt Me Before Enabling All Controls with Minimal Restrictions.

✦ **Macro Settings:** Macros (described in Book VI) are programs that you can write to automate objects in your Access database. We like to leave the Macro Settings option set to the default: Disable All Macros with Notification.

Book VIII
Programming in VBA

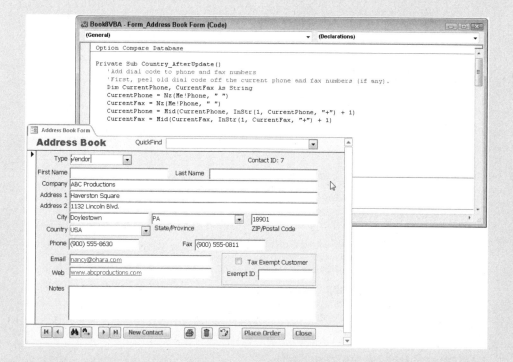

Find out about using VBA to change form controls at www.dummies.com/extras/
access2013aio.

Contents at a Glance

Chapter 1: What the Heck Is VBA? 537

Getting Acquainted with VBA Code 537
Enabling VBA Code...541
Working with Visual Basic Editor 543
Discovering Code As You Go 553

Chapter 2: Writing Code 557

Seeing How VBA Works 557
Understanding VBA Syntax 558
Writing Your Own VBA Procedures 563
Typing and Editing in the Code Window 570
Testing and Running Your Code...575

Chapter 3: Writing Smarter Code. 581

Creating Variables and Constants 581
Making Decisions in VBA Code 589
Executing the Same Code Repeatedly...595
Using Custom Functions 600

Chapter 4: Controlling Forms with VBA 605

Displaying Custom Messages..605
Opening Forms with DoCmd 608
Changing Form Controls with VBA...612
Understanding Objects and Collections...619

Chapter 5: Using SQL and Recordsets 629

Recordsets and Object Models..629
SQL and Recordsets 633
Action Queries in VBA 638
Connection Cleanup 640

Chapter 6: Debugging Your Code. 641

Recognizing Types of Program Errors..641
Fixing Compiler Errors 642
Trapping Runtime Errors..643
Dealing with Logical Errors 647

Chapter 1: What the Heck Is VBA?

In This Chapter

✔ Understanding Visual Basic for Applications (VBA) code

✔ Working with VBA code

✔ Using Visual Basic Editor

✔ Working with other people's code

Visual Basic for Applications, often abbreviated *VBA,* is a programming language that you can use to extend the functionality of Microsoft Access and other products in the Microsoft Office suite of programs. A *programming language* is a means of writing instructions for the computer to *execute* (perform). Programmers often refer to the written instructions as *code* because the instructions aren't in plain English. Rather, they're in a language that the computer can interpret and execute.

You can create sophisticated Access databases without using VBA at all. In most cases, the other objects offered by Access — tables, queries, forms, reports, and macros — offer more than enough flexibility and power to create just about any database imaginable. Once in a while, though, you want to do something that none of those other objects can do. That's where VBA comes in. If you can find no other way to accomplish some goal in Access, writing VBA code usually is the solution.

Getting Acquainted with VBA Code

So what the heck is VBA code, anyway? To the untrained eye, VBA code looks like gibberish — perhaps some secret code written by aliens from another planet. But to Access, the code represents very specific instructions on how to perform some task.

Within any given database, Access stores code in two places:

✦ **Class modules (code-behind forms):** Every form and report you create automatically contains a *class module* (also called a *code-behind form*), as illustrated in Figure 1-1. The class module for a given form or report is empty unless you place controls in that form or report that require VBA code.

Class module (code behind form)

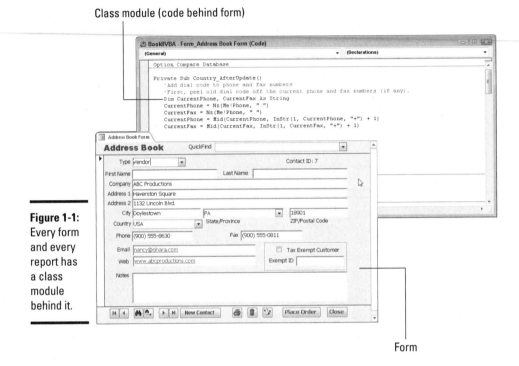

Figure 1-1:
Every form
and every
report has
a class
module
behind it.

Form

✦ **Standard modules:** Code can also be stored in *standard modules.* Code in standard modules is accessible to all objects in your database, not just a single form or report.

Opening a class module

If you want to view or change the code for a form or report's class module, first open, in Design view, the form or report to which the module is attached. Then click the (Form Design Tools) Design tab, and click the View Code button in the Tools group, shown near the mouse pointer in Figure 1-2.

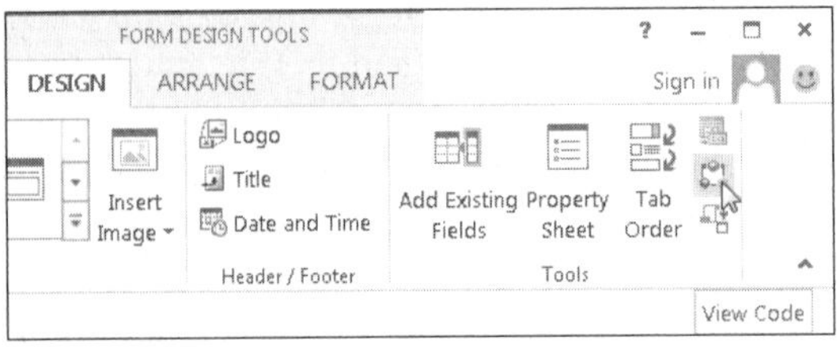

Figure 1-2:
The View
Code button.

You can also get to a class module from the Event tab of the property sheet in the Design View window. The property sheet allows you to zoom right in on the VBA code that's associated with a given control. Some controls, for example, contain code created by wizards. When you click such a control and then click the Events tab on the property sheet, the property value shows `[Event Procedure]`. When you click `[Event Procedure]`, a button with an ellipsis (three dots) appears on the right side of the property value (shown in Figure 1-3). That button is the Build button. Click it to see the code that executes in response to the selected event.

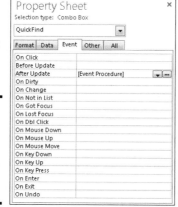

Figure 1-3:
Look for the code that executes in response to the event.

To write custom code for a control, select the control in Design view, open the property sheet, click the Event tab, click the event to which you want to attach some custom code, click the Build button, and then choose Code Builder.

After you open a module, you're taken to a separate program window called *Visual Basic Editor* (VBE), where you see the module in all its glory.

Creating or opening a standard module

Standard modules contain VBA code that isn't associated with a specific form or report. The code in a standard module is available to all tables, queries, forms, reports, macros, and other modules in your database. You won't see Module as an option when you're viewing All Access Objects in the Navigation Pane until you create at least one standard module. You have to go looking for options to create and work with modules.

To create a new module, click the Create tab. Then click the Module button in the Macros & Code group (see Figure 1-4). Visual Basic Editor opens.

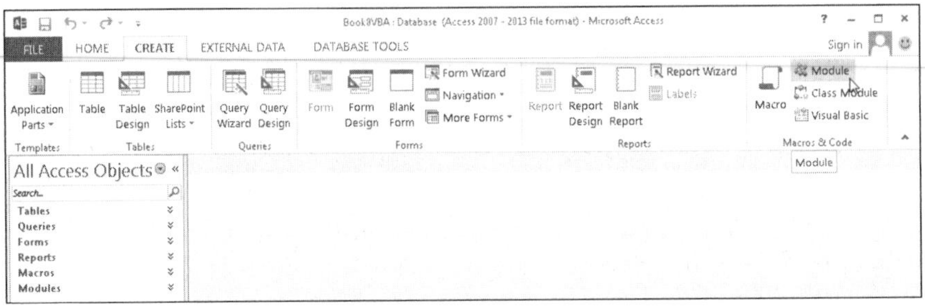

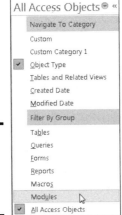

Figure 1-4:
Create
a new
module.

To show a list of modules in the Navigation Pane, click the button at the top of the Navigation Pane and choose Modules from the drop-down menu, as shown in Figure 1-5. If you've already created and saved a standard module, you can open it by double-clicking its name. If the current database contains no standard modules, you won't even see Modules as a category.

Figure 1-5:
Open a
pane to see
standard
modules.

Regardless of whether you create or open a module, you end up in Visual Basic Editor. The editor is a separate program with its own Windows taskbar button; it retains the old-style Windows look and feel, using menus instead of the Ribbon. We cover that topic in more detail later in this chapter. For now, keep in mind that you can close Visual Basic Editor and return to Access at any time by clicking the Close (X) button in the top-right corner of the editor window.

Enabling VBA Code

As with any programming language, people use VBA to create code that does good things and code that does bad things. Whenever you open a database that contains code, Access displays a warning in the Security bar. The warning doesn't mean that the database contains bad code; it just means that the database *does* contain code. Access has no way of determining whether code is beneficial or malicious; only a human can make that judgment call.

If you trust the source of that code, click the Enable Content button to make the code executable. Otherwise, the code is disabled, as are many features of Visual Basic Editor.

All modules organize their code with a Declaration section at the top followed by individual procedures, as shown in Figure 1-6. The Declaration section contains options, written in code format, that apply to all procedures in the module. Each procedure is also a chunk of VBA code that, when executed, performs a specific set of steps.

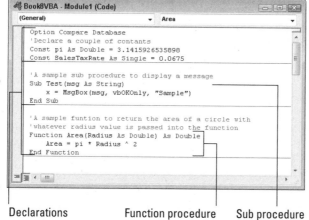

Figure 1-6: Modules consist of declarations and procedures.

Declarations   Function procedure   Sub procedure

Procedures in a module fall into two major categories: sub procedures and function procedures. Both types of procedures use VBA code to perform some task. The next sections outline some subtle differences in how and where these procedures are used.

Sub procedures

A *sub procedure* consists of one or more lines of code that make Access perform a particular task. Every sub procedure starts with the word Sub,

`Private Sub`, or `Public Sub` and ends with `End Sub`, using one of the following general structures:

```
Sub name()
    ...code...
End Sub

Private Sub name()
    ...code...
End Sub

Public Sub name()
    ...code...
End Sub
```

name is the name of the procedure, and `...code...` is any amount of VBA code.

Text that appears to be written in plain English within a module represents *programmer comments* — notes for other programmers. The computer ignores the comments. Every comment starts with an apostrophe (') and appears in a green font — unless you've changed VBE's default settings.

Function procedures

A *function procedure* is enclosed in `Function...End Function` statements, as the following code shows:

```
Function name()
    <...code...>
End Function

Public Function name()
    <...code...>
End Function

Private Function name()
    <...code...>
End Function
```

Unlike a sub procedure, which simply performs some task, a function procedure performs a task and returns a value. In fact, an Access function procedure is no different from any of the built-in functions you use in Access expressions, and you can use a custom function procedure wherever you can use a built-in procedure.

A `Public` procedure is available to all modules in Access. A `Private` procedure is available only to other procedures in the same module.

Working with Visual Basic Editor

Regardless of how you open a module, you end up in Visual Basic Editor, which is where you write, edit, and test your VBA code. VBE is separate from the Access program window. If you click outside the VBE window, the window may disappear, because whatever window you clicked comes to the front.

Visual Basic Editor retains the view that it had in previous versions of Access, with no Ribbon or Navigation Pane. In fact, VBE is similar to Microsoft Visual Studio, the integrated development environment used for all kinds of programming in Microsoft products.

Like all program windows, VBE has its own Windows taskbar button, as shown in the top half of Figure 1-7. If the taskbar is particularly crowded with buttons, the editor and Access may share a taskbar button, as shown in the bottom half of Figure 1-7. If you suddenly lose the VBE window, click its taskbar button to bring the window back to the top of the stack of program windows on your desktop.

Figure 1-7:
Taskbar buttons for Access and Visual Basic Editor.

TIP

In most versions of Windows, you can right-click the Windows taskbar and choose Show Windows Stacked from the contextual menu to make all open program windows visible onscreen without overlap.

VBE provides many tools that are designed to help you write code. Most of the tools are optional and can be toggled via VBE's View menu. Figure 1-8 shows the windows. We provide more information on each of the optional windows when they become relevant to the type of code we're demonstrating. For now, showing you how to make these windows appear and disappear is sufficient.

You can move and size most of the windows in VBE by using standard methods. You can move most windows by dragging their title bars, for example, and size windows by dragging any corner or edge. Most of the time, you won't need to have all those optional windows open to write code. Feel free to close any optional window that's open in your editor by clicking its Close (X) button. To open a window, open the View menu and choose the name of the window you want to open.

**Book VIII
Chapter 1**

What the Heck Is VBA?

Project Explorer   Code window   Locals window

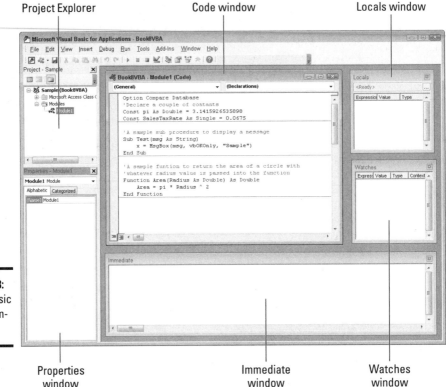

Figure 1-8:
Visual Basic
Editor com-
ponents.

Properties
window

Immediate
window

Watches
window

If you have multiple monitors connected to your computer, you can put the Access window on one monitor and the VBE window on the other.

Using the Code window

The Code window is where you type your VBA code. Similar to a word processor or text editor, the Code window supports all the standard Windows text-editing techniques. You can type text and press the Backspace and Delete keys on your keyboard to delete that text. You can press the Tab key to indent text. You can select text by dragging the mouse pointer through it. You can copy and paste text to and from the Code window. In short, the Code window is a text editor.

The Code window acts like the document window in most other programs. Click its Maximize button, shown near the mouse pointer at the top of Figure 1-9, to enlarge it. To restore it to its previous size, click the Restore Window button, shown at the bottom of that same figure.

Talkin' the talk

Programmers have their own slang terms to describe what they do. Here are a few:

✔ **Code:** The term *code,* which refers to the actual instructions written in a programming language, is always singular, like the terms *hardware* and *software.* You don't add hardware*s* and software*s* to your computer system; you add hardware and software. Likewise, you never write or cut and paste code*s;* you write or cut and paste code.

✔ **GUI:** The term *GUI* (pronounced *goo*-ey) means *graphical user interface.* Anything you can accomplish by using a mouse (that

is, without writing code) is considered to be part of the GUI. You create tables, queries, forms, reports, and macros with the GUI. You need to write code only in modules.

✔ **App:** A database may be referred to as an *app,* which is short for *application.* If a programmer says, "I created most of the app with the GUI; I hardly wrote any code at all," he means that he spent most of his time creating tables, queries, forms, reports, and macros by using the mouse and spent relatively little time typing code in VBA.

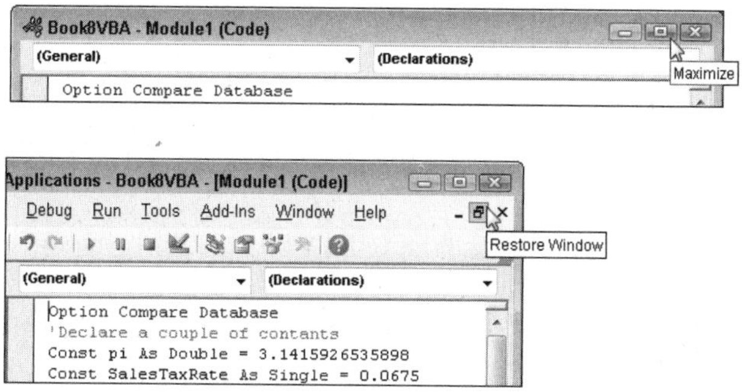

Figure 1-9:
Code window's Maximize and Restore Window buttons.

The tools in the Code window are identified in Figure 1-10 and summarized in the following list:

✦ **Object box:** When you're viewing a class module, this box shows the name of the object associated with the current code and allows you to choose a different object. In a standard module, only the word `General` appears because a standard module isn't associated with any specific form or report.

✦ **Procedure/Events box:** When you're viewing a class module, this box lists events supported by the object whose name appears in the Object box. When you're viewing a standard module, the Procedure/Events box lists the names of all procedures in that module. To jump to a procedure or event, just choose its name from the drop-down menu.

Object box   Procedure/Events box   Split box

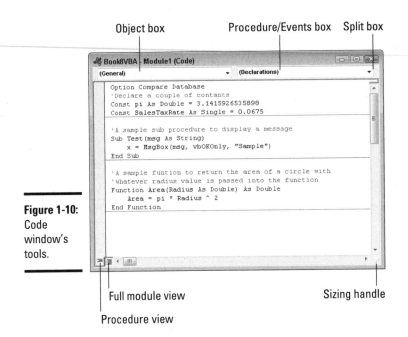

Figure 1-10:
Code
window's
tools.

Full module view   Sizing handle

Procedure view

✦ **Split bar:** This tool divvies up the screen for you. Drag the Split bar down to separate the Code window into two independently scrollable panes. Drag the Split bar back to the top of the scroll bar to unsplit the window.

✦ **Procedure view:** When clicked, the window displays only one procedure (or the declarations section) at a time. This feature is useful when you're scrolling through a long procedure and don't want to scroll past the end.

✦ **Full Module view:** When clicked, the window lets you scroll through all the declarations and procedures in the module. This feature is useful when you're browsing through a module.

✦ **Sizing handle:** Drag it to size the window. (You can drag any corner or edge as well.)

Using the Immediate window

The *Immediate window* (or *debug window)* in Visual Basic Editor allows you to run code at any time, right on the spot. Use the Immediate window for testing and debugging (removing errors from) code. If the Immediate window isn't open in VBE, you can bring it out of hiding at any time by choosing View➪Immediate Window.

When the Immediate window is open, you can anchor it to the bottom of the VBE window just by dragging its title bar to the bottom of the VBE window. Optionally, you can make the Immediate window free-floating by dragging its title bar up and away from the bottom of the VBE program window. Finally, you can dock and undock the Immediate window by right-clicking within the Immediate window and choosing the Dockable option from the contextual menu that appears.

The Immediate window allows you to test expressions, run VBA procedures you create, and perform other tasks. To test an expression, you can use the debug.print command or the abbreviated ? version, followed by a blank space and the expression. Which command you use doesn't matter, although (obviously) typing the question mark is easier. You may think of the ? character in the Immediate window as standing for *"What is . . . ?"* Typing **? 1+1** in the Immediate window and pressing Enter is like asking, "What is one plus one?" The Immediate window returns the answer to your question — 2 — as shown in Figure 1-11.

Figure 1-11:
The free-floating Immediate window solves the 1 + 1 calculation.

If you see a message about macro content being blocked, switch over to the Access program window, and click the Enable Content button on the Security bar that appears when you open a database in Access. For more information on opening databases containing macros and VBA procedures, refer to Book VI, Chapter 1.

If you want to re-execute a line that you've already typed in the Immediate window, you don't need to type that same line again. Instead, just move the cursor to the end of the line that you want to re-execute, and press Enter. To erase text from the Immediate window, drag the mouse pointer through whatever text you want to erase. Then press the Delete (Del) key, or right-click the selected text and choose the Cut option from the contextual menu.

You see many examples of using the Immediate window in later chapters of this minibook. For the purposes of this chapter, it's enough to know that the Immediate window exists and have a basic idea of how it works.

Do bear in mind that the Immediate window is just for testing and debugging. The Code window is where you type (or paste) VBA code.

Using the Object Browser

VBA code can manipulate Access objects programmatically. Remember that everything in Access is an object. Tables, forms, reports, and even single controls on forms or reports are objects. Every object that you see onscreen in Access, you can manage either interactively or programmatically. When you work with objects in the Access program window, using your mouse and keyboard, you use Access interactively — that is, you do something with your mouse and keyboard, and the object responds accordingly.

When you write code, you write instructions that tell Access to manipulate an object *programmatically,* without user intervention. You write instructions to automate some task that you may otherwise do interactively with mouse and keyboard. To manipulate an object programmatically, you write code that refers to the object by name.

All the objects that make up Access and the current database are organized in an *object model,* which comprises one or more object libraries. An *object library* is an actual file on your hard drive that provides the names of objects that VBA refers to and manipulates.

Each object consists of *classes,* and each class is a single programmable object. Each class has *members,* and some members are *properties* — characteristics of the class, such as its name or the number of items it contains. Other members are *methods,* which expose things you can do to the class programmatically.

The object model is huge, containing many libraries and classes. There's no way to memorize everything in the object model; it's just too darn big. Visual Basic Editor provides an Object Browser that acts as a central resource for finding things, as well as getting help with things in the model. It's especially useful for deciphering other people's code, like the examples you see later in this minibook.

To view the objects that VBA can access, follow these steps to open the Object Browser:

1. **Make sure that you're in Visual Basic Editor.**

2. **Click the Object Browser button in the toolbar, choose View⟹Object Browser from the menu, or press F2.**

Figure 1-12 shows the Object Browser and points out some of the major features of its window. The following list describes the browser's components:

✦ **Project/Library list:** This list allows you to choose a single library or project to work with, or <All Libraries>.

✦ **Search tools:** Use these tools to find information in the libraries.

Project/Library list   Search tools

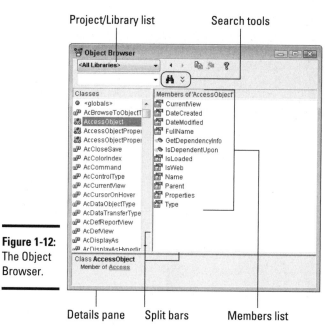

Figure 1-12:
The Object
Browser.

Details pane   Split bars   Members list

✦ **Classes list:** This list shows the names of all classes in the currently selected library or project name (or all libraries).

✦ **Members list:** When you click a name in the Classes list, this pane shows the members (properties, methods, events, functions, objects) that belong to that class.

✦ **Details pane:** When you click a member name in the Members list, the Details pane shows the syntax for using the name, as well as the name of the library to which the member belongs. You can copy text from the Details pane to the Code window.

✦ **Split bar:** Drag the Split bar left or right to adjust the size of the panes. (Drag any edge or corner of the Object Browser window to size the window as a whole.)

Searching the Object Library

For a beginning programmer, the sheer quantity of items in the Object Browser is daunting, but finding details about the prewritten code that you pick up elsewhere is useful.

Suppose that you find and use a procedure that has a DoCmd object in it, and you're wondering what this DoCmd thingy is. You can search the Object Library for information about any object, including DoCmd, by following these steps:

Book VIII
Chapter 1

What the Heck
Is VBA?

1. **In the Object Browser's Search box, type the word you're searching for.**

For this example, type **DoCmd**, as shown in Figure 1-13.

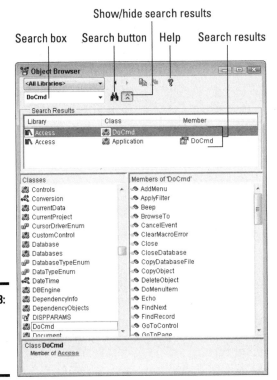

Show/hide search results

Search box   Search button   Help   Search results

2. **Click the Search button.**

The search results appear in the Search Results pane.

3. **Click the word you searched for.**

4. **Click the Help (question-mark) button on the Object Browser toolbar.**

Figure 1-14 shows the Internet help page for the DoCmd object. For the absolute beginner, even the information in the help page may be a bit advanced. As you gain experience and dig a little deeper into VBA, however, you'll find the Object Browser and help pages useful for constructing references to objects, properties, and methods from within your code.

Figure 1-14:
Help for the
DoCmd
object.

Referring to objects and collections

Objects in the object model all have a syntax that works like this: You start with the largest, most encompassing object and work your way down to the most specific object, property, or method. The process is sort of like following a path to a filename, as in C:\My Documents\MyFile.doc; you start with the largest container (disk drive C:) and go down to the next container (the folder named My Documents) and then to the specific file (MyFile.doc).

The Application object, for example, refers to the entire Access program. It includes a CurrentProject object. If you were to look up the CurrentProject object in the Object Browser and view its help window, you'd see that CurrentProject houses several collections, including one named AllForms. The AllForms collection contains the name of every form in the current database. The AllForms collection in turn supports a Count property. That property returns the number of forms in the collection.

Suppose that you have a database open, and that database contains some forms. If you go to the Immediate window, type

```
? Application.CurrentProject.AllForms.Count
```

and then press Enter, the Immediate window displays a number matching the total number of forms in the database.

At the risk of confusing matters, typing the following line in the Immediate window returns the same result:

**Book VIII
Chapter 1**

**What the Heck
Is VBA?**

```
? CurrentProject.AllForms.Count
```

The shortened version works because the `Application` option is the default parent object used if you don't specify a parent object before `CurrentProject`. (The `Application` object is the parent of `CurrentProject` because `CurrentProject` is a member of the `Application` object library.)

The bottom line is that when you see a bunch of words separated by dots in code, such as `CurrentProject.AllForms.Count`, be aware that those words refer to some object. In a sense, the words are a path to the object, going from the largest object down to a single specific object, property, method, or event. You can use the Object Browser as a means of looking up the meanings of the words to gain an understanding of how the prewritten code works.

As you gain experience, you can use the Object Browser to look up information about objects, collections, properties, methods, events, and constants within your code. For now, consider the Object Browser to be a tool for discovering VBA as you go.

Choosing object libraries

Most likely, the object libraries that appear automatically in the Object Browser's Project/Library drop-down menu are all you need. Should a given project require you to add some other object library, however, follow these steps to add it:

1. **Choose Tools⇨References in Visual Basic Editor.**

   The References dialog box opens.

2. **Select any library in the list.**

   In the unlikely event that you need a library that isn't in the list — but you know that you stored it on your hard drive — click the Browse button, navigate to the folder that contains the object library you need, click its name, and then click the Open button.

3. **Click OK when you've selected all the object libraries that you need.**

   The Project/Library list in the Object Browser now includes all the libraries that you selected in the References dialog box.

Closing Visual Basic Editor

When you're done working in Visual Basic Editor, you can close it by using whichever of the following techniques is most convenient for you:

✦ Choose File⇨Close, and return to Microsoft Access from the VBE main menu.

✦ Click the Close button in the top-right corner of the VBE program window.

✦ Right-click the Visual Basic Editor button on the taskbar and then choose the Close Window option from the contextual menu.

✦ Press Alt+Q.

Access continues to run even after you close the VBE window.

Discovering Code As You Go

Most beginning programmers start by working with code that they pick up elsewhere, such as code generated by code wizards or copied from a website. You can also create VBA code without writing it by converting any macro to VBA code.

Converting macros to VBA code

Any macro that you create in Access can be converted to VBA code. Converting macros to code is easier than writing code from scratch. Suppose that you need to write some code because a macro can't do the job, and say that a macro can do 90 percent of the job. If you create the macro and convert it to VBA code, 90 percent of your code is already written. You just have to add the other 10 percent (which is especially helpful if you can't type worth beans).

See Book VI, Chapter 1 for information on how macros work and how to create them.

Suppose that you click the Create tab and then click the Macro button in the Macros & Code group on the Ribbon (see Figure 1-15) to create a new macro. The macro can be as large or as small as you want.

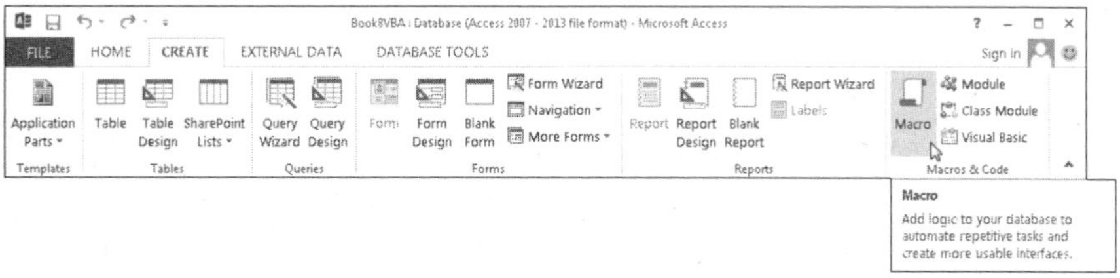

Figure 1-15:
Create a
new macro.

· Book VIII
Chapter 1

What the Heck
Is VBA?

Figure 1-16 shows a simple macro that displays a message onscreen. After you create your macro, close and save it — perhaps with the name `TinyMacro`.

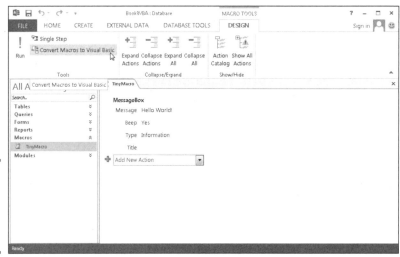

Figure 1-16:
Sample
Tin-
yMacro
macro.

When you convert a macro to VBA code, you actually convert all the macros in the macro group to code. To perform basic conversion of a macro to VBA, follow these steps:

1. **Open the macro in Design view.**

2. **Click the (Macro Tools) Design tab and then click the Convert Macros to Visual Basic button in the Tools group on the Ribbon, as shown in Figure 1-17.**

Figure 1-17:
Convert
Macros to
Visual Basic
button.

A dialog box appears, asking whether you want to include error-handling code or comments in the code. If you want to keep the code relatively simple, you can clear the first option and select only the second option.

3. **Click the Convert button.**

4. Click OK when your conversion is complete.

To see the name of the converted macro, expand the Modules category, as shown in Figure 1-18. The name of the module is `Converted Macro` - followed by the name of the macro you converted.

Figure 1-18:
A macro converted to a module.

To see the converted macro as VBA code, double-click its name. Like all VBA code, the code from the converted macro opens in the VBE Code window, as shown in Figure 1-19.

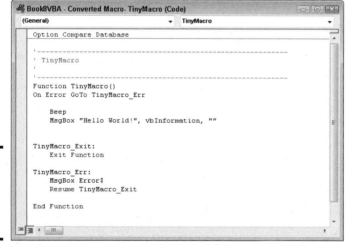

Figure 1-19:
Converted macro in the Code window.

```
Option Compare Database


' ------------------------------
' TinyMacro
'
' ------------------------------
Function TinyMacro()
On Error GoTo TinyMacro_Err

    Beep
    MsgBox "Hello World!", vbInformation, ""


TinyMacro_Exit:
    Exit Function

TinyMacro_Err:
    MsgBox Error$
    Resume TinyMacro_Exit

End Function
```

Book VIII Chapter 1

What the Heck Is VBA?

Copying and pasting code

Many VBA programmers post examples of their own code on their web pages. When you come across some sample code that you want to incorporate into your own database, retyping it all into Visual Basic Editor isn't necessary. Instead, just use standard Windows copy-and-paste techniques to copy the code from the web page to VBE.

Suppose that you come across some code on a web page that you want to use in your own database. Here's what to do:

1. **On the web page, drag the mouse pointer through the code you want to copy to select it; then press Ctrl+C to copy the selected code to the Windows clipboard.**

2. **Back in Access, create a new module or open the existing module in which you want to place the code.**

3. **In the Code window, click where you want to put the copied code.**

4. **Paste the code at the cursor position by pressing Ctrl+V.**

Bear in mind that just pasting code into the Code window doesn't make the code do anything. Most code examples are based on a sample database. Just dropping an example into your database may not be enough to get it to work.

When you copy and paste from a web page, you may get some HTML tags, weird characters, weird spacing, and so on. If that happens, you can copy the code from the page and paste it into a simple text editor like Notepad first. That method should get rid of any unusual tags and characters. Then copy and paste the text from the Notepad document into VBE's Code window.

Even if you do find an example that's generic enough to work in any database, however, the code won't actually do anything until some event in your database triggers it. In Book VIII, Chapter 2, we look at the many ways that you can trigger code.

Chapter 2: Writing Code

In This Chapter

- ✓ Understanding VBA and its syntax
- ✓ Writing custom VBA procedures
- ✓ Entering and editing code in the Code window
- ✓ Putting your custom procedures to the test

Writing Visual Basic for Applications (VBA) code is different from writing in English or any other human language. When you write in English, presumably you're writing for other human beings who speak the same language. Even if your English isn't so great (bad spelling, poor grammar), your recipients probably can still figure out what your message means. Humans have flexible brains that can figure things out based on context.

That's not so for computers. Computers don't have brains and can't figure out anything based on context. When you write code, a computer does exactly what the code tells it to do. If the computer can't read and process a statement, the procedure stops running, and an error message appears onscreen.

Before you start writing custom code, you need to know about syntax. You need to know what resources are available for finding the syntax for the tasks you want to program. Finally, you need to know at least some basic techniques for testing your code to see whether it's going to work — before you try putting it to use.

Seeing How VBA Works

VBA code is organized in *procedures*. Each procedure contains any number of lines of code called *statements*. Each statement instructs VBA to perform some action. The procedure sits in its module, doing nothing, until some event calls the procedure.

When a procedure is called, statements *execute* (run) one at a time. VBA fully executes the first statement and then fully executes the second statement, and so on, until it reaches the End Sub or End Function statement, which marks the end of the procedure. At that point, the code stops executing. Figure 2-1 summarizes how procedures work.

```
Function IsOpen(strFormName As String) As Boolean

    'Declare an Access Object named myObject.
    Dim myObject As AccessObject
    'Set myObject to passed form name.
    Set myObject = CurrentProject.AllForms(strFormName)

    'If myObject is open (loaded)...
    If myObject.IsLoaded Then
        '...and is not in Design View (acCurViewDesign)...
        If myObject.CurrentView <> acCurViewDesign Then
            '...then return True.
            IsOpen = True
        End If
    End If
'If IsOpen isn't assigned a value in this procedure,
'IsOpen() automatically returns False.
End Function
```

Figure 2-1:
Code
execution
from top to
bottom.

You can alter the top-to-bottom flow of execution by using loops and decision-making code, as we describe in Chapter 3 of this minibook.

Understanding VBA Syntax

You can't just write text that looks like VBA code. Like all languages, including English, VBA has strict rules of syntax, and each statement within a procedure must follow those rules. *Syntax* defines the order in which words must be placed so that a statement makes sense. The following sentence — which is English, by the way, and not VBA — doesn't make sense because grammar rules are broken (similar to the way that they're mangled in some of those e-mails we get):

moon the yapped sullen dog at irritating the.

If we rearrange the letters and words of that sentence so that they follow the correct rules of syntax for the English language, the sentence makes sense:

The irritating dog yapped at the sullen moon.

The rules of VBA syntax are more rigid than the rules of human language. Even the slightest misspelling or missing punctuation mark causes a statement to fail.

Most statements start with a *keyword,* which is a word that has a specific meaning in VBA. As soon as you type a complete keyword followed by a space, you typically see a brief Quick Info *syntax chart* for the keyword. Figure 2-2 shows an example. If you don't see the syntax chart, you can right-click the keywords and choose Quick Info from the contextual menu.

Figure 2-2:
A Quick
Info syntax
chart.

A Quick Info syntax chart doesn't give you any details; instead, it just guides you through the process of typing the entire statement according to the rules of syntax. For detailed information on each item in the syntax chart, you have to look in the help system. Here are several ways to get help for a keyword:

✦ Select the keyword in the Code window, and press Help (F1).

✦ Search the Object Browser for the keyword, and use the browser's help system as described in Chapter 1 of this minibook.

When you get to the help page, you see a description of the keyword. You also see a syntax chart similar to the one in Quick Info, but you get a lot more information, including the meaning of each part, acceptable values for each part, one or more examples, and perhaps links to related help pages. Figure 2-3 shows a small portion of the help page for the MsgBox keyword. Use the scroll bar on the right side of the page to scroll through it all.

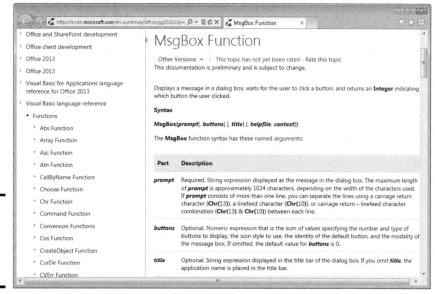

Figure 2-3:
Help page
for the
MsgBox
keyword.

Here are the most important things to know about syntax charts:

+ In the Quick Info syntax chart, boldface indicates the part that you're about to type.

+ Items in square brackets are optional and can be omitted from the statement you're typing.

+ Never type the square brackets in your statement.

+ If you skip an optional part, you must still type the comma.

Arguing with VBA

Each part that follows the keyword is generally referred to as an *argument*. Most arguments are actually expressions, similar to expressions used in calculated controls. A *string expression* can be a literal string enclosed in quotation marks (such as `"Smith"` or `"Jones"`); the name of a field; or, for that matter, the name of a variable that contains a string, such as `[LastName]` (which refers to a field in a table).

We describe variables in Chapter 3 of this minibook.

A *numeric expression* can be anything that results in a valid number. `10` is a valid numeric expression, as is `2*5` (two times five), as is the name of a field or variable that contains a number.

Given all this information, take a look at some `MsgBox` statements that follow the rules of syntax and are considered to be valid:

```
MsgBox("Slow, children at play")
```

The preceding statement is valid because the one-and-only required named argument — the `Prompt` argument — is included. When executed, the `MsgBox()` statement displays that prompt, as shown in Figure 2-4.

Figure 2-4:
Result of
`MsgBox`
statement.

As you scroll through help for the `MsgBox` function, you'll find many ways to use that function. The following statement, for example, is perfectly valid syntax for the `MsgBox` keyword. `vbYesNo` is the setting that tells the box to display Yes and No buttons (and replaces the placeholder text buttons in the `MsgBox` syntax chart), and `"Question"` is literal text that appears in the title bar of the message box (and replaces the placeholder text title in the same chart).

```
x = MsgBox ("Are we having fun yet?", vbYesNo, "Question")
```

That variation displays the message shown in Figure 2-5 and stores the user's answer to the question in a variable named x. (We talk about variables in the next chapter.)

Figure 2-5:
Result of
MsgBox
function
with three
arguments.

You can combine two or more options for the Buttons argument by using a plus sign (+). The preceding MsgBox statement uses the vbYesNo and vbQuestion constants to specify that the box show a question-mark icon as well as the Yes/No buttons:

```
x = MsgBox ("Are we having fun yet?", vbYesNo + vbQuestion, "Question")
```

When executed, the preceding statement shows the box in Figure 2-6. Unlike the one in the preceding example, this new box shows a question-mark icon because of the + vbQuestion added to the second argument.

Figure 2-6:
MsgBox
with a
question-
mark icon.

Although you have some flexibility in how you express values for arguments, you have almost no flexibility in terms of the order in which you place the arguments within a statement. If you want to use just the first and third arguments in a syntax chart, such as the Prompt and Title arguments of the MsgBox function, you still need to include a comma for the second argument to make clear that the last argument is the title, as in the following example:

```
x = MsgBox("Howdy", , "I am the Title")
```

The first comma after the "Howdy" prompt shows the start of the second argument. No argument appears between the two commas, because you're not using an argument there. The second comma shows that the next argument, Title (hence, the text "I am the Title" appears in the title bar of the message box), is actually the third one. Because no value is provided for the Buttons argument, the box shows only the default OK button.

Knowing module level from procedure level

As you work with the VBA help windows and syntax charts, you often come across the terms *module level* and *procedure level*. These terms refer to the location of code within the module. Simply stated, anything that's defined near the top of the module above the first Function or Sub procedure is a *module-level declaration*. Anything defined within a procedure is said to be a *procedure-level declaration,* as illustrated in Figure 2-7.

Module level

```
Option Compare Database
Const pi As Double = 3.1415926535898
Const SalesTaxRate As Single = 0.0675

Sub Test()
    Dim x As Integer
    x = MsgBox("Are we having fun yet?", vbYesNo)
End Sub

Function Area(radius As Double) As Double
    Area = pi * radius
End Function
```

Figure 2-7: Module level and procedure level.

Procedure level

All procedures that you add to a module should be placed below the declarations section of the module. When you see one or more Option statements at the top of a module, make sure that any procedures you add to the module start below all the Option statements at the top of the module.

Declaring module options

When you create a new standard module, it has just one declaration at the top. Typically, that declaration reads Option Compare Database, which doesn't seem to make any sense, and frankly, changing or deleting it is extremely unlikely. The declaration actually has meaning, however:

✦ **Option:** The word Option tells the VBA to set an option. The specific option to set is the Compare option (covered next).

✦ **Compare:** The Compare option tells VBA what rules to use when comparing values.

✦ **Database:** The word Database means to use the same rules that
   the rest of the database uses when comparing values. Using the same
   rules is always a good idea; otherwise, things could get very confusing.
   Nevertheless, two other options (Binary and Text) are available:

   • *Option Compare Binary:* The Binary option tells VBA to con-
      sider uppercase letters to be smaller than lowercase letters when it
      compares strings. (With Option Compare Database, VBA consid-
      ers uppercase and lowercase letters to be equal.)

   • *Option Compare Text:* The Text option tells VBA to use the sort
      order of your system's *locale* (the country and spoken language of your
      location) to compare strings. This option may be useful when you're
      creating a database to be used in non–English-speaking countries.

Writing Your Own VBA Procedures

All the code that you write is contained within procedures. A *procedure* is
a single chunk of code that performs a series of actions when called. A *sub
procedure* always begins with a Sub statement or a Private Sub statement
and ends with an End Sub statement. A *function procedure* begins with a
Function statement and ends with an End Function statement.

Chapter 1 of this minibook discusses sub and function procedures in detail.

You can add new procedures to class modules or standard modules. How
you do so depends on where you want to place the procedure.

Creating a new standard procedure

A procedure in a standard module is available to all Access objects and isn't
tied to any particular control or event. To create a new procedure in a
standard module, follow these steps:

1. **Create a new standard module, as described in Book VIII, Chapter 1.**

   or

   **Open an existing module by double-clicking its name in the
   Navigation Pane.**

2. **Choose Insert⇨Procedure in Visual Basic Editor.**

   The Add Procedure dialog box opens, as shown in Figure 2-8.

Figure 2-8:
Add
Procedure
dialog box.

3. **In the Name field, type a name for the procedure.**

   The name can be anything you choose, but it must start with a letter and can't contain any blank spaces.

4. **In the Type section, choose Sub to create a sub procedure or Function to create a function procedure.**

   The Property option has to do with creating custom objects, which isn't relevant to the topic at hand.

5. **In the Scope section, choose Public (to make the procedure available to all Access objects) or Private (to make the procedure visible only to the current module).**

   If you're not sure whether to choose Public or Private, choose Public.

   Private procedures generally are used only in class modules, not standard modules.

6. **Select the All Local Variables As Statics check box if you want to ensure that variables in the procedure retain their values between calls.**

   If you're not sure what to do with this option, your best bet is to leave it unselected.

7. **Click OK.**

   You see a new, empty procedure in the Code window.

If you chose the `Function` procedure type in Step 4, the procedure looks something like this:

```
Public Function name()

End Function
```

If you chose the `Sub` procedure type in Step 4, the code looks something like this:

```
Public Sub name()

End Sub
```

name is the name you typed in the Add Procedure dialog box.

Creating a procedure through the Add Procedure dialog box isn't really necessary. You can just type the Function statement or Sub statement in the Code window, and VBA automatically adds the corresponding End Function or End Sub statement.

The statements that the Add Procedure dialog box adds to the module use only the bare-minimum number of optional arguments supported by the Function and Sub statements. Depending on what the procedure does, you may need to define some additional arguments, as discussed in "Passing arguments to procedures," later in this chapter.

Creating a new event procedure

Recall that an event procedure is already tied to some event, such as clicking a button on a form. If you want to create a new event procedure for a control on a report or form, follow these steps:

1. **In Design view, open the form or report that contains the control for which you want to create a new procedure.**

In the Navigation Pane, right-click the object's name and choose Design View from the contextual menu.

2. **Select the control for which you want to create a procedure.**

3. **Click the Event tab in the property sheet.**

If the property sheet isn't open, right-click the selected control, choose the Properties option from the contextual menu, and then click the Event tab.

4. **Click the event that should trigger the procedure into action and then click the Build button that appears.**

If the selected control is a button, for example, and you want a user to click that button to trigger the procedure, click the On Click event and then click its Build button.

The Choose Builder dialog box opens.

5. **Select Code Builder from the list and then click OK.**

The class module for the form or report opens in Visual Basic Editor, with the cursor resting in a new procedure.

The name of the new procedure is a combination of the control's name and the event that triggers the procedure. The name is the one that appears at the top of the All tab of the property sheet. If you right-click a button named MyButton and then build the procedure from the On Click event on the Event tab of the property sheet, the procedure looks like this:

```
Private Sub MyButton_Click()

End Sub
```

Passing arguments to procedures

When you create your own expressions in Access, you often use built-in functions that are capable of accepting arguments. A built-in UCase() function, for example, takes any string of text as an argument. The argument is text that you hand over to the function to operate on. The function does its thing on the argument and then returns the results.

To pass an argument to a built-in function, you place it in the parentheses after the function name. If you're passing a literal string, you must enclose that string in quotation marks. Suppose that you type the following in the Immediate window of Visual Basic Editor:

```
? UCase("howdy world")
```

In this example, UCase() is the function, and "howdy world" is the argument — the value being passed to the function. The UCase() function returns that same chunk of text with all the letters converted to uppercase: HOWDY WORLD.

When you create your own procedures, you can define what arguments, if any, the procedure is capable of accepting. If you create a function procedure, you can also define what the procedure returns. (A sub procedure doesn't return a value.)

If you look at the syntax chart for the Sub statement and take away some of the optional stuff from that chart, you see that the syntax for the Sub statement looks something like this:

```
Sub name [(arglist)]

End Sub
```

What's with the simplified syntax?

Many optional arguments available in VBA statements represent advanced concepts that are difficult to describe out of context. This book often shows a simplified version of the syntax for a given statement, focusing on those arguments that you need to use or are likely to want to use. When you compare the simplified syntax shown in this book with the actual syntax shown in the Visual Basic Editor help pages, you may see differences. Don't be alarmed. We haven't made a mistake.

Using the simplified syntax in this book allows you to discover VBA programming in a manner that focuses on the most basic — and most important — stuff first. You can work your way to the more advanced — and mostly optional — stuff as needed. The simplified syntax may well be all you ever need to use when writing your own code.

The simplified syntax for the `Function` statement (with some of the optional stuff removed) is similar:

```
Function name [(arglist)] As type

End Function
```

In both cases, *arglist* is optional, as indicated by the square brackets. But even the optional *arglist* has a syntax, the simplified version of which is

```
name [As type]
```

name is a name you make up. You can list multiple arguments by separating their names with commas.

The *type* component specifies the data type of the data. Like Access tables, VBA supports multiple data types. These data types are similar (but not identical) to data types defined for fields in the structure of a table. The `String` data type in VBA, for example, is similar to the Text data type in an Access table, in that both contain text.

Table 2-1 lists the VBA data types that work best with Access. The Storage Size column shows how many bytes each data type assumes. The Declaration Character column shows an optional character used at the end of a name to specify a data type. (The name `PersonName$`, for example, defines `PersonName` as containing a string.) In the real world, though, you really needn't concern yourself too much with those columns. The first two columns in the table provide the information you really need to know.

**Book VIII
Chapter 2**

Writing Code

Table 2-1		**VBA Data Types**	
Data Type	*Acceptable Values*	*Storage Size*	*Declaration Character*
Boolean	True (−1) or False (0)	2 bytes	
Byte	0 to 255	1 byte	
Currency	−922,337,203,685,477.5808 to 922,337,203,685,477.5807	8 bytes	@
Date	January 1, 100, to December 31, 9999	8 bytes	
Double	−1.79769313486231E308 to −4.94065645841247E-324 for negative values; 4.94065645841247E-324 to 1.79769313486232E308 for positive values	8 bytes	#
Integer	−32,768 to 32,767	2 bytes	%
Long	−2,147,483,648 to 2,147,483,647	4 bytes	&
Object	Name of any object	4 bytes	
Single	−3.402823E38 to −1.401298E-45 for negative values; 1.401298E-45 to 3.402823E38 for positive values	4 bytes	!
String (fixed length)	Any text from 1 to 65,400 characters in length	10 + string length	$

You define the names and data types of arguments within the parentheses that follow the name of the procedure. Separate the name from the data type by using the word As. The following example Sub statement defines a sub procedure named SampleSub(). That sub procedure accepts two arguments: a single-precision number named Amount and a string named Payee.

```
Sub SampleSub(Amount As Single, Payee As String)
...code...
End Sub
```

Unlike a sub procedure, a function procedure can return a value. You define the data type of the returned value after the parentheses and the word As. The returned data doesn't need a name — just a data type. The following example Function statement defines a function procedure named IsOpen(). That function accepts one argument: a string. The name

`FormName` refers to that passed string within the function. The function returns either a `True` or `False` value (the Boolean data type).

```
Function IsOpen(FormName As String) As Boolean
    ...code...
End Function
```

Don't bother to type either of the preceding procedures, because they don't actually do anything. They just demonstrate the syntax of the `Sub` and `Function` statements. Figure 2-9 further points out the purposes of the various components of the sample `Function` statement.

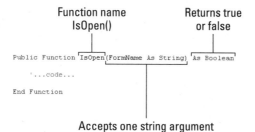

Function name
IsOpen()

Returns true
or false

Figure 2-9:
Components
of a sample
function
procedure.

```
Public Function IsOpen(FormName As String) As Boolean
    '...code...
End Function
```

Accepts one string argument

Returning a value from a function

Any function can return a value. To define the value that a function returns, you use the following syntax within the body of the function:

```
functionName = value
```

`functionName` is the name of the function, and `value` is the value that the function returns. Following is an example:

```
Function WithTax(AnyNumber As Currency) As Currency
    WithTax = AnyNumber * 1.065
End Function
```

Multiplying a number by 1.065 is equivalent to adding 6.5 percent sales tax to that number. Do this little trick with any sales tax rate. To add 7.75 percent sales tax, for example, you would multiply by 1.0775.

The `WithTax()` function is a complete VBA procedure that actually works. If you type it in a standard module, you can use it anywhere in your database just as you would a built-in function. You could even test it in the Immediate window. After you type the `WithTax` function in the Code window, for example, you can type the following in the Immediate window and press Enter:

```
? WithTax(10)
```

The Immediate window displays `10.65` because 10 times 1.065 equals 10.65. Figure 2-10 shows the function and the Immediate window.

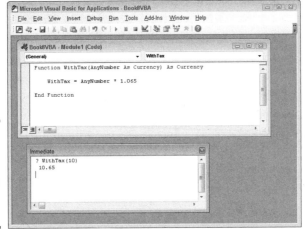

Figure 2-10:
Sample function tested in the Immediate window.

Typing and Editing in the Code Window

For a procedure to actually do anything, it has to contain some valid VBA code. As you type statements in the Code window, Visual Basic Editor offers a little help along the way. Figure 2-11 shows an example. As you type your line of code and get to a place where only certain words are allowed, a drop-down menu appears to let you know what those words are. This autocomplete feature is *IntelliSense,* which assists you in writing code.

Figure 2-11:
Drop-down menu of acceptable words.

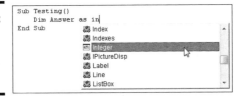

As you continue to type, the drop-down menu moves down to the first item that matches what you've typed so far. Rather than type the whole word, you can type until the selected item in the drop-down menu matches what you intend to type; then press Enter. The word in the menu replaces what you've typed so far. Choosing a word from the drop-down menu saves you some typing and also ensures that the word is spelled correctly.

Taking shortcuts in the Code window

While typing in the Code window, you can use the various shortcut keys listed in Table 2-2 to navigate, make changes, and so on. Most of the shortcut keys are identical to those in other text-editing programs and word processors.

Table 2-2	Code Window Shortcut Keys
Action	*Shortcut Key*
Move cursor right one character	→
Select character to right	Shift+→
Move cursor right one word	Ctrl+→
Select to end of word	Ctrl+Shift+→
Move cursor left one character	←
Select character to left of cursor	Shift+←
Move cursor left one word	Ctrl+←
Move cursor to start of line	Home
Select text to start of line	Shift+Home
Move cursor to end of line	End
Select text to end of line	Shift+End
Move cursor up a line	↑
Move cursor down a line	↓
Move cursor to next procedure	Ctrl+↓
Move cursor to previous procedure	Ctrl+↑
Scroll up one screen	PgUp
Scroll down one screen	PgDn
Go to top of module	Ctrl+Home
Select all text to top of module	Ctrl+Shift+Home
Go to bottom of module	Ctrl+End
Select all text to bottom of module	Ctrl+Shift+End
Cut selection	Ctrl+X
Copy selection	Ctrl+C
Paste	Ctrl+V
Cut current line to clipboard	Ctrl+Y
Delete to end of word	Ctrl+Delete
Delete character or selected text	Delete (Del)

(continued)

Table 2-2 *(continued)*

Action	Shortcut Key
Delete character to left of cursor	Backspace
Delete to beginning of word	Ctrl+Backspace
Undo	Ctrl+Z
Indent line	Tab
Outdent line	Shift+Tab
Find	Ctrl+F
Replace	Ctrl+H
Find next	F3
Find previous	Shift+F3
View Object Browser	F2
View Immediate window	Ctrl+G
View Code window	F7
View shortcut menu	Shift+F10 (or right-click)
Get help with selected word	F1
Run current sub procedure	F5
Stop code execution	Ctrl+Break

Typing comments

When typing VBA code, you can mix in programmer comments (usually called *comments* for short). A *comment* is plain-English text for human consumption only. VBA ignores all comments and processes only the code. As such, comments are optional. The purpose of adding a comment is simply to jot down notes within the code as a future reminder to yourself or to other programmers working on the same project.

The first character of a comment must be an apostrophe ('). In the Code window, comments appear as green text. Each comment is on its own line or follows a line of VBA code. Never put VBA code to the right of a comment on the same line, because VBA assumes that all text after the apostrophe (on the same line) is just a comment and ignores everything to the right of the apostrophe.

Breaking lines of code

Unlike a word processor, in which long lines of text are word-wrapped (broken between words as necessary), text in Visual Basic Editor never wraps. You (and Access) really need to be able to see each line independently. If Visual

Basic Editor were to word-wrap, you wouldn't know exactly where one line ends and the next one begins.

Sometimes, you end up typing a statement that extends beyond the right border of the window. The line in Figure 2-12 that begins with `AnyText = ` is actually much longer than it appears. Most of the line is invisible, cut off at the right margin. The statement works as is. Still, you may want to see the entire statement when you're writing, testing, or modifying your code.

Figure 2-12:
Line starting with `AnyText=` is cut off in window.

If you want to break a single long statement into two or more lines, you must insert a *continuation character* (an underscore _) at the end of the line just before you press Enter to break the line. Essentially, the continuation character tells Access, "The line break that follows isn't the end of this statement. Rather, I want to break up this lengthy line." Figure 2-13 shows the lengthy line broken into three shorter lines with continuation characters.

Figure 2-13:
Line starting with `AnyText=` broken into three lines.

Although you can use a continuation character to break a statement into two or more lines, you can't break a literal string in the same manner. A *literal string* is text enclosed in quotation marks, as in the following example:

```
SomeChunk = "A literal string is text in quotation marks"
```

If you try to break a literal string into two lines by using a continuation character, as the following example does, you get an error message:

```
SomeChunk = "A literal string is & _
text in quotation marks"
```

To break a literal string, you need to terminate the top line with a quotation mark ("), followed by an ampersand (&) and then the continuation character (_). On the next line, enclose the entire second half of the literal text in quotation marks, as the following example shows:

```
SomeChunk = "A literal string is" & _
" text in quotation marks"
```

Because breaking lines is entirely optional, you may never have to concern yourself with the nitpicky details of breaking lines within literal text. When you cut and paste code written by someone else, however, you may find that the programmer broke up lengthy lines to make them more readable. Just be aware that an underscore character (_) at the end of a line means "The line below is a continuation of this line, not a new and separate statement."

When you break literal strings, be sure to include a space between the last word of the line you're breaking and the first word of the next line. Putting the space at the start of each line makes it easy to double-check for the necessary space characters between words.

Dealing with compile errors

Each statement in VBA code must be syntactically correct and complete, and it must be on its own line or broken correctly across several lines with continuation characters. If you press Enter to end the line before you type a complete, syntactically correct statement, an error message appears onscreen.

Figure 2-14 shows what you see if you type **MsgBox("Hello World"** and press Enter. The `MsgBox()` statement requires a closing parenthesis, which is missing in this example, so the editor displays an error message. In the Code window, the faulty line is shown in red.

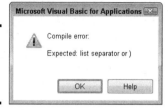

Figure 2-14:
Sample
compile
error.

The compile error means that the line you typed can't be translated to instructions that Access can perform. Access can compile and execute only syntactically correct and complete statements. The message `Expected: list separator or )` tells you that Access expected to find either a comma (to separate the first argument from the second) or a closing parenthesis.

The box displaying the error message contains two buttons:

✦ **OK:** Closes the error message box so that you can type the correction

✦ **Help:** Provides some general information about the type of error discovered and provides some suggestions for fixing the problem

Regardless of which button you click, you need to correct the statement before it can work correctly. After you type the correct statement and press Enter, the error message no longer appears, and the line no longer displays in red.

Testing and Running Your Code

A completed procedure is generally called from some object, such as a button on a form. As you write code, however, you may want to make sure that it will work before you start attaching a procedure to objects in your database. You can use the Immediate window to run the procedure right on the spot. The syntax you use depends on whether you're testing a sub procedure or function, as well as on whether the procedure accepts arguments.

Testing sub procedures

To test a sub procedure that accepts no parameters, you simply type the name of the sub procedure in the Immediate window and then press Enter. The following procedure accepts no parameters and displays a message box when called:

```
Sub ShowThanks()
   MsgBox ("Thank you")
End Sub
```

To test the preceding procedure, simply type its name (without the parentheses) in the Immediate window, as follows:

```
ShowThanks
```

The procedure switches to the Access window and shows a message. Then close the message box and switch back to Visual Basic Editor to continue writing code.

If a sub procedure accepts arguments, follow the procedure name with a blank space and the value to pass to the sub procedure. The following example sub procedure accepts one argument:

```
Sub WarnUser (msg as String)
    x = MsgBox(msg, vbCritical, "Warning")
End Sub
```

Access assumes that the passed parameter is a string. To test the procedure, you need to pass some text to it. Type the following in the Immediate window and then press Enter to test this procedure:

```
WarnUser "Don't move!"
```

When you press Enter, the procedure executes, displaying a message box in the Access window. Close the message box to return to Visual Basic Editor.

If a procedure accepts more than one argument, separate the arguments with commas. The following procedure accepts two string arguments:

```
Sub TakeTwo(msg as String, tBar As String)
    x = msgbox(msg, vbOKOnly, tBar)
End Sub
```

To test the procedure, you need to pass two parameters to it from the Immediate window, as in this example:

```
TakeTwo "Hello World", "Sample"
```

A message box opens, containing the text "Hello World" and a single OK button, and "Sample" appears in the title bar. The result is the same if you execute this statement directly:

```
x = msgbox("Hello World", vbOKOnly, "Sample")
```

Running sub procedures from Access

The real goal of a sub procedure, of course, is to run from within Access when appropriate. Sub procedures in a class module usually are tied to a control on the corresponding form or report. To actually run a procedure, open the corresponding form or report, and trigger the event that causes the code to run. If the code is attached to the `On Click` event of a button on a form, for example, you need to open the form in Form view and then click the button that runs the code.

Calling a procedure from another procedure

Any VBA procedure can call another procedure, using exactly the same syntax used to test the procedure in the Immediate window. If the sub procedure accepts no arguments, just call the procedure by name. If the sub procedure does contain arguments, include the passed values in the command.

You can use the `Call` keyword in front of the procedure name as a reminder that you're calling some other procedure, but the `Call` keyword is optional.

Figure 2-15 shows two sub procedures: one named `SampleSub()` and the other named `SecondSub()`. The `SampleSub()` procedure includes a `Call` statement that calls on `SecondSub()` to do its job. Following is what happens when you execute `SampleSub()`:

Figure 2-15:
One sub procedure calls another.

```
Sub SampleSub()
     Statement1A
     Statement2A
     Call SecondSub("Howdy World")
     Statement3A
     Statement4A
End Sub

Sub SecondSub(AnyText As String)
     Statement1B
     Statement2B
End Sub
```

1. *Statement1A* and *Statement2A* in `SampleSub()` are executed.

2. The `Call SecondSub ("Howdy World")` statement is executed, causing *Statement1B* and *Statement2B* in `SecondSub()` to be executed.

3. The `End Sub` statement at the end of `SecondSub()` returns control to the next line in the calling procedure: *Statement3A*.

4. *Statement3A* and *Statement4A* in `SampleSub()` are executed next.

5. The `End Sub` statement at the end of the `SampleSub()` procedure is executed, and no more VBA code is executed.

Running sub procedures from macros

You can also call VBA sub procedures from macros, although technically, a macro calls only a function procedure, not a sub procedure. You have two choices if you still like to have a macro call a sub procedure:

✦ Convert the sub procedure to a function procedure.

✦ Write a function procedure that calls the sub procedure and then call the function procedure from the macro.

Converting a sub procedure to a function procedure is a simple matter of changing the `Sub` keyword at the top of the procedure to `Function` and the `End Sub` statement at the bottom of the procedure to `End Function`.

If you want to leave the procedure as is and call it from a function, place the call to the sub procedure within a function procedure. When executed, the following `DoMySub()` function procedure calls the `MySub()` sub procedure:

```
'The sub procedure below is named MySub()
Sub MySub()
    MsgBox ("MySub Ran")
End Sub

'Function procedure below calls MySub sub procedure.
Function DoMySub()
    Call MySub
End Function
```

To run `MySub` from a macro, choose `RunCode` as the macro action. Then type the name of the function procedure — in this example, `DoMySub()` — as the action argument for the `RunCode` action, as shown in Figure 2-16.

Figure 2-16:
Run a function procedure (which runs the sub procedure) from a macro.

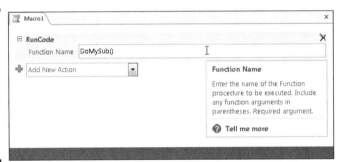

For details on defining macro actions, see Book VI, Chapter 1.

Testing function procedures

Unlike sub procedures, which return no value, function procedures always return a value. To test a function from the Immediate window, use the ? (*"What is . . . ?"*) symbol followed by the function name — and if necessary, use the values that pass to the function.

The following example custom function accepts no arguments and returns the day of the week when it's called:

```
Function Today() As String
    Today = WeekDayName(Weekday(Date))
End Function
```

To test the function, type the following in the Immediate window and press Enter:

```
? Today()
```

The Immediate window displays the value returned by the function. If you ran the test on a Monday, the function would return

```
Monday
```

The following function procedure accepts a single number as an argument (and returns a number):

```
Function Area(radius As Double) As Double
    Area = 3.141592654 * (radius ^ 2)
End Function
```

To test the function, call it with the ? symbol and pass some number to it, as in this example:

```
? Area(10)
```

The Immediate window displays the value returned by the function, as the following shows:

```
314.1592654
```

If the function accepts multiple arguments, you just separate the arguments with commas, as you do when using the Access built-in functions.

Using function procedures in Access

When you create a function procedure in VBA, you can use that function any-place within the database where you use a built-in function. Wherever you use an expression in Access, that expression can contain built-in functions, custom function procedures, or both. Here are some examples:

✦ In an expression used in the Control Source property of a calculated control on a form or a report

✦ In an expression that defines a calculated field in a select query

✦ In an expression in the Update To row of an update query

✦ In an expression used in a macro

✦ As a custom action called from a macro, such as the example shown in Figure 2-16, earlier in this chapter

In Access, function procedures generally are easier to use than sub procedures. Calling a function procedure from within any expression is easy. Many prewritten custom VBA code examples that you can find on the web are organized into function procedures rather than sub procedures.

Chapter 3: Writing Smarter Code

In This Chapter

✔ Using variables and constants to store temporary data

✔ Having your code make decisions

✔ Executing code over and over

✔ Managing data with custom VBA functions

*L*ike all programming languages, Visual Basic for Applications (VBA) offers certain concepts and statements designed to allow you to write the code necessary to make a computer do — well, *anything*. Those concepts and statements are the subject of this chapter.

We must point out, though, that the underlying VBA concepts described in this chapter aren't unique to VBA. Virtually all programming languages are built around these same concepts. If you aspire to know how to program in any language — Java, JavaScript, C++, C#, VBScript, or whatever — the concepts that you discover in this chapter apply equally to most programming languages.

Creating Variables and Constants

Within a procedure, you define and use variables. A *variable* is a name — a placeholder — for any data that may change. You make up your own variable names. Choose names that indicate what information the variables contain so you don't have to wonder later.

A variable name must begin with a letter, can't contain spaces or punctuation, and can't be the same as any built-in keyword.

Unlike data stored in a table, data stored in a variable isn't permanent. Data stored in a variable is fleeting and exists for only as long as VBA needs the information contained within the variable.

Creating variables

You can create variables in VBA code in a couple of ways: create them on the fly or define them in advance.

The quick-and-dirty way is to simply make up a variable name and assign a value by following the name with an equal sign (=) and the value to be stored in the variable. The following VBA statements define three variables named x, y, and ExtPrice. The variable x stores the number 10; the variable y stores the number 9.99; and the variable ExtPrice stores the result of multiplying the contents of x by the contents of y (or 99.9, by the time all three lines are executed):

```
x = 10
y = 9.99
ExtPrice = x * y
```

All these statements are examples of *implicit variable declarations* — which basically means that you make up variables as you go.

Explicit variable declarations, as the name implies, require you to assign a data type to each variable before you assign values to variables. Explicit variable declaration is a little more work than implicit variable declaration, but your code runs more smoothly and efficiently because Access doesn't have to figure out the best data type to use when it encounters the data lurking in the variable.

Two steps go into using a variable explicitly:

1. You *define* (or *declare*) the variable, which gives the variable a data type.

2. After the variable exists, you assign a value, using the same syntax as for implicit declarations: *variableName = value.*

The command for defining a variable explicitly is Dim, which is short for *dimension.* Thinking of Dim as standing for *define in memory* may be easier, however, because variables exist only in the computer's random access memory (RAM). The simplified syntax for the Dim statement looks like this:

```
Dim varname [As type] [,...]
```

varname is a name of your own choosing, and *type* refers to one of the acceptable VBA data types or object types. The data types that you assign to variables in a Dim statement are the same as those that you use to define arguments in a Function or Sub statement.

The comma and ellipsis in the syntax chart mean that you can define multiple variables, separated by commas, within a single statement. The following example statement declares one variable, named ReportName, as a string (textual data):

```
Dim ReportName As String
```

The following sample `Dim` statement declares two variables: a string named `ReportName` and a long integer named `Qty`. Then the lines after the `Dim` statement assign a value to each variable, using the standard `variable Name = value` syntax:

```
Dim ReportName As String, Qty As Long
ReportName = "Sales Summary Report"
Qty = 50
```

Understanding the scope and lifetime of variables

Every variable and constant has a scope and a lifetime.

The *scope* of a variable defines the procedures to which the variable is visible. You determine the scope of a variable when you declare the variable. Variables declared at the beginning of a module (before the first procedure in the module) can be *private* (visible only to procedures within the same module) or *public* (visible to all procedures in all modules). These variables have *module-level scope.*

If you use the `Public` keyword (rather than `Dim`) to declare a variable at the module level, the variable is visible to all procedures in all modules. On the other hand, if you use a `Dim` or `Private` statement to define a variable at the module level, the variable is private to the module. All procedures defined within the same module can see the variable, but the variable is invisible to procedures defined in other modules.

When you define a variable within a procedure, that variable has *procedure-level scope,* meaning that the variable is *private* (visible only) to the procedure in which it is defined. Only the procedure in which the variable is defined can see, and use, the variable.

Figure 3-1 shows a module containing several variables declared with `Dim`, `Private`, and `Public` keywords. Comments in the code describe the scope of the variables declared within the module, as follows:

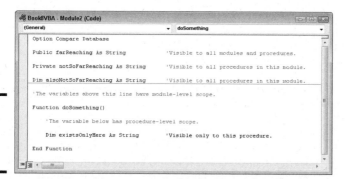

Figure 3-1:
Scopes
of sample
variables.

+ **Public farReaching As String:** The variable named farReaching is visible to all procedures in all modules because it's declared by using the Public keyword.

+ **Private notSoFarReaching As String and Dim alsoNotSoFar Reaching As String:** These variables are visible to all procedures in the same module but aren't visible to procedures defined in other modules. Dim and Private have the same meaning in this context.

+ **Dim existsOnlyHere As String:** Because this variable is declared within a procedure, the variable is visible only to that procedure.

The *lifetime* of a variable defines how long a variable retains a value. When you open a database, variables defined at the module level of standard modules are created and can be assigned a new value at any time. The lifetime of such variables is lengthy. These variables exist and can contain values for the entire session, from when you open the database to when you close it.

Variables declared with a Dim keyword at the procedure level have a much shorter lifetime. The variable retains its value for only as long as the procedure runs. A second call to the same procedure re-creates the variables and assigns new values to them.

Although it's rare to do so, sometimes you may want to make one or more variables retain their values between calls to the procedure. You may have a variable that keeps track of how many times the procedure is called, for example. In that case, you can use the Static keyword, rather than Dim, to declare the variable or variables. The following statement defines a static variable named howMany, which stores an integer (whole number):

```
Static howMany as Integer
```

You can make all variables declared within a procedure static by preceding the Sub or Function keyword with Static. All variables defined within the following procedure are static because the Static keyword in front of the word Function makes all that procedure's variables static:

```
Static Function myFunction()
    'Both variables below are static
    Dim var1 As String
    Dim var2 As Byte
End Function
```

If you find variable scope and lifetime terribly confusing, you rarely need to be so picky about the scope and lifetimes of variables. In fact, if you never use the Public, Private, or Static keywords in any code you write, chances are that the code will still work perfectly; the default scope and lifetime assigned to a variable through the Dim statement usually are exactly what you need. Exceptions are few and far between, and they aren't likely to show up until you start developing huge, complex databases.

Defining constants

A *constant* is similar to a variable, in that it has a name, a data type, and a value. Unlike a variable (whose contents can change at any time), a constant has a fixed value. Constants are often used to assign a short name to some value that must be used repeatedly throughout the code but never changed.

To declare a constant, you use the `Const` keyword. The simplified syntax for the `Const` keyword is

```
Const name [As type]=value [, name [As type]=value]...
```

You define the name, data type (`type`), and value of the constant on a single line. The rules for coming up with a name are the same as those for a variable: It must start with a letter, can't contain blank spaces or punctuation, and can't be the same as a VBA keyword.

As an example of creating a constant, the following statement defines a constant named `pi` as a double-precision number containing the value `3.141592654`:

```
Const pi As Double = 3.141592654
```

You can declare multiple constants in a single `Const` statement by separating them with commas. The following example statement declares two constants: a number named `x` of the Byte data type, with a value of `10`, and a string named `myName`, containing the text `"Billy"`:

```
Const x As Byte = 10, myName As String = "Billy"
```

Constants tend to be private to the modules in which they're defined. If you want to ensure that a constant is available to all objects and all modules within the database, precede `Const` with the `Public` keyword, as follows:

```
Public Const pi As Double = 3.141592654
```

Organizing variables into arrays

An *array* is a collection of variables organized into a list or table. Each item's name is the same, but each array has one or more subscripts that uniquely identify each item in the array based on its position in the array. The *subscript* is one or more numbers, enclosed in parentheses, that follow the name. If `Colors` is the name of an array, for example, `Colors(0)` (pronounced *colors sub zero)* is the first item in the list, `Colors(1)` is the second item in the list, and so on.

In a sense, an array is like a database table in that the data can be organized into rows and columns. Also, you can use VBA to manipulate data stored in tables. The only time you really want to use an array is when you work with a small amount of data that either never changes or changes only while the code is running. The data in an array is defined in code, not in a table, so getting to the data stored in the array isn't easy.

The syntax for declaring an array is almost identical to that for creating a variable, but you need to define the number of *dimensions* in the array and the number of *elements* in each dimension of the array. An array can have up to 60 dimensions and virtually any number of elements within each dimension. The basic syntax for declaring an array with the Dim statement is

```
Dim varname[([subscripts])] [As type] [,varname[([subscripts])]] [As type]] . .
```

In this statement,

+ *varname* is the name assigned each element in the array.

+ *subscripts* is the number of elements in each dimension, with the dimensions separated by commas. It can contain the optional keyword To to specify the starting and ending subscripts.

+ *type* is any valid VBA data type.

All arrays are zero-based unless you specify otherwise, which means that the first item in the array has a subscript of 0 (zero) rather than 1. The number of elements specified is actually one less than the total number of elements that the array contains.

The following Dim statement declares a one-dimensional array named Colors that contains four string elements (numbered 0, 1, 2, and 3):

```
Dim Colors(3) as String
```

The following lines of code show how you can then assign a value to each element in the array. Because the first item always has a subscript of 0, you actually place four items in the array rather than three:

```
Colors(0) = "black"
Colors(1) = "red"
Colors(2) = "blue"
Colors(3) = "green"
```

Having the first element in an array start with 0 can be counterintuitive for us humans, because we tend to think of the first item in a list as being number 1. You can force the first element to be 1 by specifying a range (rather than a number) of elements in the Dim statement. The following Dim statement declares an array of three elements, with subscripts ranging from 1 to 3. The lines after the Dim statement assign values to each of those elements:

```
Dim Colors(1 To 3) as String
Colors(1) = "red"
Colors(2) = "blue"
Colors(3) = "green"
```

If you want all your arrays to start at 1 rather than 0, another alternative is to simply put the following statement in the `Declarations` section of the module, before the first procedure in the module:

```
Option Base 1
```

After you add the `Option Base 1` statement to the top of a module, all arrays within that module start at 1 rather than 0. Thus, the `Dim Colors(3)` statement creates an array of three elements numbered 1, 2, and 3, as you expect. There is no `Colors(0)` when the optional base for arrays is set to 1 via the `Option Base 1` module declaration.

Working with multidimensional arrays

A *multidimensional array* offers more than one subscript per name. The simplest example is a two-dimensional array, which you can envision as a table. The first subscript in a two-dimensional array represents the element's row position in the array, and the second subscript represents the element's column position in the array. In the following example array, `State(3,2)` refers to row 3, column 2 in the `States` array, which contains `"AZ"`:

```
State(1,1)  = "Alabama"              State(1,2)  = "AL"
State(2,1)  = "Alaska"               State(2,2)  = "AK"
State(3,1)  = "Arizona"              State(3,2)  = "AZ"
State(50,1) = "Wyoming"              State(50,2) = "WY"
```

The `Dim` statement that creates a two-dimensional array named `States`, with 50 row elements and 2 column elements, is shown with the following statement. If you use the `Option Base 1` statement in the `Declarations` section, the starting number for each array is 1:

```
Dim States (50,2) as String
```

The code that *populates* the array (that is, assigns a value to each variable) looks like this:

```
State(1,1)  = "Alabama"
State(1,2)  = "AL"
State(2,1)  = "Alaska"
State(2,2)  = "AK"
State(3,1)  = "Arizona"
State(3,2)  = "AZ"
...
State(50,1) = "Wyoming"
State(50,2) = "WY"
```

Although many programming languages support multidimensional arrays, you won't use them in Access very often. Instead, you can use a table to store lists and tables of data and then use Access code to extract data from that table as needed.

Following naming conventions for variables

Some programmers use *naming conventions* to identify the data type of a variable as part of the variable's or constant's name. The naming conventions are optional; you don't have to use them. A lot of VBA programmers follow them, though, so you're likely to see them in any code you happen to come across.

The idea behind a naming convention is simple. When you define a new variable, make the first three letters of the name (referred to as the *tag)* stand for the type of variable or object. The following line creates an Integer variable named intMyVar, where int is short for *integer:*

```
Dim intMyVar As Integer
```

The tag added to the front of the name doesn't affect how the variable is stored or how you can use it. The tag serves only as a reminder that MyVar is an Integer.

Table 3-1 summarizes the tags that you'll most likely encounter when reading other people's code. In the Sample Declaration column of the table, the italicized word *Name* means that you can use any variable name of your own choosing.

Table 3-1   Naming Conventions Used among VBA Programmers

Tag	Stands For	Sample Declaration
bln	Boolean data type	Dim bln*Name* As Boolean
byt	Byte data type	Dim byt*Name* As Byte
cur	Currency data type	Dim cur*Name* As Currency
dbl	Double data type	Dim dbl*Name* As Double
dtm	Date/Time data type	Dim dtm*Name* As Date
int	Integer data type	Dim int*Name* As Integer
lng	Long Integer data type	Dim lng*Name* As Long
sng	Single data type	Dim sng*Name* As Single
str	String data type	Dim str*Name* As String
var	Variant data type	Dim var*Name* As Variant

Making Decisions in VBA Code

Decision-making is a big part of programming, because most programs need to be smart enough to figure out what to do in various circumstances. Often, you want your code to do one thing if such-and-such is true and to do something else if such-and-such is false. You use conditional expressions to determine whether something is true or false. A *conditional expression* is one that generally follows the syntax

```
Value ComparisonOperator Value
```

where *Value* is some chunk of information and the *ComparisonOperator* is one of those listed in Table 3-2.

Table 3-2	Comparison Operators
Operator	*Meaning*
=	Equal to
<	Less than
<=	Less than or equal to
>	Greater than
>=	Greater than or equal to
<>	Not equal to

The expression

```
[Last Name] = "Smith"
```

compares the contents of the Last Name field with the string "Smith". If the [Last Name] field does, indeed, contain the name Smith, the expression is (or *returns*) True. If the [Last Name] field contains anything other than Smith, the expression is (returns) False.

Another example is the following statement:

```
[Qty] >= 10
```

The content of the Qty field is compared with the number 10. If the number stored in the Qty field is 10 or greater, the expression returns True. If the number stored in the Qty field is less than 10, the expression returns False.

You can combine multiple conditional expressions into one by using the logical operators summarized in Table 3-3.

Table 3-3	Logical Operators
Operator	*Meaning*
and	Both values are True.
or	One value is True, or both values are True.
not	Value is not True.
xor	Exclusive or: One value is True, but both values aren't True.

The following conditional expression requires that the [Last Name] field contain "Smith" and the [First Name] field contain "Janet" for the entire expression to be True:

```
[Last Name] = "Smith" and [First Name] = "Janet"
```

An example of an expression that returns True if the State field contains NJ or NY is the following:

```
[State] = "NJ" or [State] = "NY"
```

Using If...End If statements

You can have VBA code make decisions as the code is running, and you can enable this feature in several ways. One method is to use the If...End If block of code. The syntax for If...End If looks like this:

```
If condition Then
    [statements]...
[Else
    [statements]...
End If
```

condition is an expression that results in True or False, and statements refers to any number of valid VBA statements. If the condition proves to be True, the statements between Then and Else execute, and all other statements are ignored. If the condition proves to be False, only the statements after the Else statement execute, as illustrated in Figure 3-2.

As an example, imagine that a State variable contains some text. The following If...End If block checks whether the State variable contains NY. If the State variable does contain NY, the TaxRate variable receives a value of 0.075 (7.5%). If the State variable doesn't contain NY, the TaxRate variable receives a value of 0.

```
If State="NY" Then
    TaxRate=0.075
Else
    TaxRate=0
End If
```

If *Condition* proves True, do these statements

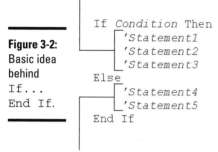

Figure 3-2:
Basic idea
behind
If...
End If.

```
If Condition Then
    'Statement1
    'Statement2
    'Statement3
Else
    'Statement4
    'Statement5
End If
```

If *Condition* proves False, do these statements

You have a little bit of flexibility in using If...End If. If only one line of code executes for a True result and only one line executes for a False result, you can put the whole statement on a single line and omit the End If statement, as follows:

```
If State="NY" Then TaxRate=0.075 Else TaxRate=0
```

Because you can use any built-in function in VBA, and because Access supports the use of the IIf() *(Immediate If)* function, you can also write the preceding statement as an expression:

```
TaxRate = IIf([State]="NY",0.075,0)
```

In the block format, you can also write code that tests for more than just two possible conditions by using the optional ElseIf statement. Suppose that the Reply variable stores a string of text. If Reply contains the word "Yes", your code does one thing. If Reply contains "No", your code does something else. If Reply contains neither "Yes" nor "No", you want your code to do something else instead. You could set up an If...End If block to test for and respond to all three conditions, as follows:

```
If Reply = "Yes" Then
    statements for "Yes" reply
ElseIf Reply="No" Then
    statements for "No" reply
Else
    statements for any other reply
End If
```

When the code has to choose a decision from among many possibilities, you may find that using a Select Case...End Select block is easier. For details, see "Using a Select Case block," later in this chapter.

Nesting If...End If statements

What if you have more than two possible scenarios? No problem — you can nest `If...End If` blocks, meaning that you can put one complete `If...End If` block inside another `If...End If` block. In the code shown in Figure 3-3, for example, the innermost statements execute only if `Condition1` and `Condition2` result in `True`.

Executed only if Condition1 and Condition2 are both true

```
If Condition1 Then

    If Condition2 Then

        ...statements
        statements...

    End If

End If
```

Figure 3-3:
Nested
`If...`
`End If`
blocks.

You can see why the nested `If...End If` statements work if you look at what happens when either test proves to be `False`:

✦ If `condition1` proves to be `False`, all code down to the last `End If` statement is skipped. The inner `If...End If` block isn't seen or executed.

✦ If `condition1` proves to be `True` but `condition2` proves to be `False`, all the statements in the nested block are ignored. The innermost statements still don't execute.

✦ If both `condition1` and `condition2` prove to be `True`, no code is skipped, and the innermost statements execute normally.

You can nest `If...Else...End If` blocks as deeply as you want, but you have to make sure that each block has its own `End If` statement.

Using a Select Case block

What if you have more than two or three cases to check for? Suppose that you need to perform different statements depending on which of ten product types a customer ordered. You could nest a lot of `If...End If` blocks, but that code would be confusing. Luckily, Access provides a better way.

A `Select Case` block of code performs a particular set of instructions, depending on some value. Typically, the value is a number that represents some previous selection, and it's stored in a variable or field in a table. The basic syntax of a `Select Case` block of code looks like this:

```
Select Case value
    [Case possibleValue  [To possibleValue]
        [statements]]
    [Case possibleValue [To possibleValue]
        [statements]]...
    [Case Else
        [statements]]
End Select
```

value is some value (such as a number), and *possibleValue* is any value that could match the value. You can have any number of Case *possibleValue* statements between the Select Case and End Select statements. Optionally, you can include a Case Else statement, which specifies statements that execute only if none of the preceding Case *possibleValue* statements proves to be True.

Each Case statement can have any number of statements below it. When the code executes, only those statements after the Case statement that match the *value* at the top of the block execute. Figure 3-4 shows the idea.

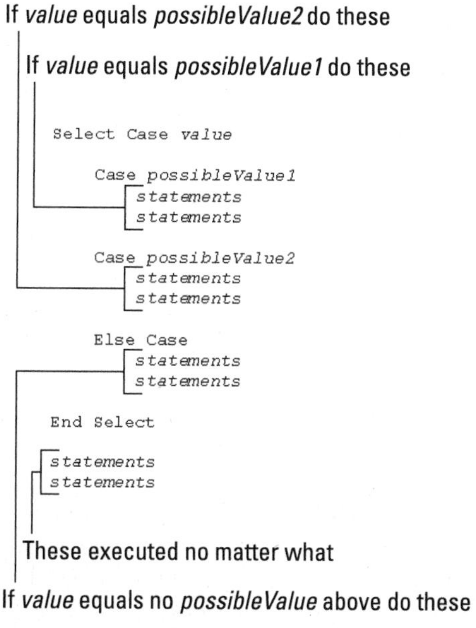

Figure 3-4: A Select Case... End Select block.

Suppose that you create a custom option group named WhereTo and a command button named OKButton on a form like the one in Figure 3-5. When the user chooses an option and clicks OK, you want to have the appropriate form open.

Figure 3-5:
Option
group and
button on a
form.

Figure 3-5:
Option
group and
button on a
form.

Button named OKButton

In the class module for that form, a sub procedure named OKButton_ Click() executes whenever someone clicks OK. The sub procedure, shown in Figure 3-6, opens a form, exits Access, or does nothing, depending on what's selected in the WhereTo option group.

Figure 3-6:
Sub pro-
cedure to
handle OK
Button_
click().

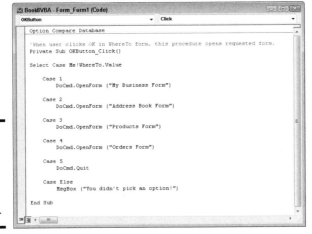

```
Option Compare Database

'When user clicks OK in WhereTo form, this procedure opens requested form.
Private Sub OKButton_Click()

Select Case Me!WhereTo.Value

    Case 1
        DoCmd.OpenForm ("My Business Form")

    Case 2
        DoCmd.OpenForm ("Address Book Form")

    Case 3
        DoCmd.OpenForm ("Products Form")

    Case 4
        DoCmd.OpenForm ("Orders Form")

    Case 5
        DoCmd.Quit

    Case Else
        MsgBox ("You didn't pick an option!")

End Sub
```

The OKButton_Click() procedure does its job this way. When the procedure is called, the following statement executes first:

```
Select Case Me!WhereTo.Value
```

This statement uses the Me!WhereTo.Value expression to refer to the value of the WhereTo option group on the form. The word Me! is used mainly in class modules to refer to the form or report to which the class module is attached. Me!WhereTo.Value is a number from 1 through 5 when the code executes. If no option is selected, Me!WhereTo.Value equals Null. In that case, the code after the Case Else statement executes.

If you omit the Case Else statement from the sample code, no code within the Select Case...End Case block executes when Me!WhereTo.Value contains something other than a number from 1 through 5. Execution continues normally at the first line after the End Case statement, however.

You can use the optional To keyword of the Case statement to specify a range of values to compare against. In the following code, statements after Case 1 To 9 execute only if SomeNumber contains a value from 1 through 9. Statements after Case 10 To 99 execute only if SomeNumber contains a value from 100 through 999, and so on.

```
Select Case SomeNumber
    Case 1 to 9
        Statements for when SomeNumber is between 1 and 9
    Case 10 to 99
        Statements for when SomeNumber is between 10 and 99
    Case 100 to 999
        Statements for when SomeNumber is between 100 and 999
End Select
```

The ranges used in a Case statement include the endpoints. For example, Case 1 to 9 includes 1, 2, 3, 4, 5, 6, 7, 8, and 9.

Executing the Same Code Repeatedly

Occasionally, you want to execute one or more VBA statements multiple times. Suppose that you write some VBA statements that need to operate on each record in a table, and the table contains 1,000 records. You have two choices: Write each set of statements 1,000 times, or create a loop that repeats a single set of statements 1,000 times. Needless to say, typing the statements once rather than 1,000 times saves you a lot of time. A loop is your best bet.

Using Do...Loop to create a loop

The Do...Loop block is one method of setting up a loop in code to execute statements repeatedly. Two syntaxes for using Do...Loop exist. The first syntax evaluates the condition of the loop, as follows:

```
Do [{While | Until} condition]
    [statements]
    [Exit Do]
    [statements]
Loop
```

The second syntax provides the option of defining the condition at the bottom of the loop, using this syntax:

```
Do
    [statements]
    [Exit Do]
    [statements]
Loop [{While | Until} condition]
```

As an example of the first syntax, the code in the following `Do Until` loop executes once for each record in a recordset named `rst`. (A recordset, as discussed in Chapter 5 of this minibook, is the VBA equivalent of a table in Access.)

```
'Example assumes recordset named rst already exists.
rst.MoveFirst
Do Until rst.EOF()
    Debug.Print rst.Fields("Product Name")
    rst.MoveNext
Loop
```

Here's how the loop works: The `rst.MoveFirst` statement moves the cursor to the first record in the table. At that point, `EOF()` (which stands for *end of file*) is `False` because `EOF()` means "past the last record in the table." Because the cursor is at the first record, `EOF()` is `False`.

Within the loop, the `rst.MoveNext` statement moves the cursor to the next record in the table. `EOF()` remains `False` until `rst.MoveNext` executes a sufficient number of times to have visited every record in the table. After visiting the last record, `rst.MoveNext` moves the cursor to the end of the file — past the last record. When the cursor is past the last record, `EOF()` becomes `True`, and the loop doesn't repeat anymore. Instead, Access resumes executing your code normally at the first statement after the `Loop` statement.

Using the alternative syntax, in which you define the condition at the bottom rather than at the top of the loop, you can construct the same sort of loop as follows:

```
'Example assumes recordset named rst already exists.
rst.MoveFirst
Do
    Debug.Print rst.Fields("Product Name")
    rst.MoveNext
Loop Until rst.EOF()
```

You'll notice one subtle difference between setting the loop condition at the top of the loop and setting it at the bottom of the loop. Access checks the condition *before* the loop executes for the first time (and each time thereafter). When you set the condition at the top of the loop, none of the statements in the loop may execute. Forgetting about recordsets and tables for the moment, consider the following more generic example:

```
Counter = 101
Do While Counter < 100
    Counter = Counter +1
Loop
'Statements below the loop.
```

Because `Counter` already has a value of `101` when the `Do While Counter < 100` statement executes, the looping condition is `False` right off the bat. Thus, everything between the `Do While` and `Loop` statements is skipped completely, and code execution resumes at the statements after the loop.

In the following code, the looping condition, `While Counter < 100`, moves to the bottom of the loop:

```
Counter = 101
Do
    Counter = Counter +1
Loop While Counter < 100
'Statements below the loop.
```

In the preceding loop, `Counter` receives a value of `101`. The `Do` statement doesn't specify a condition for starting the loop, so the `Counter = Counter + 1` statement within the loop executes. Then the `Loop While Counter < 100` condition proves to be `False` (because `Counter = 102` by then), so code execution continues at the statements after the `Loop` statement at the bottom of the loop.

In short, when you define the condition for the loop at the top of the loop, the code within the loop may not execute at all, but if you define the condition at the bottom of the loop, the code within the loop executes at least once.

Using While...Wend to create a loop

The `While...Wend` loop is similar to `Do...Loop`, but it uses the simpler (and less flexible) syntax shown in the following code:

```
While condition
    [statements]
Wend
```

`condition` is an expression that results in a `True` or `False` value, and `statements` is any number of VBA statements, all of which execute with each pass through the loop.

The condition is evaluated at the top of the loop. If the condition proves to be `True`, all lines within the loop execute (down to the `Wend` statement), and the condition at the top of the loop is evaluated again. If the condition proves to be `False`, all statements within the loop are ignored, and processing continues at the first line after the `Wend` statement.

Using For...Next to create a loop

When you want to create a loop that keeps track of how many times the loop repeats, you can use the `For...Next` block of statements. The syntax for a `For...Next` loop is as follows:

Book VIII
Chapter 3

Writing Smarter
Code

```
For counter = start To end [Step step]
    [statements]
    [Exit For]
    [statements]
Next [counter]
```

In this syntax,

✦ *counter* is any name you want to give to the variable that keeps track of passes through the loop.

✦ *start* is a number that indicates where the loop should start counting.

✦ *end* is a number that indicates when the loop should end.

✦ *step* (optional) indicates how much to increment or decrement *counter* with each pass through the loop. If *step* is omitted, *counter* increments by 1 with each pass through the loop.

✦ *statements* is any number of VBA statements that execute with each pass through the loop.

Figure 3-7 shows a simple example of a For...Next loop within a sub procedure. This loop starts at 1 and increments the Counter variable by 1 with each pass through the loop. The loop continues until Counter reaches a value of 10, at which point the loop is done and processing continues at the first line after the Next statement. Within the loop, the Debug.Print statement simply prints the current value of the Counter variable to the Immediate window.

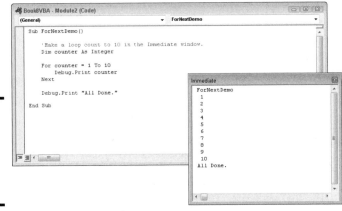

Figure 3-7:
A simple
For...
Next loop
in a sub
procedure.

Figure 3-7 shows the result of testing the procedure in the Immediate window. As you can see, the Counter value displays once with each pass through the loop. Then processing continues at the lines that use Debug. Print to display the words "All Done."

Note: If you change the loop so that it counts from 2 to 10 and adds 2 (rather than 1) to Counter with each pass through the loop, the code looks like the following:

```
For counter = 2 to 10 Step 2
    Debug.Print counter
Next
```

Running the preceding loop displays the following in the Immediate window:

```
2
4
6
8
10
All Done.
```

Looping through an array

You can use the Counter variable for a For...Next loop as the subscript for elements in an array. You can use the LBound() (lower boundary) and UBound() (upper boundary) functions to automatically return the lowest and highest subscripts in the array. You can use those values as the *start* and *end* values in the For... statement. The following code creates an array of four elements and assigns a value — a color name — to each element in the array. The For...Next loop that follows the array prints the contents of each array element by using the Counter value as the subscript for each pass through the loop.

```
Sub LoopArrayDemo()
    'Declare a variable and an array.
    Dim counter As Integer
    Dim Colors(3) As String

    'Fill the array.
    Colors(0) = "Black"
    Colors(1) = "Red"
    Colors(2) = "Green"
    Colors(3) = "Blue"

    'Create a loop that shows array contents.
    For counter = LBound(Colors) To UBound(Colors)
        Debug.Print Colors(counter)
    Next

End Sub
```

Book VIII
Chapter 3

Writing Smarter Code

In the For statement, LBound(Colors) and UBound(Colors) automatically fill in the lowest and highest subscript numbers. On the first pass through the loop, the Debug.Print statement prints the contents of Colors(0). On the second pass through the loop, Debug.Print displays the contents of Colors(1), and so on until all array elements print.

Analyzing each character in a string

You can also use a `For...Next` loop to look at each character in a string. First, be aware that these two built-in Access functions help with the loop:

+ **Len(*string*):** Returns the length of a string in number of characters

+ **Mid(*string, start, length*):** Returns a portion of *string* starting at character *start* that's *length* characters long

As an example, if *string* is `"Hello World"`, `Len(string)` returns 11, because there are 11 characters in `"Hello World"` (counting the blank space that separates the two words). The expression `Mid(string,7,3)` returns a substring of *string* that starts at the seventh character and is three characters in length. In this case, that substring would be `Wor`, because W is the seventh character, and the returned substring is three characters in length.

Text-handling functions are described in more detail in Book III, Chapter 2.

To create a loop that looks at each character in a string one at a time, start the loop at 1 and end it at `Len(string)`. Within the loop, use `Mid(string, counter, 1)` to isolate the single character at the position indicated by `Counter`. A simple loop that prints each character from the string named `strFull` in the Immediate window looks like this:

```
Sub LookAtEachCharacter()
    'Declare a couple of string variables.
    Dim strFull As String, thisChar As String

    'Give strFull a value.
    strFull = "Hello World"

    'Now isolate and display each character from strFull.
    For Counter = 1 to Len(StrFull)
        thisChar = Mid(strFull,Counter,1)
        Debug.Print thisChar
    Next

End Sub
```

The `For Each...Next` loop is a slight variation on the `For...Next` loop, and it's discussed in Chapter 4 of this minibook.

Using Custom Functions

Access has many built-in functions that you can use in expressions. One of the beauties of VBA is that it allows you to create your own custom functions, commonly referred to as *user-defined functions,* or *UDFs.* After you create such a function in a standard module, you can use it throughout your database as you would a built-in function.

To illustrate, we show you a function that converts numbers (like 123.45) to words (like One Hundred Twenty Three and 45/100). It's handy for printing checks. This function also requires using a little bit of everything that VBA has to offer — variables, arrays, loops, and decision-making — so it works as an example of how programmers combine all aspects of programming languages to come up with solutions to problems. Comments throughout the function explain what's going on, but it's not important to understand everything about how the function works. Rather, this function is just an example of what a large custom function might look like.

To create a custom function that's accessible to all objects in a database, you have to put the function in a standard module. Listing 3-1 shows the NumWord() custom function used to convert numbers to words as it would appear in a module below the words Option Compare Database.

Listing 3-1:   NumWord() Custom Function

```
'Declare variables for NumWord to use
Dim English As String, strNum As String
Dim Chunk As String, Pennies As String
Dim Hundreds As Integer, Tens As Integer
Dim Ones As Integer, LoopCount As Integer
Dim StartVal As Integer, TensDone As Boolean
Dim EngNum(90) As String

'NumWord converts a number to its words,
'Useful for printing checks.
Function NumWord(AmountPassed As Currency) As String

    'Just bail out if no valid check amount passed.
    If AmountPassed <= 0 Then
        NumWord = "Void"
        Exit Function
    End If

    'Set up the array of words for numbers.
    EngNum(0) = ""
    EngNum(1) = "One"
    EngNum(2) = "Two"
    EngNum(3) = "Three"
    EngNum(4) = "Four"
    EngNum(5) = "Five"
    EngNum(6) = "Six"
    EngNum(7) = "Seven"
    EngNum(8) = "Eight"
    EngNum(9) = "Nine"
    EngNum(10) = "Ten"
    EngNum(11) = "Eleven"
    EngNum(12) = "Twelve"
    EngNum(13) = "Thirteen"
    EngNum(14) = "Fourteen"
    EngNum(15) = "Fifteen"
    EngNum(16) = "Sixteen"
    EngNum(17) = "Seventeen"
    EngNum(18) = "Eighteen"
    EngNum(19) = "Nineteen"
```

(continued)

Listing 3-1 *(continued)*

```
EngNum(20) = "Twenty"
EngNum(30) = "Thirty"
EngNum(40) = "Forty"
EngNum(50) = "Fifty"
EngNum(60) = "Sixty"
EngNum(70) = "Seventy"
EngNum(80) = "Eighty"
EngNum(90) = "Ninety"

'** Copy amount passed to a string with leading zeroes.
strNum = Format(AmountPassed, "000000000.00")

'** Put last two digits in Pennies variable for later use.
Pennies = Mid(strNum, 11, 2)

'Set starting values for some local variables.
English = ""
LoopCount = 1
StartVal = 1

'** Now do each 3-digit section of number.
Do While LoopCount <= 3
    Chunk = Mid(strNum, StartVal, 3)     '3-digit chunk
    Hundreds = Val(Mid(Chunk, 1, 1))     'Hundreds portion
    Tens = Val(Mid(Chunk, 2, 2))         'Tens portion
    Ones = Val(Mid(Chunk, 3, 1))         'Ones portion

    '** Do the hundreds portion of 3-digit number
    If Val(Chunk) > 99 Then
        English = English & EngNum(Hundreds) & " Hundred "
    End If

    '** Do the tens & ones portion of 3-digit number
    TensDone = False
    '** Is it less than 10?
    If Tens < 10 Then
        English = English & " " & EngNum(Ones)
        TensDone = True
    End If

    '** Is it a teen?
    If (Tens >= 11 And Tens <= 19) Then
        English = English & EngNum(Tens)
        TensDone = True
    End If
    '** Is it evenly divisible by 10?
    If (Tens / 10) = Int(Tens / 10) Then
        English = English & EngNum(Tens)
        TensDone = True
    End If
    '** Or is it none of the above?
    If Not TensDone Then
        English = English & EngNum((Int(Tens / 10)) * 10)
        English = English & " " & EngNum(Ones)
    End If

    '** Add the word "Million" if necessary
    If AmountPassed > 999999.99 And LoopCount = 1 Then
        English = English + " Million "
    End If
```

```
'** Add the word "Thousand" if necessary
If AmountPassed > 999.99 And LoopCount = 2 Then
    English = English + " Thousand "
End If

'** Do pass through next three digits
LoopCount = LoopCount + 1
StartVal = StartVal + 3
Loop

'** Done: Return English with Pennies/100 tacked on
NumWord = Trim(English) & " and " & Pennies & "/100"
End Function
```

You can test any custom function you create right in the Immediate window. To test the `NumWord()` function, for example, you'd use a question mark followed by a space and then `NumWord` with some number you want to convert to words. Suppose that you type the following and press Enter:

```
? NumWord(123456.78)
```

`NumWord()` does its thing and spits back the result:

```
One Hundred Twenty Three Thousand Four Hundred Fifty Six and 78/100
```

In real life, of course, you'd most likely use `NumWord()` in a database that has the capability to print checks. Suppose that in the same database as the `NumWord()` function, you have a table like the one in Figure 3-8 that contains information for writing checks.

Figure 3-8:
Table of data for printing checks.

Payables				
CheckID	PayTo	CheckNumb	CheckAmount	DatePrinted
1	Tori Pines	1001	$1,331.47	4/1/2013
2	Marilou Midcalf	1002	$123,456.78	4/1/2013
3	Wilma Wannabe	1003	$76,543.00	4/6/2013
4	Frankly Unctuous	1004	$644.45	4/7/2013
5	Margaret Angstrom	1005	$19.37	5/1/2013
6	Margie McDonald	1006	$782.35	5/2/2013
7	Hortense Higglebott	1007	$6.23	5/9/2013

Next, you need to create a report format that can print on preprinted checks. Most of the controls on that report come straight from the table, except that you need one calculated control to print the check amount in words. That calculated control uses the expression `=NumWord(CheckAmount)`. In other words, it uses the `NumWord()` function in the same way that you use a built-in Access function. Figure 3-9 shows what that report design looks like.

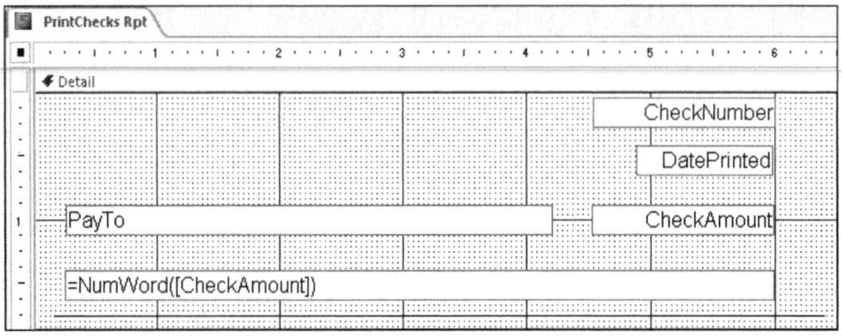

Figure 3-9:
Report
format for
printing
checks.

The tricky part is getting all the boxes on the report to line up correctly with areas on the preprinted checks, but you deal with that part in the report design. VBA is out of the loop on that aspect. The NumWord() function just saves you from having to handwrite the check amounts in words on all the printed checks.

Chapter 4: Controlling Forms with VBA

In This Chapter

✔ Displaying and responding to custom messages

✔ Opening a form with the DoCmd object

✔ Making changes in form controls

✔ Using objects and collections in code

*W*hen you create a database for other people to use, making things as automatic as possible is to your advantage. The more automated your overall database is, the less likely *users* — the people who actually use the database — are to make mistakes (even if one of those users is you!). This chapter explores some techniques for using Visual Basic for Applications (VBA) to display custom messages to users, to automatically open and close forms, to change form controls, and more.

Displaying Custom Messages

In your day-to-day work with your computer, programs occasionally pop little messages onscreen to ask you questions, such as "Are you sure you want to delete . . .?" You can click the Yes or OK button to delete, or click the No or Cancel button to change your mind. You can add similar custom messages to your database.

Displaying a message box

As we discuss in Chapter 2 of this minibook, VBA can display custom messages. By using a variable and the MsgBox() function, you can display a question and then have VBA perform some task based on the user's answer to that question. The syntax for creating such an interactive message box is

```
Dim myVar as Byte
myVar = MsgBox(prompt[, buttons] [, title])
```

The Dim statement defines a variable as the Byte data type — a number in the range of 0 to 255. *myVar* is any variable name of your choosing, *prompt* is the text of the message, and *title* is the text to appear in the title bar of the message. The *buttons* argument is a constant or sum of constants specifying the buttons and icons to show in the box, as summarized in Table 4-1.

Table 4-1   Constants Used for the MsgBox Buttons Argument

Constant	Description
vbOKOnly	Display OK button only.
vbOKCancel	Display OK and Cancel buttons.
vbAbortRetryIgnore	Display Abort, Retry, and Ignore buttons.
vbYesNoCancel	Display Yes, No, and Cancel buttons.
vbYesNo	Display Yes and No buttons.
vbRetryCancel	Display Retry and Cancel buttons.
vbCritical	Display Critical icon.
vbQuestion	Display Question icon.
vbExclamation	Display Warning icon.
vbInformation	Display Information icon.

The following example statement shows a message box that contains a Question icon and Yes and No buttons:

```
Dim myVar as Byte
myVar = MsgBox("Are you sure?",vbYesNo+vbQuestion)
```

Figure 4-1 shows the message box that the code displays when executed.

Figure 4-1:
Sample
MsgBox
message.

When someone clicks a button in the message box, the variable (myVar, in this example) receives a value. That value tells you which button the person clicked, as summarized in Table 4-2.

Table 4-2	Values That MsgBox Passes to the Variable	
Button Clicked	*Variable Receives*	*Numeric Value*
OK	vbOK	1
Cancel	vbCancel	2
Abort	vbAbort	3
Retry	vbRetry	4
Ignore	vbIgnore	5
Yes	vbYes	6
No	vbNo	7

Responding to what the user clicks

By using decision-making code, you can have your VBA procedure do something when someone clicks a button on your message box, based on the contents of the myVar variable. The sample message box displays a Yes button and a No button. If the user clicks the Yes button, myVar contains vbYes (or 6). If the user clicks the No button, myVar contains vbNo (or 7). The skeletal structure of the code that decides what to do — based on the button clicked (where Do these statements can be any number of VBA statements) — is shown in Listing 4-1.

Listing 4-1: Message-Box Response Code in Which a Constant Refers to myVar

```
'Show a message box with Yes and No buttons.
Dim myVar as Byte
myVar = MsgBox("Are you sure?",vbYesNo+vbQuestion)
'Decide what to do next based on button clicked in box.
If myVar = vbYes Then
    'Do these statements if Yes
Else
    'Do these statements if No
End If
```

You can use either the constant or the numeric value to refer to the contents of the myVar variable. The code in Listing 4-2 works exactly the same way as the code in Listing 4-1.

Listing 4-2:   Message-Box Response Code in Which a Numeric Value Refers to myVar

```
'Show a message box with Yes and No buttons.
Dim myVar as Byte
myVar = MsgBox("Are you sure?",vbYesNo+vbQuestion)
'Decide what to do next based on button clicked in box.
If myVar = 6 Then
    'Do these statements if Yes
Else
    'Do these statements if No
End If
```

If you need three buttons, you can use a `Select Case` statement to choose what to do. The code in Listing 4-3 displays a message box with Yes, No, and Cancel buttons. The `Select Case` block of code decides what to do based on the button that was clicked. (Again, `Do these statements` represents any number of VBA statements.)

Listing 4-3:   Message-Box Response Code for Three Buttons

```
 'Show a message box with Yes, No, and Cancel buttons.
Dim myVar as Byte
myVar = MsgBox("Overwrite?",vbYesNoCancel+vbQuestion)
'Decide what to do next based on button clicked in box.
Select Case myVar
    Case vbYes
        'Do these statements if Yes clicked
    Case vbNo
        'Do these statements if No clicked
    Case vbCancel
        'Do these statements if Cancel clicked
End Select
```

Message boxes are handy for presenting short messages or asking the user questions. Often, though, you want your code to open an entire form.

Opening Forms with DoCmd

Although you can access countless objects in VBA, the DoCmd object (pronounced *do command*) is one of the easiest and handiest for manipulating Access objects. The DoCmd object gives you access to all the commands — including options on all menus, Ribbon groups, and shortcut menus — in the Access program window. The basic syntax of a DoCmd statement is as follows:

```
DoCmd.methodName(arglist)
```

methodName is any method that's supported by the DoCmd object, and *arglist* represents required and optional arguments that a given method accepts.

As with any VBA keyword, as soon as you type **DoCmd** in the Code window, a menu of acceptable words that you can type next appears, as shown in Figure 4-2. Use the scroll bar on the right side of the list to see all your options.

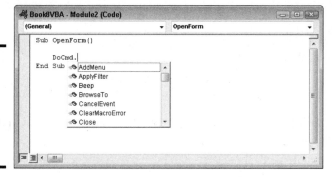

Figure 4-2:
Sample
drop-down
menu that
appears as
you type in
VBA.

You can also use the VBA help system to find more information on the DoCmd object and its methods. Type **DoCmd** in the code window and then press F1 to get help with that object.

Finding umpteen ways to open a form

Although many methods are available in the DoCmd object, the OpenForm method provides a good example. The syntax of the OpenForm method is

```
DoCmd.OpenForm FormName, [View], [FilterName], [WhereCondition], [DataMode],
    [WindowMode], [OpenArgs]
```

In this syntax,

✦ *FormName* represents the name of the form that you want to open.

✦ *View* represents the view in which you want to open the form, using the built-in constants:

  • acNormal: Form view. Use this view if you omit the *View* argument in the statement.

  • acDesign: Design view.

  • acLayout: Layout view.

  • acFormDS: Datasheet view.

  • acFormPivotChart: PivotChart view.

  • acFormPivotTable: PivotTable view.

  • acPreview: Print Preview.

✦ *FilterName* specifies the name of a query within the current database, which limits records displayed by the form. If this variable is omitted, no query filter is applied.

✦ *WhereCondition* represents an expression; enclosed in quotation marks, that specifies records to include. If this variable is omitted, all records are available. Entering a *WhereCondition* such as **"[State] = 'CA'"** displays only records that have CA in the State field.

✦ *DataMode* specifies the data entry mode in which the form opens, using one of the following constants:

  • acFormatPropertySettings: Opens the form in its default view, as specified in the form's AllowEdits, AllowDeletions, AllowAdditions, and DataEntry properties. If you don't specify a DataMode argument in the statement, this setting is used by default.

  • acFormAdd: Opens the form with the capability to add new records enabled and the cursor in a new, empty record.

  • acFormEdit: Opens the form with the capability to edit records contained within the table.

  • acFormReadOnly: Opens the form in read-only mode so that the user can only view — not change — the data.

✦ *WindowMode* specifies the appearance of the form window upon opening, using any of the following options:

  • acWindowNormal: Opens the form in its normal view. If you omit this argument, acWindowNormal is the setting that's applied automatically.

  • acDialog: Opens the form by using a fixed-size, dialog-box-style border.

  • acHidden: Opens the form so that the code can have access to the form's controls and data but doesn't make the form visible onscreen.

  • acIcon: Opens the form minimized to an icon in the Access program window.

✦ *OpenArgs* can be used to pass data to the form's class module, where other code can use it.

When you type a DoCmd.OpenForm statement in the Code window, the Quick Info syntax chart keeps you posted on which argument you're currently typing (by showing that argument in boldface). When you get to an argument that requires a constant, the Code window displays a drop-down menu of acceptable constants. You can just double-click, rather than type, the constant that you want to use.

Look at some examples of using the OpenForm method of the DoCmd object. The following line opens a form named Products Form:

```
DoCmd.OpenForm "Products Form"
```

Macros and the DoCmd object

Access macros (see Book VI) use the `DoCmd` object to carry out most of their actions. Often, you can use macros to write a series of `DoCmd` statements without the complexities of typing each statement manually. Create a macro to do whatever you want your code to do; then convert the macro to VBA code, as we discuss in Chapter 1 of this minibook. When you open the converted macro in Visual Basic Editor, you see that most, if not all, of its actions are converted to `DoCmd` statements. Then you can cut and paste those statements into some other procedure that you're writing or just add any necessary code to the converted macro.

Because no optional arguments are specified, no filter is applied, and all other optional settings take on their default values. Opening the form by double-clicking its name in the Navigation Pane accomplishes the same thing.

The following statement opens a form named `Products Form`, displaying only those records in which the `Selling Price` field contains a number greater than `100`:

```
DoCmd.OpenForm "Products Form", , , "[Selling Price] > 100"
```

The following statement opens a form named `Sales Tax Calcs` with the `Window Mode` property set to the dialog-box style:

```
DoCmd.OpenForm "Sales Tax Calcs", , , , , acDialog
```

As you can see, the `DoCmd` object offers a lot of flexibility in specifying how you want to open a form. The same is true of many other methods of the `DoCmd` object. These few examples don't even come close to showing all the variations. The important things are knowing that the `DoCmd` object exists and that you can perform many Access actions on objects within your database.

Closing a form with DoCmd

Just as you can open a form with `DoCmd`, you can use `DoCmd` to close it. The syntax for closing an object with `DoCmd` is

```
DoCmd.Close(ObjectType, ObjectName, Save)
```

Each argument in the syntax represents the following:

✦ *ObjectType*: The type of object that you want to close expressed with one of the available constants, such as `acForm`, `acReport`, `acTable`, and `acQuery`

✦ *ObjectName*: A string expression that identifies an object currently open

✦ *Save*: One of the following constants:

* acSaveNo: Closes the object without saving any changes

* acSavePrompt: (Default) Displays the standard Do you want to save... message so the user can choose whether to save

* acSaveYes: Saves all changes to the form and then closes it

If you want to close a form from code and save the user's changes without prompting, use the following syntax:

```
DoCmd.Close acForm, formName, acSaveYes
```

formName is the name of the form that you want to close. If you want a line of code to close a form named Products Form, the syntax is

```
DoCmd.Close acForm, "Products Form", acSaveYes
```

Changing Form Controls with VBA

When a form is open, you can use VBA code to change the contents and even the appearance of the form, from the big picture down to the individual controls. Suppose that you have a form that includes a control for choosing a payment method. When the user chooses a payment method, you want to enable or disable other controls on the form based on the selected payment method. Alternatively, you may want to autofill some other controls on the form or even make some controls visible or invisible, depending on which payment method the user selected.

Figure 4-3 shows a few examples. When the user selects Cash, the Paid field is marked True, and all other fields are disabled. When the user selects Credit Card, the fields for entering credit card information are enabled. When the user selects Purchase Order, the P.O. Number control is enabled, and the Paid check box is cleared.

Figure 4-3:
Enabling/
disabling
controls
with VBA.

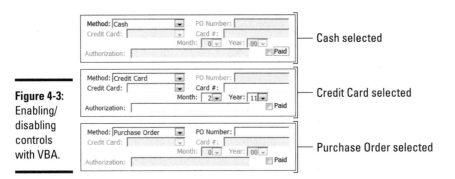

Within VBA, use the following syntax to change a control's property:

```
ControlName.PropertyName = Value
```

ControlName is the complete name of a control on an open form, *PropertyName* is the name of the property that you want to change, and *Value* is the new value for the property. A dot separates the control name from the property name. The complete name means that the name has to contain both the name of the form and the name of the control. In a class module, however, you can use the keyword Me to stand for the form name. The keyword Me means "the form to which this class module is attached."

Some cool control properties

To make a control invisible, use the following syntax:

```
Me.ControlName.Visible = False
```

To make the control visible, use the syntax

```
Me.ControlName.Visible = True
```

To disable a control so that it's dimmed and doesn't respond to mouse clicks or keyboard presses, set the control's Enabled property to a False value:

```
Me.ControlName.Enabled = False
```

To set the control back to its normal Enabled status, use this syntax:

```
Me.ControlName.Enabled = True
```

Why not just show everything?

In case you're wondering why we don't show all the methods of the DoCmd object — or all the objects, properties, and methods available in all the object libraries — the truth of the matter is that there'd be too many words. No, we're not too lazy to type that many words. Rather, there aren't enough pages in this entire book to hold that many words.

The sheer quantity of information makes remembering every detail of every VBA statement and object nearly impossible, so it wouldn't do much good to print that information here anyway. Even professional programmers spend a lot of time looking up the syntax of keywords and objects in the help system (or the Object Browser). The sooner you become fluent in using Visual Basic Editor's help system or the Object Browser, or both, the better off you'll be. See Chapters 1 and 2 of this minibook for more information on the Object Browser and VBA help.

**Book VIII
Chapter 4**

**Controlling Forms
with VBA**

To change the value (contents) of a control, set the control's Value property equal to the value you want to put in that control. Here's the syntax:

```
Me.ControlName.Value = desiredValue
```

The *desiredValue* part has to be an appropriate data type for the control. Suppose that a form control named Paid is bound to a Yes/No field in the underlying table. The following statement makes that control True, thereby putting a check mark in its check box:

```
Me.Paid.Value = True
```

To clear that check mark, use

```
Me.Paid.Value = False
```

To insert new text into a text box, use the standard syntax, but enclose the new text in quotation marks. If the current form has a Text Box control named Product Name that's bound to a Text field, the following statement puts the text in quotation marks in that control:

```
Me.ProductName.Value = "9-Passenger Lear Jet"
```

To increase or decrease a value in a numeric field, set the Value property of its control to an expression that does the appropriate math. Suppose that a form contains a UnitPrice control that's a Currency field. The following statement increases that control's current value by 10 percent:

```
Me.UnitPrice.Value = 1.10 * Me.UnitPrice.Value
```

Examples of controlling properties

Now take a look at how you might use the preceding techniques to control what happens to controls in the payment-method example shown near the start of this chapter. Figure 4-4 shows those controls on a form, in Design view, so that you can see the actual control names. The Label control, named ExpireLabel, doesn't show a name, so we point that one out in the figure. We also select that control — and show its property sheet — so that you can see its Name property and some of the other properties it offers. The property sheet for a control is how you find out exactly what properties the control offers.

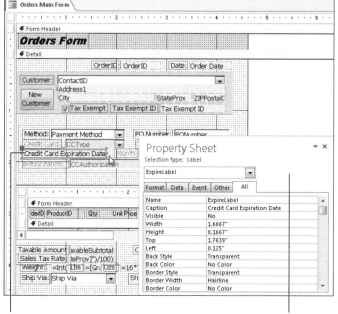

Figure 4-4:
Properties
of a form
control
in Design
view.

Selected control (ExpireLabel)   Properties of selected control

The payment-method control in the example is named `Payment Method`.
It's a combo box that allows the user to choose one of four possible payment
methods: Cash, Check, Credit Card, and Money Order. As soon as the user
makes a selection from that combo box, you want some VBA code to change
some other controls. In particular, you want it to disable controls that aren't
relevant to the selected payment method. You can also have it mark the
`Paid` field as `False` when Purchase Order is selected. Just as an example,
for this exercise, have it hide the `ExpireLabel` control when the user
selects anything except Credit Card.

So the first question is when to execute this custom VBA code. The `After`
`Update` event is the best event for this situation, because it occurs after a
new value is selected and any validation criteria for the field have already
been met. In this case, you click the `Payment Method` control (in Design
view) to select it. If the property sheet isn't already open, right-click that
control and choose Properties from the contextual menu. Click the Event tab
on the property sheet. Click the `After Update` event; click its Build button;
and then choose the Code Builder in the dialog box that appears, as illustrated
in Figure 4-5.

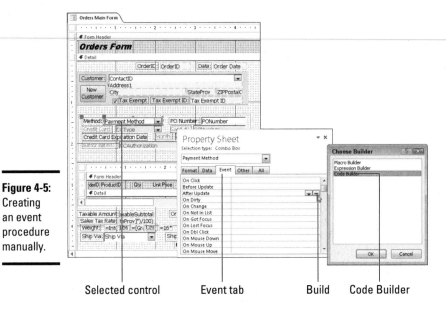

Selected control   Event tab   Build   Code Builder

Figure 4-5:
Creating
an event
procedure
manually.

After you select Code Builder and click OK in the Choose Builder dialog box, the class module for the form opens. The first and last lines of the procedure are already typed for you. In this example, the lines look like this in the module:

```
Private Sub Payment_Method_AfterUpdate()

End Sub
```

When you're writing the procedure, be sure to put all the lines between the `Private Sub` and `End Sub` statements. Listing 4-4 shows the necessary code. To make things even fancier, the listing code throws in a few `DoCmd.GoToControl` statements to position the cursor on the control that the user is likely to type in next. The statement `DoCmd.GoToControl "CCType"`, for example, means "Move the blinking cursor to the control named `CCType`."

Listing 4-4: An Event Procedure

```
Private Sub Payment_Method_AfterUpdate()
    'First, disable controls and hide the label,
    'to create a simple starting point.
    Me.CheckNo.Enabled = False
    Me.PONumber.Enabled = False
    Me.CCType.Enabled = False
    Me.CCNumber.Enabled = False
    Me.CCExpireMonth.Enabled = False
    Me.CCExpireYear.Enabled = False
```

```
   Me.CCAuthorization.Enabled = False
   Me.ExpireLabel.Visible = False

   'Now selectively show and enable controls,
   'and fill the Paid field, based on the
   'contents of the Payment Method control
   Select Case Me.[Payment Method].Value

       'If selection is Cash...
       Case "Cash"
          Me.Paid.Value = True

       'If selection is Check...
       Case "Check"
          Me.CheckNo.Enabled = True
          Me.Paid.Value = True
          'Move cursor to CheckNo control
          DoCmd.GoToControl "CheckNo"

       'If selection is Credit Card...
       Case "Credit Card"
          Me.CCType.Enabled = True
          Me.CCNumber.Enabled = True
          Me.CCExpireMonth.Enabled = True
          Me.CCExpireYear.Enabled = True
          Me.CCAuthorization.Enabled = True
          Me.ExpireLabel.Visible = True
          Me.Paid.Value = True
          'Move cursor to CCType control
          DoCmd.GoToControl "CCType"

       'If selection is Purchase Order...
       Case "Purchase Order"
          Me.PONumber.Enabled = True
          Me.Paid.Value = False
          'Move cursor to PONumber control
          DoCmd.GoToControl "PONumber"

   End Select
End Sub
```

The code and comments should be fairly easy to read. For starters, the sub procedure name, `Payment_Method_AfterUpdate()`, tells you that this code executes after a user makes a selection from the `Payment Method` control and Access accepts that change.

The first lines below the `Sub` statement disable most controls and hide the expiration label, just so that you know the status of each control before the `Select Case` statement executes.

Looks can be deceiving

When you create a lookup field, what you see in that field may not match what Access actually stored in the field. You may have a `ContactID` field that shows a customer name in the format `Jones, Hank`, but Access actually stored that person's `ContactID` as a number (perhaps `39` or whatever).

VBA sees what Access sees — the `ContactID` number in the preceding example, not the name. Any code you write needs to take that fact into consideration. To create an `If` statement that makes a decision based on the contents of the `ContactID` field, use something like this:

```
If Me.ContactID.Value = 39
```

If you use the following statement instead, the code either generates an error message or perhaps doesn't give you the result that you think it should:

```
If Me.ContactID.Value =
"Jones. Hank"
```

You can add a `Debug.Print` statement to your code and run it from the Immediate window to see what type of data is stored in a control. The following example displays the content of the `ContactID` control:

```
Debug.Print Me.ContactID.
Value
```

If that content is a number, you know that the `ContactID` field in every record contains a number.

The `Select Case Me.[Payment Method].Value` statement uses the value (contents) of the `Payment Method` control to make a decision about which controls to enable and make visible. When the `Cash` option is selected, only this code is executed, filling the Paid check box with a check:

```
Case "Cash"
    Me.Paid.Value = True
```

When the `Check` option is selected, the following lines execute to enable the `CheckNo` control, place a check in the Paid check box, and move the cursor to the `CheckNo` control:

```
Case "Check"
    Me.CheckNo.Enabled = True
    Me.Paid.Value = True
    'Move cursor to CheckNo control
    DoCmd.GoToControl "CheckNo"
```

And so it goes, each `Case` statement modifying certain controls and positioning the cursor based on the current value of the `Payment Method` control.

After you type the code, close the Code window and Visual Basic Editor to return to your form. Then save the form, open it in Form view, and try out your code.

If you have difficulty with your own code, you may find some of the debugging techniques described in Chapter 6 of this minibook useful for diagnosing and fixing problems.

Understanding Objects and Collections

Working with controls on a form or report from within a class module is greatly simplified by the `Me` keyword, which refers to the form or report to which the class module is attached. Things become more complicated when you write code in standard modules. In a standard module, the keyword `Me` doesn't refer to anything because the module isn't attached to any particular form or report. The moment you step outside a class module, you have to think more in terms of object models.

As we hope that you know, just about everything you work with in Access is an object. Tables, queries, and forms are all objects. Some objects are very much alike; tables are alike in that they all contain data. Forms are alike in that they all present data from tables in a certain format. A group of like objects forms a *collection*. All the tables within your database, for example, represent that database's tables collection.

In some cases, a single object may be a collection as well. A single form is one object in the collection of forms, but it's also a collection in its own right — a collection of controls. Each control on a form is also an object in its own right, but even a single control is a collection. A control has lots of properties, as you can see on any control's property sheet in Design view. Figure 4-6 shows that a collection is a bunch of objects that have something in common and that any given object can also be a collection.

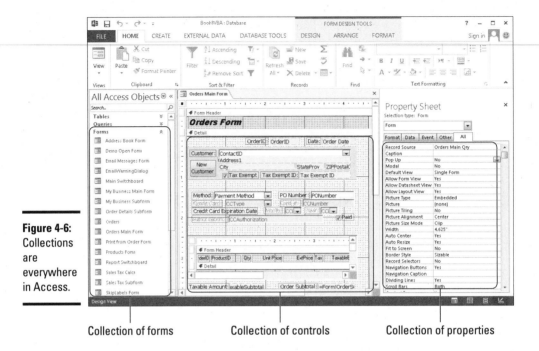

Figure 4-6:
Collections are everywhere in Access.

Collection of forms   Collection of controls   Collection of properties

Working with properties, methods, and events

All objects have some combination of properties, methods, and events. Objects in the real world as well as objects in Access have properties, methods, and events. You can describe a car in terms of its properties (make, model, size, color, and so on), methods (you drive a car), and events (you press the brake pedal, which causes a series of actions that slow the car). Getting back to Access, those terms are defined as follows:

✦ **Property:** A *property* of an object (or collection) is some characteristic of that object, such as size, color, or font.

✦ **Method:** A *method* is something that you can do to the object. Every form has an Open method and a Close method because you can open and close forms. (The DoCmd object that we mention earlier in this chapter provides access to the methods provided by most Access objects.)

✦ **Event:** An *event* is something that happens to an object. When you click a button on a form, you trigger its On Click event (or Click event).

Virtually everything in Access is an object that has properties, methods, and events. If you open a form in Design view, you can click any control to see its properties in the property sheet. If the property sheet isn't open, press Alt+Enter, or right-click a control and choose Properties from the contextual menu.

Many objects support methods. If you right-click a form name in the Navigation Pane, for example, you see a contextual menu like the one shown in Figure 4-7. Most of the items you see on the menu are methods — things you can do to the object.

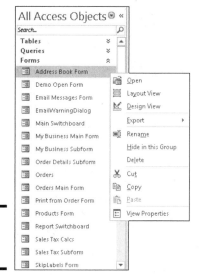

Figure 4-7:
Form methods.

When you're working in VBA, of course, the visual interactive tools that Access offers — tools such as contextual menus and property sheets — aren't visible. In VBA, you write code to access collections, objects, properties, methods, and events.

Referring to objects and collections

Manipulating an object through VBA code starts with a two-step process:

1. Declare an object variable (by using `Dim`) as the appropriate object or collection type.

2. Set the object variable (by using the `Set` keyword) to a specific object or collection within your database.

The syntax of the statements for performing those two steps looks like this:

```
Dim anyName As objectType
Set anyName = specificObject
```

anyName is a variable name of your choosing, the *objectType* is one of the keywords shown in the first column of Table 4-3, and *specificObject* represents a specific named object.

**Book VIII
Chapter 4**

**Controlling Forms
with VBA**

Table 4-3	Common Types for Object Variables
Object Type	*Use to Declare*
AccessObject	Any type of Access object in AllForms, AllReports, and other collections
Form	A form
Report	A report
Control	A control on a form or report
Property	A property of an object
Recordset	A group of records (see Chapter 5 of this minibook)

At the highest level of the object model, you can use the AllForms, AllReports, and other collections contained within the CurrentProject object to refer to any form or report — even forms and reports that aren't open. Each object in those collections has a general type called AccessObject.

For a detailed explanation of the CurrentProject object and the collections that it supports, look up the CurrentProject object in Visual Basic Editor's help system, and examine the CurrentProject Object link.

If you want to create a reference to a form named Products Form, in code, and give that form a short variable name like myForm, declare myForm as an AccessObject. Then set that variable's value to the form by using the syntax Set myForm = CurrentProject.AllForms("FormName"), as follows:

```
Dim myForm As AccessObject
Set myForm = CurrentProject.AllForms("Products Form")
```

After the code runs, the variable named myForm refers to the form named Products Form.

Naming conventions for object variables

In this chapter, we use the letters my at the start of variable names just to provide some consistency. Some programmers, however, follow other naming conventions, replacing the letters my with a tag that represents the object type to which the variable refers. If an object variable refers to an AccessObject, programmers may use obj as the first letters of an object variable name, as in Dim objForm as AccessObject. Or they may use ctl as

the first letters of an object variable that refers to a control, as in Dim ctlProductID as Control.

Naming conventions are especially useful in large projects in which many programmers work with code, because the conventions help identify the object types that variables refer to. Naming conventions are optional, though, so don't feel that you must use them in your own code.

Seeing whether a form is open

You can create a custom VBA function that uses a collection and an object variable. You can prevent your code and macros from opening multiple copies of a form. The name of this custom function is isOpen(), as shown in Figure 4-8.

Figure 4-8:
The isOpen() function determines whether a form is open.

```
Book/VBA - Module2 (Code)
(General)                                    isOpen

Option Compare Database
Option Explicit

Function isOpen(ByVal strFormName As String) As Boolean
'Return True if the specified form is open in Form View or Datasheet View
    isOpen = False
    Dim myForm As AccessObject
    Set myForm = CurrentProject.AllForms(strFormName)
    If myForm.IsLoaded Then
        If myForm.CurrentView <> acCurViewDesign Or myForm.CurrentView <> acCurViewLayout Then
            isOpen = True
        End If
    End If
End Function
```

The isOpen() function is stored in a standard module rather than a class module, so you can access it freely from anywhere in your database.

You use the isOpen() custom function just as you would a built-in function by passing a form name to the function, as follows:

```
isOpen("Products Form")
```

When called, the isOpen() function returns True if the specified form is open or False if the specified form is closed. The first statement of the isOpen() function is

```
Function isOpen(FormName As String) As Boolean
```

which defines the name of the function as isOpen, accepting a single string value that is referred to as FormName within the procedure. This custom function returns either True or False (a Boolean value).

The ByVal keyword, used in front of an argument name in a Sub or Function statement, passes the value directly instead of as a reference to the object. ByVal, although optional, can speed processing.

The next line sets the initial value to be returned by the function to False. Later code in the procedure turns that value to True if the form is open in Form or Datasheet view:

```
isOpen = False
```

The next line in the code declares an object variable named `myForm` and sets its type to `AccessObject`:

```
Dim myForm As AccessObject
```

The next line makes the `myForm` object variable refer to the specific form, based on the name that passes to the function:

```
Set myForm = CurrentProject.AllForms(strFormName)
```

If you call the function by using `isOpen("Products Form")`, the variable name `myForm` refers to the `Products Form` after the line is executed.

The next statement uses the built-in `IsLoaded` property to determine whether the form is open. If the form is open, `IsLoaded` returns `True`. If the form is closed, `IsLoaded` returns `False`.

```
If myForm.IsLoaded Then
```

If (and only if) the form is indeed open, the next statement uses the `CurrentView` property to see whether the form is currently open in Design view or Layout view. (`CurrentView` is a property of all form objects; `acCurViewDesign` is a constant that means "currently open in Design view"; `acCurViewLayout` is a constant that means "currently open in Layout view.")

```
If myForm.CurrentView <> acCurViewDesign And _ myForm.CurrentView <>
    acCurViewLayout Then
```

If (and only if) the form is open — but not open in Design view or Layout view — the following statement sets `isOpen` to `True`. If the form isn't open or is open in Design view or Layout view, the next line doesn't execute, so `isOpen` retains its original value of `False`.

```
isOpen = True
```

The rest of the procedure just contains an `End If` statement for each `If` block and the `End Function` statement to mark the end of the procedure.

To see some practical uses of the custom `isOpen()` function, imagine that you've already added that custom function to a standard module in your database. Now you want to use the function to see whether a form is open before you execute code to open that form. In particular, you want the code to see whether `Products Form` is open — and, if it isn't, to go ahead and open the form. Use the following code to open a form:

```
'Open Products Form, but only if it isn't open already.
If Not isOpen("Products Form") Then
    DoCmd.OpenForm "Products Form"
End If
```

Suppose that you want a procedure to close the form, but you want to make sure that the form is indeed open before using DoCmd.Close to close the form. In that case, use these statements:

```
'Close Products Form if it is currently open.
If isOpen("Products Form") Then
    DoCmd.Close acForm, "Products Form", acSaveNo
End If
```

In a macro, you can use isOpen() to ensure that the macro doesn't try to open a form that's already open. You can also use isOpen() to make sure that a form is open before you close it, as shown in Figure 4-9.

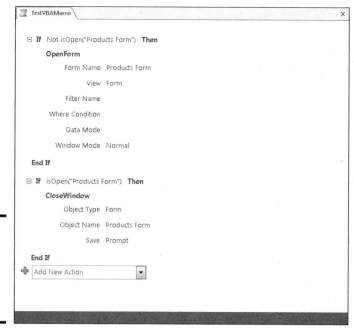

Figure 4-9:
Using the
IsOpen
function in
a macro
condition.

Looping through collections

Access provides a slight variation on the For...Next loop known as the For Each...Next loop, which is designed specifically to repeat once for each item within a collection. With each pass through the loop, the object variable used in the For Each...Next loop refers to the next object in the collection. The syntax of the For Each...Next loop is

```
For Each element In collection
    [statements]
[Exit For]
    [statements]
Next [element]
```

element is an object variable of the appropriate type for the collection, *collection* is the name of a collection, and *statements* is any number of statements to be executed within the loop.

Whether you ever need a For Each...Next loop in your own code depends on how fancy your code gets. If you use other people's code, however, you may come across an occasional For Each...Next loop, so you need to have an idea of what that loop does.

You may recall from "Referring to objects and collections," earlier in this chapter, that the AllForms collection in the CurrentProject object contains all the forms in the current database. Each form in the collection is a type of AccessObject.

TIP

The Forms collection contains only the forms that are open. The AllForms collection includes both closed and open forms.

In Listing 4-5, the Dim statement declares an object variable named myForm as an AccessObject. Then a For Each...Next loop loops through the AllForms collections and prints the Name property of every form in the database.

Listing 4-5:   Looping Through the AllForms Collection

```
Dim myForm as AccessObject
For Each myForm In CurrentProject.AllForms
    'Code to be performed on every form.
    Debug.Print myForm.Name
Next
```

Running the code in Listing 4-5 prints the name of each form in the current database to the Immediate window.

A form is a collection in its own right — a collection of controls. To set up a loop that looks at each control on a form, you first need to make sure that the form is open. Then define an object variable as the Control element type. The collection name used in the For Each...Next loop needs to be a specific open form.

The code snippet in Listing 4-6 opens a form named Products Form. The Dim statement creates an object variable, named myCtl, as the generic Control type of object. The For Each...Next loop specifies all the controls on the current form as the collection. With each pass through the loop in Listing 4-6, the Debug.Print statement prints the name of the current control.

Listing 4-6:   Looping Through the Controls

```
DoCmd.OpenForm "Products Form"
Dim myCtl as Control
For Each myCtl In Forms![Products Form]
    'Code to be performed on every control goes below.
    Debug.Print myCtl.Name
Next
```

A control is also a collection: A collection of properties defines the control's name, contents, appearance, type, and behavior. If you want to set up a loop that accesses each property that a control supports, first ensure that the form is open. With that task accomplished, define an object variable of the Property type, and use the specific control's name as the collection name in the For Each...Next loop, as Listing 4-7 shows.

Listing 4-7:   Looping Through the Properties

```
DoCmd.OpenForm "Products Form"
Dim myProp as Property
For Each myProp In Forms![Products Form].[Product Name]
    'Code to be performed on every control goes below.
    Debug.Print myProp.Name & " = " & myProp.Value
Next
```

The first line opens a form named Products Form. The next line defines an object variable named myProp as the Property type. Then the For Each...Next loop displays the name and value of every property for the Product Name field.

Using With...End With

If you need to change a whole bunch of properties associated with an object, you can save a little typing by using a With...End With block. The syntax of the block is

```
With objectName
    .property = value
End With
```

objectName is the name of an open object or the object variable name that points to the object, .property is a valid property for that object, and value is the value you want to assign to that object. Assuming that myCtl refers to a control on an open form, as in Listing 4-8, you can use a With myCtl...End With block to change several properties of that control.

Listing 4-8: Using a With myCtl...End With Block to Change a Control's Properties

```
Dim myCtl As Control
Set myCtl = myForm.[Selling Price]
With myCtl
    .Visible = True
    .SpecialEffect = Flat
    .FontBold = True
    .Value = 1.1 * myCtl
End With
```

The With...End With block changes the Visible property of the Selling Price control to True, sets its Special Effect property to Flat, sets its font to bold, and increases the value stored in that field by 10 percent.

As in the case of the For Each...Next loop, the With...End With statement is optional — not something that you must use in any code you write. Our main purpose is to take the mystery out of it in case you should ever come across With...End With in someone else's code.

Chapter 5: Using SQL and Recordsets

In This Chapter

✔ Creating recordsets

✔ Using SQL to create recordsets

✔ Running action queries from VBA code

*W*orking with data in tables and queries through Visual Basic for Applications (VBA) is — in a word — weird. You don't exactly work with a table or query directly in VBA. Instead, you work with a recordset. As the name implies, a *recordset* is a set of records. A recordset can be all the records in a given table, all the records in the results of a query involving two or more tables, or a subset of particular records from any table or query. In other words, a recordset can contain any records from any tables you want.

Recordsets and Object Models

Because Access offers two object models for the purpose of working with recordsets, you may find recordsets to be confusing. One object model is DAO (Data Access Objects); the other is ADO (ActiveX Data Objects). The DAO model is the older of the two. DAO works only with Access tables. ADO, the newer of the two, works either with Access tables or external data sources, such as Oracle and Microsoft SQL Server.

At first glance, you may think, "Well, I'll never use external data sources, so I'll stick with the DAO object model." Picking an object model isn't that simple, though. Microsoft currently favors the newer ADO model, meaning that ADO will continue to grow and get better while DAO remains in maintenance mode, which generally spells doom for a technology. If a technology is in maintenance mode today, that fact pretty much guarantees that it won't exist in the not-too-distant future.

Given the bias of Microsoft, we stick with ADO in this book. To ensure that the stuff that we do in this chapter works on your computer, make sure the ADO object model is loaded in your copy of Access. To do so, open Visual Basic Editor, choose Tools⇨References to open the References dialog box, and select the Microsoft ActiveX Data Objects 6.1 Library option (see Figure 5-1). If you don't see that option, you'll have to scroll down to find it.

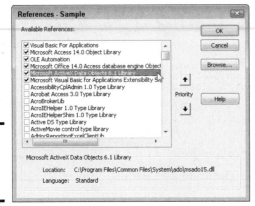

Figure 5-1:
The
References
dialog box.

Because ADO is evolving quickly, you'll likely find several versions of the ActiveX Data Objects Library in your References dialog box. Select only the most recent one — the one with the highest version number. Then click OK.

Creating quick and easy recordsets

If your goal is to create a recordset that contains all the fields and records from a single table in your database, the job is fairly straightforward. Just type the following code, exactly as shown, in a procedure, but replace *tableName* with the name of the table that you want to open:

```
Dim myConnection as ADODB.Connection
Set myConnection = CurrentProject.Connection
Dim myRecordset as New ADODB.Recordset
myRecordset.ActiveConnection = myConnection
myRecordset.Open "tableName", , adOpenStatic, adLockOptimistic
```

If you don't yet know how to type code in a procedure, see Chapter 2 of this minibook.

After all the lines execute, the `myRecordset` object variable refers to all the fields and records in whatever table you specified as `tableName` in the last line of code.

Understanding ADO recordset properties and methods

Most ADO recordsets support the following methods, which allow you to manipulate the data in the recordset with VBA code:

✦ **.AddNew:** Adds a new, blank record to the recordset

✦ **.MoveFirst:** Moves the cursor to the first record in the recordset

✦ **.MoveNext:** Moves the cursor to the next record in the recordset

✦ **.MovePrevious:** Moves the cursor to the previous record in the recordset

+ **.MoveLast:** Moves the cursor to the last record in the recordset

+ **.Move *numrecords, start*:** Specifies the number of records to move through and the starting point

+ **.Open:** Opens a new recordset

+ **.Close:** Closes a recordset

+ **.Update:** Saves any changes made to the current row of a recordset

+ **.UpdateBatch:** Saves all changes made to the current recordset

Following are some properties you can use to determine the number of records in a recordset, as well as the current position of the cursor within the recordset:

+ **.RecordCount:** Returns the total number of records in the recordset

+ **.AbsolutePosition:** Returns a number indicating which row the cursor is in (1 for the first record, 2 for the second record, and so on)

+ **.BOF (Beginning of File):** Returns True when the cursor is above the first record in the recordset

+ **.EOF (End of File):** Returns True when the cursor is past the last record in the recordset

Looping through a recordset

When a recordset is open, you can use a loop to step through each record within it. As an example, Figure 5-2 shows some code that creates a recordset named myRecordset. The While...Wend loop steps through each record in the recordset — one record at a time — and then prints the record's position and the contents of the first couple of fields in each record.

Figure 5-2:
Sample sub procedure loops through records in a recordset.

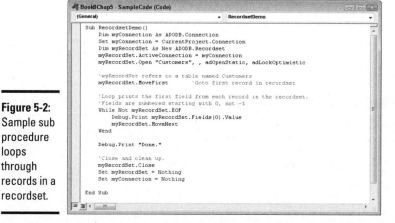

```
Sub RecordsetDemo()
    Dim myConnection As ADODB.Connection
    Set myConnection = CurrentProject.Connection
    Dim myRecordSet As New ADODB.Recordset
    myRecordSet.ActiveConnection = myConnection
    myRecordSet.Open "Customers", , adOpenStatic, adLockOptimistic

    'myRecordSet refers to a table named Customers
    myRecordSet.MoveFirst        'Goto first record in recordset

    'Loop prints the first field from each record in the recordset.
    'Fields are numbered starting with 0, not -1
    While Not myRecordSet.EOF
        Debug.Print myRecordSet.Fields(0).Value
        myRecordSet.MoveNext
    Wend

    Debug.Print "Done."

    'Close and clean up.
    myRecordSet.Close
    Set myRecordSet = Nothing
    Set myConnection = Nothing

End Sub
```

**Book VIII
Chapter 5**

Using SQL and Recordsets

The code in Figure 5-2 isn't exactly simple. The sections that follow, how-ever, shed some light on some of its meanings.

Flip to Chapter 3 of this minibook for details on `While...Wend` loops.

Defining a recordset's cursor type

When you open a table in Datasheet or Form view, you see the blinking cursor, and you can use your mouse or keyboard to move it around freely. In recordsets, you can choose among different types of cursors. The *cursor* is a pointer to the current record in the recordset. The type of cursor has noth-ing to do with how the cursor looks, because in a recordset, you can't see the cursor (or the data)! Rather, the cursor type in a recordset defines how the cursor behaves within the recordset.

You can define a recordset's cursor type in two ways:

✦ Change the recordset's `CursorType` property by using the following syntax:

`recordsetName.CursorType = constant`

recordsetName is the name of the recordset, and *constant* is one of the constants listed in the first column of Table 5-1.

You must define the recordset's cursor type before opening a recordset.

✦ Specify the cursor type when opening the recordset by using this syntax:

`myRecordset.Open "tableName/SQL", , CursorType`

tableName/SQL is the name of the table in the current database or a valid SQL statement (which we discuss in a moment), and *CursorType* is one of the constants listed in Table 5-1.

Many cursor type options are relevant only to multiuser databases. When you're working with a single-user database, the `adOpenStatic` setting is the easiest to work with.

Table 5-1		Recordset Cursor Types
Constant	*Name*	*Description*
adOpen Dynamic	Dynamic Cursor	This constant allows unrestricted cursor movement. You can modify data in the recordset. Changes made by other users in a multiuser setting are reflected in the recordset.
adOpen Static	Static Cursor	The recordset is a nonchanging version of the table. Changes made by other users have no effect on the recordset.

Constant	Name	Description
adOpen Forward Only	Forward-Only Cursor	This constant is the same as Static Cursor, but the cursor moves only forward through the table. This setting is the default if you don't specify a cursor type.
adOpen Keyset	Keyset Cursor	This constant is like Dynamic Cursor, but records added by other users aren't added to the record-set. Records deleted by other users are inaccessible to your recordset.

The .RecordCount and .AbsolutePosition properties return correct values only when you're using a Static Cursor type, which is another reason why we use adOpenStatic as the cursor type in our examples. When you're using a Dynamic Cursor, .RecordCount and .AbsolutePosition always return -1, because the number and positions of the records in the recordset may change — which could cause you to accidentally change the wrong record(s).

Using field names in recordsets

In a recordset, each *record* is a collection of fields. You can refer to fields by their positions in the record. myRecordset.Fields(0) refers to the first field in the record, myRecordset.Fields(1) refers to the second field, and so on. You can also refer to fields by their names. The syntax is

```
myRecordset.Fields("fieldname")
```

fieldname is the name of the field as defined in the table. You must type the fieldname exactly as it appears in the table's Design view (including spaces).

SQL and Recordsets

You don't have to base a recordset on a single table; you can base it on a query, if you like. You can't use the query's name in the myRecordset.Open statement, however, because only table names are allowed there. If you want to base a recordset on a query, you need to use the query's SQL statement to create the query.

SQL (pronounced *see*-quel) stands for *Structured Query Language*. You can't get very far in database management without hearing some reference to SQL, because SQL is *the* standard language for extracting information from data stored in Access, Microsoft SQL Server, Oracle, and a whole bunch of other database products.

As a language, SQL can get fairly complex. The syntax of a basic SQL statement looks something like this:

```
SELECT fields1 FROM table(s) [WHERE criterion] [ORDER BY fields2]
```

`fields1` represents a list of fields from the table (or * for all fields); `table(s)` represents the name of the table (or tables) where the data are stored; `criterion` represents an expression that filters records (such as `State="CA"`); and `fields2` represents fields to use for sorting the records. The `WHERE` and `ORDER BY` portions are optional.

Writing SQL statements

Writing SQL statements is fairly easy after a bit of practice. Don't worry — you rarely need to write them by hand. Every time you create a query by using Design view, you actually write a SQL statement. The fields that you choose for the query are the fields that get included in the recordset, although only those fields that have a check mark in the Show check box are actually included. The `FROM` table, from which you select records, is plainly visible at the top of the grid. The Sort row defines the `ORDER BY` clause. The Criteria row specifies the `WHERE` clause, as illustrated in Figure 5-3.

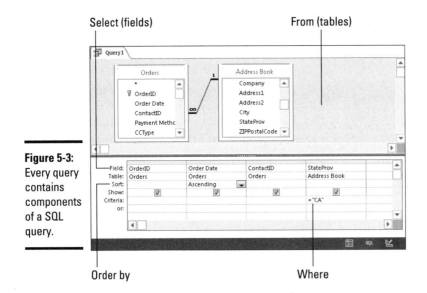

Select (fields)   From (tables)

Figure 5-3: Every query contains components of a SQL query.

Order by   Where

To see the SQL statement for any query you create, right-click the title bar or document tab of your query (in Design view), and choose the SQL View option from the contextual menu. Alternatively, click Results on the (Query Tools) Design tab of the Ribbon, and choose View➪SQL View. You see the SQL statement that the query uses to get the data specified, as shown in Figure 5-4. The SQL statement may already be selected (highlighted); copy it to the clipboard, if you want, by pressing Ctrl+C.

Figure 5-4:
Sample SQL
statement
produced by
a query.

```
Query1
SELECT Orders.OrderID, Orders.[Order Date], Orders.ContactID, [Address Book].StateProv
FROM [Address Book] INNER JOIN Orders ON [Address Book].ContactID = Orders.ContactID
WHERE ((([Address Book].StateProv="CA")))
ORDER BY Orders.[Order Date];
```

If the SQL statement isn't already selected, drag the mouse pointer through the entire SQL statement to select it and then press Ctrl+C. After you copy the SQL statement to the clipboard, you can paste it into a `myRecordset.Open` statement in VBA code where indicated by the SQL statement here:

```
myRecordset.Open "SQL statement here", , CursorType
```

Unfortunately, just pasting the SQL statement isn't quite enough to get the job done. You have to change some things in the VBA code, as follows:

+ Remove the semicolon (`;`) from the end of the SQL statement.

+ If the pasted SQL statement breaks across multiple lines, gather the lines together into one long line (or break up the line by using the continuation character, as we discuss in the next section).

+ If the SQL statement contains any double quotation marks (`"`), replace them with single quotation marks (`'`).

Take a look at Figure 5-4, earlier in this chapter, for an example of a big SQL statement. The first step is selecting the SQL statement by dragging the mouse pointer through it until you highlight all the text. Then press Ctrl+C, or right-click the highlighted text and choose Copy from the contextual menu to put a copy of the SQL statement on the clipboard.

Within your procedure in the Code window, type the `recordset.Open` statement, followed by two sets of double quotation marks. Place the cursor between the two quotation marks, as in the following example (where the | character represents the cursor):

```
myRecordset.Open "|"
```

Press Ctrl+V to paste the SQL statement between the quotation marks.

The cursor lands at the end of the SQL statement, just to the right of the semicolon at the end of the statement. Press Backspace to delete the semi-colon.

If the SQL statement breaks into multiple lines, you need to unbreak it. Move the cursor to the end of the first line. If a quotation mark is at the end of the first line, delete it. Then press the Delete (Del) key to delete the line break and bring the next line up to the current line. Leave a blank space between any whole words. Repeat this process until the entire SQL statement is one big, long line in the Code window.

Finally, look through the SQL statement for any double quotation marks. Don't disturb the quotation marks surrounding the whole SQL statement. Just change any double quotation marks within the statement

```
WHERE ((([Address Book].StateProv)="CA")) ORDER BY
```

to single quotation marks:

```
WHERE ((([Address Book].StateProv)='CA')) ORDER BY
```

When everything is clean, the Code window accepts the statement without displaying any red lines (lines with code that VBA doesn't recognize) or `Compile Error` messages.

Breaking up long SQL statements

In the preceding section, we say that to make a copied SQL statement work in your code, you have to treat it as one extremely long line. An alternative to the one-extremely-long-line approach is to store the SQL statement as a string variable and then use that variable name in your `myRecordset.Open` statement. Within the code, build the lengthy SQL statement by joining short chunks of text.

The first step is declaring a string variable, perhaps named *mySQL*, to store the SQL statement, as the following variable shows:

```
Dim mySQL As String
```

Assign the SQL statement to the string. Use the following rules to assign the SQL statement:

✦ Each chunk is fully enclosed in quotation marks.

✦ If a blank space is after a word, leave that blank space in the line.

✦ Follow each line with an ampersand (&) character (the join-strings operator), a blank space, and the continuation character (_).

✦ Use the variable name in the `recordset.Open` statement.

You still have to convert any embedded double quotation marks to single quotation marks and then remove the ending semicolon.

The following example shows an original SQL statement. (Just imagine that the code stretches out as one long line, which the margins of this book prevent us from showing.)

```
SELECT Orders.*, [Address Book].* FROM [Address Book] INNER JOIN Orders ON
    [Address Book].ContactID = Orders.ContactID WHERE ((([Address Book].
    State)="NY")) ORDER BY Orders.[Order Date];
```

The following statements show some VBA code to store that SQL statement in a mySQL string variable. The myRecordset.Open statement creates the recordset from the SQL statement.

```
'Form a SQL statement from "chunks".
Dim mySQL As String
mySQL = "SELECT Orders.*, [Address Book].* FROM [Address Book]" & _
    " INNER JOIN Orders ON [Address Book].ContactID = Orders.ContactID" & _
    " WHERE ((([Address Book].State)='NY'))" & _
    " ORDER BY Orders.[Order Date]"
'Fill the recordset with data defined by the SQL statement.
myRecordset.Open mySQL, , adOpenStatic, adLockOptimistic
```

Notice a few essential characteristics of this code:

✦ Each chunk of the SQL string is enclosed in double quotation marks.

✦ The blank space after a word is included at the beginning of each subsequent line.

✦ The ampersand and continuation characters, separated by single blank spaces, end each line.

✦ The myRecordset.Open statement uses the mySQL variable name in place of the lengthy SQL statement.

Figure 5-5 shows how the preceding SQL string looks in the Code window.

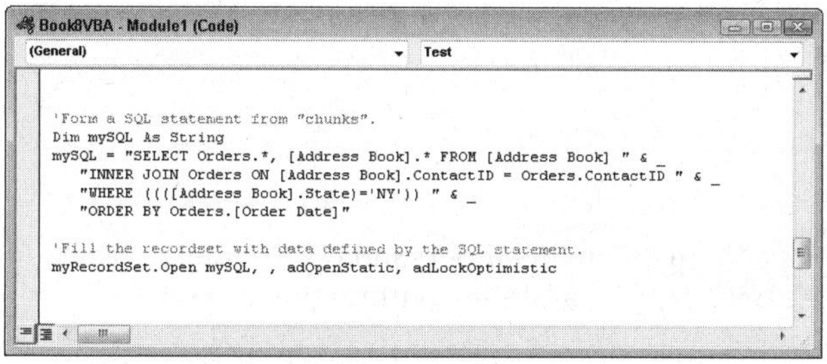

Figure 5-5:
A SQL
statement
stored in a
String
variable
named
mySQL.

Action Queries in VBA

Everything about SQL that we've discussed so far in this chapter involves *select queries* — queries that select data from tables to display but don't alter the data from the tables in any way. In this section, we discuss *action queries,* which actually change the contents of tables.

Book III, Chapter 3 introduces the update and append forms of action queries.

Creating an action query

To execute an action query from VBA, you don't need to define a recordset or use a `Recordset.Open` statement. Instead, use the `RunSQL` method of the `DoCmd` object as follows:

```
DoCmd.RunSQL SQLstatement
```

When you compose the SQL statement for an action query, follow the same rules that you do for a select query, as described in "SQL and Recordsets," earlier in this chapter. Figure 5-6 shows a sample action query to update records in Design view and SQL view.

Design view

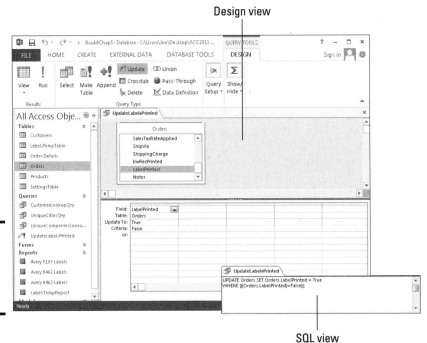

Figure 5-6:
An update query in Design and SQL views.

SQL view

In the VBA Code window, store the SQL statement in a string variable, and follow the `DoCmd.RunSQL` statement with that variable name. In the following example, `mySQL` is the name of the variable that stores the SQL statement:

```
Sub RunUpdateQry()
    'Declare a string variable named mySQL
    Dim mySQL As String
    'Store an action SQL statement in the mySQL variable.
    mySQL = "UPDATE Employees SET Employees.[Country/Region] = 'USA'" & _
        " WHERE (((Employees.[State/Province])='WA'))"
    'Run the action query.
    DoCmd.RunSQL mySQL
End Sub
```

Turning off warnings

Normally, when you run an action query (from Access or from VBA), Access displays a warning before the query actually runs, stating that you're about to change records in a table — which gives you a chance to change your mind. In many cases, though, you won't want that warning to appear. If you know that the query does what it purports to do, and you're writing code for other people to use, presenting a warning message that your users may not know how to respond to is pointless.

To prevent that warning from appearing when your code executes and to enable the query to run without asking for permission, use the `SetWarnings` method of the `DoCmd` object to disable the warnings. In Figure 5-7, the code includes a `DoCmd.SetWarnings False` to turn off permission-asking just before executing a `RunSQL` statement. Then the code turns the normal warning messages back on (`DoCmd.SetWarnings True`) after the query runs.

Figure 5-7: Code used to execute action query without warning messages.

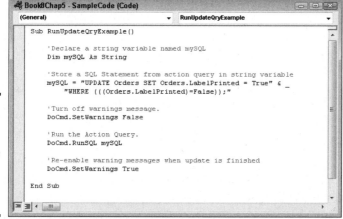

When you run an update, append, make a table, or delete a query from within a VBA procedure, use the query's SQL statement as the argument to a `RunSQL` statement in your code.

Connection Cleanup

Before your procedure ends, you may want to close both the recordset and the active connection to the local tables to prevent those objects from remaining open after your code moves on to other tasks. To close a recordset, follow the recordset's name with a `.Close` method, as in the following example:

```
myRecordset.Close
```

To terminate the connection to the local tables in the database and remove the recordset and connection objects from the computer's memory, set each one to the keyword `Nothing`, as shown here:

```
Set myRecordset = Nothing
Set myConnection = Nothing
```

So that's what SQL and recordsets are all about in VBA. Will there ever come a time where you *need* to write all this complex code to perform some task? It depends on how complex your database projects are. One thing is for sure, though: If you ever inherit a database that someone else wrote, and you come across a bunch of code with SQL statements and recordsets, the information in this chapter will at least help you better understand what's going on with that code.

Chapter 6: Debugging Your Code

In This Chapter

✔ **Identifying types of errors**

✔ **Figuring out how to solve compiler errors**

✔ **Trapping and fixing runtime errors**

✔ **Digging out logical errors**

*I*nstant gratification is rare in the world of programming. Nobody writes perfect code every time. Usually, coding takes some trial and error: You write a little code, test it, find and fix any *bugs* (errors), write a little more, test a little more, and so on until the code is fully *debugged* (free of errors) and runs smoothly every time. With the help of some debugging tools built into Visual Basic for Applications (VBA) and Visual Basic Editor, you usually can track down, and fix, any problems that are causing your code to fail.

Recognizing Types of Program Errors

Many things can go wrong in the process of writing code, especially for a beginner. Being able to identify what type of error you're dealing with is helpful. The three types of errors that all programmers have to contend with are

✦ **Compiler errors:** A problem with the code prevents the procedure from running at all. Messages alerting you to compiler errors often appear right in the Code window — such as when you type a faulty VBA statement and press Enter before you catch the goof.

✦ **Runtime errors:** The code compiles without error but fails to run properly in practice, often because of a problem in the environment. If a procedure assumes that a certain form is already open in Form view, for example, but that form isn't open, the code *crashes* — stops running — before the procedure completes its task.

✦ **Logical errors:** The code compiles and runs without displaying any error messages, but the code doesn't do what it's supposed to do.

Fortunately, Visual Basic Editor contains tools that help you track down, catch, and fix all these errors. We start with compiler errors because you have to fix them before the code can do anything at all.

Fixing Compiler Errors

When you write code, the stuff that you're writing is referred to as *source code.* Before your code executes, VBA compiles your source code to an even stranger language that the computer executes very rapidly. You never actually see that compiled code; humans work only with source code. If a problem in the source code prevents compilation, though, you definitely see an error message.

Most compiler errors happen immediately. If you type just **DoCmd.** and press Enter, you get a compiler error. The DoCmd. statement alone on a line isn't enough for VBA to compile the line. You need to follow DoCmd. with some method that's specific to the DoCmd object.

Not all compiler errors are caught the moment that you press Enter. Furthermore, code may be in your database (or project) that's never been compiled. When you call the code, it compiles on the spot and then executes. That extra step slows performance.

To compile all the code in a database (or project), both to check for errors and to improve performance, follow these steps:

1. **If you're currently in the Microsoft Access window, go to Visual Basic Editor.**

When you're in the Microsoft Access window, you can press Alt+F11 to switch quickly to Visual Basic Editor.

2. **Choose Debug⇨Compile *name* (where *name* is the name of the current database or project) in Visual Basic Editor.**

This command compiles all the code in all standard and class modules. If any errors lurk anywhere, you see a compile-error message box. The message provides a brief, general description of the problem, as in the example shown in Figure 6-1.

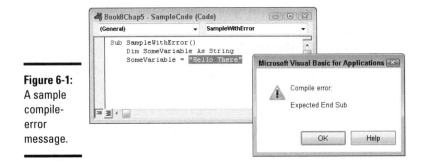

Figure 6-1:
A sample compile-error message.

The location of the error is highlighted in blue. The message box in Figure 6-1, for example, shows that the compiler was expecting an End Sub statement after the blue highlight. You can click the Help button for more information about the error, although in this example, the fix is pretty easy. Every sub procedure needs an End Sub statement, and one of the procedures in this module has no End Sub statement. Click OK to close the error message box; then type the missing End Sub statement after the blue highlight.

When you can choose Debug➪Compile *name* without seeing any error messages, you know that all your code is compiled and free of compiler errors. The Compile command is *disabled* (dimmed) because no uncompiled code is left to compile. Any remaining errors are runtime or logical errors.

Trapping Runtime Errors

Some VBA errors may be caused by events in the environment rather than in the code. Here are a couple of examples:

✦ Your code performs some operation on data in an open form. If the form isn't open when the code executes, code execution stops, a runtime error occurs, and an error message pops up onscreen.

✦ An expression performs division using data from a table, and the divisor ends up being 0 (zero). Because dividing a number by 0 doesn't make sense, code execution stops, a runtime error occurs, and an error message appears.

If people who know nothing about Access use the database that you create, the error messages that pop up onscreen aren't likely to help those users much. What you want to do is anticipate what kinds of errors may occur, *trap* them (that is, tell Access to let you know when they happen), and fix them when they occur. To do this, you add an error handler to your code. An *error handler* is a chunk of code within the procedure that intercepts the error and fixes the problem without stopping code execution or displaying an error message.

Creating an error handler

To create an error handler, the first order of business is adding an On Error statement to your code — preferably just after the Sub or Function statement that marks the beginning of the procedure. You have three ways to create an On Error statement:

✦ **On Error GoTo** *label:* When an error occurs as a statement runs, code execution jumps to the section of code identified by *label* within the same procedure.

✦ **On Error Resume Next:** If an error occurs as a statement runs, that statement is ignored, and processing continues with the next line of code in the procedure.

✦ **On Error GoTo 0:** This statement cancels any previous On Error GoTo or On Error Resume Next statements, so VBA handles future runtime errors rather than your own code.

You can use the Resume statement in any error-handling code to tell VBA exactly where to resume code execution after the runtime error occurs. The syntax for the Resume statement can take any of the following forms:

✦ **Resume:** Causes VBA to re-execute the statement that caused the error. You want to use this statement only if the error-handling code fixed the problem that caused the error in the first place. Otherwise, executing the same statement again causes the same error again.

✦ **Resume Next:** Causes execution to resume at the first statement after the statement that caused the error. The statement that caused the error doesn't execute at all.

✦ **Resume *label*:** Causes execution to resume at the specified *label*.

In addition to the On Error statements, VBA includes a helpful object known as an ErrObject, which stores the error message that pops up onscreen when an error occurs. Each of those built-in error messages has its own number and text. The ErrObject stores that number and text, so you can write code to identify the error and work around it.

The ErrObject has several properties. The two main ones, which are essential to understand first, are

✦ **Err.Number:** Returns either the number (integer) of the error that occurred or 0 for no error

✦ **Err.Description:** Returns the textual description of the error that occurred as a string

The ErrObject also supports a couple of methods whose jobs can be summed up like this:

✦ **Err.Raise(errNo):** Causes the error specified by errNo to occur. This method generally is used for testing error-handling code. (No practical reason exists to intentionally cause an error in actual working code.)

✦ **Err.Clear():** Clears all current properties of the ErrObject. (Err. Number returns to 0, Err.Description returns to a null string, and so on.)

Code created by control wizards and macro conversions may already have error-handling code written into it. Fortunately, you can easily enter such code in any procedure that you write. As a rule, you want the `On Error GoTo` `label` statement to execute early in the procedure. That way, no matter where an error occurs in the procedure, execution passes to the error handler.

The label text can be any text at all, provided that it starts with a letter and contains no blank spaces. Using the word `Err` and an underscore, followed by the procedure name and a colon, is customary. (The colon is mandatory.)

Place the error-handling code at the bottom of the procedure, just before the `End` function or `End Sub` statement. You also need to place an `Exit Sub` statement before the error handler to prevent code execution from reaching the error-handler code when no runtime error occurs.

Because you can't anticipate every conceivable runtime error, having the error handler display the error number and error description is best; that way, at least you know what caused the error. The following example shows an error message, where *[main body of code]* stands for all the code that makes up the actual procedure:

```
Sub myProcedure()
On Error GoTo Err_myProcedure
    [main body of code]
Exit_myProcedure:
    Exit Sub 'Returns control to whomever called procedure.
'Error handler starts below.
Err_myProcedure:
    Msg = Err.Description & " - " & Err.Number
    MsgBox Msg
    Resume Exit_MyProcedure
End Sub
```

The following list details what happens when a runtime error occurs while code in *[main body of code]* executes:

✦ **On Error GoTo Err_MyProcedure:** Because this statement tells VBA to transfer execution to the `Err_MyProcedure` label, execution doesn't stop cold. Instead, execution continues at the first line after the `Err_MyProcedure` label.

✦ **Msg = Err.Description & " - " & Err.Number:** This statement creates a string of text that contains the description of the error and the error number.

✦ **MsgBox Msg:** This statement displays the error message text and number in a message box with an OK button. Code execution stops until the user clicks the OK button in the message box.

✦ **Resume Exit_MyProcedure:** This statement causes execution to resume at the first line after the `Exit_MyProcedure` label.

✦ **Exit Sub:** This statement causes the procedure to exit without any further error messages.

Error-handling code by itself doesn't fix the error or allow the procedure to continue its job. If an error does occur, you see the message (text) and the number that identifies that message, so you can add code to your custom error handler to fix the problem and resume code execution normally.

Suppose that the main body of the code is trying to move the cursor into a control named Company on the current form, using the statement DoCmd. GoToControl "Company". If you run the procedure when the form that contains the Company field isn't open, a runtime error occurs. The error handler displays the message box shown in Figure 6-2. Code execution stops because nothing in the error handler takes care of the problem.

Figure 6-2:
A sample message displayed by an error handler.

The error description and number (2046) display in the error message. In this particular example, the GoToControl action isn't available because the form that the code expects to be open isn't open. The solution is to come up with a means of making sure that the appropriate form is open before the code executes.

Fixing runtime errors

One way to handle the problem is to use an If...End If block (or Select Case...End Select block) to provide a solution to error 2046. Because error 2046 tells you that a form the code expects to be open is in fact closed, the solution is to open the appropriate form, as in the following example:

```
[code above handler]
Err_MyProcedure:
    'Trap and fix error 2046.
    If Err.Number = 2046 Then
       DoCmd.OpenForm ("Address Book Form")
       Resume    'Try again now that form is open.
    End If
    'Errors other than 2046 still just show info and exit.
    Msg = Err.Description & " - " & Err.Number
    MsgBox Msg
    Resume Exit_MyProcedure
End Sub
```

Preventing runtime errors

A cleaner, more elegant solution to the problem, though, is to rewrite the procedure so that the runtime error can't possibly occur. In the following example, the procedure starts by checking to see whether the required form is already open. If it's not, the procedure opens the form before the DoCmd. GoToControl statement executes.

```
Sub myProcedure1()
    On Error GoTo Err_myProcedure

    'Make sure Address Book form is open.
    If Not isOpen("Address Book Form") Then
        DoCmd.OpenForm "Address Book Form", acNormal
    End If

    'Now move the cursor to the Company field.
    DoCmd.GoToControl "Company"
Exit_myProcedure:
    Exit Sub
Err_myProcedure:
    Msg = Err.Description & "-" & Err.Number
    MsgBox (Msg)
End Sub
```

The isOpen() function used in the preceding example isn't built into Access. See Chapter 4 of this minibook for a description of the isOpen() function.

Dealing with Logical Errors

When your code is free of compile and runtime errors, Access executes every statement perfectly — which doesn't necessarily mean that the code does exactly what you intended. If you were thinking one thing but wrote code that does something else, an error in the logic of the code occurs — a *logical error*.

Logical errors can be tough to pinpoint because when you run a procedure, everything happens so fast. You'll find it helpful to slow things down and watch what happens while the procedure runs. Several tools in Access can help with that task.

Watching things happen

You can use the Debug.Print statement anywhere in your code to print the value of a variable, a constant, or anything else. Because all output from the Debug.Print statement goes to the Immediate window, those statements don't disrupt the normal execution of your procedure.

Imagine writing a procedure that's supposed to make some changes in all the records in a table with the help of a loop embedded in your code. When you run the procedure, though, the expected result doesn't happen. You can put a Debug.Print statement inside the loop to display the current value of some counting variable within the loop, as in this example:

```
Function Whatever()
    [code]
    For intCounter = LBound(myArray) To UBound(myArray)
        'Show value of intCounter with each pass through loop
        Debug.Print "intCounter = " & intCounter
    [Code]
    Next
    [maybe more code]
End Function
```

If you run the procedure with the Immediate window open, the Immediate window displays something like this:

```
intCounter = 0
intCounter = 1
intCounter = 2
etc.
```

If some problem exists with the loop's conditional expression (the logic that makes the loop repeat *x* times), you may just see something like the following:

```
intCounter = 0
```

The preceding output tells you that the loop repeats only once, with a value of 0. You need to go back into the code, figure out why the loop isn't repeating as many times as you expect, fix that problem, and then try again.

After you solve the problem, remove the Debug.Print statements from the code, because they serve no purpose after the debugging phase is done. Optionally, you can comment out the Debug.Print statement by adding an apostrophe to the beginning of its line, thereby making it appear to VBA to be a comment. After you comment out a statement, it's no longer executed in the code. To reactivate the Debug.Print statement in the future, uncomment it by removing the leading apostrophe.

Slowing procedures

Another way to check for logical errors in code is to slow things way down to see exactly what's happening, step by step, while the procedure runs. To do this, you set a breakpoint at the line of code, right where you want to start slowing things down.

If you want the entire procedure to run slowly, you can set the breakpoint in the first line of the procedure (the `Sub` or `Function` statement). To set a breakpoint, right-click the line where you want to set the breakpoint and then choose Toggle⇨Breakpoint from the contextual menu, as shown in Figure 6-3. The line where you set the breakpoint is highlighted in red and has a large red dot to the left.

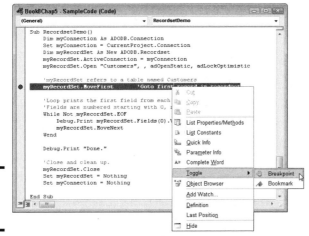

Figure 6-3:
Setting a breakpoint.

You can also open the Locals window to watch the values of variables change as the code is running in break mode. (After you set a breakpoint, the code runs in break mode, or one line at a time.) To open the Locals window, choose View⇨Locals Window in Visual Basic Editor. Like other windows in Visual Basic Editor, the Locals window can be docked to the Visual Basic Editor program window or dragged away from the window border to become free-floating.

After you set a breakpoint, just run the code normally. Before executing a line of code, VBA highlights the line in yellow that's about to execute and shows an arrow to the left of that line. You have three choices at that point:

✦ To execute only the highlighted line, press F8 or choose Debug⇨Step Into.

✦ To skip the highlighted line without executing it, press Shift+F8 or choose Debug⇨Step Over.

✦ To bail out of break mode, press Ctrl+Shift+F8 or choose Debug⇨Step Out.

Some types of runtime errors cause VBA to go into break mode automatically. You see the yellow highlight line when that happens.

While your code executes, the highlight moves from line to line. Each time an executed statement changes the value of a variable, the Locals window updates to reflect that change, as shown in Figure 6-4.

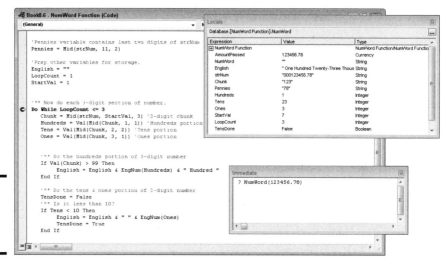

Cleaning up

When you finish debugging or just want to start over with a clean slate, do one of the following:

✦ To clear the Locals window, right-click any text within the window and choose the Reset option from the contextual menu that appears.

✦ To clear all breakpoints from your code, choose Debug⇨Clear All Breakpoints.

You can also close the Locals window by clicking the Close button in the window's top-right corner.

Book IX
Going Beyond Access

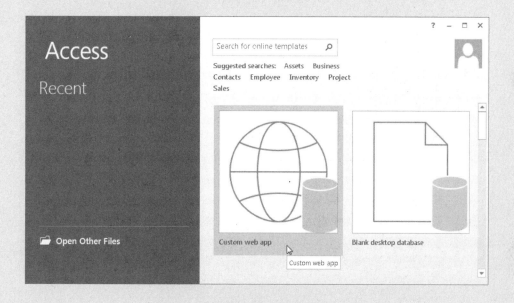

Contents at a Glance

Chapter 1: Automation with Other Office Programs **653**

Understanding Automation 653

Working with Object Libraries 654

Adding Contacts to Outlook 657

Merging Data with a Word Document 661

Exporting Data to Excel 666

Chapter 2: Using Access As a Front End to SQL Server **671**

What Is SQL Server? 671

Using ODBC 672

Finding Alternatives to Access Data Projects 682

Chapter 3: Using Access with SharePoint. **685**

What Is SharePoint? 685

Using a SharePoint List As a Data Source 686

Building a Custom Web App 692

Designing Custom Web Apps 695

Chapter 1: Automation with Other Office Programs

In This Chapter

✔ Getting up to speed on Automation

✔ Working with Object Libraries

✔ Adding a contact to Outlook

✔ Merging data with a Word document

✔ Exporting data to Excel

*I*n Book VIII, we show you Visual Basic for Applications (VBA) and present some of the wonderful ways you can take control of your Access database. You can use VBA to open and close forms, print reports, loop through tables and change data, and modify form properties.

Well, VBA isn't there just for Access. You can also use VBA to control other Microsoft Office applications, including Outlook, Excel, Word, and PowerPoint. With VBA, the possibilities are virtually endless when you consider what some advanced users do in these Office applications on a daily basis. This chapter explains Automation and gives several examples of how Access can interact with other Office programs.

Understanding Automation

Automation (with a lowercase *a*) came about during the Industrial Revolution to replace tasks performed by humans with faster, more efficient methods. Phone operators no longer plug and unplug wires manually to make connections; large systems handle connections automatically. People don't do all the work of assembling cars on assembly lines; industrial robots now handle the bulk of the duties. We humans just get in the way.

In the world of VBA, *Automation* (with a capital *A*) refers to the capability of a program to *expose* itself (make itself available) to VBA so that VBA can control it behind the scenes, with little or no human interaction. Humans just slow the process anyway. Other programming languages (such as VB.NET, C++, and C#) use Automation as well, but because VBA is the language of Access, we focus in this chapter on using VBA.

Automation with other Microsoft Office programs works only when you have those programs installed on your computer. If you don't have Word, Excel, or Outlook installed, you won't be able to control them from Access.

Working with Object Libraries

To use VBA to control another program, you need to have access to that program's object library. Each program has its own properties and methods that allow VBA to control it. Just as each object (such as a form, text box, or button) has its own properties and methods, each application — including Access — has a set of properties and methods, collectively referred to as the *object library*.

To access another program's object library, you first have to tell VBA where to find it. To add an object library to your VBA project, choose Tools⇨References in Visual Basic Editor and then add the desired object libraries, as shown in Figure 1-1.

For more information on using Visual Basic Editor, see Book VIII, Chapter 1.

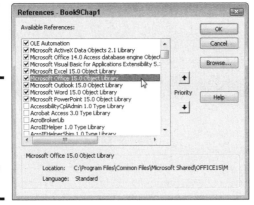

Figure 1-1:
Choose object libraries from the References dialog box.

In Figure 1-1, we chose Microsoft Excel 15.0 Object Library, Microsoft Office 15.0 Object Library, Microsoft Outlook 15.0 Object Library, Microsoft Word 15.0 Object Library, and Microsoft PowerPoint 15.0 Object Library. Selected items appear at the top of the list when you open the References dialog box, so they may not always appear in the same order.

If you have multiple versions of a program installed on your computer (Excel 2007 and Excel 2013, for example), you see different versions of the Excel object library in the References dialog box (refer to Figure 1-1). If you're sure that you'll be working only in the latest version, choose the version with the highest number. Applications in Office 2013 are version 15.0, whereas applications in Office 2010 are version 14.0.

Exploring object libraries

After adding a reference to a program's object model, you can explore that program's objects, properties, and methods through the Object Browser. To open the Object Browser from Visual Basic Editor, choose View➪Object Browser or press F2. When you open the Object Browser, it shows the objects for everything VBA has access to. To limit the list to a specific library, choose the library's name from the Project/Library drop-down menu in the top-left corner of the Object Browser window. In Figure 1-2, we chose Excel to show only the classes and members related to Microsoft Excel, and then chose Application from the list of Classes to display the members of the Application class.

For more information on object models and object libraries, see Book VIII, Chapter 1.

Figure 1-2:
Use the
Object
Browser
to view a
program's
object
model.

Each application exposes a lot of objects to VBA — way too many for you (or any sane person) to remember. We don't have enough room in this book to define every property and every method for each Office application. We'd probably need a book just for each application, which wouldn't make too many trees very happy, would it? Instead, you have to be able to get the information you need when you need it.

To find out more about a selected object, property, or method in the Object Browser, click the Help icon — the yellow question mark — in the Object Browser window (refer to Figure 1-2).

Using the Application object

Each application exposes its own set of objects to VBA, but one object that all applications have in common is `Application`. The `Application` object exposes a program's objects, properties, and methods to VBA. When a program is open, its objects are available to VBA. If VBA opens a Word document, for example, everything in that Word document is also exposed. VBA can do anything in the Word document that a human can do from the Word Ribbon.

To take control of an application, you first have to create an instance of the application in VBA. Creating an *instance* is basically the same as opening the program from the Windows Start menu. When you start Microsoft PowerPoint on your computer, for example, you're creating an instance of PowerPoint on your computer.

To create an instance of an application in VBA, you have to declare a variable that references that object. The variable can have any name you like, but you should attempt to give it a meaningful name. The syntax for declaring an object variable is

```
Dim objectVariable as New program.Application
```

For more information on declaring and using variables, see Book VIII, Chapter 3.

The *objectVariable* in the preceding example is the name of the variable. The *program* is a reference to one of the Office applications (such as Word, Excel, or Outlook). The `Application` part refers to the `Application` object of that program. The `New` keyword ensures that VBA creates a new instance of the program. Here are some examples of declaring new instances of the Office programs:

```
Dim XL as New Excel.Application
Dim Wrd as New Word.Application
Dim Olk as New Outlook.Application
Dim PPT as New PowerPoint.Application
```

After you declare the object variable for the desired program, you can control that program. To take control of the program, you must open the program from VBA. The syntax for opening a program in VBA is

```
Set objectVariable as CreateObject("program.Application")
```

where the *objectVariable* is the same name you specified in the Dim statement and *program* is the name of the application. When you use the Dim statements described in this section, the corresponding Set statements for opening the applications are

```
Set XL as CreateObject("Excel.Application")
Set Wrd as CreateObject("Word.Application")
Set Olk as CreateObject("Outlook.Application")
Set PPT as CreateObject("PowerPoint.Application")
```

To control another program with VBA, you must first add the program's object library to VBA, using the References dialog box (refer to "Working with Object Libraries," earlier in this chapter).

In the next few sections, you see how Access can share information with Outlook, Word, and Excel — oh, my!

Adding Contacts to Outlook

Suppose that you're working on an Access program, and your users suggest that it would be a good idea to give them the capability to add contacts from the Access database to Microsoft Outlook. You could be mean and tell them to type the contacts themselves, or you can impress them by adding a button to a form that lets them add the current contact to their Outlook contacts.

Adding the contact button and code

Consider the form shown in Figure 1-3. This form is a basic customer contact form that you might find in any of your applications, with one exception: the addition of an Add to Outlook Contacts button.

Figure 1-3: Changing an Access form to let users add contacts to Outlook.

frmCustomerContact			
Customers			
CustID	1	Country	USA
FirstName	Tori	Phone	555-1212
LastName	Pines	Fax	(618)555-4343
Company	Arbor Classics	Email	Tori@arborclassics.com
Address1	345 Pacific Coast Hwy	DateEntered	7/21/2012
City	Del Mar	TaxExempt	☑
StateProv	CA	TaxExemptID	323-40-4039
ZIPCode	98765		Add to Outlook Contacts

Record: 1 of 35 · No Filter · Search

Now, just adding the button doesn't accomplish much; you also have to add code to the button's Click event procedure. In the form's Design view, double-click the button to show the property sheet, click the Event tab, click the ellipsis button to the right of the On Click event property, and then click Code Builder to open Visual Basic Editor to the button's Click event procedure. The code looks something like this:

```
Private Sub cmdOutlook_Click()

  'Open Instance of Microsoft Outlook
  Dim Olk As Outlook.Application
  Set Olk = CreateObject("Outlook.Application")

  'Create Object for an Outlook Contact
  Dim OlkContact As Outlook.ContactItem
  Set OlkContact = Olk.CreateItem(olContactItem)

  'Set Contact Properties and Save
  With OlkContact
    .FirstName = Me.FirstName
    .LastName = Me.LastName
    Me.Email.SetFocus
    .Email1Address = Me.Email.Text
    .CompanyName = Me.Company
    .BusinessAddressStreet = Me.Address1
    .BusinessAddressCity = Me.City
    .BusinessAddressState = Me.StateProv
    .BusinessAddressPostalCode = Me.ZIPCode
    .BusinessTelephoneNumber = Me.Phone
    .BusinessFaxNumber = Me.Fax
    .Save
  End With

  'Let User know contact was added
  MsgBox "Contact Added to Outlook."

  'Clean up object variables
  Set OlkContact = Nothing
  Set Olk = Nothing

End Sub
```

This example may look like a lot of code, but it's really just a series of small steps. In layman's terms, this procedure creates and sets a variable for the Outlook application, creates and sets a variable for an Outlook contact, sets the properties of the Outlook contact object to values from the form, saves the Outlook contact, displays a message box, and cleans up the object variables. In the following section, we give you a detailed look at this example.

Examining the contact-form code

The first two statements below the first comment declare an object variable named `Olk` and set it to an open instance of Microsoft Outlook:

```
'Open Instance of Microsoft Outlook
Dim Olk As Outlook.Application
Set Olk = CreateObject("Outlook.Application")
```

The `Application` object for Outlook lets you create items within Outlook, just as though you'd opened Outlook and navigated through the program. The second comment and the next two lines are as follows:

```
'Create Object for an Outlook Contact
Dim OlkContact As Outlook.ContactItem
Set OlkContact = Olk.CreateItem(olContactItem)
```

These lines declare an object variable named `OlkContact` and create that contact by using the `CreateItem` method of the Outlook Application object. This code is VBA's way of clicking Contacts and then clicking the Click Here to Add a New Contact line at the top of the Outlook window.

Now look at the next block of code:

```
'Set Contact Properties and Save
With OlkContact
   .FirstName = Me.FirstName
   .LastName = Me.LastName
   Me.Email.SetFocus
   .Email1Address = Me.Email.Text
   .CompanyName = Me.Company
   .BusinessAddressStreet = Me.Address1
   .BusinessAddressCity = Me.City
   .BusinessAddressState = Me.StateProv
   .BusinessAddressPostalCode = Me.ZIPCode
   .BusinessTelephoneNumber = Me.Phone
   .BusinessFaxNumber = Me.Fax
   .Save
End With
```

The `With...End With` block of code sets the properties of the Outlook `ContactItem`. The `ContactItem` object has many properties that you can see via the Object Browser. This example uses only a few of these properties and sets them to the values from the form. Everything that uses the `Me` keyword reads a value from the form shown in Figure 1-3, earlier in this chapter.

The last few statements tell the user that the contact was added and reset the object variables.

The one tricky part of the code lies in how Access stores an e-mail address. Access doesn't just store the e-mail address as text; it stores additional information along with the e-address. So when VBA finds the e-mail address on the form, you want it to read only the text component of the e-mail address field. To direct VBA to read this property on the form, you must use the `SetFocus` method of the Email text box to make sure that the control *has the focus* — that is, the cursor is in that field.

The `Save` method of the `ContactItem` object saves the contact in Outlook. The remaining code displays a message to let you know that the contact was added to Outlook; then it cleans up the variables before the `Click` event procedure ends. Figure 1-4 shows the contact in Outlook.

The code in this section and throughout this chapter is designed to show you how to use the object libraries of other Office components. Error messages may appear for various reasons, such as null values or typos. For more information on handling errors in VBA, see Book VIII, Chapter 6.

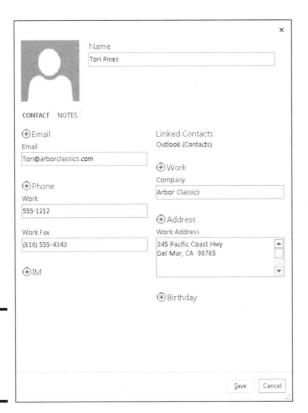

Figure 1-4:
A contact added to Outlook from VBA.

Outlook's object library exposes many more objects and methods than we describe here. You can do anything from VBA that you can do from the Outlook program, such as compose and send e-mail messages, create and schedule calendar items, and build tasks and to-do lists. To find out more about these objects, properties, and methods, open the Object Browser, and choose Outlook from the Project/Library drop-down menu in the top-left corner.

Merging Data with a Word Document

Microsoft Word is probably the most widely used word-processing program in the world, if not the universe. If you have Microsoft Office installed, you almost certainly have Word installed as well. Many people in any given work environment know how to use and edit Word documents, but they may not know how to create and modify an Access report. Using Automation, you can enable some users to edit the body of a form letter in Word and then print that letter from Access. This section shows you how.

To control Word 2013 with VBA, you must first add the Microsoft Office Word 15.0 Object Library to VBA by using the References dialog box (see "Working with Object Libraries," earlier in this chapter).

Creating a Word template

To put data from Access in a Word document, you have to tell Access where in the Word document to put that data. One method is to create bookmarks in the Word document; later, Access can replace these bookmarks with data from the database. A bookmark in Word is just a placeholder. If you do this in a Word template file (.dotx file), you can easily create new documents based on this template.

First, use Word to create a new document, and format the document however you want. You can add a company logo and other letterhead information, and type the body of the letter. This task should be pretty easy. When you save the file, choose File⇨Save As to open the Save dialog box, and from the Save As Type drop-down menu, choose Word Template (*.dotx).

Viewing and inserting bookmarks

When you get the document ready, you need to add bookmarks where you want the data from Access to go. Bookmarks in Word are usually hidden, so you need to start by displaying them so that you can see what you're doing. Follow these steps:

1. **In Microsoft Word, choose File⇨Options.**

2. **Click the Advanced option on the left side of the Word Options window.**

3. **Scroll down to the Show Document Content section, and select the Show Bookmarks option.**

4. **Click OK.**

   Now you can insert bookmarks into your Word template.

5. **Move the cursor to where you want the bookmark to appear in the Word document.**

6. **Type a short, meaningful name for the bookmark.**

   The name can't contain spaces or punctuation, and it must start with a letter.

7. **Select the text by double-clicking the name you just typed, and copy it to the clipboard by pressing Ctrl+C.**

8. **On the Word Ribbon, click the Insert tab and then click Bookmark in the Links group.**

   The Bookmark dialog box appears, as shown in Figure 1-5.

Figure 1-5: Adding bookmarks to a Word template (`.dotx`) file.

9. **Paste the typed name into the Bookmark Name field by pressing Ctrl+V.**

10. **Click the Add button to create the bookmark.**

    Square brackets appear around the text to indicate the bookmark.

For this example, create three bookmarks — `CurrentDate`, `AccessAddress`, and `AccessSalutation` — and then save the `.dotx` file in the same folder as your database.

Adding the merge button

Now that the Word template is ready to go, create another button on the Customer form that sends data from the form to Word. You might call it Send Welcome Letter, as shown in Figure 1-6.

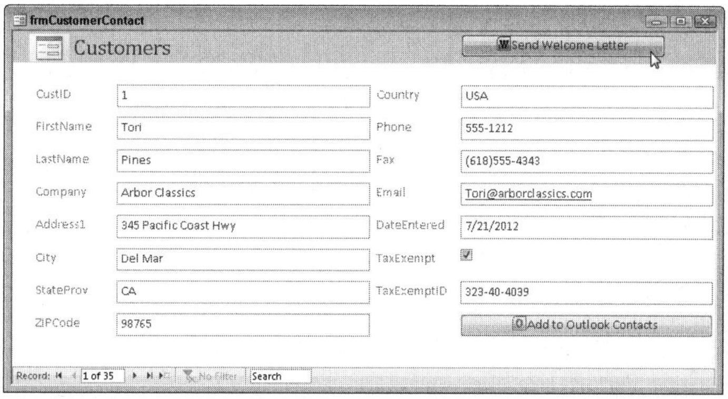

Figure 1-6:
Adding another button to send data to Word.

Entering the merge code

When the button is on the form, you can add the following code to this button's `Click` event procedure to send the data to the Word document:

```
Private Sub cmdWord_Click()

  'Declare Variables
  Dim sAccessAddress As String
  Dim sAccessSalutation As String

  'Build sAccessAddress
  sAccessAddress = FirstName & " " & LastName & _
    vbCrLf & Company & vbCrLf & Address1 & _
    vbCrLf & City & ", " & StateProv & "  " & ZIPCode

  'Build sAccessSalutation
  sAccessSalutation = FirstName & " " & LastName

  'Declare and set Word object variables
  Dim Wrd As New Word.Application
  Set Wrd = CreateObject("Word.Application")

  'Specify Path to Template
  Dim sMergeDoc As String
  sMergeDoc = Application.CurrentProject.Path & _
    "\WordMergeDocument.dotx"

  'Open Word using template and make Word visible
```

```
Wrd.Documents.Add sMergeDoc
Wrd.Visible = True

'Replace Bookmarks with Values
With Wrd.ActiveDocument.Bookmarks
  .Item("CurrentDate").Range.Text = Date
  .Item("AccessAddress").Range.Text = sAccessAddress
  .Item("AccessSalutation").Range.Text = sAccessSalutation

End With

'Open in Print Preview mode, let user print
Wrd.ActiveDocument.PrintPreview

'Clean Up code
Set Wrd = Nothing

End Sub
```

Again, this example has a lot of code, but that code breaks down into several
sections. It declares the variables you're going to use, sets the address and
salutation variables, opens Word (using the template you created), replaces
the bookmarks with values from Access, and shows the Print Preview view
for the document. The following section takes a closer look at some key
components of this code.

Examining the merge code

After declaring the string values, you set the sAccessAddress variable to
a concatenated string of values from the form. You use the line-continuation
character (an underscore) as well as the vbCrLf keyword, which starts a
new line in the string variable, as follows:

```
'Build sAccessAddress
sAccessAddress = FirstName & " " & LastName & _
  vbCrLf & Company & vbCrLf & Address1 & _
  vbCrLf & City & ", " & StateProv & "  " & ZIPCode
```

You also build the sAccessSalutation variable by combining the first-
name and last-name fields from the form, with a space in between:

```
'Build sAccessSalutation
sAccessSalutation = FirstName & " " & LastName
```

Next, use the syntax described in "Using the Application object," earlier in this chapter, to open an instance of Microsoft Word. Here's the code:

```
'Declare and set Word object variables
Dim Wrd As New Word.Application
Set Wrd = CreateObject("Word.Application")
```

After opening an instance of Word, set the location of the Word template that created earlier (see "Creating a Word template," earlier in this chapter). You use the `Path` property of `Application.CurrentProject` to get the location and then concatenate it with the filename. For this example, we named the Word template file `WordMergeDocument.dotx`, as follows:

```
'Specify Path to Template
Dim sMergeDoc As String
sMergeDoc = Application.CurrentProject.Path & _
    "\WordMergeDocument.dotx"
```

This code assumes that you saved the Word template file in the same folder as the Access database.

Next, use the `Add` method of the `Application.Documents` object to create a new document based on the template file. After creating a new Word document, set the `Visible` property of the `Wrd` object to true, letting the user see Word. When you open Word from VBA, it's invisible to the user unless you specify otherwise, as follows:

```
'Open Word using template and make Word visible
Wrd.Documents.Add sMergeDoc
Wrd.Visible = True
```

After viewing the document, use the `Bookmarks` collection within the `ActiveDocument` to add the values from Access. Replace the `CurrentDate` bookmark with the system date, using the `Date()` function. Then replace the `AccessAddress` and `AccessSalutation` bookmarks with the variables set earlier in the code, as follows:

```
'Replace Bookmarks with Values
With Wrd.ActiveDocument.Bookmarks
  .Item("CurrentDate").Range.Text = Date
  .Item("AccessAddress").Range.Text = sAccessAddress
  .Item("AccessSalutation").Range.Text = sAccessSalutation
End With
```

Finally, switch to Print Preview view, and clean up the code in Word. Figure 1-7 shows the document with the bookmarks replaced by data from Access.

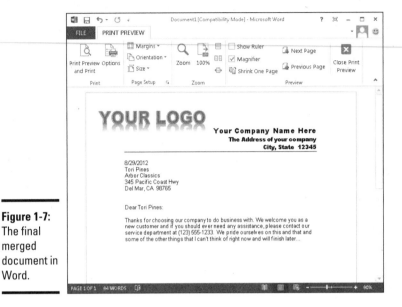

Figure 1-7:
The final
merged
document in
Word.

Just like the Outlook object library, the Word object library contains many
more properties and methods that allow you to control Word as though you
were clicking the various Ribbon commands and typing in the Word window.
For assistance on all of these commands, use the Object Browser (choose
View➪Object Browser or press F2 in Visual Basic Editor).

Exporting Data to Excel

Many Office users who are familiar with Excel just don't understand the
power and flexibility of Access, and many executives are used to viewing
and printing tables of data from an Excel spreadsheet. So even though you're
convinced that everyone in your organization (and, perhaps, the world)
should use Access instead of Excel, you'll still come across quite a few
people who'd rather see the data in Excel than open an Access database.

Sure, you can export data to Excel (or other formats) from the Export group
on the External Data tab, but that task requires one of those pesky humans
to know what to do. As a compromise, you can automate the process by
writing VBA code to export the data — and do several formatting tasks as well.

Adding the export button and code

Pretend that you're going to create a spreadsheet of phone numbers in the
Customer table. You also want to add a meaningful title that includes the

date when the phone numbers were exported. You can create a button any-where in your application to do this, so we'll just show you the code:

```
'Declare and set the Connection object
Dim cnn As ADODB.Connection
Set cnn = CurrentProject.Connection

'Declare and set the Recordset object
Dim rs As New ADODB.Recordset
rs.ActiveConnection = cnn

'Declare and set the SQL Statement to Export
Dim sSQL As String
sSQL = "SELECT FirstName, LastName, Phone FROM Customers"

'Open the Recordset
rs.Open sSQL

'Set up Excel Variables
Dim Xl As New Excel.Application
Dim Xlbook As Excel.Workbook
Dim Xlsheet As Excel.Worksheet

Set Xl = CreateObject("Excel.Application")
Set Xlbook = Xl.Workbooks.Add
Set Xlsheet = Xlbook.Worksheets(1)

'Set Values in Worksheet
Xlsheet.Name = "Phone List"
With Xlsheet.Range("A1")
   .Value = "Phone List " & Date
   .Font.Size = 14
   .Font.Bold = True
   .Font.Color = vbBlue
End With

'Copy Recordset to Worksheet Cell A3
Xlsheet.Range("A3").CopyFromRecordset rs

'Make Excel window visible
Xl.Visible = True

'Clean Up Variables
rs.Close
Set cnn = Nothing
Set rs = Nothing
Set Xlsheet = Nothing
Set Xlbook = Nothing
Set Xl = Nothing
```

As you can see, the code is starting to grow. It's not out of control, but procedures commonly grow to pages in length. Don't be afraid; as long as you break code into small chunks, it's not so hard to understand. The following section gives you the breakdown for this code.

The code in this section requires the ActiveX Data Objects Library to be selected in the References dialog box. For more information on ActiveX, see Book VIII, Chapter 5.

Examining the export code

The first chunk of code sets up the `Recordset` object with a simple SQL `Select` statement that gets the first name, last name, and phone number from the `Customers` table, as follows:

```
'Declare and set the Connection object
Dim cnn As ADODB.Connection
Set cnn = CurrentProject.Connection

'Declare and set the Recordset object
Dim rs As New ADODB.Recordset
rs.ActiveConnection = cnn

'Declare and set the SQL Statement to Export
Dim sSQL As String
sSQL = "SELECT FirstName, LastName, Phone FROM Customers"

'Open the Recordset
rs.Open sSQL
```

For more information on using recordsets and creating SQL statements in VBA code, see Book VIII, Chapter 5.

The next chunk of VBA code initializes the Excel objects so that you can manipulate them. You have three objects to declare when you're working with Excel: `Application`, `Workbook`, and `Worksheet`. By default, when you open Excel from the Start menu, the program opens to a new workbook, and each workbook contains at least one worksheet. Here's the code:

```
'Set up Excel Variables
Dim Xl As New Excel.Application
Dim Xlbook As Excel.Workbook
Dim Xlsheet As Excel.Worksheet

Set Xl = CreateObject("Excel.Application")
```

After opening the Excel Application object, use the Add method of the Workbooks collection to create a new workbook stored in the Xlbook variable, as follows:

```
Set Xlbook = Xl.Workbooks.Add
```

After adding a new Workbook to the Excel Application, set the Xlsheet variable to the first Worksheet of the Workbook object, using the Worksheets collection:

```
Set Xlsheet = Xlbook.Worksheets(1)
```

Now that the worksheet is initialized and set, it's time to start playing around. First, set the Name of the worksheet to something other than Sheet1. Then change cell A1 to a meaningful heading that includes the date, and format the cell to use a larger, bolder, more colorful font, as follows:

```
'Set Values in Worksheet
Xlsheet.Name = "Phone List"
With Xlsheet.Range("A1")
   .Value = "Phone List " & Date
   .Font.Size = 14
   .Font.Bold = True
   .Font.Color = vbBlue
End With
```

Now it's time to take the data from the Recordset object and put it into the spreadsheet. There's no looping through the recordset here; just use the CopyFromRecordset method to copy the contents of a recordset into a particular range of cell. For this example, copy the data from the recordset starting with cell A3, as follows:

```
'Copy Recordset to Worksheet Cell A3
Xlsheet.Range("A3").CopyFromRecordset rs
```

Finally, make the Excel application visible so that you can see your data in Excel (as shown in Figure 1-8), and clean up the variables.

You can add much more code to this routine to fully customize the look of the spreadsheet. You can change the column widths, change the cells' background colors, and sort the data.

If you can perform a task with the mouse and keyboard in the Excel window, you can find a way to do it with VBA.

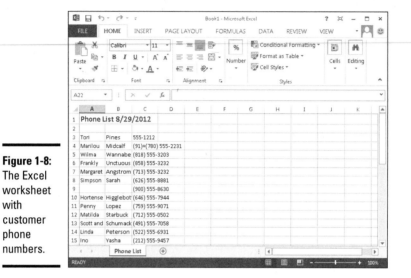

Figure 1-8:
The Excel worksheet with customer phone numbers.

Automating Access with other Office programs can seem overwhelming at first, but when you know where to find help and examples, you'll be well on your way to beefing up your Access applications — and relying less and less on other humans to perform these tasks.

Chapter 2: Using Access As a Front End to SQL Server

In This Chapter

✔ **Understanding SQL Server**

✔ **Using ODBC to connect to SQL Server**

✔ **Living without Access Data Projects**

*A*ccess is more than just a relational database; it's also a robust development environment where you can create queries to view and manipulate subsets of data, build forms to view your data in an easy-to-read format, and generate reports to print your data on paper. You can even create macros and Visual Basic for Applications (VBA) code to perform common tasks and routines automatically. The data itself, however, resides in the Access tables.

When you're building your beautiful applications, you aren't limited to working exclusively in Access. You can use Access as a front end to several data sources. In Book II, Chapter 4, we show you how to import and link to data from several data sources, such as Excel and Outlook. In this chapter, we demonstrate how to connect to and use data from other relational databases, such as Microsoft SQL Server.

What Is SQL Server?

SQL Server is a relational database management system (RDBMS) produced by Microsoft, just like Access. SQL Server was built to serve primarily as a database engine, and it has much higher hardware requirements to achieve faster performance than a database designed for the desktop, such as Access. You must purchase SQL Server from Microsoft — usually, at a high cost — to achieve maximum benefits. For large companies with lots and lots of data, the purchase is a no-brainer. For individuals and smaller companies, the cost involved will probably break the bank.

SQL Server is a *client/server* database, which means that at least two computers are involved — sometimes three, four, or a hundred. The network computer on which SQL Server is installed and running is (you guessed it) the *server;* the computers running Access (or another program that's retrieving data) are the clients. The client/server architecture allows the client computers to focus on displaying the data to the end user while the server computer retrieves, inserts, updates, and deletes data. Client/server databases like SQL Server are optimized to deal with data and perform tasks on large sets of data much faster than Access can.

The Internet is a perfect example of client/server computing. It's nothing more than a bunch of servers networked together and a bunch of client computers using their web browsers to retrieve and update information on these servers. In fact, many of these server computers use SQL Server to store data.

Plenty of client/server databases besides SQL Server are on the market, and Access can link to and import data from several of them, including Oracle, Sybase, and MySQL (to name just a few). If your organization uses any of these databases, and you need to connect to them, you'll have to talk to the system administrator and refer to the documentation for these databases to gain access to the servers.

Using ODBC

ODBC (*Open Database Connectivity,* for short) is a standard method for communicating with a database management system. ODBC was created to allow programs to communicate with different databases regardless of the manufacturer or the construction of the database engine. Think of ODBC as being a translator that speaks many languages. Access has to know one language, and ODBC talks to the other databases.

Access uses ODBC to connect to a variety of data sources, including dBASE, Excel, Paradox, Visual FoxPro, Oracle, and (of course) SQL Server. After Access connects to these data sources, it can communicate with all of them in the same way, all because of ODBC.

Connecting to SQL Server with ODBC

We could spend all day writing about client/server computing and the intricacies of the ODBC architecture, such as how it allows programmers to add drivers for databases that aren't currently supported. Honestly, though, you don't need to know any of that to use ODBC to connect to a SQL Server database. Sure, it helps to know a little bit about these topics, but you don't have to be an expert.

To connect to a SQL Server database, click the ODBC Database button in the Import & Link group on the External Data tab of the Ribbon, as shown in Figure 2-1.

Downloading SQL Server Express Edition

If you have access to a full-blown version of Microsoft SQL Server, or if one is running in your company (or basement) already, consider yourself lucky. But if you're trying to get familiar with SQL Server and haven't hit the lottery lately, you can download a scaled-down version for free. This version slices and dices just like the full version of SQL Server, but it has a

database-size limitation. As of this printing, you can download it at www.microsoft.com/express/database.

Alternatively, because Microsoft likes to change its URLs more often than gas stations change their prices, you can just do an Internet search for *SQL Server Express download.*

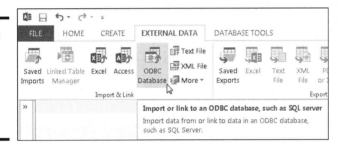

Figure 2-1:
Linking to an ODBC database from the Access Ribbon.

When the Get External Data – ODBC Database dialog box opens, Access gives you two choices: import or link to the data. Because you're using Access as a front end to manipulate data in SQL Server, select the option to link to the data source (as shown in Figure 2-2), and click OK. If you import the data, you'll get a snapshot of the data at the time you performed the import, and any changes you make won't be reflected in SQL Server.

For further assistance on when to import data and when to link to data in another data source, see Book II, Chapter 4.

Next, the Select Data Source dialog box opens, as shown in Figure 2-3. This dialog box lets you choose an existing ODBC data source or create a new one. After you create a connection to a particular database, it appears in the list. If you're connecting to a data source for the first time, you have to create a new data source.

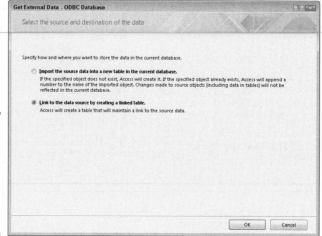

Figure 2-2:
Select the
Link To
option when
you're using
Access as a
front end.

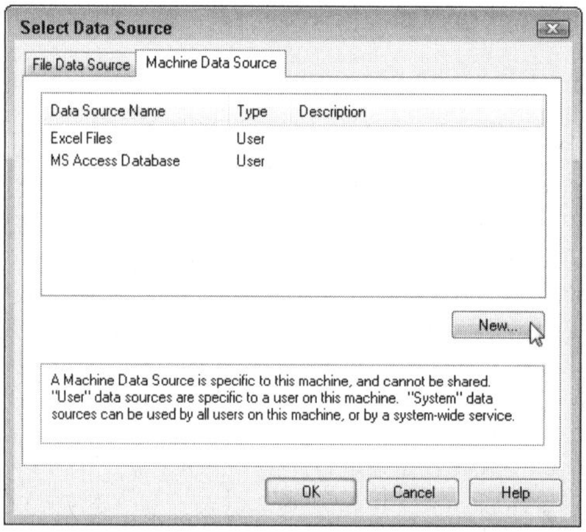

Figure 2-3:
Create or
select a
data source.

You can create a *file data source,* which is a file that can be shared with other computers and may reside somewhere on your company's network, or you can create a *machine data source,* which is specific to the computer you're working on. If you're using the data source only on your computer, creating a machine data source is the better option. Follow these steps to create your data source:

1. **Click the Machine Data Source tab of the Select Data Source dialog box (refer to Figure 2-3) and then click the New button below the list of data sources to open the Create New Data Source dialog box.**

This dialog box lets you create a *user data source,* which can be used only by the current user, or a *system data source,* which can be used by any users of the machine. If many users log in to this computer, creating a system data source is the better option because you won't have to create one for each user.

To create a system data source, you must be logged in to the computer with administrative rights. If you don't have administrative rights, you won't be allowed to create a system data source.

2. **Select User Data Source or System Data Source and then click Next to display the list of ODBC drivers, as shown in Figure 2-4.**

   The list contains all the available ODBC drivers installed on your computer. Some may appear to be in other languages, such as Spanish or German.

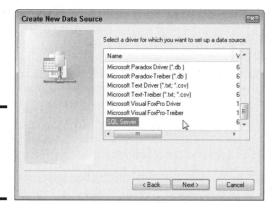

Figure 2-4:
Select the
correct
ODBC
driver.

If you're connecting to a database and don't see a specific driver in the list, you may have to download and install it. Search the Internet for your database, entering the phrase *ODBC driver* after the database name (*Oracle ODBC driver, MySQL ODBC driver,* and so on).

3. **Scroll down and click the SQL Server driver, and then click Next to display the confirmation page for creating a new data source.**

4. **Click Finish to start another wizard for configuring the SQL Server data source (see Figure 2-5).**

Figure 2-5:
Enter the
user-friendly
name and
the SQL
Server
name.

5. **Enter a name, description, and server for the data source.**

   Specifically, fill out the following fields:

   • *Name:* Enter whatever name you want to give the data source. The
     name you enter here is what Access will use to refer to the ODBC
     connection. (Keeping the name short and memorable is helpful, in
     case you need to create it on another computer.)

   • *Description:* Type something more descriptive than just the name so
     that later, you'll know what the data source connects to. You might
     enter a description like *Contact Database on SERVER1,* for example.

   • *Server:* In this field, enter the pertinent server name or IP address,
     followed by the name of the server you want to connect to. If you
     don't know the address or name of the server, contact the database
     administrator for help.

   If your network has registered servers, you can simply choose one from
   the Server drop-down menu.

6. **When you finish filling out these fields, click Next to display a screen
   that lets you configure how you log in to the server (see Figure 2-6).**

7. **Make one of the following choices and then click Next:**

   • *With Windows NT Authentication Using the Network Login ID:* Choose
     this option if the username and password for the server match the
     username and password you use to log in to your computer.

   • *With SQL Server Authentication Using a Login ID and Password Entered
     by the User:* Choose this option if you have a separate username and
     password for SQL Server. If you choose this option, enter the login ID
     and password at the bottom of the dialog box.

   When you click Next, you see a slew of additional options for connecting to the server, as shown in Figure 2-7. The only option you need to be
   concerned with is the first one.

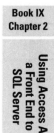

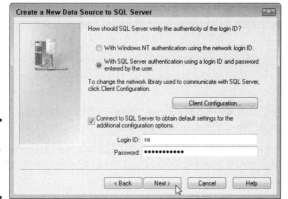

Figure 2-6:
Choose how
to log in to
SQL Server.

Figure 2-7:
Selecting
the default
database.

8. Select the Change the Default Database To check box, choose the desired database from the drop-down menu, and then click Next.

If you'd like to find out about the other options that are available, click the Help button.

If you click Next, and the wizard won't let you continue because your server name is wrong or the login fails, make sure that you've typed everything correctly. If so, check with your system administrator to make sure that you have the necessary login rights.

9. In the next screen of options, make any changes you want or accept the default settings; then click Finish.

Usually, the default settings on this page of the wizard are okay, but if you want to know more about these options, click the Help button.

The ODBC Microsoft SQL Server Setup confirmation dialog box appears, displaying the settings that you've entered over the past few minutes.

10. At the bottom of the dialog box, click the Test Data Source button to make sure that all the settings, login IDs, and passwords are entered correctly.

If you click this button and see the message TESTS COMPLETED SUCCESSFULLY!, you did a good job. If not, go back and tweak your settings.

11. When you have a successful connection, click OK in the ODBC Microsoft SQL Server Setup dialog box.

You're taken back to the initial Select Data Source dialog box (refer to Figure 2-3, earlier in this chapter); this time, the data source you created appears.

12. Select your new data source, and click OK.

Just when you thought that no more windows would appear, you're prompted to log in to SQL Server again. If you're one of the lucky ones using Windows NT Authentication, you get to skip ahead to Step 14.

13. If you're using SQL Server Authentication as described earlier in Step 7, enter the login ID and the password, and click OK.

The Link Tables dialog box appears, as shown in Figure 2-8. This dialog box is where you select which tables to link to. The dialog box also lists a bunch of system tables that you normally don't see; you can ignore these tables.

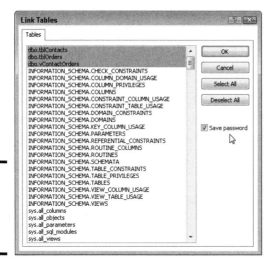

Figure 2-8:
Selecting tables and views to link to.

14. **Select the tables you want to link to.**

You can click the Select All button to select all the tables, but if you have a lot of tables to select and don't want to use all the system tables, forget about using the Shift key to select a range. Instead, click the first table you want to select; then alternate pressing the down-arrow key and the spacebar until you reach the last table you want to link to.

In addition to seeing the tables from SQL Server, you see the views. A *view* in SQL Server is the same as a select query in Access; it just returns data. When you link to a view in SQL Server, that view appears as a table in Access. Opening a SQL Server view in Design view shows you only the list of fields, not the criteria or source tables.

15. **(Optional) Select the Save Password check box if you want Access to remember the password when you connect.**

If you leave this check box deselected, users of the database will have to know the password to log in to SQL Server. Consider the security and sensitivity of the data when you set this option. If you choose to save the password, Access lets you know that it cannot encrypt the password and gives you the option to change your mind.

16. **Click OK.**

Access begins linking to the tables in SQL Server that you selected in Step 14.

You may be prompted to select a unique identifier for some of the tables, particularly if the view is an SQL Server view. Just click the unique identifier for each table, and you're on your way.

When Access is done linking to the tables, they appear in the Navigation Pane, as shown in Figure 2-9. Instead of the table icons that you're used to seeing, each table has an icon with an arrow, indicating that the table is linked.

Figure 2-9:
SQL Server
tables and
views in the
Navigation
Pane.

If you don't see arrows in the icons next to the table names, you probably chose to import the tables instead of linking to them. No problem — just delete the tables, click the ODBC Database button in the Import & Link group on the External Data tab of the Ribbon, and start over (unless, of course, you meant to import the tables).

When you attach a table from an ODBC data source, Access adds a prefix to the table's name, which is dbo_ by default (short for database owner). This prefix indicates the owner of the table in SQL Server. If you don't want to see the SQL tables with the prefix, simply right-click the table, choose Rename from the contextual menu, and give the linked table a new name.

Using linked tables in Access

Now that you have these tables from SQL Server appearing inside Access, what do you do with them? Well, you use them just as you use any other local tables in Access. You can build queries, forms, reports, macros, and modules that reference these tables, just as you do in the other eight minibooks.

The main difference is that you can't alter the structure of a linked table. If you need to add a field or change a field size, you have to log in to SQL Server to perform that operation.

You can mix and match tables in your Access database. To see how this process works, create a few local tables for data that doesn't need to be on the server, connect to a several different databases, and gain access to the data from one .accdb file. The possibilities are endless when you know where all this data resides.

Maintaining linked tables

Different things can cause the links to an ODBC database to break. The server may change locations, someone may change the structure of the SQL Server table or database, or you may move the .accdb file to another machine. Whatever the reason, if the link is broken, you'll know: The tables won't display any data, or you get an error when opening a linked table.

To fix this problem, click the Linked Table Manager button in the Import & Link group on the External Data tab of the Ribbon, select all the linked tables, select the Always Prompt for New Location check box in the bottom-left corner of the dialog box, and then click OK. The Select Data Source dialog box opens (refer to Figure 2-3, earlier in this chapter). Select the existing data source or create a new data source to correct the problem.

For more information on using the Linked Table Manager, see Book II, Chapter 4.

ODBC allows you to use data from any number of data sources, including SQL Server. Just one simple button on the Ribbon opens your world and a variety of options. Whether you're in a small company with one server or a large organization with multiple servers around the world, you can use Access to connect to these databases and build eye-catching front-end applications to view and manipulate this data.

Using pass-through queries

Pass-through queries let you send commands directly to an ODBC database server. By using a pass-through query, you work directly with the server tables instead of having the Microsoft Jet Database Engine process the data. Sometimes, however, the Jet Database Engine can't process the information or criteria you're entering in the query window. A pass-through query lets you interact directly with SQL Server (or any other ODBC-linked database).

To create a pass-through query, click the Query Design button in the Queries group on the Create tab of the Ribbon. When the Show Table dialog box appears, click Close without selecting any tables. Then click the Pass-Through button in the Query Type group on the (Query Tools) Design tab of the Ribbon, as shown in Figure 2-10.

Figure 2-10:
Creating a pass-through query.

Access gets rid of the fancy query-builder interface and shows you a blank area where you can type any SQL statement you want. You must know the native syntax of SQL Server (or the ODBC database you're working with) to have a successful result.

The following example SQL Select statement shows all the records from the SQL table `tblContacts` in which the `LastName` field starts with `J`:

```
SELECT * FROM tblContacts WHERE LastName Like 'J%'
```

Notice that this query uses the name of the table from SQL Server, not the name assigned in the Access Navigation Pane. Because SQL Server processes this query, it doesn't care what you called the query in Access. Also, instead of using an asterisk (*) for a wildcard character, this query uses a percent sign (%). Again, because the query gets passed through directly to SQL Server, you must use the syntax that SQL Server recognizes.

To run a pass-through query, simply click the Run button in the Results group of the (Query Tools) Design ribbon.

If you typed the same SQL statement in a non–pass-through query, the Access equivalent would be

```
SELECT * FROM dbo_tblContacts WHERE LastName Like 'J*'
```

In the preceding Access example, you must use the table name as it appears in the Navigation Pane — with the dbo_ prefix. This query wouldn't work as a pass-through query, because dbo_tblContacts doesn't exist on the server.

When you're using pass-through queries, always type the SQL statement with the syntax that the ODBC data source recognizes. Also, use the table names as they appear on the server.

Finding Alternatives to Access Data Projects

If you're a user of Access 2000 through 2010, you may be familiar with *Access Data Project* (ADP) files — Access data files that provide access to SQL Server databases. Access 2013 drops support for the ADP format, and Microsoft recommends one of the following alternatives:

+ **Continue using the same version of Access.** ADPs continue to work in earlier versions of Access. They won't work, however, with newer versions of SQL Server such as SQL Server 2012 and SQL Server Azure.

  If you upgrade (or your organization upgrades) to versions of SQL Server newer than your current version of Access knows about, your ADPs will no longer function properly.

+ **Convert to an Access Custom Web App.** In Access 2013, you can import your tables into a new Access app, and Access automatically creates forms for your application. You can extend the functionality of the base forms that Access creates for you so that other people can use your application on the web. Although some of the functionality that you use in ADPs may no longer be available, expect Microsoft to continue to focus improvements in the product on this application type.

  Book IX, Chapter 3 covers Custom Web Apps.

+ **Convert to a linked desktop database.** Access 2013 continues to support creating desktop databases in .accdb file format. You can convert your application to the .accdb format — including all your existing forms and reports — and leave the data in SQL Server. Then you can link to the SQL Server database by using linked tables, and your application will continue to operate.

For more information on using linked tables in an Access database, see "Using ODBC," earlier in this chapter.

✦ **Create a hybrid application.** If your application is large, and you don't want to convert everything at the same time, you can import your data into an Access app and link to the SQL Server database from an .accdb file. This method allows you to migrate gradually, adding forms and functionality to your Access app over time while maintaining your client application as an .accdb file with tables linked to the SQL Server database behind the Access app.

✦ **Upgrade to the .NET Framework.** Your application may be complex enough for you to consider moving to a more robust development platform, such as the .NET Framework. SQL Server is designed to make it easy for you to use the database infrastructure you've already created and extend the functionality of your application without having to significantly rewrite your code.

When you're working with data from SQL Server (or another data source), the data is coming from somewhere other than Access. After you establish the connection to the server and the database, you can build the rest of your Access objects — forms, reports, macros, and modules — to create a robust front end to a SQL Server database.

Chapter 3: Using Access with SharePoint

In This Chapter

✓ **Understanding SharePoint**

✓ **Getting data from a SharePoint list**

✓ **Creating a Custom Web App**

*U*nless you've been living under a rock for the past 20 years, you're probably aware of the Internet — the all-encompassing network of information at your fingertips. The popularity of the Internet has soared more than anyone can imagine. Twenty years ago, did you think that parents and grandparents would ever need a reason to have computers in their houses? This change is due mainly to the convenience of e-mail and social networking sites like Facebook and Twitter — and let's not leave out shopping!

But what does the Internet mean to Microsoft Access? Until recently, it hasn't meant too much to Access users. With SharePoint, however, Microsoft built — and continues to enhance — a wonderful collaborative tool for sharing information with users around the world. Access takes advantage of this information in some interesting, yet limited, ways. In this chapter, we explore using this information from Access, as well as creating a rich user interface for use on a SharePoint site.

What Is SharePoint?

According to Microsoft, *SharePoint* — the short name for *Microsoft Office SharePoint Server* — is "an integrated suite of server capabilities that can help improve organizational effectiveness by providing comprehensive content management and enterprise search, accelerating shared business processes, and facilitating information-sharing across boundaries for better business insight. Additionally, this collaboration and content management server provides IT professionals and developers with the platform and tools they need for server administration, application extensibility, and interoperability."

Huh? Basically, SharePoint is another product from Microsoft that some IT person must set up and administer so that its users can access information stored on that server. SharePoint allows you to set up lists of contacts and other information, create calendars, share documents, and have discussions on a message-board–style interface. SharePoint is Microsoft's vision for sharing information, and Access is fully capable of using SharePoint to share and manage this information.

To use SharePoint, you must have access to a SharePoint server. If you work for a medium-size to large organization, chances are good that the organization uses one or more SharePoint servers for collaboration. If not — and if you can't afford the cost of installing and maintaining your own SharePoint server — you can rent one from a SharePoint hosting site. Just open your favorite Internet browser and search for *SharePoint hosting;* then get out your credit card, and start sharing.

Using a SharePoint List As a Data Source

A *SharePoint list* is a table in which SharePoint stores its data. Just like an Access table, a SharePoint list contains columns or fields that define the items and rows that house the information. From the Access interface, you can create new lists on a SharePoint server or link to an existing list.

Creating a new SharePoint list

If you want to create a SharePoint list on the server — one that the SharePoint administrators and developers didn't already create — you can do so from within Access. To create a new SharePoint list, follow these steps:

1. **Click the SharePoint Lists button in the Tables group on the Create tab of the Ribbon.**

Access displays a drop-down menu of choices, as shown in Figure 3-1.

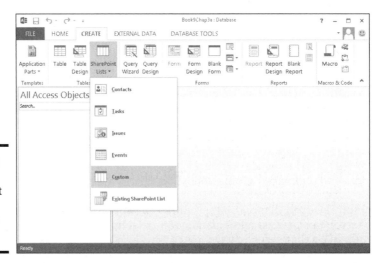

Figure 3-1: Using SharePoint lists from the Create tab.

SharePoint allows you to choose from five types of lists:

- *Contacts:* Create a contacts list when you want to manage information about people with whom your team works, such as customers and partners.

- *Tasks:* Create a tasks list when you want to track a group of work items that you or your team members need to complete.

- *Issues:* Create an issues list when you want to manage issues or problems. You can assign, prioritize, and follow the progress of issues from start to finish.

- *Events:* Create an events list when you want a calendar-based view of upcoming meetings, deadlines, and other important events.

- *Custom:* Create a custom list when you want to specify your own columns.

Each of these five options walks you through the steps of creating a new SharePoint list. (We discuss the menu's sixth option — Existing SharePoint List — in "Linking to an existing SharePoint list," later in this chapter.) If you choose Contacts, the Create New List dialog box for a Contacts list appears, as shown in Figure 3-2.

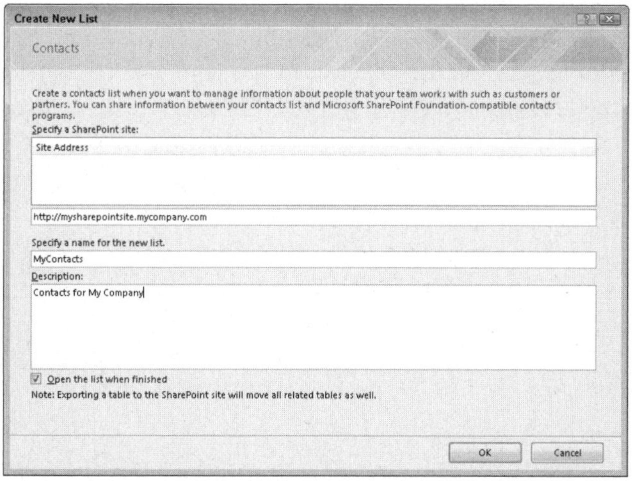

Figure 3-2:
Creating
a new
Contacts
list.

2. In the Specify a SharePoint Site text box, type the address of the SharePoint server.

This address typically looks like the URL of an Internet site. You need to get this information from your SharePoint administrator or your SharePoint hosting site.

After you specify a site in Access, it appears in the Site Address list of the Create dialog box whenever you create and manage a list.

3. **In the Specify a Name for the New List text box, type a name for the list.**

   If you're creating a catalog of products for your company, for example, you might give the list a name such as Catalog.

4. **Enter a description of the new list.**

   Don't be too wordy, but type something that will be meaningful to others who use this new list.

5. **Select the Open the List When Finished check box if you'd like Access to open the list after you create it, or deselect the check box if you want to create the list without opening it afterward.**

6. **After you enter all the information for the new list, click OK.**

   Access shows a login screen for the SharePoint server you specified in Step 2.

   Depending on the configuration of your SharePoint site, you may have to log in to your site before you can continue.

7. **If prompted, enter the username and password for this SharePoint site and then click OK.**

   If you selected the Open the List When Finished option in Step 5, the new list appears in the Access window, and a linked table appears in the Navigation Pane, as shown in Figure 3-3.

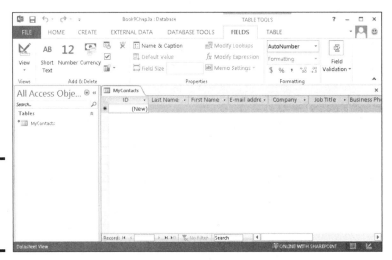

Figure 3-3:
The new SharePoint list in Access.

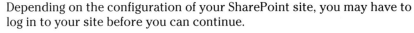

After you create the SharePoint list from Access, you can add and modify data just as you would with any other local or linked table. The changes you make will be accessible to anyone else who has access to the SharePoint site.

To make changes in the design of the SharePoint list, right-click the table name in the Navigation Pane and choose More Options⇨Modify Columns and Settings from the contextual menu. The Customize page on the SharePoint site loads in a new browser window, in which you can use the SharePoint tools to modify the list's structure.

Linking to an existing SharePoint list

If your SharePoint site already contains lists (usually created by a SharePoint administrator or developer) that you want to get information from and make changes in, you want to link to those SharePoint lists. To link to an existing SharePoint list, follow these steps:

1. **Click the SharePoint Lists button in the Tables group on the Create tab on the Ribbon (refer to Figure 3-1, earlier in this chapter).**

2. **Choose Existing SharePoint List from the drop-down menu.**

    The Get External Data – SharePoint Site Wizard loads.

3. **Enter or choose a SharePoint site at the top of the first screen.**

    As with linking to other external data sources, you're prompted to import the data into your database or link to the data source in a linked table. If you import the data, you get a snapshot of the list at the time you perform the import, and any changes you make won't be reflected on the SharePoint server. If you choose to link to the data source, you see the data that other users enter and modify — and they see your changes too.

    For further assistance on when to import data and when to link to data in another data source, see Book II, Chapter 4.

4. **Click Next to display the list of SharePoint lists to link to (as shown in Figure 3-4) or import.**

5. **Click the check box to the left of each list that you want to link to and then click OK in the bottom-right corner of the screen.**

    The SharePoint lists that you chose to link to appear in the Access Navigation Pane as linked tables, just as they appear in Figure 3-3, earlier in this chapter. If you chose to import the lists, the data is stored in local Access tables, and the standard Access table icon (without an arrow) appears next to the table names.

Figure 3-4:
Choosing
the
SharePoint
lists to
link to.

You may notice that when you create a new list or link to an existing list, some other linked tables appear in the Access Navigation Pane. If these lists are linked in SharePoint, they also need to be part of the Access database that's manipulating them. So don't be alarmed if you see linked tables that you didn't create or select. Access is smart enough to know that you need them; it just brings these lists along for the ride and shows them as linked tables.

Moving an existing database to SharePoint

If you've already taken the time to build an Access database with tables, queries, forms, and reports that all work together and are automated with modules and macros, you don't have to reinvent the wheel in SharePoint. Access provides a tool that moves your existing tables to SharePoint and links them to the Access database.

To move your database to a SharePoint site, follow these steps:

1. **Click the SharePoint button in the Move Data group on the Database Tools tab of the Ribbon.**

   The Export Tables to SharePoint Wizard launches.

2. **In the first wizard screen, enter the SharePoint site where you'll place these tables as SharePoint lists.**

   If you've used your SharePoint site before, the address appears in the list of available sites. If you're moving these tables to a site that's not in the list, type the new site information in the provided text box.

3. **Click Next.**

If SharePoint requires additional authentication, you're prompted for the login information for the SharePoint site.

Depending on the configuration of your SharePoint site, you may have to log in to your site before you can continue.

4. **If prompted, enter your username and password, and click OK.**

Access creates the SharePoint lists, moves the data from Access to these lists, and then links these lists to the Access database. If everything goes smoothly, Access displays a message that the tables have been shared successfully (see Figure 3-5).

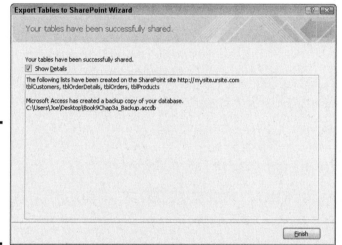

Figure 3-5:
Success
in moving
Access
tables into
SharePoint
lists.

5. **Click the Show Details check box of the confirmation window to show the summary of what Access did.**

You see that Access created new lists on the specified SharePoint site and made a backup copy of the original database.

6. **Click Finish.**

Your database opens, displaying the linked tables in addition to your other database objects.

If something goes wrong — if Access can't move the tables to the SharePoint site or other issues occur during the process — the wizard creates a table called Move to SharePoint Site Issues that lists the issues that prevented the tables from being moved. Just open this table in Datasheet view to review and correct these issues as they're found.

By linking tables to a SharePoint site, you can create front ends for an existing SharePoint site or give users access to data from your database in SharePoint. These users don't even have to have Microsoft Office Access installed to edit the data in a SharePoint list; they just need access to the list on the SharePoint site.

Building a Custom Web App

If you work through Chapters 1 and 2 of this minibook, you see how to create a rich, data-driven Windows application that you or your company can use to track all kinds of information. One day, you can build a database that tracks your music collection at home, and the next day, you can work on a database that tracks sensitive corporate data (so that you can continue to finance a music collection that's large enough to require a database).

Like many Access developers before you, you're probably thinking, "Wow, it would be great to put this database online so I can access it from anywhere." With the release of Microsoft Access 2013 and SharePoint 2013, you can. This capability comes at a cost, however: You have some limitations on the formatting and structure of the database. The first big limitation is that you must use SharePoint 2013 Enterprise Edition to deploy this application. We discuss other limitations throughout the rest of this chapter.

Defining a Custom Web App

An Access database consists of several objects: tables, queries, forms, reports, and macros. In Access 2013, you have the option of storing these database objects locally in an `.accdb` file or storing them on a SharePoint 2013 server as a Custom Web App. A *Custom Web App* is a new application model that allows you to store Access objects on a SharePoint server and make them available to users without Microsoft Access.

Custom Web Apps allow you to deploy solutions to anyone who has an Internet connection and a web browser. These apps use SQL Azure or SQL Server to allow you to share data over the Internet with SharePoint.

 If you spent the time to find out about web databases in Access 2010, you need to rethink the process in Access 2013. Web databases in Access 2010 were Microsoft's first attempt at moving an Access database to the web. In Access 2013, Custom Web Apps replace the old functionality and are a huge leap forward when paired with SharePoint 2013.

Meeting the requirements for a Custom Web App

To create a Custom Web App, you need the following:

✦ Access 2013 (obviously!)

✦ A SharePoint 2013 development environment

SharePoint 2013 is a robust server-based software package that requires Windows Server and SQL Server to operate fully. Most Access users don't have the capability — or pocketbook — to set up this type of environment. If you work for a company that has SharePoint 2013, you're in luck. You can work with the system administrator to get the web address and login information for the SharePoint site.

If you don't have the luxury of being able to use an existing SharePoint 2013 site, other options are available:

✦ **Use a SharePoint hosting company.** Search the web for *SharePoint hosting,* and make sure that the company you choose supports the Access 2013 Custom Web App.

✦ **Sign up for Office 365.** Office 365 is Microsoft's cloud-based service that allows you to use Microsoft Office products anywhere. Several plans are available; just make sure that the plan you sign up for includes a SharePoint 2013 site.

Regardless of which option you choose to use for SharePoint 2013, make sure that you have a website URL (such as `http://sharepoint.company.com`), a username, and a password.

Creating a Custom Web App

When you have access to a SharePoint 2013 server, you can create your Custom Web App by following these steps:

1. **On the Microsoft Access main screen, click the Custom Web App option (shown in Figure 3-6).**

The Custom Web App window launches.

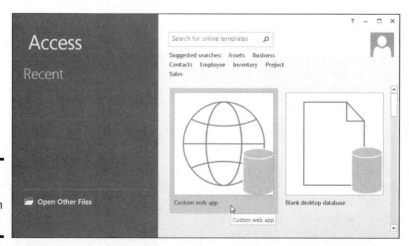

Figure 3-6:
Creating a
new Custom
Web App.

2. **Enter the app name and the web location (the SharePoint 2013 web address), as shown in Figure 3-7, and then click Create.**

The Windows Security dialog box launches if SharePoint requires further authentication.

If a message box appears, stating that an error occurred in the client while attempting to connect to communicate with the server, double-check the web location to ensure that it matches what the SharePoint administrator specified.

3. **If prompted, enter a username and password for the SharePoint server (see Figure 3-8), and then click OK.**

Access displays a progress indicator, creates your app, and then displays your Custom Web App.

Figure 3-8:
Enter a
username
and
password
for the
SharePoint
server.

After Access creates your app, you can customize it by adding tables, queries, forms, macros, and data macros.

Designing Custom Web Apps

As we mention in the preceding section, Custom Web Apps don't represent all the functionality of a desktop `.accdb` database file. Because of these limitations, you'll notice a different interface when you work within such an app (see Figure 3-9).

Ribbon

Launch App button   Add Tables tab   Sharepoint site

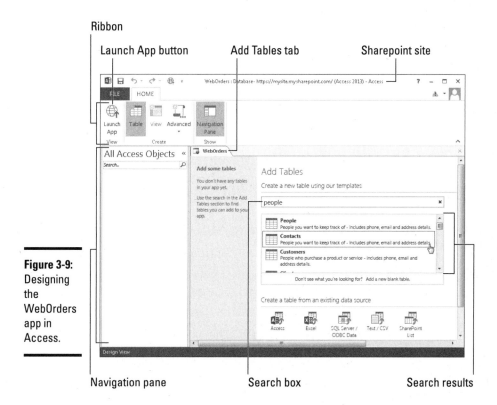

Figure 3-9:
Designing
the
WebOrders
app in
Access.

Navigation pane   Search box   Search results

Some key differences between the desktop `.accdb` and the Custom Web App are

- ✦ The title bar shows the web address of the SharePoint site.
- ✦ The Ribbon has only the File and Home tabs. Additional object-specific tabs appear when you design these objects.
- ✦ The Create group appears on the Home tab instead of on its own tab.
- ✦ Forms are also called views.
- ✦ The Add Tables tab allows you to create new tables in your app.
- ✦ The Launch App button lets you view your app in a browser.

Adding tables

Just like its desktop counterpart, a Custom Web App stores data in tables. These tables are stored in SQL Server or SQL Azure via the connection made with SharePoint 2013. Creating tables in an app is similar to creating tables in an `.accdb` file.

For more information on designing tables, using the various field types and properties, and editing data, see Book II.

Adding a table from a template

The easiest way to add a table to your app is to create one by using a template. Access offers a few templates for various types of information. You can add tables to store information for people, orders, vendors, issues, and many other items.

To add a table from an existing template, follow these steps:

1. **Click the Table button in the Create group on the Home tab of the Ribbon.**

   The Add Tables tab appears, listing the name of the app as the tab's title (refer to Figure 3-9, earlier in this chapter).

2. **In the search box, enter the type of information you'd like to track.**

   Access displays a list of templates that match the information you're looking for.

3. **Select the template that you want to add to your app.**

   Access adds the table to your app, along with associated views (forms). These objects appear in the Navigation Pane. Access also adds a pane to the Add Tables tab that shows the table's name with a star to the left.

4. **On the Add Tables tab, click the table name to display the different views (see Figure 3-10).**

   In the example shown in Figure 3-10, Access created the Contacts table, along with Contacts List view, Contacts Datasheet view, and By Group view. Click the view buttons to see the different views.

When you're working with apps, Access displays a lot of information onscreen. You may have to show or hide the Navigation Pane and use the scroll bars to see all the available options — or buy yourself a gigantic monitor.

Table names   View buttons

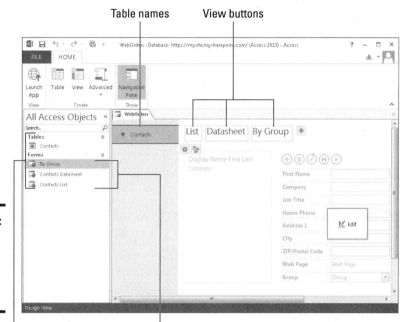

Figure 3-10:
Displaying
the new
table's
views
(forms).

Objects in Navigation pane   Views Access creates automatically

Adding a new blank table

If you don't see a template for information you want to track, you're free
to create a table from scratch. You can define the fields, data types, and
description, just as you do in a desktop database.

To create a custom table, follow these steps:

1. **Click the Table button in the Create group on the Home tab of the
    Ribbon.**

    The Add Tables tab appears, displaying the name of the app as the tab's
    title (refer to Figure 3-9, earlier in this chapter).

2. **Click the Add a New Blank Table link.**

    Access displays the table designer, along with the (Table Tools) Design
    tab.

3. **Enter field names, data types, and optional descriptions for the fields
    you want to track.**

4. **Click the Save button on the Quick Access toolbar.**

    The Save As dialog box appears.

5. **Enter a table name, and click OK.**

Access saves the table and creates the List and Datasheet views (see Figure 3-11).

(Table Tools) Design tab   Design view   Table Close button

Figure 3-11:
Creating a
new blank
table.

6. **Click the table's Close button.**

Access closes the table.

As you continue to add tables to your app, they appear in the Navigation Pane and on the app's main tab with a star to the left.

Launching your app

As you build your app, it's wise to take a look at how it's going to look to the end user. Custom Web Apps are designed to be used in a web browser, so you should review your app every now and then to be sure it's what you want to create.

To launch your app on the Internet, click the Launch App button in the View group on the Home tab of the Ribbon (refer to Figure 3-9, earlier in this chapter). Access launches your browser to display your app (see Figure 3-12).

Depending on the configuration of your SharePoint site, you may have to log in to your site before you see your app in the browser. Work with your SharePoint administrator to determine the best method for allowing users to access the site without a username and password.

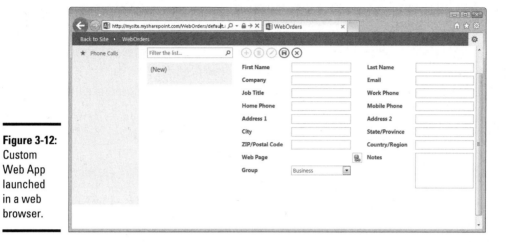

Figure 3-12:
Custom
Web App
launched
in a web
browser.

Entering data in your app

After you launch your app, you may want to give it a test drive to see how it operates. When the app is launched, you can navigate to the view in which you'd like to enter data. Simply fill out the fields in the form, and click the Save button on the mini toolbar to save the data (see Figure 3-13).

Figure 3-13:
Entering
data in a
Custom
Web App's
list view.

Access automatically adds the mini toolbar to the app's views. Depending on where you are in the app, Access automatically enables and disables these buttons. Access adds these buttons for you:

✦ Add (plus sign) navigates to a new record.

✦ Delete (trash can) deletes the current displayed record.

✦ Edit (pencil) switches the view from read-only mode to edit mode so modifications can occur.

✦ Save (disk) saves the current changes to the record.

✦ Cancel (x) cancels changes made to the edited record without saving.

Unlike with forms in a desktop database, you must switch the web page from view mode to edit mode to make changes. To make changes in a record, for example, you must first click the Edit button.

For information on modifying the mini toolbar and on the layout of the views, see "Editing views," later in this chapter.

Navigating your app

When adding tables to your app, Access automatically creates a few views for you. These views present your data in different formats:

✦ **List view** shows your data from a single record on a form, similar to the desktop database's form view.

✦ **Datasheet view** presents the data in a tabular format, similar to the desktop database's datasheet view in a table or form.

✦ **By Group view** (shown in Figure 3-14) shows the data with grouping on the left and a list view on the right. Clicking the record in the list view on the right displays a pop-up window where you can review the record.

When you're creating tables in a Custom Web App, Access automatically adds the navigation and views required to edit the data in these tables. After you add tables to the app, the app is functional on the web.

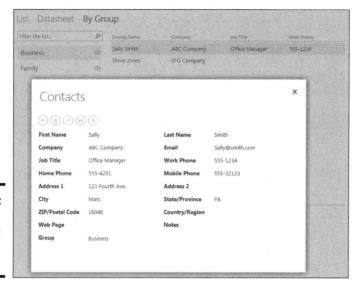

Figure 3-14:
Navigating
to the app's
By Group
view.

Editing views

Access tries to expedite app development by creating views for you.
Although that feature is a big help in getting started, it doesn't always create
exactly what you want. Just as you do when editing forms in a desktop database, you can modify the design and layout of the views — and even create
your own view from scratch.

You use the web browser to view, edit, and manipulate data in your app. To
make changes in the design of the objects (such as tables and views), make
sure that you're using Access.

To download the database package, click the gear icon in the upper-right
corner of the SharePoint web page (in the browser), and then click the
Customize in Access menu. Then save the file (an .accdw file). You can
store this .accdw file locally and open the file in Access to make changes to
your Custom web app.

To change the layout and edit an existing view, follow these steps:

1. **Navigate to the view you want to edit and then click the Edit button
    that appears (see Figure 3-15).**

    Access opens Design view (see Figure 3-16).

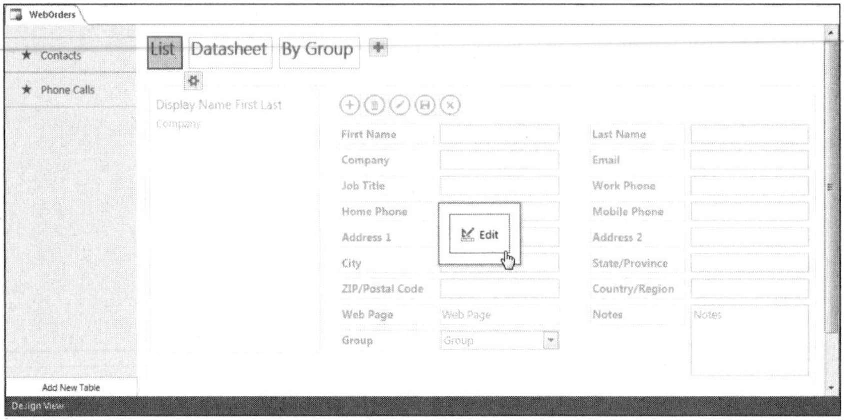

Figure 3-15:
Selecting which view to edit.

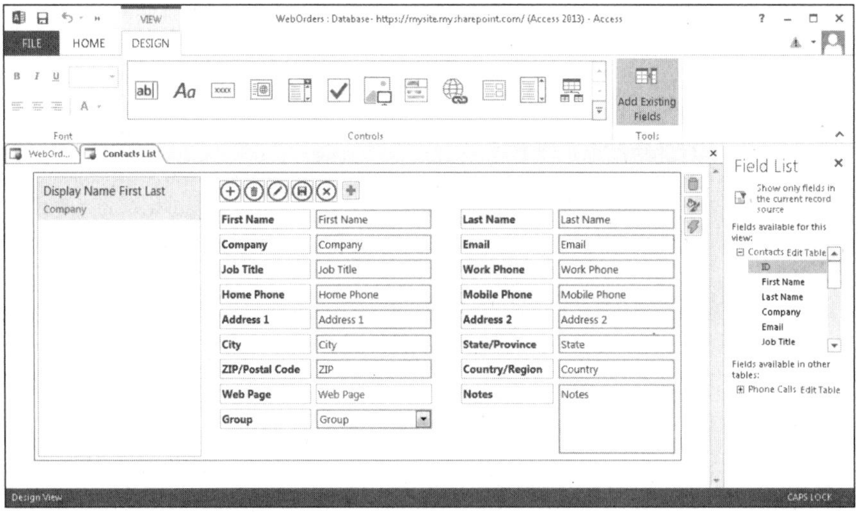

Figure 3-16:
Editing a view in Design view.

2. To move a control, hover over it until the cursor changes to a four-headed arrow; then drag the control to the new location.

3. To resize a control, hover over the edge of the control until the cursor changes to a double-headed arrow; then drag the edge to resize.

4. To modify additional properties of a control, click the control to highlight it and then click one of the three icons that appear (see Figure 3-17).

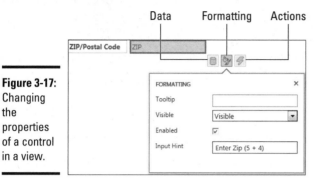

Figure 3-17:
Changing
the
properties
of a control
in a view.

To modify visual properties (such as font size, color, and alignment) of
the selected control, for example, click the buttons in the Font group on
the (View) Design tab on the Ribbon.

The list of properties and event properties available in an app is smaller
than the list available in a desktop database. A text box control in a desktop
database has a property sheet that goes on and on and on, for example,
whereas in a Custom Web App, the list is much shorter (see Table 3-1).

Table 3-1	**Properties and Events of a Text Box Control**	
Data	*Formatting*	*Actions*
Control Name	Tooltip	On Click
Control Source	Visible	After Update
Default Values	Enabled	
	Input Hint	

For more information on designing forms in Design view and on adding and
moving controls (such as fields, buttons, and visual elements), see Book IV.

Adding actions

Making your app do stuff is the true power of using a database. Any database can store information and present that information to the user, but if
you want something to happen when a user performs a certain action, such
as clicking a button or entering data in a field, it's your job as app creator to
make that action happen.

Adding an action to a view

To add a macro to an event property of a control on the form, follow these steps:

1. **Click the control to highlight it and then click the Actions icon (refer to Figure 3-17, earlier in this chapter).**

Access displays the Actions window.

2. **Click the Action button for which you'd like to add a macro.**

Access opens a new tab where you can design the macro (see Figure 3-18).

Figure 3-18:
Adding a
macro to
a control's
action.

3. **Build the macro by adding actions.**

For more information on creating and designing macros, see Book VI.

4. **Click the Save button in the Close group on the (Macro Tools) Design tab of the Ribbon.**

Access saves the macro.

5. **Click the Close button in the Close group on the (Macro Tools) Design tab of the Ribbon.**

Access closes the macro tab and returns to the view's design tab.

6. **Click Save in the Quick Access toolbar.**

Access saves your changes.

To see all your changes in action, click the Launch App button in the View group on the Home tab of the Ribbon. Just make sure that you save your changes before you launch your app in a web browser.

The list of macros available in a Custom Web App is smaller than the list available in a desktop database (see Table 3-2).

Table 3-2	Macros Actions Available in a Custom Web App	
Comment	GoToControl	RunMacro
Group	GoToRecord	SaveRecord
If	MessageBox	SetProperty
Change View	NewRecord	SetVariable
ClosePopup	OpenPopup	StopMacro
DeleteRecord	RequeryRecords	UndoRecord
EditRecord	RunDataMacro	

Customizing the mini toolbar

When Access creates the views, it adds a mini toolbar with Add, Delete, Edit, Save, and Cancel buttons. To customize the toolbar, you simply open the view in Design view and customize the buttons:

✦ To remove one of the buttons that Access added, click once to select the button and then press the Delete key.

✦ To change the order of the buttons, click and drag them to new locations.

✦ To add a new button, click the plus sign to the right of all the buttons; click the new button; and then click the Data Properties icon to customize the button (Control Name, Tooltip, Icon, or On Click macro).

For information about the properties of a control, see "Editing views," earlier in this chapter.

Creating a data macro

A data macro doesn't run when a user does something. Instead, the data macro runs when something happens at the table level. Just as you can in a desktop database — but with fewer options available — you can add macros to the events listed in Table 3-3.

Table 3-3	Data Macro Events
Event	*Description*
On Insert	After a new record has been added to this table
On Update	After any field in a record in this table has been updated
On Delete	After a record in this table has been deleted

For more information on creating and designing data macros, see Book VI, Chapter 2.

To create a data macro that runs when a record is added to the table, follow these steps:

1. **Right-click a table name in the Navigation Pane and choose Design View from the contextual menu.**

    Access displays the table in Design view.

2. **Click the On Insert button in the Events group on the (Table Tools) Design tab of the Ribbon.**

    Access opens a new tab to design the macro, similar to the tab shown in Figure 3-18, earlier in this chapter.

3. **Build the macro by adding new actions.**

4. **Click the Save button in the Close group on the (Macro Tools) Design tab of the Ribbon.**

    Access saves the macro.

5. **Click the Close button in the Close group on the (Macro Tools) Design tab of the Ribbon.**

    Access closes the macro tab and returns to the view's design tab.

6. **Click Save in the Quick Access toolbar.**

    Access saves the changes to the table.

Adding queries

Select queries allow you to show subsets of table data, perform calculations, and show summary information. Fortunately, you can create many of the same queries in a Custom Web App that you can in a desktop database. Unfortunately, action queries are unavailable in Custom Web Apps.

To create a select query, follow these steps:

1. **Click the Advance button in the Create group on the Home tab of the Ribbon.**

2. **Choose Query from the drop-down menu that appears.**

    Access displays the new query tab in Design view and displays the Show Table dialog box.

3. **Select the tables that you want to use in the query, and click Add to add them to the query.**

4. **Click the Close button.**

    Access closes the Show Table dialog box and displays the query designer.

5. **Add fields, calculated fields, and so on to the Query by Example (QBE) grid.**

   Access saves the macro.

6. **Click the View button in the Results group on the (Query Tools) Design tab of the Ribbon.**

   Access displays the query's results.

7. **Click Save in the Quick Access toolbar.**

   Access saves the changes to the query.

For more information on creating and designing select queries, see Book III, Chapters 1 and 2.

Using Access with SharePoint allows you to store table data — through SharePoint lists — on an external server and view them in Access. SharePoint users can also view and manipulate the data, which allows you to create desktop apps that use data shared by other SharePoint users who may not have Access.

Appendix: Installing Microsoft Access

*I*f Microsoft Access 2013 is already on your computer, you don't need to read this appendix unless you want to change something related to your current installation. If Microsoft Access 2013 isn't on your computer, you need to install it before you can use it. The program doesn't come free with Windows; you have to purchase it separately.

If you've just bought Access new, don't even think about throwing away the packaging until after the installation is complete. Also, never throw away the product key (see the next section). You never know when you might need to reinstall the program again, and you'll need that key to do so.

Installing Access from a Disc

To install Access 2013, you need a Microsoft Office Professional 2013 or Microsoft Access 2013 disc and the 25-character product key that came with it (included in the packaging). To get started with the installation, follow these steps:

1. **If you're currently using any programs, save your work and close the programs.**

   You don't need to close programs whose icons appear in the notification area — just the application programs on the desktop.

2. **Insert your Microsoft Office Professional or Microsoft Access disc into your computer's CD or DVD drive.**

3. **Wait a minute for the installation program to start.**

   If no program starts automatically, choose Start⇨Computer, right-click the icon for your CD or DVD drive, choose the Open AutoPlay option from the contextual menu, and click the option to install or run the program from your media.

   You may see some security warnings asking for permission to proceed. These standard warnings appear whenever you install any program. It's okay to proceed with the installation.

   The Microsoft Software License Agreement appears next, containing the usual legalese about licensing.

4. **Read the agreement (yeah, sure), which says you won't sell or give away copies of the program; then select the I Accept the Terms of This Agreement check box, and click Continue.**

   The next page you see depends on whether you have an earlier version of Access or other Office programs installed on your computer. If you do, proceed to Step 5. If you don't have a previous version of Access or other Office programs, skip to Step 7.

5. **Choose the Upgrade or Customize option.**

   Before you choose an option, keep these points in mind:

   - *Upgrade:* Your current versions of Access and any other programs you're installing will be replaced by the new 2013 versions, which means that you can't use the old versions anymore.

   - *Customize:* You can opt to keep your old versions and still have the new 2013 versions, too — not a bad idea if you want to use features of these older versions that are slightly different from those in 2013.

6. **Do one of the following:**

   - If you chose Upgrade in Step 5, click the Upgrade button, follow any remaining onscreen instructions to completion, and ignore the steps that follow.

   - If you chose Customize in Step 5, your first decision is whether to remove all previous versions, keep all previous versions, or just replace certain ones.

   If you want to keep your previous version of Access, be sure to choose Keep All Previous Versions. Alternatively, you can choose the option to remove only certain programs, but be sure to clear the Access check box.

   After you make your choice, the installation options appear. Skip to Step 8.

7. **If you don't have an earlier version of Access or another Office program on your computer, choose Install Now or Customize.**

   Here's what these options do:

   - *Install Now:* The program installs with Microsoft's default settings.

   - *Customize:* You can choose which programs and features of the software you want to install.

   After you make your choices, the installation options appear.

8. **To install all of Microsoft Access 2013, click the Installation Options tab, click the drop-down menu for Microsoft Access, and choose Run All from My Computer, as shown in Figure A-1.**

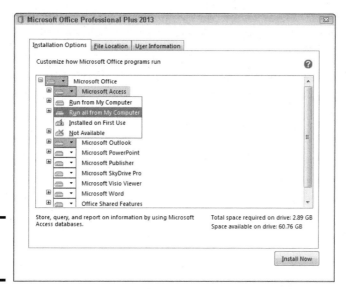

Figure A-1:
Installation
options.

If you're installing a full Microsoft Office suite, you can make similar selections for other programs.

Selections that you make in this step don't override any selections that you made in Steps 5 and 6 concerning upgrading or keeping old versions.

Each time you choose Run from My Computer to install a component, the Total Space Required on Drive indicator (in the bottom-right corner of the Installation Options window) shows how much hard drive space the program will use compared with available disk space (shown in the Space Available on Drive indicator).

9. **(Optional) Click the File Location tab, and choose a different location for the installed programs.**

    It isn't necessary to change the file location to keep previous versions of programs. Use that tab only if you have some other good and compelling reason to store the installed programs on another drive or in a folder other than the Program Files folder.

10. **(Optional) Click the User Information tab, and enter information about yourself.**

    Some programs use user information to identify you as the author or reviser of documents.

11. **Click Install Now in the bottom-right corner of the window, and follow the onscreen instructions.**

12. **Wait.**

The rest of the process is largely automatic. If you see any additional onscreen instructions, follow them, but the installation should proceed on its own from this point forward. When it's done, you see a Continue Online option. It's a good idea to choose that option, because the services you see online may prove to be valuable resources for future information, but if you skip the opportunity now, it's no big deal. You can register for online services at any time.

If you see a Delete Installation Files option, it's best to leave it alone. The installation files make it easy to install any components that you may have skipped on the first pass. If you choose this option, you can still install those components; you just need to insert the original disc to do so.

Be sure to store your original disc and product key in a safe place where you can easily find them in the future. You just never know when a bad disk crash or nasty virus will force you to reinstall Access (or Office) from scratch!

Installing Access from Office 365

Office 365 is basically an Internet-based version of Office. It adds more power and accessibility to the Office you already know by making collaboration and communication with others easier. By combining Office with Office 365, you can work on complete solutions that allow you and your colleagues to view and edit documents and data from almost anywhere.

The first step is signing up for an Office 365 account or getting the information regarding your Office 365 account from your organization. When you obtain the necessary login credentials, you're ready to go.

Microsoft is known for continuously changing and updating information on its products. For more information on the plans and options available in Office 365, open your favorite search engine, and search for "Office 365."

To install Access from Office 365, follow these steps:

1. **Log in to your Office 365 account.**

   Use the login credentials supplied when you signed up for your account, or get them from your organization.

2. **Navigate to the Admin page, and click the Software option.**

   The software page loads (shown in Figure A-2). This page is where you can install the latest version of various available Office programs — including Access.

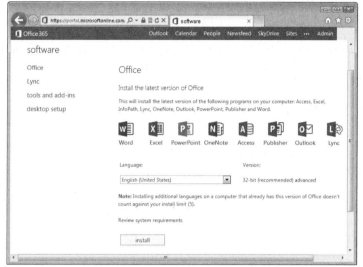

Figure A-2:
Installing
Access from
Office 365.

3. **Click Install, and follow the instructions on the screen.**

   Because there are no discs with Office 365, your browser downloads the installation program. Make sure that you have a relatively high-speed connection; otherwise, you could find yourself twiddling your thumbs for a while.

4. **Run the executable (.exe) file that downloaded in Step 3.**

   The Office installation loads.

5. **Click Next.**

   The installation walks you through an introduction to Office 365 and then prompts you to sign in to your account.

6. **Sign in to your account, and follow the onscreen instructions to configure and set up your Office environment.**

The installation options for online services tend to change often, so it's impossible to keep this printed book current. The good folks at Microsoft, however, made it rather easy to install Office by following the onscreen prompts. We recommend becoming familiar with Office 365 before signing up and installing Office.

Activating Access

Microsoft requires *product activation,* which is a process designed to prevent people from installing their products on more computers or devices than the license agreement allows. The first time you start Access (or some other Office program), you're prompted to activate the product. Follow these steps to activate Access:

1. **Start Microsoft Access by choosing Start⇨All Programs⇨Microsoft Office 2013⇨Access 2013.**

   The first time you start Access, the Activate Office screen appears. You can activate your copy in several ways, depending on how you or your company purchased the product:

   - *Microsoft Account:* Use this option to sign in by using a Microsoft account for SkyDrive, Xbox LIVE, Outlook.com, or another Microsoft service.

   - *Organizational Account:* Use this option to sign in with an account provided by your company or school to use with Office 365 or other Microsoft services.

   - *Enter a Product Key Instead:* Use this option if you're installing from a disc or from a network location that requires a product key.

2. **Select an option in Step 1 to activate Access.**

   If you select Microsoft Account or Organizational Account, be sure to have the necessary information (such as username and password) available.

   If you select Enter a Product Key Instead, obtain the product key from your packaging material or your organization, and enter it in the screen provided (shown in Figure A-3).

×

Enter your product key

Your product key is 25 characters and is typically found in your product packaging

See product key examples
Sign in with an active account instead

[   ]   [Install]

Figure A-3:
Enter the
product key.

When Microsoft came out with product activation, many people were alarmed that Microsoft would spy on them, correlating their Access use with their personal information and making other appalling invasions of their privacy. As it turns out, product activation doesn't do any of those things. Product activation is unconnected with *product registration,* a process in which you give Microsoft your name and address. Activation just connects your Office product key with your computer(s) so that no one else can install your Office license on his or her computer(s). Go ahead and activate Office with no worries!

Repairing, Reinstalling, or Uninstalling Access

If something bad happens to your hard drive, and you can't start Access on your computer, you may have to reinstall or repair it. Alternatively, if you chose to omit some optional components, you may change your mind later and want to install them. Here's how:

1. **Close Access and all other Office programs.**

2. **Navigate to your list of installed programs in either of these ways:**

   - In Windows 7, choose Start⇨Control Panel⇨Programs⇨Programs and Features.

   - In Windows 8, move the cursor to the bottom-right or top-right corner of the Home screen or Desktop to reveal the Search, Share, Start, Devices, and Settings icons. Click the Settings icon on the menu that appears; then choose Control Panel⇨Programs⇨Programs and Features.

3. **Click the Microsoft Access 2013 or Microsoft Office Professional 2013 option (whichever contains your Access installation).**

4. **Click the Change button.**

5. **In the next screen, choose one of these options:**

   - *Add or Remove Features:* This option displays a window similar to the one shown in Figure A-1, earlier in this chapter. Choose which features of Access (and other Office programs) you want to install on or remove from your computer.

   - *Repair:* This option attempts to repair a damaged installation of Access or Office. What might damage an installation, you may ask? All those nasty viruses, Trojan horses, and Internet worms can cause various things to go wrong with your computer.

   - *Remove:* This option removes Access or Office from your computer.

   - *Enter a Product Key:* This option lets you enter a new product key if yours expires or becomes invalid. It may expire if you're using a trial edition of Office that's good for a short period.

6. **If a repair operation doesn't work, you may have to remove Access (or Office) and reinstall it from scratch.**

   You'll need to search through your desk and dig out your CD and product key first.

Index

Symbols & Numerics

- (dash), input mask character, 163
- (subtraction operator), 225
! (exclamation point)
  action queries, 257
  formatting Text field, 117
  input mask characters, 163
" " (quotation marks)
  inserting text into text box, 614
  literal strings, 574
  literal text, 224
  passing string, 566
  SQL statement, 635–637
  zero-length strings, 242
(pound character)
  defining number format, 114
  delimiting values, 239
  hyperlinks, 87–89
  input mask characters, 163
  Like operator, 173
#Div/0! error message, 368
#Error error message, 368
#Name? error message, 368
$ (dollar sign), defining number format, 114
% (percent symbol), defining number format, 114
& (ampersand character)
  and operator, 408
  breaking literal string, 574
  breaking up SQL statement, 636–637
  formatting Text field, 117
  input mask characters, 163
  keyboard shortcuts for command buttons, 485
  printing reports, 408
  string concatenation, 225, 242
* (asterisk character)
  From option, QBE grid, 268–269
  inserting field into design grid, 204
  Like operator, 173
  matching part of field, 131
  multiplication operator, 225

... (ellipsis), defining multiple variables, 582
. (period character)
  defining number format, 114
  input mask characters, 163
/ (slash character)
  division operator, 225–226
  input mask characters, 163
: (colon character)
  expressing literal times, 239
  input mask characters, 163
; (semicolon character)
  input mask characters, 163
  pasting SQL statement, 635
? (question mark character)
  input mask characters, 163
  Like operator, 173
  testing function from Immediate window, 578–579
@ (at symbol), 117
[] (square brackets)
  field names in expressions, 226
  formatting Text field, 117
  syntax charts, 560
\ (backslash character), 163
^ (caret symbol)
  exponentiation operator, 225
  key-assignment macros, 468
_(underscore symbol)
  continuation character, 573, 636–637
  field names in SQL environments, 73
{ } (curly brackets), 468
¯ key, choosing from drop-down menu, 83
+ (plus sign)
  addition operator, 225
  combining options for argument, 561
  key-assignment macros, 468
  subdatasheets, 102
< (less than sign)
  formatting Text field, 117
  grouping data in report, 393
  input mask characters, 163
  less than operator, 209, 245, 589
< > (angle brackets), 231–232

<> (not equal to operator), 209, 245, 589

<= (less than or equal to operator), 209, 244–245, 589

= (equal sign)
  equal to operator, 209, 245, 589
  variables, 582

> (greater than sign)
  formatting Text field, 117
  greater than operator, 209, 245, 589
  grouping data in report, 393
  input mask characters, 163

>= (greater than or equal to operator), 209, 245, 589

∞ (infinity symbol)
  detail tables, 176–177, 181
  referential integrity, 184, 216

0 (zero)
  defining number format, 114
  input mask characters, 163
  leading, 58
  versus null values, 236–237
  zero-based arrays, 586–587

1 character
  as base for arrays, 587
  detail tables, 176
  referential integrity, 184, 216

' (apostrophe symbol), comments, 572

, (comma symbol)
  for arguments in statement, 561–562
  declaring multiple constants, 585
  defining multiple variables, 582–583
  defining number format, 114
  input mask characters, 163
  listing multiple arguments, 567
  multivalue lookup fields, 212–213

'' (single quotation marks), SQL statements, 635

3-D charts, 443

3-D View, Microsoft Graph, 455

9 character, input mask characters, 163

A

a character, 163

A character
  AutoKeys macro, 468
  input masks, 163

abbreviations, 51, 94–96

Abs(number) function, 233

.AbsolutePosition property, 631, 633

.accdb files
  .accde files versus, 530
  Custom Web App versus, 695
  general discussion, 21
  linking to SQL Server database from, 683
  new databases, 62–63

.accde files, 514, 516, 529–532

.accdw files, 701

Access
  compatibility with older versions, 21
  importing data from database, 153–154
  installing, 709–716
  saving database in different version, 21
  starting program, 17–19

Access Data Project (ADP) files, 682–683

Access for Developers website, 34

Access Help window, 34

Access Web website, 34

Access Window, 22–25

accessibility, 143

AccessObject keyword, 622

Account command, Backstage view, 33

Account Options dialog box, 33

acDesign constant, 609

acDialog constant, 610

acFormAdd constant, 610

acFormatPropertySettings constant, 610

acFormDS constant, 609

acFormEdit constant, 610

acFormPivotChart constant, 609

acFormPivotTable constant, 609

acFormReadOnly constant, 610

acHidden constant, 610

acIcon constant, 610

acLayout constant, 609

acNormal constant, 609

acPreview constant, 609

acSaveNo constant, 612

acSavePrompt constant, 612

acSaveYes constant, 612

Action Catalog, 463–465

action queries
append queries, 265–267
delete queries, 267–270
general discussion, 12, 191
make-table queries, 262–265
new, 255–258
overview, 255
update queries, 258–262
in VBA, 638–640
actions
changing order, 464–465
Custom Web App, 703
general discussion, 462–464
specifying arguments to, 464
specifying for macro, 460
viewing all possible, 474
Actions list, Command Button Wizard, 349
Activate Office screen, 714
activating Access, 713–714
Active content disabled security
warning, 20
ActiveX Data Objects (ADO)
object model, 629–631
ActiveX Settings option, Trust Center, 533
acWindowNormal constant, 610
Add & Delete section, Ribbon, 77
Add a Place option, Ribbon interface, 19
Add button, mini toolbar, 700
Add method, 665
Add New Action box, macros, 463
Add option, Spelling dialog box, 94
Add or Remove Features option, Change
Access Installation screen, 715
Add Procedure dialog box, 563–565
Add Tables tab, Ribbon, 696
Add to Outlook Contacts button, 657–658
add-ins, 508–509
Add-Ins settings, Trust Center, 533
addition operator (+), 225
.AddNew method, 630
addresses
hyperlinks, 88–89
postal, 79
ADO (ActiveX Data Objects) object model,
629–631

Adobe Reader, 423
adOpenDynamic constant, 632–633
adOpenForwardOnly constant, 633
adOpenKeyset constant, 633
adOpenStatic constant, 632
ADP (Access Data Project) files, 682–683
Advanced button, Ribbon, 131
Advanced Filter/Sort feature, 128,
132–135, 190
After Delete event, 479
After Insert event, 479
After Update event, 479, 484
aggregate columns, 285–286
aggregate functions
calculating group subtotals and report
totals, 406–407
Crosstab queries, 277–278
general discussion, 379–381
total rows, 104
aligning
controls, 329
forms, 331–334
All Records option, record-locking feature,
520–521
AllForms collection, 626
Allow Additions property, 310
Allow Datasheet View property, 309
Allow Default Shortcut Menus setting, for
current database, 526
Allow Deletions property, 310
Allow Edits property, 309–310
Allow Full Menus setting, for current
database, 526
Allow Multiple Selections check box,
Lookup Wizard, 169
Allow Zero Length property, 159
ampersand character (&)
breaking literal string, 574
breaking up SQL statement, 636–637
formatting Text field, 117
input mask characters, 163
keyboard shortcuts for command
buttons, 485
printing reports, 408
string concatenation, 225, 242

Analyze Performance button, Ribbon, 506

And operator, 131, 245

AND operator, 173, 210–211

and operator, 590

angle brackets (< >), 231–232

antivirus software, 20

apostrophe ('), 572

Append dialog box, 266

append queries, 256, 265–267

Append To row, query grid, 266–267

appending data, 144

Application command, Command Button Wizard, 349

Application Icon setting, for current database, 525

Application object, 656–657, 668–669

Application options, for current database, 525–526

Application Parts, 75–76, 309

Application Title setting, for current database, 525

Apply Filter macro action, 462

apps, 545

APR value, 235

area charts, 446–448

arguments

functions in expressions, 227

interval, 241

macros, 460–461

passing to procedures, 566–569

specifying for action, 464

syntax, 231, 560–562

testing procedures, 576

arrays

looping through, 599

multidimensional, 587

organizing variables into, 585–587

ascending order, sorting in

Advanced Filter/Sort feature, 134

combo boxes, 342

general discussion, 121–122

by name or company, 249

queries, 205–206

records in report, 394

associated labels, 327–328

asterisk character (*)

From option, QBE (Query by Example) grid, 268–269

inserting field into design grid, 204

Like operator, 173

matching part of field, 131

multiplication operator, 225

at symbol (@), 117

Attachment data type, 39, 89–91

Attachment fields, 59, 112, 355–357

attachments, 91, 355–357

Attachments dialog box, 90–91, 356–357

Auto Order button, Tab Order dialog box, 337

AutoCorrect feature, 94–96

AutoExec macro, 467, 491

AutoKeys macro, 468

AutoLookup queries, 191, 217–218

Automation

adding contacts to Outlook, 657–661

exporting data to Excel, 666–670

general discussion, 653–654

merging data with Word document, 661–666

object libraries, 654–657

AutoNumber data type, 39–40

AutoNumber fields

append queries, 265

assigning unique number to each record in table, 52

general discussion, 111–112

as primary key in master table, 56

secret keys, 61

sorting data, 123

autonumbering records, 52

Available Fields list, Form Wizard dialog box, 297

Available Fields list box, Simple Query Wizard, 195

Avg() function, 379

Avg operation, 252

axes, 455

Axis setting, in charts, 440

B

`Back Style` property, 372
back-end databases, 16, 513–518, 532
Background Image button, Ribbon, 335
backgrounds
  chart, 453–454
  colors, 98–99
  form, 335
  report, 409
backslash character (\), 163
Backstage View, 17–19, 32–33
backups, 16, 256, 500–503
bar charts, 443–446
`Beep` macro action, 462
`Before Change` event, 479
`Before Delete` event, 479
`Before Update` event, 484
BETWEEN operator, 209
`Between` operator, 245
`Binary` option, 563
blank fields, 122
Blank Form button, Ribbon, 291, 303
Blank Report button, Ribbon, 390
`bln` tag, 588
`.BOF` property, 631
boldface type, 560
bookmarks, 661–662
`Boolean` data type, 568
Boolean expressions, 474
Boolean values, 57
`Bound Column` property, 344
bound controls, 317
Bound object frame control button,
  Ribbon, 320
bound subreports, 409–410
boxes, in forms, 335
brackets
  angle (<>), 231–232
  curly [{}], 468
  square ([]), 117, 226, 560
breaking
  field, 147
  line, 572–574, 635–637, 648–650
  page, 420–421

Browse for File option, Insert Hyperlink
  dialog box, 88
Browse the Web option, Insert Hyperlink
  dialog box, 88
Browsed Pages option, Insert Hyperlink
  dialog box, 88
browsers, 698–699
bubble charts, 450
bugs, 641
Build button, Design view window, 539
Builder button, Ribbon, 108, 199
Built-In Functions folder, Expression
  Builder, 229
Button control button, Ribbon, 319, 492
button macros, 484–486
buttons
  adding to Quick Access toolbar, 25
  customizing mini toolbar, 705
  Ribbon, 24
`buttons` argument, `MsgBox()` function,
  605–606
By Group view, 700–701
`byt` tag, 588
Byte data type, 568
Byte setting, Number fields, 115
`ByVal` keyword, 623

C

`C` character, input masks, 163
caching options, 527
calculated controls
  in form footer, 381–383
  formatting, 371–372
  general discussion, 366–368
  naming, 408
`Calculated` data type, 39
Calculated field type, 60
calculated fields
  adding to table, 85–86
  Expression Builder, 228–229
  filtering records, 254
  formatting in queries, 233–236
  general discussion, 112, 222–224
  null values, 236–237

calculated fields *(continued)*
  query containing, 246–247
  in reports, 407
  sorting by name or company, 249
calculated values
  general discussion, 365–366
  placing on form or report, 369
  sorting records, 406
calculations
  dates, 370
  displaying datasheet with split form,
    372–373
  displaying values depending on
    conditions, 371
  expressions, 368–369
  for Number and Currency fields, 58
  numbers, 369–370
  overview, 365
  in queries, 221–224
  storing, 60
  subforms, adding subtotals and totals
    from, 379–384
  subforms, displaying detail records with,
    373–378
  subtotals, 254
  text, 370–371
Call keyword, 577
Can Grow property, 413
Can Shrink property, 413–414
Cancel button, mini toolbar, 700
Cancel option, Spelling dialog box, 94
cancelling typing, 36
capitalization
  AutoCorrect Exceptions dialog box, 95–96
  field names in SQL environments, 73
  formatting Short Text, Long Text, and
    Hyperlink fields, 326
Caption property
  command button, 353
  labels, 323–324
  naming forms, 307
  Table Design view, 109
caret symbol (^)
  exponentiation operator, 225
  key-assignment macros, 468

Cascade Deleting Related Records option,
    referential integrity, 178–179, 181
Cascade Update Related Fields option,
    referential integrity, 178–179, 181
cascading deletes, 55
cascading updates, 54–55
Case statements, 593–595
Categories list, Command Button
    Wizard, 349
Category fields, 79
CBool(expression) function, 235
CByte(expression) function, 235
CCur(expression) function, 235
CDate() function, 240
CDate(expression) function, 235
CDbl(expression) function, 235
CDec(expression) function, 235
cells, pasting data into multiple, 141
Change options, Spelling dialog box, 94
Character Map, 91–92
characters
  analyzing each in string, 600
  input masks, 163
  special, 91–92, 122
Characters to Copy box, Character Map
    window, 92
Chart Options dialog box, 453–454
Chart Wizard, 438–443, 448–449
charts
  bar, 443–446
  bubble and XY scatter plots, 450
  changing data to be charted, 455–456
  changing how data is graphed, 454–455
  Chart Wizard, 438–443
  creating manually, 450
  data bars, 435–437
  formatting with colors, legends, and
    titles, 453–454
  line and area, 446–448
  modifying existing, 451–453
  pie and doughnut, 448–449
Check Box button, Ribbon, 320, 335
check boxes
  changing settings, 82–83
  option groups, 346–348

putting check mark in, 614
Yes/No fields, 335, 345
Check for Truncated Number Fields
setting, for current database, 526
CInt(expression) function, 235
class modules, 537–539
classes, 548
Classes list, Object Browser, 548–549
Clear Cache on Close setting, for current
database, 527
Click event procedures
contact button, 658
sending data to Word document, 663
Click to Add drop-down menu, 85–86
Click to Add heading, table datasheets, 77
client/server databases, 671–672
clipboards
keyboard shortcuts, 35–36
Office, 139–140
task pane, 139
Windows, 138–139
CLng(expression) function, 235
Close button, forms, 350–351
Close command, Backstage view, 33
.Close method, 631
CloseWindow macro action, 462
cloud services, 693
code. *See also* debugging code; forms; VBA
(Visual Basic for Applications)
Code window, 570–575
compiling, 642–643
contact button, 657–661
copying and pasting, 555–556
custom functions, 600–604
decision-making, 589–595
executing repeatedly, 595–600
exporting data to Excel, 666–670
general discussion, 537, 545
merging data with Word document,
663–666
overview, 557, 581
procedures, 563–570
syntax, 558–563
testing and running, 575–580
variables and constants, 581–588
VBA, 553–556, 557–558

Code Builder, 615–616
Code Page option, Import Specification
dialog box, 149
Code window
breaking lines of code, 572–574
comments, 572
compile errors, 574–575
displaying converted macro, 555
overview, 570
shortcut keys, 571–572
VBE, 544–546
code-behind forms, 537–539
codes, 51, 59–60
collections
determining whether form is open,
623–625
looping through, 625–627
properties, methods, and events, 620–621
referring to, 551–552, 621–622
With...End With block, 627–628
colon character (:)
expressing literal times, 239
input mask characters, 163
colors
background, 98–99
charts, 453–454
formatting Text field, 117
forms, 331–334
numeric formats, 114–115
reports, 409
themes, 310
column charts, 443–444
Column Count property, 344
Column Headings property, 286
Column Heads property, 344
column selector, 204
Column Widths property, 344
columnar reports, 391
columns
aggregate, 285–286
amount of information stored in, 72
changing width, 99–100
in control layout, 304–305
editing query, 204
freezing, 101
headings, 279–282

columns *(continued)*
  hiding, 101
  inserting and deleting, 100
  inserting field into design grid, 204
  of labels, 428–429
  placing calculated value on form or
    report, 369
  rearranging, 99
  in report, 419
  sorting manually, 286
  subform, 377
Combo box control button, Ribbon, 319
combo box controls
  changing properties, 344–345
  Combo Box Wizard, 341–344
  general discussion, 323
  overview, 339–341
  simple setup, 341
combo boxes, 82–83, 164, 354–355
comma symbol (,)
  for arguments in statement, 561–562
  declaring multiple constants, 585
  defining multiple variables, 582–583
  defining number format, 114
  input mask characters, 163
  listing multiple arguments, 567
  multivalue lookup fields, 212–213
Command Button Wizard, 349, 351–352,
  492–493
command buttons
  Close, 350–351
  creating on form, 484–485
  customizing, 353
  displaying related form, 351–352
  overview, 348–349, 491–492
  printing current record, 352
  to run macros, 493–494
  using form as main menu, 362–363
comments
  Code window, 572
  macros, 465
  programmer, 542
Comments template, 76
Compact on Close setting, for current
  database, 525

compacting databases, 499–500
companies, sorting by, 248–249
`Compare` option, 562
comparison operators
  built-in, 245
  decision-making, 589
compatibility
  ADP files, 682
  converting databases, 503–504
  front-end and back-end database files, 515
  importing data from applications, 143
  with older Access versions, 21
compile errors, 574–575, 641–643
compiled code, 530
Computer option, Ribbon interface, 19
concatenating
  fields, 408
  strings, 242
conditional calculations, 408
conditional execution, 474–476
conditional expressions, 589–590
conditional formatting, 333–334, 436–437
Conditional Formatting Rules Manager
  dialog box, 333–334
`conditionalExpression` argument,
  `IIf()` function, 244
conditions, values depending on, 371
cone column charts, 443
connections
  cleaning up, 640
  between tables, 45
`Const` keyword, 585
constants
  defining, 585
  message-box response code, 607
  `MsgBox()` function `buttons` argument,
    605–606
contact button, 657–661
`ContactItem` object, 659–660
contacts
  adding to Outlook, 657–661
  importing from Outlook, 150–151
Contacts lists, SharePoint, 687
Contacts template, 76
continuation character (_), 573, 636–637

continuous forms, 290, 299, 308–309

Control keyword, 622

control layouts
  adding and deleting rows
    and columns, 304
  general discussion, 301
  Layout view, 304–305
  lining up controls, 328–329
  moving or resizing control, 327–328
  overview, 326
  rearranging fields, 302
  removing, 327

Control Source property
  calculated controls, 366–367
  combo and list boxes, 344
  general discussion, 322–323
  mailing labels, 428

controls
  adding to control layout, 305
  binding to data in record source, 323
  calculated, 366–368, 371–372
  changing properties of, 627–628, 702–703
  changing value, 614
  chart, 442, 451–452
  disabling, 613
  displaying Attachment fields, 355–357
  displaying text, numbers, and dates,
    323–326
  editing reports, 396–397
  enabling, 613
  event procedures, 565–566
  form, 317–320, 483–489, 612–619
  general discussion, 290, 313, 315–316
  looping through, 626–627
  making invisible, 613
  making visible, 613
  navigation, 362
  new, 320–321
  page break, 420–421
  referring to on subform, 381
  report, 317–320
  setting properties, 321–323
  subform, 378
  tabbed forms, 358–360
  to total subform, 381–384

Controls button, Ribbon, 317–318, 321

conversion functions, 234–235

Convert All Picture Data to Bitmaps
    setting, for current database, 526

Convert Macros to Visual Basic button,
    Ribbon, 554

Copy button, Ribbon, 138

copying data
  general discussion, 31
  importing by, 137–142
  keyboard shortcut, 35

corrupted databases, 58

Count check boxes, Summary Options
    window, 196

Count() function, 379, 407

Count operation, 252

counter fields, 117

Counter variable, 597–599

Create a New Data Source to SQL Server
    dialog box, 675–677

Create Data Macros button, Design-view
    Ribbon tools, 108

Create Digital Certificate dialog box,
    472–473

Create Named Macro event, 479

Create New List dialog box, SharePoint,
    687

Create tab, Ribbon, 23, 31

Created Date grouping option, Navigation
    Pane, 26–27

criteria
  Crosstab queries, 284
  dates, times, text, and values, 208
  filtering by form, 131–132
  general discussion, 12, 125
  including in query, 197
  lookup fields in, 211–212
  multiple, 210–211
  operators in, 208–210
  update queries, 262

Criteria row
  joining multiple criteria for one
    field, 210
  query design grid, 201

Crosstab queries
  aggregate columns, 285–286
  aggregating data, 277–278
  criteria, 284
  in Design view, 282–284
  general discussion, 12, 191
  multiple fields for row headings, 284–285
  overview, 277
  sorting data, 286
Crosstab Query Wizard, 278–282
crosstabs, 14
`CSng(expression)` function, 235
`CStr(expression)` function, 235
cur tag, 588
curly brackets [{}], 468
`Currency` data type, 39, 71, 97, 568
Currency fields
  controls, 326
  formatting, 113–115, 233–236
  general discussion, 111
  null values, 237
  storing information, 59
  Text fields versus, 58
Currency Number format, 113
Current Database page, Access Options
  dialog box, 524
Current Folder option, Insert Hyperlink
  dialog box, 88
`CurrentProject` object, 622
`CurrentView` property, 624
cursors
  controlling movement in form, 336–337
  Expression Builder, 230
  in recordsets, 632–633
`CursorType` property, 632
Custom grouping option, Navigation
  Pane, 26–27
Custom lists, SharePoint, 687
Custom Web Apps
  .accdb files versus, 695
  actions, 703–706
  defining, 692
  entering data, 699–700
  launching, 698–699
  navigating, 700–701
  new, 693–694
  overview, 692, 695
  queries, 706–707
  requirements, 692–693
  tables, 696–698
  views, 701–703
Customer Experience Improvement
  Program, 18
customizing
  Access, 710
  data, 142
Cut button, Ribbon, 138
cutting data, 84, 137–142
`CVar(expression)` function, 235
cylinder column charts, 443

D

DAO (Data Access Objects) object model,
  629
dash (-), input mask characters, 163
data bars, 435–437
data entry
  AutoCorrect feature, 94–96
  general discussion, 71–72
  validating data during, 170–173
data macros, 14, 460, 478–481, 705–706
Data setting, in charts, 440
data sources
  ODBC, 673–676
  SharePoint lists, 686
data tables, 454
data tasks, 429, 432–433
`Data Type` property, 158
data types
  adding fields to datasheet, 77–78
  append queries, 265
  choosing, 56, 110–112
  cutting and pasting data, 140
  general discussion, 38–39
  specifying, 71
  VBA, 567–569
data validation, 159–164, 360–361
Database File Types options, Backstage
  View, 21

`Database` option, 563

database server programs, 511

Database Splitter Wizard, 514–516

Database Tools tab, Ribbon, 23

databases. *See also* relational databases

  add-ins, 508–509

  analyzing and documenting, 504–508

  Backstage View, 32

  backups, 500–503

  blank, 501

  compacting and repairing, 499–500

  converting, 503–504

  creating main-menu form to appear upon opening, 490–491

  designing, 38, 46

  desktop, 682–683

  exporting objects, 501–503

  front and back end, 513–518

  general discussion, 9

  granting access to specific users, 532

  grouping objects, 26–27, 28

  guidelines, 15–16

  importing data from, 153–154, 311–312

  keyboard shortcuts, 35–36

  main menus, 361

  make-table queries, 264

  moving to SharePoint, 690–692

  multiple, 43

  multiple users, 21

  normalizing, 41

  opening, 19–22, 469–474

  opening form automatically upon opening, 363

  order for setting up, 46

  overview, 499

  planning for, 10

  reasons for using, 10

  renaming, 63

  running macro upon opening, 467, 527

  sample, 21–22, 53

  saving attached files, 91

  saving in different Access version, 21

  from scratch, 61–63

  SharePoint, 701

  tables and fields in, 74–76

  from template, 63–64

  user settings, 524–527

  viewing objects in, 29–30

data-integrity rules, 159

`DataMode` variable, 610

Datasheet Formatting dialog box, 98–99

Datasheet option, Ribbon, 292, 300

Datasheet view

  `Attachment` fields, 90

  calculations in queries, 222–223

  choosing between Design view and, 75

  creating new table, 70–71

  displaying query results, 353

  forms, 294

  inserting columns, 100

  keystrokes to enter and edit data, 83

  moving columns, 99

  navigating Custom Web App, 700

  queries, 189

  renaming fields, 73

  viewing form fields in datasheet, 309

  viewing query, 197

  viewing tables, 68–70

datasheets

  adding total row, 103–104

  changing default formatting for new tables, 101

  changing fonts, 97

  changing row height, 100

  columns, 99–101

  cutting and pasting data, 140–141

  displaying with split form, 372–373

  editing hyperlinks in, 86–87

  filtering data, 121, 125–135

  finding and replacing data, 123–125

  formatting, 96–101

  formatting fields, 97

  forms versus, 289

  general discussion, 70

  gridlines and background color, 98–99

  Microsoft Graph, 452

  navigating, 81–82

  overview, 80, 121

  query, 217–218

  Rich Text, 97–98

  sorting rows, 121–123

  spell checking, 92–94

datasheets *(continued)*
  testing existing data, 173
  for update query, 259–260
  viewing, 80–81
Date and Time button, Ribbon, 358
date arithmetic calculations, 238
Date data type, 568
Date Delimiter option, Import Specification
    dialog box, 149
Date fields
  controls, 326
  grouping in report, 393
Date() function, 232, 238, 240
Date Last Changed field, 53
Date Order option, Import Specification
    dialog box, 149
Date Updated field, 53
DateAdd() function, 240–241
DateDiff() function, 240–241
dates
  adding to report, 402
  calculating, 370
  in criteria, 208
  Crosstab queries, 278–281
  formatting, 330–331, 370
  grouping in chart, 441, 444
  typing today's, 36
Date/Time data type, 39
Date/Time fields
  filtering, 128–130
  formatting, 116
  general discussion, 111
  X-Axis setting in bar chart, 444
Date/Time functions, 239–241
Date/Time option, Crosstab Query
    Wizard, 281
DAvg function, 380
Day() function, 240
dbl tag, 588
dbo_ prefix, table names, 680, 682
DCount function, 380
debug window, Visual Basic Editor, 546–547
debugging code
  compiler errors, 642–643
  general discussion, 641

logical errors, 647–650
overview, 641
runtime errors, 643–647
Debug.Print statement
  logical errors, 647–648
  viewing type of data stored in control, 618
Decimal Places property, 331
Decimal setting, Number fields, 116
Decimal Symbol option, Import
    Specification dialog box, 149
decimals
  formatting display, 97
  storing percentages, 60
decision-making
  expressions, 243–247
  If...End If statements, 590–592
  overview, 589–590
  Select Case blocks, 592–595
declarations
  modules, 541
  variables, 582
decrypting databases, 529
Default Value property
  avoiding GIGO, 158
  form controls, 361
default values, setting, 57
Default View property
  displaying multiple records, 309
  reports, 388–389
defining variables, 582
Definition Only option, Import Objects
    dialog box, 154
Del key, AutoKeys macro, 468
Delete button, mini toolbar, 700
Delete Columns button, Ribbon, 200
Delete option, contextual menus, 182
delete queries, 256
Delete row, QBE (Query by Example) grid,
    268–269
Delete Rows button, Ribbon, 108, 200
deleting
  objects, 31
  records, 267–270
Delimited Option
  Import Text Wizard, 146–147
  Link Text Wizard, 146–147

delimiting values, 239
dependency information, viewing, 505
descending order, sorting in
  Advanced Filter/Sort feature, 134
  combo boxes, 342
  general discussion, 121–122
  groups, 404
  queries, 205–206
  records, 394
Description field, Create a New Data
    Source to SQL Server dialog box, 676
descriptions, of fields, 106
design grid
  inserting table, 203–204
  selecting fields for queries, 192–193
Design tab
  Access Options window, 101
  Ribbon, 316
Design view
  action queries, 638
  calculations in queries, 222
  changing forms, 314
  changing size of panes, 200
  choosing between Datasheet view and, 75
  creating data macro as part of table,
    478–481
  creating tables in, 105–107
  Crosstab queries, 282–284
  defining primary key, 117–118
  displaying data from different tables, 215
  displaying or hiding table names, 202
  editing reports, 396–397
  editing view in, 701–702
  formatting fields with field properties,
    113–117
  forms, 294
  general discussion, 198–200
  indexing fields, 118–119
  input masks, 160
  joining tables, 214–215
  keyboard shortcut, 35
  macros, 462
  modifying chart, 451
  modifying existing forms and reports,
    300–301

navigating, 202
overview, 105, 198
printing table designs, 119–120
queries, 189–190, 191–194
query design grid, 201
refining table, 107–112
reports, 388–389, 409–410
saving tables, 73–74
sorting by name or company, 249
tables in, 201
viewing properties of subform controls,
    378
viewing query, 197
viewing tables, 68–70
designing databases
  adding tables for codes and
    abbreviations, 51
  choosing primary keys for each table,
    51–53
  cleanup, 56–57
  eliminating redundant fields, 47
  identifying data, 46
  linking tables, 53–55
  organizing fields into tables, 47–50
  overview, 46
  table names, 55–56
desktop databases, 682–683
detail queries, 194–195
Detail section
  forms, 357
  reports, 397–399
detail tables
  cascading deletes, 55
  cascading updates, 54–55
  general discussion, 43
  one-to-many relationships, 176
  referential integrity, 54
Details option, Navigation Pane, 27
Details pane, Object Browser, 548–549
DFirst function, 380
diagnostic programs, 18
dialog boxes, editing hyperlinks in, 87–89
dictionaries, 92–93
digital certificates, 473
digital signatures, 470, 472–474

Dim command
  defining variable at module level, 583–584
  explicit variable declarations, 582–583
  multidimensional arrays, 586–587
Dim keyword, 621–622
dimensions, in arrays, 586
discs, installing from, 709–712
Display Form setting, for current database, 525, 527
Display Navigation Pane setting, for current database, 526
Display Status Bar setting, for current database, 525
division operator (/), 225–226
DLast function, 380
DLookup function, 380
DMax function, 380
DMin function, 380
DoCmd object, 608–612
Document Window Options, for current database, 525
Documenter dialog box
  general discussion, 64, 508
  printing table designs, 119–120
documenting databases, 508
documents, tabbed, 30, 525
dollar sign ($), defining number formats, 114
Do...Loop loops, 595–597
domain aggregate functions, 380
Don't Display Lists When More Than This Number of Records Is Read setting, for sample database, 527
doThis argument, IIf() function, 243
.dotx files, 661–662
Double data type, 568
double quotation marks (""), SQL statements, 635–637
Double setting, Number fields, 115
doughnut charts, 448–449
drivers, 675
drop-down menus, 82–83, 164, 354–355
DSum function, 380
dtm tag, 588
duplicate values
  cutting and pasting data, 140
  finding with query wizard, 272–275
  hiding, 275, 408

duplicating entries, 36
Dynamic Cursor type, 632–633
dynamic datasheets, 189–190
dynasets, 217

E

Edit button, mini toolbar, 700
Edit Hyperlink dialog box, 87–89
Edit List button, Input Mask Wizard, 161
edit mode, 84
Edit Named Macro event, 479
Edit Relationships dialog box
  general discussion, 182
  setting referential integrity between two tables, 180
Edited Record option, record-locking feature, 521
EditRecord action, 480
elements, in arrays, 586
ellipsis (...), defining multiple variables, 582
Else sections, If blocks, 476
elseDoThis argument, IIf() function, 243
ElseIf sections, If blocks, 476
ElseIf statement, 591
e-mail
  exporting report, 431–432
  linking to address, 88
  storing address in Access, 660
embedded macros, 460, 482, 484–485
Enable Content button, Search Online Templates search box, 64
Enable Data Integrity option, Lookup Wizard, 167
Enable Design Changes for Tables in Datasheet View setting, for current database, 526
Enable Layout View setting, for current database, 525, 527
Enabled property, 487, 614
encrypting databases, 528–529
End Function statement, 563
End key, datasheets, 82
End Sub statement, 563
EndDate value, 238–239

Enter a Product Key Instead option, Activate Office screen, 714

Enter a Product Key option, Change Access Installation screen, 715

Enter key, navigating datasheets, 81

Enter Parameter Value dialog box, 250–251

.EOF property, 631

equal sign (=)
  equal to operator, 209, 245, 589
  variables, 582

Eqv operator, 245

Err.Clear() property, 644

Err.Description property, 644

Err.Number property, 644

ErrObject object, 644

error handling, 495, 643–646

error messages
  coding, 645–646
  compile errors, 574–575
  troubleshooting expressions, 368
  when communicating with SharePoint server, 694

errors
  compiler, 641–643
  general discussion, 641
  logical, 647–650
  runtime, 643–647

Err.Raise(errNo) property, 644

Esc key, cancelling entries, 83

Euro Number format, 113

event procedures, 565–566, 615–617

Event tab, property sheets, 482–483, 539

event-driven macros, 477

events
  data macro, 705
  form, 482–484
  general discussion, 477, 620–621
  triggering data macro, 479–481

Events lists, SharePoint, 687

Excel
  exporting data to, 666–670
  importing data from, 141–142
  sending reports to, 429–430
  spreadsheet compatibility, 143

Exceptions button, AutoCorrect dialog box, 95–96

exclamation point (!)
  action queries, 257
  formatting Text field, 117
  input mask characters, 163

exclusive mode, 518–519

executing code, 537, 557–558, 595–600

Exit Sub statement, 645

Expected:list separator or) error message, 575

explicit variable declarations, 582

exponentiation operator (^), 225

Export – Excel Spreadsheet dialog box, 429–430, 432–433

export button, adding to application, 666–668

Export dialog box, 155, 502

Export Tables to SharePoint Wizard, 690–691

exporting data
  automatically, 432–433
  database objects, 501–503
  to Excel, 666–670
  general discussion, 154–155
  overview, 137
  from query, 219
  reports, 429–435
  saving steps, 423
  Word mail merge, 156

Expression argument, SetTempVar action, 494

Expression Builder
  adding calculated field to table, 86
  buttons in Design view, 199
  calculated controls, 367
  Expression box, 229
  general discussion, 228–229

expressions
  checking, 368
  dates, 370
  decision-making, 243–247
  field names in, 226
  on forms and reports, 366

expressions *(continued)*
  function procedures in, 579
  functions in, 227
  literal dates and times, 239
  manipulating text, 242
  numeric, 369
  operators in, 224–226
  overview, 224
  passing to functions, 231
  in select query, 260
  testing with VBE Immediate window, 547
  text, 370
  troubleshooting, 368–369
  viewing long, 367
  zooming in on, 224
ExtendedDate value, 239
Extensible Markup Language
    (XML) files, 432
External Data tab, Ribbon, 23, 144
ExtPrice field, 222–223

F

F1 key, AutoKeys macro, 468
F4 key, opening drop-down menus, 83
Fail option, On Error action, 495
field breaks, 147
Field Information option, Import
    Specification dialog box, 149
Field List pane, 303, 316
field lists, 180, 301
field names
  appending data, 144
  changing, 73
  choosing, 72–73
  in criteria, 208
  in expressions, 226
  inserting field into design grid, 203–204
  passing to functions, 231
  in recordsets, 633
field properties
  avoiding GIGO, 158
  Design view, 69
  formatting, 113–117
  general discussion, 107

  overview, 113
  setting field size, 115–116
Field row
  query design grid, 201, 266–267
  zooming in on expressions, 224
Field Size property
  avoiding GIGO, 158
  formatting, 114–117
  general discussion, 115–116
field templates, 75, 78–80
field types
  choosing, 78
  overview, 57
  Short Text versus Long Text, 57–58
  storing, 59–61
  Text versus Number or Currency, 58
  Text versus Yes/No, 57
Field Width dialog box, 99–100
fields. *See also* lookup fields
  adding and deleting, 109, 110, 302
  appending data, 144
  avoiding multiple identical, 49–50
  calculated, 85–86, 222, 228–229
  captions, 109
  changing format, for query, 206–207
  for chart, 439–440
  choosing data type, 56
  combining, 52–53
  for combo box, 342–343
  copying in Design view, 109
  creating by clicking button, 77–78
  creating new control by dragging, 317–320
  Crosstab queries, 282
  cutting and pasting data, 140
  data types, 38–39
  data validation rules, 56
  defining in Design view, 106
  defining with Like operator, 173
  descriptions, 106
  determining whether value
      has changed, 481
  displaying empty or long, 413–414
  displaying form with
      command button, 351
  displaying in report, 392
  eliminating redundant, 47

filtering multiple, 130–132
Find box, 354–355
finding duplicate records, 272–275
finding unmatched records, 271
formatting, 97, 113–117
general discussion, 11–12, 70
hiding, 206
indexing, 57, 118–119
inserting into design grid, 203–204
lookup, 164–170
mailing labels, 426–427
moving in Design view, 110
naming, 48, 55–56
new, 71–72
organizing into tables, 47–50
overview, 37–38, 76–77
for pie and doughnut charts, 448–449
primary key fields for tables, 40
for queries, 192–193
quick-starting table with field
    templates, 78–80
rearranging with control layout, 302
in record source, 290
required, 56
setting size, 115–116
sorting by, 205, 405
spell checking, 92–94
subform, 375–376
for summary queries, 194–195
tables in database and, 74–76
testing for empty, 248
using multiple for row headings in
    Crosstab queries, 284–285
viewing previous value of edited, 481
Fields tab, Ribbon, 71, 80–81
File button, Ribbon, 74
file data sources, 674
File Name dialog box, 62
File tab, Ribbon, 19, 23
files
  linking to, 88
  storing, 59
Filter button, Ribbon, 127, 130, 134
Filter by Form feature, 130–132

Filter by Group section, Navigation
    Pane, 26–27
Filter Lookup options, for sample
    database, 527
Filter Name argument, macro
    actions, 464
Filter property, 127
Filtered/Unfiltered indicator,
    datasheets, 127
filtering data
  Advanced Filter/Sort feature, 132–135
  based on calculated fields, 254
  general discussion, 126–127
  multiple fields, 130–132
  overview, 125–126
  printing forms, 312
  quick filters, 128–129
  by selection, 129–130
  types of filters, 127–128
FilterName variable, 610
financial functions, 232–233
Find and Replace dialog box, 123–125, 259
Find boxes, 354–355
Find Duplicates Query Wizard, 272–275
Find Next option, Find and Replace dialog
    box, 124–125
Find Unmatched Query Wizard, 270–272
Find What option, Find and Replace dialog
    box, 124
finding data, 123–125
FindNextRecord macro action, 462
FindRecord macro action, 462
First() function, 379
First Name field, sorting by, 248–249
First operation, 252
first-level subdatasheets, 102
Fixed Number format, 114
Fixed Width Option
  Import Text Wizard, 146–147
  Link Text Wizard, 146–147
folders
  shared, 512–513
  trusted locations, 470–472
Font button, Zoom dialog box, 84

fonts
  changing, 97
  character sets in Character Map, 92
  forms, 331–334
  themes, 310
footers
  calculated control in, 381–383
  forms, 357–358
  hiding or displaying for group in report,
    404
  reports, 398
For Each...Next loops, 625–627
Force New Page property, 420
Fore Color property, labels, 487
foreign key fields
  AutoLookup query, 218
  general discussion, 43
  linking tables, 53–54
  Long Integer Number field as, 56
  one-to-many relationships, 176
  referential integrity, 178
Form button, Ribbon, 291, 293–294
Form Design button, Ribbon, 291
Form Footer sections, of forms, 358
Form Header sections, of forms, 358
Form keyword, 622
Form Operations commands, Command
    Button Wizard, 349
Form view
  editing data, 295–296
  general discussion, 294
  previewing changes in form, 314
  subform, 377
  tab order, 336–337
  testing changes in form, 305
Form Wizard
  adding button to Ribbon, 291
  general discussion, 296–299
  headers and footers, 357–358
Format field property, 158–159
Format Painter, 333
Format property
  adding current date to report, 402
  Boolean values, 57
  changing format of query field, 207

defining numeric format to depend on
    value, 114–115
formatting Date/Time and Text fields,
    116–117
Format tab, Ribbon, 316
formatting
  calculated fields in queries, 233–236
  changing default for new tables, 101
  charts, 453–454
  conditional, 333–334
  copying, 333
  data bars, 436–437
  datasheet, 96–101
  dates, 330–331, 370
  with field properties, 113–117
  with input masks, 159–164
  Number and Currency fields, 58
  numbers, 330–331, 369–370
  query field, 206–207
  reports, 407–408, 418–422
  text, 370–371
Formatting buttons, Ribbon, 97
FormName variable, 609
forms
  changing controls with VBA, 612–619
  changing dynamically, 487–489
  changing in Design view, 314–317
  check boxes for Yes/No fields, 335
  combo and list boxes, 339–345
  command buttons, 348–353
  configuring, 305–310
  control layouts, 326–329
  controlling cursor movement, 336–337
  controls, 317–323, 330
  copying to reports, 409
  creating with wizards, 296–300
  custom messages, 605–608
  designing, 318
  determining whether open, 623–625
  displaying attachments, 355–357
  displaying text, numbers, and dates,
    323–326
  displaying with command button,
    351–352
  with filter, 135

filtering by, 128, 130–132
Find box, 354–355
fonts, colors, and alignment, 331–334
formatting numbers and dates, 330–331
general discussion, 12–13, 290–292
headers and footers, 357–358
Layout view, 301–305
lines, boxes, and backgrounds, 335
main menu, 361–363, 490–494
modifying existing, 300–301
new, 293–296, 313–314
objects and collections, 619–628
opening and closing with DoCmd object, 608–612
opening automatically when database opens, 363
opening upon opening database, 467
option groups, 345–348
overview, 289–290, 313, 339, 605
placing calculated value on, 369
printing, 312
relationship between reports and, 290, 388–389
running macros in, 482–487
spell checking, 92–94
split, 372–373
storing, 310–312
tabbed, 358–360
validating data, 360–361
Yes/No fields, 345
Forms group buttons, Ribbon, 291
For...Next loops, 597–600
Four Digit Years option, Import Specification dialog box, 149
Freeze Fields option, contextual menus, 101
From option, QBE (Query by Example) grid, 268–269
FROM table, 634
front end databases. *See also* SQL Server
Database Splitter Wizard, 514–516
distributing copies, 516–517
general discussion, 16
overview, 513
relinking tables, 517–518
splitting database, 513–514
Full Module view, Code window, 546
function procedures
in Access, 579–580
general discussion, 563–564
modules, 542
running sub procedure from macro, 578
syntax, 568–569
testing, 578–579
Function statement, 563, 567
functions
aggregate, 379–381
custom, 600–604
in expressions, 227
help with, 230–231
nesting, 232, 371
passing arguments to built-in, 566
returning values from, 569–570

G

General Number format, 113, 233–234
Get External Data – Access Database dialog box, 311
Get External Data dialog box, 144–145
Get External Data – ODBC Database dialog box, 673
Get External Data – SharePoint Site Wizard, 689
GIGO (garbage in, garbage out)
general discussion, 15–16
lookup fields, 164–170
overview, 157
tools for avoiding, 158–159
validating and formatting data with input masks, 159–164
validating data during entry, 170–173
GoTo statement, 643–644
GoToControl macro action, 462
graphical user interface (GUI), 545
graphs. *See* charts

greater than or equal to operator (>=)
  decision-making, 589
  general discussion, 209, 245
greater than sign (>)
  formatting Text field, 117
  greater than operator, 209, 245, 589
  grouping data in report, 393
  input mask characters, 163
gridlines, 98–99, 454
grids, 315
Group, Sort, and Total pane, 403–407
Group by operation, 252
Group By value, 254
Group dialog box, 441, 444
Group on line, Group, Sort, and Total
    pane, 403
Grouping Footer section, of reports,
    398–399
Grouping Header section, of reports,
    398–399
Grouping Intervals dialog box, 393–394
grouping operator [( )], 225
grouping sections, in reports, 402–405,
    406–407
groups, Ribbon, 24
GUI (graphical user interface), 545

H

handles, 327, 451
headers, 357–358, 398, 404
headings
  Crosstab queries, 279, 284–285
  sorting manually, 286
Help button
  error message boxes, 575
  Expression Builder, 230
help system
  functions, 230–231
  general discussion, 18
  keyboard shortcut, 35
  keywords, 559
  Object Browser, 550–551
  online, 34
hidden fields, 140
Hide Duplicates property, 408

hiding fields, 101, 206
Home key
  datasheets, 82
  Design view, 202
Home tab, Ribbon, 23, 80
horizontal scroll bar
  navigating datasheet, 81
  in Print Preview window, 417
hosting, SharePoint, 693
Hour() function, 240
HTML documents
  compatibility, 143
  exporting data to, 155
  exporting report as, 432
hybrid applications, 683
Hyperlink Address property, 325
Hyperlink Builder, 89
Hyperlink button, Ribbon, 319, 325
hyperlink controls, 323–326
Hyperlink data type, 39
Hyperlink fields, 86–87, 112
hyperlinks, 86–89

I

Icon option, Navigation Pane, 27
ID fields, 70–71
If blocks, 475–476, 488–489
If statements, 618
If...End If blocks, 646
If...End If statements, 590–591, 592
If-Then blocks, 475–476
if-then calculations, 371
If-Then-Else blocks, 476
Ignore All option, Spelling dialog box, 94
Ignore Field option, Spelling dialog box, 94
Ignore Nulls index property, 119
Ignore option, Spelling dialog box, 94
IIf() function
  comparisons in, 244–245
  decision-making, 591
  displaying values depending on
      conditions, 371
  general discussion, 243–244
  printing reports, 408

sales tax example, 246–247

sorting by name or company, 249

Image control type, 320

Immediate If function, 243–244

Immediate window

  logical errors, 647–648

  testing function procedure, 578–579

  testing functions, 569–570, 603

  testing sub procedure, 575–576, 598–599

  VBE, 546–547

immediate-if() function, 371

Imp operator, 245

implicit variable declarations, 582

Import Objects dialog box, 153–154, 311–312

Import Specification dialog box, 148

Import Spreadsheet Wizard, 149–150

Import Text Wizard, 146–148

Import Wizard, 142

importing data

  from Access database, 153–154

  cleaning up, 152

  cutting, copying, and pasting, 137–142

  forms and reports, 311–312

  general discussion, 142

  linking to data or, 142–153

  ODBC, 673–674

  overview, 137

IN operator, 209

In operator, 245

Indexed property, 118–119, 159

Indexes button, Design-view Ribbon tools, 108

Indexes window, 118–119

indexing fields, 57, 118–119

infinity symbol (∞)

  detail tables, 176–177, 181

  referential integrity, 184, 216

Info command, Backstage view, 32–33

inner joins, 215–216, 272

Input Mask property

  avoiding GIGO, 158–159

  form controls, 361

  manually creating input mask, 162–163

Input Mask Wizard, 110, 160–162

input masks

  formatting calculated text box, 371

  formatting data, 159–164

  validating data, 162–164

Ins key, AutoKeys macro, 468

Insert Above button, Ribbon, 304

Insert Below button, Ribbon, 304

Insert Columns button, Ribbon, 200

Insert Hyperlink dialog box, 87–88, 325

Insert Left button, Ribbon, 304

Insert page break control button, Ribbon, 319

Insert Right button, Ribbon, 304

Insert Rows button, Ribbon, 108, 200

Insert Subdatasheet dialog box, 103

installation files, 712

installing Access

  activating, 713–714

  from disc, 709–712

  from Office 365, 712–713

  overview, 709

  repairing, reinstalling, or uninstalling, 715

instances of applications, 656

InStr() function, 243

int tag, 588

Integer data type, 568

Integer setting, Number fields, 115

IntelliSense feature, 570

Internet

  client/server computing, 672

  Custom Web App, 692

  help pages, 34, 550–551

  launching Custom Web App, 698–699

  scanning downloaded files for viruses, 20

The Internet For Dummies, 20

interval arguments, 241

Int(number) function, 233

Is Not Null criterion, 208

Is Null criterion, 208, 272

IsLoaded property, 624

IsNull() function, 248

isOpen() function, 623–625

Issues lists, SharePoint, 687

Issues template, 76

J

Join field, 218
join lines, 181
Join Properties dialog box, 215–216
join tables
  choosing type of join and setting join
    properties, 215–216
  in Design view, 214–215
  inner, 272
  referential integrity, 180–181, 183–184
  selecting multiple items in lookup field,
    169
Join Type button, Edit Relationships dialog
    box, 182
junction tables
  general discussion, 45
  linking tables, 54
  many-to-many relationships, 182–183

K

key fields. *See* primary key fields
key-assignment macros, 467
keyboard shortcuts
  cancelling entry, 83
  changing check box settings or choosing
    from drop-down menu, 82–83
  Code window, 571–572
  command buttons, 485
  cutting, copying, and pasting, 138
  deleting or copying control, 330
  Design view, 202
  editing data, 83, 85
  entering data, 83–84
  general discussion, 34–36
  navigating datasheet, 81, 82
  navigating forms, 296
  to object, 28, 32
  switching views, 30
  undoing actions, 318
keys. *See* primary key fields
KeyTips, 34–35
keywords, 558–559

L

L character, input masks, 163
Label button, Ribbon, 319, 324, 390
label controls, 323–324
labels
  associated, 327–328
  error handlers, 643–645
  mailing, 424–429
  option groups, 346, 348
  turning into hyperlink labels, 325
.laccdb file extension, 522
landscape orientation, printing reports, 419
Language option, Import Specification
    dialog box, 149
LANs (local area networks)
  multiuser access, 511
  security, 524
Last() function, 379
Last Name field, sorting by, 248–249
Last operation, 252
Launch App button, Ribbon, 704
Layout view
  adding and deleting rows and columns,
    304
  control layouts, 304–305
  creating navigation form, 362
  editing reports, 396–397
  fields, 302
  forms, 294
  modifying existing forms and reports,
    300–301
  new form, 303–304
  overview, 301–302
  reports, 388–389
  settings, 525, 527
  trying out form, 305
layouts
  forms, 315–316
  reports, 315–316, 395–396
LBound() function, 599
LCase() function, 243
LDB files, 522
leading zero (0), 58, 149
Left() function, 243

left outer joins, 215–216

left-aligned controls, 329

legends, in charts, 442, 453–454

Len() function, 243, 600

less than or equal to operator (<=)
  comparisons in IIf() function, 244–245
  decision-making, 589
  general discussion, 209

less than sign (<)
  formatting Text field, 117
  grouping data in report, 393
  input mask characters, 163
  less than operator, 209, 245, 589

Leszynski naming convention, 56

letters, sorting, 122

Levine, John R., 20

lifetimes of variables, 584

Like operator, 173, 245

LIKE operator, 209

Limit to List property, 167, 345

line breaks
  in code, 572–574
  slowing procedures, 648–650
  SQL statement, 635–637

line charts, 446–448

Line control button, Ribbon, 319

lines, in forms, 335

Link Child Fields property, 378, 412

Link Master Fields property, 378, 412

Link Spreadsheet Wizard, 149–150

Link Tables dialog box, 678

Link Text Wizard, 146–148

Link Wizard, 142

Linked Forms option, Form Wizard dialog box, 298

Linked Table Manager, 151–152, 517–518, 680

linking
  database to table, 43
  desktop databases, 682–683
  to existing SharePoint list, 689–690
  to ODBC data source, 673–674
  password-protected database, 529
  refining links, 54–55
  tables, 53–55, 517–518, 689–690

linking to data
  cleaning up imported data, 152
  compatible applications, 143
  contacts from Outlook, 150–151
  getting external data, 144–146
  with Import Spreadsheet and Link Spreadsheet wizards, 149–150
  making data available, 142–143
  managing links, 151–152
  overview, 142
  running and scheduling saved imports, 153
  text or spreadsheet, 146–149

links, 86–89

List box control button, Ribbon, 319

list box controls, 323, 339–345

List option, Navigation Pane, 27

List Rows property, 344

List view, 700

lists. *See* SharePoint

literal dates, 239

literal strings, 574

literal text, 224, 242

literal times, 239

literal values, 231

lng tag, 588

LoanAmount field name, 235

local area networks (LANs)
  multiuser access, 511
  security, 524

Local Indexed Fields setting, for sample database, 527

Local Non-Indexed Fields setting, for sample database, 527

locales, 563

Locals window, 649–650

locking
  databases, 529–532
  information files, 522
  records, 519–522

Log Name AutoCorrect Changes setting, for current database, 526

logical errors, 641, 647–650

logical expressions, 207

logical operators, 245, 589–590

logical values, 57

Logo button, Ribbon, 358

Long data type, 568

Long Integer setting, Number fields, 56, 115

Long Text data type, 38

Long Text fields

  general discussion, 111

  Short Text fields versus, 57–58

  in text boxes, 325–326

  wrapping onto additional lines, 413

Look In option, Find and Replace dialog box, 124

lookup fields. *See also* fields

  allowing multiple selections, 168–169

  combo boxes, 341

  in criteria, 211–212

  Design-view Ribbon tools, 108

  Lookup Wizard, 165–168

  modifying lookup list, 170

  overview, 164

  queries with multivalue, 212–213

  viewing type of data stored in, 618

lookup lists, 170

Lookup Wizard, 39, 112, 165–168

loops

  analyzing each character in string, 600

  through arrays, 599

  through collections, 625–627

  Do...Loop, 595–597

  For...Next, 597–599

  overview, 595

  through recordsets, 631–632

  While...Wend, 597

Lowe, Doug, 524

M

machine data sources, 674

Macro Builder, 480

Macro button, Ribbon, 460, 553

Macro Name option, On Error action, 495

Macro Settings option, Trust Center, 533

macros

  attaching to tables, 478–481

  blocked content, 547

  converting to VBA code, 553–555

  in Custom Web App, 704

  data, 705–706

  DoCmd object and, 611

  dynamically changing form, 487–489

  for forms, 322

  general discussion, 14, 460

  main-menu forms, 490–494

  opening databases containing, 469–474

  overview, 459, 477

  running conditionally, 474–476

  running in forms, 482–487

  running sub procedures from, 577–578

  running with command button, 353

  stand-alone, 460–469

  temporary variables, 494–495

mail merges, 156, 431

mailing labels, 425–429

main forms, 381–383

main menus, 361

main reports, 412

main-menu forms, 490–495

maintenance, importing data, 142

Make Submacro Block option, contextual menus, 466

Make Table dialog box, 263–264

make-table queries, 256, 262–265

malicious code, 64

Manage Data Tasks dialog box, 153

many-to-many relationships

  general discussion, 42, 44–46, 176

  linking tables, 54

  referential integrity, 182–184

margins, 419–422

master tables

  AutoNumber field as primary key in, 56

  cascading deletes, 55

  cascading updates, 54–55

  general discussion, 43

  one-to-many relationships, 175–176

  referential integrity, 54

Match Case option, Find and Replace dialog box, 124

Match option, Find and Replace dialog box, 124
matching
  keys, 176
  part of field, 131
math
  calculations in queries, 221–224
  date and time calculations, 238–241
  decision-making expressions, 243–247
  Expression Builder, 228–232
  expressions, 224–227
  flexible parameter queries, 249–251
  formatting calculated fields in queries, 233–236
  manipulating text with expressions, 242–243
  null values, 236–237
  overview, 221
  sorting by name or company, 248–249
  testing for empty fields, 248
  totals, subtotals, and averages, 252–254
Max() function, 379
Max operation, 252
Maximize button, Code window, 544–545
.mdb files, 21, 63, 532
Me keyword, 619
Members list, Object Browser, 548–549
merge button, 663
merging data, with Word documents, 661–666
MessageBox macro action, 462
messages, custom, 605–608
methods, 548, 620–621
Me!WhereTo.Value expression, 594
mice, navigating datasheets with, 81
Microsoft Account option, Activate Office screen, 714
Microsoft Graph, 450, 452–455
Microsoft Help system, 18
Microsoft Office Trusted Location dialog box, 471–472
Microsoft Support website, 34
Microsoft Technet website, 34
Mid() function, 243, 600
Min() function, 379
Min operation, 252

mini toolbar, 699–700, 705
Minimize the Ribbon button, Ribbon, 24
minus sign (-)
  subdatasheets, 102
  subtraction operator, 225
Miscellaneous commands, Command Button Wizard, 349
MOD operator, 226
Modal Dialog option, Ribbon, 292, 300
Modified Date grouping option, Navigation Pane, 26–27
Modify Lookup button, Ribbon, 108, 167
Modify the Query Design option, Summary Options window, 196
Module button, Ribbon, 539
module-level declarations, 562
module-level scope, 583
modules
  class, 537–538
  converting macro to, 555
  general discussion, 15
  options, 562–563
  standard, 538
money, storing, 59–60
MonthName() function, 240
months, sorting by, 205
More Fields button, Ribbon, 78
More Forms button, Ribbon, 292
More Pages view, Print Preview, 417
.Move numrecords, start method, ADO recordsets, 631
Move to SharePoint Site Issues table, Export Tables to SharePoint Wizard, 690–691
.MoveFirst method, ADO recordsets, 630
.MoveLast method, ADO recordsets, 631
.MoveNext method, ADO recordsets, 630
.MovePrevious method, ADO recordsets, 630
Msg = Err.Description & " - " & Err.Number statement, 645
MsgBox() function, 605–607
MsgBox keyword, 559
MsgBox Msg statement, 645
MsgBox() statements, 560–561
multidimensional arrays, 587

Multiple Items option, Ribbon, 292, 299
multiplication operator (*), 225
multiuser access
  exclusive mode, 518–519
  front end and back end databases,
    513–518
  overview, 511–512
  programming locks, 521–522
  record-locking feature, 519–521
  shared folders, 512–513
multiuser databases, 21
mvps.org, 56
myForm object variable, 624
myRecordset.Open statement, 636–637
myVar variable, 607

N

Name argument, SetTempVar action, 494
Name AutoCorrect feature, 73, 526
Name fields, 79, 676
Name property, 330
named macros, 481
names
  displaying or hiding, for table, 202
  inserting field into design grid, 203–204
  parameters, 250
  query, 219, 229
  sorting by, 248–249
  storing, 59–60
naming
  calculated controls, 408
  constants, 585
  controls, 323, 330, 368
  databases, 63
  fields, 55–56, 72–73
  forms, 307
  macros, 461–462
  new databases, 62
  pages, 359
  prefixes, 56
  procedures, 566
  tables, 55–56
  variables, 581
naming conventions, for variables, 588, 622

Navigation button, Ribbon, 292, 319
navigation buttons, on forms, 310
Navigation Buttons property, 310
navigation forms, 361–363
Navigation options, for current database,
    526
Navigation Options dialog box, 28
Navigation Pane
  choosing object size and details, 27–28
  displaying list of modules, 540
  displaying table or query in Datasheet
    view, 80
  forms, 293–294
  general discussion, 22
  grouping database objects, 26–27, 28
  hiding and showing, 35
  listing reports in database, 388
  managing forms and reports, 311
  for multiuser access, 516
  overview, 25
  searching for object, 29
  sorting objects in, 29
  SQL Server tables, 679
  viewing tables, 68
nesting
  functions, 232, 371
  If...End If statements, 592
.NET Framework, 683
Networking For Dummies, 524
Never Cache setting, for current database,
    527
New command, Backstage view, 33
New database option, Ribbon, 62
New Formatting Rule dialog box, 334,
    436–437
New Record buttons, Ribbon, 82
Next option, On Error action, 495
nine character (9), input masks, 163
No Locks option, record-locking feature,
    519–520
No value, 118
normalizing databases, 41
not equal to operator (<>), 209, 245, 589
NOT operator, 173
Not operator, 245

not operator, 590
Now() function, 240, 402
null values
  finding records with, 208
  general discussion, 236–237
  testing for empty fields, 248
Number data type, 39
Number fields
  controls, 326
  filtering, 128, 130
  formatting, 113–115
  general discussion, 111
  grouping in report, 393
  sorting, 121–122
  storing information, 59
  versus Text fields, 58
numbering
  automatically, 52
  pages in reports, 401–402
numbers
  calculating, 369–370
  in criteria, 208
  formatting, 97, 330–331, 369–370
  option groups, 346
  storing, 59–60
  summarizing numeric field in chart, 441
numeric expressions, 560
numeric values, 608
NumWord() custom function, 601–604
Nz() function, 236

O

Object box, Code window, 545–546
Object Browser
  looking up meanings of words in code, 552
  VBE, 548–549
  viewing project's object model, 655–656
Object data type, 568
object dependencies, 505–506
Object Dependencies button, Design-view
    Ribbon tools, 108
object libraries, 548, 552, 654–657
Object Library, 549–551

Object Linking and Embedding
    (OLE), 39, 320
object models, 548, 629–633
Object Name argument, macro
    actions, 464
Object Type grouping option, Navigation
    Pane, 26–27
object variables, 621–622
ObjectName variable, 611
object-oriented systems, 11
objects
  choosing size and details, 27–28
  creating, deleting, renaming, copying,
    and printing, 31–32
  determining whether form is open,
    623–625
  displaying properties, 35
  forms, 12–13
  grouping, 26–27, 28
  keyboard shortcuts, 36
  looping through collections, 625–627
  macros, 14
  modules, 15
  in object model, 551–552
  overview, 11, 619–620
  properties, methods, and events, 620–621
  queries, 12
  referring to, 621–622
  reports, 13–14
  searching for, 29
  shortcuts to, 32
  sorting in Navigation Pane, 29
  tables, 11–12
  viewing, 29–30
  With...End With block, 627–628
Objects That Depend on Me option, Object
    Dependencies pane, 505
Objects That I Depend On option, Object
    Dependencies pane, 506
ObjectType variable, 611
ODBC (Open Database Connectivity)
  compatibility, 143
  connecting to SQL Server with, 672–682
  linked tables, 680
  pass-through queries, 681–682

ODBC Database button, Ribbon, 672–673

ODBC Fields setting, for sample database, 527

Office, 18

Office 365, 693, 712–713

Office clipboard, 139–140

Office Professional, 709

OK button, error message boxes, 575

OKButton_Click() sub procedure, 594

OLE (Object Linking and Embedding), 39, 320

OLE data type, 39, 58, 59

On Click event
  contact button, 658
  general discussion, 484

On Click property, 353, 486–487, 493

On Dbl Click event, 484

On Delete event, 705

On Enter event, 484

On Error action, 495

On Error GoTo Err_MyProcedure statement, 645

On Error statements, 643–645

On Exit event, 484

On Insert event, 705

On Not in List event, 484

On Update event, 705

1 character, as base for arrays, 587

one-to-many relationships
  considering before running delete query, 268
  displaying detail records with subform, 373–374
  general discussion, 41, 42–43, 175–177
  linking tables, 53–54
  lookup fields, 164
  separate table for individual items, 49–50

one-to-one relationships, 42–44, 54

online help system, 34

Open command, Backstage view, 33

Open Database Connectivity (ODBC)
  compatibility, 143
  connecting to SQL Server with, 672–682
  linked tables, 680

overview, 672

pass-through queries, 681–682

Open Form button, main-menu form, 492

.Open method, ADO recordsets, 631

Open statement, 636–637

Open the Query to View Information option, Summary Options window, 196

OpenArgs variable, 610

OpenForm macro action, 462

OpenForm method, 608–609, 610–611

OpenQuery macro action, 462

OpenReport macro action, 462

OpenTable macro action, 462

operators
  in criteria expressions, 208–210
  data validation, 172–173
  in expressions, 224–226
  filtering by form, 131
  logical expressions, 207

Optimize button, Performance Analyzer, 507

Option Base 1 statement, 587

Option button control button, Ribbon, 320

option buttons, 345–348

Option Compare Binary declaration, 563

Option Compare Database declaration, 562

Option Compare Text declaration, 563

option groups, 319, 345–348

Option statements, 562–563

Options command, Backstage view, 33

Options dialog box, 101

Options option, Spelling dialog box, 94

Or operator, 131, 245–246

OR operator, 173, 210–211

or operator, 590

Or rows, 201, 210

ORDER BY clause, 634

Order By property, 308

order of precedence, 224–227

Organizational Account option, Activate Office screen, 714

outer joins, 215–216

Outlook
  compatibility, 143
  exporting contacts to, 657–661
  importing contacts from, 150–151
  sending reports to, 431–432
overlapping windows, 30, 525
overwrite mode, 84

p

page breaks, 404, 420–421
Page Down key
  datasheets, 81–82
  Design view, 202
Page Footer section, of reports, 398,
    400–402
Page Header section, of reports, 398,
    400–402
page numbers, for reports, 401–402
Page Setup dialog box, 428–429
Page Setup tab, Ribbon, 416–417
Page Up key, datasheets, 81–82
page-level locking, 521
pages
  controlling which receive headers and
    footers, 402
  general discussion, 358–360
  viewing multiple in Print Preview,
    417–418
paper orientation, for reports, 419–420
paper sizes, for reports, 419–420
paper-clip icon, Attachment fields, 90
parameter queries, 191, 249–251
Parameters button, Ribbon, 200
parentheses [()]
  controlling order of precedence, 225–227
  conversion functions, 235
  defining name and data type for
    argument, 568
  function syntax, 231
  grouping operator, 225
  passing argument to built-in function, 566
  subscripts, 585
passing, 227
pass-through queries, 681–682
Password input mask character, 163

Password Required dialog box, 529
passwords
  decrypting database, 529
  encrypting database, 528–529
  LAN, 524
  opening password-protected
    database, 529
  SQL Server, 679
  Windows, 524
Paste Append command, Ribbon, 140
Paste button, Ribbon, 138
pasting objects
  general discussion, 31
  importing data, 137–142
  keyboard shortcut, 36, 84
Path property, 665
pathnames, 59
Payment Type fields, 79
PDF (Portable Document Format) files
  compatibility, 143
  printing reports, 423–424
Percent Number format, 114
percent symbol (%), defining number
    formats, 114
percentages
  formatting display, 97
  specifying data type, 71
  storing, 60
  viewing top values, 205–206
Perform AutoCorrect setting, for current
    database, 526
Performance Analyzer, 506–507
period character (.)
  defining number format, 114
  input mask characters, 163
Phone fields, 79
phone numbers, storing, 59
Picture property, command button, 353
Picture Property Storage Format setting,
    for current database, 526
pictures
  in Attachment field, 356
  background, 335
  command button, 353
  storing, 59
pie charts, 448–449

pivot charts, 443

placeholders
  input masks, 162
  text in angle brackets, 231–232

plus sign (+)
  addition operator, 225
  combining options for argument, 561
  key-assignment macros, 468
  subdatasheets, 102

Pmt() function, 235

Pmt(rate, nper, po[,fv[, type]])
    function, 233

populating arrays, 587

Portable Document Format (PDF) files,
    423–424

portrait orientation, printing reports, 419

postal codes, 51, 59, 163

pound character (#)
  defining number format, 114
  delimiting values, 239
  hyperlinks, 87–89
  input masks, 163
  Like operator, 173

precedence, 224–227

prefixes, for object names, 56

Preserve Source Image Format setting, for
    current database, 526

Preview Report button, main-menu
    form, 492

Primary index property, 119

Primary Key button, Design-view Ribbon
    tools, 108

primary key fields
  append queries, 265
  AutoNumber fields, 56, 112
  choosing whether or not to define, 106
  data types, 38–39
  defining, 117–118
  for each table, 51–53
  general discussion, 40, 43
  linking tables, 53–54
  lookup fields, 166, 211–212
  one-to-many relationships, 175–176
  overview, 37–38
  referential integrity, 178
  secret keys, 61
  for tables, 40

primary sort keys, 205

Print command, Backstage view, 33

Print dialog box, 418–419

Print option, Ribbon, 32

Print Preview
  charts, 442
  keyboard shortcut, 32
  reports, 388–389, 415–418

Print Report button, main-menu form, 492

Print Table Definition dialog box, 119–120

printing
  current record, 352
  filtered table, 134
  forms, 312
  information from subreport on main
      report, 412
  matching records from form, 486–487
  objects, 31–32, 36
  only data from report, 422
  Relationships window, 184–185
  reports, 13–14, 352, 407–408, 422–424
  selecting printer, 418–419
  table designs, 119–120

PrintInvoiceOrReceipt submacro,
    486–487

PrintPreview macro action, 462

Priority fields, 79

Private keyword, 583–584

Private procedures, 542, 564

Private Sub statement, 563

private variables, 583

Procedure view, Code window, 546

Procedure/Events box, Code window,
    545–546

procedure-level declarations, 562

procedure-level scope, 583

procedures
  calling from another procedure, 577
  event, 565–566
  general discussion, 557–558
  modules, 541
  overview, 563
  passing arguments to, 566–569
  returning value from function, 569–570
  slowing, 648–650
  standard, 563–565

product activation, 713–714

product registration, 714
`ProductID` field, 253–254
program errors, 641
Program Flow group, Action Catalog, 465
programmatically manipulating
    objects, 548
programmer comments, 542
programming languages, 537
programs
  opening in VBA, 656–657
  separating data from, 16
Project/Library list, Object Browser,
    548–549
`Prompt` argument, 560–561
properties
  changing with `With...End With` block,
    627–628
  general discussion, 548, 620–621
  looping through, 627
`Property` keyword, 622
Property Sheet button, Ribbon,
    108, 192, 200
property sheets
  combo or list box, 344–345
  controls, 614–619
  Design-view Ribbon tools, 108
  forms, 301, 306–307
  general discussion, 316
  modifying chart, 451–452
  reports, 301, 306–307, 399–400
  setting control properties, 321–322
  specifying sort order, 286
  split forms, 373
protecting data. *See* referential integrity
Prototype Label list, Label Wizard, 426
`Public` keyword, 583–585
`Public` procedures, 542, 564
public variables, 583
pyramid column charts, 443

Q

QBE (Query by Example) grids
  Advanced Filter/Sort feature, 132–133
  Delete row, 268–269
  flexible parameter queries, 250
  general discussion, 198

`Qty` field, 221–223
queries
  action, 638–640
  adding tables, 203
  calculating in, 221–224
  calculating subtotals, 254
  chart, 456
  criteria, 207–213
  Custom Web App, 706–707
  Design view, 191–194, 198–202
  displaying results in Datasheet view, 353
  editing, 204–207
  by example, 207–208
  filtering data, 127
  formatting calculated fields, 233–236
  general discussion, 12, 190–191
  inserting field into design grid, 203–204
  making report, 390–396
  multiple related tables, 213–216
  names, 229
  overview, 189–190
  parameter, 249–251
  pass-through, 681–682
  placing calculated value on form or
    report, 369
  query datasheets, 217–218
  as record source for subform, 375
  saving, 219
  Simple Query Wizard, 194–197
  SQL statements, 634–635
  as subdatasheet, 102–103
  viewing, 197
query datasheets, 217–218
query fields, 206–207
Query Parameters dialog box, 250
Query Tools Design Tab, Ribbon, 199
Query Type buttons, Ribbon, 199, 258
query wizards, 255, 270–275
question mark character (?)
  input masks, 163
  `Like` operator, 173
  testing function from Immediate window,
    578–579
Quick Access toolbar, 24–25
quick filters, 128
Quick Info, 558–560
Quick Print option, Ribbon, 32

Quick Start Application Parts, 75
Quick Start fields, 78–79
quotation marks (" ")
  inserting text into text box, 614
  literal strings, 574
  literal text, 224
  passing string, 566
  SQL statement, 635–637
  zero-length strings, 242
quotation marks, single (' '), SQL
  statements, 635

R

ranges, Case statements, 595
Rathbone, Andy, 513, 524
RDBMS (relational database management
  systems), 671
read-only forms, 309–310
Recent Files option, Insert Hyperlink dialog
  box, 88
Recent option, Ribbon interface, 19
Record box, datasheets, 82
Record Navigation commands, Command
  Button Wizard, 349
record numbers, 82
Record Operations commands, Command
  Button Wizard, 349
record selector, 72, 310
Record Source property, 307–308
record sources
  binding control to data in, 323
  for chart, 438
  general discussion, 290, 307–308
  split forms, 372
  subform, 375–376
.RecordCount property, ADO recordsets,
  631, 633
record-locking feature, 519–521
record-navigation buttons, 82
records. *See also* rows
  adding calculated field to table, 85–86
  adding duplicate, 353
  Attachment data type, 89–91
  autonumbering, 52

controlling order, 308
deleting, 91, 134, 267–270
displaying multiple, 308–309
displaying with subform, 373–374
editing data, 84–85
entering data automatically with
  keystrokes, 83–84
entering special characters, 91–92
fields, 37–38
filtering based on calculated fields, 254
finding duplicate, 272–275
finding unmatched, 270–272
general discussion, 11–12, 70
grouping, 402–405
hyperlinks, 86–90
keyboard shortcut, 35
limiting with criteria, 207–213
macro to run when added to table, 706
numbering automatically, 40
overview, 82–83
printing, 352, 486–487
saving current, 353
setting page breaks, 420
sorting in report, 394, 405–406
specifying validation rules, 170
specifying which to include when opening
  form, 610
summarizing, 380
Recordset keyword, 622
Recordset object, 668–669
recordsets
  action queries in VBA, 638–640
  closing, 640
  connection cleanup, 640
  defining cursor type, 632–633
  field names, 633
  looping through, 631–632
  object models and, 629–633
  overview, 629
  properties and methods, 630–631
  SQL and, 633–637
Rectangle button, Ribbon, 319, 335
Redo button, Quick Access toolbar, 25
redundant information, 47
References dialog box, 552, 629–630, 654

referential integrity
  avoiding unmatched records, 272
  Cascade Deleting Related Records option,
      178–179
  Cascade Update Related Fields option,
      178–179
  displaying data from different tables, 216
  editing and deleting relationships,
      181–182
  general discussion, 54, 175
  with many-to-many relationships, 182–184
  overview, 177–178
  Relationships window, 179–180
  setting between two tables, 180–181
relational database management systems
    (RDBMS), 671
relational databases
  designing database, 46–57
  field types, 57–60
  general discussion, 10
  new, 61–64
  overview, 37
  relationships, 40–46
  storing single facts, 60–61
  tables, fields, and keys, 37–40
relational operators, 209
relationships
  between Application Part and existing
      table, 75–76
  considering before running delete
      query, 268
  displaying data from different tables, 215
  general discussion, 41–42
  lookup fields, 167–168
  many-to-many, 44–46
  one-to-many, 42–43
  one-to-one, 43–44
  overview, 40–41, 175–177
  printing Relationships window, 184–185
  referential integrity, 177–184
  subdatasheets, 101–103
  subform, 373–374, 376–377
  Table pane, 201
  among tables in database, 504
Relationships button, Design-view Ribbon
    tools, 108

Relationships window
  adding table, 179–180
  choosing type of join and setting join
      properties, 215–216
  opening, 179
  printing, 184–185
  setting referential integrity between two
      tables, 181
  viewing relationships among tables in
      database, 504
Remove Layout button, Ribbon, 327
Remove Link option, Insert Hyperlink
    dialog box, 88
Remove option, Change Access Installation
    screen, 715
Remove Personal Information from File
    Properties on Save setting, for current
    database, 525
Remove Sort button, Ribbon, 121–122
Rename/Delete Macro button, Design-view
    Ribbon tools, 108
renaming objects, 31
Repair option, Change Access Installation
    screen, 715
repairing Access, 715
Replace All button, Find and Replace
    dialog box, 125
Replace button, Find and Replace dialog
    box, 125
Replace With option, Find and Replace
    dialog box, 125
replacing data, 123–125
Replication ID setting, Number fields, 116
Report button, Ribbon, 390
Report Design button, Ribbon, 390
Report Design screen, 184
report designs, 13–14
Report Footer section, of reports, 398
Report Header section, of reports, 398
`Report` keyword, 622
Report Operations commands, Command
    Button Wizard, 349
report selector, 399
Report view, 388–389, 409–410
Report Wizard, 390–396

reports
  configuring, 305–310
  controls, 317–320, 438–439
  copying forms to, 409
  creating automatically, 389–396
  custom functions, 603–604
  designing, 318
  displaying empty or long fields, 413–414
  editing in Layout and Design view,
    396–397
  with filter, 135
  formatting, 407–408
  formatting page, 418–422
  general discussion, 13–14, 252
  grouping data, 392–393
  mailing labels, 424–429
  modifying existing, 300–301
  overview, 387, 415
  placing calculated value on, 369
  printing, 352, 422–424
  relationship between forms and, 290,
    388–389
  sections, 397–407
  sending to application, 429–435
  subreports, 409–412
  themes, 310
  viewing, 414, 415–418
Reports group, Ribbon, 390
Requery macro action, 462
Required property, 159, 170
response code, 607–608
Restore Window button, Code
    window, 544–545
Resume Exit_MyProcedure
    statement, 645
Resume Next statement, 644
Resume statement, 644
Return (Top Values) button, Ribbon,
    200, 205–206
Ribbon
  Design-view tools, 107–108
  hiding and showing, 24, 35
  minimizing, 24
  navigating tabs, 23–24
  navigating without mouse, 34–35
  overview, 23

Ribbon Name setting, for current
    database, 526
Rich Text, 97–98
Rich Text data type, 39, 58
Rich Text Format (RTF) files, 430–431
Rich Text option, text boxes, 98
Right() function, 243
right outer joins, 215–216
right-aligned controls, 329
Round(number[,decimals]) function,
    233
Row Height dialog box, 100
Row Source property, 344
Row Source setting, chart controls, 455–456
Row Source Type property, 344
row sums, 281
rows. *See also* records
  changing height, 100
  in control layout, 304–305
  Crosstab queries, 284–285
  headings, 279–282
  identifying in combo box, 343
  joining multiple criteria, 211
  of labels, 428
  sorting, 121–123
RTF (Rich Text Format) files, 430–431
Run button, Ribbon, 199, 256–257
Run Macro button, main-menu form, 492
Run Query button, main-menu form, 492
RunCode macro action, 462, 578
RunMacro macro action, 463
RunMenuCommand macro action, 463
running sums, 408
RunSQL method, 638–639
runtime errors, 641–647

S

sales taxes, 246–247
sample databases, 21–22
Save All button, Attachments
    dialog box, 91
Save As button, Attachments dialog box, 91
Save As command, Backstage view, 33
Save As dialog box, 219

Save As option, Import Specification dialog box, 149
Save button
  mini toolbar, 700
  Quick Access toolbar, 25
  Ribbon, 73
Save command, Backstage view, 33
Save method, 660
Save variable, 612
saved exports, 154
saved imports, 153
SaveRecord macro action, 463
saving
  advanced filter, 134
  attached files, 91
  databases, 21
  filters, 127
  forms, 305, 310, 318, 409
  macros, 461–462
  objects, 36
  queries, 193, 219
  records, 296
  reports, 310, 318, 409
  tables, 73–74
scheduling saved imports, 153
Scientific Number format, 114
scopes, of variables, 583
screen tips, hyperlinks, 88–89
scroll bars
  datasheet, 81
  form, 310
  in Print Preview window, 417
Scroll Bars property, 310
Search bar, Navigation Pane, 29
Search box, datasheets, 123
Search Fields As Formatted option, Find and Replace dialog box, 125
Search Online Templates search box, 63–64
Search option, Find and Replace dialog box, 124
Search tools, Object Browser, 548–549
searching
  finding and replacing data, 123–125
  Object Library, 549–551
  for objects, 29
  for text, 35

second-level subdatasheets, 102
secret keys, 61
sections, of reports
  adding page headers, footers, and numbers, 400–402
  calculating group subtotals and report totals, 406–407
  grouping records, 402–405
  overview, 397–399
  page breaks, 420–421
  setting properties, 399–400
  sorting records, 405–406
security
  Active content disabled warning, 20
  back-end databases, 514
  enabling VBA code, 541
  locking database as .accde file, 529–532
  one-to-one relationships, 43
  opening databases containing macros, 469–474
  overview, 523
  passwords, 528–529
  SharePoint server, 694
  SQL Server, 679
  Trust Center, 532–533
  user settings, 524–527
  Windows, 523–524
Select Case blocks, 592–595
Select Case statement, 608
Select Case...End Select blocks, 646
Select Data Source dialog box, 673–674
select queries
  action queries versus, 255
  in Custom Web App, 706–707
  general discussion, 190–191
  View and Run buttons, Ribbon, 256
Select statements, 668, 681
Selected Fields list, Form Wizard dialog box, 297
selecting items
  cells, 141
  deselecting, 35–36
  filtering by selection, 128
  multiple, in lookup field, 168–169
  in wizard, 34

SelectObject macro action, 463
semicolon character (;)
  input masks, 163
  pasting SQL statement, 635
Send Object As dialog box, 431
Series setting, in charts, 440, 446
Server field, Create a New Data Source to
    SQL Server dialog box, 676
servers, 671, 686
Set Database Password dialog box, 528
Set keyword, 621–622
Set statements, 657
SetField action, 480
SetFocus method, 660
SetProperty macro action, 463
SetTempVar action, 494
SetValue action, 489
SetWarnings method, 639–640
Shape Outline button, Ribbon, 335
shared folders, 512–513
shared mode, 518–519
SharePoint
  caching options, 527
  compatibility, 143
  Custom Web App, 692–694
  general discussion, 685–686
  hosting companies, 693
  lists, as data source, 686–692
  overview, 685
SharePoint Lists button, Ribbon, 75
SharePoint Server. See SharePoint
Short Text data type, 38
Short Text fields
  general discussion, 110–111
  Long Text fields versus, 57–58
  in text boxes, 325–326
  wrapping onto additional lines, 413
Shortcut Menu Bar setting, for current
    database, 526
shortcuts. See keyboard shortcuts
Show All Actions button, Ribbon, 489
Show Date Picker property, 331
Show Grand Total option Group, Sort, and
    Total pane, 406

Show Group Subtotal As % of Grand Total
    option Group, Sort, and Total pane, 406
Show List Values In options, for sample
    database, 527
Show row, query design grid, 201
Show Subtotal in Group Footer option
    Group, Sort, and Total pane, 406
Show Subtotal in Group Header option
    Group, Sort, and Total pane, 406
Show Table dialog box
  adding table to query, 203
  adding table to Relationships window, 180
  buttons in Design view, 199
  creating query in Design view, 191–192
Show Windows Stacked option, contextual
    menus, 543
ShowAllRecords macro action, 463
Shutter Bar Open/Close button, Access
    window, 25
signing databases, 472–474
Simple Query Wizard, 190, 194–197
simplified syntax, 567
Single data type, 568
Single Form property, 309
single quotation marks (' '), SQL
    statements, 635
Single setting, Number fields, 115
Sizing handle, Code window, 546
SkyDrive, 19, 59
slash character (/)
  division operator, 225–226
  input mask characters, 163
Snap to Grid feature, 318, 329
sng tag, 588
software page, Office 365, 712–713
Sort buttons, Ribbon
  sorting query, 205–206
  sorting rows, 121–122
Sort row, query design grid, 201, 205–206
sorting
  data in Crosstab queries, 286
  fields, 166
  filtered table, 134
  by name or company, 248–249
  in Navigation Pane, 29

Number and Currency fields, 58
query, 205–206
records, 308, 342, 394, 405–406
rows, 121–123
Text fields, 58
source code, 642
Source Object property, subform
  controls, 378
spacebar, changing check-box settings, 83
spacing
  adding spaces to text expressions, 242
  breaking literal string, 574
  breaking SQL statement, 636–637
  control layouts, 304–305
  controls, 329
  eliminating extra when printing reports,
    408
  rows on labels, 428
  sorting spaces, 122
  in table and field names, 48
special characters, 91–92, 122
Special Effect property, 372
Specs option, Import Specification dialog
  box, 149
spell checking, 35, 92–96
Spelling button, Ribbon, 92
Split bar
  Code window, 546
  Object Browser, 548–549
Split Form Datasheet property, 373
Split Form option, Ribbon, 292, 300
Split Form Orientation property, 373
Split Form Printing property, 373
Split Form Size property, 373
Split Form Splitter Bar
  property, 373
split forms, 290, 372–373
SQL (Structured Query Language), 73, 197,
  633–637
SQL Server
  alternatives to ADP files, 682–683
  Express Edition, 673
  general discussion, 671–672
  ODBC, 672–682
  overview, 671

SQL statements, 681
SQL view, 197
Sqr() function, 227
square brackets ([])
  field names in expressions, 226
  formatting Text field, 117
  syntax charts, 560
square roots, 227
Stacked control layout, 301
stacking windows, 543
stand-alone macros
  actions, 462–465
  comments, 465
  naming, saving, and editing, 461–462
  overview, 460–461
  running in form, 482
  submacros, 465–467
standard modules, 538–540, 601
Standard Number format, 114
standard procedures, 563–565
Start and End Dates fields, 79
StartDate value, 238–239
statements, 557
Static Cursor type, 632–633
Static keyword, 584
Status fields, 80
StDev operation, 252
storage
  guidelines, 15
  importing data, 142
storing
  forms and reports, 310–312
  names, money, and codes, 59–60
  pictures and files, 59
  single fact, 60–61
str tag, 588
String (fixed length) data type, 568
string concatenation operator (&), 225
string expressions, 560
string variables, 636–637
strings, 242, 600
Structured Query Language (SQL), 73, 197,
  633–637
structures, storing information
  based on, 15

sub procedures
    For...Next loop in, 598
    general discussion, 563–565
    modules, 541–542
    running from Access, 576–578
    syntax, 568–569
    testing, 575–576
Sub statement, 563, 566–567
subaddresses, 89
subdatasheets, 101–103
Subform Wizard, 374–375
subforms
    adding subtotals and totals from, 379–384
    creating forms with Form Wizard, 298
    displaying detail records, 373–378
    general discussion, 289
    viewing properties of controls, 378
Subform/subreport control button,
    Ribbon, 320
submacros
    assigning macros to keys, 468–469
    general discussion, 465–467
    hiding unneeded controls on form,
      488–489
    overview, 467
    running macro when database opens, 467
subreports
    controls, 409
    exporting reports, 430
    new, 411–412
    overview, 409–410
    printing information on main report, 412
subscripts, 585, 587
subsets, 43, 189
subtotals
    adding from subform, 379–384
    calculating in query, 254
    for group in report, 404, 406–407
subtraction operator (–), 225
Suggestions list, Spelling dialog box, 93
Sum() function, 379, 407
Sum operation, 252
Summarize dialog box, 441, 445
Summary Options dialog box, 195–196,
    394–395
summary queries, 191, 194–195

Symantec, 473
syntax
    arguments, 560–562
    declaring module options, 562–563
    functions, 230–231
    general discussion, 558–560
    module-level declarations versus
      procedure-level declarations, 562
    returning value from function, 569
    simplified, 567
syntax charts, 558–560
system data sources, 675

T

Tab control button, Ribbon, 319
Tab key
    Design view, 202
    navigating datasheet, 81–82
tab order, of forms, 336–337
tabbed documents, 30, 525
tabbed forms, 358–360
Table Analyzer Wizard
    analyzing imported data, 148, 150
    cleaning up imported data, 152
    general discussion, 64
Table button, Ribbon, 74–75
table definitions, 73
Table Design button, Ribbon, 74–75
Table Design view, 109, 157
Table Names button, Ribbon, 200
Table pane
    Crosstab queries, 283
    general discussion, 198, 201
    joining tables in Design view, 215
Table property sheet, 102
Table row
    append queries, 266–267
    query design grid, 201
Table tab, Ribbon, 81
tables
    adding field in Design view, 109
    adding to query, 203
    adding to Relationships window, 179–180
    adding total row to datasheet, 103–104

analyzing and documenting design, 64
attaching macros, 478–481
AutoCorrect, 94–96
Caption property, 109
changing default formatting, 101
choosing data type, 110–112
choosing type of join and setting join properties, 215–216
for codes and abbreviations, 51
creating new with make-table queries, 262–265
custom functions, 603
Custom Web App, 696–698
data types, 38–39
datasheets, 80–82, 96–101
in Design view, 105–107, 109, 110, 201
displaying or hiding name, 202
fields, 74–80
Find Unmatched Query Wizard, 270–272
general discussion, 11
imported, 146
joining, 214–215
linking, 53–55
locking, 520–521
macro to run when record added, 706
making report, 390–396
many-to-many relationships, 182
moving data from one to another with append queries, 265–267
moving field, 110
multiple related, 213–214
naming, 48, 55–56
new, 70–74
new databases, 62–63
organizing fields into, 47–50
overview, 37–38, 67–68
primary keys, 40, 51–53
printing, 119–120
as record source for subform, 375
records, 82–92
refining, 107–112
relationships, 40–46, 504
relinking, 517–518
selecting view, 696–697

setting referential integrity between two, 180–181
spell checking, 92–94
from SQL Server, 678–680
subdatasheets, 101–103
templates, 75–76
values for combo or list box, 340, 342
viewing, 68–70
Tables and Related Views grouping option, Navigation Pane, 26–27
Tables group, Ribbon, 74–75
Tables heading, Navigation Pane, 68
tabs, Ribbon, 23–24
Tabular control layout, 301
Tag fields, 80
tags, 588, 622
taskbar buttons, 543
Tasks lists, SharePoint, 687
Tasks template, 76
taxes, 246–247
templates
    adding tables from, 696–697
    creating sample database from, 21–22
    databases from, 63–64
    field, 75, 78–80
    table, 75–76
    Word, 661
temporary variables, 494–495
Test Validation Rules button, Ribbon, 108, 173
testing code, 575–580
text
    calculating, 370–371
    in criteria, 208
    entering in angle brackets, 231–232
    finding, 35
    formatting, 370–371
    labels, 323–324
    manipulating with expressions, 242
text box controls
    calculated text boxes, 366–367
    general discussion, 319, 323–324
    Number, Currency, and Date fields, 326
    page numbers in reports, 401–402
    placing calculated value on form or report, 369

text box controls (*continued*)
  properties and events, 703
  Short Text and Long Text fields, 325–326
  for summary information in report, 406–407
text boxes
  calculated, 371–372
  data bars, 436
  displaying empty fields, 413–414
  displaying long fields, 413
  inserting text, 614
Text fields
  filtering, 128, 130
  formatting, 116–117
  grouping in report, 393
  versus Number or Currency fields, 58
  sorting, 121–122
  storing phone numbers and postal codes, 59
  Yes/No fields versus, 57
text files
  compatibility, 143
  exporting report as, 432
Text Formatting tools, Ribbon, 97–98
Text functions, 243
Text option, 563
text qualifiers, 146
Text to Display option, Insert Hyperlink dialog box, 88
themes, 310
3-D charts, 443
3-D View, Microsoft Graph, 455
Time Delimiter option, Import Specification dialog box, 149
time formats, 163
Time() function, 238, 240
Time/Date fields, 196
times
  adding to report, 402
  in criteria, 208
  Crosstab queries, 278–281
Title button, Ribbon, 358
titles
  charts, 453–454
  on forms, 323
  report, 404
To keyword, 595

toggle buttons
  option groups, 346–348
  Ribbon, 319
  Yes/No fields, 345
toolbars
  mini, 699–700, 705
  options for current database, 526
tooltips, buttons on Ribbon, 24
top values, 205–206
Total On option Group, Sort, and Total pane, 406
Total row
  calculations in queries, 253
  query design grid, 201
total rows, adding to datasheet, 103–104
totals
  adding from subform, 379–384
  displaying, for groups in report, 404
  printing information from subreport on main report, 412
  for report, 406–407
Totals button
  Home tab, 104
  Ribbon, 200, 253
Totals option, contextual menus, 253
totals queries, 191, 194, 252–254
Track Name AutoCorrect Info setting, for current database, 526
trapping errors, 643
trendlines, for charts, 455
Trim() function, 243
troubleshooting expressions, 368–369
Trust Center, 257, 471, 532–533
trusted locations, 470–472
Try It box, Input Mask Wizard, 161
Two Pages view, Print Preview, 417
type component, 567
Type option Group, Sort, and Total pane, 406
typos, 35, 92–96

U

UBound() function, 599
UCase() function, 243

UDFs (user-defined functions), 600–604
unavailable items, 55
unbound controls, 317, 347
unbound forms, 362–363, 490
Unbound Object Frames, 320, 451
unbound subreports, 409–410
UNC (universal naming convention)
    paths, 145
underlined text, in hyperlinks, 89
underscore symbol (_)
    continuation character, 573, 636–637
    field names in SQL environments, 73
Undo button
    Quick Access toolbar, 25, 318
    Ribbon, 83
Undo Last option, Spelling dialog box, 94
undoing actions, 36
Unfreeze All Fields option, contextual
    menu, 99, 101
Unhide Columns dialog box, 101
Unhide Fields option, contextual
    menus, 101
uninstalling Access, 715
Unique property
    avoiding GIGO, 159
    indexes, 119
Unique Records property, 275
Unique Values property, 275
Unit Price field, 221–223
universal naming convention (UNC)
    paths, 145
.Update method, ADO recordsets, 631
update queries, 256, 258–262
Update To rows, 260–262
.UpdateBatch method, ADO
    recordsets, 631
updates
    to .accde file, 530–532
    automatic, 18
upgrading Access, 710
URLs, linking to, 88
U.S. Postal Service zip-code database, 51
Use Access Special Keys setting, for
    current database, 525

Use the Cache Format That Is Compatible
    with Microsoft Access 2010 and Later
    setting, for current database, 527
Use Windows-Themed Controls on Forms
    setting, for current database, 525
user data sources, 675
user settings, for databases, 524–527, 532
user-defined functions (UDFs), 600–604
users, multiple. *See* multiuser access
Users template, 76

V

validating data
    during entry, 170–173
    in forms, 360–361
    with input masks, 159–164
    rules, 56
Validation Rule property, 158, 170–171,
    361
validation rules, 157, 170–173
Validation Text property, 171–172, 361
Value field, Crosstab queries, 282–283
Value property
    for control, 614
    multivalue lookup fields, 213
values
    assigning to variable, 582–583
    combining in bar chart, 445
    for combo or list box, 340, 342
    in criteria, 208
    displaying those depending on
        conditions, 371
    in lookup field drop-down menu, 165
    option groups, 346
    passed to variable by MsgBox() function,
        606–607
    returning from function, 569–570
    sorting groups in reports, 404
Var operation, 252
var tag, 588

variables
  general discussion, 581–583
  instances of applications, 656
  naming conventions, 588
  organizing into arrays, 585–587
  scope and lifetime, 583–584
  static, 584
  temporary, 494–495
  values passed by MsgBox()
    function to, 607
VBA (Visual Basic for Applications). *See
    also* code; forms
  action queries in, 638–640
  changing form controls, 612–619
  code, 553–556
  data types, 567–569
  enabling, 541–542
  general discussion, 15, 459, 537–540,
    557–558
  locking databases, 530
  overview, 537
  procedures, 563–570
  syntax, 558–563
  VBE, 543–553
VBA modules, 322
vbAbort constant, 607
vbAbortRetryIgnore constant, 606
vbCancel constant, 607
vbCritical constant, 606
VBE (Visual Basic Editor)
  choosing object libraries, 552
  closing, 552–553
  Code window, 544–546
  compiling code, 642–643
  general discussion, 539–540
  Immediate window, 546–547
  Object Browser, 548–549
  overview, 543–544
  referring to objects and collections,
    551–552
  searching Object Library, 549–551
vbExclamation constant, 606
vbIgnore constant, 607
vbInformation constant, 606
vbNo constant, 607

vbOK constant, 607
vbOKCancel constant, 606
vbOKOnly constant, 606
vbQuestion constant, 560–561, 606
vbRetry constant, 607
vbRetryCancel constant, 606
vbYes constant, 607
vbYesNo constant, 560–561, 606
vbYesNoCancel constant, 606
versions, Access
  ADP files, 682
  compatibility, 21
  databases, 21, 503, 515
  upgrading or customizing, 710
vertical scroll bar
  navigating datasheet, 81
  in Print Preview window, 417
View argument, macro actions, 464
View button, Ribbon
  action queries, 256
  forms, 295
  general discussion, 199
  switching views, 30, 70, 217
  viewing data in datasheet, 80
  viewing datasheet with data selected by
    query, 193
View By option, Navigation Pane, 27
View Code button, Design view
    window, 538
View menu, Visual Basic Editor (VBE), 543
View variable, 609
views
  adding actions, 704–705
  editing, 701–703
  general discussion, 29
  switching, 30
viruses, 20, 470
Visible property
  macro controls, 487
  subforms, 383
  Word, 665
Visual Basic Editor (VBE)
  choosing object libraries, 552
  closing, 552–553

Code window, 544–546
compiling code, 642–643
general discussion, 539–540
Immediate window, 546–547
Object Browser, 548–549
overview, 543–544
referring to objects and collections, 551–552
searching Object Library, 549–551
Visual Basic for Applications (VBA). *See also* code; forms
action queries, 638–640
changing form controls, 612–619
code, 553–556
data types, 567–569
enabling, 541–542
general discussion, 15, 459, 537–540, 557–558
locking databases, 530
overview, 537
procedures, 563–570
syntax, 558–563
VBE, 543–553

W

warnings, disabling, 639–640
web addresses, 325
web applications, 682
Web browser control control button, Ribbon, 319
Web Display Form setting, for current database, 525
web links, 86–89
web pages
copying and pasting code, 555–556
linking to, 88
web services, caching options, 527
WeekDay() function, 232
Welcome screen, 17
WHERE clause, 634
Where Condition argument, 464, 486
Where option, QBE (Query by Example) grid, 268–269

WhereCondition variable, 610
WhereTo options, on forms, 594
While...Wend loops, 597, 631–632
Width property, for reports, 422
wildcard characters, 173
WindowMode variable, 610
windows
moving focus, 35
overlapping, 30, 525
stacking, 543
VBE, 543–544
Windows 7, 512, 715
Windows 7 For Dummies, 513, 524
Windows 8, 512, 715
Windows 8 For Dummies, 513
Windows clipboard, 138–139
Windows Explorer, 63
Windows security, 473–474, 523–524
Windows Vista, 512
Windows Vista For Dummies, 513, 524
Windows XP, 512
Windows XP For Dummies, 513, 524
With SQL Server Authentication Using a Login ID and Password Entered by the User option, Create a New Data Source to SQL Server dialog box, 676
With Windows NT Authentication Using the Network Login ID option, Create a New Data Source to SQL Server dialog box, 676
With...End With blocks, 627–628
WithTax() function, 569–570
wizards
Combo and List Box, 341–344
Crosstab Query, 278–282
forms, 296
general discussion, 33–34
Lookup, 39
navigation forms, 361
query, 255, 270–275
Subform, 374–375
Word
mail merge, 156
sending reports to, 430–431
template, 661

Word documents
  compatibility, 143
  merging data with, 661–666
Workbook object, Excel, 668–669
Worksheet object, Excel, 668–669
Wrd object, 665
Write Conflict dialog box, 520
writing data, 72

X

x-axes, in charts, 440, 444, 447–448
XML (Extensible Markup Language) files
  compatibility, 143
  exporting report as, 432
Xor operator, 245
xor operator, 590
XPS (XML Paper Specification) files
  compatibility, 143
  general discussion, 423–424
XY scatter plots, 450

Y

y-axes, in charts, 440, 445, 447–448
year numbers, in criteria, 208
Yes (Duplicates OK) value, 118
Yes (No Duplicates) value, 118
Yes/No data type, 39

Yes/No fields
  check boxes for, 335
  display options, 345
  general discussion, 112
  Text fields versus, 57
Young, Margaret Levine, 20

Z

zero-length strings, 242
zero (0)
  defining number format, 114
  input mask characters, 163
  leading, 58
  versus null values, 236–237
  zero-based arrays, 586–587
zip codes
  defining with Like operator, 173
  input mask, 163
  storing, 59
  validating, 51
Zoom control, 417
Zoom dialog box
  columns, 72
  viewing all data in cell, 84–85
  viewing long expressions, 367–368
  zooming in on expressions, 224